Mike Meyers'

CompTIA A+™

# CERTIFICATION PASSPORT

(Exams 220-1001 & 220-1002)

SEVENTH EDITION

# Mike Meyers
# Mark E. Soper

New York   Chicago   San Francisco   Athens
London   Madrid   Mexico City   Milan
New Delhi   Singapore   Sydney   Toronto

McGraw-Hill Education is an independent entity from CompTIA® and is not affiliated with CompTIA in any manner. This publication and accompanying media may be used in assisting students to prepare for the CompTIA A+ exams. Neither CompTIA nor McGraw-Hill Education warrants that use of this publication and the accompanying media will ensure passing any exam. CompTIA and CompTIA A+ are trademarks or registered trademarks of CompTIA in the United States and/or other countries. All other trademarks are trademarks of their respective owners.

McGraw-Hill Education books are available at special quantity discounts to use as premiums and sales promotions, or for use in corporate training programs. To contact a representative, please visit the Contact Us pages at www.mhprofessional.com.

**Mike Meyers' CompTIA A+™ Certification Passport, Seventh Edition (Exams 220-1001 & 220-1002)**

Copyright © 2020 by McGraw-Hill Education. All rights reserved. Printed in the United States of America. Except as permitted under the Copyright Act of 1976, no part of this publication may be reproduced or distributed in any form or by any means, or stored in a database or retrieval system, without the prior written permission of publisher, with the exception that the program listings may be entered, stored, and executed in a computer system, but they may not be reproduced for publication.

All trademarks or copyrights mentioned herein are the possession of their respective owners and McGraw-Hill Education makes no claim of ownership by the mention of products that contain these marks.

1 2 3 4 5 6 7 8 9    LCR    24 23 22 21 20

Library of Congress Control Number: 2019957595

ISBN    978-1-260-45502-1
MHID      1-260-45502-5

| | | | |
|---|---|---|---|
| **Sponsoring Editor** | **Acquisitions Coordinator** | **Proofreader** | **Composition** |
| Tim Green | Emily Walters | Rick Camp | Cenveo Publisher Services |
| **Editorial Supervisor** | **Technical Editor** | **Indexer** | **Illustration** |
| Janet Walden | Christopher Crayton | Ted Laux | Cenveo Publisher Services |
| **Project Manager** | **Copy Editor** | **Production Supervisor** | **Art Director, Cover** |
| Harleen Chopra, | William McManus | James Kussow | Jeff Weeks |
| Cenveo® Publisher Services | | | |

Information has been obtained by McGraw-Hill Education from sources believed to be reliable. However, because of the possibility of human or mechanical error by our sources, McGraw-Hill Education, or others, McGraw-Hill Education does not guarantee the accuracy, adequacy, or completeness of any information and is not responsible for any errors or omissions or the results obtained from the use of such information.

The *Additional Resources* icon art, first appearing on page xlii, is licensed from Shutterstock/Aayam 4D.
The *Caution* icon art, first appearing on page xlii, is licensed from Shutterstock/Arcady.
The *Exam Tip* icon art, first appearing on page xlii, is licensed from Shutterstock/Katrina Lee.
The *Note* icon art, first appearing on page xlii, is licensed from Shutterstock/MD. Delwar hossain.

*We dedicate this book to our students, past, present, and future.*
*You're why we do what we do!*

# About the Authors

**Mike Meyers**, lovingly called the "AlphaGeek" by those who know him, is the industry's leading authority on CompTIA A+ certification. He is the president and co-founder of Total Seminars, LLC, a provider of computer and network repair seminars, books, videos, and courseware for thousands of organizations throughout the world. Mike has been involved in the computer and network repair industry since 1977 as a technician, instructor, author, consultant, and speaker.

Author of numerous popular PC books and videos, including the best-selling *CompTIA A+ Certification All-in-One Exam Guide*, Mike is also the series editor for the highly successful *Mike Meyers' Certification Passport* series, and the *Mike Meyers' Guide To* series, published by McGraw-Hill.

As well as writing, Mike has personally taught (and continues to teach) thousands of students, including U.S. senators, U.S. Supreme Court justices, members of the United Nations, every branch of the U.S. Armed Forces, most branches of the U.S. Department of Justice, and hundreds of corporate clients, academic students at every level, prisoners, and pensioners.

E-mail: michaelm@totalsem.com
Twitter/Skype/Most IMs: desweds

**Mark Edward Soper** is a technology multitool, equally adept at technical writing and training on topics ranging from Windows and Microsoft Office to self-service help desk, hardware, and certification. Mark has been working with technology since the days of the Commodore 64, Franklin Ace, Atari 800XL, and IBM PC. In the process of authoring/co-authoring over 40 books, contributing to many more, and writing hundreds of magazine and website articles and blog entries, he has built many versions of experimental computers known collectively as "FrankenPC" and torn them down and built them back up again.

Mark is also very comfortable at the controls of a camera, doing much of his own photography over the years for book illustrations, writing two books on digital photography, and specializing in railroads, airshows, travel, and family subjects.

Mark has taught computer troubleshooting, Microsoft Windows, networking, digital photography, photo editing, and Microsoft Office to thousands of students across the United States and has developed training courses for universities and institutions. Mark originally worked with Mike in the 1990s when both worked for the same company as computer trainers and appreciates the opportunity to work together again!

E-mail: mark@markesoper.com
Facebook: Sopertech
Twitter: Sopertech
Website: www.markesoper.com

## About the Editor-in-Chief

**Scott Jernigan** wields a mighty red pen as editor-in-chief for Total Seminars. With a Master of Arts degree in medieval history, Scott feels as much at home in the musty archives of London as he does in the warm computer glow of Total Seminars' Houston headquarters. After fleeing a purely academic life, he dove headfirst into IT, working as an instructor, editor, and writer. Scott has written, edited, and contributed to dozens of books on computer literacy, hardware, operating systems, networking, and certification. His latest book (aside from the one in your hands) is *Computer Literacy: Your Ticket to IC³ Certification*. Scott co-authored the best-selling *CompTIA A+ Certification All-in-One Exam Guide*, the *Mike Meyers' CompTIA A+ Guide to Managing and Troubleshooting PCs*, and the *Mike Meyers Guide to CompTIA Security+, Second Edition* (all with Mike Meyers). He has taught computer classes all over the United States, including stints at the United Nations in New York and the FBI Academy in Quantico, Virginia.

## About the Technical Editor

**Chris Crayton**, MCSE, is an author, technical consultant, and trainer. He has worked as a computer technology and networking instructor, information security director, network administrator, network engineer, and PC specialist. Chris has authored several print and online books on PC repair, CompTIA A+, CompTIA Security+, and Microsoft Windows. He has also served as technical editor and content contributor on numerous technical titles for several of the leading publishing companies. He holds numerous industry certifications, has been recognized with many professional teaching awards, and has served as a state-level SkillsUSA competition judge.

## About Total Seminars

Total Seminars provides certification training services to thousands of schools, corporations, and government agencies. Total Seminars produces the #1-selling CompTIA A+ and best-selling CompTIA Network+ certification books, and develops training materials such as the TotalTester for superior exam preparation. You can find Total Seminars on the Web at www.totalsem.com.

# Contents at a Glance

# Contents

# Acknowledgments

As with every book, a lot of work from a lot of people went into making this happen.

Our acquisitions editor, Tim Green, kept us on track with kind words and pointy sticks. Always a pleasure working with you!

Our acquisitions coordinator, Emily Walters, did an outstanding job acquiring and coordinating . . . with gentle yet insistent reminders for us to get stuff to her on a timely basis. Fun project and we look forward to the next one!

Michael Smyer provided great photographs for the book, and Ford Pierson added his incredible illustrations. Mark Soper also shot a lot of new photographs for this edition. Thanks guys!

Bill McManus did great work as our copy editor. He transformed every awkward stumble of language into a grammatical gem.

Our technical editor, Chris Crayton, took what some would describe as gleeful delight in pointing out every technical error he found. But since he helped us fix every error, too, we won't hold it against him. Thanks, once again, for your technical expertise.

The layout team at Cenveo Publisher Services did a remarkable job, putting the prose and pictures into printable form, that you get to enjoy now!

Finally, thanks to our proofreader, Rick Camp, for catching every last error. There's no error too big or small—he'll find them all. Thank you.

Great work, team!

Mark also wants to thank Mike for the opportunity to work together on the latest generation of CompTIA A+ certification, Mark's family (many of who love to "talk tech" at family get-togethers), and Jesus the Messiah, who has blessed Mark and his family in countless ways over the years.

# Introduction

## Your Passport to Certification

Hello! I'm Mike Meyers, president of Total Seminars and author of a number of popular certification books. On any given day, you'll find me replacing a hard drive, setting up a website, or writing code. The book you hold in your hands is part of a powerful book series called the *Mike Meyers' Certification Passports*. Every book in this series combines easy readability with a condensed format—in other words, it's the kind of book I always wanted when I went for my certifications. Putting a huge amount of information in an accessible format is an enormous challenge, but I think we have achieved our goal and I am confident you'll agree.

I designed this series to do one thing and only one thing—to get you the information you need to achieve your certification. You won't find any fluff in here. We packed every page with nothing but the real nitty-gritty of the CompTIA A+ certification exams.

My personal e-mail address is michaelm@totalsem.com. Please feel free to contact me directly if you have any questions, complaints, or compliments.

## Your Destination: CompTIA A+ Certification

This book is your passport to CompTIA A+ certification, the vendor-neutral industry standard certification for PC hardware technicians, the folks who build and fix PCs. To get CompTIA A+ certified, you need to pass two exams, 220-1001 and 220-1002. Past CompTIA A+ exams used friendly names like "Essentials" and "Practical Application," but these terms don't apply anymore.

### The CompTIA A+ Exams

The 220-1001 exam concentrates on five areas: Mobile Devices, Networking, Hardware, Virtualization and Cloud Computing, and Hardware and Network Troubleshooting. This exam focuses on your understanding of the terminology and hardware technology used in each of the five subject areas.

The 220-1002 exam works the same way, covering Operating Systems, Security, Software Troubleshooting, and Operational Procedures. The 1002 exam is very Windows focused—installing, updating, maintaining, troubleshooting, and more. The other operating systems covered—macOS, Linux, iOS, and Android—get more of a big-picture view. Security and troubleshooting—Windows and applications—make up half the exam questions.

Speaking of questions, each exam consists of up to 90 questions. Each exam takes 90 minutes. You must score at least 675 on a scale of 100–900 to pass exam 220-1001 (Core 1) and at least 700 on a scale of 100–900 to pass exam 220-1002 (Core 2). Remember, you must pass **both** exams to achieve your CompTIA A+ certification.

## Question Types and Examples

Both of the exams are extremely practical, with little or no interest in theory. When you take the exams, you will see three types of questions: multiple choice, drag-and-drop matching, and performance based (simulation).

The following is an example of the type of multiple-choice question you will see on the exams:

> A company is planning to upgrade its Fast Ethernet network to Gigabit Ethernet. The existing network uses a mixture of Cat 5, Cat 5e, and Cat 6 cables. Which of the following needs to be performed during the upgrade process?
>
> **A.** Replace all cables with Cat 6
>
> **B.** Keep the same cables
>
> **C.** Replace Cat 5 with Cat 5e or Cat 6
>
> **D.** Replace all cables with Cat 5e

The best answer is C, Replace Cat 5 with Cat 5e or 6. The cable standards mentioned in Answer A and D support Gigabit Ethernet, but since some parts of the network already use these cables types, it is not necessary to replace them. You might also see multiple-response questions, essentially multiple choice with more than one correct answer.

Drag-and-drop questions involve dragging and dropping a picture onto the relevant text. For example, you might see the words "HDMI" and "DisplayPort," and then two video port illustrations next to them. You would need to drag the HDMI illustration onto the word "HDMI," then drag the other illustration onto the word "DisplayPort."

Performance-based (simulation) questions ask you to re-create a real process used by techs when working on PCs. You might be asked to copy a file or change a setting in Control Panel, but instead of picking a multiple-choice answer, your screen will look like a Windows desktop and you will follow the provided instructions, just like you were using the real thing.

Always read the questions very carefully, especially when dealing with performance-based and multiple-choice questions with two or more correct responses. Remember to look for the *best* answer, not just the right answer. Check the CompTIA website for the most up-to-date exam information, as CompTIA does make changes.

## Signing Up for Your CompTIA A+ Certification Exams

So, how do you sign up to take the CompTIA A+ certification exams? As this book went to press, the procedure looks like this:

Go to https://home.pearsonvue.com/CompTIA. Click the Sign in button or, if you don't already have a Pearson VUE account, click Create account and create one. Then, click View Exams, select the 1001 or 1002 exam (you must pass both), select your preferred language, review the details, and click Schedule this Exam. Enter your username and password, choose an exam center, date, and time, and provide payment or an exam voucher when required. Repeat this process to schedule the other exam. Be sure to see the Pearson VUE website for the latest details.

A single exam voucher purchased directly from the CompTIA website is $219. However, there are many sources, including Total Seminars (Mike's home base online!), that offer discounts. Some vendors offer bundles that include a free retest voucher. Take it from me, you might like the opportunity to have a "mulligan" if you get test jitters!

CompTIA A+ certification can be your ticket to a career in IT or simply an excellent step in your certification pathway. This book is your passport to success on the CompTIA A+ certification exams.

## Your Guides: Mike Meyers and Mark Edward Soper

You get a pair of tour guides for this book—both me and Mark Edward Soper. I've written numerous computer certification books—including the best-selling *CompTIA A+ Certification All-in-One Exam Guide* and the *CompTIA Network+ Certification All-in-One Exam Guide*. More to the point, I've been working on PCs and teaching others how to make and fix them for a very long time, and I love it! When I'm not lecturing or writing about PCs, I'm working on PCs!

Mark has written or co-authored many technology books on certification, Windows, self-service help desk and troubleshooting, home networking and automation, digital photography, and more, including *Mike Meyers' CompTIA A+ Guide to Managing and Troubleshooting PCs Lab Manual, Sixth Edition (Exams 220-1001 & 220-1002)*. Mark has also taught computer repair and troubleshooting, Microsoft Office, Microsoft Windows, and other topics. Go into his office and you'll see the latest "FrankenPC," a couple of future candidates, and a wide variety of desktop and laptop computer parts.

## About the Book

This *Passport* is divided into "Domains" that follow the exam domains. Each Domain is further divided into "Objective" modules covering each of the top-level certification objectives. The goal is to facilitate accelerated review of the exam objectives in a quick-review format that will allow you to quickly gauge what you can expect to be tested on. Whether you want a last-minute review or you have enough experience that you don't need full coverage of every topic, this format is designed for you. This isn't meant to be a course in a book, but we hope you will find the *Passport* helpful as you prepare for your exams. If you find you need more in-depth coverage of the exam topics, we suggest using Mike's *CompTIA A+ Certification All-in-One Exam Guide, Tenth Edition* to supplement your studies.

We've created a set of learning elements that call your attention to important items, reinforce key points, and provide helpful exam-taking hints. Take a look at what you'll find:

- Each Domain begins with a **Domain Objectives** list of the official CompTIA A+ exam objectives, which correspond to the titles of the individual Objective modules in that Domain. The structure of each Objective module is based on the sub-objectives listed under the corresponding exam objective.

- The following elements highlight key information throughout the modules:

 **EXAM TIP**    The Exam Tip element focuses on information that pertains directly to the exam. These helpful hints are written by authors who have taken the exam and received their certification—who better to tell you what to worry about? They know what you're about to go through!

**Cross-Reference**

This element points to related topics covered in other Objective modules or Domains.

 **ADDITIONAL RESOURCES**    This element points to books, websites, and other media for further assistance.

 **CAUTION**    These cautionary notes address common pitfalls or "real world" issues.

 **NOTE**    This element calls out any ancillary, but pertinent information.

- **Tables** allow for a quick reference to help quickly navigate quantitative data or lists of technical information:

| Video Cable Type | Standard Name | Reduced-size Version | Signal Types Supported | Notes |
|---|---|---|---|---|
| VGA | Video Graphics Array | N/A | Analog video | VGA displays can be connected to HDMI, DVI-I, and DisplayPort ports with suitable adapters. |
| HDMI | High Definition Multimedia Interface | Mini-HDMI | HD video and HD audio | Video signal is compatible with DVI. |

- Each Objective module ends with a brief **Review**. The review begins by repeating the official exam objective number and text, followed by a succinct and useful summary, geared toward quick review and retention.
- **Review Questions and Answers** are intended to be similar to those found on the exam. Explanations of the correct answer are provided.

# Online Content

For more information on the practice exams and other bonus materials that are included with the book, please see the "About the Online Content" appendix at the back of this book.

After you've read the book, complete the free online registration and take advantage of the free practice questions! Use the full practice exam to hone your skills and keep the book handy to check answers.

When you're acing the practice questions, you're ready to take the exam.

*Go get certified!*

# What's Next?

The IT industry changes and grows constantly, and so should you. Finishing one certification is just a step in an ongoing process of gaining more and more certifications to match your constantly changing and growing skills. Remember, in the IT business, if you're not moving forward, you are way behind!

Good luck on your certification! Stay in touch.

Mike Meyers, Series Editor
*Mike Meyers' Certification Passport*

# CompTIA A+
# Exam 220-1001

# Mobile Devices

DOMAIN 1.0

## Domain Objectives

- **1.1** Given a scenario, install and configure laptop hardware and components
- **1.2** Given a scenario, install components within the display of a laptop
- **1.3** Given a scenario, use appropriate laptop features
- **1.4** Compare and contrast characteristics of various types of other mobile devices
- **1.5** Given a scenario, connect and configure accessories and ports of other mobile devices
- **1.6** Given a scenario, configure basic mobile device network connectivity and application support
- **1.7** Given a scenario, use methods to perform mobile device synchronization

## Objective 1.1 Given a scenario, install and configure laptop hardware and components

Although an increasing number of laptops have no user-replaceable parts, there are still many existing and new models from a variety of manufacturers that will need replacement keyboards, upgraded RAM or mass storage, or other types of upgrades. This objective gives you the "inside story" on what to expect.

## Hardware/Device Replacement

Laptops can break, but when they do, the problem is usually a component that can be replaced.

The most common replacements (or upgrades) include keyboards and other input devices, hard drives, and RAM, but there are several additional components that you might be called upon to swap out. Many of these components can be seen in Figures 1.1-1 and 1.1-2.

### Cross-Reference

Be sure to follow ESD precautions while performing laptop component replacements or upgrades. See Part II, Domain 4.0, Objective 4.4 for details.

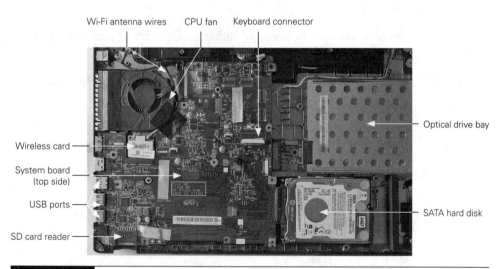

**FIGURE 1.1-1** The top side of a typical system board

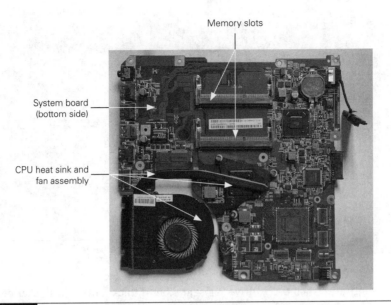

**FIGURE 1.1-2**  The bottom side of a typical system board.

 **CAUTION**  Before attempting any laptop hardware or component replacement, look for its service manual online. Because laptops vary so much from brand to brand and model to model, the steps vary a great deal and if you don't use proper procedures to disassemble a laptop, you might end up with more problems than when you started!

## Keyboard

Replacing a laptop keyboard varies in difficulty from model to model. With some laptops, removing the old keyboard can be as easy as removing a retaining screw from the bottom of the laptop and pushing the keyboard up. However, some models require that almost all other components be removed before the keyboard can be removed.

 **NOTE**  If a laptop keyboard fails and can't be replaced right away, connecting a USB keyboard, USB wireless receiver for a keyboard, or Bluetooth keyboard will usually work. Only a few very old laptops use the equally venerable PS/2 keyboard port.

## Hard Drive

The term *hard drive* is used for a variety of mass storage devices using magnetic or solid-state technologies. You can replace a hard disk drive (HDD), solid-state drive (SSD), or solid-state hybrid drive (HHD or SSHD) easily in any recently manufactured traditional laptop; it's

**FIGURE 1.1-3**     The 2.5-inch and 3.5-inch drives are mostly the same.

almost certainly a 2.5-inch SATA drive (most are 7 mm thick, but a few thicker drives won't fit into some laptops). Otherwise, no difference exists between 2.5-inch drives and their larger 3.5-inch brethren (see Figure 1.1-3).

Hard drive replacement is a little different on laptops than on desktops: find the hard drive hatch—either along one edge or on the bottom—and remove the screws (see Figure 1.1-4).

Remove the old hard drive, detach its mounting hardware, and install the mounting hardware on the new drive. The mounting hardware might include brackets, shock bumpers, or a protective cover over the drive's circuit board (see Figure 1.1-5).

Next, slide the new drive into its place (see Figure 1.1-6), making sure it is firmly connected to the drive interface and secured in place. Reattach the hatch, boot the computer, and install an OS if necessary.

 **NOTE**     Some laptops require the user to remove many components before upgrading the drive. Try to avoid upgrading these systems.

**FIGURE 1.1-4**     Removing the drive compartment hatch. Some laptops, like this one, use a single cover for access to hard drives and RAM.

Shock bumpers    Protective cover    Bumper attachment screws

| **FIGURE 1.1-5** | The mounting hardware on this hard drive must be removed and attached to the new drive so it will fit properly in the computer. |

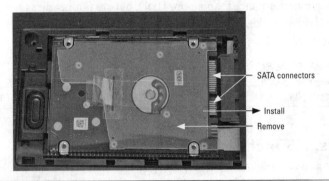

SATA connectors

Install

Remove

| **FIGURE 1.1-6** | Inserting a replacement drive |

## SSD vs. Hybrid vs. Magnetic Disk

One of the best laptop upgrades is to an SSD from a magnetic disk (HDD). It's less storage for the money, but SSDs are faster, lighter, quieter, cooler, use less power, and lack mechanical parts easily damaged by bumps, drops, and travel. SSDs are available in both the traditional 2.5-inch laptop form factor and smaller form factors, most notable the M.2 design. Some laptops, like the one shown in Figure 1.1-7, can use both. M.2 SSDs are available in two types: those that emulate SATA drives, and versions known as NVMe drives. These connect to the PCIe bus, which is much faster than the SATA bus.

**EXAM TIP**   Make sure you are familiar with installing and configuring SSDs, hybrid drives, and magnetic hard disk drives.

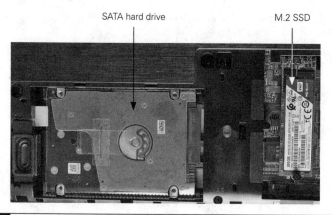

SATA hard drive                                                        M.2 SSD

**FIGURE 1.1-7**    A laptop with both SATA and SSD drives.

*Hybrid drives* combine a traditional magnetic HDD mechanism with a small onboard SSD. They provide faster performance than a pure HDD, but are not nearly as fast or durable as a pure SSD. Hybrid drives make sense when you need high capacity (up to 2 TB) more than you need maximum speed.

**Cross-Reference**

To learn more about hard disk drives, SSDs, and hybrid drives, see Part I, Domain 3.0, Objective 3.4.

### 1.8 inch vs. 2.5 inch

2.5-inch HDDs and SSDs dominate laptop designs. 1.8-inch HDDs have fallen out of favor as flash memory usurps their role in portable music players and other small portables. These days, 1.8-inch HDDs are quite rare. If you encounter one, it almost certainly will be in an older portable on the small end of the scale.

## Memory

Traditional laptops have upgradeable memory (RAM) slots; other portables may not. Remember that portable RAM has its own SO-DIMM form factors (though you may see them in some compact all-in-one desktops). Older systems may have 200-pin DDR or DDR2 SO-DIMMs. Most current systems use 204-pin DDR3 or DDR3L (lower-voltage) SO-DIMMs or 260-pin DDR4 SO-DIMMs (see Figure 1.1-8).

**Cross-Reference**

For more about laptop and desktop RAM types and specifications, see Part I, Domain 3.0, Objective 3.3.

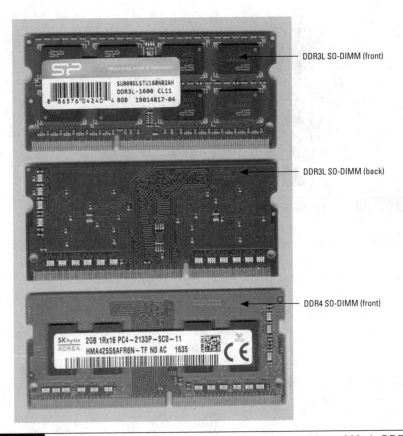

DDR3L SO-DIMM (front)

DDR3L SO-DIMM (back)

DDR4 SO-DIMM (front)

**FIGURE 1.1-8** 204-pin DDR3L SO-DIMMs (front and back) compared to a 260-pin DDR4 SO-DIMM

 **EXAM TIP** Memorize the SO-DIMM form factors—and the associated memory technologies—for the CompTIA A+ 220-1001 exam.

When installing RAM, just like with a desktop, protect yourself and the portable by removing all power and taking ESD precautions. With portables, this includes removable batteries. If the portable has built-in batteries, consult the manufacturer's resources to check if and how you can safely work on it.

 **CAUTION** Some portables have both built-in and removable batteries.

**FIGURE 1.1-9**    Removing a RAM panel

Once you know you can work safely, consult the manufacturer's website or manual to confirm what kind of RAM the portable requires. Next, check the existing RAM configuration to confirm what you need to buy. To go from 4 GB to 8 GB, for example, you need to know if the portable has one 4-GB module or two 2-GB modules. You should also match the clock speed and timing of the existing module.

Second, locate the RAM slots. Depending on the system, the RAM slots might be under the same panel that you remove to access the hard drive (refer to Figure 1.1-4), or under a separate panel (see Figure 1.1-9) on the bottom of the portable. Then you push out the retaining clips and the RAM stick pops up (see Figure 1.1-10). Gently remove the old stick of RAM and insert the new one by reversing the steps.

Retaining clips

RAM swings up after
retaining clips are released

**FIGURE 1.1-10**    Releasing the RAM

Some portables (and desktops) have shared memory that enables the video card to borrow regular system RAM, providing performance comparable to its mega-memory alternative at a much lower cost. Unfortunately, the term "shared" is a bit misleading: the video card reserves this memory, and performance can suffer if the system runs out.

Some CMOS utilities can change the amount of shared memory, while others can just toggle the setting. In both cases, more system RAM will improve overall performance when the OS and CPU get more usable RAM; the upgrade can also improve video performance if the system either shares a percentage of all RAM or lets you adjust the amount.

**EXAM TIP**    RAM and hard drives are usually the easiest components to replace.

## Smart Card Reader

*Smart card readers* read smart card chips, such as those embedded in ID badges, and are built into some portable devices designed for use in enterprise and business networks. Smart card readers can be used as part of two-factor authentication for device login: password/username plus a smart card. To replace a defective internal smart card reader, the system must be partly or completely disassembled. Smart card readers use a ribbon cable to connect to the motherboard.

Many organizations that use two-factor authentication with smart cards use external smart card readers that plug into USB ports. To replace a USB smart card reader, simply uninstall the drivers, disconnect the reader, install drivers for the new reader, and connect it.

## Optical Drive

If an optical drive is part of a modular system, you can just pop out the old drive and pop in a new one. Some optical drives use a securing screw or slider on the bottom of the computer to hold the drive in place. If it's part of the internal chassis, you're looking at a full dissection.

## Wireless Card/Bluetooth Module

A wireless card/Bluetooth module is sometimes relatively easy to swap, as it may be accessible from the panel covering the hard drive and/or RAM. Before choosing an upgrade, make sure you check out the supported models, as an unsupported card won't be recognized by your system. If you upgrade a wireless expansion card, remember to reattach the antenna leads coming from the display in the correct locations. Depending on the age of the system, the wireless card might use a Mini-PCIe (refer to Figure 1.1-1) or M.2 form factor.

**EXAM TIP**    Make sure you are familiar with the form factors used for wireless cards/Bluetooth modules.

## Cellular Card

An internal *cellular card* uses a separate slot from the wireless card, typically a mini-PCIe or an M.2 card. If you need to replace the card, be sure to use a card made for your specific mobile device configuration, and be sure to note the correct locations for the antenna leads.

## Video Card

Most laptops have CPU-integrated video. However, some business and gaming laptops have separate (discrete) *display adapters* that use the MXM (Mobile PCI Express Module) standard. These video cards are not sold at retail, but are sometimes available from eBay or other secondary sources as pulls from working systems.

 **ADDITIONAL RESOURCES**   To learn more about MXM cards, generations, and available GPUs, go to https://graphicscardhub.com and search for "MXM Graphics Card Types, Models & MXM GPU List."

## Mini PCIe

Some portables have true expansion slots such as *Mini-PCIe* (see Figure 1.1-11) and M.2 for add-on cards. As with RAM, remove power and avoid ESD. If you upgrade a wireless expansion card, remember to reattach the antenna.

## Screen

Removing the screen is required when performing extensive or complete disassembly of a laptop. Aside from finding the connection points and removing the proper screws, you need to note the connection points for the display and any antennas or other devices (such as webcams

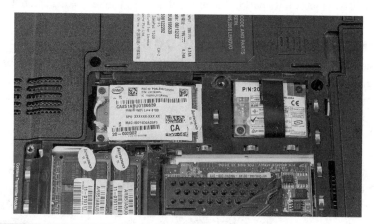

**FIGURE 1.1-11**   Mini-PCIe expansion slot on a laptop

or microphones) in the frame. Older touchscreen laptops might use a separate touchscreen layer, while newer touchscreens incorporate the touchscreen with the regular display, so only a single connector is needed.

## DC Jack

Replacing the DC jack, which might be soldered to the main board, requires extra love. If it's soldered, you'll need to strip the laptop to the bare metal, unsolder the old part, and solder the new part. CompTIA can't expect a CompTIA A+ technician to know how to do this stuff, but may expect you to know if it *can* be done. Fortunately, many newer laptops don't use a soldered connector.

## Battery

When a portable computer's battery life between charges falls below an acceptable level, get a manufacturer or aftermarket replacement battery with the same specifications. This should be a simple swap replacement (if the battery isn't built in), but if the new battery fares no better, you may have an inadequate or malfunctioning charging system.

## Touchpad

Replacing the touchpad usually requires extensive disassembly of a laptop. The touchpad might be wired to the motherboard by a separate ribbon cable from the keyboard or the keyboard connector might also be used for the touchpad. Both variations use zero insertion force (ZIF) connectors.

 **EXAM TIP**   Make sure you are familiar with the levels of difficulty for replacing different components.

## Plastics/Frames

A portable's components are secured by a variety of plastic, metal, and rubber parts, known collectively on the CompTIA A+ 220-1001 exam as *plastics/frames*. These too can be replaced, if you can find a suitable replacement. Start with the device model, and use manufacturer or third-party resources to find the part number; be careful, and don't just eyeball it by searching for a part that looks the same. A tiny part can set you back a silly sum if it's sold only in a larger assembly.

## Speaker

Replacing the internal speaker(s) on a laptop can be simple or a total pain, depending on where the speaker connects. Some speakers are mounted on the outside of the chassis: you just pry off the cover, pull out the little speaker, disconnect the cable, and reverse the process for the replacement. If the speaker is inside the chassis, you need to dismantle the portable.

## System Board

Some repairs go as far as stripping down the portable to the bare chassis, which is best left to portable repair specialists. You open a portable by peeling away layers either from the top down through the keyboard, or from the base up; both techniques demand systematic attention to tiny parts, screws, and connectors.

### Cross-Reference

To learn more about the four-step disassembling process for proper reassembly of mobile devices, see Part I, Domain 5.0, Objective 5.5.

Figure 1.1-12 illustrates a typical laptop after removing the keyboard. Before the system board (motherboard) can be accessed, the optical drive, ribbon cables, and a number of screws must be removed.

## CPU

Replacing the CPU on a portable takes a lot more work than replacing RAM or a Mini-PCIe expansion card. Before you start, make sure the CPU is replaceable—some vendors use surface-mounted CPUs. Once again, start by removing all power and remove the parts (layers) needed to access the CPU. It might be necessary to flip over the system board to access the CPU. Next, you will need to remove an elaborate heat sink and fan assembly (refer to Figure 1.1-2). The heat sink might cover both the CPU and chipset. Unscrew the assembly and lift out the CPU. Replace it with another CPU, apply thermal paste, and reattach the assembly. Reconnect the fan power connector and you're ready to reassemble the laptop. Take a quick look at the cooling fan, though. If it's like the one shown in Figure 1.1-2, it could use some canned air!

**FIGURE 1.1-12**    A typical laptop partially disassembled

# REVIEW

**Objective 1.1: Given a scenario, install and configure laptop hardware and compo-
nents**   Laptop hardware and component issues you might deal with include the following:

- Keyboard, replacement
- Hard drive (2.5 inch), removal and installation
  - Use an SSD (2.5 inch or M.2) if you can to improve performance and durability
- Memory (SO-DIMM) types, removal and installation
- Smart card reader
- Optical drive, removal and installation
- Wireless card/Bluetooth module, removal and installation
- Cellular card, removal and installation
- Video card (MXM used by some laptops)
- Mini-PCIe, removal and installation
- Screen, removal and installation
- DC jack, removal and installation
- Battery, removal and installation
- Touchpad, removal and installation
- Plastics/frames, care in disassembly
- Speaker, removal and installation
- System board, disassembly process
- CPU, removal and installation

# 1.1 QUESTIONS

1. Your client wants you to upgrade the RAM, wireless cards, and storage in a collection
   of laptops from different vendors. Which of the following do you need to perform the
   work successfully? (Choose all that apply.)

   **A.** Service manual for each model

   **B.** Specialized tools

   **C.** Specifications

   **D.** All of the above

2. You are specifying the components you want in a killer gaming laptop. Which of the
   following standards provides the best opportunity for high-performance mass storage?

   **A.** SATA

   **B.** USB

   **C.** M.2

   **D.** Mini-PCIe

3. Which of the following laptop components typically requires the least disassembly to swap or upgrade?
   A. Hard drive
   B. RAM
   C. CPU
   D. Smart card reader

4. Your client wants to switch from SATA hard disk to SATA SSD storage in their fleet of laptops. Which of the following advice is most likely to be correct?
   A. Buy M.2 drives because all laptops have M.2 slots.
   B. SSDs are no faster than hard disk drives, so don't bother switching.
   C. Replacing hard disk drives with SSDs can provide better performance.
   D. SSDs are more fragile than hard disk drives.

5. Your client has stripped components from retired laptops to use for replacements in more recent laptops. Which of the following is most likely to be compatible with a newer laptop?
   A. Hard drive
   B. RAM
   C. Wireless card
   D. Optical drive

## 1.1 ANSWERS

1. **D**   A service manual provides detailed teardown and reassembly instructions; specialized tools help you open cases without breaking parts; and specifications inform you of standard features and supported upgrades.

2. **C**   M.2 drives using NVMe are the fastest mass storage devices.

3. **B**   Most laptops with upgradeable RAM have the modules under an easy-to-remove panel on the bottom of the case.

4. **C**   SSDs in the SATA form factor provide faster performance than SATA hard disk drives.

5. **A**   As long as a SATA 2.5-inch hard drive will physically fit into a laptop, it can be used as a replacement (a few hard drives are too thick for some laptops, but that is rare).

## Objective 1.2 Given a scenario, install components within the display of a laptop

Laptop displays are thin, but they're very complex on the inside. Most contain components such as webcams, wireless antennas, touchscreens, and microphones, all of which you need to know how to install as a CompTIA A+ technician.

# Types of Laptop Displays

Laptops come in a variety of sizes and at varying costs. One major contributor to the overall cost is the LCD or OLED screen size, which typically ranges from 10.1 inches to 17.3 inches, though some screens are just over 20 inches. Compared to desktop displays, the biggest difference is that the laptop's LCD or OLED frame may contain a Wi-Fi antenna, webcam, and microphone.

## LCD

A *liquid crystal display (LCD)* uses a separate backlight. Older models, now mostly retired, used fluorescent tubes for backlighting. Newer models use LEDs for backlighting.

## OLED

*Organic LED (OLED)* displays don't use a separate backlight and provide superior display quality. Laptops using OLED technology were introduced in early 2019.

# Wi-Fi Antenna Connector/Placement

There are two ways to service a broken laptop display: replace the entire display assembly, or swap the display panel only while retaining the existing frame, Wi-Fi antennas, webcam, and microphone. Because the same panel can work in a wide variety of laptop models, finding a compatible display panel is easier than finding a compatible display assembly, and purchasing only a panel is less expensive than purchasing an assembly. In a few cases, it might be possible to switch screen types (from matte to glossy, for example). When swapping the panel only, take particular care to note the *placement* of component wires and how they are routed around the panel.

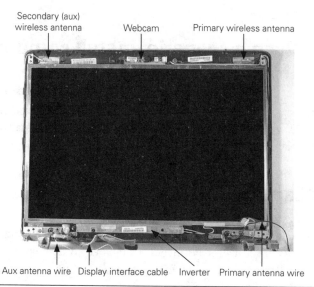

Secondary (aux) wireless antenna    Webcam    Primary wireless antenna

Aux antenna wire    Display interface cable    Inverter    Primary antenna wire

**FIGURE 1.2-1**    Wi-Fi antennas and other components in a typical laptop display panel

**EXAM TIP**    Expect a question or two on the A+ 220-1001 exam involving a typical scenario that requires replacement of the screen or components in the screen; for example, a cracked display panel, digitizer/touchscreen failure, Wi-Fi antenna malfunction, and so on. Note that CompTIA's specific language for the antenna is *WiFi antenna connector/placement* (although the industry-standard term is *Wi-Fi*). This refers to the wireless antenna wires (pun intended!) that run along the top and sides of the screen assembly and connect to the Wi-Fi card.

When swapping a display assembly, it's important to note how the Wi-Fi antenna wires are connected to the wireless card. Even if you are only swapping a panel, you might need to move the wires out of the way. When necessary to move them, it's important to properly position the Wi-Fi antenna wires around the panel and reconnect them to the wireless card. If they are pinched or broken, the laptop's Wi-Fi will stop working.

Figure 1.2-1 illustrates the position of Wi-Fi antenna wires and other components in a typical laptop display assembly.

# Webcam

The webcam (refer to Figure 1.2-1) is also built into the display assembly. The webcam can be replaced if it stops working. However, it's usually easier to replace a failed webcam with a USB version. If you decide to replace the webcam, be sure to note how it is attached to the display assembly and connected to the system board.

# Microphone

Some laptops include a microphone in the screen assembly, while others place the microphone in the base of the laptop. If the laptop has a microphone in the screen assembly, be sure to disconnect it before swapping the screen assembly, and be sure to reconnect it during the replacement process.

# Inverter

Laptops that use older LCDs screens with cold cathode fluorescent lamp (CCFL) backlighting require an inverter to convert DC power to AC power to power the backlight (refer to Figure 1.2-1). If the inverter fails, the screen will be extremely dim (use a flashlight to see if the screen still works). Replacing an inverter is a relatively easy and inexpensive repair to make because it is accessed from the bottom of the display assembly and is a plug-in component.

# Digitizer/Touchscreen

Older laptops often used a separate digitizer/touchscreen layer, making repairs both expensive and more complicated. (A *digitizer* refers to the component that provides the "touch" part of a touchscreen. The digitizer's fine grid of sensors under the glass detects your finger touch and signals the OS its location on the grid.) Recent touchscreen laptops typically use display panels with integrated touchscreens, making the process of swapping the panel easier.

# REVIEW

**Objective 1.2: Given a scenario, install components within the display of a laptop**   A typical laptop display assembly includes the following:

- LCD panel (standard) or OLED panel (only very recent laptops)
  - LCD has a fluorescent or LED backlight
  - OLED has no backlight
- Wi-Fi antenna wires
- Webcam
- Microphone (might be built into the base on some models)
- Inverter, but only on older LCD screens with fluorescent backlights
- Digitizer/touchscreen (might be a separate display panel layer on older models)

## 1.2 QUESTIONS

1. Your client has a cracked laptop screen, but the laptop still works. Which of the following might be the most cost-effective solution?
   A. Replace the display panel
   B. Replace the display assembly
   C. Replace the laptop
   D. Replace the laptop with a desktop

2. Your client decided to have a laptop display assembly swapped. Now, the wireless doesn't work. Which of the following is the most likely cause?
   A. Webcam plugged into wireless card
   B. Wi-Fi card not reconnected to wireless antennas
   C. New assembly not compatible with current wireless card
   D. Wi-Fi wires broken during swap

3. A user reports that the laptop isn't displaying anything. However, when you plug in an external display, the laptop can be used. Which of the following would you check first?
   A. Digitizer
   B. Microphone
   C. Inverter
   D. Wi-Fi antennas

4. The wireless antennas in a laptop display assembly are usually located where?
   A. Lower left and right corners of the display
   B. Bottom center of the display
   C. Top center of the display
   D. Top left and right corners of the display

5. Your client uses a laptop for live chats with her salesforce, but her webcam has failed. The weekly chat is in two hours. What should you do?
   A. Arrange for an express swap of her display assembly
   B. Connect a USB webcam
   C. Reimage a spare laptop
   D. Advise her to cancel the chat

## 1.2 ANSWERS

1. **A**  Replace the display panel. The other components in the display assembly are working, so replacing only the panel is likely to be cheaper and probably faster than swapping the entire display assembly.

2. **B**  The Wi-Fi card is in the laptop base, so the wireless antenna wires must be disconnected to swap a display assembly. It's easy to forget to reattach them.

3.  **C**   Check the inverter (on laptops so equipped). When it fails, the built-in display becomes extremely dim.

4.  **D**   The antennas usually are located in the upper left and right corners of the display assembly.

5.  **B**   A USB webcam will work fine, may have better image quality than the built-in webcam, and can be installed and configured in plenty of time for the meeting.

## Objective 1.3   Given a scenario, use appropriate laptop features

Laptops are designed to squeeze a lot of power into a small space. To do so, many of them include a variety of specific features, from special function keys to rotating screens. This section reviews the options you might encounter.

## Special Function Keys

Laptop keyboards use the QWERTY key layout, just like regular keyboards (see Figure 1.3-1), but some laptop manufacturers get "creative" with the size and placement of other keys. Most use a *Function (fn) key* to enable other keys to double as media controls, hardware feature toggles, a number pad, and so on. Collectively, these are called *special function keys*.

**EXAM TIP**   Be sure to know the types of special function keys listed in Table 1.3-1. Keep in mind that there are no standards for special function keys, so don't be surprised if different models from the same vendor, let alone different brands, have different arrangements of special function keys.

**FIGURE 1.3-1**   Keyboard comparison

Table 1.3-1 describes these keys and provides typical examples of several. Press the FN key plus the additional key shown to perform the special function listed.

 **NOTE**    Some laptops set up the special functions as the primary use for the keys and require the user to press the FN key to use a key for its traditional purpose (for example, FN-F1 to get help, and so on). Look at the color of the FN key text and compare it to the markings on the keyboard to figure out when you need to use the FN key.

**TABLE 1.3-1**    Typical Laptop Special Function Keys

| Special Function Key | Usage | Example |
|---|---|---|
| Dual displays | Switches between built-in and external displays, or turns on both displays | F5 |
| Wireless (on/off) | Enables/disables Wi-Fi | F3 |
| Cellular (on/off) | Enables/disables cellular | |
| Volume settings | Adjusts volume | |
| Screen brightness | Adjusts screen brightness | F2   F3 |
| Bluetooth (on/off) | Enables/disables Bluetooth | |
| Keyboard backlight | Enables/disables keyboard backlight | F9 |
| Touchpad (on/off) | Enables/disables touchpad | F7 |
| Screen orientation | Changes screen orientation | |
| Media options (fast forward/rewind, play/pause, stop) | Controls media playback | Pg Dn   End   Home   Pg Up |
| GPS (on/off) | Enables/disables GPU | |
| Airplane mode | Enables/disables Airplane mode | |

**FIGURE 1.3-2**   Port replicator (bottom) versus docking station (top)

# Docking Station

Business-oriented laptops can connect (Transformers style) with *docking stations* that provide a host of single- and multi-function ports. The typical docking station uses a proprietary connection but adds ports or devices not present on the original laptop, such as a network port, optical drive, and so on (see Figure 1.3-2, top device).

# Port Replicator

A *port replicator* provides a permanent home for video, network, and audio cables that you would otherwise attach to and detach from a laptop as you move it around. Port replicators typically connect to the highest-bandwidth port (such as USB 3.0/3.1 or Thunderbolt) and subdivide the bandwidth among port devices. Figure 1.3-2 shows a typical port replicator for a MacBook Pro or Air compared with a docking station for a Microsoft Surface Pro.

**EXAM TIP**   The difference between port replicators and docking stations is sometimes unclear. For purposes of the CompTIA A+ 220-1001 exam, a docking station connects to a proprietary port, while a port replicator connects via a standard port. The Microsoft Surface Dock shown in Figure 1.3-2 is a true docking station because it plugs into the proprietary charging/docking port on the Surface Pro and adds a network port. The third-party port replicator for macOS-based laptops connects to a Thunderbolt 2 port on a MacBook, MacBook Air, or MacBook Pro.

# Physical Laptop Lock and Cable Lock

A *laptop lock* (also called a *cable lock*) loops around a solid object and locks to the small security hole on the side of the laptop (see Figure 1.3-3).

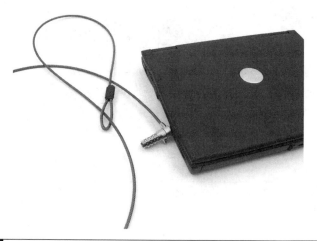

**FIGURE 1.3-3**   Cable lock

# Rotating/Removable Screens

A *convertible* laptop uses one of several mechanisms to "convert" into something you can use like a tablet. Some have removable screens that become standalone tablets (leaving behind any hardware built into the keyboard half), and others use innovative hinges that enable you to open the screen until it's flush with the bottom of the laptop; flip the screen to expose it when the laptop is closed; or pop the screen up from a default tablet position, revealing a keyboard. CompTIA refers to these screens as *rotating*.

A *hybrid* laptop/tablet has a tablet form factor that integrates with a detachable keyboard, which may double as a cover (see Figure 1.3-4). The line between a hybrid tablet that can attach to a keyboard and a convertible laptop with a removable tablet screen is hard to draw, so focus on what is lost when you use the tablet portion alone: if you just lose a keyboard, it's a hybrid.

**FIGURE 1.3-4**   Microsoft Surface Pro with its keyboard cover

# REVIEW

**Objective 1.3: Given a scenario, use appropriate laptop features**    Laptops might feature some or all of the following:

- Special function keys vary from model to model and are used to control laptop functions such as
    - Dual displays switch between built-in and external displays
    - Wireless (on/off)
    - Cellular (on/off)
    - Volume settings adjust internal or external speakers
    - Screen brightness adjusts internal display
    - Bluetooth (on/off)
    - Keyboard backlight might be on/off or have multiple brightness levels
    - Touchpad (on/off)
    - Screen orientation change from landscape (default) to portrait
    - Media options (fast forward/rewind) for A/V playback
    - GPS (on/off)
    - Airplane mode turns off all wireless/cellular connections
- Docking station is supported on some business-oriented laptops to provide additional types of ports or features.
- Port replicator is a device that connects to a high-bandwidth port (USB 3.0, USB 3.1, or Lightning) to provide additional ports of the same types as those onboard.
- Physical laptop and cable locks connect to supported laptops to help prevent theft.
- Rotating/removable screens are used on convertible and 2-in-1 laptops.

# 1.3 QUESTIONS

1. You are providing phone support for a user who wants to switch from her laptop's built-in display to an external display. Which of the following should you do first?

    **A.** Ask the user to describe the symbols on the special function keys to determine the correct key(s) to use

    **B.** Tell the user to use the same key combination that you use on your laptop

    **C.** Tell the user to check the laptop's instruction manual

    **D.** Tell the user to try pressing combinations of the FN key and different keys at random until she finds the correct combination

2. Your client is concerned about unauthorized Bluetooth connections to his laptop, but he can't find a function key to control Bluetooth. Which of the following is the best advice to give?

   **A.** Keep looking for the Bluetooth key

   **B.** Use Airplane mode to turn off Bluetooth

   **C.** Use the operating system to manage Bluetooth

   **D.** Unplug the Bluetooth adapter

3. Your client wants to buy laptops that can be expanded with additional ports not found in the base unit. The types of laptops your client is considering are designed to use which of the following?

   **A.** Port replicator

   **B.** USB hub

   **C.** MXM

   **D.** Docking station

4. While teaching a Microsoft Excel class, you instruct your students to press the F2 key to edit a formula. Some of your students must press and hold an additional key on their laptops to edit a formula. Which of the following keys would they need to press?

   **A.** ALT

   **B.** FN

   **C.** CTRL

   **D.** SPACE

5. Your client is a traveling salesperson on a business call and has forgotten the keyboard for her hybrid laptop at home. Which of the following is *not* a likely workaround?

   **A.** Onscreen keyboard

   **B.** Bluetooth keyboard

   **C.** PS/2 keyboard

   **D.** USB keyboard

## 1.3 ANSWERS

1. **A**   Looking at the keyboard markings is the first (and usually best) way to figure out the keys to use. The instruction manual is also helpful, but is often not available. You might need to prompt the user to describe some symbols to you.

2. **C**   Bluetooth, whether built-in or provided with a USB adapter, can be managed via the operating system.

3. **D**   A docking station provides features not found in the base unit. For example, the Microsoft Surface Dock for Surface Pro includes a Gigabit Ethernet port (the Surface Pro itself doesn't have one).

4. **B**   Some laptops use the special function keys as the primary function for function keys. On those computers, the user must hold down the FN key along with F2 to edit an Excel formula.

5. **C**   A PS/2 keyboard port is found on a few old laptops and some desktops, but not on hybrid laptop/tablet computers.

 **Compare and contrast characteristics of various types of other mobile devices**

In this objective, you learn about other popular devices from tablets and smartphones to wearables, GPS devices, and VR/AR headsets. Compared to laptops, mobile devices such as tablets and smartphones are lighter, generally no more than two pounds; are designed to fit in your hand, pocket, or purse; have a touch or stylus interface rather than an attached keyboard; are sealed units with no user-replaceable parts; use mobile operating systems. Wearables are wristwatch-sized devices. Some monitor vital signs, while others also display incoming e-mails and messages, as well as display time/date. GPS devices provide navigational assistance for drivers, boaters, flyers, bikers, and walkers. VR/AR headsets provide immersive 3-D for gaming and work applications.

> **EXAM TIP**   Be sure you understand the differences between smartphones and tablets, and can identify the unique features of wearable and GPS devices.

## Smartphones

In 2007, Apple introduced the first iPhone *smartphone*: a small, touchscreen-equipped computer with great support for backups, synchronization, and third-party apps, all piggybacking on a decades-old voice communication device called a "cell phone." Smartphones continually fold in new features as they move to the center of the trend toward ever-present connectivity and seamless data access across all our devices. The rear of a typical smartphone is shown in Figure 1.4-1.

Phones with larger screens are occasionally known as "phablets," such as the Samsung Note series and iPhone X Max and iPhone 11 Pro Max.

Compared to tablets, smartphones offer these advantages:

- More portability
- More connectivity options (cellular as well as wireless and Bluetooth)

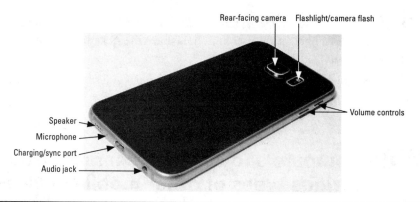

**FIGURE 1.4-1** Typical smartphone (rear view)

# Tablets

Tablets are very similar to smartphones; they run the same OSs and apps, and use the same multitouch touchscreens. From a tech's perspective, tablets are like large smartphones that use Wi-Fi instead of cellular connections in most cases. Whereas a typical smartphone screen is around 5 inches, tablets run around 7 to 12 inches (see Figure 1.4-2).

Compared to smartphones, tablets offer these advantages:

- Larger screens
- Louder speakers

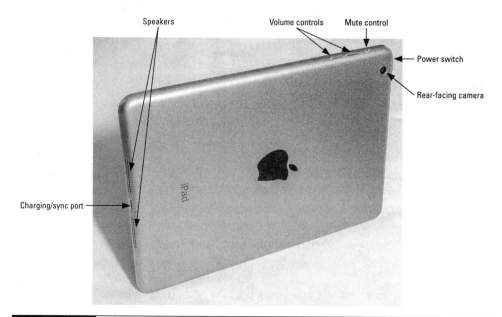

**FIGURE 1.4-2** Typical tablet (rear view)

| FIGURE 1.4-3 | Apple Watch |

# Wearable Technology Devices

As the name indicates, wearable technology devices are designed to be worn by users, which is accomplished by integrating tiny, limited computers with novel interfaces and a featherweight OS that leverages a host device (often a smartphone) for heavy lifting. The wearable devices listed in the CompTIA A+ 220-1001 objectives—smart watches, fitness monitors, and VR/AR headsets—seamlessly gather data (such as how active the device user is) and create new interfaces that integrate data and technology with the natural flow of daily life.

## Smart Watches

A *smart watch* connects to a smartphone to make tasks such as controlling music playback, providing fitness tracking, connections to contact lists and calendars, and checking e-mail, texts, notifications, time, and weather easier. Figure 1.4-3 shows a typical smart watch, the Apple Watch.

## Fitness Monitors

Common fitness monitor (aka fitness tracker) features include counting your steps using accelerometers, registering your heart rate through sensors, using the GPS network to track your exercise, and vibrating to prompt you to keep up with fitness goals. The two most popular fitness monitor formats are fobs that clip to your body and perform simple functions such as tracking your steps, and more sophisticated fitness wristbands (see Figure 1.4-4) that provide advanced features such as GPS tracking and heart-rate monitoring.

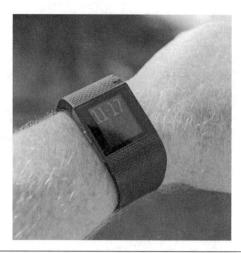

**FIGURE 1.4-4**   Mike's battered Fitbit Surge

## VR/AR Headsets

Virtual reality (VR) headsets, which create a 3-D world for gamers, have become a popular technology for both console and PC gamers. VR headsets create an immersive experience by mounting two high-resolution screens into a headset that blocks external visual sensory input. The latest VR goggles use organic light-emitting diode (OLED) technology to power the tiny, high-resolution stereo panels, while older models use LCD technology.

Mobile versions of VR headsets, such as the Samsung Gear VR, use a smartphone for computing power, while more powerful tethered models, such as the HTC Vive, are connected to a console game or a PC with a high-performance CPU and video card. A few models, such as the Oculus Quest, are standalone headsets, providing powerful 3-D rendering and motion control without tethering cables.

Augmented reality (AR) is also known as mixed reality. AR headsets combine transparent lenses with overlays that enable you to see 3-D objects in the real world, using beamsplitter, mirrors, or waveguide technologies. Although AR can be used for gaming, most AR is designed for use in work environments, such as projecting step-by-step visual guides for repairs, identifiers for people or objects in a crowd, showing how a new piece of furniture would look in a room, and much more.

**ADDITIONAL RESOURCES**   For a useful review of VR technologies and representative models, go to www.pcmag.com and search for "The Best VR Headsets." And, learn more about AR, VR, and mixed reality at www.realitytechnologies.com.

Microsoft has teamed up with several PC vendors to add this technology to Windows 10 games.

# E-readers

To give the obvious definition, an *e-reader* is a device designed for reading electronic books (e-books). The traditional e-reader uses e-paper screen technology to present a low-power grayscale screen that is eye-friendly and enables days or weeks of reading on a charge, and the typical user interface is a simple touch (see Figure 1.4-5) or button interface for obtaining, reading, and annotating e-books. Additional books can be downloaded via Wi-Fi.

 **EXAM TIP**   The popular Amazon Kindle and Barnes & Noble Nook e-reader lines have spawned reader apps and full-fledged tablets, but don't confuse either with a standalone e-reader.

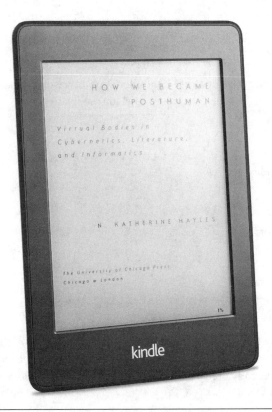

**FIGURE 1.4-5**   Kindle Paperwhite e-reader

# GPS

*Global Positioning System (GPS)* is based on 24 satellites that transmit their location and time to earth-based GPS receivers. The most common purpose-built GPS device is the navigational aid that mounts on a vehicle's dash or windshield, and you can buy the equivalent for boats, airplanes, bicycles, and more. There are even hand-held versions tailored to scuba diving, hiking, hunting, and so on—they have features that better suit them to their niche, such as preloaded special-purpose maps, waterproofing, impact resistance, route memory, bookmarking, stored locations, low-power use, simple replaceable batteries, other useful sensors or tools, and so on.

GPS support is also built into smartphones and smart watches, where it is used along with Bluetooth (when enabled), Wi-Fi hotspots, and cellular towers to determine your location. This feature, known as Location Services in iOS and Location in Android, can be accessed by mapping apps and other apps. However, apps can't use this information unless you provide permission.

 **ADDITIONAL RESOURCES**    To learn more about iOS Location Services, go to https://support.apple.com and search for Location Services.

# REVIEW

**Objective 1.4: Compare and contrast characteristics of various types of other mobile devices**    Mobile devices other than laptops include the following:

- Tablets
- Smartphones
- Wearable technology devices
    - Smart watches
    - Fitness monitors
    - VR/AR headsets
- E-readers
- GPS

## 1.4 QUESTIONS

1. You are preparing for a 15-hour flight and intend to spend most of the time reviewing *Mike Meyers' CompTIA A+ Certification Passport* and then maybe reading a novel. Your carry-on is already pretty full. Which of the following would best help you achieve your goals?

    **A.** Load e-book versions on your laptop and make sure its battery is fully charged

    **B.** Overstuff your carryon with bulky books and hope it doesn't get checked at the gate for an additional fee

    **C.** Load e-book versions on your e-reader

    **D.** Load e-book versions on your smartphone

2. You're playing a game that overlays 3-D figures over what you see around you. What is this an example of?

    **A.** Smart watch

    **B.** Augmented reality

    **C.** Virtual reality

    **D.** None of the above

3. A smart watch needs which of the following to work?

    **A.** Smartphone

    **B.** VR headset

    **C.** GPS

    **D.** E-reader

4. Which type of mobile device is available in specialized versions for airplanes, boats, hunting, hiking, and scuba diving?

    **A.** Smart phone

    **B.** Smart watch

    **C.** E-reader

    **D.** GPS

5. A tethered VR headset connects to which of the following?

    **A.** Smartphone

    **B.** PC or console

    **C.** GPS

    **D.** Tablet

## 1.4 ANSWERS

1. **C** An e-reader will enable you to read both fiction and nonfiction books, with minimal bulk and a comfortable screen size. Compared to laptops, e-readers have long battery life, so a 15-hour flight is no problem.

2. **B** Augmented reality combines real-world, real-time scenes with 3-D objects.

3. **A** A smart watch connects to a smartphone, which sends/receives messages and phone calls, updates calendars, and so on.

4. **D** GPS devices are available in many different variations for different types of uses.

5. **B** A tethered VR headset relies on the GPU in a PC or console for 3-D rendering.

### Objective 1.5 Given a scenario, connect and configure accessories and ports of other mobile devices

Mobile devices are small and portable, but thanks to a variety of wired and wireless connections, they can also be versatile. In this objective, you are introduced to the main types of accessories available for mobile devices and the ways in which they can be connected.

## Connection Types

Mobile devices have many of the same types of connections and options as desktop devices do. These include wired ports, wireless devices, and accessories.

### Wired

Wired connections can be used for data synchronization and transfer to a larger computer, for charging, and for tethering to share a cellular connection. You need to be able to identify several wired connection types for the CompTIA A+ 220-1001 exam.

#### Micro-USB/Mini-USB/USB-C

The most common family of wired connections used for mobile devices is the USB family. Recent and current Android smartphones and tablets use USB-C connectors. However, older phones used the micro-USB (USB-on-the Go) connector.

Apple now uses USB-C for its third generation of iPad Pro tablets released in November 2018, replacing the Lightning connector it had used previously. Figure 1.5-1 compares USB-C to micro-USB and Lightning cables.

> **Cross-Reference**
>
> To learn more about these cables, their features, and how they are used, see Part I, Domain 3.0, Objectives 3.1/3.2.

**FIGURE 1.5-1**    From left to right, USB-C, micro-USB, and Lightning cables

## Lightning

Starting with the iPhone 5, iPod Touch (5th generation), and iPod Nano (7th generation) in 2012, Apple began to use the proprietary Lightning connector for charging and sync. It continues to use Lightning for most mobile devices. However, with Apple's decision to switch to USB-C for its third-generation iPad Pro tablets, Lightning might eventually be replaced.

## Tethering

Both Android and Apple mobile devices support *tethering*, in which the device's USB or Lightning connector is used to share its cellular connection with another device via its USB connector.

## Proprietary Vendor-specific Ports (Communication/Power)

Before the advent of standardized USB mini and micro ports for communications and power, early smartphones and feature phones used a wide variety of proprietary connectors. Many third-party chargers included a variety of adapters for the different brands' proprietary connectors. Before Apple adopted the current Lightning proprietary connector, it used a proprietary 30-pin connector for charging its early mobile devices.

# Wireless

Mobile devices use Wi-Fi and cellular for network connectivity, as discussed in the next section covering objective 1.6, but their wireless connectivity options also include technologies for convenient short-range communication.

## NFC

*Near Field Communication (NFC)* uses chips embedded in mobile devices that create electromagnetic fields when these devices are close to each other or touching each other (typical ranges are anywhere from a very few centimeters to only a few inches). The fields can be used to exchange contact information, small files, and even payment transactions through stored credit cards using systems like Apple Pay and Google Pay.

The exact features supported by a smartphone are determined by the OS. For example, Apple supports NFC only for Apple Pay, while Android smartphones also support file transfer.

## Bluetooth

*Bluetooth* is a short-range wireless technology that can be used for PAN (personal area networking), connections to wireless speakers, mice, and keyboards, and connections to headsets, microphones, and wearables. (The process of pairing Bluetooth devices so that they can communicate is described in the next section covering objective 1.6.). Bluetooth implementations in mobile devices generally have a range of no more than 10 meters (about 33 feet).

### IR

*Infrared (IR)* is an old and slow wireless technology that was once used for printing and file transfer. Smartphones that include IR support can be used as universal remotes for TVs by installing the appropriate app.

## Hotspot

Many smartphones and tablets with cellular support can share their cellular Internet connection with other devices by enabling a *hotspot*. The hotspot feature turns the device into a wireless router with an SSID and password. By sharing that information with Wi-Fi enabled devices, they can connect to the Internet. The range of a hotspot connection varies according to the Wi-Fi standard used by the smartphone and the location (outdoors has a longer range than indoors).

 **EXAM TIP**   Be able differentiate the wireless connection types, including NFC, Bluetooth, IR, and hotspot.

# Accessories

Although mobile devices have many built-in features, they can use accessories to provide even more functionality. The following sections describe the accessories you need to understand for this objective.

## Headsets

Headsets can connect to mobile devices via traditional 3.5-mm mini-jacks, USB, or wirelessly via Bluetooth. Headsets designed for use with smartphones or gaming include microphones.

## Speakers

Mobile devices often have very small speakers with limited power. To increase volume and make it easier for groups to hear music, connect external speakers via 3.5-mm speaker jacks or wirelessly via Bluetooth.

## Game Pads

Game pads, traditionally used with PC and console games, are also available for Android and iOS mobile devices. They use Bluetooth wireless connectivity. If you are looking for a controller for an iPhone, MFi (made for iPhone) controllers are your best bet.

## Extra Battery Packs/Battery Chargers

A mobile device becomes a paperweight without a battery charger. While most laptops have easily removable batteries, tablets and smartphones must rely on built-in batteries, AC or

| **TABLE 1.5-1** | External Battery Pack Comparison | |
|---|---|---|
| **Charger Type** | **Smartphone/Tablet** | **Smartphone** |
| Input voltage/amp | 5-V DC/2 A | 5-V DC/1 A |
| Output voltage/amp | 5-V DC/2.1 A | 5-V DC/1.5 A |
| Capacity (mAh) | 10,000 | 4000 |

12-V DC battery chargers, or portable battery packs. Phones designed to use wireless charger pads support the Qi standard.

 **NOTE**   The Qi standard is the de facto safe wireless charging standard. It was developed by the Wireless Power Consortium (www.wirelesspowerconsortium.com). Qi provides from 5 to 15 watts of power to small personal electronic devices, including tablets, smartphones, and mice.

External battery packs for charging mobile devices typically use a micro-USB or USB-C connector to charge the internal battery, and then one or two USB Type-A ports for charging smartphones or tablets. A port with 2.1 amp or higher output can charge a tablet or a smartphone. Battery packs are rated in mAh (milliampere-hour). The higher the rating, the more devices it can recharge before it must be recharged itself. Table 1.5-1 compares the markings on two typical battery packs. Note that chargers made for tablets have higher amp output than chargers made only for smartphones.

## Protective Covers/Waterproofing

Smartphones and tablets are very vulnerable to impact and water damage. Although some recent models now have water-resistant designs, impact damage is a threat for all models. For maximum protection, the best protective covers combine a flexible rubber lining with covers over I/O ports to guard against water damage and a hard-external shell. Some include a clear protective overlay for the screen.

 **NOTE**   Look for a device's IP rating (Ingres Protection rating) for water resistance. IP68 and IP67 are most resistant to water.

## Credit Card Readers

Credit card readers from Square and other vendors make it possible for smartphone and tablet users to accept credit and debit cards at bazaars, farmers' markets, and other venues.

Most readers plug into the 3.5-mm audio jack, but some vendors also offer credit card readers for Lightning devices or offer adapters for connecting Lightning or USB-C to the 3.5-mm audio jack.

## Memory/MicroSD

Some Android and Windows mobile devices feature expandable storage by including a microSD card slot (most also support microSD HD and microSD XC versions). Depending on the operating system, the additional storage can be used for data or for programs.

# REVIEW

**Objective 1.5: Given a scenario, connect and configure accessories and ports of other mobile devices**    Mobile devices feature various types of connections and accessories.

- Wired connections include
  - Micro-USB
  - Mini-USB
  - USB-C
  - Lightning
  - Proprietary
- Wireless connections include
  - NFC
  - Bluetooth
  - IR
  - Hotspot
- Accessories include
  - Headsets
  - Speakers
  - Game pads
  - Extra battery packs
  - Battery chargers
  - Protective covers/waterproofing
  - Credit card readers
  - Memory (microSD)

## 1.5 QUESTIONS

1. Which of the following chargers supports both tablets and smartphones and has the largest capacity?
   - **A.** 1.5-amp output, 2000 mAh
   - **B.** 2.1-amp output, 5600 mAh
   - **C.** 1.5-amp output, 10,000 mAh
   - **D.** 2.1-amp output, 10,000 mAh

2. Bluetooth can be used for which of the following accessories? (Choose all that apply.)
   - **A.** Headset
   - **B.** Battery pack
   - **C.** Game pad
   - **D.** Speaker

3. Your supervisor asks you about using a smartphone to make a payment at a convenience store. Which feature needs to be activated?
   - **A.** USB
   - **B.** Tethering
   - **C.** NFC
   - **D.** Hotspot

4. Your client has just purchased a new model iPad Pro. Which type of charge/sync cable does she need to use?
   - **A.** Lightning
   - **B.** USB-C
   - **C.** Thunderbolt
   - **D.** 30-pin

5. You're getting ready to sell your artwork and want to be able to accept payment by credit cards via your older Android phone. What type of connection will you use for your card reader?
   - **A.** Lightning
   - **B.** USB-C
   - **C.** 3.5-mm audio jack
   - **D.** Mini-USB

## 1.5 ANSWERS

1. **D** 2.1-amp output supports both smartphones and tablets, and 10,000 mAh is the highest battery capacity of those listed.

2. **A C D** Bluetooth cannot be used for battery charging but works with Bluetooth-equipped speakers, headsets, game pads, and other input/output devices.

3. **C**   Near Field Communication (NFC) can be used for cardless payment at convenience stores.

4. **B**   The newest iPad Pro models have switched from Lightning to USB-C.

5. **C**   Android phones use the 3.5-mm audio jack for credit card readers.

## Objective 1.6 Given a scenario, configure basic mobile device network connectivity and application support

In this objective, you learn how to configure cellular, e-mail, and other mobile connectivity.

## Wireless/Cellular Data Network (Enable/Disable)

The default settings for wireless (Wi-Fi) and cellular data networks on a smartphone or cellular-equipped tablet is on. However, you can also share or disable these functions.

### Hotspot

A mobile *hotspot* device creates a Wi-Fi network to share its cellular data connection (3G, 4G, 4G LTE, or 5G) with other Wi-Fi devices. Wireless providers sell standalone hotspot devices for their network, but many smartphones and tablets with cellular access can act as hotspots. Just enable the cellular data connection and toggle the hotspot setting to broadcast the Wi-Fi network and serve as a router between it and the cellular network (see Figure 1.6-1); configure a password to limit access. Some people use the term *tethering* as a synonym for *hotspot*.

### Tethering

Tethering more properly describes the use of a USB port to share a cellular connection with just one device. To enable tethering, connect a device via USB to your smartphone, open the Tethering or Mobile Hotspot and Tethering menu, and enable USB tethering.

Both mobile hotspots and tethering are cost-effective ways to give additional devices cellular Internet access on an occasional basis.

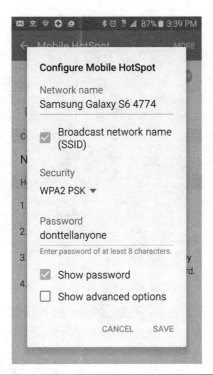

**FIGURE 1.6-1**  Configuring an Android phone as a portable hotspot

# Airplane Mode

*Airplane mode* (see Figure 1.6-2) is simply a hardware or software switch that turns off all cellular and wireless services, including Bluetooth. The aptly named mode disables these features so passengers can comply with restrictions protecting aircraft instruments from interference, although it's also a shortcut for turning off communication functions.

**FIGURE 1.6-2**  Airplane mode enabled on Android 7

**TABLE 1.6-1** Bluetooth Setup Process

| Step | What It Does |
|---|---|
| Enable Bluetooth | Turns on Bluetooth connectivity. |
| Enable pairing | Enables the device to find and be found by other Bluetooth devices. |
| Find a device for pairing | Locates and lists nearby Bluetooth devices available to pair with (headset, keyboard, etc.). |
| Enter the appropriate pin code or press a button on the device. | Makes the pairing connection between the Bluetooth host and device. |
| Test connectivity | Confirms that the devices can communicate. Use the Bluetooth device to play music, record audio, type, etc. |

# Bluetooth

As discussed in the previous objective, Bluetooth is a popular way to connect many different types of accessories. Table 1.6-1 covers the process of using Bluetooth on a mobile device.

 **EXAM TIP** Given a scenario, know the setup process for Bluetooth pairing.

# Corporate and ISP E-mail Configuration

The process of setting up e-mail on a mobile device has the same steps as when you set up e-mail on a laptop or desktop computer. The difference is that with iOS or Android, you set up e-mail through the Accounts section of Settings rather than with an e-mail client. All e-mail clients use either POP3 or IMAP protocols to receive mail. If you use a web browser to check your e-mail, you are using webmail.

## POP3

POP3 (Post Office Protocol 3) e-mail's default setting is to download messages from the server to the device. If you leave this feature enabled, the messages you receive on your phone will be stored only on your phone and the messages you receive on other devices, such as your computer, will be stored only on those devices, scattering your e-mails across devices.

Instead of using this default, leave your messages on the e-mail server. However, keep in mind that if you receive loads of e-mail every day, you will need to delete it from the server so that your e-mail box doesn't overflow. If you can use IMAP to check your e-mail instead of POP3, you're much better off for two reasons: your e-mail stays on the server and POP3 is not secure.

## IMAP

IMAP (Internet Message Access Protocol) is far better than POP3 for mobile users to access e-mail. With IMAP, not only do your messages stay on the server, regardless of which device you use to access them, but you can set up folders to organize your mail. IMAP also supports webmail. Your e-mail provider decides which protocol to use, IMAP or POP3, but the good news is that POP3 is fading away.

**EXAM TIP**   Simple mail transfer protocol (SMTP) is used by both POP3 and IMAP to send e-mail.

## Port and SSL Settings

If you need to manually set up an e-mail account, you might need to provide the appropriate port settings for the protocols your e-mail provider uses. Table 1.6-2 provides the original and secure port settings for these e-mail protocols.

If you are unable to use automatic setup for your e-mail account, it's because you need to enter nonstandard port or secure e-mail settings. To get the specific settings needed for your account, contact your e-mail provider.

## S/MIME

*S/MIME (Secure/Multipurpose Internet Mail Extensions)* is a popular standard for encrypting e-mail. To be able to send or receive S/MIME e-mail, you must purchase an S/MIME certificate from a cybersecurity provider such as Comodo, install it, and configure it.

**ADDITIONAL RESOURCES**   To learn more about getting an S/MIME certificate, go to https://ssl.comodo.com and search for "S/MIME."

**TABLE 1.6-2**   E-mail Protocol Port Reference

| E-mail Protocol | Original TCP Port | Secure TCP Port(s) |
|---|---|---|
| SMTP | 25 | 465 or 587 |
| POP3 | 110 | 995 |
| IMAP | 143 | 993 |

# Integrated Commercial Provider E-mail Configuration

The CompTIA A+ 220-1001 objectives want you to know about this whale of a phrase: *integrated commercial provider e-mail configuration*. iOS, Android, and Windows mobile devices have baked-in e-mail service from the OS developer. iOS devices integrate perfectly with iCloud, Apple's one-stop shop for e-mail, messaging, and online storage. Android devices assume a Gmail account, so they feature Gmail/Inbox front and center. Windows devices integrate Microsoft Exchange Online e-mail. Mobile devices also support corporate and ISP e-mail. Almost every mobile device also enables you to add other e-mail providers as well, such as Yahoo or Microsoft Outlook.com.

 **EXAM TIP** Be familiar with integrated commercial provider e-mail configuration settings for Google's Inbox (Inbox by Gmail), Yahoo, Exchange Online, and iCloud.

## iCloud

To configure iCloud on Apple devices, go through the Settings app, then the Passwords & Accounts option (see Figure 1.6-3). Tap the Add Account option for the default e-mail options (see Figure 1.6-4). For a Microsoft Exchange Server e-mail account, tap the appropriate option

**FIGURE 1.6-3** The Passwords & Accounts screen on the iPhone (iOS 12.x)

**FIGURE 1.6-4**    The default e-mail accounts in iOS

and enter the e-mail address, domain, user name, password, and description. Apple's suggested options skip POP3 and IMAP4; to find them, tap the Other option on the initial Add Account screen. When prompted, choose POP3 or IMAP4 and type in addresses for the sending (SMTP) and receiving servers.

## Google/Inbox

Android devices assume you'll have a Gmail account as your primary account, so you'll often find the Gmail icon on the home screen (see Figure 1.6-5). If you prefer to use other e-mail accounts (Exchange, POP3, or IMAP), tap the Email icon, tap the Menu button, tap the Settings (gearbox) icon, and tap Add Account. Configure it with the server names, port number and security type, such as SSL or TLS (see Figure 1.6-6).

## Exchange Online

To set up a Microsoft Exchange Online account, open the Accounts menu in your iOS or Android device's Settings app. Select Add Account and select Exchange. You can choose Automatic or Manual setup. If you select Manual, choose your e-mail account type, enter your password, incoming and outgoing server names, and any additional information required by the provider.

**FIGURE 1.6-5** Gmail app icon (top right) on the home screen

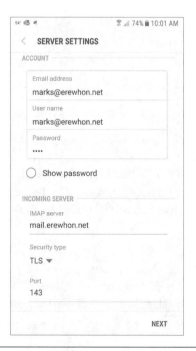

**FIGURE 1.6-6** Setting up a secure IMAP4 account

## Yahoo

To set up a Yahoo account, open the open the Accounts menu in your iOS or Android device's Settings app. Select Add Account and select Yahoo. Enter your username and password.

# PRI Updates/PRL Updates/Baseband Updates

As mobile devices travel, they frequently have to pass through areas that don't have strong signals, or into areas that the carrier does not service, and maintain connection by roaming on another carrier's network. Your phone's firmware gets occasional updates to its *Preferred Roaming List (PRL)*, a priority-ordered list of other carrier networks and frequencies, sent via your phone's cellular connection (called baseband updates, or over-the-air updates) or through normal OS updates. Updates to the PRL are also sent to cell towers. As the PRL is updated, devices can roam further from their own providers' coverage area.

Code division multiple access (CDMA) devices may also receive *product release instruction (PRI)* updates that modify a host of complex device settings. Don't worry about specifics, here—but a device may need PRI updates if the network is evolving during the lifetime of the device, the device is moving to a new network, or the device has a new owner.

 **EXAM TIP**   PRL and PRI updates are handled automatically during firmware/OS updates. They are only for CDMA networks. No one but the nerdiest of nerds will ever see these updates.

# Radio Firmware

Radio firmware updates are provided by the broadband vendor (with Android phones) or by Apple (with iOS phones). Follow the directions from the vendor to install these updates.

# IMEI vs. IMSI

What's the difference between IMEI and IMSI?

 **EXAM TIP**   Know that an IMEI identifies the device and an IMSI identifies the user of the device.

- The 15-digit *International Mobile Equipment Identity (IMEI)* number uniquely identifies a Global System for Mobile Communications (GSM) mobile device (including 4G LTE and LTE-Advanced). Carriers can use the IMEI number, which is often printed inside the battery compartment, to block a device from the network (for example, if the device owner notifies the carrier that the device has been lost or stolen).

- The *International Mobile Subscriber Identity (IMSI)* number, included on the SIM, represents the actual user associated with the SIM. This number can be used to unlock a phone or to ensure a stolen phone isn't misused.

 **NOTE**   The Integrated Circuit Card Identifier (ICCID) uniquely identifies a subscriber identity module (SIM). The SIM, which authenticates the subscriber to the network, can usually be moved from phone to phone with no problems.

# VPN

A *virtual private network (VPN)* securely connects a remote client and the corporate infrastructure, or a branch office and the corporate office. VPNs create an encrypted tunnel through an unsecure network such as the Internet. The most popular ways to set up a VPN use either a combination of the Layer 2 Tunneling Protocol (L2TP) and IPsec, or Secure Sockets Layer (SSL)/Transport Layer Security (TLS).

Using the L2TP/IPsec method, you configure a client (see Figure 1.6-7) to match server settings (the UDP port, usually 1701, must be open), connect to the corporate network, and then use network applications, such as your e-mail client, and map shares and drives as if you

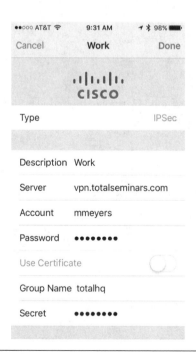

**FIGURE 1.6-7**   Configuring a VPN

were actually connected onsite to the corporate infrastructure. An SSL/TLS-based VPN typically connects through a web browser via the standard SSL/TLS port (TCP 443) instead of a specially configured client, but lacks direct

# REVIEW

**Objective 1.6: Given a scenario, configure basic mobile device network connectivity and application support**   Wireless/cellular data network features that can be enabled or disabled include the following:

- Hotspot
- Tethering
- Airplane mode

Bluetooth setup has the following steps:

1. Enable Bluetooth.
2. Enable pairing.
3. Find a device for pairing.
4. Enter the appropriate pin code.
5. Test connectivity.

E-mail features to understand include

- POP3 e-mail is not recommended for portable devices because it downloads new messages off the server by default to your current device. If you use both mobile and desktop computers to check your e-mail, different messages will be stored on each device.
- IMAP keeps messages on the server and allows you to organize them into folders. It also supports webmail.
- Standard port and SSL/TLS settings can be changed by e-mail providers, in which case you need to configure the settings manually.
- S/MIME e-mail encryption requires the user to install an S/MIME certificate.
- Integrated commercial provider e-mail accounts that are available include iCloud, Google/Inbox (Gmail), Exchange Online, and Yahoo.
- PRI, PRL, and baseband updates are provided by cellular carriers.
- Radio firmware is provided by the broadband or device vendor.
- IMEI is a unique identifier for GSM devices.
- IMSI is the user associated with a SIM.
- A VPN (virtual private network) enables secure connections over the Internet, even over unsecure public connections.

## 1.6 QUESTIONS

1. Your client's smartphone has been lost and is presumably stolen. Which of the following can the carrier use to prevent others from using the phone?

    **A.** IMEI

    **B.** SIM

    **C.** VPN

    **D.** Bluetooth

2. Your firm is considering trying a service that would set up secure Wi-Fi connections while users are working from a coffee shop or hotel lobby. Which of the following is being considered?

    **A.** Bluetooth

    **B.** IMSI

    **C.** VPN

    **D.** iCloud

3. Which of the following enables you to use your mobile device for reading without interfering with aviation navigation systems?

    **A.** GPS

    **B.** Airplane mode

    **C.** IMSI

    **D.** Exchange

4. You are getting ready to try out a new Bluetooth headset for your smartphone. After you enable Bluetooth and turn on the headset, which of the following do you need to do to use the headset?

    **A.** Tether the headset

    **B.** Connect to the hotspot in the phone

    **C.** Pair the headset with the phone

    **D.** Run a program

5. You are helping a user at a company that runs its own e-mail server to configure a smartphone to use it. Which of the following would you select to start the process?

    **A.** Yahoo

    **B.** Gmail

    **C.** Outlook

    **D.** None of the above

## 1.6 ANSWERS

1. **A**  The IMEI number can be given to the provider to block the phone from being used by unauthorized people.

2. **C**  A virtual private network (VPN) creates a secure "tunnel" for running Wi-Fi on a public network.

3. **B**  Airplane mode turns off all radios (cellular, Wi-Fi, Bluetooth) but keeps the device on.

4. **C**  You must pair a new Bluetooth device with your mobile device before you can use it.

5. **D**  A private e-mail account doesn't use these settings. Instead, you would enter the correct settings manually.

# Objective 1.7  Given a scenario, use methods to perform mobile device synchronization

People generally want their contacts and calendars to match across their devices, so for the CompTIA A+ 220-1001, you need to know how to configure mobile devices to synchronize data to maintain one set of contacts, one e-mail inbox, one calendar, and so forth. Smartphones and tablets use local machines or cloud-based servers to *synchronize*, or *sync*, personal documents, Internet bookmarks, calendar appointments, social media data, e-books, and even location data.

## Synchronization Methods

We used to sync to a desktop (uphill, in the snow!) with bundled software that only handled contacts—but it beat not syncing. Now, you can wirelessly sync contacts, media files, apps, and even OS updates.

### Synchronize to the Cloud

Each vendor has its own cloud technology to store personal data from your mobile device: Apple iCloud, Microsoft OneDrive, and Google Drive. Independent cloud providers such as Dropbox enable you to store and even share files.

You can sync to the cloud from any wireless connection, but be wary of syncing over unsecure public wireless networks. Finally, once your data is in the cloud, you no longer fully control it. You are at the mercy of the limits, security mechanisms, and privacy policies of your provider.

## Synchronize to the Desktop

Synchronizing your data to a computer gives you full control of storing, encrypting, and protecting your own data, but you must be able to connect to your computer. For Windows users, SyncToy, despite its cutesy name, is a powerful file sync app. If you're looking for cross-platform (Windows, Linux, macOS) file sync, check out FreeFileSync.

 **ADDITIONAL RESOURCES** Learn more about SyncToy at www.microsoft .com. Learn more about FreeFileSync and other file sync apps at www.capterra.com; search for "file sync."

## Synchronize to the Automobile

Synchronizing your smartphone to your auto's entertainment system enables you to use it for hands-free, voice-activated calling. However, many vehicles disable the pairing function while the car is in motion. Before you head out on a trip across town or across the country, take a few minutes to figure out how to pair your smartphone with your auto's entertainment system via Bluetooth. Do it before starting out, and you can drive and use your phone hands-free.

 **ADDITIONAL RESOURCES** For tips and how-to's, go to www.lifewire.com and search for "Pair a Cell Phone with Your Car."

# Types of Data to Synchronize

You can synchronize many types of data, depending on the apps you use (examples in parentheses):

- Contacts (Facebook, e-mail)
- Applications (app store)
- E-mail
- Pictures (OneDrive, iCloud, Dropbox, Google Drive)
- Music (OneDrive, iCloud, Dropbox, Google Drive)
- Videos (OneDrive, iCloud, Dropbox, Google Drive)
- Calendar (Google Calendar, Apple Calendar, Outlook.com, Exchange)
- Bookmarks (browsers)
- Documents (OneDrive, iCloud, Dropbox, Google Drive)
- Location data (Google Maps, MapQuest)
- Social media data (Facebook, Twitter, Instagram, and so on)

- E-books (Amazon Kindle, Barnes & Noble Nook)
- Passwords (password managers such as LastPass)

# Mutual Authentication for Multiple Services (SSO)

It's hard to tell what CompTIA expects from this phrase, but a properly coded app on a modern mobile device can use single sign-on (SSO) to let you log in with another account you're probably already logged into, such as Google, Apple ID, Facebook, or Twitter.

 **EXAM TIP** Single sign-on is an authentication method that allows you to access multiple apps and websites by logging on only once with a single set of credentials (username and password).

# Software Requirements to Install the Application on the PC

Some types of synchronization happen automatically. For example, if you use a web-based password-management app, it's always available to you. Microsoft synchronizes settings for Windows 10 for any user with a Microsoft account. It doesn't matter what device you use when you're posting on social media. However, file synchronization to cloud storage apps, as opposed to built-in synchronization in specific apps, doesn't happen magically.

Although you can perform cloud file synchronization with your browser, it's easier to install the appropriate apps and configure them with your account information. To do so, your systems must meet the software requirements of the apps you plan to synchronize. For example, the OneDrive desktop sync app works with 32-bit or 64-bit versions of Windows 7 or later, macOS 10.12 or later, or Windows Server 2008 R2 or later. The OneDrive mobile app for iOS requires iOS 11.3 or later. The OneDrive mobile app for Android requires Android 6.0 or later.

 **ADDITIONAL RESOURCES** Check the https://support.office.com website to learn more about OneDrive requirements. Check the https://help.dropbox.com website to learn about Dropbox requirements. Check the https://support.google.com website to learn about Google Drive requirements.

# Connection Types to Enable Synchronization

To synchronize with cloud service providers, you must connect to the Internet. To synchronize to your computer, you must have a local or network connection to the drive(s) or devices you want to synchronize. To synchronize to your automobile, you must enable Bluetooth and pair your smartphone and car entertainment system.

**EXAM TIP**    Know the connection types to use, the types of data you can synchronize, and the methods (to cloud, to computer, to automobile).

# REVIEW

**Objective 1.7: Given a scenario, use methods to perform mobile device synchronization**    Synchronization methods include

- To the cloud
- To the desktop
- To the automobile

The types of data you can synchronize include

- Contacts
- Applications
- E-mail
- Pictures
- Music
- Videos
- Calendar
- Bookmarks
- Documents
- Location data
- Social media data
- E-books
- Passwords

You can use SSO to connect to a service such as Google, Apple ID, Facebook, or Twitter. Your system must meet the software requirements to install a sync application on your PC. You must be able to connect to the cloud (Internet) for cloud synchronization, to drives or networks for computer synchronization, or via Bluetooth to your auto's entertainment system for automobile synchronization.

# 1.7 QUESTIONS

1. Which service could you use for document and photo synchronization?

    **A.** Facebook

    **B.** Kindle

    **C.** Twitter

    **D.** iCloud

2. Your client forgot to install the OneDrive app on her new smartphone before leaving on a business trip and now needs to retrieve files from her cloud account. Which of the following would be the best workaround to recommend to her?

    **A.** Ask the administrative assistant to e-mail the files

    **B.** Use FTP to retrieve the files

    **C.** Use the phone's browser

    **D.** Worry and fret over lack of connection

3. You and your supervisor are driving a rental car to a meeting and are trying to sync one of your phones to the entertainment system. It doesn't work. What's the most likely reason?

    **A.** Different versions of Bluetooth

    **B.** Pairing disabled while vehicle in motion

    **C.** Must use a proprietary cable

    **D.** Can't pair a car you are renting

4. To save time on your next trip, you looked up the directions to the restaurants you want to visit and stored them using Google Maps on your tablet. However, when you try to look up the directions on your smartphone, they're not available. What is the most likely cause?

    **A.** You must log into Google Maps to get stored directions.

    **B.** You forgot to e-mail them to yourself.

    **C.** You must sync your phone to the GPS in your car.

    **D.** Your tablet and smartphone don't use the same operating system.

5. Your client wants to use the OneDrive mobile app for iOS but can't install it. Which of the following would you check first?

    **A.** Amount of free space on the iOS device

    **B.** Whether blocking of Microsoft apps in the app store is enabled

    **C.** Whether the user has a Microsoft account

    **D.** Which iOS version is installed

## 1.7 ANSWERS

1. **D**   iCloud can be used for document and photo sync.

2. **C**   OneDrive supports file sync through web browsers.

3. **B**   Some vehicles don't support pairing while the vehicle is in motion, so pull over and try it again.

4. **A**   You must log into Google Maps to get stored directions

5. **D**   An old version of iOS will prevent the OneDrive mobile app from installing. Chances are it won't even be listed in the user's app store until the device is updated.

# Networking

DOMAIN
2.0

## Domain Objectives

- **2.1** Compare and contrast TCP and UDP ports, protocols, and their purposes
- **2.2** Compare and contrast common networking hardware devices
- **2.3** Given a scenario, install and configure a basic wired/wireless SOHO network
- **2.4** Compare and contrast wireless networking protocols
- **2.5** Summarize the properties and purposes of services provided by networked hosts
- **2.6** Explain common network configuration concepts
- **2.7** Compare and contrast Internet connection types, network types, and their features
- **2.8** Given a scenario, use appropriate networking tools

**Objective 2.1** **Compare and contrast TCP and UDP ports, protocols, and their purposes**

The Transmission Control Protocol (TCP) and User Datagram Protocol (UDP) are two key components of a TCP/IP network. Although both are used to transport information, they differ in several important ways, as you will learn in this objective.

## Ports and Protocols

Protocols handle data transfer details, such as how to pack and unpack data with protocol-specific *packet* formats. The most famous protocol is the *Transmission Control Protocol/Internet Protocol (TCP/IP)* used by most modern networks, including the Internet—though TCP/IP is technically a big group of protocols. Let's look at a simple example.

**NOTE**   The terms *packet* and *frame* get used interchangeably quite often, but they actually mean different things. A *frame* is used in Ethernet networks, and a *packet* is used in TCP/IP networks such as the Internet.

TCP and UDP both use port numbers to identify the type of connection being used. Table 2.1-1 provides a quick reference to application protocols and the TCP port numbers they use. Table 2.1-2 provides a quick reference to utility protocols (protocols that are hidden "behind the scenes" protocols) and the TCP and UDP port numbers they use.

**TABLE 2.1-1**   Application Protocols

| TCP Port Number | Application Protocol | Function |
|---|---|---|
| 21 | FTP (File Transfer Protocol) | File transfer |
| 22 | SSH (Secure Shell) | Encrypted terminal emulation |
| 23 | Telnet | Terminal emulation (not secure) |
| 25 | SMTP (Simple Mail Transfer Protocol) | Outgoing e-mail |
| 80 | HTTP (Hypertext Transfer Protocol) | Web pages (not secure) |
| 110 | POP3 (Post Office Protocol 3) | Incoming e-mail |
| 143 | IMAP (Internet Message Access Protocol) | Incoming e-mail |
| 443 | HTTPS (HTTP Secure, HTTP over SSL) | Secure web pages |
| 3389 | RDP (Remote Desktop Protocol) | Remote Desktop |

**TABLE 2.1-2**   Utility Protocols

| Port Number | Protocol Type | Utility Protocol | Function |
|---|---|---|---|
| 53 | UDP | DNS (Domain Name Service) | Allows the use of DNS naming |
| 67, 68 | UDP | DHCP (Dynamic Host Configuration Protocol) | Automatic IP addressing provided by a DHCP server |
| 137, 138 | UDP | NetBIOS/NetBT (NetBIOS over TCP/IP) | Enables legacy (pre-TCP/IP) apps to run on TCP/IP networks |
| 137, 139 | TCP | NetBIOS/NetBT (NetBIOS over TCP/IP) | Enables legacy (pre-TCP/IP) apps to run on TCP/IP networks |
| 161, 162 | UDP | SNMP (Simple Network Management Protocol) | Remote management of network devices |
| 389 | TCP | LDAP (Lightweight Directory Access Protocol) | Querying directories |
| 445 | TCP | SMB/CIFS (Server Message Block/Common Internet File Sharing) | Windows naming/folder sharing and cross-platform file sharing |
| 427 | TCP/UDP | SLP (Service Location Protocol) | Services discovery protocol |
| 548 | TCP | AFP (Apple File Protocol) | macOS file services |

 **EXAM TIP**   Be able to identify the various TCP and UDP ports and associated protocols.

 **NOTE**   Apps with network support use many additional TCP and UDP ports. To see a comprehensive real-time report on TCP and UDP activity on a computer running Windows, download the free LiveTcpUdpWatch utility from NirSoft.

# TCP vs. UDP

TCP accomplishes the reliable transfer of data with communication rules that require both machines to acknowledge each other to send and receive data. Thus, TCP is referred to as a connection-oriented protocol.

UDP is much faster because it lacks these checks—which is fine if your data can tolerate some errors or the chance of errors is low. For example, speed might be more important than a few dropped packets for a Voice over IP call or video chat. Because UDP simply sends data without checking to see if it is received, it is referred to as a connectionless protocol.

When data moving between systems must arrive in good order, we use the connection-oriented *Transmission Control Protocol (TCP)*. If it's not a big deal for data to miss a bit or two, then the connectionless *User Datagram Protocol (UDP)* is the way to go. Most TCP/IP applications use TCP (that's why we don't call it UDP/IP) because it transfers data reliably.

# REVIEW

### Objective 2.1: Compare and contrast TCP and UDP ports, protocols, and their purposes

- Application protocols use TCP ports to perform functions such as file transfer, terminal emulation, web page transfers, and remote desktop connections.

- TCP ports are connection-oriented, meaning that both ends of a connection must acknowledge the connection. TCP connections are more reliable but slower than UDP connections.

- Utility protocols use primarily UDP ports, as well as some TCP ports, to perform functions such as file and directory services, folder sharing, and services discovery.

- UDP ports are connectionless, meaning that a service using UDP does not verify that the connection is working. UDP connections are faster but less reliable than TCP connections.

## 2.1 QUESTIONS

1. An incorrect firewall setting results in port 110 being blocked. Which of the following services will not work until the port is unblocked?

   A. Secure web pages

   B. Receiving POP3 e-mail

   C. Remote desktop

   D. Upgrading to Windows 10

2. A computer that uses automatic IP addressing relies on which of the following ports?

   A. 21

   B. 25

   C. 143

   D. 67, 68

3. All information is transmitted over the Internet in which of the following?

   A. Frame

   B. Archive

   C. Packet

   D. Zip file

4. Sometimes, for greater security, e-mail providers change the default ports used for sending and receiving e-mail. If an e-mail provider changes from port 143 to a different port, which of these services would need to be configured to use the new port?

   **A.** POP3

   **B.** SMTP

   **C.** IMAP

   **D.** HTTP

   **E.** Zip file

5. A user reports that she can connect to normal websites (HTTP://), but not to secure websites (HTTPS://). Which port is being blocked by a firewall?

   **A.** 80

   **B.** 445

   **C.** 25

   **D.** 443

## 2.1 ANSWERS

1. **B**    The default port used by POP3 to receive e-mail is 110.

2. **D**    The ports used by the DHCP service for automatic IP addressing are 67 and 68.

3. **C**    All Internet traffic is broken into packets that are reassembled at the destination.

4. **C**    IMAP normally uses port 143.

5. **D**    443 is the port used for HTTPS (secure HTTP).

**Objective 2.2** ## Compare and contrast common networking hardware devices

Networks are all about interconnecting computing devices (also called hosts) so they can communicate. More specifically, your *local host* can communicate with *remote hosts* in order to access the *resources* (such as printers, files, web pages, and so on) those systems share, and to share its own resources. In a given exchange, the system providing a resource is the *server*, and the system using the resource is the *client*; when we call an entire system a server, what we really mean is that the system's primary job is serving some resource(s) to clients.

In order for a variety of different devices to share resources over a network, the network components need a shared connectivity standard, an addressing method clients and servers can use to find and communicate with each other, and shared software protocols that each system in an exchange understands. Let's look at many of the concepts and components that come together to form a network.

| **FIGURE 2.2-1** | A switch and two laptops connected by UTP cable |

## Ethernet

The dominant shared connectivity standard on modern networks, *Ethernet*, defines every-thing needed to get data from one system to another. Ethernet has evolved through hundreds of *Ethernet flavors* over the years—and most modern network speeds are expressed as *10BaseT*, *100BaseT (Fast Ethernet)*, and *1000BaseT (Gigabit Ethernet)*, which respectively run at 10, 100, and 1000 Mbps. Individual hosts have a network adapter that connects to a central switch with a segment of *unshielded twisted pair (UTP)* cable (see Figure 2.2-1), which is limited to 100 meters for most cable types.

### Cross-Reference

To learn more about Ethernet cable and standards, see Part I, Domain 3.0, Objectives 3.1/3.2.

 **NOTE** Gigabit Ethernet is common on current desktops and laptops, but 10-Gigabit Ethernet (10GbE or 10GigE) is common for server-to-server links. Most 10GigE connections use fiber optic cable.

## Routers

A router is a device that connects LANs to a WAN (see Figure 2.2-2). Hosts send signals for destinations outside of the LAN to the router, which routes traffic between networks.

| **FIGURE 2.2-2** | Two broadcast domains connected by a router—a WAN |

**FIGURE 2.2-3** Two broadcast domains—two separate LANs

# Switches

Switches connect hosts on a *local area network (LAN)* and pass signals between them. Switches memorize the MAC address of each device to smartly repeat signals to the appropriate host. A group of computers connected by one or more switches is a *broadcast domain* (see Figure 2.2-3).

**EXAM TIP** A LAN is a group of networked computers within a few hundred meters of each other, whereas a *wide area network (WAN)* is a group of computers on multiple LANs connected with long-distance technologies.

## Managed

A *managed switch* is a switch in which each port can be configured with different settings. For example, you can set a single managed switch to function as two or more virtual LANs (VLANs), control quality of service (QoS) settings on a per-port basis, and more.

## Unmanaged

An *unmanaged switch* is the type of switch sold for small office/home office (SOHO) use, such as the one shown in Figure 2.2-1. It has no management features, and all devices connected to it are in the same LAN.

**EXAM TIP** Be ready to identify the various networking hardware devices. Know the differences between routers, managed switches, and unmanaged switches.

# Hub

An Ethernet *hub* resembles a switch, but takes a signal from one *port* and blindly broadcasts it out the others. This slows down traffic, and to make matters worse, hubs subdivide the total bandwidth of the network by the number of connected devices. Take, for example, a 100Base-T (Fast Ethernet) network. Use a switch, and you get the full 100-Mbps speed to each port. Replace that switch with a hub, and if you have four devices connected, the effective speed per port is only 25 Mbps. Don't use Ethernet hubs (USB hubs, on the other hand, are very useful.)

### Cross-Reference

Learn more about USB hubs in Part I, Domain 3.0, Objectives 3.1/3.2.

# Access Points

An *access point (AP)* centrally connects wireless network nodes into a wireless LAN (WLAN) in the same way a switch connects wired devices into a LAN. Many APs also act as high-speed switches and Internet routers (see Figure 2.2-4). APs are sometimes referred to as *wireless APs (WAPs)*.

**FIGURE 2.2-4**   Device that acts as access point, switch, and router (inset shows ports on back side)

# Cloud-based Network Controller

A *cloud-based network controller* is a network appliance that enables the creation and management of a wireless mesh network, such as a private or public network in a hotel, convention center, shopping mall, or apartment complex. A typical cloud-based network controller has onboard storage for caching and uses compatible gateways and repeaters and cloud-based management software.

 **NOTE**   Some cloud service providers that offer cloud-based network controllers include CloudTrax (which purchased Open Mesh in 2018 and is now owned by Datto Networks) and Ubiquiti.

# Firewall

*Firewalls* generally protect an internal network from unauthorized access to and from the Internet at large with methods such as hiding IP addresses and blocking TCP/IP ports, but firewalls at internal boundaries can also help limit the damage a compromised node can do to important resources. *Hardware firewalls* are often built into routers (or standalone devices), whereas *software firewalls* run on individual systems.

Hardware firewalls protect your LAN from outside threats by filtering packets before they reach your internal machines. You can configure a SOHO router's firewall from the browser-based settings utility (see Figure 2.2-5). Hardware firewalls use *stateful packet inspection (SPI)* to inspect individual packets and block incoming traffic that isn't a response to your network's outgoing traffic. You can even disable ports entirely, blocking all traffic in or out.

# Network Interface Card

A network interface card (NIC) was originally an add-on card that connected a computer to an Ethernet or other wired network. Although most computers and network devices use integrated wired or wireless network connections instead of a card, the term NIC is used for both network cards and integrated network adapters. Older computers can use PCI-based NICs, while current computers can use PCIe NICs, such as the wireless NIC shown in Figure 2.2-6.

If a computer needs an upgrade to a faster or more capable NIC, it's usually easier to use a USB NIC, such as the wireless NIC shown in Figure 2.2-7. For tablets or other computers that have USB 2.0, 3.0, or 3.1 ports but no Ethernet ports, use a USB to Ethernet adapter, such as the one shown in Figure 2.2-8.

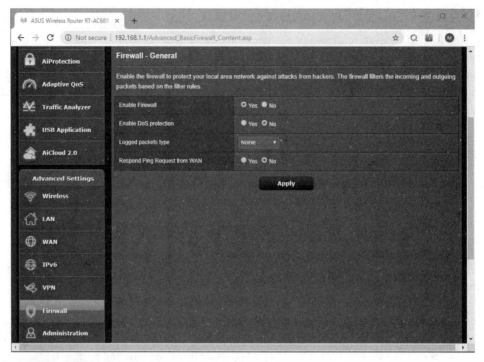

**FIGURE 2.2-5** The firewall settings in an ASUS router

**FIGURE 2.2-6** Wireless PCIe add-on NIC

**FIGURE 2.2-7** External USB wireless NIC

**FIGURE 2.2-8** External USB to Ethernet adapter

Each network adapter (or NIC) has a 48-bit built-in binary *media access control (MAC) address* that uniquely identifies it; before a NIC sends data out, it chunks it into transmission-friendly *frames* (see Figure 2.2-9) that are tagged with the MAC address of the sender and recipient and include information the receiver can use to detect errors. A *switch* uses the MAC address to send frames to the correct host.

 **NOTE** Cyclic redundancy check (CRC) is a common mechanism for detecting data transmission errors.

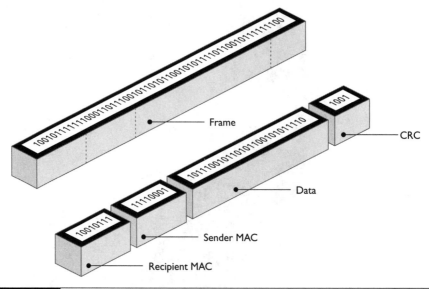

Frame

CRC

Data

Sender MAC

Recipient MAC

**FIGURE 2.2-9**   Generic frame

# Repeater

To increase the range of a wireless network, you can install extra APs for devices to roam between, replace stock antennas with higher-gain versions, use a signal booster, or use *wireless repeaters/extenders* to receive and rebroadcast the Wi-Fi signal. Wireless mesh networks include two or more repeaters.

# Cable/DSL Modem

The most common type of broadband connection for a SOHO network is either a cable modem or a DSL modem. Read on to discover the differences.

## DSL Modem

A digital subscriber line (DSL) modem connects to a standard RJ-11 telephone line, enabling the conversion of high-speed digital signals to and from the telephone line. DSL modems frequently are combined with wireless routers and are referred to as *DSL gateways*.

DSL speeds vary widely from location to location because the greater the distance from the DSL modem to the telephone company's central switch, the slower the performance.

**Cross-Reference**

To learn more about DSL service, see the "DSL" section in Objective 2.7, later in this domain.

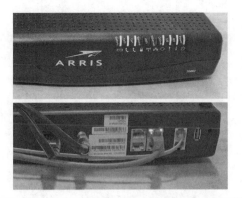

**FIGURE 2.2-10** | Cable modem with VoIP telephone support

## Cable Modem

Cable uses regular RG-6 or RG-59 cable TV lines to provide upload speeds from 1 to 20 Mbps and download speeds from 6 Mbps to 1+ Gbps. *Cable Internet* connections are theoretically available anywhere you can get cable TV. The cable connects to a cable modem that itself connects (via Ethernet) to a small home router or your NIC. Some cable modems also include support for VoIP telephony, such as the one shown in Figure 2.2-10.

## Bridge

A *bridge* connects two different media types (such as UTP and fiber optic) and converts signals between them.

## Patch Panel

A *patch panel* (shown in Figure 2.2-11) has a row of permanent connectors for horizontal cables on the back and a row of female port connectors on the front, enabling you to use short stranded-core UTP *patch cables* (shown in Figure 2.2-12) to connect the patch panel to

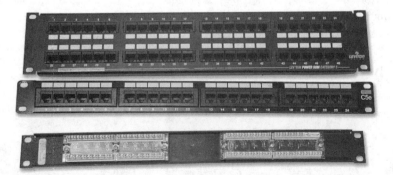

**FIGURE 2.2-11** | Typical patch panels

FIGURE 2.2-12    Typical patch cable

the switch. Premade patch cables make it simple to get multiple colors for organization and often come with booted (reinforced) connectors.

 **NOTE**    A patch cable is a specific length (usually short, but can be up to 100 feet) of cable terminated at each end with a plug or socket. Also called a patch cord.

# Power over Ethernet (PoE)

Most network hardware—including APs—draw power from an electrical outlet. Advanced APs and networked devices such as security cameras can instead run on electricity supplied by a *Power over Ethernet (PoE) injector* or *PoE switch*. Both types of devices enable a standard Ethernet cable to carry power as well as signals.

## Injectors

A PoE injector (also known as a midspan) is plugged into a standard Ethernet cable coming from a switch and a source of AC power. The injector adds the power to the Ethernet cable running from the injector to the PoE device.

## Switch

A PoE switch detects whether connected devices are standard Ethernet devices or PoE devices. It supplies power to PoE devices, but does not supply power to standard Ethernet devices.

 **EXAM TIP**    Be clear about the differences between PoE (power carried over Ethernet wiring) and EoP (Ethernet signals carried over power lines).

**FIGURE 2.2-13**   An EoP bridge plugged into an AC power outlet

# Ethernet over Power

An *Ethernet over Power (EoP)* bridge connects UTP cable to your building's power infrastructure, enabling you to have wired connections where it would be difficult to run new cable. EoP devices are used in pairs: connect one to each end of the connection, such as one near a switch and the other near a workstation. Figure 2.2-13 illustrates a typical EoP bridge connected to an AC power outlet.

# REVIEW

### Objective 2.2: Compare and contrast common networking hardware devices

- Network hardware devices are based on Ethernet, which is available in several speeds ranging from 10 Mbps to 1000 Mbps or more.
- A router connects a local area network (LAN) to a wide area network (WAN).
- A switch transfers data directly between the transmitting and receiving devices on the network.
- A managed switch allows each port to be configured with different settings, including different LAN settings, while an unmanaged switch has no settings. Switches have replaced hubs, which broadcast data to all devices and are much slower.

- An access point (AP) is the wireless counterpart to a switch. A wireless router typically incorporates the features of an AP and a switch.
- A cloud-based network controller enables existing wireless networks to be managed and used as a single wireless mesh network.
- A firewall is a device or app that examines network traffic and blocks unwanted traffic.
- A network interface card (NIC) enables a device to connect to a network. Many devices have built-in NICs.
- A repeater relays wireless signals to devices outside the range of the current AP or router.
- Cable and DSL modems are popular broadband Internet connection technologies. DSL can use phone lines.
- A bridge connects two different media types so they can work together.
- A patch panel is used for wired Ethernet cable connections to a single location. A patch cable is used to run patch panel wires to a switch.
- Power over Ethernet (PoE) is used to provide power to Fast Ethernet devices that need power but don't have power at their locations. An injector is used to add power, and a PoE switch is used to provide power only to PoE devices.
- An Ethernet over Power (EoP) bridge sends Ethernet signals over power lines in a building, and EoP devices are used in pairs.

## 2.2 QUESTIONS

1. Company A wants to create two separate networks in a building but only wants to use a single point of connection. Which of the following does the company need?

   **A.** Unmanaged switch

   **B.** Router

   **C.** Hub

   **D.** Managed switch

2. To avoid the expense of adding network cable or the uncertainty of wireless signals in a building with brick walls, which of the following would you use to add a network connection?

   **A.** Router

   **B.** PoE

   **C.** EoP

   **D.** Hub

3. Company B has just moved into a new building and has found an existing Internet connection that use RG-6 wiring. Which of the following is being used?

   **A.** Cable

   **B.** DSL

   **C.** PoE

   **D.** Router

4. Your client is a company that has two locations in the same city, both of which
   locations get their Internet service from the same provider in the same city. Both
   locations use the same type of service, but one location has service that is about three
   to five times faster than the other. What type of service is most likely being used?

   **A.** Cable

   **B.** Satellite

   **C.** DSL

   **D.** PoE

5. What feature of all network adapters can be used to determine which device a frame is
   sent from or going to?

   **A.** IP address

   **B.** MAC address

   **C.** Switch port

   **D.** Router

## 2.2 ANSWERS

1. **D**   A managed switch can be used to create multiple networks.

2. **C**   Ethernet over Power (EoP) sends Ethernet signals over power lines in a building.

3. **A**   RG-6 is a type of wiring used for cable Internet and cable TV.

4. **C**   DSL service varies widely in speed because its speed is dependent upon the
   distance from a client site to the central switch (central office) used by the phone
   company; longer distances have slower connections.

5. **B**   Every network adapter, including those built into other devices, has a unique
   48-bit MAC address.

Objective 2.3 **Given a scenario, install and configure a
basic wired/wireless SOHO network**

Setting up a small office/home office (SOHO) network is a great way to learn how networking works while also bringing the benefits of networking, such as easy file sharing and more
flexible printing, into your home or small office. The principles and methods you learn in this
section will work on any workgroup network.

# Router/Switch Functionality

The heart of most SOHO networks is a wireless router, such as the one shown earlier in Figure 2.2-4. Wireless routers actually combine three functions into a single device: a router, switch, and AP. Simply plug your computer into any of the LAN ports on the back and then plug the cable from your Internet connection into the port labeled Internet or WAN.

After the wireless router is connected to a computer and to the Internet, you can configure it as discussed in the following sections. We will discuss each of the functions separately, beginning with the AP.

# Access Point Settings

Each AP includes a web server that hosts a browser-accessible configuration utility (see Figure 2.3-1) at the AP's default IP address (often 192.168.1.1). The configuration utility prompts you to log in with an administrator password, which you create during installation or find in the AP's documentation.

 **NOTE**   Configuration utilities vary by vendor and model.

**FIGURE 2.3-1**    ASUS wireless router setup screen

Current APs come with web-based utilities that guide you through the initial setup, but manual setup isn't too hard. Here's a checklist:

- Install available firmware updates.
- Give the configuration utility a secure administrator password.
- Configure a unique SSID and consider disabling SSID broadcast.
- Modern WAPs should select a channel/frequency (also known as a control channel) automatically (see Figure 2.3-2), but you may still need to configure it to match other WAPs or use a quieter, less congested channel, based on a survey with a wireless analyzer.

**Cross-Reference**

For more information about channels, see the "Channels" section at the end of this objective.

**Cross-Reference**

To learn more about wireless (Wi-Fi) analyzers, see the "Wi-Fi Analyzer" section in Objective 2.8, later in this domain.

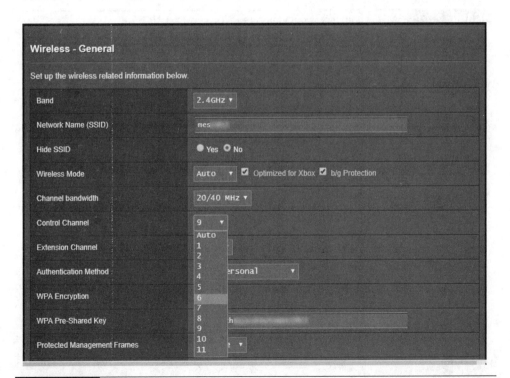

**FIGURE 2.3-2**   Changing the channel

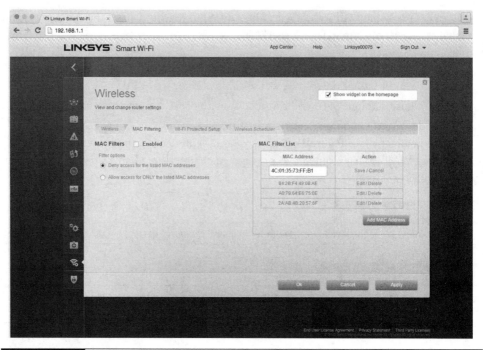

**FIGURE 2.3-3** MAC filtering configuration screen for a Linksys AP

- Dual-band WAPs can separately enable or disable the 2.4-GHz and 5-GHz networks. Most setups use both bands for compatibility, but you can disable one band if interference makes it unreliable and all of your devices support the other band.

- Configure MAC filtering (see Figure 2.3-3) if you have known MAC addresses to allow or deny. Some routers support MAC filtering on both wired and wireless connections, while others, such as the one shown in Figure 2.3-3, support this feature only for wireless networks.

- Enable the best available security/encryption mode on the AP and generate or enter the security key or password (see Figure 2.3-4).

- If you absolutely must use older equipment that only supports WEP, it should have an option to generate encryption keys; select the highest available encryption level, enter a unique *passphrase*, and click the Generate button or its equivalent. Document these settings and either export the encryption keys to removable media or write them down as well; wireless clients will need this information to connect.

 **EXAM TIP** WEP is easily cracked. Given a scenario on the A+ exam (or in the field), choose WPA2; if that is not an option, choose WPA.

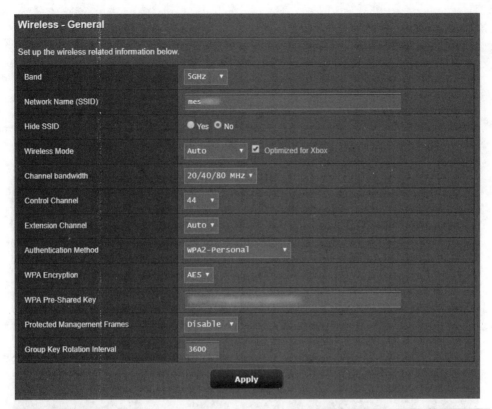

**FIGURE 2.3-4**   5-GHz properties panel for an ASUS AP with WPA2 Personal with AES selected

- WPA and WPA2 are configured similarly. Use WPA/WPA2 Personal for SOHO networks. WPA/WPA2 Enterprise requires a special server (called a *RADIUS server*) for serious security in larger business environments. Mixed network mode supports WPA clients on a WPA2-encrypted WAP; only use it if you must support WPA devices.

 **EXAM TIP**   Pre-Shared Key (PSK) is a more technical name for WPA/WPA2 Personal.

# IP Addressing

There are two IP address settings you need to make on your router: First, make sure your router is configured with the correct IP address setting from your ISP. In most cases, your router will receive an IP address automatically. However, if the ISP has provided a static IP address, enter it in your WAN configuration. Next, unless the devices connecting to your router will have manual IP addresses, enable the DHCP server built into your router (see Figure 2.3-5). You can specify what range of IP addresses to assign automatically.

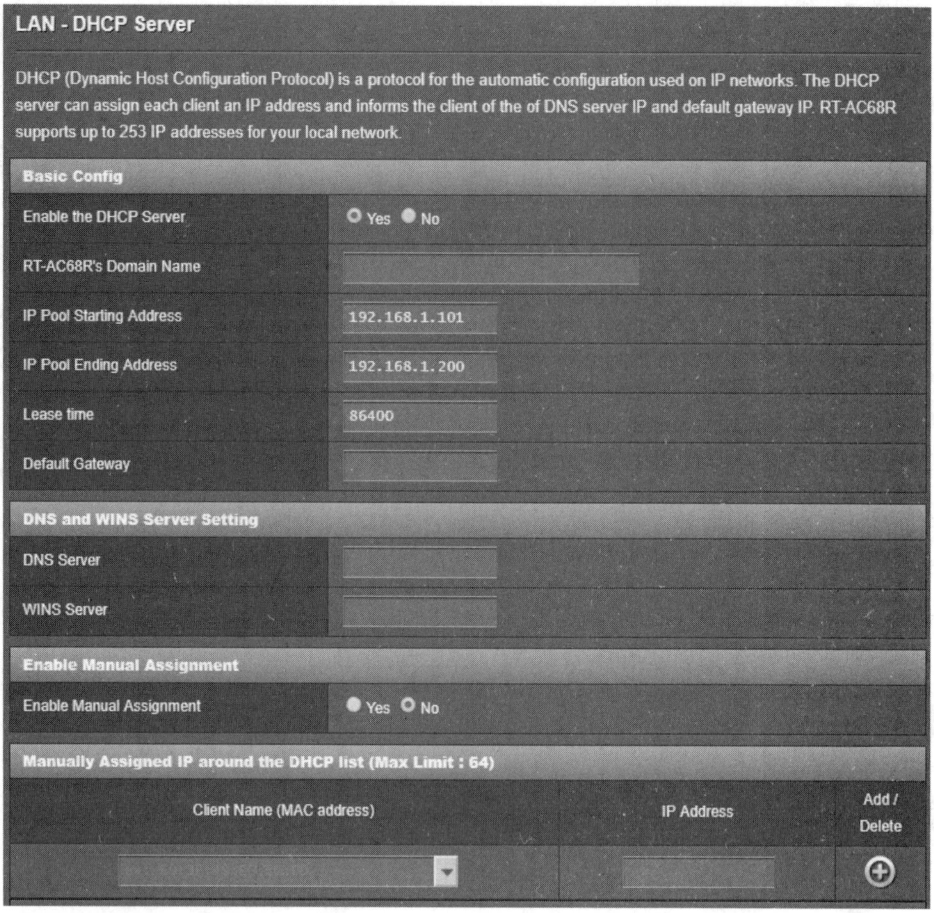

**FIGURE 2.3-5**    DHCP server settings in an ASUS router

# NIC Configuration

Although both wired and wireless NICs offer many configuration options, most of them are not needed in a typical network. The available settings vary according to the network type.

## Wired

Generally, wired networks should be configured to use auto-negotiation (see Figure 2.3-6) for network speed and duplex settings. Auto-negotiation enables the NIC to cope with any network settings without the need to reconfigure the NIC.

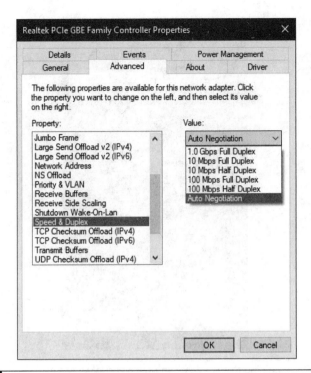

**FIGURE 2.3-6**   Viewing speed/duplex settings for a Gigabit Ethernet NIC

**EXAM TIP**   *Full duplex* enables the NIC to send/receive data simultaneously, while *half duplex* sets the NIC to send or receive in separate operations.

## Wireless

At one time, wireless clients needed to know the wireless channel and encryption type used by the AP. However, this is no longer necessary. To connect to a wireless network using Windows, open the network icon in the taskbar, select (or enter, in the case of a hidden wireless network) the correct SSID, and enter the password (encryption key) as prompted (see Figure 2.3-7). The channel and encryption type are set automatically. With macOS, open the AirPort status icon, click Turn AirPort On, select the correct SSID, and enter the password as prompted. With Linux, use the ifconfig, iwconfig, and dhclient command-line utilities to set up your connection.

**ADDITIONAL RESOURCES**   For more information about connecting to a wireless network with Linux, go to www.wikihow.com and search for the article "How to Set up a Wireless Network in Linux."

**FIGURE 2.3-7**    Connecting to a wireless network using Windows 10

# End-user Device Configuration

Devices that you connect to a SOHO network, such as external drives, IP cameras, mobile devices, printers, scanners, multifunction devices (printer/scanner/fax/copier), need the following configuration settings:

- **Wired network**    Select Wired Network or Ethernet as the connection type.
- **Wireless network**    Select Wireless or Wi-Fi as the connection type, and provide the SSID and encryption key (if any).

 **NOTE**    These devices might be configured through on-device setup dialogs (as with printers and multifunction devices) or with a web browser built into the device. See the device documentation for details.

After the device is configured, it should appear on the network and be selectable for printing, scanning, and so on.

## Cross-Reference

See Objective 2.6 later in this domain for more information.

# IoT Device Configuration

The Internet of Things (IoT) is a broad category of devices that are used to monitor and control HVAC, security, and home entertainment, such as *thermostats, light switches, security cameras, door locks,* and *voice-enabled, smart speakers/digital assistants.* To communicate via the Internet, these devices also need to be configured. Here are the basic configuration methods for these devices (other than smart speakers/digital assistants, discussed separately next) after they are installed:

- **Wi-Fi devices**   After installation, connect the device to your Wi-Fi network, install the companion app on your smartphone, set up an account, and use the app to configure your device. On some devices, you might need to temporarily connect to a Wi-Fi network on the device during the installation process.
- **Z-Wave devices**   After installation, set up the device category on your Z-Wave controller, then follow the vendor's procedure to connect the device to your controller. Install the companion app on your smartphone and use it to configure the device.
- **Bluetooth low-energy devices**   After installation, install the companion app on your smartphone. Pair the device and use the app for initial configuration.

## Voice-enabled, Smart Speaker/Digital Assistant

Smart speaker/digital assistant technology can be incorporated into operating systems or into hardware. These devices respond to voice commands and, using an Internet connection, can answer questions, activate lights, play music, play video, and more.

To use a digital assistant installed on a computer or mobile device, the computer or device must be connected to the Internet, and the user must enable the digital assistant app.

To use a smart speaker, the speaker must be paired to a computer or mobile device using its host app. If the smart speaker will be used with other hardware, such as home automation products, you need to choose compatible home automation products, set up the speaker to work with each specific device (a process known as "enabling the skill" with Alexa), and pair the speaker with the device.

# Cable/DSL Modem Configuration

The basic configuration process for a cable or DSL modem is relatively simple:

1. Make sure you know the MAC (hardware) address for your modem; check the side, back, or bottom of the unit.
2. Make sure you know your ISP account information.
3. Connect the modem to the appropriate signal cable (coaxial cable for cable modem, phone cable for DSL).
4. Connect an Ethernet cable from the modem to a computer.
5. Connect the power cable for the modem to AC power and to the modem.

6. Turn on the modem.

7. After the signal lights on the modem indicate that the connection is live, go to the vendor's web page to test and/or register your modem or account. Depending upon your ISP, you might need to call the ISP to register your modem.

If the modem also includes a wireless gateway or router, that must also be configured.

# Firewall Settings

Although larger business networks and enterprise networks have separate firewall appliances, routers used for small-office/home-office (SOHO) uses have built-in firewalls. Just like a software firewall, a hardware firewall is designed to block unwanted inbound traffic. However, because the router's firewall is designed to work with different devices that might require different types of access, it has many additional options. These are covered in the following sections.

## DMZ

The incredibly dangerous demilitarized zone (DMZ) setting excludes specific devices from firewall protection, enabling all incoming traffic (and any attacks therein). Don't use it. If you need to provide a different level of access to a particular device, set up the device with a static IP address and use port forwarding.

## Port Forwarding

*Port forwarding* (see Figure 2.3-8) enables you to open a port in the firewall and direct incoming traffic on that port to a specific IP address on your LAN.

## NAT

Routers use *Network Address Translation (NAT)* to present an entire LAN of computers to the Internet as a single machine. All anyone on the Internet sees is the *public* IP address your ISP gives you—not private addresses assigned to devices on your LAN—effectively firewalling LAN nodes from malicious users on the vast untrusted WAN that is the Internet.

 **EXAM TIP**   Dynamic NAT (DNAT) can share more than one routable IP address among devices on your LAN. Also called pooled NAT.

## UPnP

A lot of networking devices designed for the residential space use a feature called *universal plug and play (UPnP)* to find and connect to other UPnP devices. This feature enables seamless interconnectivity at the cost of somewhat lower security, so disable it if you don't need it.

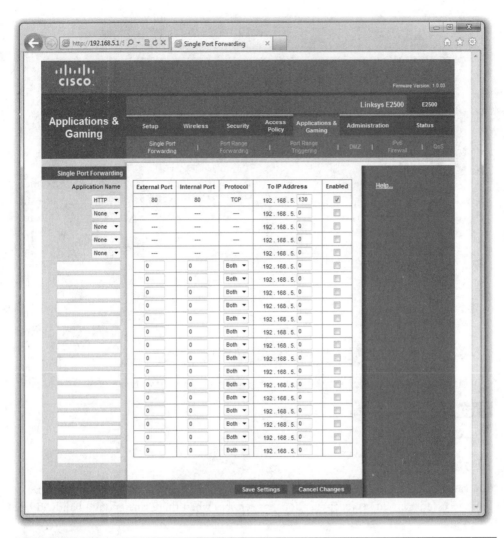

**FIGURE 2.3-8**    Port forwarding configured to pass HTTP traffic to a web server

# MAC Filtering/Whitelist/Blacklist

Most APs support MAC address filtering to limit access to your wireless network using the physical, hard-encoded MAC address of each wireless network adapter. A table stored in the WAP—the *access control list (ACL)*—lists MAC addresses permitted *(white list)* or excluded *(black list)* from the wireless network.

**EXAM TIP**    Given a scenario on the A+ exam, you should be able to identify and configure settings for DMZ, port forwarding, NAT, UPnP, and MAC filtering.

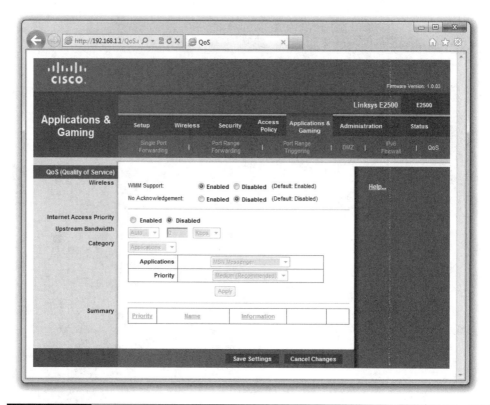

**FIGURE 2.3-9**    QoS configuration

# QoS

You can configure *Quality of Service (QoS)* on your router (see Figure 2.3-9) to prioritize or limit access for certain users, applications, or services when there isn't enough bandwidth to go around.

# Wireless Settings

The essential settings needed for an AP, a wireless router, or a wireless gateway include *encryption type* and *channels* (QoS, another important setting, is covered in the previous section).

## Encryption

Encryption is used to protect wireless data from eavesdropping. Currently, there are three encryption standards supported by Wi-Fi: WEP, WPA, and WPA2. WPS is a setup method that makes it easier to use WPA or WPA2 encryption.

# WEP

Wired Equivalent Privacy (WEP) encryption was meant to secure wirelessly transmitted data with standard 40-bit encryption; many vendors also support 104-bit encryption (which some advertise as 128-bit). Unfortunately, WEP contains some serious security flaws. Shortly after it was released, hackers demonstrated that WEP could be cracked in a matter of minutes using readily available software. It's better than nothing, but it only stops casual snooping; it will not deter a serious attacker. Because WEP uses one key for all clients, other members of the network can read your packets.

# WPA

Wi-Fi Protected Access (WPA) is a sort of interim security protocol upgrade for WEP-enabled devices. WPA uses the *Temporal Key Integrity Protocol (TKIP)* to protect from many attacks WEP was vulnerable to by providing a new encryption key for every packet sent. Other security enhancements include encryption key integrity-checking and user authentication through the industry-standard *Extensible Authentication Protocol (EAP)*.

# WPA2

The full IEEE 802.11i standard, WPA2, is the preferred way to lock down wireless networks. WPA2 uses the *Advanced Encryption Standard (AES)*, among other improvements, to secure the wireless environment. Current WAPs and wireless clients support (and require) WPA2, and most access points have a "backward compatible" mode for the handful of devices that still need WPA.

# WPS

The developers of Wi-Fi created *Wi-Fi Protected Setup (WPS)* to make secure connections using WPA or WPA2 easier for novice users to configure with a button (see Figure 2.3-10), password, or code. For example, you could connect a WPS-capable WAP and wireless printer by pressing the WPS button on the printer and then on the WAP within a set time. Sadly, WPS codes are very easy for a program to guess. The only protection is disabling WPS; check the WAP manufacturer's website for instructions.

 **EXAM TIP**   Be familiar with WEP, WPA, WPA2, TKIP, and AES because you might be called upon to explain the differences between WEP, WPA, and WPA2 or to identify which encryption type is used with WPA and which with WPA2.

**FIGURE 2.3-10**   WPS button on an e2500 router

## Channels

802.11-based wireless networks use one of two radio bands for sending and receiving data: 2.4 GHz and 5 GHz. Each band is comprised of a range of frequencies that are divided up into channels.

2.4-GHz channels range from 1 to 11 in most world areas. Unfortunately, only channels 1, 6, and 11 do not overlap with each other. The combination of a few non-overlapping channels and the crowded 2.4-GHz range can cause 2.4-GHz networks to be slow.

5-GHz channels are more numerous (13) and more widely spaced, enabling all channels to be usable.

As mentioned in the "Access Point Settings" section earlier in this objective, modern WAPs should select a channel/control channel/frequency automatically (refer back to Figure 2.3-2), but you may still want to configure it manually to use a quieter channel, based on a survey with a wireless analyzer.

# REVIEW

### Objective 2.3: Given a scenario, install and configure a basic wired/wireless SOHO network

- A wireless router is the foundation for a SOHO network, as it combines a router, a switch, and a wireless AP. It is managed through a browser-based interface.

- The router has two IP address settings to configure: enter (or confirm) the IP address used to connect to the broadband Internet device, and enable the DHCP server used to provide IP addresses to connected devices.

- To connect a wireless NIC, select the SSID and enter the encryption key (if used).

- To configure an end-user device such as external drives, IP cameras, mobile devices, printers, scanners, multifunction devices (printer/scanner/fax/copier), select the network type, then enter the SSID and encryption key if you choose a wireless connection.

- IoT device configurations for thermostats, light switches, security cameras, and door locks, vary according to whether they use Wi-Fi, Z-Wave, or Bluetooth for initial configuration.

- You must pair voice-enabled digital assistants and smart speakers with devices as part of their setup.

- During the process of setting up a cable or DSL modem, make sure you have a working connection with the ISP before completing the setup process.

- DMZ, port forwarding, NAT, UPnP, MAC filtering, and whitelist/blacklist firewall settings all affect network security.

- QoS improves network performance for priority data.

- Wireless encryption types from least to most secure are WEP, WPA (TKIP encryption), and WPA2 (AES encryption).

- WPS for easy push-button configuration is not secure and should not be used.
- Channels 1–11 are used for 2.4-GHz wireless networks; however, only 1, 6, and 11 are recommended for normal use.
- 5-GHz wireless networks have non-overlapping channels, making configuration easier than with 2.4-GHz networks.

## 2.3 QUESTIONS

1. Company C is setting up its own wireless network instead of using a contractor. Which of the following does the company need to configure to provide IP addresses automatically?

   **A.** AES

   **B.** TKIP

   **C.** WEP

   **D.** DHCP

2. The term Internet of Things (IoT) applies to a wide variety of devices. Which of the following categories is not considered an IoT category?

   **A.** Streaming video playback

   **B.** Lighting

   **C.** Security

   **D.** Thermostats

3. Company D is setting up a web server on its network. Which of the following router settings will enable the company to safely host the web server while protecting other devices with the router's built-in firewall?

   **A.** NAT

   **B.** Port forwarding

   **C.** DMZ

   **D.** QoS

4. A wireless network that is using the old WEP encryption standard because of legacy equipment on the network has a lot of unauthorized use. Until the network can be upgraded to use WPA2-compliant devices, the client wants to allow only authorized devices to use the network by checking their MAC addresses. Which of the following describes what the client wants to create?

   **A.** Blacklist

   **B.** Red flag list

   **C.** Whitelist

   **D.** ACL

**5.** Your client is confused about how the devices on a network that connects to the Internet receive their IP addresses. Which of the following router functions do you need to explain to help the client understand this process?

   **A.** DNS

   **B.** Port forwarding

   **C.** Blacklist

   **D.** DHCP

## 2.3 ANSWERS

**1.** **D**   DHCP supplies IP addresses to connected devices.

**2.** **A**   Streaming video playback is a function of complex devices such as smart TVs; IoT devices are used to perform low-power and simple tasks.

**3.** **B**   Port forwarding enables inbound connections of a particular type (such as web page requests on HTTP port 80) to be routed to a particular device.

**4.** **C**   A whitelist allows only devices with listed MAC addresses to use the network.

**5.** **D**   DHCP is the router function that provides IP addresses to connected devices.

**Objective 2.4**   # Compare and contrast wireless networking protocols

Wireless networking is dominated by *radio frequency (RF)* technologies, in particular the 802.11 (Wi-Fi) standards (sometimes also referred to as WiFi, such as in the CompTIA A+ exam objectives), but you still need to be familiar with infrared, Bluetooth, and cellular standards.

## 802.11 Standards

The IEEE 802.11 wireless Ethernet standard, better known as *Wi-Fi*, defines how devices can communicate with data broadcast in small chunks spread over available frequencies within the 2.4-GHz and/or 5-GHz bands (which are further divided into discrete *channels*). The original 802.11 standard has been extended to the 802.11a, 802.11b, 802.11g, 802.11n, and 802.11ac variations—newer standards (except for 802.11a) are backward compatible with their predecessors.

**EXAM TIP**   Be very familiar with the 802.11 wireless standards speeds, distances, and frequencies.

**802.11a**   Despite the "a" on the end, it's newer than 802.11b. It runs in the faster 5-GHz band, but its range suffers compares to 802.11b, and the use of the 5-GHz band makes it incompatible with both older and newer Wi-Fi devices unless they support 5 GHz (802.11n and 802.11ac).

**802.11b**   The first wireless networking standard to take off; its main downside is that it uses the 2.4-GHz band already crowded with baby monitors, garage door openers, microwaves, and wireless phones.

**802.11g**   Achieves the range of 802.11b and the speed of 802.11a, and maintains backward compatibility with 802.11b.

**802.11n**   Introduced two new antenna technologies: multiple in/multiple out (MIMO), which increases speed by requiring all but handheld devices to use more than one of up to four antennas; and transmit beamforming, which adjusts the signal based on each client's location. Also introduced optional dual-band support for both 2.4 GHz and 5 GHz, which means some 802.11n devices are backward compatible with 802.11a.

**802.11ac**   Expands on 802.11n technology by adding more streams, speed, and wider bandwidth. Technically, 802.11ac only uses the 5-GHz band, but it too includes optional dual-band support. It introduces an updated MIMO called Multiuser MIMO (MU-MIMO) that enables a WAP to broadcast to multiple users simultaneously.

Table 2.4-1 compares the important characteristics of the 802.11 versions.

**TABLE 2.4-1**   Comparison of 802.11 Standards

|  | 802.11a | 802.11b | 802.11g | 802.11n | 802.11ac |
|---|---|---|---|---|---|
| **Max. Throughput** | 54 Mbps | 11 Mbps | 54 Mbps | 100+ Mbps | 1+ Gbps |
| **Max. Range** | 150 feet | 300 feet | 300 feet | 300+ feet | 300+ feet |
| **Frequency Band** | 5 GHz | 2.4 GHz | 2.4 GHz | 2.4 and 5 GHz | 5 GHz (ac routers also support 2.4 GHz) |
| **Security** | SSID, MAC filtering, WEP, WPA, WPA2 | SSID, MAC filtering, WEP, WPA, WPA2 (later hardware) | SSID, MAC filtering, WEP, WPA, WPA2 | SSID, MAC filtering, WEP, WPA, WPA2 | SSID, MAC filtering, WEP, WPA, WPA2 |
| **Compatibility** | 802.11a | 802.11b | 802.11b, 802.11g | 802.11b, 802.11g, 802.11n, (802.11a in some cases) | 802.11a, 802.11b, 802.11g, 802.11n |
| **Communication Mode** | Ad hoc or infrastructure | Ad hoc or infrastructure | Ad hoc or infrastructure | Ad hoc or infrastructure | Ad hoc or infrastructure |

**NOTE** Infrastructure mode is the normal mode for Wi-Fi devices, in which they communicate with each other via an AP. Ad hoc mode enables Wi-Fi devices to connect directly with each other, a feature typically used for sharing a printer or a multifunction device.

# Frequencies: 2.4 GHz, 5 GHz

Wi-Fi supports two different frequency bands: *2.4 GHz* and *5 GHz* (listed as 2.4Ghz and 5Ghz in the CompTIA objectives). These frequencies differ in the number of available channels and, consequently, in ease of configuration.

# Channels

The number of channels available in a 5-GHz wireless network is more than the number of channels available in a 2.4-GHz network. A 5-GHz network has the following non-overlapping channels using the standard 40-MHz width (twice the width of 2.4-GHz channels): 38, 46, 54, 62, 102, 110, 118, 126, 134, 134, 142, 151, 159.

When 80-MHz wide channels are used, available non-overlapping channels are 42, 58, 106, 122, 138, 155.

When 160-MHz wide channels are used, available non-overlapping channels are 50, 114.

 **ADDITIONAL RESOURCES** To learn more about 5-GHz Wi-Fi channels, go to www.accessagility.com and look up "Introduction to 5 GHz WiFi Channels" on their blog.

# 1–11

If your wireless router or AP supports only channels 1–11 or 1–13 (Japan/Europe), it supports only the 2.4-GHz wireless band. Unfortunately, the frequencies used mean that most channels overlap, causing slowdowns when in use. To avoid congestion, use channels 1, 6, and 11 if you use the standard 20-MHz channel width; 40-MHz channels are available on 802.11n, but channel 3 is the only non-overlapping channel when 40-MHz channels are used.

 **ADDITIONAL RESOURCES** For more information, go to www .electronics-notes.com and search for the article "Wi-Fi Channels, Frequencies, Bands & Bandwidths."

**FIGURE 2.4-1** External USB Bluetooth adapter, keyboard, and mouse

# Bluetooth

*Bluetooth* creates small wireless networks ideal for wearable devices, audio headsets, and automotive entertainment systems that connect to your smartphone; linking two computers in a quick-and-dirty wireless *personal area network (PAN)*; and input devices such as keyboards and mice (see Figure 2.4-1) as well as mobile device headsets and speakers. Most connections are ad hoc, but Bluetooth access points also exist.

 **ADDITIONAL RESOURCES** Bluetooth can also be used for certain IoT applications. For a discussion of Bluetooth strengths and weaknesses in IoT uses, go to www.iotforall.com and search for "Bluetooth IoT Applications: From BLE to Mesh."

Bluetooth has grown faster and more secure over the years, but speed isn't Bluetooth's big selling point—reliable low-power communication is. Bluetooth resists interference by hopping between 79 frequencies in the 2.45-GHz range around 1600 times a second. Bluetooth enables wearables and peripherals to save much-needed power with three power-use classes, as shown in Table 2.4-2.

**TABLE 2.4-2** Bluetooth Classes

|  | Max. Power | Max. Range |
|---|---|---|
| Class 1 | 100 mW | 100 meters |
| Class 2 | 2.5 mW | 10 meters |
| Class 3 | 1 mW | 1 meter |

Let's look at what has changed over the years:

- The first generation (versions 1.1 and 1.2) supports speeds around 1 Mbps.
- The backward-compatible second generation (2.0 and 2.1) increases speed to around 3 Mbps with Enhanced Data Rate (EDR).
- With the optional High Speed (+ HS) feature, the third generation (3.0) tops out at 24 Mbps by transferring data over an 802.11 Wi-Fi connection after initial Bluetooth negotiation.
- Called Bluetooth Smart, the fourth generation (4.0, 4.1, 4.2) focuses on better support for "smart" devices by reducing cost and power use, and improving speed and security. The most interesting addition is IP connectivity so Bluetooth devices can skip the smartphone and talk directly to a Bluetooth-enabled AP.
- Bluetooth 5 (fifth-generation Bluetooth) is optimized for IoT devices such as smart speakers, lights, and so on. Bluetooth 5 provides options for trading greater speed for reduced range or changing packet sizes.

 **EXAM TIP** Be aware of the differences between Bluetooth and Wi-Fi (ranges, signaling, AP versus direct connection, and so on).

# NFC

*Near field communication (NFC)* uses chips embedded into mobile devices that create and communicate with tiny electromagnetic fields, limiting range between NFC-enabled devices to a few inches. NFC can exchange contact information, small files, and even payment transactions with stored credit cards using systems such as Apple Pay and Google Pay.

# RFID

*Radio frequency identification (RFID)* is used to identify and track the location of objects. It combines RFID scanners that use electromagnetic fields with RFID tags that respond when moved through a scanner field. RFID tags consist of a microchip and antenna; they are often used for theft prevention and inventory tracking.

# Zigbee

Zigbee (also known as ZigBee) is a popular IoT standard for home automation and security. It is based on the IEEE 802.15.4 wireless networking standard, but unlike Wi-Fi, Zigbee is designed for short-range interchange of sensor data at a data rate of about 250 Kbps, using 2.4 GHz or lower frequencies. A Zigbee network must include at least one Coordinator and one or more Zigbee devices. Zigbee devices support mesh networking, and many of them are battery powered, thanks to the low voltage needed to run Zigbee. To connect complex Zigbee networks such as cluster tree or mesh networks together, Zigbee routers are used. Zigbee works with Amazon Alexa.

 **ADDITIONAL RESOURCES**  To learn more about Zigbee, see the Zigbee Alliance website at https://zigbee.org.

## Z-Wave

Z-Wave is a home automation and security standard developed by Zensys and currently managed by the Z-Wave Alliance. Z-Wave runs in the 908.42-MHz frequency and uses a wireless hub to connect to Z-Wave devices. Z-Wave also supports mesh topologies.

 **ADDITIONAL RESOURCES**  To learn more about how Zigbee and Z-Wave compare, go to http://thesmartcave.com and search for the article "Z Wave Vs ZigBee: Which Is Better for Your Smart Home?"

Up to 232 Z-Wave devices can be in a single Z-Wave network. Z-Wave uses very little power, so some Z-Wave devices run on battery power, while others plug into AC outlets. The Z-Wave Alliance certifies Z-Wave compatible devices.

 **ADDITIONAL RESOURCES**  To learn more about Z-Wave, see the Z-Wave website at www.z-wave.com or the Z-Wave Alliance website at https://z-wavealliance.org.

## Cellular Standards: 3G, 4G, LTE, 5G

*3G* is the general term for third-generation cellular data services. 3G hit the market in the early 2000s, and typically offers maximum data rates of at least 144 Kbps. However, most implementations of 3G run at much faster speeds. Although most wireless networks now support its successor, 4G, 3G is still in use in some areas.

 **ADDITIONAL RESOURCES**  To see how sparsely populated areas have lagged behind urban areas in cellular network generations, look at the 3G Network Comparison map available at www.cellularmaps.com.

**FIGURE 2.4-2**  Real-world LTE speed test

*4G* is the general term for fourth-generation cellular data services. 4G began to roll out during the early 2000s. Originally, there were several competing 4G standards, but *Long Term Evolution (LTE)*, also known as 4G LTE, is the current standard. Although LTE claims to run at up to 300 Mbps download and 75 Mbps upload, real-world performance is typically lower, as shown in Figure 2.4-2.

*5G* is short for fifth-generation cellular data services. 5G is much faster than 4G (up to 20-Gbps peak speeds), offers lower latency for gaming, and uses small short-range wireless antennas on buildings rather than the large antenna towers used by 4G LTE and older networks. Note that the so-called 5GE network from AT&T is actually a new name for their gigabit-class 4G LTE network. True 5G networks require users to get new smartphones.

**EXAM TIP**  Be able to compare and contrast the various cellular technologies.

**ADDITIONAL RESOURCES**   If you ever wondered why you can't always reuse an existing cellular phone when you switch carriers, here's why: Two competing digital cellular standards, Global System for Mobile Communications (GSM) and code division multiple access (CDMA), emerged in the early 1990s and have continued to evolve since. Most of the world uses GSM, as well as AT&T and T-Mobile. However, CDMA is supported by Sprint, Verizon, and US Cellular. The industry is phasing out GSM and CDMA in the wake of 4G LTE and the introduction of 5G. To learn more, go to www.pcmag.com and search for "CDMA vs. GSM: What's the Difference?"

# REVIEW

### Objective 2.4: Compare and contrast wireless networking protocols

- Wi-Fi standards from slowest to fastest include 802.11b, 802.11a, 802.11g, 802.11n, and 802.11ac. 802.11a and 802.11ac are 5-GHz standards, and 802.11n has an optional 5-GHz feature. All others are 2.4 GHz. 802.11ac is backward compatible with 2.4-GHz networks.
- 2.4-GHz Wi-Fi networks use channels from 1 to 11, but only channels 1, 6, and 11 don't overlap.
- 5-GHz Wi-Fi networks can use 13 non-overlapping channels.
- Bluetooth is a short-range network used for data interchange or connections with keyboards, mice, and headsets.
- NFC is used for touchless payments and data interchange with smartphones.
- RFID is used for inventory tracking and theft prevention.
- Zigbee is a popular IoT standard for home automation and security. Z-Wave is also aimed at this market, but differs in several ways.
- 3G, 4G, and 5G are the most recent cellular data services, with 4G LTE being the dominant one. 5G is available in only a few cities at present.

## 2.4 QUESTIONS

1. Company E is replacing its aged 802.11g wireless network with newer hardware. Which of the following would provide the fastest speed and also support older devices?
   - **A.** 802.11a
   - **B.** 802.11ac
   - **C.** 802.11n
   - **D.** 802.11b

2. Company F is installing Bluetooth mice and keyboards in its meeting room, which is about 8 meters from front to back. The computer will be at the back of the room. Which Bluetooth standard is the minimum needed to have the range necessary?

   **A.** Bluetooth Class 2

   **B.** Bluetooth Class 1

   **C.** Bluetooth 4.2

   **D.** Bluetooth Class 3

3. Company G is having a huge problem with theft in its warehouse. Which of the following technologies does it need to implement to track inventory and help prevent theft?

   **A.** NFC

   **B.** Z-Wave

   **C.** RFID

   **D.** 4G LTE

4. Your client wants to use multiple devices that can relay radio signals to and from each other as part of their smart home. What is this category of technology called?

   **A.** Wi-Fi

   **B.** Hotspot

   **C.** Bluetooth

   **D.** Mesh

5. A co-worker wants to use a smartphone to make payments instead of digging through a wallet or purse for a credit card. What feature needs to be enabled?

   **A.** NFC

   **B.** Z-Wave

   **C.** Wi-Fi

   **D.** Mesh

## 2.4 ANSWERS

1. **B**    802.11ac is the fastest wireless standard in use and is also backward compatible with older hardware.

2. **A**    Bluetooth Class 2 devices have a maximum range of up to 10 meters.

3. **C**    RFID chips on merchandise and scanners at entrances, exits, and restrooms will help reduce theft.

4. **D**    A mesh network uses multiple devices that can wirelessly connect directly with each other. Several smart home technologies use mesh networking, including Zigbee and Z-Wave, among others.

5. **A**    Near field communication (NFC) is used for cardless payment systems such as Apple Pay or Google Pay.

**Objective 2.5** ## Summarize the properties and purposes of services provided by networked hosts

Network hosts can be used as servers to provide file, print, and other types of services; as network appliances, to provide security and network protection features; and as embedded and legacy devices to provide ATM, traffic light, machine control, and other specialized services.

## Server Roles

A server is any computer or device that provides services to connected devices. Depending on the size and types of networks in use, some servers are built into devices such as routers, and computers on the network perform server roles. The following sections describe these roles.

**EXAM TIP**   Know the various server roles by name and function. For example, know that a syslog server is used to store (log) events and can send alerts to administrators.

## Web Server

A *web server* runs software designed for serving websites. For example, the Microsoft Internet Information Services (IIS) functionality is available as an optional feature of Windows Server and business-oriented editions of Windows 7, Windows 8/8.1, and Windows 10. Most Linux distributions include Apache or Nginx web servers. Apache can also be used on macOS.

## File Server

A *file server* stores files that are used by other computers or devices on a network. For SOHO or small business networks, you can enable file sharing on Windows, Linux, or macOS computers. However, larger networks use dedicated file server computers. File servers generally feature very large high-speed storage devices and high-performance network adapters.

## Print Server

A *print server* manages a network print queue for printers that are attached to the server or are connected directly to the network. Depending on the network, a single physical server might be used for both file and print server tasks or separate servers might be used.

## DHCP Server

A Dynamic Host Configuration Protocol server *(DHCP server)* provides IP addresses, default gateways, and other network settings such as DNS server addresses to connected devices. Typically, a DHCP server's function is incorporated into a device such as a router on a SOHO network. However, larger networks might use dedicated DHCP servers.

## DNS Server

A Domain Name Service server *(DNS server)* maintains a database of IP addresses and their matching host names. When a host name, such as www.totalsem.com, is entered into a web browser, the DNS server used by that system matches www.totalsem.com to the appropriate IP address.

DNS servers are provided by ISPs as well as by public DNS services such as Google DNS or OpenDNS. Although your device typically is configured with DNS servers by the DHCP server, it is possible to manually configure the DNS servers you prefer.

## Proxy Server

A *proxy server* is an intermediary between its users and the resources they request. Applications send requests to the proxy server instead of trying to access the Internet directly, and the proxy server fetches the resources on behalf of the users. This enables the proxy server to monitor usage; restrict access to or modify insecure or objectionable content; cache, compress, or strip out resources to improve performance; and more. Enterprise proxy servers are usually implemented as software running on a multipurpose server.

## Mail Server

A *mail server* sends or receives mail. Incoming servers (where you check for new mail) typically use *Post Office Protocol version 3 (POP3)* or *Internet Message Access Protocol version 4 (IMAP4)*, while outgoing servers (where you send mail) use *Simple Mail Transfer Protocol (SMTP)*. These addresses come from your e-mail provider (usually your ISP, company, school, or other organization).

## Authentication Server

An *authentication server* is used to verify the identity of a user after the user has logged in to a network. Some examples of authentication servers include RADIUS servers used by WPA and WPA2 encryption on corporate networks and servers that inspect RSA tokens provided by users with RSA key fobs.

## Syslog

*Syslog* is a protocol that network devices use to send event messages to a server that logs them for viewing. The syslog server can send alerts that can be reviewed by network administrators.

Syslog is not natively supported on Windows, but third-party software can be used to convert messages from Windows apps into syslog-compatible messages.

 **ADDITIONAL RESOURCES**   To learn more about syslog, see the article "Understanding Syslog: Servers, Messages & Security" at www .networkmanagementsoftware.com.

# Internet Appliance

Internet appliances are special-purpose devices that are incorporated into networks, typically to provide various types of network security. The following sections provide a brief overview of the types of Internet appliances you need to know for the CompTIA A+ 220-1001 exam.

## IDS

An *intrusion detection system (IDS)* inspects packets from within the network to look for active intrusions or threats (such as viruses, illegal logon attempts, or a disgruntled employee running a vulnerability scanner) that are already behind the firewall. If it finds something suspicious, it will do some combination of the following: log it, contact an administrator, and enlist help from other devices such as a firewall.

## IPS

The more powerful *intrusion prevention system (IPS)* sits directly in the flow of traffic, enabling it to stop an ongoing attack dead in its tracks (or even fix packets on the fly), but network bandwidth and latency take a hit. Additionally, if the IPS goes down, it may take the network link with it.

 **EXAM TIP**   Know the purposes of and understand the differences between Internet appliances such as UTM, IDS, IPS, and end-point management server. For example, an IDS can identify threats and send alerts. However, the more powerful IPS can actually act on the threat and possibly stop it!

## UTM

Modern dedicated firewall/Internet appliances are built around providing *unified threat management (UTM)*, which bundles other security services such as IPS, VPN, load balancing, anti-malware, and more.

 **EXAM TIP**   Many security appliances include context-based rules called Data Loss Prevention (DLP) to avoid data leaks. DLP scans outgoing packets and stops the flow if they break a rule.

### End-point Management Server

An *end-point management server* centralizes the management of all types of end-user devices, including desktops, laptops, and mobile devices. It can provide security, access to enterprise apps for mobile devices, and a consistent user interface for managed devices.

## Legacy/Embedded Systems

Networked devices don't necessarily look like computers. Many are, but you can find narrow-purpose computers or servers embedded in all sorts of machines and other equipment—CompTIA calls these *legacy/embedded systems*. It can be easy to overlook networked devices embedded in this equipment, but they may represent massive investments your network must remain compatible with. Some examples of legacy/embedded systems include machine controllers, digital watches, digital music players, traffic light controllers, aviation equipment, bank ATMs, and so on. If these systems are running operating systems that are no longer supported with security or other patches (such as Windows XP), they represent a significant security threat.

## REVIEW

**Objective 2.5: Summarize the properties and purposes of services provided by networked hosts**

- Web servers run software that serves websites.
- File servers store files and folders for use on the network.
- Print servers manage network print queues.
- DHCP servers provide IP addresses to connected devices.
- DNS servers handle DNS/IP address lookups.
- Proxy servers reroute requests for Internet content to their own copy of that content or block requests.
- Mail servers send and receive mail.
- Authentication servers verify a user's identity.
- The syslog protocol is used to send event messages to a server where they can be logged and viewed.
- Internet appliance categories include IDS, IPS, UTM, and end-point management servers, all of which can be used to protect the network.
- Legacy/embedded systems such as ATMs and machine controllers represent a significant security threat if their operating systems are no longer being patched.

## 2.5 QUESTIONS

1. Microsoft IIS and Apache are examples of which type of server?

   **A.** DHCP server

   **B.** File server

   **C.** Web server

   **D.** Print server

2. Company H is setting up a RADIUS server as part of its wireless network. This server will perform which of the following tasks?

   **A.** Mail server

   **B.** Authentication server

   **C.** Proxy server

   **D.** Print server

3. Company J wants to install an Internet appliance that will provide protection as well as load balancing and VPN services. Which of the following categories has the device they need?

   **A.** IPS

   **B.** DLP

   **C.** IDS

   **D.** UTM

4. Your client's network is able to receive mail but unable to send it. Which of the following is not working?

   **A.** SMTP

   **B.** UTM

   **C.** Authentication server

   **D.** DNS server

5. Your department is considering an Internet appliance. Which of the following is the most likely reason to get one?

   **A.** Print serving

   **B.** Security

   **C.** Wireless AP

   **D.** Web server

## 2.5 ANSWERS

1. **C**   These are examples of web servers.

2. **B**   A RADIUS server is used for authentication on a WPA or WPA2 Wi-Fi enterprise network.

3. **D** UTM is unified threat management, which includes broad protection against threats and bundles network security services

4. **A** SMTP (Simple Mail Transfer Protocol) is used to send e-mail messages. If this protocol is disabled or blocked, e-mail cannot be sent.

5. **B** Internet appliances are used to provide additional security features to an Internet connection.

## Objective 2.6 Explain common network configuration concepts

To enable a network to work properly, an IP address must be assigned to each device on the network, a mechanism must be available for translating between website names and IP addresses, and methods must exist for connecting different networks to each other. This objective explains these features.

## IP Addressing

A network address must uniquely identify the machine, and it must locate that machine within the larger network. In a TCP/IP network, an *IP address* identifies a device and the network on which it resides.

There are two versions of Internet Protocol (IP): IPv4 and IPv6. The following sections cover their essentials features and differences.

**EXAM TIP** Know the differences between IPv4 and IPv6. For example, an IPv4 address uses 32 bits while an IPv6 address uses 128 bits.

An *Internet Protocol version 4 (IPv4)* address is expressed in *dotted-octet notation*—four sets of eight binary numbers (octets) separated by periods. The binary form (11001010.00100010 .00010000.00001011) isn't human-friendly, so we usually use a decimal form (202.34.16.11).

**Cross-Reference**

IPv4 also uses subnets to subdivide networks. To learn more, see the "Subnet Mask" section in this objective.

An IPv4 loopback address is the address assigned to the adapter inside a computer or device. Each device has the same loopback address (127.0.0.1) because it is used for testing, not for routing data. If you cannot ping your computer's loopback address, you have a problem with your IP configuration.

The 32-bit IPv4 standard offers 4 billion addresses; this seemed like plenty in the beginning, but the Internet Engineering Task Force (IETF) had to develop a replacement, *Internet Protocol version 6 (IPv6)*, to support enough addresses for the foreseeable future. IPv6 notation uses up to eight colon-separated groups (unofficially called *fields* or *hextets*), each containing a hexadecimal number between 0000 and FFFF.

**EXAM TIP**   Homegroups require IPv6, though it's enabled by default.

IPv6 has "up to" eight groups because there are two ways to shorten the written form:

- Leading zeros can be dropped per group, so 00CF becomes CF and 0000 becomes 0.
- Once per address, you can omit any number of consecutive all-zero groups, leaving just the two colons at either end.

Here's a full IPv6 address followed by a shorter form applying these rules:

2001:0000:0000:3210:0800:200C:00CF:1234
2001::3210:800:200C:CF:1234

**EXAM TIP**   IPv6 addresses can also use lowercase letters. For example, fedc::cf:0:ba98:1234/64. Most discussions of IPv6 use uppercase, but you might encounter either lowercase or uppercase notation on the exam.

OS developers have two options for the last 64 bits of an IPv6 address. The method Windows uses is to generate a random value when you activate a NIC and never change it. Linux and macOS use the other method: build it from the MAC address of the NIC (called the *Extended Unique Identifier, 64-bit*, or *EUI-64*).

IPv6 adapters also have a loopback address that can be used for testing. The full address is 0000:0000:0000:0000:0000:0000:0000:0001/128. It is usually abbreviated as ::1/128 (using the two-colon abbreviation for consecutive all-zero groups).

# IPv4 vs. IPv6

As you have seen, IPv4 and IPv6 differ in many ways. Table 2.6-1 helps you compare the differences.

| **TABLE 2.6-1** | IPv4 vs. IPv6 | |
|---|---|---|

| Feature | IPv4 | IPv6 |
|---|---|---|
| Number of bits in IP address | 32 bits | 128 bits |
| Address format | Four groups of dotted octets | Eight fields of hex numbers |
| Zero compression | N/A | Yes. You can use :: to replace one or more contiguous fields of zeros |
| Address example | 192.168.0.1 | 2001:0000:0000:3210:0800:200C:00CF:1234 or 2001::3210:800:200C:CF:1234 |
| Loopback address | 127.0.0.1 | 0000:0000:0000:0000:0000:0000:0000:0001/128 or ::1/128 |
| Maximum number of public IP addresses | Over 4 billion ($2^{32}$) | Over 340 undecillion ($2^{128}$) |

## Dynamic

In DHCP, which Windows uses by default, systems receive their IP address, subnet mask, default gateway address, and DNS address from the *DHCP server* automatically. This is also known as dynamic IP address assignment. To see the current IP properties sheet:

1. Open the Control Panel and select Network and Sharing Center.
2. Click Change Adapter Settings.
3. Click the Local Area Connection link.
4. Click Properties.
5. Click Internet Protocol Version 4.
6. Click Properties.

See Figure 2.6-1 for a typical example of dynamic IP addressing.

## APIPA

If the system is configured to obtain an address automatically but can't do so, the OS will use *Automatic Private IP Addressing (APIPA)* to set a 16-bit subnet mask (255.255.0.0) and randomly choose an address from 169.254.0.1 to 169.254.255.254. The system will broadcast this random address on the subnet and use it if no other system responds. An APIPA address cannot be used for Internet access.

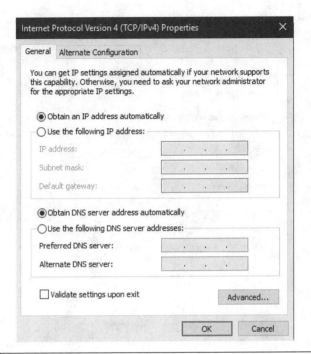

**FIGURE 2.6-1**   Network adapter configured to get IP address from DHCP server

**EXAM TIP**   If your system can communicate with other systems on your local network but can't reach the Internet, chances are the DHCP server is down and you have been assigned an APIPA address. You can find out if you are using an APIPA address by running ipconfig.

## Link Local

When a computer running IPv6 boots, it gives itself a *link-local address*, the equivalent to IPv4's APIPA address. Because APIPA is a fallback in IPv4, the use of an APIPA address can indicate a loss of network connectivity or a problem with the DHCP server; IPv6 systems always have a link-local address. The first 64 bits of a link-local address are always FE80:0000:0000:0000 (which shortens to FE80::).

## Static

A static IP address is an IP address that is manually assigned. Typically, static IP addresses are used in networks for systems that must always have the same IP address because they are used as servers or because they use different protocol settings than other devices on the network.

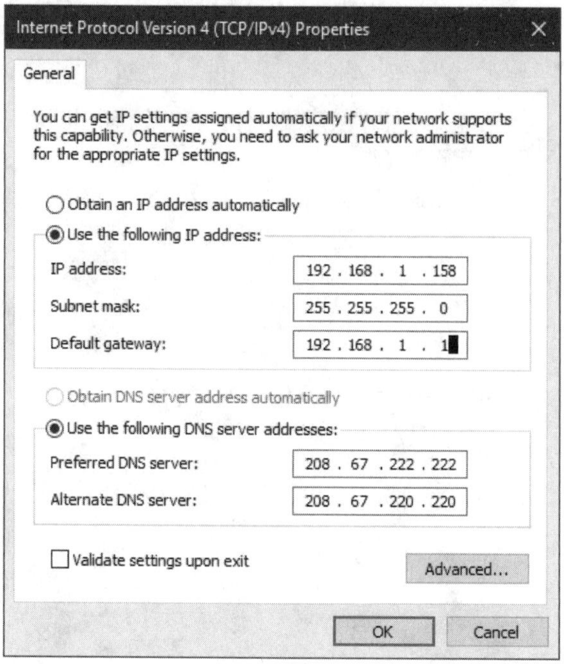

Internet Protocol Version 4 (TCP/IPv4) Properties ☒

General

You can get IP settings assigned automatically if your network supports this capability. Otherwise, you need to ask your network administrator for the appropriate IP settings.

○ Obtain an IP address automatically

● Use the following IP address:

| IP address: | 192 . 168 . 1 . 158 |
| Subnet mask: | 255 . 255 . 255 . 0 |
| Default gateway: | 192 . 168 . 1 . 1▮ |

○ Obtain DNS server address automatically

● Use the following DNS server addresses:

| Preferred DNS server: | 208 . 67 . 222 . 222 |
| Alternate DNS server: | 208 . 67 . 220 . 220 |

☐ Validate settings upon exit

[ Advanced... ]

[ OK ] [ Cancel ]

**FIGURE 2.6-2** Network adapter configured with a static IP address

When a static IP address is used, the IP address, subnet mask, default gateway, and DNS servers must also be assigned. See Figure 2.6-2 for a typical example.

 **EXAM TIP** Know the various IP addressing concepts, including static, dynamic, APIPA, and link local. Practice using the ipconfig and ipconfig /all commands at a command prompt and see if you can identify any of these IP address assignments.

# DNS

The *Domain Name Service (DNS)* matches IP addresses to host names. Each device on an IP network must have access to at least one DNS server to be able to connect to host names. DNS values are typically assigned by the DNS server, but can also be manually entered (refer to Figures 2.6-1 and 2.6-2 for examples).

# DHCP

The *Dynamic Host Configuration Protocol (DHCP)* assigns unique IP addresses to each device on a network. The default setting for Windows and macOS devices is to use DHCP-assigned IP addresses.

## Reservations

A *DHCP reservation* is a DHCP-supplied IP address that never changes. It is meant for devices whose IP address needs to remain constant; for example, a print server. DHCP reservations are created on the DHCP server. This feature is available in DHCP servers as well as in some SOHO routers.

**EXAM TIP**   What's the difference between a static IP address and a reservation? A static IP address is configured at the client and the DHCP reservation is created at the server.

# Subnet Mask

Part of an IPv4 address identifies the network (the network ID), and the rest identifies the local computer (the host ID, or host). NICs use a *subnet mask* to indicate which part identifies the network ID and which identifies the host by blocking out (masking) the network portion. A 255 group is in the network ID, and zeros are in the host ID. Because the first three subnet mask octets in the following example are 255, the network ID is 192.168.4 and the host ID is 33:

> IP address: 192.168.4.33
> Subnet mask: 255.255.255.0

Computers on the same LAN must have the same network ID and unique host IDs. Two computers with the exact same IP address create an *IP conflict*; they won't be able to talk to each other, and other computers won't know where to send data. An IPv4 address can't end with 0 or a 255, so our sample network supports 254 addresses from 192.168.4.1 to 192.168.4.254.

**EXAM TIP**   Know the basic differences between subnet mask notation formats.

Originally, subnet masks fell into A, B, or C "classes," where Class C was 255.255.255.0, Class B was 255.255.0.0, and Class A was 255.0.0.0. One Class B network ID left two full octets (16 bits) for 64,534 unique host IDs ($2^{16} - 2$). This system is long gone, but it's still common to see subnet masks expressed in one to three groups of 255.

The current *Classless Inter-Domain Routing (CIDR)* system works well in binary—where you make subnets with any number of 1s in the mask—but these octets tend to look odd to new techs when presented in decimal (see Table 2.6-2).

| TABLE 2.6-2 | CIDR Subnets | | |
|---|---|---|---|

| Binary | Decimal | IDs | Shorthand |
|---|---|---|---|
| 11111111.11111111.11111111.00000000 | 255.255.255.0 | 254 | /24 |
| 11111111.11111111.11110000.00000000 | 255.255.240.0 | 4094 | /20 |

**EXAM TIP** With CIDR, techs write shorthand for how many binary 1s a mask has. A mask with 24 1s is /24 in shorthand—pronounced *whack twenty-four*.

IPv6 still has subnets, but we append the "/x" from CIDR with the IP address itself: FEDC::CF:0:BA98:1234/64.

# Gateway

A gateway is a link connecting two networks. When a computer uses DHCP for its IP address, it receives the default gateway's IP address as part of its settings. However, if you configure a device's IP address manually, you must provide the default gateway's IP address yourself. The default gateway on most private networks is an address such as 192.168.0.1 or 192.168.1.1.

To see the current IP address, subnet mask, default gateway, and DNS servers in Windows, open a command prompt and use the command **ipconfig /all**. Scroll to the current Local Area Connection after running the command (a typical example is shown in Figure 2.6-3). The comparable command in Linux and macOS is **ifconfig**.

```
C:\Users\Mark E. Soper>ipconfig /all

Windows IP Configuration

    Host Name . . . . . . . . . . . . : Tiger-Athlon
    Primary Dns Suffix  . . . . . . . :
    Node Type . . . . . . . . . . . . : Hybrid
    IP Routing Enabled. . . . . . . . : No
    WINS Proxy Enabled. . . . . . . . : No

Ethernet adapter Local Area Connection:

    Connection-specific DNS Suffix  . :
    Description . . . . . . . . . . . : Realtek PCIe GBE Family Controller
    Physical Address. . . . . . . . . : C8-60-00-14-D3-FB
    DHCP Enabled. . . . . . . . . . . : Yes
    Autoconfiguration Enabled . . . . : Yes
    Link-local IPv6 Address . . . . . : fe80::6c5a:c90d:4169:13da%21(Preferred)
    IPv4 Address. . . . . . . . . . . : 192.168.1.154(Preferred)
    Subnet Mask . . . . . . . . . . . : 255.255.255.0
    Lease Obtained. . . . . . . . . . : Sunday, August 18, 2019 9:53:48 PM
    Lease Expires . . . . . . . . . . : Tuesday, August 27, 2019 1:36:55 PM
    Default Gateway . . . . . . . . . : 192.168.1.1
    DHCP Server . . . . . . . . . . . : 192.168.1.1
    DHCPv6 IAID . . . . . . . . . . . : 231235584
    DHCPv6 Client DUID. . . . . . . . : 00-01-00-01-1A-6C-94-27-C8-60-00-14-D3-FB
    DNS Servers . . . . . . . . . . . : 208.67.222.222
                                        208.67.220.220
    NetBIOS over Tcpip. . . . . . . . : Disabled
```

| FIGURE 2.6-3 | Using ipconfig /all to display the current IP address, subnet mask, default gateway, and DNS servers on the author's PC |
|---|---|

**EXAM TIP**   Make sure you know how to use ipconfig /all and how to identify the settings displayed by ipconfig /all. Practice using ipconfig and ipconfig /all on different computers.

# VPN

A *virtual private network (VPN)* sets up endpoints at each end of an encrypted tunnel between computers or networks to join them into a private network as if they were on a directly connected LAN (though they obviously won't perform like it). In order to pull this trick off, the endpoint on each LAN gets its own LAN IP address and is responsible for handling traffic addressed to and from the remote network (see Figure 2.6-4).

**NOTE**   When your mobile or portable device connects to an untrusted Wi-Fi hotspot, you can connect to another network with a VPN and do all of your browsing (or other work) through the secure tunnel.

To create a VPN connection in Windows 7, click Start, type **VPN** in the Search bar, and press ENTER. In Windows 8/8.1/10, type **VPN** at the Start screen and select *Manage virtual private networks (VPN)* on 8/8.1 or *VPN settings* on 10. Enter your VPN server information, which your network administrator will most likely provide, in the resulting dialog box (see Figure 2.6-5). This creates a virtual NIC that gets an IP address from the DHCP server back at the office.

To set up a VPN connection in macOS, open System Preferences | Network, click Add, choose VPN, select the VPN type, the server address, account name, and authentication settings, and click OK. Click Connect to connect.

To set up a VPN connection in Linux, check the distro's documentation.

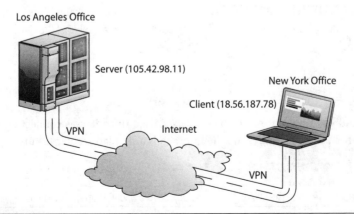

**FIGURE 2.6-4**   Typical VPN tunnel

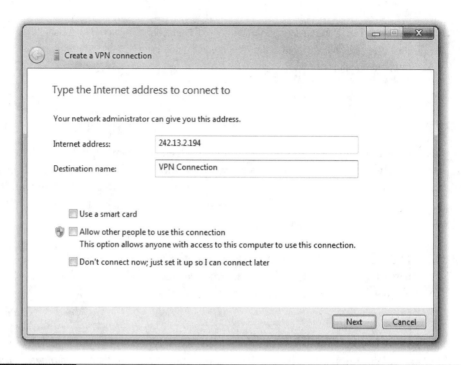

**FIGURE 2.6-5**    VPN connection in Windows

# VLAN

A *virtual local area network (VLAN)* is a subsection of a physical network that is partitioned from the rest of the physical network at the Data Link layer (OSI Layer 2) and is used as a separate physical network. VLANs can be created with managed switches. For example, a 48-port managed switch could be subdivided into six eight-port VLANs.

 **ADDITIONAL RESOURCES**    To learn more about VLANs, go to www .lifewire.com and search for the article "What Is a Virtual LAN (VLAN)?"

# NAT

Network Address Translation, which conceals private IP addresses connecting to a route and displays only a public IP address on the Internet, is a standard router feature.

**Cross-Reference**

For more about NAT, see the "NAT" section in Objective 2.3, earlier in this domain.

# REVIEW

### Objective 2.6: Explain common network configuration concepts

- A dynamic IP address is received from a DHCP server by a device on the network.
- An APIPA address is generated if the DHCP server cannot be reached.
- A link-local address is IPv6's equivalent to an APIPA address.
- A static IP address is an address that is manually assigned.
- If a static IP address is assigned, a DNS server must also be assigned.
- A DHCP reservation is a DHCP-supplied IP address that doesn't change.
- IPv4 uses dotted-octet notation and a subnet mask.
- IPv6 uses up to eight groups of numbers and supports methods to shorten its address.
- NICs use a subnet mask to indicate which part of an IP address identifies the network ID and which identifies the host by blocking out (masking) the network portion.
- A gateway is a link connecting two networks.
- A VPN is a virtual private network. It enables secure connections over an unsecure network such as the Internet.
- A VLAN is a collection of ports that act as a separate physical network; it requires a managed switch.
- NAT protects private network addresses from being revealed to the Internet.

## 2.6 QUESTIONS

1. A user cannot connect to the Internet. When you ask her for her current IP address, she tells you it is 169.254.0.18. Which of the following is not working?

   **A.** APIPA

   **B.** Static IP

   **C.** Link-local

   **D.** DHCP

2. You are reconfiguring up a system using IPv4 and a static IP address after its original settings were deleted. The subnet mask was recorded using the CIDR shorthand of /24. Which of the following decimal subnet masks should you enter when entering the IPv4 address?

   **A.** 255.255.255.0

   **B.** 192.168.1.1

   **C.** 255.255.0.0

   **D.** 2001::3210:800:200C:CF:1234

3. Company K has a sales force that typically uses insecure hotel and coffee-shop wireless networks. Which of the following should you advice they start using to enhance security?

   **A.** VLAN

   **B.** VPN

   **C.** NAT

   **D.** IPv6

4. A DHCP-provided IP address that never changes is known as which of the following?

   **A.** IP permanency

   **B.** IP reservation

   **C.** Link-local

   **D.** APIPA address

5. Your client wants to buy a single switch to create three separate wired networks. What type of networks does the client want to create?

   **A.** VPN

   **B.** Link-local

   **C.** VLAN

   **D.** IPv6

## 2.6 ANSWERS

1. **D**    A 169.254.x.x address is generated when the DHCP server cannot be reached.

2. **A**    /24 is the CIDR shortcut for 255.255.255.0.

3. **B**    A VPN is a virtual private network, which creates a secure "tunnel" for carrying network traffic through insecure connections.

4. **B**    An IP reservation is an address set up by a DHCP server that doesn't change.

5. **C**    A VLAN is a group of ports on a managed switch that performs as if it's on a separate network from other ports on the switch.

**Objective 2.7**  **Compare and contrast Internet connection types, network types, and their features**

There are many different methods for connecting to the Internet and many different network types. They work together to connect devices into networks ranging in size from small LANs to worldwide networks.

# Internet Connection Types

Objective 2.2 earlier in this domain briefly discussed the concept of a bridge that translates signals from one network media to another. When you want to connect a LAN to the Internet, what you're looking for is a bridge between that LAN and one of the data transmission media available in your house or building. No matter how you slice it, you need hardware that can connect your computer, LAN, or WLAN to this other media and you need software that speaks to this hardware—but where these components are located varies.

**EXAM TIP**   Make sure you can explain the differences between these Internet connection types: cable, DSL, dial-up, fiber, satellite, ISDN, cellular, tethering, mobile hotspot, and line-of-sight (fixed) wireless.

In general use we call this hardware a *modem*, even though vanishingly few of them are true modulator/demodulators that create a bridge to *analog* transmission media. Sometimes we install the hardware and software both into a host computer (in which case the computer itself serves as part of the bridge); other times, the software is built into the hardware device, which itself connects directly to a standard RJ-45 jack on our computer or router. The following sections explain the many types of Internet connections.

**NOTE**   Each OS has settings to share a direct Internet connection with the LAN or other systems; Windows systems use Internet Connection Sharing (ICS).

## Cable

Cable uses regular RG-6 or RG-59 cable TV lines to provide upload speeds from 5 to 35+ Mbps and download speeds from 15 to 1000+ Mbps. *Cable Internet* connections are theoretically available anywhere you can get cable TV. The cable connects to a cable modem that itself connects (via Ethernet) to a small home router or your network interface card (NIC).

## DSL

*Digital subscriber line (DSL)* connections to ISPs use standard telephone lines, but special equipment on each end creates always-on Internet connections at much greater speeds than dial-up. To set up a DSL connection, connect a DSL receiver (shown in Figure 2.7-1) from the ISP to the telephone line. A tech or knowledgeable user then configures the DSL modem and router with settings from the ISP.

**FIGURE 2.7-1**    A DSL receiver

 **NOTE**    The most common forms of DSL are *asynchronous (ADSL)* and *synchronous (SDSL)*. ADSL lines differ between slow upload speed (such as 384 Kbps, 768 Kbps, or 1 Mbps) and faster download speed (usually 3 to 15 Mbps). You can pay more for SDSL to get the same upload and download speeds. DSL encompasses many such variations, so you'll often see it referred to as *x*DSL.

Service levels for DSL can vary widely. At the low end of the spectrum, speeds are generally in the single digits—less than 1 Mbps upload and around 3 Mbps download. Where available, more recent *x*DSL technologies can offer competitive broadband speeds measured in tens or hundreds of megabits per second.

## Dial-up

Dial-up Internet links use the first ubiquitous data network—the telephone system. In traditional dial-up, connection software on a computer uses an analog modem. An internal version for desktop computers is shown in Figure 2.7-2.

An external modem is shown in Figure 2.7-3. With either type, the modem is used to dial (as in, dial a phone) the ISP, where it begins translating between digital information and analog sound to negotiate a connection. At 56 Kbps download and up to 48 Kbps upload, dial-up is glacial when compared to the newest connection standards.

**FIGURE 2.7-2**   An internal modem

**FIGURE 2.7-3**   An external USB modem

You can create a new connection from within the OS. You'll need to provide one or more dial-up telephone numbers for the ISP as well as your user name and password; the ISP should give you this information along with any configuration options specific to their system. In Windows 7, for example, you can click *Set up a new connection or network* from the Network and Sharing center applet, select Connect to the Internet, and enter the dial-up connection details (as shown in Figure 2.7-4).

If you have to troubleshoot a traditional modem, keep in mind what it is and how it works. The user needs a dial tone, and they may need to configure a prefix to "dial out" if they're in an office or hotel. They may not be able to test their connection while they speak with you. They can manually dial the number (or listen in) and confirm another computer answers it. If you've double-checked everything, including connection numbers and user credentials, it's time to call the ISP to troubleshoot Dial-up Networking settings.

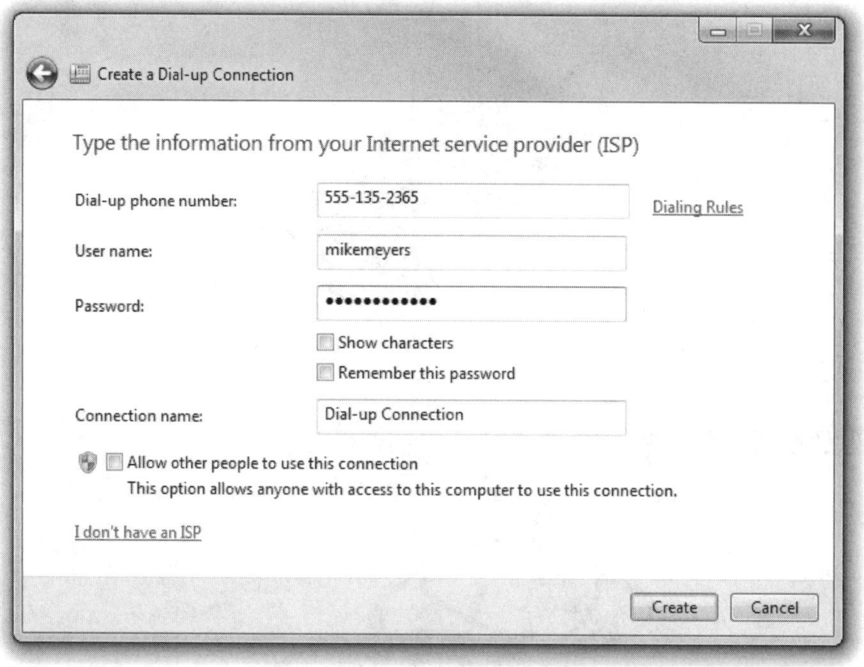

Create a Dial-up Connection

Type the information from your Internet service provider (ISP)

Dial-up phone number:    555-135-2365                          Dialing Rules

User name:               mikemeyers

Password:                ••••••••••••

☐ Show characters
☐ Remember this password

Connection name:         Dial-up Connection

☐ Allow other people to use this connection
This option allows anyone with access to this computer to use this connection.

I don't have an ISP

Create    Cancel

**FIGURE 2.7-4**    Creating a dial-up connection in Windows 7

## Fiber

DSL providers have developed very popular fiber-to-the-node (FTTN) and fiber-to-the-premises (FTTP) services that provide Internet (and more). FTTN connections run from the provider to a box in your neighborhood, which connects to your home or office via normal coaxial or Ethernet cable. FTTP runs from the provider straight to a home or office, using fiber the whole way.

AT&T Internet FTTN services start with download speeds up to 100 Mbps and upload speeds up to 20 Mbps. AT&T also offers 300 Mbps and 1 Gbps FTTP services.

 **ADDITIONAL RESOURCES**    To learn more about the many DSL, hybrid, and fiber Internet speed tiers that AT&T offers, go to currently.att.yahoo.com, search for "AT&T speed tiers," and click the AT&T - Speed Tiers link.

Verizon's Fios FTTP service provides upload and download speeds from 100 Mbps to 500 Mbps and its Fios Gigabit connection runs at up to 940 Mbps download and 880 Mbps upload. Google Fiber offers a 1 Gbps upload/download service in a few cities nationwide.

Cable TV providers are also using fiber to push speeds to 1 Gbps.

# Satellite

*Satellite* connections beam data to a professionally installed satellite dish at your house or office (with line-of-sight to the satellite). Coax connects the satellite to a receiver or satellite modem that translates the data to Ethernet, which can connect directly to your router or the NIC in your computer.

Real-world download speeds in clear weather run from a few to about 25 Mbps; upload speeds vary, but are typically a tenth to a third of the download speed. They aren't stunning, but satellite can provide these speeds in areas with no other connectivity.

 **NOTE** Keep in mind *satellite latency*—usually several hundred milliseconds (ms). It isn't highly obvious for many purposes, but can affect real-time activities like gaming or video/voice calls.

# ISDN

On all-digital telephone lines, you may be able to get *integrated services digital network (ISDN)* dial-up, which uses a terminal adapter (TA) that closely resembles a dial-up modem. ISDN uses 64-Kbps channels in two common configurations: basic rate interface (BRI), which combines two channels for 128-Kbps bandwidth, and primary rate interface (PRI), which combines 23 channels for 1.544 Mbps. Most ISPs that formerly offered ISDN are now offering some form of DSL, which is substantially faster.

# Cellular

Cellular Internet connections are available in 3G, 4G, and, in a few locations, 5G, as discussed in the "Cellular Standards: 3G, 4G, LTE, 5G" section in Objective 2.4, earlier in this domain. In addition to being available in smartphones, cellular connections are also available for tablets and laptops as an additional wireless feature alongside the usual Wi-Fi and Bluetooth connections.

## Mobile Hotspot/Tethering

A *mobile hotspot* device creates a Wi-Fi network to share its cellular data connection (3G, 4G, 4G LTE, or 5G) with other Wi-Fi devices. Wireless providers sell standalone hotspot devices for their network, but many smartphones and tablets can act as hotspots. Just enable the cellular data connection and toggle the hotspot setting to broadcast the Wi-Fi network and serve as a router between it and the cellular network (see Figure 2.7-5); configure a password to limit access.

Sharing a smartphone or tablet's data connection is also called *tethering* when a USB cable is used, a term you'll see carriers use to indicate different rules, rates, and restrictions on data consumed this way.

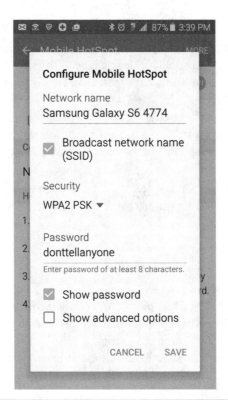

**FIGURE 2.7-5**   Configuring an Android phone as a portable hotspot

**CAUTION**   Keep in mind that open hotspots aren't encrypted, so attackers can monitor your connection. Check with your vendor to determine whether its hotspots are open or encrypted.

## Line-of-sight Wireless Internet Service

*Line-of-sight wireless Internet service* (also known as *fixed wireless*) is a popular choice in some smaller cities and nearby rural areas where cable or DSL Internet services are not available. This type of service uses high-powered, directional antennas to connect to fixed locations up to about eight miles away. Speeds can vary from as little as 256 Kbps to as much as 20 Mbps or more, depending upon distance and your ISP.

**ADDITIONAL RESOURCES**   To learn more about this type of service, enter **Broadbandnow fixed wireless** into a search engine such as Google or DuckDuckGo.

# Network Types

With more network types than ever before, the CompTIA A+ 220-1001 and 220-1002 exams expect you to know the differences between LANs, WANs, and many more. See the following sections for a brief introduction to the types you need to know.

 **EXAM TIP**   Make sure you can explain the differences between these network types: LAN, WAN, PAN, MAN, and WMN.

## LAN

A *local area network (LAN)* is a group of networked computers within a few hundred meters of each other. LAN connections typically use wired Ethernet or Wi-Fi.

## WAN

A *wide area network (WAN)* is a group of computers on multiple LANs connected with long-distance technologies. The Internet is a WAN.

## PAN

A *personal area network (PAN)* is a short-range network typically using Bluetooth. It is used to interchange data between personal devices such as smartphones, tablets, and laptops.

## MAN

A *metropolitan area network (MAN)* is a network larger than a LAN but smaller than a WAN. The term MAN is often used to refer to city-wide or campus-wide networks that use fiber optic or fixed-base wireless networks.

## WMN

A *wireless mesh network (WMN)* connects wireless access points or network adapters to each other in such a way that each access point can forward data to the next access point or adapter. WMN technology is now available for use in homes and small offices to enable wireless coverage without dead spots or the use of conventional wireless repeaters.

# REVIEW

### Objective 2.7: Compare and contrast Internet connection types, network types, and their features

- Cable uses RG-59 or RG-6 cable and runs faster than DSL or dial-up.
- Traditional DSL uses phone lines, but newer types also incorporate cable or fiber optic lines for greater speed.
- Dial-up works over any conventional phone line and is by far the slowest Internet connection type.
- Fiber is used by many DSL and cable TV providers to improve speed and carry more information.
- Satellite Internet can provide service to remote locations outside the reach of other Internet service types, but it is much slower and can be affected by weather conditions.
- ISDN is largely outdated for Internet service, although it is still used for telephone service.
- Cellular connections work anywhere a smartphone is used but have data caps. A mobile hotspot or a smartphone with mobile hotspot support can share its connection with others wirelessly. A tethered connection is similar but uses USB.
- Line-of-sight wireless Internet uses directional antennas for connections, and is popular in rural and suburban areas outside the reach of DSL or cable.
- LAN = local area network
- WAN = wide area network
- PAN = personal area network
- MAN = metropolitan area network
- WMN = wireless mesh network

## 2.7 QUESTIONS

1. You are working with a client who needs Internet access but lives too far away from the city to use DSL or cable TV. They live on top of a hill. They need quick response and expect to use 15 GB or more of data per month. Which of the following Internet services would you recommend investigating?

   **A.** Satellite

   **B.** Cellular

   **C.** FTTP

   **D.** Line-of-sight fixed wireless

2. Your client has an old laptop with an RJ-11 port and an RJ-45 port built in. It does not have wireless capabilities. Without buying or renting another component, which of the following Internet connection types is this laptop ready to use?

   **A.** DSL

   **B.** Dial-up

**C.** Cable

**D.** Fiber

3. You are at a client's location preparing to install an update to Windows. Their Internet connection goes down. Which of the following is the best choice to use to install the update immediately?

**A.** DSL

**B.** Dial-up

**C.** Mobile hotspot/tethering

**D.** ISDN

4. Your client wants to build a network that will connect locations in various parts of a medium-sized city with each other. Which type of network does the client want to create?

**A.** MAN

**B.** WAN

**C.** LAN

**D.** PAN

5. Your company is considering upgrading its DSL service to a faster service. Which of the following types of services is likely to be the fastest?

**A.** Cable

**B.** FTTN

**C.** Satellite

**D.** FTTP

## 2.7 ANSWERS

1. **D** Line-of-sight fixed wireless, if available, is the best choice because it has no data caps and, unlike satellite, has quick response (fast ping rate).

2. **B** The RJ-11 port indicates the laptop has a dial-up modem. Dial-up requires no additional equipment, only an account with a dial-up ISP.

3. **C** The mobile hotspot/tethering option supported by many smartphones would enable you to perform the update on-site.

4. **A** A metropolitan area network (MAN) connects locations in a single city that might be separated by some blocks of distance.

5. **D** Fiber to the premises (FTTP) will be the fastest, since the fiber is connecting directly to the home or office.

**Objective 2.8** # Given a scenario, use appropriate networking tools

Whether you build, repair, or troubleshoot wired or wireless networks, you need to understand how to use the networking tools covered in this section.

 **EXAM TIP** Make sure you understand the uses for the tools: crimper, cable stripper, multimeter, tone generator and probe, cable tester, loopback plug, punchdown tool, and Wi-Fi analyzer.

## Crimper and Cable Stripper

For a patch cable, use stranded UTP cable matching the Cat level of your horizontal cabling. If you use cable with a lower Cat level than your existing cable, the network might run more slowly. The basic tool is a RJ-45 *crimper* (see Figure 2.8-1) with built-in *cable stripper* (also known as a wire stripper) and *wire snips*. Stranded and solid-core cable require different crimps; make sure you have the right kind. First, cut the cable square with the RJ-45 crimper

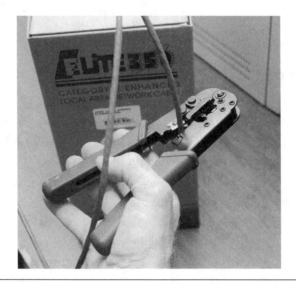

**FIGURE 2.8-1** Crimper

**FIGURE 2.8-2**   Properly stripped cable

or scissors; then use the built-in cable stripper to strip a half inch of plastic jacket off the end of the cable (see Figure 2.8-2). Once the cable is stripped, you're ready to wire the connector.

## Multimeter

The CompTIA A+ 220-1001 exam objectives include multimeters in networking tools. Multimeters are a bit of a Swiss Army knife for testing anything that carries a current. You can certainly use a multimeter to test whether a dead switch is connected to a good outlet, for example. In a pinch, you can use one to test cables you don't have a regular tester for—but this is often tedious; a multimeter should be your last resort for testing network cable.

## Tone Generator and Probe

Even in well-planned networks that don't turn into a rat's nest of cable, labels fall off and people miscount which port to label. In the real world, you may have to locate or *trace* cables and ports to test them.

Network techs use a *tone generator and probe* (see Figure 2.8-3). The *tone generator* connects to the cable with alligator clips, tiny hooks, or a network jack, and it sends an electrical signal along the wire. The *tone probe* emits a sound when it is placed near the cable carrying this signal.

**FIGURE 2.8-3** Fox and Hound, a tone generator and probe made by Triplett Corporation

## Cable Tester

A *cable tester* (shown in Figure 2.8-4) is used to verify the individual wires in TP cable are properly located and connected. When testing cables, be sure to test patch cables as well as cable runs in the walls. To do so, unplug the patch cable from the PC, attach a cable tester, and

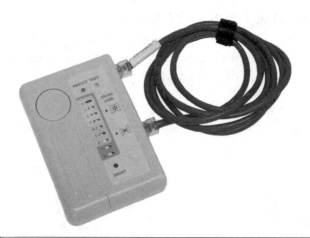

**FIGURE 2.8-4** Typical cable tester

go to the communications room. Unplug the patch cable from the switch and plug the tester into that patch cable.

A specialized device used for cable testing is a time-domain reflectometer (TDR) tester such as the Fluke MicroScanner. A TDR measures impedance (resistance) in network cabling. If the tester measures any impedance, something is wrong with the cable.

# Loopback Plug

A bad NIC can cause a length of network cable to appear to have failed. However, the NIC's female connector is easy to damage. To determine if the card is bad, diagnostics provided by the OS or NIC manufacturer may include a *loopback test* that sends data out of the NIC to see if it comes back. A *loopback plug* (see Figure 2.8-5) is attached to the NIC's RJ-45 cable port and it loops transmit lines back to receive lines. If the same data is received as sent, the NIC port works. If not, the NIC needs repair or replacement

**FIGURE 2.8-5**   Loopback plug

# Punchdown Tool

With a typical horizontal cabling run, you'll connect the work-area end to the back of a wall outlet with a female connector, and the telecommunications-room end will connect to the back of a patch panel's female connector. You typically use a *punchdown tool* (see Figure 2.8-6) to connect the cable to a *110 block* (also called a *110-punchdown block*), which is wired to the female connector. The punchdown tool forces each wire into a small metal-lined groove (shown in Figure 2.8-7), where the metal lining slices the cladding to contact the wire.

**FIGURE 2.8-6**    Punchdown tool

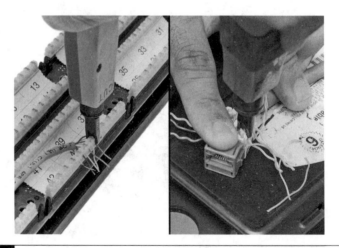

**FIGURE 2.8-7**    Punching down a patch panel (left) and modular jack (right)

 **NOTE**    The UTP connectors in outlets and patch panels also have Cat levels—for example, don't hamstring a good Cat 6 installation with outlets or patch panels that have a lower Cat level (Cat5e or Cat5 in this example).

A work-area wall outlet (see Figure 2.8-8) consists of one or two female jacks, a mounting bracket, and a faceplate.

**FIGURE 2.8-8**   Typical work area outlet

# Wi-Fi Analyzer

Which Wi-Fi channels are currently in use? How strong are the signals? To find out, you can use your Android or iOS smartphones with a free or paid Wi-Fi analysis app, available from many vendors on the Google Play or Apple App stores. Figure 2.8-9 illustrates how a typical Wi-Fi analysis app (Wifi Analyzer app for Android from Farproc) shows activity on 2.4- and 5-GHz bands. After you review the information, you might want to change the channel(s) used by your router.

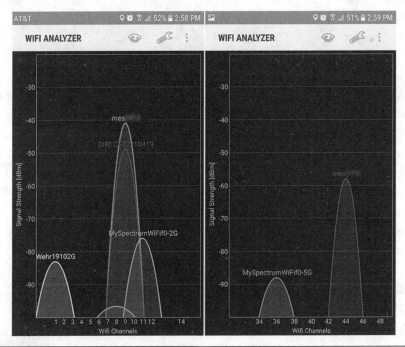

**FIGURE 2.8-9**   Typical 2.4-GHz (left) and 5-GHz (right) router activity as captured by Wifi Analyzer from Farproc

# REVIEW

**Objective 2.8: Given a scenario, use appropriate networking tools**

- A crimper is used to attach a connector to a UTP cable.
- A wire/cable stripper is used to remove the outer sheath from the cable to expose the UTP wires.
- A multimeter can be used to test individual cable strands.
- A tone generator and probe (also known as a toner or toner probe) is used to find the specific cable for labeling or testing.
- A cable tester tests specific wires in a cable.
- A loopback plug checks the condition of a NIC port.
- A punchdown tool is used to connect the wires in a cable to a 110-punchdown block.
- Wifi Analyzer is an app you can run on Android smartphones to display signal strength and network usage for Wi-Fi networks.

# 2.8 QUESTIONS

1. Your client is reporting problems with some of their network cables. Unfortunately, none of the cables are labeled and the client's wiring closet is a mess. Which of the following should you use to help label the client's cables?

   **A.** Multimeter

   **B.** Tone generator and probe

   **C.** Crimper

   **D.** Loopback plug

2. After labeling the cables for your client, you discover that one of the cables is connected to a workstation that can't connect to the Internet. To help determine if the problem is actually the NIC, which of the following would you use?

   **A.** Loopback plug

   **B.** Multimeter

   **C.** Cable tester

   **D.** Tone generator and probe

3. Your client's 2.4-GHz network once ran very quickly. However, several new houses have been built nearby and network performance is now very poor. Which of the following would help determine if different settings are needed?

   **A.** Mobile hotspot

   **B.** Cable tester

   **C.** Punchdown tool

   **D.** Wi-Fi analyzer

4. You are preparing to build some network patch cables for a Gigabit Ethernet network. Which of the following do you *not* need to use for this task?

   **A.** Punchdown block

   **B.** RJ-45 crimper

   **C.** Wire stripper

   **D.** Connector matching cable type

5. After an office remodeling project, some segments of your client's wired network are slow. The exiting computers, switches, and routers were retained, but additional patch panels were installed. What might have gone wrong during the process? (Choose two.)

   **A.** Incorrect Cat level in patch panels

   **B.** Loopback plugs left connected to some workstations

   **C.** Incorrect Cat level in patch cables

   **D.** Hub used on some network segments

## 2.8 ANSWERS

1. **B**   A tone generator and probe helps determine which wire is which.

2. **A**   A loopback plug is attached to the NIC's RJ-45 cable port and it loops transmit lines back to receive lines. If the same data is received as sent, the NIC port works. If not, the NIC needs repair or replacement.

3. **D**   A Wi-Fi analyzer displays the activity on the 2.4-GHz band by channel and router name.

4. **A**   A punchdown block is not used for patch cables. It is used for cables wired into a wall.

5. **A C**   Using patch cables or punchdown blocks with Cat levels lower than the previous network hardware could slow down the network; for example, using Cat 5 (100 Mbps) instead of Cat 5e (1000 Mbps) hardware.

# Hardware

DOMAIN 3.0

**Objective 3.1** **Explain basic cable types, features, and their purposes**

**Objective 3.2** **Identify common connector types**

Although USB dominates external device connections, many other types of cables and connectors are used with laptops, desktops, and mobile devices, including network, video, and audio. In the following sections, you learn what they do and how to tell them apart from each other.

 **NOTE**    Because cables and connectors are closely related, we have combined the coverage of these two objectives.

## Network Cables and Connectors

Network cables are used to connect computers and devices to wired networks ranging from LANs to the Internet. Network cables are available in three categories: twisted pair (Ethernet and phone), fiber, and coaxial (RG-59 and RG-6). Network cables use connectors ranging from RJ-45 and RJ-11 to BNC and various fiber types.

Let's look at cables and connectors used for Ethernet first.

### Ethernet

Ethernet cable is twisted-pair cable, which is comprised of eight tiny cables arranged in four wire pairs. Table 3.1/3.2-1 compares the characteristics of the major categories of Ethernet cable in use: Cat 5, Cat 5e, and Cat 6. These cables use RJ-45 connectors.

**TABLE 3.1/3.2-1**    Ethernet Cable Types Compared

| Category | Maximum Data Speed Supported | Network Types Supported | Connector Used |
|----------|------------------------------|-------------------------|----------------|
| Cat 5 | 100 Mbps | Fast Ethernet (100-Mbps Ethernet) and slower | RJ-45 |
| Cat 5e | 1000 Mbps | Gigabit Ethernet (1000-Mbps Ethernet) and slower | RJ-45 |
| Cat 6 | 1000 Mbps | Gigabit Ethernet (1000-Mbps Ethernet) up to 100-meter segments; 10 Gbps (10,000-Mbps Ethernet) up to 55-meter segments | RJ-45 |

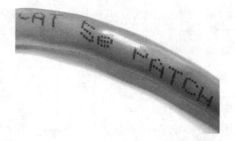

FIGURE 3.1/3.2-1 Cat 5e Ethernet cable

 **EXAM TIP**   Although most Ethernet installations used twisted-pair cabling, Ethernet can also be carried over fiber optic cables and formerly used coaxial cable. In other words, an Ethernet network does not necessarily require Ethernet cable!

Most Ethernet cables are marked with the Cat number, as shown in Figure 3.1/3.2-1.

The maximum distance for a single Cat 5, 5e, or 6 cable run is 100 meters (about 328 feet). To go further, use repeaters.

## Cross-Reference

To learn more about network devices used with Ethernet, see Part I, Domain 2.0, Objective 2.2.

## RJ-45

Network interfaces come in several varieties. Most network interface cards (NICs) and motherboards have an 8-wire RJ-45 port (see Figure 3.1/3.2-2). RJ-45 connectors look like wide RJ-11 telephone connectors and plug into the female RJ-45 ports in the same manner that RJ-11 telephone cables plug into a modem.

**FIGURE 3.1/3.2-2**   An RJ-45 connecter and port

**NOTE** A network interface card (NIC) enables a computer to connect to a network. Techs call them NICs, even when the network adapter is built into a motherboard and thus is distinctly lacking in "card-ness."

## Unshielded Twisted Pair

*Unshielded twisted pair (UTP)* cabling consists of 22–26 AWG wire twisted into color-coded pairs. Each wire is insulated, and then the group is encased in a common jacket. The ANSI/ TIA 568 standards specify several UTP categories that define maximum data transfer speeds (or *bandwidth*); these are printed on the cable. UTP is the predominate type of cable used in 10/100/1000Base T Ethernet installations.

## Shielded Twisted Pair

The wire pairs in *shielded twisted pair (STP)* are wrapped in shielding to protect them from electromagnetic interference (EMI). STP is rare because few cables run in EMI-heavy settings such as a shop floor crowded with electric motors.

## Plenum

Each horizontal cabling run is usually Cat 5e or better UTP. Most of the cabling runs in the *plenum* space, the space above the ceiling, under the floors, or in the walls.

This has two implications:

* If the PVC (polyvinyl chloride) protective jacket on standard network cables burns, it produces dangerous fumes that can spread quickly via the plenum space. Instead, we must use more expensive plenum-grade cable with a fire-retardant jacket.
* The protection afforded by the plenum space means we can use faster solid-core UTP cable with a single fragile solid wire, instead of slower, damage-resistant stranded-core UTP with a bundle of tiny wire strands that don't conduct as well.

## 568A/B

If you wire your own connectors, you can technically order the wires however you like if you use the same pairings on each end, but you should pick either the ANSI/TIA 568A (T568A) or the ANSI/TIA 568B (T568B) standard—and save yourself time later by keeping good records. The pins in UTP are numbered (as shown in Figure 3.1/3.2-3), but each matching wire just has a standardized color, as detailed in Table 3.1/3.2-2.

## RJ-11

Dial-up and DSL modem ports look identical to traditional wired telephone jacks and use two-wire *RJ-11* telephone cables and connectors (see Figure 3.1/3.2-4). The locking clips on

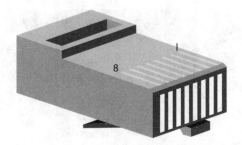

**FIGURE 3.1/3.2-3** RJ-45 pin numbers

**TABLE 3.1/3.2-2** UTP Cabling Color Chart

| Pin | T568A | T568B | | Pin | T568A | T568B |
|-----|-------|-------|---|-----|-------|-------|
| 1 | White/Green | White/Orange | | 5 | White/Blue | White/Blue |
| 2 | Green | Orange | | 6 | Orange | Green |
| 3 | White/Orange | White/Green | | 7 | White/Brown | White/Brown |
| 4 | Blue | Blue | | 8 | Brown | Brown |

the male RJ-11 connectors secure the cable into the port. Most modems also have an output port for a telephone.

**FIGURE 3.1/3.2-4** RJ-11 connectors on a modem

# Fiber

Fiber optic cable uses light to transmit Ethernet network frames, which makes it immune to electrical problems such as lightning, short circuits, and static. Fiber optic signals also travel 2000 meters (2 km) or more. Most fiber Ethernet networks use 62.5/125 multimode fiber optic cable. Fiber optics are half-duplex; data flows only one way, so fiber connections require two cables.

**FIGURE 3.1/3.2-5**   ST (left), SC (center), and LC (right) fiber connectors

The most common fiber connectors are ST, SC, and LC (see Figure 3.1/3.2-5). Other fiber connectors that you might see are FDDI, MT-RJ, and FC.

**EXAM TIP**   It's not important to memorize the different types of fiber optic connectors.

If you want to use fiber optic cabling, you need a fiber optic switch and fiber optic network cards. Regardless of fiber's impressive theoretical speed and range, real-world fiber networks are limited to the speed and distance specified by their respective Ethernet standard. The record single-mode transmission way back in 2011 was 100 terabits per second over 100 miles, but you won't find Ethernet standards anywhere near that (yet). Multimode networks run from 10 to 10,000 Mbps up to ~600 meters.

**NOTE**   Fiber networks use laser or LED light sources. In single mode, lasers pulse single bursts over long distances at incredible speeds. Multimode fiber carries multiple simultaneous LED signals using different reflection angles within the core of the cable. These reflection angles disperse over long distances, limiting multimode to relatively short distances.

## Coaxial

Coax consists of a core cable, surrounded by insulation, covered with a shield of braided cable (see Figure 3.1/3.2-6) to eliminate interference, and wrapped with a protective cover. Early versions of Ethernet ran on coaxial cable instead of UTP, and coax lives on for cable modems and satellite connections.

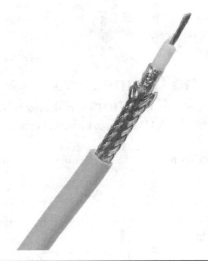

**FIGURE 3.1/3.2-6** Typical coax

There are hundreds of RG ratings for coax, but you just need to know *RG-59* and *RG-6* for the CompTIA A+ 220-1001 exam; the RG rating is marked on the cable. Both have a 75-ohm impedance and are used in cable television, but RG-59 is thinner and can't carry data as far as RG-6, which is the standard for HD video. Coax generally tops out around 100 Mbps. Recommended maximum length without using amplifiers is about 400 meters.

 **EXAM TIP** Be sure you are familiar with the various network cable types. As CompTIA specifically lists under objective 3.1 for network cables, know their speed and transmission limitations.

## BNC

Very old NICs might have a bayonet-style coax connector called a BNC connector (see Figure 3.1/3.2-7), used for 10Base2 or Thinnet (10 Mbps) Ethernet networking. You won't

**FIGURE 3.1/3.2-7** BNC connector and terminator used on 10Base2 network cards

see these connectors on working systems, but you might on the exam! Maximum segment length is 185 meters (about 606 feet).

## Video Cables and Connectors

Video cables connect displays, monitors, HDTVs, and projectors to your computer's video card or onboard video port. Table 3.1/3.2-3 provides an overview of these cables and connector types.

Figure 3.1/3.2-8 illustrates some of these video cables and Figure 3.1/3.2-9 illustrates most of these video ports.

**TABLE 3.1/3.2-3**   Video Cables

| Video Cable Type | Standard Name | Reduced-size Version | Signal Types Supported | Notes |
|---|---|---|---|---|
| VGA | Video Graphics Array | N/A | Analog video | VGA displays can be connected to HDMI, DVI-I, and DisplayPort ports with suitable adapters. |
| HDMI | High Definition Multimedia Interface | Mini-HDMI | HD video and HD audio | Video signal is compatible with DVI. |
| DVI | Digital Visual Interface | N/A | HD video | DVI-I (analog/digital) and DVI-D (digital) signals are compatible with HDMI; the rare DVI-A supports analog displays only. |
| DP | DisplayPort | Mini DisplayPort (mDP) | HD video and HD audio | Video signal is compatible with DVI and HDMI. |

**FIGURE 3.1/3.2-8**   Typical HDMI, Mini-HDMI, DP, and mDP cables/connectors (left to right)

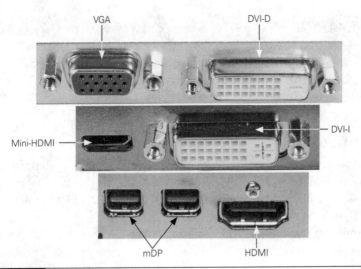

**FIGURE 3.1/3.2-9**  Typical video ports

# Multipurpose Cables

Modern computers use one or more multifunction ports to connect a host of useful peripherals. All newer machines have universal serial bus (USB) ports, and some have additional ports such as Thunderbolt. Mobile devices have USB or Lightning ports.

## Lightning

With the iPhone 5, Apple replaced its older 30-pin connector with its proprietary 8-pin Lightning connector (see Figure 3.1/3.2-10), which can be inserted in both up and down orientations—it's not "keyed" to a single orientation. Licensed Lightning connectors have a small verification chip, and knock-off cables without it typically won't work or will have only limited use.

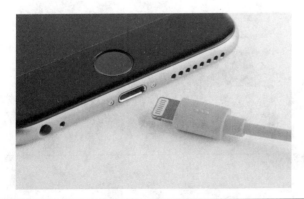

**FIGURE 3.1/3.2-10**  Lightning connector

**EXAM TIP**    The Apple Lightning standard is the poster child for *proprietary vendor-specific ports and connectors*. Only iOS devices use Lightning for communication and power. Android and Windows mobile devices typically use industry-standard, vendor-neutral ports and connectors.

## Thunderbolt

Intel and Apple developed the *Thunderbolt* interface as a high-speed alternative to existing technologies such as USB and FireWire to connect peripherals via PCIe and DisplayPort simultaneously, combining their capacity. Consult Table 3.1/3.2-4 for the basics on each version of the Thunderbolt standard.

Thunderbolt can use copper or fiber cabling, though the fiber optic cables are still pretty rare. The copper cables can run up to 3 meters (whether a single cable, or chained). Optical runs can extend much farther—up to 60 meters—but optical cables of that length are several hundred dollars, and you'll need another way to power the device.

The only way to tell the difference between a standard DisplayPort and a Thunderbolt 1 or 2 port (see Figure 3.1/3.2-11) is that the latter has a little lightning bolt symbol next to it—and you'll need the same trick to tell a Thunderbolt 3 port apart from a regular USB Type-C port.

**TABLE 3.1/3.2-4**    Thunderbolt Standards

| Standard | Connector | Maximum Speed | Cable Length |
|---|---|---|---|
| Thunderbolt 1 | Mini DisplayPort | 10 Gbps | 3 m (copper) / 60 m (fiber) |
| Thunderbolt 2 | Mini DisplayPort | 20 Gbps | 3 m (copper) / 60 m (fiber) |
| Thunderbolt 3 | USB Type-C | 40 Gbps | 3 m (copper) / 60 m (fiber) |

**FIGURE 3.1/3.2-11**    Thunderbolt 2 port

# USB

*USB (universal serial bus)* is a large family of hot-swappable connectors that, as the name implies, can be used to interface almost anything to a PC or mobile device. USB works with IT essentials such as keyboards, mice, joysticks, microphones, scanners, printers, modems, tablets, and digital cameras as well as eccentric office gadgets such as lap warmers, cup heaters, personal fans, and many more.

The core of USB is the USB host controller, an integrated circuit normally built into the chipset. It acts as the interface between the system and every USB device that connects to it. The USB root hub is the part of the host controller that makes the physical connection to the USB ports. A USB host controller is the boss (the master) of any device (the slave) that plugs into that host controller. The host controller performs two tasks: sending commands and providing power to connected USB devices. The host controller is upstream, controlling devices connected downstream to it. The host controller is shared by every device plugged into it, so speed and power are reduced with each new device.

You can add extra USB ports to a system using either a USB expansion card or a USB hub (see Figure 3.1/3.2-12). USB hubs come in powered and bus-powered varieties. Powered USB devices have their own power plug, whereas bus-powered USB devices do not and instead draw their power from the USB bus. Too many bus-powered devices on a bus-powered hub can cause problems, so it's best to use powered hubs in such situations.

 **ADDITIONAL RESOURCES**  For more information about USB, visit www.usb.org.

USB devices are *hot-swappable*, which means that you can connect or disconnect them at any time without powering down your computer. USB technology lets you use hubs to connect up to 127 devices to a single host controller on your computer.

 **EXAM TIP**  For the CompTIA A+ 220-1001 exam, you need to know that you can connect 127 devices to a single USB port. But for real-life, on-the-job situations, it's a bad idea to hit this maximum. Some applications reserve bandwidth, and you could wind up with quite a mess. Too much of a good thing isn't good!

**FIGURE 3.1/3.2-12**  Typical USB hub

**TABLE 3.1/3.2-5**   USB Standards

| Name | Standard | Maximum Speed | Cable Length |
|------|----------|---------------|--------------|
| Low-Speed USB | USB 1.1 | 1.5 Mbps | 3 meters |
| Full-Speed USB | USB 1.1 | 12 Mbps | 3 meters |
| Hi-Speed USB | USB 2.0 | 480 Mbps | 5 meters |
| SuperSpeed USB | USB 3.0, renamed USB 3.1 Gen 1 | 5 Gbps | 3 meters* |
| SuperSpeed USB 10 Gbps SuperSpeed+ USB | USB 3.1 Gen 2 | 10 Gbps | 3 meters* |

\* USB 3.*x* doesn't specify a limit, but interference can make longer cables slower. Try to keep cables under 2 meters, and avoid going over 3 meters.

There have been several generations of USB standard, along with a number of connector types; let's start with the standards. Table 3.1/3.2-5 provides a quick reference to help you sort them out.

USB offers many connector types that are interchangeable among the many versions, for the most part. Whether a PC has a USB 1.1 or USB 2.0 port, for example, you can plug a Type-A connector into it. (Type-A is the ubiquitous rectangular connector type that's been around for two decades and is notorious for plugging into the port in whichever orientation is the reverse of your first attempt.) USB 3.*x* uses separate and clearly marked ports and connectors. The USB 3.0 standard suggests that the ports should be colored blue to differentiate them from earlier versions, although this is not universally followed. The latter ports are usually black. You can still plug older USB devices into a USB 3.0 port, but they will run at the slower speeds. You can also plug USB 3.0 devices into an older USB port, but they will also run at the slower speeds.

Table 3.1/3.2-6 lists the common USB connectors and their purposes. Note that "keyed" means the plug fits into the socket in only one direction.

**TABLE 3.1/3.2-6**   USB Connection Types

| Connector | Plug Type | Plugs Into... |
|-----------|-----------|---------------|
| Type-A | Keyed | Computers |
| USB 3.0/3.1 Standard-A | Keyed | Computers |
| USB 2.0 Type-B | Keyed | Larger peripherals |
| USB 2.0 Mini-B | Keyed | Smaller peripherals |
| USB 2.0 Micro-B | Keyed | Tiny peripherals |
| USB 3.0/3.1 Micro-B | Keyed | Tiny peripherals |
| USB Type-C | Reversible | Computers and peripherals |

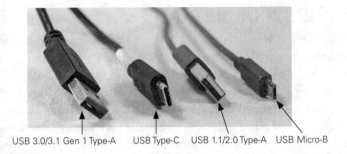

USB 3.0/3.1 Gen 1 Type-A    USB Type-C    USB 1.1/2.0 Type-A    USB Micro-B

**FIGURE 3.1/3.2-13** USB Type-A, Type-C, and Micro-B cables

Figures 3.1/3.2-13 and 3.1/3.2-14 illustrate connector types discussed in Table 3.1/3.2-6.

 **EXAM TIP** CompTIA uses the term USB-C for what others call USB Type-C. CompTIA also uses the term Micro-USB for USB Micro-B and Mini-USB for USB Mini-B. You might see either form on the exam.

The *USB Type-C* connector is now being used on the latest Android smartphones and tablets, on Apple's latest iPad tablets, as well as on many desktop and laptop computers. Like the Lightning connector, the USB Type-C connector is not keyed, making it easier to buy interoperable cables. USB-C is a form factor, not a specification. USB-C ports might run at USB 3.1 Gen 2, USB 3.1 Gen 1, or USB 2.0 speeds; check the device's specifications to find out.

 **EXAM TIP** You will likely see micro- and mini-USB, USB Type-C, and Lightning mobile device connection types on the exam. Know their characteristics and differences.

USB 1.1/2.0 Mini-B    USB 1.1/2.0 Type-B    USB 3.0/3.1 Gen 1 Micro-B    USB 3.0/3.1 Gen 1 Type-B

**FIGURE 3.1/3.2-14** USB 2.0 and USB 3.0 Type-B and Micro-B cables

# Serial (RS-232) Cable

Most peripherals connect via some type of USB port, but a few desktop systems still include support for specialized peripheral cables, such as the serial (RS-232) cable.

The RS-232 cable is a programmable interface that supported many types of slow-speed peripherals, including dial-up modems, early mice, and early printers. RS-232 ports use a 9-pin DB-9 connector and use software configuration to set up the port to communicate with the devices attached to the other end of the cable. USB ports can be used to connect to serial devices through a USB-RS-232 adapter. Figure 3.1/3.2-15 illustrates an RS-232 port and an RS-232 modem cable connector.

**FIGURE 3.1/3.2-15**   RS-232 port and cable connector

# Hard Drive Cables

CompTIA A+ 220-1001 exam objective 3.1 refers to "hard drive cables," but it's important for you to realize that these cable types are also used by other types of mass storage devices, such as SSDs, optical drives, and tape drives. Different types of cables are used by different types of hard drive and mass storage devices.

## SATA and eSATA

Advanced Technology Attachment (ATA) drives have been around for over three decades, though *serial ATA (SATA)* is the one used for current hard drives and optical drives. SATA creates a point-to-point connection (see Figure 3.1/3.2-16) between a SATA device, such as a hard drive or optical drive, and the SATA controller.

A SATA device's stream of data traverses a thin 7-wire cable that can reach up to a meter; speeds depend on which version of the SATA standard is in use. The versions—1.0 (1.5 Gbps), 2.0 (3 Gbps), and 3.0 (6 Gbps)—have a maximum throughput of 150 MBps, 300 MBps, and 600 MBps, respectively.

**FIGURE 3.1/3.2-16**   SATA power (wide) and data (narrow) cables and drive connectors

*External SATA (eSATA)* extends the SATA bus to external devices at the same speed as the internal SATA bus. The connector (see Figure 3.1/3.2-17) is similar to internal SATA but is keyed differently; it supports cables up to 2 meters outside the case and is hot-swappable.

 **EXAM TIP**   If you encounter the term *hot-swappable* on the exam, keep in mind that a hot-swappable drive will be recognized even if it is connected, swapped, or replaced while the system is running.

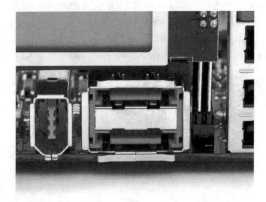

**FIGURE 3.1/3.2-17**   eSATA connectors (in center of photo)

# IDE

*Integrated Drive Electronics (IDE)* is the name used on the CompTIA A+ exam for what is also known as ATA or Parallel ATA (PATA) drives. These drives use a 40-wire flat ribbon cable to connect one or two drives to a host adapter built into a motherboard or an add-on card.

**FIGURE 3.1/3.2-18** 80-wire (left) and 40-wire (right) IDE cables

IDE interfaces are found on legacy systems, although a few more-recent computers that use SATA for hard drives also use IDE for optical drives. Figure 3.1/3.2-18 shows an 80-wire IDE cable and an older, slower 40-wire IDE cable.

 **EXAM TIP**   Although CompTIA uses the term IDE on the exam, the interface is more often referred to as PATA or ATA/IDE by the industry. They're the same thing, so be prepared!

## SCSI

*Small Computer System Interface (SCSI)* refers to a large family of internal and external drive and device connectors. Internal SCSI devices such as tape drives and hard drives are used only by servers, and connect via 50-wire or 68-wire flat cables that resemble wider versions of IDE cables. External SCSI devices use bulky round cables ranging from 25 pins to 68 pins. Each SCSI device is assigned an ID number, enabling multiple devices to be connected to a single host adapter using daisy-chaining. Unless you work with servers, it's unlikely you will encounter a SCSI host adapter or device in the field.

 **NOTE**   SCSI has largely been replaced by Serial Attached SCSI (SAS) for servers and storage arrays. SAS-3, the latest version, runs at up to 12 Gbps. SAS interfaces also support SATA drives. There are over a dozen SAS connector types, some of which resemble bulked-up SATA interfaces.

## Molex

Internal hard drives also need power. For IDE (ATA, PATA) drives, the 4-pin Molex power connector is the standard choice. Molex can also be adapted to provide power for other types of devices and is often used for case fans.

The smaller Berg (aka mini) power connector is used primarily by floppy drives. Figure 3.1/3.2-19 compares Molex and Berg power connectors.

**FIGURE 3.1/3.2-19** Molex and Berg power connectors

# Adapters

Adapters and converters enable you to connect devices in interesting ways. You can use a cable with DVI on one end and HDMI on the other end, for example, to plug into a DVI port on the video card and the HDMI socket on the monitor. These devices fall into two broad categories based on the problems they solve: connecting one type of video cable or port to another, and connecting almost anything to USB.

## DVI to HDMI, DVI to VGA

Adapters and converters for video take two primary forms: relatively small devices that fit at one end of a cable, converting it to the desired interface, and cables with built-in converters that have different connectors on each end. The former are more flexible, but the latter are easier to use. Figure 3.1/3.2-20 illustrates a DVI-to-HDMI cable, and Figure 3.1/3.2-21 illustrates a DVI-to-VGA adapter.

**FIGURE 3.1/3.2-20** DVI-to-HDMI cable

**FIGURE 3.1/3.2-21**    DVI-to-VGA adapter enables a DVI-I port to work with VGA displays.

## USB to Ethernet

There are many USB adapters for different types of devices, but the most common one is the USB to Ethernet (RJ-45) adapter, as it enables computers without Ethernet ports to connect to a twisted-pair Ethernet network (see Figure 3.1/3.2-22).

 **NOTE**    Other USB adapters you might encounter include PS/2 to USB, USB A to USB B, USB to Bluetooth, USB to Optical Drive, and USB to Wi-Fi.

**FIGURE 3.1/3.2-22**    USB to Ethernet adapter enables a USB port to connect to an Ethernet network.

# REVIEW

### Objective 3.1: Explain basic cable types, features, and their purposes
### Objective 3.2: Identify common connector types

- The most common type of network cable is Ethernet, commonly available in Cat 5, 5e, and 6 speed grades.
- Ethernet uses the RJ-45 connector.
- Plenum-grade cables are designed for use in plenum (air spaces) and are fire-resistant.
- UTP cables are used in the vast majority of 10/100/1000BaseT networks.
- STP cables are shielded for use in areas of EMI and typically are used only in such environments.
- The 568A and 568B cable standards for connecting the RJ-45 connector to UTP cable differ in their use of white/green, green, orange, and white/orange wires.
- An RJ-11 connector resembles an RJ-45 connector but is smaller and is used for telephone-based Internet service (dial-up or DSL).
- Coaxial cable is used for cable TV and Internet. RG-6 is the most common type, but RG-59 may be found in older installations.
- A coaxial cable that uses BNC, such as 10Base2 Ethernet, has a T-shaped BNC connector that cables are attached to; if the connector is at the end of the cable run, a terminator is used in place of one of the cables.
- Fiber optic cabling can be used for Ethernet network, and common connectors include ST, SC, and LC.
- VGA carries analog signals.
- DVI-I carries digital and analog signals and can be adapted to VGA.
- DVI-D carries digital signals only.
- HDMI carries HD video and audio signals. Mini-HMDI is a reduced-size version of HDMI.
- DisplayPort also carries HD video and audio signals. Mini DisplayPort is a reduced-size version of DisplayPort.
- Lighting is used for data transfer and charging by recent iOS devices.
- Thunderbolt is a very high-bandwidth video and storage standard that uses Mini DisplayPort or USB-C depending upon version.
- USB is available in speeds from 12 Mbps (USB 1.1) up to 10 Gbps (USB 3.1 Gen 2).
- USB Type-A ports connect to computers or hubs.
- USB Type-A, Mini-B, and Micro-B ports connect to devices.
- USB On the Go is used by many Android tablets and smartphones.
- USB-C is the first unkeyed USB form factor and works for both computers and devices.

- RS-232 serial ports for older types of slow-speed peripherals use a 9-pin DB-9 connector.
- SATA is used for mechanical and SSD hard drives, optical drives, and tape drives (on servers).
- IDE was also called PATA and was formerly used for mechanical hard drives and optical drives.
- SCSI is a large family of daisy-chained storage and scanning peripherals that are found in servers, but not PCs. The latest version of SCSI is called Serial Attached SCSI or SAS.
- Adapters such as DVI-to-HDMI, USB-to-Ethernet, and DVI-to-VGA enable DVI and USB ports to handle other types of devices.
- eSATA enables the high-speed SATA bus to be used by external drives; it has been largely replaced by USB 3.0 and USB 3.1.
- Molex provides power for IDE drives and internal fans and can be adapted to provide power for SATA and floppy drives.

## 3.1/3.2 QUESTIONS

1. Company A wants to eliminate separate speakers on desktops and use speakers built into monitors. Which of the following video card standards should be specified?

   **A.** DVI-I

   **B.** DVI-D

   **C.** VGA

   **D.** HDMI

2. Company B is planning to upgrade its Fast Ethernet network to Gigabit Ethernet. In checking existing cables, the network techs have discovered that some areas were wired with Cat 5, some with Cat 5e, and some with Cat 6. Which of the following should they do as part of the upgrade process?

   **A.** Replace all cables with Cat 6

   **B.** Keep the same cables

   **C.** Replace Cat 5 with Cat 5e or Cat 6

   **D.** Replace all cables with Cat 5e

3. Company C has purchased some new computers that have USB 3.0 ports as well as a USB-C port. It wants to use the USB-C port for very fast external SSD drives. What needs to be determined first?

   **A.** Are USB-C SSD drives available?

   **B.** How fast is the USB-C port?

   **C.** Can the USB-C port work with other form factors?

   **D.** Is USB-C always running at 10 Gbps?

4. Company D wants to run coaxial cable in its offices for use with HDTV. Which of the following cable types should the company specify?

   **A.** RG-6

   **B.** STP Cat 5e

   **C.** STP Cat 6

   **D.** RG-59

5. Company E wants to purchase SuperSpeed USB drives and card readers. However, all its techs can find are devices labeled with a USB version number. Which of the following USB versions does the company need?

   **A.** USB 3.1 Gen 2

   **B.** USB 3.0

   **C.** USB 1.1

   **D.** USB 2.0

## 3.1/3.2 ANSWERS

1. **D**   HDMI carries HD audio and HD video signals.

2. **C**   Cat 5e and Cat 6 both support Gigabit Ethernet, so either could be used as a replacement for Cat 5.

3. **B**   USB-C can support USB 2.0, USB 3.0/USB 3.1 Gen 1, or USB 3.1 Gen 2 speeds. Check the system documentation.

4. **A**   RG-6 is the standard for HD video.

5. **B**   USB 3.0 is the version number for SuperSpeed USB. It is also known as USB 3.1 Gen 1.

---

**Objective 3.3**  **Given a scenario, install RAM types**

Computer users are curious people, and before long one of them is going to ask you, the learned tech, "Where are programs stored as they run?" Without hesitation, you might answer, "In system RAM, of course!"

Many computer users falsely believe that programs run directly off of the hard drive. This is rarely the case, because even the fastest hard drive can't keep up with the slowest CPU. Instead, programs must be copied to a super-fast medium that can supply the CPU with the data it needs to run an application at a speed it can use: this is the function of RAM. Launching an application loads the necessary files from the hard drive into RAM, where the CPU can access the data to run the program.

**NOTE** Technically, you can use a hard drive or flash drive as *virtual memory* to expand available RAM, but these devices are not nearly as fast as RAM, and it isn't quite the same as running a program from where it is stored on a hard drive.

RAM was once a precious commodity, and even a small upgrade cost hundreds of dollars. These days, it's not very expensive to add more RAM, and it is often the best upgrade for a sluggish system. This doesn't mean that you can just grab any type of RAM; you've got to match the motherboard with the right type of RAM, running at the right speed. Manufacturers have produced RAM in many physical form factors (sometimes called *packages*) and technologies over the years. This section looks at the types of RAM covered in objective 3.3 of the CompTIA A+ 220-1001 exam.

# Desktop RAM

Desktop computers use a type of RAM known as *dual inline memory modules (DIMMs)*. The latest systems use DDR4 DIMMS, but you also need to know about DDR2 and DDR3 DIMMs for the 220-1001 exam.

## DDR2

DDR2 DIMMs have a flat connector along the bottom with 240 pins. The previous memory type, DDR, also has a flat connector with 240 pins. To distinguish DDR2 from DDR, note that DDR2 modules have their alignment notch located slightly to the left from where it is found on DDR modules (see Figure 3.3-1).

The big speed increase from DDR2 compared to regular DDR comes by clock-doubling the input/output circuits on the chips (instead of speeding up the memory itself) and adding special 4-bit buffers (sort of like a cache). Table 3.3-1 shows common DDR2 speeds.

 **NOTE** The *PC2-####* that often follows the name of a DDR2 stick—such as *DDR2-400 (PC2-3200)*—refers to the data throughput possible with that particular stick. A DDR2-400 stick, therefore, has a bandwidth of 3.2 GB per second (GBps). PC3 refers to DDR3, and PC4 refers to DDR4.

**TABLE 3.3-1**  DDR2 Speeds

| Core RAM Clock Speed | DDR I/O Speed | DDR2 Speed Rating | PC Speed Rating |
| --- | --- | --- | --- |
| 100 MHz | 200 MHz | DDR2-400 | PC2-3200 |
| 133 MHz | 266 MHz | DDR2-533 | PC2-4200 |
| 166 MHz | 333 MHz | DDR2-667 | PC2-5300 |
| 200 MHz | 400 MHz | DDR2-800 | PC2-6400 |
| 250 MHz | 500 MHz | DDR2-1000 | PC2-8000 |

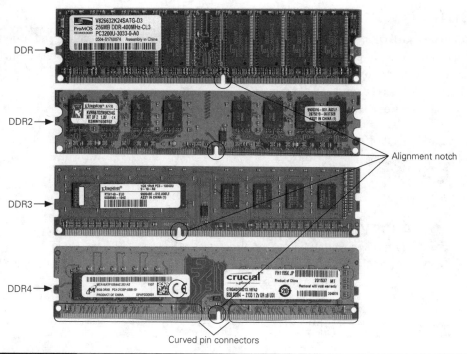

DDR

DDR2

Alignment notch

DDR3

DDR4

Curved pin connectors

**FIGURE 3.3-1**   DDR, DDR2, DDR3, and DDR4 DIMMs compared

Typical sizes of DDR2 DIMM sticks range from 512 MB up to 4 GB.

# DDR3

DDR3 boasts higher speeds, more efficient architecture, and around 30 percent lower power consumption than DDR2. Desktop DDR3 uses a 240-pin DIMM (slotted differently than 240-pin DDR2 or DDR); the sticks are not interchangeable (refer to Figure 3.3-1).

DDR3 doubles the size of the prefetch buffers from 4 bits to 8 bits, giving its bandwidth a huge boost when reading contiguous data. Table 3.3-2 lists common DDR3 speeds. Many DDR3 systems support dual- and triple-channel memory configurations.

Typical sizes of DDR3 DIMM sticks range from 1 GB up to 8 GB.

**TABLE 3.3-2**   DDR3 Speeds

| Core RAM Clock Speed | DDR I/O Speed | DDR3 Speed Rating | PC Speed Rating |
|---|---|---|---|
| 100 MHz | 400 MHz | DDR3-800 | PC3-6400 |
| 133 MHz | 533 MHz | DDR3-1066 | PC3-8500 |
| 166 MHz | 667 MHz | DDR3-1333 | PC3-10667 |
| 200 MHz | 800 MHz | DDR3-1600 | PC3-12800 |
| 233 MHz | 933 MHz | DDR3-1866 | PC3-14900 |
| 266 MHz | 1066 MHz | DDR3-2133 | PC3-17000 |

## DDR4

Compared to DDR3, DDR4 offers higher speeds, more efficient architecture, and around 20 percent lower power consumption. Desktop DDR4 uses a 288-pin DIMM that has a slight curve on both ends of its motherboard connector (refer to Figure 3.3-1).

Table 3.3-3 lists common DDR4 speeds.

Typical sizes of DDR4 DIMM sticks range from 4 GB up to 64 GB.

 **EXAM TIP** You should be familiar with the various RAM speeds for DDR2, DDR3, and DDR4.

 **ADDITIONAL RESOURCES** To familiarize yourself with the many RAM standards and specifications for both desktops and laptops, visit www.crucial.com. Pay special attention to descriptions such as module size, package, and features. Be sure to check out Crucial's memory compatibility tools while you're there.

**TABLE 3.3-3** DDR4 Speeds

| Core RAM Clock Speed | DDR I/O Speed | DDR4 Speed Rating | PC Speed Rating |
|---|---|---|---|
| 200 MHz | 800 MHz | DDR4-1600 | PC4-12800 |
| 233 MHz | 933 MHz | DDR4-1866 | PC4-14900 |
| 266 MHz | 1066 MHz | DDR4-2133 | PC4-17066 |
| 300 MHz | 1200 MHz | DDR4-2400 | PC4-19200 |
| 333 MHz | 1333 MHz | DDR4-2666 | PC4-21333 |
| 366 MHz | 1466 MHz | DDR4-2933 | PC4-23466 |
| 400 MHz | 1500 MHz | DDR4-3000 | PC4-24000 |
| 433 MHz | 1600 MHz | DDR4-3200 | PC4-25600 |

## Handling and Installing DIMM Sticks

Proper RAM handling and installation procedures prevent damage to your system. This section reviews the proper way to handle desktop RAM and how to install it.

RAM is extremely sensitive to ESD, so take precautions while transporting, handling, and installing it. Always store RAM in anti-static bags or sleeves when it's not installed on a computer, and keep it labeled with the type, size, and speed so that you can identify it later. Wear an anti-static wrist strap and ground yourself before working with RAM. Don't take a RAM stick out of its bag before you actually need to install it. Handle RAM by the edges, and avoid touching the contacts or circuits.

**FIGURE 3.3-2**   Properly seating a DIMM module

To install DIMM modules, first power down the computer and unplug it from the AC outlet. DIMM sticks fit into their sockets vertically. You'll note on the motherboard that the guide notches on the sockets match up to the notches on the RAM (refer back to Figure 3.3-1) to prevent you from inserting it the wrong way. Make sure that the RAM retention clips at either end of the socket are pushed completely outward.

Hold the RAM stick by the edges, position it above the RAM socket, and press it straight down into the slot with gentle pressure (see Figure 3.3-2). When the RAM is fully inserted, the retention clips will rotate into the retention notches on each end of the stick. Snap the clips firmly into place, and you're done.

Barring ESD, not a lot can go wrong. The main thing to look for is improper seating. If the retention clip doesn't engage fully, your RAM stick isn't inserted completely. Note that DDR2/DDR3 sockets typically use a retention clip on both ends, while DDR4 sockets use a retention clip on one end and a fixed guide rail on the other end. Double-check the positioning, and insert the RAM again. If it doesn't go in easily, it's not in the right position.

To remove a DIMM, push the retention clip(s) on the socket outward. These clips act as levers to eject the stick partially so that you can then pull it all the way out.

# Laptop RAM

Laptops use DDR2, DDR3, and DDR4 RAM, just as desktops do, but laptop RAM is packaged in a smaller form factor known as *small-outline DIMM*, or *SO-DIMM* (sometimes spelled without the hyphen, SODIMM, as in the exam objectives). Thus, DIMMs and SO-DIMMs are not interchangeable with each other (see Figure 3.3-3). Note that some all-in-one and small form factor desktop computers also use SO-DIMMs.

The performance characteristics of SO-DIMM modules using a given memory technology are similar to those of DIMM modules using the same technology; thus the information

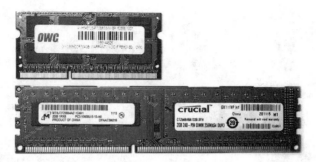

**FIGURE 3.3-3**    SO-DIMM module (top) and DIMM module (DDR3) compared

in Tables 3.3-1, 3.3-2, and 3.3-3 apply to both DIMM and SO-DIMM modules. Figure 3.3-4 shows the position of the alignment notch in the DDR2, DDR3, and DDR4 SO-DIMMs.

- **DDR2 SO-DIMM**    DDR2 SO-DIMM is packaged in a 200-pin module, such as the one shown in Figure 3.3-4.
- **DDR3 SO-DIMM**    DDR3 SO-DIMM is packaged in a 204-pin module, such as the one shown in Figure 3.3-4. Note that some DDR3 SO-DIMMs use low-voltage DDR3 memory.

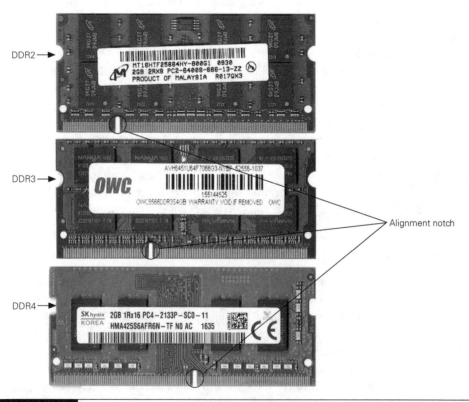

**FIGURE 3.3-4**    DDR2, DDR3, and DDR4 SO-DIMMs compared

These modules are called DDR3L SO-DIMM. Check the specifications for a specific device to determine if it uses standard-voltage (DDR3) or low-voltage (DDR3L) memory.

- **DDR4 SO-DIMM** DDR4 SO-DIMM is packaged in a 260-pin module, such as the one shown in Figure 3.3-4. A DDR4 SO-DIMM module is slightly wider than previous SO-DIMM types.

**EXAM TIP** Memorize the DIMM and SO-DIMM form factors—and the associated memory technologies—for the CompTIA A+ 220-1001 exam. Be prepared for questions that require you to know the number of pins to differentiate between DIMM and SO-DIMM modules.

## Handling and Installing SO-DIMM Sticks

Just like with a desktop, protect yourself and the portable by removing all power and protect the SO-DIMM modules by using proper ESD avoidance techniques. With portables, removing power includes disconnecting removable batteries. If it has built-in batteries, consult the manufacturer's resources to check if and how you can safely work on it.

**NOTE** Some portables have both built-in and removable batteries.

Once you know you can work safely, confirm what kind of RAM you need by checking the manufacturer's website or manual. Next, check the existing RAM configuration to confirm what you need to buy. To go from 4 GB to 8 GB, you need to know if the portable has one 4-GB module or two 2-GB modules.

Second, locate the RAM slots. They're often both behind a panel (see Figure 3.3-5) on the bottom of the portable, but sometimes they're separated.

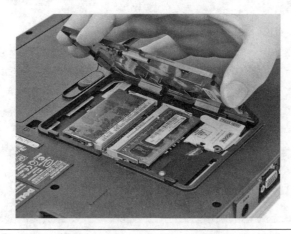

**FIGURE 3.3-5** Removing a RAM panel

**FIGURE 3.3-6** Releasing the RAM

Then you press out on the retaining clips and the RAM stick pops up (see Figure 3.3-6). Gently remove the old stick of RAM and insert the new one by reversing the steps.

## Confirming RAM Installation

Once you've installed RAM, confirm that the computer recognizes it by booting up and checking the RAM count message or by looking in the UEFI/BIOS setup utility (see Figure 3.3-7).

**FIGURE 3.3-7** Confirming RAM installation by checking total memory in UEFI BIOS Utility

Modern systems automatically detect the RAM size and configure the system accordingly. You rarely need to reconfigure these RAM settings. You can also verify the amount of installed RAM from within the operating system—for example, in any version of Windows, simultaneously press the WINDOWS LOGO and PAUSE keys to bring up the System Properties applet.

# Performance Configurations for Desktop and Laptop

Current desktop and laptop motherboards use multichannel memory configurations to increase memory performance. With a 64-bit data bus, DIMMs deliver 64 bits of data at a time. That's pretty logical! This is a *single memory channel*. Memory controllers can be designed to use two channels simultaneously, a *dual-channel* configuration. As you'd expect, *triple-channel* and *quad-channel* configurations use three and four channels, respectively.

In dual-channel mode, the memory controller's 128-bit-wide data path uses two DIMMs per bank. In triple-channel mode, the 192-bit-wide data path requires three DIMMs per bank. On multichannel systems, the DIMM slots for a given bank are typically the same color. Use identical RAM sticks to populate a bank for multichannel memory modes. Always check the motherboard or system book for details.

 **EXAM TIP**  Know the differences between single-, dual-, and triple-channel memory. Quad-channel memory isn't listed in the objectives.

Motherboards that support a multichannel mode can also run in the lower-channel modes, but you'll get the best performance using the highest mode the motherboard supports.

# Error-correcting Memory

High-end, mission-critical systems often use special *error-correcting code (ECC)* RAM. This type of RAM uses special circuitry to detect and, in some cases, correct errors in data. ECC RAM contains circuitry that not only detects errors, but corrects them on the fly without interrupting system processes. ECC RAM is common on performance-enhanced workstations and servers.

# Parity vs. Non-parity RAM

The older *parity RAM* used a dedicated parity chip mounted on the RAM stick that added an extra bit—the parity bit—to each byte of data. Parity checking protected early desktop computers from early DRAM's relatively high failure rate, but today's DRAM is so dependable that few computers still support parity.

Note that the computer's motherboard and basic input/output system (BIOS) must be designed to support either parity or ECC RAM; this support can usually be disabled in the UEFI/BIOS setup utility to use regular RAM.

# REVIEW

### Objective 3.3: Given a scenario, install RAM types

- Desktop RAM uses the DIMM form factor. It is available in DDR2, DDR3, and DDR4 types.
- DIMMs are installed by lining up the module with the appropriate RAM slot and pressing it down until the DIMM locks into place.
- Laptop RAM uses the SO-DIMM form factor. It also is available in DDR2, DDR3, and DDR4 types.
- SO-DIMMs are installed by lining up the module with the appropriate RAM slot at an angle, pushing the module into the slot, and pivoting the top of the module until it locks into place.
- Single-channel memory accesses a single DIMM as a channel.
- Dual-channel memory accesses two DIMMs as a channel for greater bandwidth.
- Triple-channel memory accesses three DIMMs as a channel for even greater bandwidth.
- DIMM slots on multichannel systems for a given bank are typically the same color. Use identical RAM sticks to populate a bank for multichannel memory modes.
- Error-correcting code (ECC) RAM contains circuitry that not only detects errors, but corrects them on the fly without interrupting system processes.
- Parity memory includes an additional bit for each eight bits of data to detect errors, while non-parity memory uses data bits only with no error detection function.
- Parity checking protected early desktop computers from high failure rate, but today's DRAM is so dependable that few computers still support parity.

## 3.3 QUESTIONS

1. How many pins does a stick of DDR3 DIMM RAM use?
   A. 108 pins
   B. 186 pins
   C. 205 pins
   D. 240 pins

2. What is stored in RAM?
   A. Currently running programs
   B. Programs that aren't running
   C. Nothing
   D. Hardware information

3. How many pins does a stick of DDR4 SO-DIMM RAM use?
   A. 200 pins
   B. 260 pins

   **C.** 204 pins

   **D.** 240 pins

4. You are adding RAM to a dual-channel system that has one 4-GB module to upgrade it to 8 GB. Which of the following do you need to confirm before you buy more RAM?

   **A.** The current stick's brand of RAM

   **B.** The current stick's speed of RAM

   **C.** The current stick's type of RAM

   **D.** All of the above

5. You are purchasing 288-pin RAM to upgrade computers in your organization. What type of RAM are you purchasing?

   **A.** DDR2 DIMM

   **B.** DDR4 SO-DIMM

   **C.** DDR4 DIMM

   **D.** DDR3 SO-DIMM

## 3.3 ANSWERS

1. **D** DDR3 DIMM memory uses a 240-pin connector, but the keying is not the same as with DDR2.

2. **A** RAM is the workspace used by programs as they are running. Programs that are not running are located on a local or network storage device.

3. **B** A DDR4 SO-DIMM has a 260-pin connector (a DDR4 DIMM has a 288-pin connector).

4. **D** To run the computer in dual-channel mode for better speed, the new module must be identical to the old, so all of these factors must be matched.

5. **C** A 288-pin module is a DDR4 DIMM.

 **Objective 3.4** **Given a scenario, select, install, and configure storage devices**

The storage industry is in a period of massive transformation, with flash memory technologies rapidly replacing optical and magnetic media. Nevertheless, you will encounter optical, solid-state, magnetic, and flash media in your work as a tech, and all four types are important parts of this objective.

# Optical Drives

*Compact disc (CD)*, *digital versatile disc (DVD)*, and *Blu-ray Disc (BD)* drives use lasers to read (and sometimes to write or burn) data on shiny *optical discs*. Riding the popularity of these formats for delivering music, movies, video games, and software, writable versions of all three technologies have been used to back up and archive data. The capacity and speed of optical media have not kept pace with other technologies, and its popularity is fading.

Internal optical drives generally use the SATA interface, and you'll learn about installing SATA drives of all types later in this objective. External optical drives typically connect to USB ports, and installation is simple: plug them in any they're ready to go.

## Optical Media Formats

Optical media comes in three main styles: read-only, write-once, and rewritable. Current optical *combo drives* read and write to many optical media types, though you should always check compatibility, especially with older drives.

CD media types include

- CD-ROM (read-only pressed media)
- CD-R (recordable media)
- CD-RW (rewriteable media)

There are many DVD media types, but the ones you need to know for the CompTIA A+ 220-1001 exam include

- DVD-ROM (read-only pressed media)
- DVD-RW (rewriteable media)
- DVD-RW DL (dual-layer rewriteable media)

 **ADDITIONAL RESOURCES**  To learn about other types of DVD media, see the www.lifewire.com website and search for "DVD+R and DVD-R."

Blu-ray Disc media types include

- BD-ROM (pressed read-only media)
- BD-R (recordable media)
- BD-RE (rewriteable media)

 **NOTE**  Optical discs use a unique *Compact Disc File System (CDFS)*, more accurately called the *ISO 9660 file system*. The International Organization for Standardization (ISO) provides standards for many technologies.

| **TABLE 3.4-1** | Common DVD/Blu-ray Disc Capacities in DVD-Industry Gigabytes | |
| --- | --- | --- |

| | **Single Layer** | **Dual Layer** |
| --- | --- | --- |
| **Single-sided DVD** | 4.7 GB | 8.5 GB |
| **Double-sided DVD** | 9.4 GB | 17.1 GB |
| **Blu-ray Disc** | 25 GB | 50 GB |
| **Mini Blu-ray Disc** | 7.8 GB | 15.6 GB |

## Optical Media Capacity

CDs come in 650-MB or 700-MB capacity, and Table 3.4-1 shows DVD and Blu-ray Disc capacities.

## Optical Speeds

Though relatively slow, newer optical drives are much faster than the first 150-KBps CD-ROM drive. Modern drives list up to three speeds (in order: read, rewrite, and write) per media using a "number times" format such as 40×. It's simple math: to find throughput in KBps, expand 40× and multiply (40 × 150 = 6000). A CD-RW lists all three speeds in a format such as 48×32×52× (write speed, rewrite speed, read speed).

DVD drives read, write, and rewrite DVDs nine times faster than 150 KBps, so a 1× DVD drive and disc have a throughput of 1.32 MBps. DVD drives read and write CDs even faster, so they often list an extra set of CD speeds.

A 1× Blu-ray Disc drive has a speed of 4.5 MBps; Blu-ray Disc burners can write to BD-R media at speeds up to 54 MBps (12×), rewrite BD-RE discs at speeds up to 9 MBps (2×), and read BD-ROM discs as fast as 36 MBps (8×). Blu-ray Disc burners can also burn to CD and DVD media and often list three sets of speeds.

# Magnetic Hard Drives

Devices that encode and decode data on magnetic media have had a long run as the dominant long-term digital data storage technology, but the writing is on the wall. Now that floppy drives and tape drives have been retired from the CompTIA A+ exams, the last magnetic media type standing is the hard disk drive.

## Hard Disk Drives

Traditional *hard disk drives (HDDs)* store data magnetically on spinning platters, using fast-moving actuator arms with read/write heads that are controlled by a servo motor (see Figure 3.4-1). The important properties are physical size, storage capacity, spindle speed, cache size, and interface.

**FIGURE 3.4-1**    Inside a hard drive

Most modern HDDs are *2.5* or *3.5* inches wide and have storage capacities measured in gigabytes (GB) or terabytes (TB). HDD size relates to capacity: 2.5-inch drives, primarily used in laptops and in external storage that is powered by a USB or Thunderbolt port, presently top out around 2 TB, whereas 3.5-inch drives, used in desktop and servers and in external storage powered by an AC adapter, exceed 10 TB.

 **EXAM TIP**    Know the HDD spindle speeds and the drive categories represented.

Drives with higher spindle speed seek faster but consume more power and generate more heat and noise; Table 3.4-2 shows common HDD spindle speeds with typical use. Cache size, measured in megabytes (MB), affects the drive's sustained throughput.

**TABLE 3.4-2**    Typical HDD Spindle Speeds

| Spindle Speed | Typical Purpose | Drive Type |
|---|---|---|
| 5,400 RPM | Standard for portable computers | SATA, IDE |
| 7,200 RPM | Standard for desktop computers | SATA, IDE |
| 10,000 RPM | Enthusiast and server computers | SAS, SCSI |
| 15,000 RPM | Enterprise servers | SAS |

# Hybrid Drives

Hybrid drives, also known as hybrid hard drives (HHDs) and solid-state hybrid drives (SSHDs), combine a standard HDD mechanism with a small onboard solid-state drive (SSD). Performance of hybrid drives is faster than HDDs but slower than SSDs. They are available in capacities up to 2 TB.

 **NOTE**   Computers running macOS use a somewhat similar technology called a *Fusion Drive*, which uses separate hard drive and SSD components. With Fusion Drive, macOS decides which information is stored in the SSD.

# Solid-State Drives

The SSD, which uses flash memory chips to store data, is running the HDD out of town. SSDs weigh less, have no moving parts, seek faster, have higher throughput, consume less power, produce less heat, have better shock resistance, and last longer than HDDs. For a time HDDs retained a price and capacity advantage, but as SSDs catch up in capacity, the only advantage left is cost.

Most consumer SSDs use a SATA 2.5-inch hard drive format or an M.2 flash drive format. M.2 SSDs use two different internal data bus designs: SATA or NVMe. The original form factor used for SSDs is SATA 2.5-inch. Figure 3.4-2 compares a SATA 2.5-inch drive with an M.2 drive.

 **NOTE**   Confused by all of the *xx*D acronyms yet? *Hard drive* and *hard disk* were traditionally synonyms, but in this book, aside from the term "hybrid hard drive," we use *hard drive* as an umbrella term including HDD, SSD, and HHD.

**FIGURE 3.4-2**   SATA (top) and M.2 (bottom) SSDs

## M.2 Drives

M.2 drives (referred to as "M2" drives in objective 3.4) are small SSDs that are included in many laptops and tablets as well as a large number of desktop computers. The M.2 slot is used primary for SSDs, but is also used for some Wi-Fi and Bluetooth radios in some laptops.

Some M.2 drives use the SATA interface internally for data transfer, but the newest development in SSDs is NVMe.

## NVMe

*Non-Volatile Memory Express (NVMe)* enables SSDs to run at much faster speeds than the poky SATA speeds originally developed for mechanical drives and used by SATA and standard M.2 SSDs. NVMe uses PCIe lanes for communication.

NVMe drives transfer data at 2.5–3 times the speeds of SATA and standard M.2 SSDs. They are available in either M.2 or PCIe form factors. NVMe drives are more expensive than other SSDs, but offer much higher speeds.

 **EXAM TIP**   The M.2 form factor supports both NVMe-compatible and SATA-compatible SSDs. You might encounter a question that asks about the differences, so keep in mind that NVMe is faster but doesn't work in all M.2 slots.

# Flash

Flash memory, which uses solid-state technology similar to that found in SSDs, has displaced other data storage technologies. You need to know about two flash memory families: USB thumb drives and memory cards.

*USB thumb drives* contain a standard USB connection, and *memory card* is a generic term for a number of different tiny cards that are used in cameras, tablets, and other devices. Both of these types can show up as drives in modern operating systems, but they have different jobs. USB thumb drives have replaced virtually all other rewritable removable media as the way people transfer files or keep copies of important programs.

## SD Card

Many small devices such as digital cameras and smartphones store data on flash memory cards. The most popular format is Secure Digital (SD) and its smaller siblings, shown in Figure 3.4-3, mini-SD (also known as miniSD) and micro-SD (also known as microSD). Most devices support a single format, though some smaller cards fit into a converter that itself fits a larger slot. SD cards are available in capacities exceeding 2 TB.

 **ADDITIONAL RESOURCES**   To learn more about the different form factors, speeds, and capacities of SD cards, see www.sdcard.org.

**FIGURE 3.4-3**   Assortment of SD memory cards

Other popular formats include

- **CompactFlash (CF)**   Capacities up to 512 GB and are used primarily in professional digital SLR cameras. CF cards are also available for network and other non-storage applications.
- **Extreme Digital (xD) Picture Card**   xD Picture Card memory cards have capacities up to 2 GB. They were used by many older Olympus and Fujifilm cameras, but have been replaced by other formats, most notably SD.

 **EXAM TIP**   Be familiar with the differences between SD, CF, and xD cards, including capacities, smaller versions, and current uses.

# Installing Storage Devices

There are two types of interfaces used for internal storage devices on recent systems: SATA and M.2. The following sections explain how to install devices that use these interfaces.

## Installing SATA Drives

There used to be a few catches when installing SATA drives; these days, just connect the power, plug in the controller cable (see Figure 3.4-4), and wait for the OS to automatically detect the drive. The keying on SATA controller and power cables makes it impossible to install either incorrectly.

Since motherboards come with many SATA connectors, how does the system find the right hard drive to boot up to? That's where the BIOS/UEFI settings come into play. By default, boot order and drive letter priority follow SATA controller ID: SATA 0 is C:, SATA 1 is D:, and so on.

 **EXAM TIP**   BIOS/UEFI setup utilities enable you to change boot order easily, which is great for multi-OS computers.

**FIGURE 3.4-4**   Properly connected SATA cables

When installing optical drives, you might also need to install movie playback apps supplied with some drives. The SATA interface works the same way with any type of SATA drive.

 **NOTE**   If you need to install an IDE drive, each drive on the cable (which supports up to two drives) needs to be jumpered using a small block on the rear or bottom of the drive. With an 80-wire cable, jumper all drives as CS (cable select). With two drives on the older 40-wire cable, one should be jumpered as MA (master) and the other as SL (slave). If there is only one drive on a 40-wire cable, see the drive's documentation for details.

## Installing M.2 Drives

With any type of M.2 device, including standard SSDs, NVMe SSDs, or other types of M.2 devices used in laptops, the selection and installation processes have these steps:

1. Select a device that fits into the slot.

2. Secure the device with a mounting screw.

All M.2 cards are 22 mm wide, with lengths varying from 30 mm to as much as 110 mm. The most common size, however, is 2280 (22 mm wide, 80 mm long), as illustrated in Figure 3.4-5.

**FIGURE 3.4-5**   An M.2 2280 SSD installed and secured into an M.2 slot

# Configurations

The CompTIA A+ 220-1001 exam also expects you to know about two special drive configurations: RAID and hot-swapping. See the following sections for details.

## RAID 0, 1, 5, 10

A *redundant array of independent (or inexpensive) disks (RAID)* uses multiple hard drives to increase performance and protect data. Motherboards with built-in RAID controllers may have a BIOS/UEFI setting to enable or disable RAID (see Figure 3.4-6).

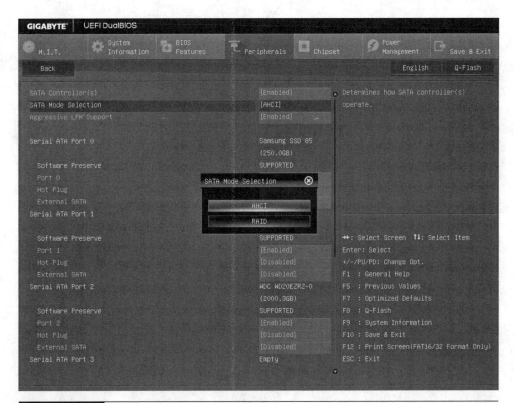

**FIGURE 3.4-6**   Settings for RAID in a UEFI BIOS

**EXAM TIP** A RAID *array* collects two or more hard drives into a logical unit. CompTIA expects you to know RAID levels 0, 1, 5, and 10.

**RAID 0: Disk striping**   Disk striping requires at least two drives. It increases performance by splitting work over multiple drives, but it does not provide redundancy to data. If any drive fails, all data is lost.

**RAID 1: Disk mirroring/duplexing**   RAID 1 arrays require at least two hard drives, although they also work with any even number of drives. RAID 1 *mirrors* data across multiple drives, providing safety at the cost of storage space (since data is duplicated; you need two 2-TB drives to store 2 TB of data).

**RAID 5: Disk striping with distributed parity**   RAID 5 distributes data and parity information evenly across all drives. This is the fastest way to provide data redundancy. RAID 5 arrays effectively use one drive's worth of space for parity, requiring a minimum of three drives. In RAID 5, three 2-TB drives provide a capacity of 4 TB, while four 2-TB drives provide a capacity of 6 GB.

**RAID 10: Nested, striped mirrors**   RAID 10 takes two mirrored pairs of drives and stripes them together. This creates an array with excellent speed and redundancy, though it takes four drives as a minimum. RAID 10 is not one of the original RAID levels, but is fairly common today.

**EXAM TIP** RAID 0 and 1 can be combined. Mirroring two striped-drive pairs results in *RAID 0+1*. Striping two mirrored-drive pairs produces *RAID 1+0*, or *RAID 10*. Arrays combining single RAID types are called *multiple RAID solutions* or *nested RAID*.

Windows 8 and later include a tool called Storage Spaces that enables you to create a number of RAID-like array varieties via software. We'll cover Storage Spaces in Part II, Domain 1.0, for CompTIA A+ 220-1002 exam candidates.

**EXAM TIP** JBOD stands for *just a bunch of disks* (or *drives*). It's a storage system with multiple independent disks, rather than RAID-organized disks. It provides no redundancy and no performance increase. You might encounter a question that contrasts JBOD with RAID, so make sure you understand the differences.

# Hot Swappable

A *hot-swappable* drive will be recognized even if it is connected, swapped, or replaced while the system is running. SATA drives that are configured as Advanced Host Controller Interface (AHCI) drives or hardware RAID in the system BIOS or UEFI firmware are hot-swappable, as are eSATA, USB, and Thunderbolt drives.

# REVIEW

### Objective 3.4: Given a scenario, select, install, and configure storage devices

- Optical discs are available in CD, DVD, and BD (Blu-ray) types.
- RW and RE discs are rewriteable.
- R discs are recordable.
- ROM discs are read-only.
- BD drives can also use DVD and CD media.
- DVD drives can also use CD media.
- Optical speeds are rated differently according to the media type, using the order write, rewrite, and read.
- SSDs are rapidly replacing HDDs for primary storage.
- A hybrid hard drive combines a small SSD with a larger HDD.
- SATA HDD, SSD, and optical drives are installed using a SATA data cable and a SATA power cable.
- M.2 drives are available in conventional (SATA SSD speed) and NVMe (2.5 to 3 times faster) types.
- M.2 drives are installed using a mounting screw provided with the motherboard that holds the drive in place and are available in various form factors, of which 2280 (22-mm wide, 80-mm long) is the most common.
- HDDs are available in 3.5-inch or 2.5-inch form factors.
- HDDs have spindle speeds of 5400 RPM, 7200 RPM, 10000 RPM, and 15000 RPM.
- 3.5-inch drives are used in AC-powered enclosures or desktops and servers.
- 2.5-inch drives are used in USB-powered enclosures or laptops.
- The most common family of flash memory cards is SD, including mini-SD and the very popular micro-SD.
- CompactFlash cards are used primarily in professional-level digital SLR cameras.
- xD cards (xD-Picture Card) were used by older Fujifilm and Olympus digital cameras.

- RAID 0 is faster than other RAID types because data is striped across two drives; it has no redundancy.
- RAID 1 mirrors the contents of one drive to the other.
- RAID 5 uses at least three drives and distributes data and recovery (parity) information across all drives.
- RAID 10 combines striping and mirroring (requiring four drives).
- Hot-swappable drives can be replaced without shutting down the system. USB, Thunderbolt, and SATA drives configured as AHCI or hardware RAID all support hot-swapping.

## 3.4 QUESTIONS

1. Your client is planning to replace 500-GB hard disks with similarly sized SSDs. Assuming compatibility, which of the following would provide the best performance?
   A. NVMe 2.5-inch
   B. NVMe M.2
   C. SATA M.2
   D. SATA 2.5-inch

2. Which of the following correctly ranks SATA drive types in order from slowest to fastest?
   A. 5400 RPM, SSHD, 7200 RPM, SSD
   B. 7200 RPM, 5400 RPM, SSD, SSHD
   C. 5400 RPM, 7200 RPM, SSHD, SSD
   D. SSD, SSHD, 5400 RPM, 7200 RPM

3. Your client wants to add an NVMe drive to its desktop systems to boost performance, but the M.2 slots in these systems don't support NVMe drives. Which of the following interfaces can be used instead?
   A. SATA
   B. PCIe
   C. SATA
   D. ISO 9660

4. Your client wants to choose a RAID array type that offers excellent speed and reliability. Which of the following is the best match for this requirement?
   A. RAID 10
   B. RAID 1
   C. RAID 5
   D. RAID 0

5. Your client accidentally purchased a micro-SD card for her digital camera instead of an SD card. Which of the following is the best way to use the card?

   **A.** Copy the data from an existing card to the new card

   **B.** Return the card to the store for the correct type

   **C.** Use an adapter with the card

   **D.** Buy a new camera that uses micro-SD cards

## 3.4 ANSWERS

1. **B**   The NVMe M.2 SSD is the fastest type of SSD.

2. **C**   5400 RPM is the slowest SATA drive, 7200 RPM is faster, SSHD is faster, and SSD is fastest.

3. **B**   NVMe drives are available in PCIe cards; NVMe uses the PCIe bus for extra speed over SATA.

4. **A**   RAID 10 combines mirroring for data protection and striping for speed.

5. **C**   SD adapters for micro-SD cards are very common, and are often bundled with micro-SD cards.

**Objective 3.5**  # Given a scenario, install and configure motherboards, CPUs, and add-on cards

Custom PC configurations and upgrades rely on a tech's ability to integrate off-the-shelf components from various sources into a working system. In this objective, you learn how to choose, install, and configure compatible motherboards, CPUs, and add-on cards.

## Motherboard Form Factor

A *form factor* defines the motherboard's size, orientation, location of built-in sockets and expansion slots, and so on. Most motherboards come in either of two form factors, ATX or ITX, though you'll probably see proprietary form factors as well. Each form factor has a few varieties. Form factors are not interchangeable, and they determine the type of power supply and case a computer can use; ATX motherboards fit into ATX cases, and ITX motherboards fit into ITX cases.

## ATX

In 1995, Intel introduced the ATX motherboard form factor (see Figure 3.5-1) to replace the aging AT form factor originally developed by IBM. The ATX form factor rearranged

**FIGURE 3.5-1** ATX motherboard

expansion slots, CPU, and RAM for easier access and enhanced performance, and to prevent long expansion cards from colliding with the CPU (a common problem in AT systems).

ATX motherboards collect ports for built-in peripherals at an I/O panel on the back of the case known as a port cluster. A sheet metal I/O shield with cutouts and labels for the ports typically covers any unused space. Figure 3.5-2 illustrates a typical port cluster from a recent system.

There have been several revisions of the ATX standards over the years. The more notable changes are new power connectors for modern, power-hungry motherboards, and updated recommendations for power supply fans and airflow.

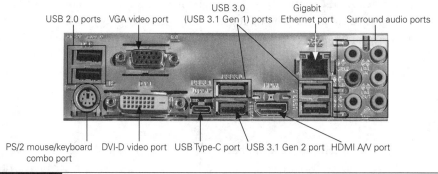

**FIGURE 3.5-2** Typical ATX port cluster

The most common versions of ATX are full-sized ATX (12 by 9.6 inches) and *microATX* (9.6 by 9.6 inches, also known as *mATX*). MicroATX shares the power connectors and basic layout with ATX but are scaled for much smaller cases. Full-sized ATX motherboards will not fit into microATX cases, though most full-sized cases support the smaller motherboards.

 **EXAM TIP**   Know that ATX is a full-sized motherboard (up to seven slots) for full-sized cases and mATX is a smaller version of ATX with up to four slots that fits into smaller or full-sized ATX cases.

# ITX

VIA Technologies created the standard for the current leader in *small form factor (SFF)* motherboards: ITX. Although the full-sized ITX design flopped, VIA created smaller form factors that fared better: Mini-ITX, Nano-ITX, and Pico-ITX.

*Mini-ITX (mITX)* is the largest and the most popular, and at a miniscule 6.7 inches square, it competes with the much larger microATX (see Figure 3.5-3). For comparison, microATX motherboards are 9.6 inches square.

If you think that's small, *Nano-ITX* at 4.7 inches square and *Pico-ITX* at 3.8 by 2.8 inches are even smaller. These tiny motherboard form factors are commonly used for embedded systems and specialized devices such as routers.

**FIGURE 3.5-3**   Mini-ITX

**EXAM TIP** ITX is the original, defunct version of the smaller and much more popular Mini-ITX (mITX) motherboard.

# Motherboard Connectors Types

Motherboards are more than the home of RAM and CPUs. Storage, video, I/O, and other types of devices are also connected to the motherboard, as you learn in the following sections. These devices are connected to each other through the slots, wires, and support chips built into the motherboard and are collectively known as the *expansion bus*.

## PCI

Intel introduced the *Peripheral Component Interconnect (PCI)* bus architecture in the early 1990s and released it into the public domain to attract manufacturers. The original PCI bus was wider (32 bits), faster (33 MHz), and more flexible than any previous expansion bus, and its self-configuration feature led to the plug and play (PnP) standard. The exceptional technology and its lack of a price tag led manufacturers to quickly replace earlier busses with PCI.

## PCIe

*PCI Express (PCIe)* is the latest, fastest, and most popular expansion bus in use today. PCI Express is still PCI, but it uses a point-to-point serial connection instead of PCI's shared parallel communication. The serial interface reduces transfer overhead and supports higher speeds without causing interference to other parts. A PCIe device's direct (point-to-point) connection to the northbridge means it does not wait for other devices.

A PCIe *lane* uses a wire each to send and receive. Better yet, each connection can use 1, 2, 4, 8, 12, 16, or 32 lanes with corresponding slots referred to as ×1, ×4, etc. Each direction of a lane runs at the following speeds depending upon the PCIe version supported by the card or device and the motherboard:

- PCIe 1.0: 2.5 gigatransfers per second (GTps)
- PCIe 2.0: 5.0 GTps
- PCIe 3.0: 8.0 GTps
- PCIe 4.0: 16.0 GTps)

 **NOTE** Pronounce lanes as "by" rather than "ex." So "by 1" and "by 16" are the correct pronunciations of ×1 and ×16.

In case of a mismatch between versions supported by the slot and the card, the slower standard is supported.

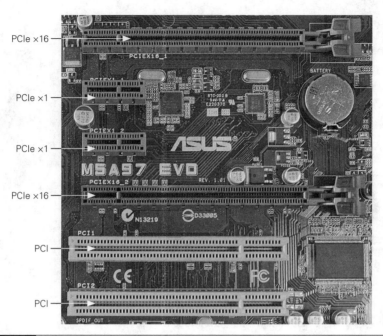

**FIGURE 3.5-4** PCIe ×16, ×1, and PCI slots

 **NOTE** A lot of laptop computers offer an internal PCIe expansion slot called PCI Express Mini Card, or Mini PCIe. It works like any PCIe expansion slot, though it's not compatible with full-sized cards.

The most common PCIe slot is the 16-lane (×16) version most video cards use, while ×1 and ×4 are the most common general-purpose PCIe slots. The first PCIe motherboards used a single PCIe ×16 slot and several standard PCI slots. Figure 3.5-4 compares PCIe and PCI slots on a typical late-model motherboard.

 **EXAM TIP** Given a scenario, be able to identify the various PCI and PCIe slots.

# Riser Card

One feature you'll see in proprietary motherboards is a special *riser card* (see Figure 3.5-5), also called a *daughter board*—part of a motherboard separate from the main one, but connected by a cable of some sort or a right-angle connector that plugs into a slot. Proprietary motherboards also have unique power connections. Proprietary motherboards, though rare today, drive techs crazy because replacement parts tend to cost more and are not readily available.

**FIGURE 3.5-5**   Riser card on an older motherboard

## Socket Types

Most desktop motherboards use sockets to accommodate different CPU models, although a few have soldered-in-place CPUs. AMD and Intel CPUs use different sockets and different internal architectures, so their CPUs are not interchangeable.

### Cross-References

For details about Intel sockets, see Table 3.5-1, and for details about AMD sockets, see Table 3.5-2; both later in this objective.

## SATA

SATA connectors on motherboards might face upward or be positioned along the front edge to face forward. Some motherboards feature ports in both positions (see Figure 3.5-6).

## IDE

Motherboards built during the transition from IDE to SATA have both types of ports (see Figure 3.5-7).

## Front Panel Connector

The *front panel connector* (see Figure 3.5-8) is used for wires such as the case power switch, power and drive activity signal lights, reset button, and more.

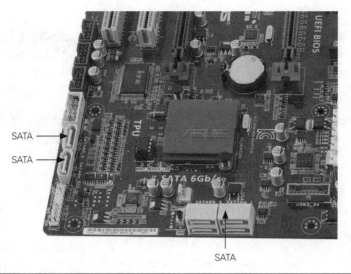

**FIGURE 3.5-6** Front-mounted and top-mounted SATA ports on a typical motherboard

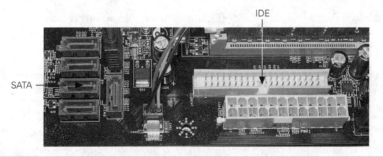

**FIGURE 3.5-7** SATA ports compared to an IDE port on a motherboard

**FIGURE 3.5-8** USB 2.0 headers, a USB 3.0 header, and a front panel connector on a typical late-model motherboard

## Internal USB Connector

*Internal USB connectors* are available in two common form factors: a USB 2.0 header is a 9-pin rectangular connector that supports two USB 2.0 ports, and a USB 3.0 header is a 19-pin rectangular connector that supports two USB 3.0 ports. Both are shown in Figure 3.5-8 along with a typical front panel connector.

 **NOTE** A USB Type-C header is considerably smaller than a USB 3.0 (USB 3.1 Gen 1) header and uses a special cable that supports a single port.

# Installing a Motherboard

When you install a motherboard, follow these guidelines:

1. Be sure to take precautions against ESD. Remember that it's very easy to damage or destroy a CPU and RAM with a little electrostatic discharge. It's also fairly easy to damage the motherboard with ESD. Always wear your anti-static wrist strap.

2. Make sure the case's brass standoff spacers match the mounting holes on the motherboard. You might need to unscrew some of them and move them around or add additional spacers.

3. Install the CPU and heat sink/fan, and RAM before you install the motherboard, to avoid cracking the motherboard.

4. Line up the I/O shield that fits between the hole for the port cluster and the motherboard from the inside of the case before fastening the motherboard into place. The ports in the port cluster will help to hold the shield in case.

5. Before fastening the motherboard into place, connect front-panel wires, fans, and front-mounted port cables. These might be difficult to access after the motherboard is secured in place.

 **CAUTION** Make sure the standoffs on the bottom of the case line up with the mounting holes. Remove any excess standoffs. Standoffs that touch the wire traces or solder points on the bottom of the motherboard will short out the motherboard when the power is turned on.

6. Fasten the motherboard into place using the appropriate screws. If possible, use a hex driver instead of a Phillips-head screwdriver to avoid tool slippage. A scratched motherboard might fail.

# BIOS/UEFI Settings

The CMOS setup utility stored in the system ROM enables you to configure important system BIOS settings stored in the CMOS chip, which is built into the chipset on most computers. These settings include CPU setup, boot sequence, power management, and a number of others, as described here.

# BIOS/UEFI

The system BIOS chip is a ROM chip that stores the system BIOS routines and CMOS setup utility. Because these are software routines that are stored on a chip, the system BIOS is an example of firmware. System ROM is often distinctively labeled with the BIOS maker's name, but can also appear as a tiny chip on the motherboard.

There's a big difference between system ROM chips and RAM: RAM is called *volatile* because it stores data only while the computer is powered. System ROM is *non-volatile* and retains data even when the system is not powered. Except for replacing the CMOS battery (described in the next section) if it dies, system ROM requires no specific maintenance.

The firmware on modern systems is the *Unified Extensible Firmware Interface (UEFI)*. Here are the essentials:

- UEFI is often associated with graphical system setup utilities, whereas traditional BIOS is associated with text-mode utilities—even on the CompTIA A+ 220-1001 exam. However, this isn't a given. You can find graphical BIOS utilities and text-mode UEFI utilities.
- UEFI supports booting to partitions larger than 2.2 TB.
- Unlike with BIOS, the UEFI setup utility can be opened from within the OS.
- UEFI supports a security feature called Secure Boot that ensures a device boots using only trusted software.

## Entering the CMOS Setup Utility

With a traditional BIOS, you can't enter the CMOS setup utility from within the OS; you must do it early in the boot process. Methods differ by maker, but instructions for entering CMOS usually appear on your monitor during bootup (see Figure 3.5-9). Watch the messages carefully or check your motherboard documentation on which key to press.

## Navigating the CMOS Setup Utility

Mouse-friendly graphical setup utilities are increasingly common, but if you find yourself in a text-mode utility, you'll navigate with the keyboard. Both interface styles typically open to a screen with information about your system, components, and settings (see Figure 3.5-10); this interface provides a good overview of your CPU, RAM, hard drives, and optical drives. Navigation instructions may vary but should be prominently displayed. Usually the ARROW keys move the cursor and the ENTER key makes selections. If you get stuck, press the F1 key to bring up a Help menu.

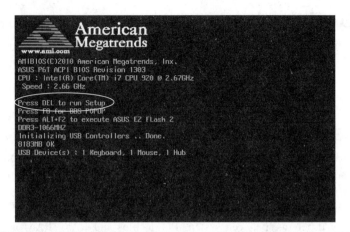

**FIGURE 3.5-9**   Each BIOS maker provides instructions for entering CMOS at bootup.

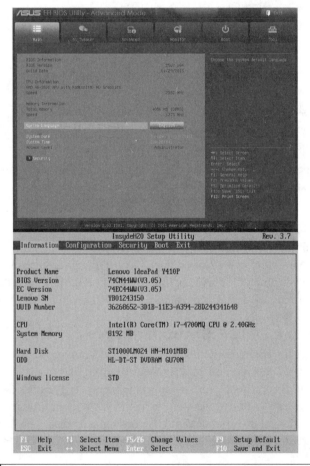

**FIGURE 3.5-10**   System information screen in graphical (top) and text-mode (bottom) setup utilities

Even though Figure 3.5-10 shows you can't count on tab names being the same on different utilities, there are still many common settings and organizational patterns that will help you to find your way. Before we dive in, there are two more navigation features to keep in mind before you decide to exit the system setup utility:

- **Save & Exit Setup**   To avoid accidents, *only* use this option when you intend to make a change and you're absolutely certain what the effect will be. Typically, selecting this option brings up a confirmation prompt such as "Are you sure you want to make these changes? Y/N."
- **Exit Without Saving**   This option discards your changes. Choosing this option brings up another "Are you sure? Y/N" confirmation prompt. Press Y to take your leave of CMOS setup without doing any damage.

 **NOTE**   There's enough variety in how tabs, menus, and options are labeled in different setup utilities that you'll inevitably find yourself hunting for what you need.

# Boot Options

The boot options (see Figure 3.5-11 for an example) hold one of the most frequently changed settings in the setup utility: the boot sequence. This setting decides which devices your system attempts to boot from and in what order. Other options you're likely to find here dictate whether the system boots from USB devices or network locations, displays detailed POST information, displays the key combination to reach the setup utility, and so on.

 **EXAM TIP**   The boot sequence is the first place to check if you have a computer that attempts to boot to an incorrect device or gives an "invalid boot device" error. If you have a USB thumb drive inserted and this CMOS setting has removable devices ahead of hard drives in the boot order, the computer will dutifully try to boot from the thumb drive.

# Firmware Updates

Techs refer to *firmware updates*, or updating system BIOS, as *flashing the BIOS*. It's a simple procedure, but it must be done correctly and without interruption: an interrupted BIOS flash usually renders the motherboard useless. Before flashing your BIOS, back up your important documents and update any system repair media. Make certain the process isn't disturbed once you start.

 **EXAM TIP**   The CompTIA A+ 220-1001 exam refers to flashing the BIOS as a *firmware update*.

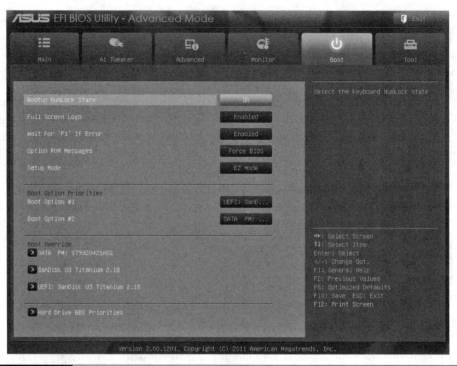

**FIGURE 3.5-11**    Boot tab in graphical setup utility

Some motherboards come with a Windows-based utility that will go to the Web, download an updated BIOS, and enable you to flash the BIOS from within Windows. When it works, it's sweet. Otherwise, BIOS makers provide flashing utilities on their websites.

## Interface Configurations

Some of the interface settings available in typical BIOS/UEFI firmware settings include

- Enable/disable ports (SATA, USB, Serial-RS-232, network, audio)
- Configure SATA settings: AHCI supports hot-swapping and full features; RAID supports RAID configurations and hot-swapping; IDE accesses drives in IDE mode (slower, no support for hot-swapping)

## Security and Security Settings

CompTIA wants you to know about several security options you might find in the setup utility, whether collected on a single tab (see Figure 3.5-12) or scattered about other menus:

- **Passwords**    When a user CMOS password is set, the system won't boot without the correct password. An administrator CMOS password restricts access to the CMOS utility itself.

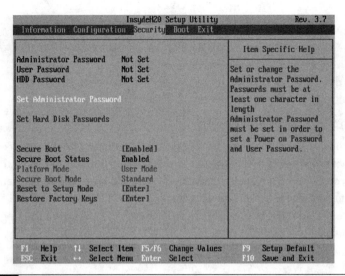

InsydeH20 Setup Utility                    Rev. 3.7

Information  Configuration  Security  Boot  Exit

                                          | Item Specific Help
Administrator Password     Not Set        |
User Password              Not Set        | Set or change the
HDD Password               Not Set        | Administrator Password.
                                          | Passwords must be at
Set Administrator Password                | least one character in
                                          | length
Set Hard Disk Passwords                   | Administrator Password
                                          | must be set in order to
                                          | set a Power on Password
Secure Boot                [Enabled]      | and User Password.
Secure Boot Status         Enabled        |
Platform Mode              User Mode      |
Secure Boot Mode           Standard       |
Reset to Setup Mode        [Enter]        |
Restore Factory Keys       [Enter]        |

F1   Help    ↑↓  Select Item  F5/F6  Change Values  F9   Setup Default
ESC  Exit    ↔   Select Menu   Enter  Select         F10  Save and Exit

**FIGURE 3.5-12**  Security tab in text-mode setup utility

**EXAM TIP**   Remember that CMOS settings—including passwords—can be wiped via the CMOS clear jumper or button, or by removing and replacing the CMOS battery.

- **Chassis intrusion detection/notification**   Most new systems have an option in CMOS that reports when the side of the case is opened, alerting techs to potential tampering.
- **Drive Protection**   Drive protection, which helps protect the system drive from unauthorized use, can be incorporated into the BIOS/UEFI firmware. Three common types include
  - **Trusted Platform Module**   The *Trusted Platform Module (TPM)* acts as a secure cryptoprocessor: a hardware platform for accelerating cryptographic functions and securely storing the associated information in tamper-resistant hardware. A common use of TPMs is accelerating and securing hard drive encryption, such as the BitLocker Drive Encryption feature of Microsoft Windows.
  - **LoJack**   If you have a LoJack-equipped computer that is stolen, LoJack enables you to track its location, install a key logger, or even remotely shut down the system.
  - **Secure Boot**   This UEFI protocol protects the system from some low-level malware and other exploits by refusing to load driver or OS software that hasn't been properly signed by a trusted party. Secure Boot requires an Intel CPU, a UEFI BIOS, and an operating system designed for it.

**EXAM TIP**    Be able to distinguish between the TPM, LoJack, and Secure Boot drive protection options for the CompTIA A+ 220-1001 exam.

## CMOS Battery

Every motherboard has a CMOS battery that enables it to retain CMOS settings when disconnected from external power. CMOS batteries fail gradually. If you notice your system clock running slow, or if you're consistently prompted to enter the date and time when you boot the PC, it's time to replace the CMOS battery. Replacing the CMOS battery (see Figure 3.5-13) is simple: slide the old one out of the bracket and slip a new one with matching voltage in its place. The real-time-clock (RTC) on the motherboard is also maintained by the CMOS battery.

**FIGURE 3.5-13**    CMOS battery

## CPU Features

CPUs have a variety of features that distinguish them from each other, including the number of cores, support for virtualization, Hyper-Threading, clock speeds, overclocking support, and integrated GPUs, as you learn in the following sections.

### Hyper-Threading

CPUs can handle multiple *processes*—opening a file, playing an MP3, and so on—nearly simultaneously by switching rapidly back and forth between *threads*, the subunits that make up a process. Many processes have only one thread, but some processes have many threads.

*Hyper-Threading Technology* is Intel's implementation of *simultaneous multithreading*, which executes multiple threads simultaneously on a single processor core to increase performance. A multithreaded processor looks like more than one CPU to the OS, but it's limited by having just one set of CPU resources. AMD's version of multithreading is simply known as simultaneous multithreading (SMT).

 **EXAM TIP** Be sure to understand the difference between Hyper-Threading Technology/SMT (in which one processor core supports multiple threads) and multicore processors (in which each CPU has two or more processor cores).

## Single-core and Multicore

Originally, all CPUs had a single processor core. CPU clock speeds hit a practical limit of roughly 4 GHz around 2002, motivating the CPU makers to combine multiple CPUs onto the same physical processor die, creating *multicore* CPUs. The first batch of multicore processors combined two CPU cores onto one chip, creating a *dual-core* architecture.

Unlike Hyper-Threading, where a single processor core shares execution resources among threads, a true dual-core CPU has two discrete processor cores, each possessing its own resources. Today's CPUs often have eight or more (see Figure 3.5-14). Most modern multicore processors also support Hyper-Threading Technology or SMT, so each core can handle multiple threads.

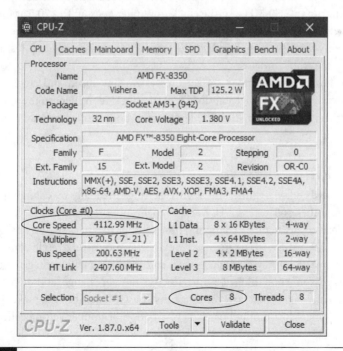

**FIGURE 3.5-14** CPU-Z showing an AMD FX-8350 with eight cores and clock speed highlighted

# Virtualization

Intel and AMD have built-in support for *virtualization*, a process that enables you to run one or more virtual computers on a single hardware computer. Early virtualization worked entirely through software. Programmers had to write a ton of code to enable a CPU designed to run one OS at a time to run more than one OS, but hardware-based virtualization enables the CPU to take on most of this burden. Virtualization is enabled through the BIOS/UEFI firmware.

**Cross-Reference**

For a comprehensive overview of virtualization, see Part I, Domain 4.0.

# Speeds

The CPU *clock speed*, or *frequency*, tells you how many calculation cycles a CPU can theoretically execute per second. One calculation cycle per second is equal to 1 hertz (Hz), but nobody measures clock cycles in hertz. Instead, we use millions or billions of calculation cycles per second, respectively called megahertz (MHz) or gigahertz (GHz), such as 1 GHz, which equals 1 billion cycles per second.

Two things determine clock speed: the maximum speed of the CPU itself and what the motherboard can handle. The CPU speed is determined by the manufacturer and set at the factory. The *system crystal*—a quartz crystal circuit that oscillates at a fixed frequency when fed current—sets the motherboard's clock speed.

Modern CPUs run at a multiple of the system clock speed. The system bus on my 4.1-GHz FX-8350 system runs at 200 MHz, so the clock multiplier goes up to ×20.5 at full load to support the maximum speed. Early CPUs ran at the speed of the bus, but engineers realized the CPU was the only thing working much of the time; if they could speed up just the CPU, they could speed up the whole process.

Old motherboards used jumpers to set the system bus speed and clock multiplier, but today's CPUs report to the motherboard via CPUID (CPU identifier) so the system bus speed and multiplier can be set automatically. Many motherboards offer manual configuration for tweaking systems.

# Overclocking

Some motherboards enable you to adjust CPU settings manually by changing a UEFI/BIOS setting or using other software; CPUs vary in their support for changes. Many enthusiasts practice *overclocking*: deliberately changing these settings to run their systems at clock speeds higher than the CPU rating, to enhance performance. A successful overclock usually takes two adjustments: increasing the system's bus speed, and increasing CPU voltage a little to provide stability. Always do only one thing at a time, document your change, and then reboot.

In addition to the slight risk of overheating, unstable CPU settings can make the UEFI/BIOS settings unreachable. Most motherboards have a button or jumper setting called *CMOS clear*

**FIGURE 3.5-15** Using the clear CMOS jumper

(see Figure 3.5-15) that resets UEFI/BIOS to default settings. Before you try overclocking, find CMOS clear and know how to use it. Always follow manufacturer recommendations and warranties before overclocking.

 **CAUTION** Overclocking might also make your system prone to system lockups, reboots, and unexpected shutdowns. Overclocking typically voids equipment warranties. Be careful!

# Integrated GPU

Computers traditionally have a discrete special-purpose microprocessor designed for video processing, known as a *graphics processing unit (GPU)*. Because graphics processors handle some tasks more efficiently than a standard CPU, integrating a GPU into the CPU enhances the overall performance of the computer and reduces its energy use, size, and cost.

Intel and AMD design their integrated GPUs a little differently. The *Intel HD Graphics* integrated into many Core i3/i5/i7/i9 processors, for example, has the CPU cores and the GPU core sharing the "last level cache," which is either L2 or L3, depending on the processor. With the AMD *accelerated processing unit (APU)*, such as the AMD Ryzen, the GPU has access to all levels of cache on the CPU.

| **TABLE 3.5-1** | Intel-based Sockets and Processors |
| --- | --- |

| Socket | CPU |
| --- | --- |
| LGA 775 | Pentium 4, Celeron, Pentium 4 Extreme Edition, Core 2 Duo, Core 2 Quad, Xeon, and many others |
| LGA 1155 | Core i3/i5/i7, Pentium, Celeron, Xeon |
| LGA 1156 | Core i3/i5/i7, Pentium, Celeron, Xeon |
| LGA 1366 | Core i7, Xeon, Celeron |
| LGA 2011 | Core i7, Core i7 Extreme Edition, Xeon |
| LGA 1150 | Core i3/i5/i7, Pentium, Celeron, Xeon |
| LGA 1151 | Core i3/i5/i7, Pentium, Celeron, Xeon |
| LGA 2066 | Core i5/i7/i9, Xeon |

# CPU Compatibility

Since no processors work in all motherboards, you should check the motherboard's documentation (or its manufacturer's website) for a chart listing the CPUs it supports. Because Intel and AMD CPUs are not pin-compatible, motherboards made since the mid-1990s support *either* Intel CPUs *or* AMD CPUs—not both. The type of CPU socket that the motherboard uses determines which model of Intel or AMD CPU you can install. Many motherboards accept more than one model of CPU. Likewise, some CPU models can fit more than one socket. Table 3.5-1 provides a reference to the Intel desktop processor sockets you're likely to encounter in the field, and Table 3.5-2 provides a reference to the AMD sockets you're likely to encounter in the field. Both vendors use zero insertion force (ZIF) sockets to hold the sockets in place.

| **TABLE 3.5-2** | AMD-based Sockets and Processors |
| --- | --- |

| Socket | Pins | CPU |
| --- | --- | --- |
| AM3 | 941 | Phenom II, Athlon II, Sempron, Opteron |
| AM3 | 942 | FX |
| AM4 | 1331 | Ryzen, some A-series, some Athlon X4 |
| TR4 | 4094 | Ryzen Threadripper |
| FM1 | 905 | A-series |
| FM2 | 904 | A-series |
| FM2+ | 906 | A-series |

**ADDITIONAL RESOURCES** To learn more about specific Intel CPU sockets and supported processors, see the Intel ARK website at http://ark.intel.com. To learn more about specific AMD CPU sockets and supported processors, see the AMD website at www.amd.com.

 **EXAM TIP** Because the CompTIA A+ exam has had pin-related questions in the past, Table 3.5-2 includes the pins for the AMD sockets. Intel socket names identify the number of pins associated with those sockets.

# Cooling Mechanism

CPUs have no moving parts (that you can see with the naked eye), but they generate considerable heat. Excessive heat causes system instability, lockups, and dead CPUs. CPU packages are made from high-tech thermal plastics and ceramics that dissipate heat, but they still can't provide enough relief without help. This help comes in the form of *active cooling* via *heat sink and fan assemblies* (see Figure 3.5-16) and *liquid cooling systems*.

## Installing a Heat Sink and Fan Assembly

Unlike the CPU socket, mounting heat sink and fan assemblies properly takes more force than you'd expect! A small flathead screwdriver will help.

 **EXAM TIP** Some systems get by on *fanless* or *passive cooling*. Smartphones and tablets are the passively cooled devices you're most likely familiar with. Passive CPU heat sinks may still rely on other fans to create good airflow in the case.

**FIGURE 3.5-16** Top of retail heat sink (left) and bottom of fan assembly (right) for an Intel CPU

Some systems use a passive heat sink assembly instead of a heat sink plus fan. These systems generally have very low-power processors that produce very little heat, such as an Intel Celeron or Atom.

Heat sink and fan assemblies for CPUs usually come as a unit; if not, attach the fan to the heat sink before installing both onto the CPU. Again, different CPUs, socket designs, and heat sinks require different installation procedures, so be sure to read the documentation. The general steps for installation are as follows:

1. If your CPU has thermal paste preapplied, remove and discard the protective tape. If not, apply a very thin film of thermal paste to the raised center of the CPU package, as shown here:

2. Align the heat sink and fan assembly's mounting bracket hardware with the mounting notches on the CPU socket.

3. With Intel stock fans, push the mounting pins in until they click in place. It's easy with the motherboard outside the case. Support the motherboard with one hand and push with the other so the motherboard does not flex.

4. For AMD fans, attach the mounting bracket to one side of the CPU socket unless you're installing a Wraith cooler. For these coolers, remove the mounting clips at each side of the socket.

5. Rotate the built-in locking lever on the opposite side to secure the assembly, as shown next. On a Wraith cooler, fasten the screws on the corners of the fan assembly into the mounting holes used by the mounting clips.

6. Finally, plug the fan's power cable into the appropriate socket or header on the motherboard. Check your motherboard documentation for information.

## Thermal Paste

Thermal paste, also known as thermal interface material (TIM), must be used between a fan and heat sink, a passive heat sink, a liquid cooling element, and the top of a CPU. OEM fan and heat sink units often include preapplied TIM that is protected with tape. The tape must be removed before installing the fan and heat sink. Otherwise, the installer must provide thermal paste and apply a thin, even coating to the top of the CPU before installing the cooling device.

## Installing a Liquid Cooling System

The essential installation steps for modern liquid cooling systems are similar:

1. Follow the manufacturer's instructions to attach the hoses from the coolant reservoir tank to the CPU cooling element and the heat exchanger unit. Confirm that all hoses are secure and crimped properly.

2. Fill the coolant reservoir with the recommended amount of distilled water.

3. Apply a small amount of thermal compound to the CPU.

4. If your liquid cooling system uses a separate CPU temperature sensor on the cooling element, attach it to the appropriate slot or groove and secure it with the supplied metal tape. Mount the cooling element to the CPU with the attached bracket and secure it in place with the tension screw (see Figure 3.5-17). Be careful not to overtighten the screw. You're ready to go!

**FIGURE 3.5-17** Cooling element mounted on CPU

# Expansion Cards

Although today's systems have many built-in ports, adding expansion cards is often necessary to provide better video performance or to add features. Although the following sections are written for Windows installations, expansion cards are also supported by macOS and Linux systems.

## Video Cards

A *video card* (or *display adapter*) handles the video chores within computing devices, processing information from the CPU and sending it to the display. It is configured the same way whether it is onboard (GPU built into the CPU) or an add-on card. When installing a card in Windows, you must install drivers and use Device Manager to confirm that it works. Then, you configure the video card in the Display Control Panel applet or with included software (see Figure 3.5-18).

### Onboard

An *onboard* video card uses the built-in graphics processing unit (GPU) found in many CPUs. Almost all laptops use onboard graphics, as well as most thick and thin client desktops. Desktop computers that support CPUs with onboard GPUs have one or more video card ports in the port cluster on the rear of the computer (refer to Figure 3.5-2 for a typical example).

### Add-on Card

A video card that goes into a PCIe slot, an *add-on card* in CompTIA terminology, probably needs additional power beyond what the slot itself provides. Midrange PCIe video cards use

**FIGURE 3.5-18** The Display dialog box from AMD Radeon Display Settings

a 6-pin PCIe power connector on the top front edge of the video card (the end pointing away from the card bracket), while high-end cards use an 8-pin version or, in some cases, two PCIe cables. Figure 3.5-19 illustrates a PCIe video card with a 6-pin power connector and a 6/8-pin PCIe power cable.

**FIGURE 3.5-19** Connecting a PCIe power cable to a PCIe video card

**FIGURE 3.5-20**  Video card with a cooling fan

The main parts of a video card are video RAM and a video processor. The video processor takes information from the video RAM and shoots it out to the monitor. Early video processors were little more than an intermediary between the CPU and video RAM, but powerful modern video cards need fans to cool their video processors (see Figure 3.5-20).

Among techs, video card discussions revolve around the GPU and RAM used. The two major GPU makers, NVIDIA and AMD, develop and sell new GPUs to card manufacturers. Let's break down a typical card name: Asus EX-RX570-O8G. Asus is the card manufacturer, RX570 is a GPU made by AMD, and O8G refers to the 8 GB of onboard memory. For more information about a card, look up the card on the vendor's website.

Low-end graphics processors are enough to write letters or run a web browser, but high-end graphics processors support intensive uses such as beautiful 3-D games, graphics rendering (3-D, animation, video), and even certain kinds of data processing (scientific research, for example) that GPUs are well suited for. Don't be shocked if someone who knows zilch about the latest games needs a system with one or more high-end GPUs—don't skimp on their hardware, and don't assume they need a GPU tailored to gaming.

## Sound Cards

Sound output is generated by the sound card and speakers. Most computers use sound chips built into the motherboard, but these often have an audible hum or buzz of interference from the rest of the motherboard (which headphones can exacerbate). In any case, speakers affect customer satisfaction much more than the sound card or built-in sound chips. Spend a little extra money to get decent speakers. If you can fit only a 2.1 set, go for a subwoofer and nice satellites (see Figure 3.5-21).

**FIGURE 3.5-21** Klipsch 2.1 speaker set

**NOTE** The numbers used to describe speaker sets—2.1, 5.1, 7.1—define the number of satellite speakers and a subwoofer. A 2.1 system, for example, means two satellites and a subwoofer. A 5.1 set, in contrast, has two front satellites, two rear satellites (for surround sound), a center channel speaker, and a subwoofer. A 7.1 set adds two additional rear satellites for sound effects to the speaker configuration used for 5.1 surround sound.

Install a sound card like you would any expansion card. Plug audio cables into the correct ports, and they should work fine. If you don't see errors but get no sound, check the Sound applet (see Figure 3.5-22) in the Control Panel to confirm the correct devices are ready, connected, set to default, and that the playback indicator shows activity on the correct device.

The 3.5-mm audio ports on the motherboard port cluster or sound card bracket aren't the only audio output. Some systems use SPDIF optical or digital ports, and the popular HDMI and DisplayPort HD video ports also output HD audio.

## Network Interface Card

The *network interface card (NIC)* links your system to the network infrastructure. Although most computers have an onboard network port for UTP Ethernet, if the computer lacks one or you need support for faster speeds or fiber optic networking, you'll need to install a USB or expansion-card NIC by following the manufacturer's instructions. Windows will automatically detect, install, and configure most NICs—you almost never need to configure a NIC manually.

**FIGURE 3.5-22** Sound applet

### Cross-Reference

To learn more about NIC configuration, see Part I, Domain 2.0, Objective 2.3.

Once the NIC is installed, connect it to the wall outlet with a patch cable that can take typical work-area abuse, such as moving equipment and an occasional kick. The work area may seem relatively simple, but the extra abuse makes it the source of most network failures. When a user can't access the network and you suspect a broken cable, start in the work area.

 **EXAM TIP** Both NICs and switches have LED *status indicators* (also called *link lights*) that can confirm your new connection. There are no real standards, but it's a safe bet that one indicates connection status; if all of them are unlit, there's no physical connection. Consult the motherboard or NIC manual to decipher other meanings.

## USB Expansion Card

If you use lots of USB devices (such as printers, scanners, external drives, or card readers), it's easy to run out of USB ports. If you don't want to use a USB hub (some devices don't work well with hubs) and you don't have any internal USB ports you can add a header cable to, add a USB expansion card to an expansion slot. Cards are available to add USB 2.0, USB 3.0, USB 3.1 Gen 2, and USB Type-C ports, enabling you to add support for faster USB standards than are already built into a computer. Most cards require additional power beyond what the expansion slot provides, so make sure you have a free power lead, or use a Y-splitter to turn one power lead into two.

## eSATA Card

An *eSATA card* enables a desktop computer that lacks eSATA ports to connect to eSATA hard drives or docking bays. As an alternative to using an eSATA card, you can attach an eSATA conversion bracket to an unused SATA port. Just be sure to configure the port as an AHCI port to enable hot-swapping.

## Installing Expansion Cards

Successful expansion card installation has four steps. First, confirm the card works with your motherboard and OS. Second, insert the card in an expansion slot properly and without damaging the card or the motherboard. Third, provide proper drivers for the specific OS. Finally, verify the card functions properly.

 **EXAM TIP**   The CompTIA A+ 220-1001 exam may ask about common cards (sound, video, and networking), legacy cards (modems), and special-purpose cards (cellular, riser, TV tuner, and video capture). The exam might even ask how to install a USB, Thunderbolt, or storage card. You install all of them using the same four steps: knowledge, physical installation, device drivers and other software, and verification.

### Step 1: Knowledge

Learn about the device you plan to install. You can check compatibility on the manufacturer's website, though most people just check the device's box. Windows-certified devices proudly display that they work with Windows.

### Step 2: Physical Installation

For installation to succeed, you must avoid damaging the card, the motherboard, or both; know how to handle a card, avoid electrostatic discharge (ESD), and remove all power from the system. Insert the card firmly and completely into an available expansion slot.

Ideally, a card should always be either in a computer or in an anti-static bag. When inserting or removing a card, hold the card only by its edges without touching the contacts or any components on the board (see Figure 3.5-23).

Use an anti-static wrist strap properly attached to the system. If you don't have one, at least touch the power supply after you remove the expansion card from its anti-static bag to put you, the card, and the computer at the same electrical potential and minimize the ESD risk.

Modern systems have a trickle of voltage to the motherboard any time the computer is plugged into a power outlet. *Always unplug the computer before inserting an expansion card!* Failure to do so can destroy the card, the motherboard, or both.

**FIGURE 3.5-23** Where to handle a card

Never insert or remove a card at an extreme angle; this can damage it. A slight angle is acceptable and even necessary to remove a card. Always secure (and ground) the card to the case with a connection screw (see Figure 3.5-24) to keep the card from coming loose and shorting out on other cards.

**FIGURE 3.5-24** Always screw down all cards.

# Step 3: Device Drivers and Other Software

Installing device drivers is fairly straightforward. If you're upgrading, uninstall the current drivers first. Next, install the *correct* drivers. If you have a problem, uninstall the new drivers or roll back to a stable one.

Check the manufacturer's website for the best possible driver. The included drivers may work fine, but there's often a newer, better driver available on the website. To know if the driver is newer, check the disc. Often the version is printed on the optical media itself; if not, load the disc and poke around. Many driver discs have an Autorun screen or Readme file that advertises the version.

 **NOTE**   Microsoft requires signed drivers to provide the most stable platform possible. You simply cannot install unsigned drivers without clunky workarounds. If you upgrade a legacy system to a newer version of Windows, make sure signed drivers exist for its hardware before upgrading.

If you install drivers and your system becomes unstable, roll back to the drivers that worked: open Device Manager, access the properties for the device you want to adjust, and click the Roll Back Driver button on the Driver tab (see Figure 3.5-25).

Some devices—notably video cards—have additional support software. These include configuration utilities that live in the Control Panel or notification area. Support software used to be a separate installation from the drivers, but most manufacturers now bundle them in one executable.

**FIGURE 3.5-25**   Driver rollback feature

**FIGURE 3.5-26**   Device Manager shows the device working properly.

## Step 4: Verification

Finally, inspect the results of the installation and verify that the device works properly. Immediately after installing, open Device Manager and confirm that Windows sees the device (see Figure 3.5-26). Assuming Device Manager shows the device with no errors, put the device through the paces by making it do whatever it is supposed to do. If you installed a printer, print something; if you installed a scanner, scan something. If it works, you're done!

# REVIEW

### Objective 3.5: Given a scenario, install and configure motherboards, CPUs, and add-on cards

- The most common motherboard form factors are ATX, microATX (mATX), and mini-ITX (mITX).
- Motherboards have port clusters at the rear of the motherboard for USB ports, audio jacks, network ports, and other built-in ports.
- PCI slots have been for the most part replaced by PCIe slots, but most motherboards still have one or two PCI slots.
- PCIe is available in versions 1, 2, 3, and 4, with each newer version running about twice as fast as the preceding version.

- PCIe uses lanes, and the most common slot types use from 1 (×1) to 16 (×16) lanes.
- Some motherboards use one or more riser cards.
- Most motherboards have at least one CPU socket.
- Motherboards support either Intel or AMD CPUs. They are not interchangeable.
- Most hard drives and optical drives connect to SATA ports.
- Some older systems in use also have IDE ports.
- Front panel connectors are used for the on/off switch, signal lights, and similar functions.
- Internal USB connectors (headers) on the motherboard can be used to add more USB ports and are available in USB 2.0, USB 3.0, and USB-C versions.
- The system BIOS is the firmware that stores the system BIOS routines for basic system configuration and the CMOS setup utility; it can be updated with a download from the motherboard maker.
- UEFI is the current firmware generation supporting hard drives over 2.2 TB and offering other benefits.
- One of the most important BIOS/UEFI settings is boot order, along with security, SATA drive, and I/O device settings.
- BIOS/UEFI security settings include passwords and drive encryption with TPM, LoJack, or SecureBoot.
- The CMOS battery enables the motherboard to retain BIOS/UEFI settings when disconnected from external power.
- Multicore processors have two or more processor cores.
- Simultaneous multithreading such as Intel Hyper-Threading or AMD SMT enables a processor core to support two execution threads, making it perform faster.
- Processor clock speed is a multiple of the system clock speed.
- Overclocking runs CPUs at faster bus and clock speeds than normal.
- Virtualization is supported by most AMD and Intel CPUs and is enabled through BIOS/UEFI firmware.
- Modern CPUs feature two or more cores, multithreading (Hyper-Threading or SMT) in some models, support for overclocking, and integrated graphics in some models.
- Intel CPUs use LGA sockets, while AMD CPUs use AM, FM, or TR sockets.
- Heat sinks with fans or liquid cooling elements are used to cool down CPUs.
- Thermal material interfacing (thermal paste or tape) is used between cooling devices and CPUs.
- Video cards use faster RAM than motherboards and most have cooling fans.
- Most video cards require extra power from a PCIe power connector.
- Sound cards and onboard sound chips support stereo or surround audio.
- SPDIF, HDMI, and DisplayPort output digital audio.
- NICs have status lights to indicate connection and speed.

- USB expansion cards and header cables enable you to add more USB ports.

- eSATA cards and eSATA-SATA conversion brackets enable you to add more eSATA ports.

- The process of installing expansion cards includes checking for compatibility (knowledge), proper physical installation (avoiding ESD and securing the card), installing device drivers, and verifying proper card operation.

## 3.5 QUESTIONS

1. You have been tasked to review motherboard form factors for a project. The number one requirement is that the motherboard be as small as possible. Which of these motherboards is the smallest?

   **A.** microATX

   **B.** Mini-ITX

   **C.** ITX

   **D.** ATX

2. Your client has selected PCIe version 3.0 graphics cards to refresh the organization's video editing workstations. However, the systems support PCIe version 2.0. Which of the following is true?

   **A.** The cards will run at PCIe 3.0 speeds.

   **B.** The motherboards must be replaced with PCIe 3.0–compatible versions.

   **C.** The cards cannot be used.

   **D.** The cards will run at PCIe 2.0 speeds.

3. You are upgrading your personal system with USB 3.0 (USB 3.1 Gen 1) devices but have run out of external ports. You need two more ports. Which of the following would provide these ports?

   **A.** USB 2.0 header cable

   **B.** USB-C header cable

   **C.** USB 3.0 header cable

   **D.** SATA-to-USB conversion cable

4. You are creating documentation for other technicians to use as they configure the UEFI firmware on new systems. Which of the following should not be in the documentation because it is incorrect?

   **A.** SATA drives cannot be configured as hot-swappable.

   **B.** USB ports can be disabled.

   **C.** The boot sequence can be changed.

   **D.** You can exit UEFI/BIOS setup without saving changes.

5. Your client wants you to install an LGA 1155 processor into a motherboard that uses an FM2 processor. Which of the following statements about these parts is correct?

   **A.** Intel parts work in AMD motherboards.

   **B.** The LGA 1155 will not fit into this motherboard.

   **C.** The FM2 processor is an older Intel processor.

   **D.** The FM2 processor has 2000 pins.

## 3.5 ANSWERS

1. **B**  The Mini-ITX (mITX) is the smallest motherboard listed.

2. **D**  When two different PCIe versions are present (slot and card), the slower version is used.

3. **C**  A USB 3.0 header cable provides two USB 3.0 ports; however, not all motherboards with USB 3.0 have headers.

4. **A**  SATA drives are hot-swappable when configured as AHCI in the UEFI/BIOS firmware.

5. **B**  LGA 1155 is an Intel CPU socket, but FM2 is an AMD CPU socket; they are not compatible.

 **Objective 3.6** # Explain the purposes and uses of various peripheral types

Many peripherals can be connected to a computer's external video, audio, and USB ports. This section presents the long list of peripherals under objective 3.6 by grouping them into three logical categories: output devices, input devices, and drives and storage devices.

 **EXAM TIP**  Be sure to know the purpose of each device in this objective.

## Output Devices

The following devices produce output on paper, as files, or as sound.

### Printer

Printers produce output on paper, envelopes, card stock, labels, or transparency media. Printers are often combined with scanners, copiers, or fax devices in both offices and homes.

Most printers used in home or office environments use laser or inkjet technologies, but thermal and impact printers are also used in some specialized environments.

**Cross-References**

To learn more about printer features, see Objective 3.10, and to learn more about printer technologies, see Objective 3.11; both later in this domain.

## Monitors

Monitors, also called displays, are connected to video cards or ports so users can view what is happening in the operating system and with running apps. Monitors formerly used CRT technology, and later LCD with fluorescent backlights, but are now based on LCD with LED backlights or organic LED (OLED) technologies. Most computers can be connected to two or more monitors.

## VR Headset

A VR (virtual reality) headset creates an immersive experience by mounting two high-resolution screens into a headset that blocks external visual sensory input. VR headsets are used in 3-D gaming and other 3-D uses that enable the user to interact with a software-created 3-D world.

## Projector

A projector connects to the same video ports used by monitors, enabling a room to see a computer presentation, documents, photos, or movies. Projectors typically use one of two display technologies—LCD or DLP—and have zoom lenses to enable the projector to work in a variety of room sizes.

### Lumens/Brightness

When selecting a projector, one consideration is the brightness of the output, measured in lumens (the higher the lumen rating, the brighter the projected image).

## Speakers

Speakers enable computers, tablets, and smartphones to double as high-quality music playback stations. Speakers can be connected via 3.5-mm analog jacks, SPDIF jacks, or Bluetooth wireless connections. Speakers built into HDTVs can be driven by HDMI or DisplayPort connections. When a different audio output is added, the sound mixer app settings need to be changed to use the new audio output.

## Headset

Headsets can be used in place of speakers for privacy and many also include microphones. Like speakers, they can be connected to 3.5-mm analog jacks or work wirelessly with Bluetooth. Some connect to USB ports.

# Input Devices

The following devices are used to input commands, text, or other types of data into a program, storage, or computer RAM.

## Mouse

Pointing devices enable us to instruct the computer to perform an action at some spot on the screen. Most computers have a mouse attached (same connection options as keyboards) with two buttons and a scroll wheel. Modern *optical mice* use light-emitting diodes (LEDs) or lasers to track and translate movement to the screen.

## Keyboard

The keyboard has been the primary computer input device since the original IBM PC several decades ago. Keyboards use wired (USB, PS/2) or wireless (Bluetooth, radio frequency [RF]) interfaces. Each OS comes with support for standard QWERTY keyboards, but extra features like multimedia controls or color-changing keys require drivers. You can adjust settings such as how fast keys repeat in the Keyboard Control Panel applet (Windows) or System Preferences (macOS). Linux supports these options, but the menu name and location differ among distros.

 **NOTE**   The eternal struggle with keyboards is keeping them clean; educate users who need a replacement not to eat or drink over it!

## Touchpad

A touchpad uses finger movements to scroll, control the cursor, and issue other commands. Touchpads typically are included only on portable computers, but standalone USB or Bluetooth touchpads are available for desktop computers.

## Signature Pad

Signature pads are devices that incorporate digitizer technology to convert users' signatures to digital. They are commonly used in banks, credit unions, or other point-of-sale locations where a signature must be captured. They are replacing paper signature slips.

## Game Controllers

You can control most modern computer games with a mouse and keyboard, but some also support joysticks, gamepads, and steering wheels. Modern controllers connect via USB, and you'll need to install drivers for complex ones. *Joysticks* (see Figure 3.6-1) mimic the iconic aircraft control stick; *gamepads* (see Figure 3.6-2) resemble gaming console controllers; *steering wheels* may come with pedals and shifters. After connecting these devices, you might need to calibrate them before they can be used.

FIGURE 3.6-1    A joystick

FIGURE 3.6-2    A gamepad

## ADF/Flatbed Scanner

A flatbed scanner is used to create digital versions of documents or photos. An auto document feeder (ADF) is built into many scanners to make scanning or copying of multiple documents faster.

 **NOTE**    A multifunction device (MFD) combines printer, scanner, and copier functionality and is considered an input/output device.

# Barcode Scanner/QR Scanner

Barcode scanners and QR scanners use lasers to read standard Universal Product Code (UPC) barcodes or Quick Response (QR) codes and are typically used with point-of-sale (POS) or warehousing systems to identify items.

# Camera/Webcam

A dedicated digital camera (see Figure 3.6-3) can offer higher quality, features tuned to the task at hand, and more room for creativity than the camera built into a smartphone.

Digital cameras typically store data on flash memory cards or internal hard drives, but may also have Wi-Fi for quick sharing. Windows and macOS both have programs for basic photo and video organization, editing, and sharing, though professional image- and video-editing software can unlock your creativity (for a price).

Unlike regular cameras, where higher quality is better, *webcams* (cameras in or mounted on computer monitors) tend to have modest, bandwidth-friendly resolutions. They often include a microphone, but you can also use a standalone mic or headset.

Windows' own webcam drivers are limited, so always install drivers supplied with a camera before you plug it in.

**FIGURE 3.6-3**    Typical dedicated digital camera

# Microphone

The computer is a great platform for recording and editing sound and music. The most common option is plugging a microphone into a microphone jack or a USB port to record your voice, make phone and video calls, coordinate with teammates in online games, and control a computer with voice commands. Musicians, however, need special hardware.

## KVM

A *keyboard, video, mouse (KVM) switch* is a hardware device that enables a single mouse, keyboard, and monitor to control multiple computers (though some KVMs reverse that capability, enabling a single computer to be controlled by multiple input devices). KVMs are useful in data centers with many rack-mounted servers and limited space. Once you connect a keyboard, mouse, and monitor to the KVM and connect the KVM to the desired computers, you can use keyboard hotkeys (such as pressing the SCROLL LOCK key twice) to toggle between computers connected to the KVM.

## Magnetic Reader/Chip Reader

Magnetic reader/chip reader attachments for smartphones and tablets enable them to be used to read credit and debit cards to accept payments via the cellular network. Magnetic reader/chip reader devices are also incorporated into point-of-sale (POS) computers for use in retail stores.

## NFC/Tap Pay Device

NFC/tap pay devices use Near Field Communication to enable payments from smartphones to payment services at gas stations and retail stores.

## Smart Card Reader

Many enterprise-level businesses use a smart-card system that requires employees to display proper credentials to obtain the correct level of access to company resources. A *smart card reader* comes in many forms, from a small device attached to a laptop computer to a panel next to a secure door, and scans chip-embedded *ID badges* or other devices.

# Drives and Storage Devices

The following peripheral devices are used to load apps, store data, or record data.

## Optical Drive Types

CD, DVD, and Blu-ray Disc (BD) drives are used to load apps, to view archival data stored on optical discs, or, when using recordable or rewriteable drives and media, to create copies of files or operating system images. Although these drives are sometimes installed into internal drive bays, most late-model laptops and some desktops use external versions instead.

## External Storage Drives

External storage drives can be used to transfer data between systems, as additional primary storage, or for data backups. The most common connection methods are USB 2.0/3.0 (for low-end flash drives and CD/DVD optical drives), USB 3.0/3.1/Type-C (for high-capacity flash drives, hard disks, SSDs, or Blu-ray Disc drives), or Thunderbolt (for hard disks or SSDs). Some external drives connect to the eSATA ports found on some older systems.

 **EXAM TIP**    Make sure you know which connection types are used by external storage drives.

# REVIEW

### Objective 3.6: Explain the purposes and uses of various peripheral types

- Output devices include printers, speakers, headsets, VR headsets, and projectors.
- Input devices include ADF/flatbed scanners, barcode/QR scanners, mice, KVM switches, keyboards, touchpads, signature pads, game controllers, camera/webcams, microphones, magnetic reader/chip readers, NFC/tap pay devices, and smart card readers.
- Storage devices include optical drives and external storage drives.

## 3.6 QUESTIONS

1. Your client cannot use a mouse and does not want to use a laptop, so your job is to choose an alternative input device. Which of the following can be used in place of a mouse?

   **A.** Touchpad

   **B.** Signature pad

   **C.** Keyboard

   **D.** Joystick

2. To enable video conferencing in privacy, your company should install which of the following components on its desktop computers?

   **A.** Speakers and camcorders

   **B.** Headsets and projectors

   **C.** Headsets and webcams

   **D.** Speakers and digital cameras

3. A client calls, complaining of no sound from his computer after replacing separate audio speakers and a VGA monitor with an HDMI display with built-in speakers. Which of the following needs to be done to hear sound again?

   **A.** New display is defective—return it to vendor for replacement

   **B.** Disable on-board sound

   **C.** Enable speakers in display with pushbutton

   **D.** Change sound mixer output to HDMI

4. Your client, a restaurant owner, wants to add support for Apple Pay to its POS systems. Which of the following types of devices is needed?

A. Signature pad

B. NFC/tap pay device

C. Magnetic reader/chip reader

D. Smart card reader

5. You are building a personal gaming system. Which of the following will not be a feature to add for this purpose?

A. Signature pad

B. VR headset

C. Game controller

D. Joystick

## 3.6 ANSWERS

1. **A**    A touchpad, whether built into a laptop keyboard or plugged into a USB port, is a very satisfactory mouse replacement for many users.

2. **C**    Headsets will help keep conference content confidential, while a webcam will enable attendees to see each other for better communication.

3. **D**    The computer will continue to route sound to the original audio jack until the new source is selected in the mixer app.

4. **B**    NFC/tap pay devices are used by device-based payment systems like Apple Pay.

5. **A**    A signature pad is useful on a POS or banking device, but has no purpose on a gaming PC.

**Objective 3.7** ## Summarize power supply types and features

Power supplies enable computers to run, and are an often-neglected cause of failures and crashes. As port-powered peripherals become more numerous and CPUs and GPUs require more power, power supplies with larger wattage ratings are becoming more important.

## Input: 115 V vs. 220 V

A desktop computer includes a power supply unit (PSU) (see Figure 3.7-1) that converts high-voltage AC power to low-voltage DC power for the computer's motherboard and devices. Its internal fan also helps cool the components and drives. When connected to a properly

**FIGURE 3.7-1**   Power supply

grounded outlet, the power supply also provides grounding for all the other equipment inside the case.

In the United States, standard AC comes in somewhere between 110 and 120 V, often written as ~115 VAC (but 115V in objective 3.7). Most of the rest of the world uses 220–240 VAC (220V in objective 3.7), so many power supplies offer a little dual-voltage switch on the back that enables you to use them anywhere. Power supplies with voltage-selection switches are referred to as fixed-input. Power supplies that you do not have to manually switch for different voltages are known as auto-switching.

 **CAUTION**   If you are using a fixed-input power supply connected to a 220–240 VAC power line, don't turn it on if the voltage selector switch is set to 115 VAC. That's a sure way to kill the power supply and possibly other components as well!

 **EXAM TIP**   The power connector for the AC plug on the back of a power supply is called an *IEC-320 connector*. CompTIA A+ 1001 exam questions might refer to the power supply as a PSU.

Power supplies come in various form factors that determine the physical size, shape, and connectors.

**ADDITIONAL RESOURCES**   To learn more about power supply form factors, see www.tomshardware.com and search for "A Basic Guide To Motherboard, Case and Power Supply Form Factors."

Power supplies also vary in output, efficiency, the number of 12-V *rails* used, and how much power each rail can supply. While a *single-rail* power supply is usually enough for an average computer, high-end systems may need a *multi-rail* power supply. In practice, avoid running too many devices off one rail in a multi-rail power supply.

**EXAM TIP**   Make sure you know the voltage ranges (~115 VAC versus ~230 VAC) supported by power supplies.

# Output: 5 V vs. 12 V

The PSU converts the high-voltage AC to low-voltage DC to power motors on devices such as hard drives and optical drives (12-V current) and onboard electronics (5-V current). The device connectors you're most likely to see are *serial ATA (SATA)*, *Molex*, and *mini* (also called *Berg*) (see Figure 3.7-2). Better power supplies have a dedicated 6- or 8-wire *PCIe* connector for PCI Express video cards (see Figure 3.7-3).

**FIGURE 3.7-2**   Mini, Molex, and SATA power connectors (left to right)

**FIGURE 3.7-3**   PCIe power connector

| FIGURE 3.7-4 | EPS12V/ATX12V connectors (left) and P1 connector (right). These use one 4-pin (P4) connector on motherboards that use a 4-pin ATX12V connector, and both on motherboards that use an 8-pin EPS12V connector. |

Power supplies connect to the motherboard with these connectors: the 20- or 24-pin (wire) *P1* connector, the primary power circuit; and a 4-wire *P4* secondary power connector or 8-wire EPS12V power connector, which typically supplies power to the CPU (see Figure 3.7-4). The power supply converts AC to DC current, so all power leads from the power supply carry DC current.

**EXAM TIP**   The 5-volt orange (sometimes gray) wire on the P1 connector is called *power good* and is used in the initial boot sequence.

Many modern ATX motherboards use an 8-pin CPU power connector, variously referred to as EPS12V, EATX12V, and ATX12V 2×4. Half of this connector will be pin-compatible with the P4 power connector; the other half may be under a protective cap.

Check the motherboard installation manual for recommendations on when to use the full 8 pins. For backward compatibility, some power supplies provide an 8-pin power connector that can split into two 4-pin sets, one of which is the P4 connector (refer to Figure 3.7-4). Although they look similar, the 8-pin CPU power connector is not compatible with the 8-pin PCIe power connector. Table 3.7-1 lists the common connectors of the ATX12V power supplies—the current standard—with their voltages and uses.

**CAUTION**   Power connectors are keyed so that you can't easily plug them in backward, but some older designs can be forced. Reversing the power on a device will fry it. Don't force a power connector.

| TABLE 3.7-1 | Power Connectors and Voltages |

| Connector | Voltages | Common Use |
|---|---|---|
| Molex | 5 V (red), 12 V (yellow) | Legacy storage and optical drives; some PCIe video cards and motherboards; case fans |
| Mini (Berg) | 5 V, 12 V | Floppy drives |
| SATA | 5 V, 12 V (3.3 V orange optional) | SATA drives |
| PCIe | 12 V | PCIe video cards |
| P1 (20-wire) | 3.3 V, 5 V, 12 V | Primary power for older ATX motherboards |
| P1 (24-wire) | 3.3 V, 5 V, 12 V | Primary power for current ATX motherboards |
| P4 and 8-pin CPU power connector | 12 V | Secondary power for current ATX motherboards |
| AUX | 3.3 V, 5 V, 12 V | Auxiliary power for old motherboards |
| Ground wire | Black | Used by all connector types |

# 24-pin Motherboard Adapter

To enable the same power supply model to work with older 20-pin ATX motherboards and modern motherboards that use 24-pin connectors, some vendors provide 24-pin motherboard adapters.

# Wattage Rating

Power supplies provide a certain *wattage* that the motherboard, drives, and fans draw on to run. That's the desired output. Power supplies also produce *harmonics*, the hum you hear when the power supply runs, that can cause problems with the power supply and other electrical devices on the circuit if not controlled.

 **EXAM TIP**  Wattage is the amount of amperage flowing at a specific voltage, usually written as W = VA.

A computer requires sufficient wattage to run properly. Every device in the system also requires a certain wattage to function. For example, a typical magnetic hard drive draws 15 W of power when accessed (SSDs use less), whereas a quad-core Intel i9-9900K CPU draws a whopping 162 W at peak usage—with average usage around 92 W. The total combined wattage needs of all devices is the minimum you need the power supply to provide.

If the power supply can't produce the wattage needed by a system, that computer won't work properly. Because most devices in the system require maximum wattage when starting, the typical outcome of insufficient wattage is a paperweight that looks like a computer. The only fixes for this situation are to remove the device or get a power supply with more wattage. Today's systems require at least 500+ watt power supplies to function.

Good computer power supplies come with *active power factor correction (active PFC)*, extra circuitry that smoothes out high-voltage AC power before passing it to the main power supply circuits to eliminate harmonics. Avoid any older and poorer power supplies without this circuitry.

Most active PFC power supplies are *auto-switching*, meaning they can detect the voltage coming from the wall and adjust accordingly. You can use an auto-switching power supply anywhere in the world, from the ~115 VAC in New York City to the ~230 in Hong Kong. This is especially important with portable computers!

# Number of Devices/Types of Devices to Be Powered

Before purchasing a new power supply, it is essential to determine the number of devices and types of devices it will power. Power supplies vary greatly in the number of Molex, SATA, and mini (Berg) connectors, and some only support only a single PCIe power connector. Molex connectors are no longer used for drives, but are frequently used to power case fans if there are not enough fan ports on the motherboard and can also be adapted to run SATA drives or devices that use mini connectors.

Try to avoid the use of splitters to run more devices than can be connected directly to a power supply. Cheap splitters that use thin wires can overheat, and even the best-quality splitters introduce additional points of potential failure into a system.

# Power Supply Installation Notes

Be careful when you work with power supplies or inside a computer. Here's why: an ATX power supply never turns off. As long as it is connected to AC power, the power supply will feed 5 V DC to the motherboard. Installing cards, chips, or memory modules to a motherboard while power is flowing could damage those components. Remember, always unplug the power supply and wait about ten seconds before you work inside the computer or disconnect the power supply for replacement!

Before you connect the power supply, you'll need to mount it inside the case with four standard case screws (see Figure 3.7-5). The only exceptions are some small or proprietary cases.

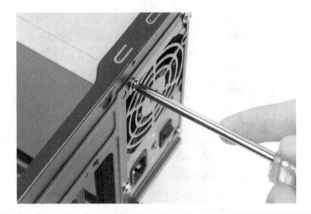

**FIGURE 3.7-5**    Power supply secured in case

# REVIEW

### Objective 3.7: Summarize power supply types and features

- Power supplies support ~115 VAC and ~230 VAC inputs, either through a sliding switch or with internal auto-switching.
- The IEC-320 connector is used for the AC plug on the rear of the power supply.
- Power supplies generally provide 5-V or 12-V power to peripherals via the SATA, Molex, and mini (Berg) power leads. PCIe power leads provide 12-V power to PCIe cards.
- P1 provides power to the motherboard using a 24-pin (newer) or 20-pin (older) keyed connector.
- Older motherboards use the P4 4-pin 12-V connector to provide power to the CPU (the power is stepped down by the motherboard); newer motherboards use the EPS12V 8-pin connector for this job.
- Higher wattage ratings in power supplies are needed when the power draw of installed and onboard devices approaches or exceeds the output of the current power supply.
- Active PFC helps eliminate harmonics for better-quality power.
- Splitters can be used to power additional devices, but it's better to use a power supply that has enough leads of the right types for your devices.
- Power supplies are typically mounted using four screws on the rear that fasten through the case wall.

## 3.7 QUESTIONS

1. Your client's 20-pin ATX power supply has failed. Which of the following can be used to enable a modern power supply to be used as a replacement?

   **A.** ATX12V adapter

   **B.** 24-pin motherboard adapter

   **C.** EPS12V adapter

   **D.** Aux adapter

2. Your company is taking several desktop computers to a European country for a long-term project. The power supplies are auto-switching, but a component with a design that varies by location is also needed. That component uses the IEC-320 connector on the power supply. Which of these is it?

   **A.** AUX adapter

   **B.** 115-230VC AC converter

   **C.** Power cord

   **D.** EPS12V adapter

3. You are providing telephone support to a new technician who is using a multimeter to check a power supply. Which of the following voltage/color combinations is incorrect?

   **A.** 12-V DC is yellow

   **B.** Black is 3.3-V DC

   **C.** Orange is 3.3-V DC

   **D.** 5-V DC is red

4. You have received a frantic call at home from a fellow gamer who has swapped her old PCIe video card for a new one and can't plug the original PCIe power cable into the new card. Which of the following is the best solution?

   **A.** Look for an 8-pin PCIe lead

   **B.** Use the 8-pin EPSV12 lead

   **C.** Cut off some power supply cables and splice in a new header

   **D.** Put the old card back in because the new one can't be used

5. You are checking out the fans built into a system that is overheating. After verifying that the system is not overclocked, you notice that there are two case fans that can't be plugged into the motherboard. Which of the following power lead types is the best candidates for use with these fans?

   **A.** Mini

   **B.** ATX12

   **C.** PCIe

   **D.** Molex

## 3.7 ANSWERS

1. **B** 24-pin motherboard adapter enables a modern 24-pin power supply to work with an older system and get the benefits of potentially higher wattage.

2. **C** The power cord varies from country to country, and IEC-320 is the designation for the power supply cable connector.

3. **B** Black is ground, not 3.3-V DC.

4. **A** Many (but not all) power supplies have both 6-pin and 8-pin PCIe power leads.

5. **D** Molex connectors are compatible with most case fans as well as with IDE hard drives and optical drives.

Objective 3.8 # Given a scenario, select and configure appropriate components for a custom PC configuration to meet customer specifications or needs

Now it's time to bring all of this component knowledge together and look at seven types of custom PCs and their typical components and configurations.

**EXAM TIP** Make sure you can identify the requirements for each custom PC configuration.

**Standard Thick Client** These systems meet the recommended requirements for running Windows (or selected OS) and standard desktop applications, such as office productivity and networking applications. Network connections are not specifically mentioned, but they are needed for operating system compatibility and updates.

**Thin Client** Thin clients are low-power computers with network connectivity that run or access an OS and applications housed on a server, leveraging the server's power. A thin client runs basic applications—to do e-mail and access the Web—and meets minimum OS requirements.

**Virtualization Workstation** A virtualization workstation is essentially the opposite of a classic thin client as it runs multiple operating systems at once through virtual machines. Correspondingly, it needs maximum RAM and a multicore CPU.

**Audio/Video Editing Workstation**   These media workstations require specialized audio and video cards; a large, fast hard drive; and multiple (dual) monitors.

**Graphic/CAD/CAM Design Workstation**   This mouthful refers to a computer built around specialized computer-aided design (CAD) software, such as AutoCAD, for designing and modeling physical objects. Such a machine needs a fast SSD, high-end video card, and maximum RAM.

**Gaming PC**   A gaming PC has similar needs to a graphics workstation, though the video card should use a high-end/specialized game-oriented GPU rather than a workstation GPU. It also needs a high-definition sound card, high-end cooling, and SSDs for storage

**Network Attached Storage Device**   A network attached storage (NAS) device has several roles, such as central file storage, print server, and streaming media machine. CompTIA specifically lists the following requirements:

- Media streaming
- File sharing
- Gigabit network interface card (NIC)
- Hard drive or RAID array using hard drives

# REVIEW

**Objective 3.8: Given a scenario, select and configure appropriate components for a custom PC configuration to meet customer specifications or needs**

- Standard thick clients meet the recommended requirements for running the selected OS and desktop applications.
- Thin clients require network connectivity and meet the minimum requirements for running the selected OS and basic applications.
- Virtualization workstations have maximum RAM and CPU cores.
- Audio/video editing workstations require specialized audio and video cards, dual monitors, and a large, fast hard drive.
- Graphic/CAD/CAM design workstations are similar to AV editing workstations but use graphics workstation cards and SSD.
- A gaming PC is similar to a graphics workstation but uses a gaming GPU, high-end cooling, and SSDs for fastest storage.
- A network attached storage device is optimized for sharing files and streaming media by using a RAID array, Gigabit NIC, and hard drive.

## 3.8 QUESTIONS

1. Your client needs to switch the role of an existing computer to be used as an A/V editing workstation. Which of the following is the least suitable candidate for upgrading?

   **A.** Thick client

   **B.** Gaming PC

   **C.** Thin client

   **D.** Virtualization workstation

2. You are examining a computer that was salvaged from a fire to determine its previous use. It contains a Gigabit Ethernet NIC and a RAID array built with four 4-TB hard disk drives. It uses onboard video and sound. What was this computer most likely used for?

   **A.** Thick client

   **B.** Virtualization workstation

   **C.** A/V editing workstation

   **D.** Network attached storage device

3. Your client has a gaming PC that is almost perfect for being used as a graphic/CAD/CAM design workstation. However, one component should be exchanged for a workstation-grade component. Which of these is it?

   **A.** Graphics card

   **B.** RAM

   **C.** Hard disk

   **D.** Keyboard

4. Your client wants to use existing computers as thin clients, so you are going through the client's excess computer inventory looking for suitable candidates. Which of the following would be the most suitable thin client for use with Windows 10 64-bit edition?

   **A.** Computer with 8 GB of RAM and a 4-TB hard disk

   **B.** Computer with Intel ATOM and 1 GB of RAM

   **C.** Computer with Intel Celeron and 2 GB of RAM

   **D.** Computer with Core i7 and a 2-TB hard disk

5. You are testing a liquid cooling system in one of your personal systems. Which of the following configurations are you most likely developing?

   **A.** Virtualization workstation

   **B.** Gaming PC

   **C.** Audio/video editing workstation

   **D.** Network attached storage device

## 3.8 ANSWERS

1.  **C**   Thin clients have low-power CPUs, minimum RAM, and sometimes lack PCIe slots suitable for video cards, so they're the least likely candidates.

2.  **D**   These are the major features of a network attached storage device. The use of onboard video and sound indicate these features are relatively unimportant to the primary task.

3.  **A**   Workstation graphics cards are optimized for 2-D/3-D CAD, while consumer graphics cards are optimized for 3-D gaming.

4.  **C**   This computer has the smallest amount of RAM supported for use with 64-bit Windows, as well as a processor that meets minimum requirements.

5.  **B**   Gaming PCs are typically overclocked, and liquid cooling is more effective for cooling than most air coolers.

 **Objective 3.9**   # Given a scenario, install and configure common devices

As part of your work, you will frequently need to install and configure common computing devices. Understanding these processes is also part of the CompTIA A+ 220-1001 exam, as you will learn in the following sections.

## Desktop

Desktop computers can be divided into two classes:

- A *thin client* is a low-power computer with network connectivity that runs or accesses an OS and applications housed on a server, leveraging the server's power. A thin client runs basic applications—to do e-mail and access the Web—and meets minimum OS requirements.
- A *thick client* meets the recommended requirements for running Windows (or selected OS) and standard desktop applications, such as office productivity and networking applications.

## Thin Client, Thick Client

Assuming the client computer has already been built and had an operating system installed, the installation and configuration steps for either type of client include

1.  Connect AC power to the power supply.
2.  For a wired client, connect network cable to the NIC.

3. Connect display, keyboard, mouse, and other peripherals.

4. Turn on the system.

5. Connect to the OS image on the network if the OS is not installed locally.

6. For a wireless connection, connect to the appropriate SSID.

7. Configure the display and other peripherals.

For additional steps, see "Account Setup/Settings."

**Cross-References**

For details about operating system installation, see Part II, Domain 1.0, Objective 1.3. For details about network configuration, see Part II, Domain 1.0, Objective 1.8. For details about connecting peripherals, see Objectives 3.1/3.2, earlier in this domain.

## Account Setup/Settings

With either type of client, you must

- Set up one or more user accounts.

**Cross-Reference**

For details about setting up users in Microsoft Windows, see Part II, Domain 2.0, Objective 2.6.

- Set up applications.

**Cross-Reference**

For details about installing applications, see Part II, Domain 1.0, Objective 1.7.

- Configure the desktop and Start menu according to company guidelines.

**Cross-Reference**

For details about setting up workstation security and account management, see Part II, Domain 2.0, Objective 2.7.

 **EXAM TIP** Make sure you know the steps required to configure desktop thick/thin clients.

# Laptop/Common Mobile Devices

Laptops and common mobile devices may require additional configuration beyond what's necessary with a thin client or thick client.

 **EXAM TIP**  Make sure you know the steps required to configure laptop and common mobile devices.

## Touchpad Configuration

Use the Settings | Devices | Mouse dialog or the Mouse applet in Control Panel for touchpad configuration. You can change sensitivity and much more in either tool, such as

- Setup for right-hand or left-hand use
- Scroll settings
- Gesture settings
- Settings to avoid phantom touches

## Touchscreen Configuration

Depending on the device, the following might need to be checked or configured:

- Multi-touch settings
- Gestures
- Scroll settings
- Calibration

In Windows, open Control Panel | Hardware and Sound | Calibrate | Touch Input to configure these options. In Linux, install the multi-touch framework recommended for your distro (Ubuntu uses uTouch) and any additional apps needed (varies by distro and framework).

## Application Installations/Configurations

Applications may need to be installed and configured with options such as

- Paid or free (reduced-feature) version installation
- Installing a standard software image using a Mobile Device Management (MDM) app
- Network and browser settings

**Cross-References**

Learn more about MDM policies in Part II, Domain 2.0, Objective 2.2. Learn more about securing mobile devices in Part II, Domain 2.0, Objective 2.8.

## Synchronization Settings

Keeping local and network files synchronized is critical to trouble-free mobile device function. Settings might include

- Setting up cloud storage and file transfer
- Specifying online/offline file access
- Installing custom file sync apps
- Configuring file sync apps and settings

**Cross-Reference**

Learn more about synchronization apps in Part I, Domain 1.0, Objective 1.7.

## Account Setup/Settings

As with thin and thick clients, you must do the following for laptops and common mobile devices:

- Set up one or more user accounts.
- Set up applications.
- Configure the icon layout or desktop and Start menu according to company guidelines.

## Wireless Settings

Wireless settings might include

- Default SSIDs
- VPN installation and configuration
- Firewall setup

**Cross-References**

Learn more about VPNs in Part I, Domain 1.0, Objective 1.6 and Part I, Domain 2.0, Objective 2.6. Learn more about firewalls in Part I, Domain 2.0, Objective 2.3. Learn more about changing SSID settings for security in Part II, Domain 2.0, Objective 2.10.

# REVIEW

### Objective 3.9: Given a scenario, install and configure common devices

- Thin and thick clients differ in amounts of RAM, hard drive size, and processor performance.

- Both require account setup, application set up, and desktop and start menu configuration.
- Laptop and mobile devices also require touchpad configuration, touchscreen configuration (when equipped), synchronization settings, and wireless settings.

## 3.9 QUESTIONS

1. Which of the following device types require(s) account and application setup?
   A. Thick client
   B. Laptops and mobile devices
   C. Thin client
   D. All of the above

2. Setting up cloud storage and file transfer is an aspect of which type of setting?
   A. Account setup
   B. Synchronization
   C. Wireless
   D. Touchscreen

3. Your client formerly used a desktop computer and is having problems with phantom touches moving the cursor on his laptop. Which configuration category needs to be performed?
   A. Touchscreen configuration
   B. Keyboard configuration
   C. Touchpad configuration
   D. Synchronization settings

4. You are creating a checklist for setting up laptop and mobile devices. Which of the following doesn't belong in the wireless settings category?
   A. Gigabit Ethernet NIC speed/duplex
   B. Default SSID
   C. VPN installation and configuration
   D. Firewall setup

5. Which of the following is a fast way to configure and install applications on standard and mobile devices?
   A. Custom file sync apps
   B. Standard software image
   C. Firewall
   D. Desktop configuration per company standards

## 3.9 ANSWERS

1. **D**    All of these device types require these settings.

2. **B**    Synchronization includes cloud storage and file transfer as well as file sync apps.

3. **C**    Touchpads can be configured to ignore phantom touches from fingers or thumbs to avoid moving the mouse pointer accidentally.

4. **A**    A Gigabit Ethernet NIC is used in wired networking, not wireless networking.

5. **B**    A standard software image contains the software and settings used by an organization, so installing it rather than making individual changes is much faster.

**Objective 3.10** Given a scenario, configure SOHO multifunction devices/printers and settings

One of the most common processes you will perform in a small office/home office (SOHO) environment is the setup and configuration of multifunction devices (MFDs) and printers. This objective guides you through the essential steps required to configure these devices. When "printer" is stated in the following sections, the instructions also apply to MFDs.

**EXAM TIP**    Make sure you know the steps required to install printers and their drivers.

## Use Appropriate Drivers for a Given Operating System

Most printers are plug-and-play devices on Windows; just plug in the printer and let Windows automatically detect and install the driver. If the system does not detect the printer, open the Devices and Printers (Windows 7 and up) applet and click Add a Printer to open the Add Printer Wizard, which enables you to install a local printer or a network printer. This distinction isn't perfect; you can use the local printer option to add network printers manually—it just doesn't automatically search for them. In Windows 10, you can also use Settings | Devices | Printers & scanners and click *Add a printer or scanner*.

macOS connects automatically with AirPrint-compatible printers or, in most cases, installs drivers for you. If you don't have an AirPrint-compatible printer, and you are connecting via USB, make sure you have updated your macOS installation so you have the latest printer drivers, then turn the printer on. Install updated drivers if prompted. To install a Wi-Fi printer that is not AirPrint-compatible, you might need to connect your printer via USB temporarily to configure it.

Linux printer installation varies with the drivers available. Many HP and Brother printers can use manufacturer-provided Linux drivers. To install other printers with typical Linux GUIs, use the Printers or System | Printers option in your desktop environment to select a printer and use the drivers provided with the GUI. The Common Unix Printer Service (CUPS) is used if printer configuration software is not provided; install it using your Linux distribution's package manager.

## Installing a Local Printer

Unless your printer is very new, or very old, you'll probably never use this option except, surprisingly, to install standalone network printers by IP address or hostname. Even here, Windows will detect most modern printers on its own, so you'll just use this if it refuses to detect yours.

In Windows 7, click *Add a local printer*. In the *Create a new port* drop-down box, select Standard TCP/IP Port. Click Next. Type the IP address here. Windows 8/8.1/10 is even simpler: if Windows doesn't automatically detect your new printer, click *The printer that I want isn't listed* and select *Add a printer using TCP/IP address or hostname*.

You'll need to manually select the proper driver (see Figure 3.10-1). Windows includes a lot of printer drivers, but you can use the Have Disk option to install from the printer's driver disc (Windows will require administrator privileges to proceed). The Windows Update button enables you to grab the latest printer drivers via the Internet.

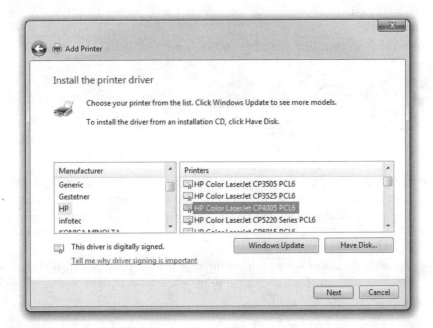

**FIGURE 3.10-1**   Selecting a printer driver for a manual printer installation

## Installing a Network Printer

When you try to install a network printer, the Add Printer Wizard will scan for available printers and usually find the one you want. Just select it, click Next, and follow the procedure just discussed to install drivers and set up the printer. You'll need to configure it manually if Windows can't find it, and the options vary if you are connected to a domain or workgroup (in homegroups, all connected printers are shared automatically if printer sharing is enabled).

In a workgroup, you can browse the network, connect to a printer by name or URL, or use a TCP/IP address or hostname. On a domain, you can search and browse by parameters such as printer features, location, and so on. Once you select a printer, you may be prompted to provide drivers using the method described earlier.

 **EXAM TIP**   Windows 7 and newer (excluding Home/Basic editions) also include the Print Management console in Administrative Tools. It enables you to view and manage printers, drivers, and Windows print servers on your system or network. Print Management's advanced features go beyond the CompTIA A+ exams, but know it centralizes (and sometimes enhances) standard Windows printer controls.

## Configuration Settings

Once the printer is installed in Windows, find it in the Devices and Printers applet, right-click it, and select Printing preferences to configure how your printer will print documents. To configure a printer in macOS, open the Print dialog, select your printer, click Show Details, and choose the options needed. To configure a printer in Linux, see the documentation for your GUI or distribution.

Options vary by device and features, but here are the ones you need to know for this objective.

 **EXAM TIP**   Make sure you know the essential configuration settings covered in this section.

**Duplex**   The duplex setting specifies whether and how to use each side of a printed page. Simple duplexing uses the front and back of each sheet in sequence, but advanced options reorient the print to account for binding on any given edge or reorder pages to support folded booklet layouts.

**Collate**   Enabling the collate option prints a full copy of a multipage document before starting the next copy. When disabled, the printer prints all copies of a page before moving to the next page.

**Orientation**   The orientation setting specifies whether to print in landscape or portrait mode.

**Quality**    Quality settings enable you to manage the tradeoffs between quality and speed, ink use, and memory use:

- The most obvious of these, *resolution*, specifies what DPI the document should be printed at.
- Some printers may let you choose some mode or quality presets that optimize printing for graphics or text, or choose to manually configure your own advanced settings.
- Some printers may have settings that reduce ink or toner used, for economic and environmental reasons.

 **NOTE**    The names and descriptions of settings that influence quality might discuss quality itself, ink or toner use, environmental friendliness, or even cost savings. As a result, quality-reducing settings may be scattered around multiple menus.

# Device Sharing

Unless multiple users in an office print documents frequently, there's no need to have a printer for every computer. There are a variety of ways to share printers, as you will see in the following sections.

## Wired

The ports built into typical printers for direct connect to a single device also make sharing possible:

- Use a *USB* switch to share a printer between two nearby computers without the need for networking; if the computer is on a network, you can share the printer as long as the host computer is running (don't forget to install file and print sharing services!).
- Very old printers use *serial* switchboxes to share printers (most of these are in museums or have been recycled, but you might run into it on the exam!).
- Use the *Ethernet* port to plug the printer into a wired network. It will have its own IP address.

## Wireless

Many printers today are ready to connect wirelessly to other computers or networks.

- A printer with *Bluetooth* is ready to connect to any computer or mobile device with Bluetooth after pairing (just make sure you have a suitable printing app for the mobile device).
- A printer with *Wi-Fi* onboard (802.11 a, b, g, n, or ac) is ready to join your wireless network, have its own IP address, and be ready to receive print jobs after configuration. The hardest part of the process may be entering the SSID and encryption key using the printer's control panel.

### Infrastructure vs. Ad Hoc

*Infrastructure* is a long name for the way that normal Wi-Fi networks work: every device, including the printer, uses an SSID to connect to an AP or router.

*Ad hoc*, on the other hand, allows for direct connection between any two Wi-Fi devices without going through a router or AP. Windows 8 and later do not officially support ad hoc connections, but you can find a variety of methods online for setting up an ad hoc connection to your printer.

### Integrated Print Server (Hardware)

You can purchase a standalone *print server* device to network one or more traditional wired printers—but you may not be able to use all features of an MFD connected this way. First, see if your router has an *integrated print server*, in which case you can plug your printer into the router's USB port.

### Cloud Printing/Remote Printing

A variety of applications such as Google Cloud Print blur the line between traditional and virtual printing. These apps install a virtual printer on your system that wraps up your document and sends it out over the Internet or other network to a cloud server, which eventually routes it to a real printer for printing—all without your system needing a driver for the target printer.

# Public/Shared Devices

Printers that are available to the public, or printers that are shared, add several additional issues to the printing process.

## Sharing Local/Networked Device via Operating System Settings

As mentioned earlier in this objective, the computer that will be sharing a printer on the network needs to have the appropriate file and printer sharing software installed before this can take place.

### TCP/Bonjour/AirPrint

If the printer will be made available to other operating systems, additional software is needed. For example, a Windows system can use Apple's Bonjour Print Service (installed alone or with iTunes) to share a connected printer with AirPrint-compatible macOS and Apple iOS devices.

To add a TCP printer in Windows, use the Devices and Printers applet and install the printer manually.

# Data Privacy

Data privacy can be enhanced by user authentication, but can be compromised by hard drive caching. Here's more about these issues.

## User Authentication on the Device

A lot of sensitive information gets printed, especially in places like schools and hospitals where strict privacy regulations apply, and safeguards need to be in place to make sure it isn't leaking out. With some types of network printers, the user must authenticate on the device after sending the print job before the job is printed. This can be done with a user code that is stored in the printer's address book or by using various authentication servers.

## Hard Drive Caching

Even with user authentication, there's still the potential for information to be taken by unauthorized users. Unfortunately, it's common for modern devices to cache documents the device prints, scans, copies, or faxes to a hard drive or other storage media (*hard drive caching* in CompTIA terminology). You may be able to disable this feature, schedule regular deletion of the cache, or manually clear the cache regularly to limit the damage a compromise could cause. It's also critical to clear this cache before disposing of the device.

# REVIEW

**Objective 3.10: Given a scenario, configure SOHO multifunction devices/printers and settings**

- Use the drivers provided by the manufacturer (preferred) or by the operating system to set up the device.
- The local printer installation process can also be used for network printers, but you must enter the network information manually.
- Layout settings include duplex, collate, orientation, and quality. Other settings might be available on some models.
- Paper settings include paper size, paper (media) type, and paper source.
- Quality settings include resolution, preset options, ink/toner saving options.
- Device sharing can use wired connections (USB, serial, Ethernet), wireless network connections (Bluetooth, Wi-Fi), print servers, or cloud printing.
- Ad hoc is a Wi-Fi alternative to connecting to the printer via an AP or wireless router (aka infrastructure), but recent versions of Windows require complex methods to set up an ad hoc setting.
- Cloud printing apps can be used to send a print job to a remote printer.

- Sharing a local printer via a network requires the use of file and printer sharing software. Bonjour allows Windows printers to be used by macOS and iOS devices.
- Data privacy can be compromised by shared printing unless user authentication is used and hard drive caches in printing devices are periodically deleted.

## 3.10 QUESTIONS

1. Adding a printer using TCP/IP address or hostname is used to add which type of printer?
   A. Laser
   B. Local
   C. Network
   D. All of the above

2. You are setting up an MFD for a user who wants to enable duplex, collating, and reverse print settings. Which category of settings needs to be configured?
   A. Paper
   B. Configuration
   C. Ad hoc
   D. Quality

3. You need to share a printer between two computers which, for security, should not be networked. Which of the following is the best solution?
   A. USB print server
   B. KVM
   C. Ad hoc wireless
   D. USB switch

4. A user in your department is unable to print to a Bluetooth printer, even though Bluetooth is enabled on the printer and her computer. Which of the following is the most likely cause?
   A. Bluetooth devices not paired
   B. No Bluetooth router
   C. Bluetooth cable is loose
   D. Firewall setup

5. After a new departmental MFD is installed, users must enter their assigned code to receive their print jobs. What is this is an example of?
   A. Hard drive caching
   B. User authentication
   C. Firewall
   D. Network printing

## 3.10 ANSWERS

1. **C**   TCP/IP or hostname indicate the printer is a network printer.

2. **B**   The layout category contains these and other settings; they are not always on a single menu.

3. **D**   A USB switch enables the USB device (such as an MFD or printer) to be shared without networking.

4. **A**   A Bluetooth printer (or other device) must be paired with a computer or mobile device before it can be used.

5. **B**   User authentication on the device helps prevent unauthorized users from seeing other users' print jobs

## Objective 3.11  Given a scenario, install and maintain various print technologies

The typical office, warehouse, or SOHO network might use one or more of several print technologies, including laser, inkjet, impact, virtual, and 3-D. In this objective, you learn how to install and maintain these leading printer technologies.

## Laser

Laser printers (see Figure 3.11-1) use *electro-photographic imaging* (known as the EP process) for quick high-quality prints. The process leverages photoconductive compounds that conduct electricity when exposed to precise laser (or cheaper LED) light.

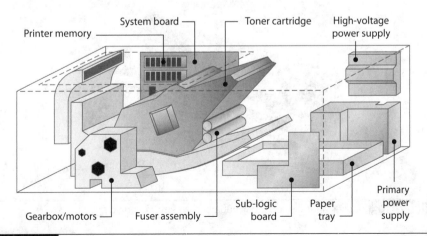

**FIGURE 3.11-1**   Components inside a laser printer

## Laser Printer Components and Features

Here are the most important laser printer components and their functions:

- The imaging drum (or photosensitive drum) is a grounded cylinder with an ungrounded coat of photosensitive compounds. When light hits these particles, their electrical charge "drains" out through the grounded cylinder. Many laser printers use a toner cartridge (see Figure 3.11-2) that contains the imaging drum and, to simplify maintenance, most of the parts that suffer "wear and tear" and need regular replacing.

- The *fuser assembly* is usually near the bottom of (but not included with) the toner cartridge and usually has two rollers (a pressure roller and a heated roller) to permanently fuse the toner to the paper. The heated roller has a nonstick coating such as Teflon to prevent toner from sticking.

- The *transfer roller* (transfer corona in older printers) applies a positive charge to the paper, so it in turn attracts toner particles from the drum. This positive charge also attracts the paper to the negatively charged drum, so a static charge eliminator removes the charge to keep the paper from wrapping around the drum.

- On single-pass color laser printers, a *transfer belt* is used to place all four colors (Cyan, Magenta, Yellow, and black) on the page at the same time.

- Paper is grabbed by the *pickup roller* from the paper tray or paper feed.

- The paper is then passed over a *separation pad* (CompTIA says *separate pads*) that uses friction to separate a single sheet from any other that were picked up.

- Printers with double-sided print capabilities also have a *duplexing assembly*, which flips the paper over after printing on the top side so the back side can be printed.

Laser printers have additional components. We will discuss these in the following section, which covers the laser print process.

**FIGURE 3.11-2**   Laser printer's toner cartridge contains the imaging drum.

# Imaging Process

Knowing the imaging process helps you to troubleshoot printing problems. If an odd line is printed down the middle of every page, for example, you know there's a problem with the photosensitive drum or cleaning mechanism, and the toner cartridge needs to be replaced. Here is the seven-step *imaging process* you need to know for the CompTIA A+ 220-1001 exam:

1. Processing
2. Charging
3. Exposing
4. Developing
5. Transferring
6. Fusing
7. Cleaning

## Step 1: Processing the Image

When you click Print in an application, the CPU processes your request and queues the print job with the *print spooler* (an area of memory), causing the spooler's printer icon to appear in the notification area. The operating system sends these jobs sequentially as the printer becomes available. Larger jobs must be broken into chunks first (which can take a while for huge documents), leaving documents further back in the queue waiting. The notification icon will go away when all jobs have gone to the printer—but you aren't out of the woods yet.

**Raster Images**    Impact printers receive data one character at a time, inkjet printers receive data one line at a time, but laser printers receive complete pages. If the page isn't already a raster image, the printer's *raster image processor (RIP)* rasterizes it to obtain a format the laser imaging unit can "paint" on the photosensitive drum. To accomplish this, the RIP needs enough memory (RAM) to process a full page.

 **EXAM TIP**    Insufficient memory usually causes memory overflow ("MEM OVERFLOW") errors, in which case you can try reducing the resolution, printing smaller graphics, or turning off RET (see the following section for more on RET). Of course, the best solution is adding RAM to the printer.

Adding more RAM won't solve every laser printer memory problem. Some data is just too complex for a RIP, as with a "21 ERROR" on an HP LaserJet, which indicates "the printer is unable to process very complex data fast enough for the print engine." If the RIP is the limiting factor, reduce the complexity of the page image (use fewer fonts, less formatting, lower-resolution graphics, and so on).

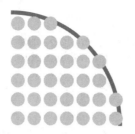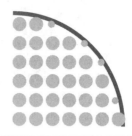

**FIGURE 3.11-3**   RET fills in gaps with smaller dots to smooth out jagged characters.

**Resolution**   Just like monitors, laser printers support different resolutions (adjusted down from the maximum the printer physically supports), with higher resolutions improving quality but requiring more memory. Common resolutions are 600 × 600 dpi and 1200 × 1200 dpi. The first number (horizontal resolution) reflects how finely the laser can focus, while the second number (vertical resolution) reflects the smallest increment the drum can turn.

Even at 300 dpi, laser printers produce far better quality than dot-matrix printers by using resolution enhancement technology (RET) to insert smaller dots that smooth out jagged curves (see Figure 3.11-3). RET uses more of the printer's RAM, so disabling RET may free enough memory to complete the print job if you get a MEM OVERFLOW error.

 **CAUTION**   Printers may convert complex memory-intensive images to lower resolutions.

## Steps 2–7: Printing the Image

Once processing (Step 1) is complete, the physical printing process can begin.

**Step 2: Charging**   The primary corona wire or primary charge roller applies a uniform negative charge (usually between ~600 and ~1000 volts) to the entire surface of the drum (see Figure 3.11-4) so it can receive a new image.

**Step 3: Exposing**   A laser (or LED) writes a positive image on the surface of the drum by forcing the photosensitive particles to release most of their negative charge.

**Step 4: Developing**   Toner is a fine powder made up of plastic particles bonded to pigment particles. These less-negative particles attract toner because they are relatively more positive than the toner particles (see Figure 3.11-5).

**Step 5: Transferring**   The transfer corona or transfer roller gives the paper a positive charge so that the negatively charged toner particles will leap from the drum to the paper.

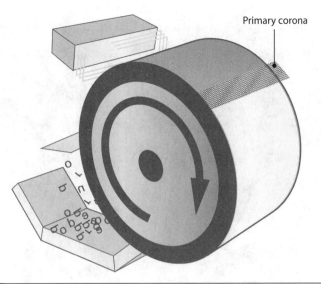

**FIGURE 3.11-4** Charging the drum with a uniform negative charge

 **EXAM TIP** Color laser printers must apply four toner colors (CMYK), which they variously accomplish by sending each page through four one-color passes, or by placing all colors onto a special *transfer belt* before transferring them to the page in one pass.

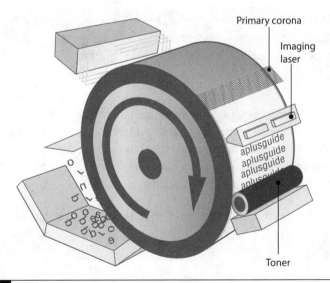

**FIGURE 3.11-5** Developing the image and applying the toner

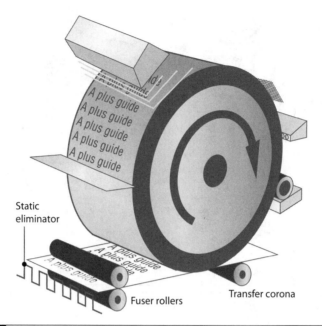

**FIGURE 3.11-6** Transferring the image to the paper and fusing the final image

**Step 6: Fusing** The mostly plastic toner particles are only attracted to the page—they still need to be fused to it. Two rollers—a heated nonstick roller and a pressure roller—melt the toner permanently into the paper. At this point, a static charge eliminator removes the paper's positive charge (see Figure 3.11-6) so the printer can eject the page.

**CAUTION** The heated roller is hot enough to melt some plastic media such as overhead transparencies, which could damage your laser printer (and void your warranty); make sure to use media designed for laser printers.

**Step 7: Cleaning** Before a new page can be printed, the drum must be returned to a clean, fresh (physical and electrical) state (see Figure 3.11-7). A rubber cleaning blade carefully scrapes residual toner from the drum and deposits it in a debris cavity or returns it to the toner cartridge, and one or more erase lamps bombard the drum with light to neutralize all surface particles by draining any remaining charge into the drum.

**NOTE** Any damage done to the drum will show up on all prints until it is replaced.

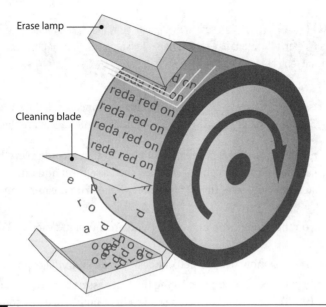

Erase lamp

Cleaning blade

**FIGURE 3.11-7** Cleaning and erasing the drum

# Laser Printer Maintenance

Unlike computer maintenance, laser printer maintenance follows a fairly well-established procedure oriented around keeping it clean and following the maintenance schedule: replace the toner, apply the maintenance kit, and clean.

> **CAUTION** All of the devices described in this objective have power supplies, but the corona in a laser printer requires extremely high voltage, making a laser printer power supply one of the most dangerous devices in computing! Turn off and unplug the printer as a safety precaution before performing any maintenance.

Over time, your laser printer builds up excess toner and paper dust or paper dander. Toner is hard to see—so the amount of paper dust is the best indicator a printer needs cleaning. If you can, take the printer outdoors and blow it out with a can of compressed air. If you must do it indoors, use a low-static vacuum designed for electronic components.

The printer's manual will specify a cleaning process, but it often leaves out the rubber rollers that guide paper through the printer; these can slip and cause jams as they build up dirt and dust. Clean them with a small amount of 90 percent or better denatured alcohol on a fibrous cleaning towel. You can also re-texture slipping rollers and separator pads by rubbing them with a little denatured alcohol on a nonmetallic scouring pad.

**CAUTION** The photosensitive drum, usually inside the toner cartridge, can be wiped clean if dirty, but be very careful—a scratch will appear on every page printed until you replace the toner cartridge.

Replacing parts according to the manufacturer's maintenance guidelines will help to ensure years of trouble-free, dependable printing from your laser printer. Here are the common tasks:

- Many laser printers or MFDs have *maintenance kits* that include everything you should replace on the same regular schedule, such as a fuser and one or more rollers or pads. You'll typically reset the page counter so the printer can prompt you when it's time again.
- Depending on the printer, you may clean (with an anti-static vacuum) or replace the ozone filter.
- Clean the fuser assembly with 90 percent or better denatured alcohol.
- A number of conditions require replacing the fuser assembly: pits or scratches on the heat roller (the Teflon-coated one containing a light bulb), an error code indicating the fuser is damaged or overheating (or merely that you've hit a preset replacement copy count), and failure of the thermal fuse that prevents overheating.

 **CAUTION** The fuser assembly melts stuff for a living; *always* let it cool down first.

- Clean the transfer corona with a 90 percent denatured alcohol solution on a cotton swab. If the wire is broken, you can replace it; most snap in or are held in by screws.
- Paper guides can also be cleaned with alcohol on a fibrous towel.

# Inkjet

*Inkjet* (or ink-dispersion) printers use a *printhead* connected to a *carriage* containing the *ink cartridges* (see Figure 3.11-8) or, on models that use refillable tanks, the printheads, to print on a staggering array of paper types.

A *belt* and motor move the assembly back and forth to cover the page. A *roller* grabs paper from a paper tray (usually under or inside the printer) or *feeder* (on the top or back of the printer) and advances it through the printer (see Figure 3.11-9). The printhead uses tiny tubes with resistors or electroconductive plates at the end to boil the ink, creating a tiny air bubble

**FIGURE 3.11-8**   Inkjet ink cartridges

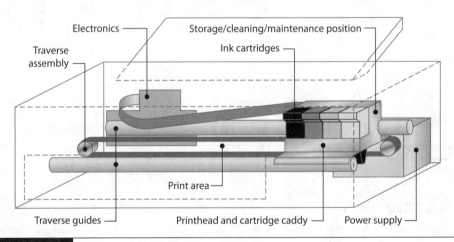

**FIGURE 3.11-9**   Inside an inkjet printer

that ejects a droplet onto the paper (see Figure 3.11-10). *Print resolution*, measured in *dots per inch (dpi)*, indicates how densely the printer lays these droplets down, and high resolution is particularly important for images. Print speed is measured in *pages per minute (ppm)*, and printers with monochrome and full-color modes typically indicate two speeds.

 **NOTE**   A *duplexing assembly* is a built-in or add-on device that flips paper to enable automatic two-sided prints. It is a common feature in inkjet and laser printers and MFDs.

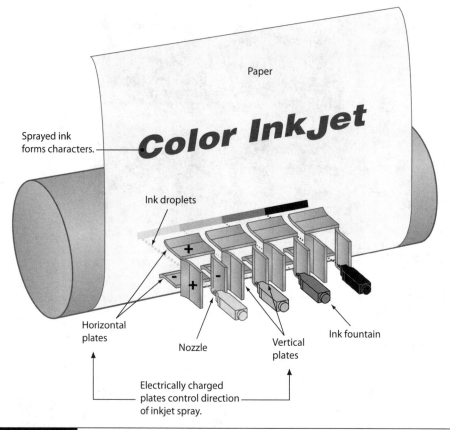

**FIGURE 3.11-10** Detail of the inkjet printhead

## Calibrate

The term calibrate has two meaning with ink jet printers. In this section, *calibrate* refers to color matching the monitor output and printer output. When what you see on your monitor and what prints differ significantly, monitor *color calibration* hardware generates an International Color Consortium (ICC) color profile that defines the color characteristics of the hardware so the OS can correct for any difference between the intended and displayed colors. Color profiles can also document the quirks of a specific printer; you can find them on the installation media, purchase one separately, or generate your own. Combined, calibrating all of your imaging devices helps harmonize what you see onscreen and on paper with the file's image data.

 **NOTE** Windows includes *Windows Color System (WCS)* to help build color profiles for use across devices. WCS is based on a newer standard Microsoft calls *color infrastructure and translation engine (CITE)*.

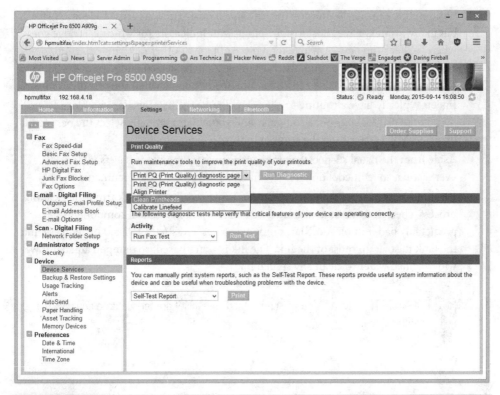

**FIGURE 3.11-11** | Inkjet printer maintenance screen

# Inkjet Maintenance

Inkjet maintenance includes cleaning heads, replacing cartridges, calibrating, and clearing jams. Inkjets generally have built-in maintenance programs that you should run from time to time to keep your inkjet in good operating order (see Figure 3.11-11). It may be hard to find; check Printing Preferences, the Start menu, and any printer management web page.

- When do you need to *clean printheads*? Ink inside the printhead nozzles has a tendency to dry out and plug them. If your printer is telling Windows that it's printing and feeding paper through, but either nothing is coming out (usually the case if you're just printing black text) or only certain colors are printing, the culprit is almost certainly dried ink clogging the nozzles. You can start the process by pressing hardware buttons or through the printer preferences menu—but just do this as needed because it uses a lot of expensive ink.

- Inkjet *cartridge replacement* varies widely from printer to printer—refer to the printer's documentation (some printers use ink reservoirs rather than cartridges). Typically you'll open a compartment on the printer and see one or more cartridges attached to the printhead. If you can't reach them, the printhead should move into an accessible position if the printer is on (don't try to force it out). They may just slide into place, but many printers have clips or slots (along with indicators for which cartridge goes where). Check the new cartridge for a piece of tape or other covering on its nozzles and contacts. Make sure you have everything properly seated and clipped before you close the lid—these parts can catch on other components when the printhead moves.

- Inkjets typically have a routine to align or *calibrate* the printheads, which can fix poor output; the printer spits out a test page, and you either manually select the best result or, on an MFD, place it on the scanner as instructed.
- Aside from the usual suspects, an inkjet may pick up too many sheets if it is overheating, so let it cool down if you have been cranking out documents.
- If your printer has an ink overflow tank or tray to catch excess ink from the cleaning process, check it from time to time—an overflow onto electrical components is predictably bad. Put on some latex or vinyl gloves and stick a twisted paper towel into the tank to soak up most of the ink. The ink is water based, so dampen a paper towel with distilled water to clean any spilled ink.

 **EXAM TIP**   Make sure you understand how inkjet printers operate and how to maintain them.

# Thermal

*Thermal* printers use a heated printhead to create a high-quality image on special or plain paper. Two types exist:

- **Direct thermal printers**   Use a *heating element* to burn dots into the surface of *special thermal paper*; these are often seen in retail receipt printers with large rolls of thermal paper housed in a *feed assembly* that automatically draws the paper past the heating element.
- **Thermal wax printers**   Work like dye-sublimation printers, but the film is coated with colored wax—no special paper required (though quality suffers because they use dithering, unlike dye-sublimation printers).

## Thermal Printer Maintenance

Direct thermal printers only need occasional cleaning and paper replacement. Turn off the printer and open it according to the manufacturer's instructions; *remove debris* and then use denatured alcohol and a lint-free cloth to *clean the heating element*. Clean the rollers with a cloth or compressed air so they can properly grip the paper. To *replace the paper*, slide off the old roll, slide on the new one, and feed the paper through the heating element.

Thermal wax printers also need wax ribbon replacement, which is similar to replacing the roll of paper; make sure to feed it past the heating element. Your printer should include instructions for installing a new ribbon.

# Impact

*Impact* printers create an image by physically striking an *ink ribbon* against the paper's surface, making them relatively slow and noisy. Impact printers are largely gone from our homes, but one kind—*dot-matrix* printers—are still common in businesses because they can print to multipart forms. *Point-of-sale (POS)* machines, for example, use special *impact paper* that can print two or more copies of a receipt. Dot-matrix printers (see Figure 3.11-12) have a *printhead* holding pins or *print wires* that strike the inked ribbon, and many use tiny sprockets to advance *tractor-feed* impact paper. *Draft-quality* printheads use 9 pins (some high-speed models use 18-pin printheads), whereas *near-letter-quality (NLQ)* printheads use 24 pins.

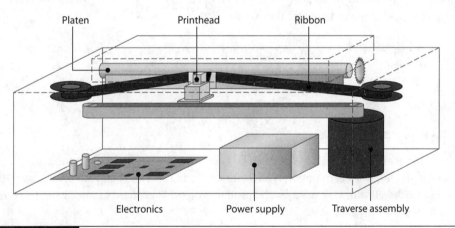

**FIGURE 3.11-12**   Inside of an impact printer

## Impact Printer Maintenance

Impact printers are near-immortal with diligent regular maintenance:

- Keep the platen (the roller or plate the pins strike against) and printhead clean with denatured alcohol.
- Lubricate gears and pulleys (but never the printhead) to specification.
- *Replace the ink ribbon* every so often.
- *Replace the printhead* if it becomes damaged.

Most impact printer paper feeds continuously from a roll or ream, so to *replace the paper*, you'll need to swap out the rolls or move the new ream into position, feed out any remaining paper, and feed in the new paper. Paper quality, debris, and improper feeding can lead to jams, which you typically clear by feeding the paper one way or the other.

**CAUTION** Check the printer's documentation first; steps to feed paper on one impact printer can easily break the feeding system on another.

# Virtual Printers

The *virtual printer* doesn't look like much, but it's still pretty similar to "real" printing. When you print to one, your system goes through all the steps to prepare the document for printing and then sends it off to a virtual printer program that converts the output from your computer into some other format and saves the result to a portable file that looks like the printed page would. It's a quick way to save anything you can print. Let's look at the virtual printers that CompTIA expects you to know for the exam.

**EXAM TIP** Make sure you understand the differences between the different virtual printer methods.

## Print to File

*Print to file*, which produces a file that can be later printed without access to the program that created it, but this is a legacy option (you'll often see it as a checkbox on your print screen) that may not work well with USB printers and produces files that are hard to work with. Use one of the other options instead.

## Print to PDF

Almost every OS can print to PDF files out of the box these days. However, Windows didn't join the party until Windows 10, so you'll need to install a virtual PDF printer on older versions of Windows. You can get one through official Adobe software or a third party.

## Print to XPS

Windows versions since Vista include the Microsoft XPS Document Writer, which creates an .xps file you can later open with the included XPS Viewer. Support in other operating systems varies, but most have third-party software available for working with XPS files. Unless you need an XPS file, a PDF file is a lot more useful with a lot more programs.

## Print to Image

This lets you save a regular image file, such as BMP, GIF, JPG, PNG, TIFF, and more. Image formats aren't the best for documents—text won't scale well and can't be easily searched/selected/copied, for example—but they are very portable. You will generally need a third-party virtual printer to print to the desired image format on a given OS.

# 3-D Printers

A new topic introduced in the CompTIA A+ 1001 exam objectives, 3-D printers are showing up in more and more places. 3-D printers turn 3-D designs into physical objects. They are used for prototyping, custom manufacturing, and modeling of 3-D objects for classrooms and for recreation.

3-D printers use melted material to create prints of three-dimensional objects. Although some 3-D printers use metal powders, the ones you are most likely to encounter in classrooms, maker spaces, and libraries use *plastic filament*.

## 3-D Printer Maintenance

The most obvious maintenance issue for a 3-D printer is the installation of the appropriate *plastic filament* for the printer and the print job.

 **ADDITIONAL RESOURCES**   To learn more about filament types, check out the https://3Dprintmanual.com website.

Beyond filament replacement, there are maintenance kits available from many 3-D printer vendors to help keep their printers working properly. Some maintenance kit features include

- Replacement Bowden tube (used by 3-D printers that have the stepper motor on the frame rather than on the printhead itself)
- Lubricant for moving parts
- Calibration card
- Nozzles
- Cooling fans

# REVIEW

## Objective 3.11: Given a scenario, install and maintain various print technologies

- Laser printers use electro-photographic imaging (known as the EP process) to print.
- The key components of a laser printer are imaging drum, fuser assembly, transfer belt, and transfer roller.
- Paper feed components on a laser printer include pickup roller, separation pad, and duplexing assembly.
- The laser printer imaging process has the following seven steps in order: processing, charging, exposing, developing, transferring, fusing, and cleaning.
- Laser printer maintenance includes replacing toner, applying a maintenance kit, calibrating the printer, and cleaning it.
- Inkjet printers use heated ink to place droplets on paper or media to print.
- Key inkjet printer components include ink cartridge, printhead, roller, feeder, duplexing assembly, carriage, and belt.
- *Calibrate* has two meanings: color matching between displays and the printer (in the context of inkjet printing), or the alignment process that is periodically recommended to make sure the printhead is printing straight vertical lines and properly formed text.
- Third-party ink should be evaluated carefully for color quality, durability, and whether it clogs printheads.
- Test prints and printhead cleaning routines help find and fix clogged printheads.
- Thermal printers use a heated printhead to print using special thermal paper or to transfer an image from a thermal wax ribbon to standard paper.
- Key components of a thermal printer include feed assembly and heating element.
- Thermal printer maintenance steps include replace paper, clean heating element, remove debris.
- Impact printers print from an inked ribbon onto single-part or multipart paper using printhead pins or wires to make a dot-matrix grid that forms letters, numbers, and shapes.
- Key impact printer components include printhead, ribbon, and tractor feed.
- Maintenance steps for impact printers include replace ribbon, replace printhead, replace paper.
- Virtual printers are software programs accessed through the printer (or occasionally the File | Save As) menu. They can save print jobs as files in PDF, XPS, and popular graphics formats such as TIFF, JPEG, and others.
- 3-D printers use a variety of plastic filament or other thermal materials to turn 3-D images into physical objects.
- The most common 3-D printer maintenance issue is filament replacement, but lubrication and replacement of tubes and print nozzles are also needed periodically.

# 3.11 QUESTIONS

1. Your client asks you to pick up some filaments before coming over to service the printer. What type of printer does your client have?

   **A.** Laser

   **B.** 3-D

   **C.** Inkjet

   **D.** Virtual

2. A direct thermal printer does not use which of the following in the print process?

   **A.** Ribbon

   **B.** Special thermal paper

   **C.** Feed assembly

   **D.** Heating element

3. You are trying to determine why a laser printing is leaving loose toner on the paper that looks like the print job but falls off the paper. Which of the following is the most likely cause?

   **A.** Processing failure

   **B.** Defective toner cartridge

   **C.** Fuser failure

   **D.** Paper feed failure

4. A user in your department is frustrated because his 20-page report is only printing on one side of the paper, and he must make 40 copies. Which component in the printer is either not enabled or not working?

   **A.** Paper feed

   **B.** Duplexing assembly

   **C.** USB

   **D.** Toner cartridge

5. A bottle of 90 percent or better denatured alcohol is a versatile cleaning product for printers. However, it should not be used to clean everything. From the following list, which item should not be cleaned with denatured alcohol?

   **A.** Transfer corona

   **B.** Platen

   **C.** Impact printhead

   **D.** Ink ribbon

## 3.11 ANSWERS

1. **B** Filaments are used in 3-D printers.

2. **A** A direct thermal printer prints directly onto special thermal paper. A thermal transfer printer uses a heat-sensitive ribbon to print onto plain paper.

3. **C** A fuser failure will cause the printed image to not stick to the paper.

4. **B** The duplexing assembly is used to print on both sides of the paper.

5. **D** If the ink ribbon is worn or faded, replace it.

# Virtualization and Cloud Computing

## Domain Objectives

- 4.1 Compare and contrast cloud computing concepts
- 4.2 Given a scenario, set up and configure client-side virtualization

## Objective 4.1 Compare and contrast cloud computing concepts

Cloud computing has become omnipresent, from online storage services and e-mail providers to integrated business apps. In this section, you learn about the different types of cloud services and how to choose the most appropriate cloud model for the work you client or organization needs to do.

# Common Cloud Models

Most people associate "The Cloud" with friendly file-storage services such as Dropbox and Google Drive—but cloud computing is about simple interfaces to a vast array of on-demand computing resources sold by Amazon (see Figure 4.1-1), Microsoft, Google, and many other companies over the open Internet. We use the servers and networks of the cloud through layers of software that add great value to the underlying hardware by making it simple to perform complex tasks and manage powerful hardware.

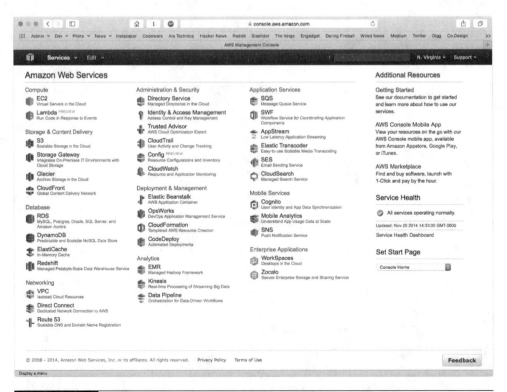

**FIGURE 4.1-1** Amazon Web Services Management Console

As end users, the web applications such as Dropbox that we associate with the cloud are actually just one of three layers of cloud services that support web applications and their developers.

As we examine the various cloud services, you should note that all of them have these features in common:

- **Cost**   Cloud services cost less than purchasing hardware, operating systems, and software.
- **Flexibility**   Cloud services are able to cope with big swings in demand.
- **Security**   Cloud services enable security to be centralized, but can also put more information at risk if best practices are not followed.
- **Administration**   Cloud services are easier to administer than traditional servers and computers.

Let's start by looking at the basis for cloud services: Infrastructure as a Service.

**ADDITIONAL RESOURCES**   For a great visualization of the differences between traditional on-premises versus IaaS, PaaS, and SaaS cloud computing, go to www.ibm.com and search for "Cloud computing defined: Characteristics & service levels."

## IaaS

Large-scale global *Infrastructure as a Service (IaaS)* cloud service providers combine virtualization's ability to minimize idle hardware, protect against data loss and downtime, and respond to spikes in demand with the power of vast data centers and massive networks. Cloud service providers (CSPs) such as Amazon Web Services (AWS) enable everyone from you to large multinational corporations to launch new virtual servers using a given OS, on demand, for pennies an hour. AWS and other CSPs provide many of the services needed to drive popular, complex web applications—unlimited data storage, database servers, caching, media hosting, and more—all billed by usage. IaaS frees us from managing hardware, but we're still responsible for configuring each virtual machine (VM) and keeping its software up to date.

## PaaS

A *Platform as a Service (PaaS)* provider such as Heroku (see Figure 4.1-2) gives programmers all the tools they need to deploy, administer, and maintain a web application. The PaaS provider starts with some form of infrastructure, which could be provided by an IaaS, and on top of that infrastructure the provider builds a *platform*: a complete deployment and management system to handle every aspect of a web application. The infrastructure underneath the PaaS is largely invisible to the developer—a PaaS service saves you even more time on setup, configuration, and maintenance (at the expense of flexibility).

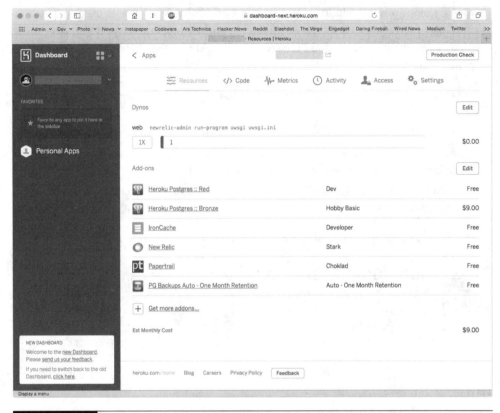

**FIGURE 4.1-2**    Heroku's management console

# SaaS

*Software as a Service (SaaS)* is the top layer of web services, accessible as web applications. Users of these web apps don't own the software—there's no installer. They use a web app through its website or native device apps. This may sound like a disadvantage, but the SaaS model provides access to necessary applications (such as word processing, presentations, spreadsheets, e-mail, flowcharting, and more) wherever you have an Internet connection, often without having to carry data or install regular updates. The monthly or yearly subscription model of many SaaS offerings makes it easier to budget and keep hundreds or thousands of computers up to date. The tradeoff to using SaaS is giving control of your data to the SaaS provider.

**EXAM TIP**    You need to know the common cloud model acronyms IaaS, SaaS, and PaaS for the CompTIA A+ 220-1001 exam. You will also see many other cloud acronyms used in the industry, such as Database as a Service (DBaaS), Desktop as a Service (DaaS), Network as a Service (NaaS), or even Anything/Everything as a Service (XaaS)!

# Public vs. Private vs. Hybrid vs. Community

Giving control of data to an SaaS provider is a major security concern for many companies, because their sensitive intellectual property or business secrets may be traveling through untrusted networks and being stored on servers they don't control. When it comes to security concerns like these (among other factors), different organizations come to different conclusions. The result is a number of terms we use to describe who owns and controls given cloud resources:

- Out on the open, public Internet, cloud services that anyone can access are the *public cloud.* When we talk about *the* cloud, we mean the public cloud. The public doesn't own it—companies such as Amazon, Google, and Microsoft do—but any individual or company can use public IaaS, PaaS, and SaaS offerings.

- Organizations that want some of the flexibility the cloud offers but need complete ownership of their data (and can afford both) can build (or contract a third party to build) an internal *private cloud.* A business could build a private IaaS that departments use to create and destroy VMs as needed, and a private PaaS to support the quick development of internal web apps such as private SaaS to meet the collaboration, planning, or time management needs of their employees.

- A *community cloud* is basically a private cloud paid for by a "community" of organizations in the same industry or with similar challenges. Imagine, for example, a community cloud for hospitals that meets the special regulatory requirements of dealing with patient data, or a cloud for military contractors that enables them to share the burden of defending against attackers sponsored by foreign states. This could be as simple as an SaaS application for tracking patient charts, or as complex IaaS and PaaS offerings.

- A *hybrid cloud* isn't really a type of cloud—it just describes blending IaaS, PaaS, and SaaS resources from the other types. For example, you could maintain your own private cloud to satisfy average demand, then launch new VMs in the public cloud as you approach your own cloud's capacity—called *cloud bursting. Hybrid cloud* can also mean integrating specific services across cloud types—a hotel chain, for example, could build a private/internal SaaS app to enable each manager to predict which bookings will likely miss because their flights got delayed or cancelled. To accomplish this, they could integrate with a third-party weather forecasting app in the public cloud and a flight-tracking app in a community cloud for the aviation industry.

**EXAM TIP**    You need to understand who can access each type of deployment model and who controls them.

# Shared Resources

One of the benefits of cloud computing is how it enhances the concept of *shared resources*. All networks feature shared resources such as storage and servers, but with cloud computing, these resources can be accessed via the Internet, not just those connected to the same LAN.

## Internal vs. External

One of the keys to sharing resources is understanding what you can do with internal and external cloud resources. Often, internal resources start with a virtual machine. The primary requirement for a VM you intend to use as a server is network connectivity, and one of the coolest features of VMs is the many different ways you can "virtually" network them. This doesn't mean just connecting them to the Internet—every hypervisor (described later under objective 4.2) has the capability to connect each of its VMs to a network in a number of different ways.

The combinations are infinite, but here are the basic options:

- Virtual machines on the same hypervisor can be internally networked (see Figure 4.1-3)—connected to a *virtual switch* (see Figure 4.1-4) inside the hypervisor—with none of their network traffic leaving the host machine.
- You can bridge the VM's NIC to the host system's NIC (connecting it to the Internet, if the LAN is connected), enabling it to get an IP address on the LAN from DHCP. By connecting the VM to the Internet, you can share resources with a cloud computing environment, IaaS, PaaS, or SaaS.

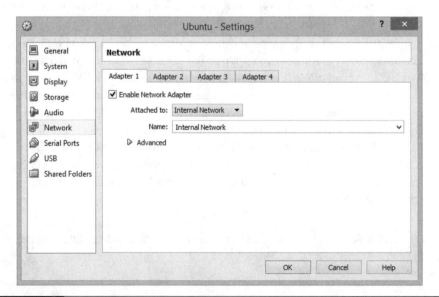

**FIGURE 4.1-3**    Configuring a VM for an internal network in VirtualBox

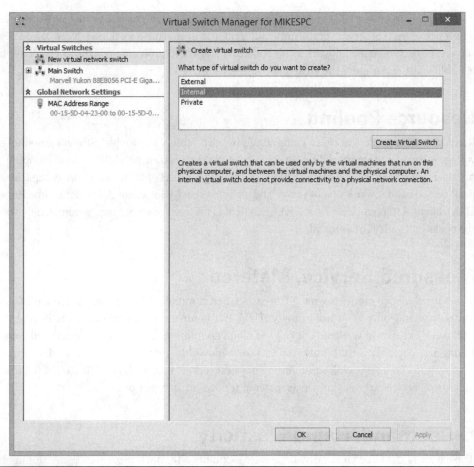

**FIGURE 4.1-4** Hyper-V's Virtual Switch Manager

**CAUTION** A VM connected using bridged networking is subject to all the same security risks as a real computer on the Internet, but it's also able to serve resources to any LAN or WAN nodes allowed to reach it.

- Just because you make a VM doesn't mean you need any kind of network. A no-network VM can be a simple place to test something quickly—or to test software that may pose a risk to your network.

The ability to network these servers on the fly means you can create a virtual LAN (VLAN) with a whole team of servers performing different jobs or sharing a workload. Need to add new servers, or rearrange the network to try something new? No problem—you don't even have to re-cable—just reconfigure the virtual network settings.

## Resource Pooling

Resource pooling refers to cloud computing providers' ability to provide different amounts of storage, server, or other shared resources to multiple clients, transparently. A cloud computing provider's resource pooling enables it to provide a higher level of server and storage capacity at peak periods and lower levels of server and storage capacity for client A (Eastern Time Zone, USA), client B (Greenwich Time, UK), and client C (Tokyo, following day) automatically with the peaks and valleys of demand.

## Measured Service, Metered

A *measured service* model is what a CSP uses when it monitors the cloud resources that customers use and bills them accordingly. Thus, if a company needs extra servers during the workweek but not on weekends, it can use cloud computing–based servers Monday through Friday and pay only for the time, capacity, or bandwidth (pricing models vary) that it uses. That way, the company avoids purchasing physical servers that would be idle part of the time. Measured services are also known as metered services or "pay per use."

## On-demand, Rapid Elasticity

The nature of cloud services provides greater flexibility and much more rapid provisioning of resources than is possible with on-premises infrastructure: the ability to use cloud resources and services *on demand* empowers customers to scale up or down rapidly to handle spikes or sags in their own demand, which is known as rapid elasticity.

For example, with traditional in-house resources, adding servers would require purchasing them, installing them, and configuring them before use, a process that can take days. By contrast, cloud services can add servers or other resources in just a few minutes.

 **EXAM TIP**   Rapid elasticity allows a customer to use more or fewer cloud resources as needed. On-demand means that a customer can access cloud resources 24/7.

# Off-site E-mail Applications

Google Mail (Gmail) and Microsoft Outlook.com are two examples of popular cloud-based off-site e-mail applications. They can be used as web-based e-mail services or can be used with popular e-mail clients such as Microsoft Office Outlook, Mozilla Thunderbird, and others. Gmail and Outlook.com are examples of SaaS.

# Cloud File Storage Services

Microsoft OneDrive, Dropbox, and Google Drive are three examples of popular cloud-based file storage services. These and similar services can be used for file backup, for file transfer, as an alternative to FTP or SFTP, and for file synchronization.

## Synchronization Apps

File synchronization apps such as Google Drive Backup and Sync, Mozy Sync, and KeepItSafe Online Backup go beyond file storage services by enabling users to sync, either on-demand or automatically, copies of files that are stored both locally on their computers and mobile devices, and remotely in the cloud. MultCloud is a cloud storage manager that performs sync and file transfer between leading cloud services such as OneDrive, Google Drive, Dropbox, Amazon Cloud Drive, and many others.

# Virtual Application Streaming/ Cloud-based Applications

*Virtual application streaming* is a technology that enables a workstation or mobile device to run cloud-based applications as if they are installed locally. Virtual application streaming enables only the relevant parts of an application to be run from cloud storage, automatically swapping program components in and out as needed. Virtual application streaming licensing is typically less expensive per user than standard software licenses, as a license is used only when the app is streamed. For example, if ten users at a time out of a fleet of 100 computers need access to program ABC, a ten-seat streaming license for ABC is likely to be much less expensive than 100 standard licenses for program ABC. Virtual application streaming is a virtualization technology rather than an example of SaaS.

## Applications for Cell Phones/Tablets

Smartphone/tablet virtual app streaming enables these mobile devices to run apps originally developed for Windows desktop operating systems. Users work with apps on their smartphone or tablet just as if they were using a desktop or laptop computer with those same apps. Some vendors also offer virtual desktops so that a Windows desktop can appear on a mobile device.

Depending upon the specific solution, users might connect via a website or by running an app on their client devices to access virtual app streaming. Examples of software that supports virtual app streaming on mobile devices include Citrix Virtual Apps (formerly XenApp) and Parallels Remote Application Server (RAS).

### Applications for Laptops/Desktops

Virtual application streaming is also useful for laptops and desktops, as it enables these devices to run software that is stored, managed, and secured remotely. One example is Microsoft Application Virtualization (App-V) for Windows 7 and later, running Win32 apps from App-V servers. Another is VMware ThinApp, supporting Windows, Terminal Server, and Citrix.

# Virtual Desktop

CompTIA uses the term virtual desktop in an odd way; we've used it the same way here, to describe a simple desktop environment on a virtual machine. In practice, a virtual desktop more commonly refers to the multiple desktop environments you can access in modern operating systems, such as clicking the Task View icon in Windows 10 and going to a second desktop.

## Virtual NIC

Virtual machines connect to physical networks by using a virtual network interface card (virtual NIC). A *virtual NIC* is a bridge created by a virtualization app to connect to a physical NIC on the host device. Whenever the VM needs to connect to another device on the network or the Internet, the request is sent to the virtual NIC, which in turn sends it to the physical NIC. Responses come back to the physical NIC, which sends them back to the virtual NIC for the appropriate VM.

 **EXAM TIP**   Understand what a virtual NIC does and how it relates to a physical NIC.

When apps that display hardware configuration, such as Windows Device Manager, are run within a VM, the virtual NICs and other virtual devices are displayed (see Figure 4.1-5). Note that the network adapter listing is the virtualized NIC; the host computer uses a different brand and model of NIC. When apps that display network connections are run from an OS that is hosting a VM, both physical and virtual NICs are displayed.

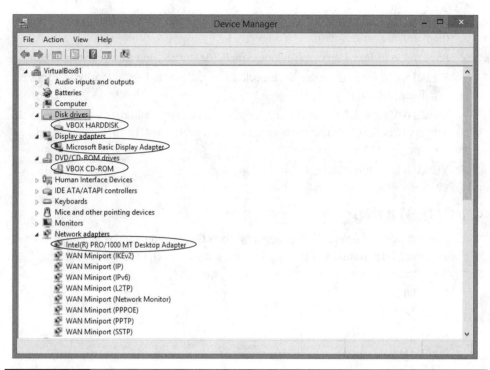

**FIGURE 4.1-5**   VirtualBox (VBOX) virtual drives and other virtualized devices shown in Device Manager

# REVIEW

### Objective 4.1: Compare and contrast cloud computing concepts

- The major types of cloud services include Infrastructure as a Service (IaaS), Platform as a Service (PaaS), and Software as a Service (SaaS).
- The public cloud refers to cloud services available to anyone.
- Private cloud services are used internally by companies.
- A community cloud is a private cloud paid for by a group of organizations or individuals.
- A hybrid cloud blends IaaS, PaaS, and SaaS resources.
- Shared resources such as VMs, cloud storage, and others can be shared via LANs (internally) or with cloud computing (externally).
- Resource pooling enables organizations to move and run VMs between different hardware as needed.
- Measured service bills cloud computing users based on bandwidth, time, or capacity used.
- The ability to add or drop cloud services as needed (on-demand self-service) enables organizations to have rapid elasticity.

- Metered service enables CSPs to offer unlimited resources to its clients but charges them only for what is used.
- Popular cloud-based services include e-mail, file storage, and file synchronization.
- Virtual application streaming enables cloud-based apps to be run locally as if they're installed locally.
- Virtual desktops (VDI) bundle an operating system, apps, and data storage for quick delivery to desktop computers as either customized (persistent VDI) or standard (non-persistent VDI) images.
- Virtual NICs connect VMs to physical networks.

## 4.1 QUESTIONS

1. Company A uses several SaaS products such as Gmail and Google Docs along with a customized private cloud for its proprietary apps. Which of the following best describes the Company A's cloud computing strategy?

   **A.** Public cloud

   **B.** Hybrid cloud

   **C.** Community cloud

   **D.** VMM

2. Company B is planning to make the same applications available via cloud or network services to desktops and tablets. Which of the following is Company B planning to implement?

   **A.** Virtual application streaming

   **B.** Private cloud

   **C.** SaaS

   **D.** Measured service

3. Your company is going to use cloud services to develop software, and the software will then be available as a cloud service. Which pairing accurately reflects what services will be used, in the correct order?

   **A.** IaaS, PaaS

   **B.** PaaS, SaaS

   **C.** SaaS, IaaS

   **D.** SaaS, PaaS

4. Which of the following in a community cloud scenario is the grouping of servers and infrastructure for use by multiple customers?

   **A.** Virtual desktop

   **B.** Synchronization apps

   **C.** Resource pooling

   **D.** Virtual application streaming

5. Your company needs access to unlimited resources to promote rapid elasticity and on-demand swings in requirements, but wants to pay only for the resources it actually uses. What arrangement is your company looking for?

   **A.** Measured service

   **B.** IaaS

   **C.** Hybrid cloud

   **D.** Metered service

## 4.1 ANSWERS

1. **B**  A hybrid cloud combines public cloud (in this case, SaaS) and private cloud solutions.

2. **A**  Virtual application streaming makes apps available to a variety of platforms via cloud or network services.

3. **B**  Platform as a Service (PaaS) is the use of a complete cloud-based software development environment. Software as a Service (SaaS) makes the software available for use via the cloud.

4. **C**  In a community cloud scenario, the cloud service provider typically implements resource pooling, which is the grouping of servers and infrastructure for use by multiple customers but in a way that is on-demand and scalable.

5. **D**  Metered service provides unlimited access to resources on a pay-for-what-you-use basis.

**Objective 4.2** **Given a scenario, set up and configure client-side virtualization**

*Virtualization* enables a single physical host computer running specialized software to create virtual machines (saved in separate files), also known as guests, that replicate other computers, each with its own operating system, settings, apps, and data. Client-side virtualization refers to running a VM on your local system (in contrast to VMs run elsewhere) regardless of whether the VM file itself might be stored locally or on a central server accessed via the network. The software used to create and manage VMs is known as a hypervisor.

**Cross-Reference**

To learn more about hypervisors, see "Hypervisor" later in this objective.

# Purpose of Virtual Machines

If you aren't familiar with virtualization, the idea can seem a little pointless at first. Why would you need to run an OS inside an OS? Here are a few of the biggest benefits:

- Going virtual enables companies to combine multiple servers onto fewer machines than in traditional computing. This offers tremendous savings on hardware purchases, electricity use, and the space used for computing.

- Because a VM is only a single file or two, a hacked system can rapidly be replaced with a snapshot (a backup) taken of the properly working VM. This is especially useful for getting critical servers back up quickly. Likewise, the minimal file numbers make it easy to duplicate a VM.

- The capability to run many operating systems on a single physical machine makes multiplatform testing and research easier and cheaper than with traditional setups.

# Resource Requirements

Any computer running Windows, Linux, or macOS will support a hypervisor, but the hypervisor will run better if your computer has hardware virtualization support. If your computer's CPU and UEFI/BIOS have this support, you can turn it on or off inside the system setup utility (see Figure 4.2-1).

 **NOTE**    More than a decade ago, both AMD and Intel added hardware virtualization support to their CPUs to enable better performance when the CPU is serving multiple operating systems. AMD's hardware virtualization feature is referred to as Secure Virtual Machine (SVM) mode or AMD-V. Intel uses the term VT-x. Intel VT-d, a separate setting from VT-x, provides directed I/O virtualization for better performance.

The other big hardware requirements are RAM and storage space. Each virtual machine needs just as much RAM as a physical one, and the host machine needs enough left over to run the hypervisor and any other software it needs to run. How much RAM is needed takes some research to figure out. Likewise, VM files eat up tons of storage space because they include everything installed on the VM—anywhere from megabytes to hundreds of gigabytes. Various online calculators for server-class virtualization are available to help you right-size physical hardware to your virtualization needs.

```
NX Mode                                    Enabled
SVM Mode                                   Enabled
    Intel Virtualization Tech             [Enabled]
    Intel VT-D Tech                       [Enabled]
```

**FIGURE 4.2-1**    UEFI firmware settings for CPU virtualization support on AMD (top) and Intel (bottom) CPUs

# Emulator Requirements

Instead of writing drivers so that every imaginable guest can use the hypervisor's virtual hardware, the hypervisor often emulates popular, widely supported hardware—devices every OS already has drivers for. For example, Oracle VM VirtualBox emulates the Intel PRO/1000 MT desktop NIC for networking and the (Southbridge) PCI to ISA bridge chip. What is the difference between virtualization and emulation?

Virtualization takes the hardware of the host system and segments into individual virtual machines. If you have an Intel system, a hypervisor creates a virtual machine that acts exactly like the host Intel system. It cannot act like any other type of computer. For example, you cannot make a virtual machine that acts like a Nintendo 3DS on an Intel system. Hypervisors simply pass the code from the virtual machine to the actual CPU.

An *emulator* is software or hardware that converts the commands to and from the host machine into an entirely different platform. In emulation performed by a hypervisor, the commands given to the virtual desktop NIC are converted into the appropriate commands used by the physical NIC. You can also use a console game emulator to run console games on a computer, such as a Super Nintendo Entertainment System emulator like Snes9X to run games made for SNES on a Windows PC.

 **EXAM TIP**  Understand that emulating another platform (using a laptop to run Sony PlayStation 4 games, for example) requires hardware several times more powerful than the platform being emulated.

# Security Requirements

A virtual machine should be kept as secure as a physical computer. After all, with network and Internet connections present on almost any VM, it can be used (or misused) in the same way as a physical computer. Different users with different levels of access should be set up on a VM that will be used by multiple users. Strong passwords should be implemented. Antivirus and anti-malware apps should be deployed and kept updated. OS updates should be performed as needed.

 **EXAM TIP**  Virtualized operating systems use the same security features as real ones. You still need to keep track of user names, passwords, permissions, and so on, just like on a normal system.

# Network Requirements

The easiest way to network a computer that will be hosting one or more VMs is with the fastest wired Ethernet supported. If you want to use wireless, a wireless NIC that uses a PCIe slot would also be suitable. Using a USB network adapter is not recommended, because of the limited support that USB devices have on most VM software.

# Hypervisor

A *hypervisor*, also known as a *virtual machine manager (VMM)*, creates, runs, and manages VMs. There are two types of hypervisors: Type 1 and Type 2.

 **EXAM TIP** Be sure to know the differences between Type 1 and Type 2 hypervisors.

A Type 1 hypervisor such as Hyper-V, VMware ESXi, and Citrix Hypervisor (formerly known as Citrix XenServer) runs directly on computer hardware in place of a standard operating system. A Type 1 hypervisor is also known as a "bare metal" hypervisor because there's no other software between it and the hardware. VMs running server operating systems are run on Type 1 hypervisors.

A Type 2 hypervisor such as Oracle VM VirtualBox or VMware Workstation is run on a standard operating system (Linux, Windows, or macOS). Thus, Type 2 hypervisors have an additional layer of software compared to Type 1 hypervisors (see Figure 4.2-2 for an example). Most types of client-side virtualization use Type 2 hypervisors.

 **NOTE** Although Hyper-V is installed after installing Windows Server or is enabled after installing Windows 8.1 or Windows 10 editions that include it, it is considered a Type 1 hypervisor. Here's why: after Hyper-V is installed/enabled, it turns the Windows edition that was installed first into a VM running under Hyper-V, and additional VMs can be created. To learn more about the differences between Hyper-V running on Windows versus Hyper-V running on Windows Server, see https://docs.microsoft.com and search for "Hyper-V."

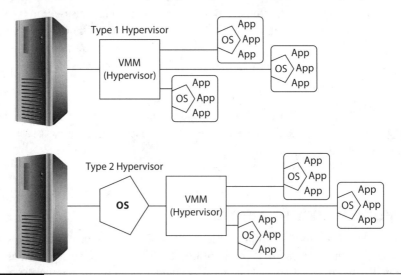

**FIGURE 4.2-2** Type 1 hypervisors (top) compared to Type 2 hypervisors (bottom)

# Installing a Hypervisor and Creating a Virtual Machine

Installing a third-party hypervisor is like installing any other software—download and execute the hypervisor software and follow its setup wizard. On a Windows 8/8.1/10 system that includes Hyper-V, you can enable it in the Windows Features dialog box (see Figure 4.2-3), which you reach via Control Panel | Programs and Features applet | *Turn Windows features on or off*. After enabling Hyper-V, reboot the system.

After you've installed the hypervisor of choice, you'll have a virtual machine manager that acts as the primary place to create, start, stop, save, and delete guest virtual machines. On pretty much any VMM, you create a new VM by clicking New | Virtual Machine and completing the wizard it opens (see Figure 4.2-4). Most hypervisors have presets to ensure your guest OS has the virtual hardware it needs.

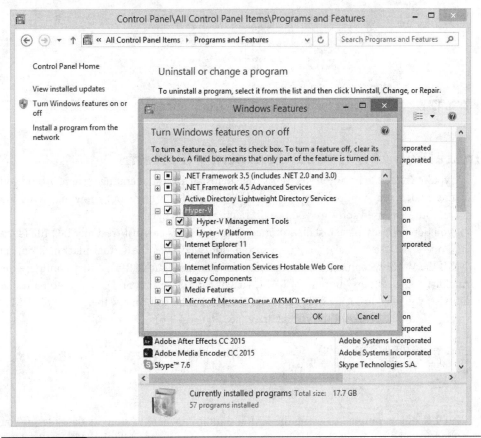

**FIGURE 4.2-3**  Enabling Hyper-V in Windows

**FIGURE 4.2-4**   Creating a new VM in Oracle VirtualBox

# Installing the Guest Operating System

Once you've created the new guest VM, it's time to install a guest operating system. Would you like to use Microsoft Windows in your virtual machine? No problem, but know that Windows (and any other licensed software you install) requires a valid license.

If you don't already have installation media, most VMMs can just treat any ISO file (such as the one you'd use to make your own installation media) as the virtual machine's optical drive. If the VMM recognizes your installation media (see Figure 4.2-5), it may configure the virtual hardware settings (amount of RAM, virtual hard drive size, and so on) automatically; otherwise, you need to set sensible values for these (you can still change them after the VM is created). Next, set the size of the virtual drive (see Figure 4.2-6).

 **EXAM TIP**   After a VM is set up, installing an operating system into it is just like installing an OS on a normal computer.

You'll also be prompted to name the VM and indicate where to store its data files. If you specified installation media, you'll also have some time to burn while the OS installs. After configuration and installation, you can stop, start, pause, or delete the VM, add or remove virtual hardware, or just interact with the OS and other software inside it.

**FIGURE 4.2-5** Installer recognizing selected installation media

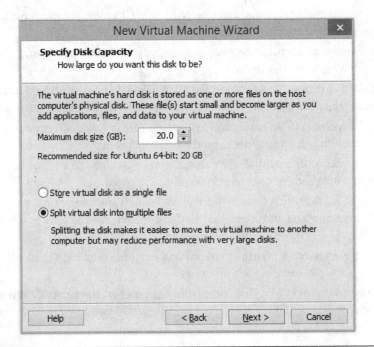

**FIGURE 4.2-6** Setting the virtual drive size

**NOTE** Use descriptive names for virtual machines, such as "64-Win7-Mark." This will save you a lot of confusion when you have multiple VMs on a single host.

Using a VM is almost exactly like using a real system, except it's contained in a window and some hotkeys differ. VMware Workstation, for example, replaces CTRL-ALT-DELETE with CTRL-ALT-INSERT by default (so you can still use CTRL-ALT-DELETE on your desktop). That, and you can adapt your *virtual desktop* to changing needs without a trip to the store: a good hypervisor can add and remove virtual hard drives, virtual network cards, virtual RAM, and so on. Keep in mind that USB drive support varies between hypervisors, and may require special settings or have limited support for USB 3.0 and faster versions.

# REVIEW

### Objective 4.2: Given a scenario, set up and configure client-side virtualization

- Virtualization enables companies to use fewer servers to perform tasks, provides for faster backup, and enables multiplatform testing on a single computer.
- For the best performance, enable the processor's hardware virtualization support in the UEFI firmware setup, and provide enough RAM and disk space for each VM as well as for the host OS or hypervisor.
- Hypervisors emulate popular chipsets, NICs, and GPUs, enabling support for a wide range of hardware without specific drivers.
- VMs require exactly the same levels of security (passwords, updates, and so on) as the physical computers they replace.
- Wired rather than wireless networks are recommended for better performance, especially when Gigabit Ethernet or faster connections are available, and easier configuration.
- Type 1 hypervisors (aka bare-metal hypervisors) are installed directly on the hardware and are typically used for VMs in production applications.
- Type 2 hypervisors are installed on an operating system, and are typically used for experimenting and educational purposes.
- Hyper-V is a Type 1 hypervisor available on business and educational versions of Windows 8 and later and is enabled through *Turn Windows features on or off* in the Programs and Features Control Panel applet.
- Other hypervisors are available from various vendors. Installing a third-party hypervisor is like installing any other software.
- After a hypervisor (VMM) is installed, the process of creating a new VM is specific to each hypervisor, but the process of installing an OS into a VM is about the same as installing that OS on a physical computer.

# 4.2 QUESTIONS

1. Company C has set up a computing lab where it plans to install VirtualBox on Linux and Windows workstations and use it to run older versions of Linux and Windows to provide customer support. Which of the following best describes how Company C is using virtualization?

   **A.** Type 1 virtualization

   **B.** Bare metal virtualization

   **C.** VMM

   **D.** Type 2 virtualization

2. When is the size of the virtual hardware (such as RAM and drive size) set during the VM creation process?

   **A.** Set automatically by the hypervisor at the start of the process

   **B.** After installing the OS into the VM

   **C.** Before installing the OS into the VM

   **D.** Before starting the VM creation process

3. Company D has set up virtualization on several late-model Intel and AMD systems running high-performance processors using the recommended settings in the hypervisor for each VM, but the VMs are running very slowly. Which of the following is the most likely cause?

   **A.** Hardware virtualization support is not enabled in the UEFI firmware.

   **B.** VMs are using too much RAM.

   **C.** Hardware virtualization support is not enabled in the OS.

   **D.** VMs are using too much disk space.

4. Customer E is running Windows 10 Pro and wants to install a Linux-based VM in Hyper-V. Which of the following must the customer do for this to work? (Choose two.)

   **A.** Turn on Hyper-V in Windows Features

   **B.** Run Windows Update

   **C.** Scan the host system for viruses

   **D.** Restart the system

5. A customer is having a problem with the network hardware on the host Windows computer for her VMs. Which of the following will help her diagnose the problem?

   **A.** Check Device Manager in each VM

   **B.** Disable/re-enable the virtual NIC in each VM

   **C.** Check Device Manager in the host computer

   **D.** All of the above

## 4.2 ANSWERS

**1.** **D** Type 2 virtualization runs within an installed operating system and relays requests to the hardware to the host operating system, whereas Type 1 virtualization directly interfaces with the computer's hardware.

**2.** **C** This information is used to set up the virtual machine, so it must be provided when the VM is created and before the OS can be installed.

**3.** **A** High-end Intel and AMD processors have support for hardware virtualization. However, if it not enabled in the firmware, virtualization will run very slowly.

**4.** **A** **D** For this to work, hardware virtualization support must first be enabled in the UEFI/BIOS. Second, Hyper-V needs to be turned on in Windows Features. Finally, enabling Hyper-V requires the system to be restarted.

**5.** **C** To solve a problem with the host's network hardware, the host's diagnostic features, such as Device Manager, must be used. The virtual NIC in each VM connects to the physical network, so the VMs can't work if the physical network connection in the host isn't working.

# Hardware and Network Troubleshooting

# Given a scenario, use the best practice methodology to resolve problems

The CompTIA *best practice methodology*, also known as the *troubleshooting methodology*, provides you with a process you can use to identify, solve, and document any technology problem.

As you apply this methodology in your day-to-day work (and to scenarios presented in the CompTIA A+ 220-1001 exam), remember to always consider corporate policies, procedures, and impacts before implementing changes.

## The CompTIA Troubleshooting Methodology

The methodology has six steps, as shown in the following table. Note that the descriptions and the bullet points are official CompTIA objectives; the other text is author comments.

| Step # | Description | Details, Tips, and Notes |
|--------|-------------|--------------------------|
| 1 | Identify the problem | • Question the user and identify user changes to computer and perform backups before making changes<br><br>• Inquire regarding environmental or infrastructure changes<br><br>• Review system and application logs<br><br>Computers, peripherals, and devices are composed of subsystems (hardware, software, and firmware), so look at all possible causes.<br><br>Conduct user interviews in a professional manner without any attempt to cast blame. |
| 2 | Establish a theory of probable cause (question the obvious) | • If necessary, conduct external or internal research based on symptoms<br><br>Check vendor and third-party websites and forums, system and peripheral documentation, and internal help desk records.<br><br>Create a list of possible causes, starting with the simple and moving to the less obvious. |

| Step # | Description | Details, Tips, and Notes |
|---|---|---|
| 3 | Test the theory to determine cause | • Once the theory is confirmed, determine the next steps to resolve problem<br><br>• If theory is not confirmed reestablish new theory or escalate<br><br>Change one item at a time and then test the device. If the device still doesn't work, restore it to its previous setting and change another item that is on the list of potential causes.<br><br>If your scope of knowledge or responsibility is limited, make sure you provide all information to the next-level tech for follow-up. |
| 4 | Establish a plan of action to resolve the problem and implement the solution | The plan should list each step necessary.<br>A backup of user data should be part of the plan of action.<br><br>You might need additional resources such as known good replacement parts. |
| 5 | Verify full system functionality and, if applicable, implement preventive measures | Making sure the system works after the solution is applied is essential, but often not performed. Preventive measures help organizations from needing to solve problems repeatedly. |
| 6 | Document findings, actions, and outcomes | Recording symptoms, solutions, and results helps minimize future outbreaks of similar problems, helps fellow techs who encounter the same issue, and helps track the troubleshooting history of a device. |

 **EXAM TIP** It is likely you will encounter exam questions directly related to the best practice troubleshooting methodology. Know it well!

# REVIEW

**Objective 5.1: Given a scenario, use the best practice methodology to resolve problems** Use the six-part CompTIA best practice methodology to troubleshoot and solve technology problems:

1. Identify the problem.

2. Establish a theory of probable cause (question the obvious).

3. Test the theory to determine cause.

4. Establish a plan of action to resolve the problem and implement the solution.

5. Verify full system functionality and, if applicable, implement preventive measures.

6. Document findings, actions, and outcomes.

## 5.1 QUESTIONS

1. After you establish a plan of action, what should you do next?
   - **A.** Test the theory
   - **B.** Verify full system functionality
   - **C.** Document findings
   - **D.** Establish a theory of probable cause

2. When should you question the obvious?
   - **A.** When identifying the problem
   - **B.** When documenting findings
   - **C.** When testing the theory
   - **D.** When establishing a theory

3. During the process of troubleshooting a printer problem, you created a document that lists the printer drivers needed, how you installed them, and how you tested the printers and systems involved. Which of the following steps did you perform?
   - **A.** Documenting findings
   - **B.** Establishing a theory of probable cause
   - **C.** Verifying full system functionality
   - **D.** Testing the theory

4. Which step of the troubleshooting methodology includes reviewing system and application logs?
   - **A.** Identify the problem
   - **B.** Establish a theory of probable cause
   - **C.** Test the theory to determine cause
   - **D.** Verify full system functionality and, if applicable, implement the solution

5. What should you always do first before implementing changes?
   - **A.** Conduct external and internal research based on symptoms
   - **B.** Implement preventive measures
   - **C.** Consider corporate policies, procedures, and impacts
   - **D.** Establish a new theory or escalate

## 5.1 ANSWERS

1. **B**   Establishing a plan of action is step 4, and verifying full system functionality is step 5.

2. **D**   Questioning the obvious is a part of establishing a theory of probably cause (step 2).

3. **A**   Documenting findings, which is the final step of the troubleshooting methodology, refers to noting in detail the solutions used and how they were applied.

4. **A**   Identifying the problem is step 1 and includes reviewing system and application logs.

5. **C**   Always consider corporate policies, procedures, and impacts before implementing a change.

**Objective 5.2** # Given a scenario, troubleshoot problems related to motherboards, RAM, CPUs, and power

Motherboards, RAM, CPUs, and power are the core components of any computer. Troubleshooting computer problems should start by looking at these subsystems.

## Troubleshooting Core Components

Troubleshooting problems with motherboards, RAM, CPUs, and power can be difficult because these components have a number of common symptoms that can have multiple causes. In this objective, you will learn about these symptoms, typical causes, and leading solutions. The following sections present each symptom listed in objective 5.2, along with a corresponding table that identifies the likely issue or issues in the left column and the corresponding solution or solutions in the right column. (The same format is used to present the subsequent objectives in Domain 5.0.)

### Unexpected Shutdowns

| | |
|---|---|
| Power Good line on power supply out of spec | Power Good is the wire at position #8 (usually gray). Normal voltage is +5-V DC. If the PG voltage drops too low, the system will reboot. |
| Overheated CPU | See the "Overheating" entry in this table for solutions. |
| Overclocked system | See the "Overheating" entry in this table for solutions. |

### System Lockups

| | |
|---|---|
| Overheating system | See the "Overheating" entry in this table for solutions. |
| Corrupt Windows files | Run System File Checker (sfc.exe) and have it replace corrupt files. |
| Corrupt temporary files | Delete the contents of \Temp folder (Windows). |
| Bad RAM | Power down the system, remove RAM, insert one stick/bank, and restart the system. If the system runs and doesn't lock up, swap RAM. If one stick/bank is the problem, replace it. |

### POST Code Beeps

| | |
|---|---|
| Bad or loose video card | Power down the system and reconnect the video card. Turn on the system and retest. If the problem persists, replace the video card. |
| Bad or missing RAM | Power down the system and check RAM. Replace bad RAM or insert new RAM, turn on the system, and retest. |

### Blank Screen on Bootup

| | |
|---|---|
| Display turned off | Turn on the display. Check the monitor power cord. |
| Bad video driver | If the display works during POST but not after the OS loads, reload the OS in Safe Mode and install an updated video driver. |

### BIOS Time and Setting Resets

| | |
|---|---|
| Bad battery on motherboard | Power down the system and replace the CMOS battery (usually a CR2032). Turn on the system, enter BIOS/UEFI firmware setup, reset date/time and settings, save changes, and restart the system. |

### Attempts to Boot to Incorrect Device

| | |
|---|---|
| Nonbootable optical disc or USB flash drive inserted | Remove nonbootable removable media and restart the system. |
| Incorrect boot sequence settings | Enter BIOS/UEFI firmware setup, reset the boot sequence to include a bootable drive, and restart the system. |
| Windows or other OS boot drive corrupt | Repair the boot drive using OS tools. |

## Continuous Reboots

| | |
|---|---|
| Power Good line on power supply out of spec | Power Good is the wire at position #8 (usually gray). Normal voltage is +5-V DC. If the PG voltage drops too low, the system will reboot. |
| Windows configured to automatically reboot after STOP (BSoD) error | Reboot Windows in Safe Mode, open Windows Explorer (Windows 7) or File Explorer (Windows 8/8.1/10), right-click Computer (Windows 7) or This PC (Windows 8/8.1/10, select Properties, Advanced System Settings, click Settings in Startup and Recovery, and uncheck Automatically Restart. Click OK, OK to close dialogs. |

## No Power

| | |
|---|---|
| Power cord not properly attached | Reattach the power cord. |
| Power switch on power supply turned off | Turn on the power supply switch. |
| Incorrect voltage setting on power supply with manual voltage switch | Turn off the power supply switch; change the switch to the correct voltage. |

## Overheating

| | |
|---|---|
| Power supply fan has failed | If the fan is not turning, shut off the system and replace the power supply. |
| Active heat sink on CPU is dirty | Clean the active heat sink fan and fins with compressed air or a computer-safe vacuum. |
| Active heat sink fan on CPU has failed or is disconnected | If the fan is not turning, shut off the system and check the fan connection to the motherboard. If the fan is connected, replace the active heat sink fan. |
| Air intakes on case are clogged | Clean the air intakes and fan. |
| Case or CPU fans turning too slowly | Use the PC Health or Hardware Monitor function in the BIOS firmware to check fan performance. |
| Overclocked system | Reset the system and memory clock speeds to the normal settings in the BIOS firmware; if the CPU is overclocked, reset its clock speed to the normal setting. |

### Loud Noise

| | |
|---|---|
| Power supply or motherboard components have failed | Check for smoke or a burning smell. Replace the burnt or smoky component. |

### Intermittent Device Failure

| | |
|---|---|
| USB device: power supply failing to provide enough power to port | Replace the power supply with a higher-rated model. Connect USB devices to the powered hub. |
| Internal drives: loose or defective power connectors or power splitters | Replace power splitters. Replace the power supply if power connectors or cables are broken or cracked. |
| Internal or external devices: power supply voltages out of spec | Use a power supply tester, the PC Health/System Diagnostics window in BIOS, or a multimeter to check power supply power levels. Replace the power supply with a higher-rated unit if power levels are out of spec. |

### Fans Spin – No Power to Other Devices

| | |
|---|---|
| Secondary power to motherboard (4/8-pin) connector loose or disconnected | Power down the system, plug in the connector, and then power up the system. |

### Indicator Lights

| | |
|---|---|
| Indicator lights not working | Power down the system, check the front panel connectors on the motherboard, and reconnect any loose ones as needed. Power up the system. |

### Smoke

| | |
|---|---|
| Component failure caused by incorrect voltage levels | Power down the system and check connectors to drives, the motherboard, and other components. Check for a burnt smell or acrid odor. Replace any damaged component. Make sure the power connectors are not backward. |

### Burning Smell

| | |
|---|---|
| Component failure caused by capacitor failure or incorrect voltage levels | See the previous entry for "Smoke." Also, check for blown, burnt, or distended capacitors. Replace damaged components. |

### Proprietary Crash Screens (BSOD/Pin Wheel)

| | |
|---|---|
| Blue Screen of Death (BSoD/STOP error): Multiple causes | Look up the STOP error code to determine the cause and solution. If the system reboots before you can read the STOP error code, see "Continuous Reboots" earlier in this table for a solution. |
| macOS pinwheel (aka Spinning Pinwheel of Death, or SPoD): Unresponsive app | Shut down the system and add RAM (if possible). Restart. Free up space on the macOS system drive to achieve 10 percent or more free space. If a particular app is unresponsive, delete its .plist file. Use Force Quit (OPTION-COMMAND-ESC) to stop an unresponsive app. |

### Distended Capacitors

| | |
|---|---|
| Swelling after installation on motherboard or components | Replace capacitors with solid capacitors (requires desolder/resolder) or replace components. |

### Log Entries and Error Messages

| | |
|---|---|
| Error messages (BSOD, other) are displayed in OS system logs. | Open event logs using OS utilities (Event Viewer in Windows, for example) and check for problems and solutions. Check error messages for problems and use the details to research solutions. |

 **EXAM TIP**   Given a scenario, be prepared to identify and troubleshoot the common systems covered in this objective and listed in the following Review section.

# REVIEW

**Objective 5.2: Given a scenario, troubleshoot problems related to motherboards, RAM, CPUs, and power**   Common symptoms of problems related to motherboards, RAM, CPUs, and power include the following:

- Unexpected shutdowns
- System lockups

- POST code beeps
- Blank screen on bootup
- BIOS time and setting resets
- Attempts to boot to incorrect device
- Continuous reboots
- No power
- Overheating
- Loud noise
- Intermittent device failure
- Fans spin – no power to other devices
- Indicator lights
- Smoke
- Burning smell
- Proprietary crash screens (BSOD/pin wheel)
- Distended capacitors
- Log entries and error messages

Keep in mind that each of these symptoms usually has multiple potential causes.

## 5.2 QUESTIONS

1. Which of the following causes for overheating can be tested in the system BIOS settings?

    **A.** Clogged air intakes

    **B.** Power supply fan failure

    **C.** Case or CPU fan speed slow

    **D.** GPU overclocking

2. What happens if a power supply is set for 230-V AC and you connect a 115-V AC line to it and turn on the computer?

    **A.** Overvoltage error appears on screen

    **B.** Computer cannot start

    **C.** Signal lights turn on but fans do not run

    **D.** Smoke and flames

3. You have tested the power supply on a computer that is continuously rebooting and the Power Good line and other voltage levels test out OK. What else should you check?

    **A.** If Windows is configured to automatically reboot after a STOP error

    **B.** If Windows always reboots automatically after a STOP error

    **C.** If the CTRL-ALT-DEL keys on the keyboard are stuck

    **D.** If the power switch on the power supply is stuck

4. What should you do if a customer's computer resets the BIOS time and settings incorrectly every time her computer is powered on?

   **A.** Reset the boot sequence order

   **B.** Check log entries and error logs

   **C.** Perform a soft reset

   **D.** Replace the CMOS battery

5. A customer reports that his computer keeps booting to an incorrect device. Which of the following will most likely remedy this situation? (Choose two.)

   **A.** Change the boot order in the BIOS

   **B.** Remove nonbootable disc or USB flash drive

   **C.** Run System File Checker (sfc.exe)

   **D.** Check front panel connectors and reconnect as needed

## 5.2 ANSWERS

1. **C**  The BIOS screen commonly called PC Health or Hardware Monitor displays fan speeds as well as system temperature.

2. **B**  The computer cannot start because the power supply is set for a voltage level twice what is being provided.

3. **A**  Windows can be configured to restart the system immediately in the event of a STOP error; to enable diagnosis of the STOP error, restart the system in Safe Mode and change this setting in System properties.

4. **D**  Power down system and replace the CMOS battery (usually a CR2032). Turn on system, enter BIOS setup, reset BIOS time and settings, save changes, and restart system.

5. **A B**  Enter BIOS setup, reset the boot sequence to include the correct bootable drive, and restart. Remove nonbootable removable media and restart system.

**Objective 5.3**  # Given a scenario, troubleshoot hard drives and RAID arrays

Hard drives and RAID arrays are where programs and data alike are stored. Solving problems with these subsystems is essential to keeping workstations and servers in order.

## Troubleshooting Storage Systems

The sections in this objective present common symptoms of storage problems, along with the typical causes and leading solutions.

### Read/Write Failure

| | |
|---|---|
| Loose data cable | Shut down the system (if an internal drive), reattach the data cable, and power up the system. |
| Bad data cable | Shut down the system (if an internal drive), replace the data cable, and power up the system. |
| Drive failure | Back up the drive, replace the drive, and restore from the backup. |

### Slow Performance

| | |
|---|---|
| Incorrect speed setting for SATA drive in BIOS/UEFI firmware setup | Check the drive specs and verify the correct SATA drive type/speed setting in BIOS/UEFI firmware setup. |
| Cable not suitable for SATA 6 Gbps | Shut down the system, replace the SATA cable with a SATA 6 Gbps cable, and restart system. |
| Bad data cable | Shut down the system (if an internal drive), replace the data cable, and power up the system. |
| Lack of RAM forcing disk thrashing (virtual memory) | Add RAM to the system. |

### Loud Clicking Noise

| | |
|---|---|
| Drive failure imminent—noise due to attempts to reread failing sectors | Back up the drive, replace the drive, and restore data from the backup. |

### Failure to Boot

| | |
|---|---|
| Drive not bootable | Change the boot order. |
| Damaged boot sector | Repair the boot sector with OS utilities. |
| Nonbootable optical or USB removable-media drives inserted | Remove nonbootable media and restart or change the boot order. |

### Drive Not Recognized

| | |
|---|---|
| Power and data cables not connected (internal) | Shut down the system, reconnect power and/or data cables, and power up the system. |
| Incorrect SATA port setting | Change the SATA port setting to non-RAID (AHCI on most recent systems). |

| USB or Thunderbolt cable disconnected | Reconnect the cable to the port and drive and retry. |
| USB port doesn't provide enough power to run drive | Plug the drive into the root hub on the system or into a self-powered hub. |
| File system not recognized by host operating system | Windows cannot use drives prepared with file systems normally used by Linux or macOS. |

### OS Not Found

| Wrong boot device selected | Change the boot order. |
| Boot files corrupt | Repair the boot sector with OS utilities. |

### RAID Not Found

| RAID controller disabled | Reenable the RAID controller in the BIOS/UEFI firmware setup or add-on card setup. |
| Bad or loose data cable | Shut down the system, reconnect the data cable, and power up the system. Replace the data cable if the problem persists. |
| Loose power cable | Shut down the system, reconnect the power cable, and power up the system. |

### RAID Stops Working

| One or more drives in array have failed | If using RAID 1, RAID 5, or RAID 10 with one failed drive, replace the drive and rebuild the array from the surviving drives. If using RAID 0 with one failed drive, replace the drive and restore data from backups (array data is lost). |

**Proprietary Crash Screens (BSOD/Pin Wheel)**   See the "Proprietary Crash Screens (BSOD/Pin Wheel)" section in the previous objective.

### S.M.A.R.T. Errors

| Hard drive prediction errors indicate drive failure imminent | Back up the drive, replace the drive, and restore data to the new drive from the backup. |

 **EXAM TIP**   Be sure to know the symptoms, meanings, and solutions covered in this objective and listed in the following Review section.

# REVIEW

**Objective 5.3: Given a scenario, troubleshoot hard drives and RAID arrays**  Hard drives and RAID arrays can have a variety of problems, symptoms of which include the following:

- Read/write failure
- Slow performance
- Loud clicking noise
- Failure to boot
- Drive not recognized
- OS not found
- RAID not found
- RAID stops working
- Proprietary crash screens (BSOD/pin wheel)
- S.M.A.R.T. errors

Keep in mind that many of these symptoms can have more than one possible cause.

## 5.3 QUESTIONS

1. A drive in a RAID 0 array stops working. After you replace the defective drive, how can you recover from this error?

   **A.** Rebuild the array from the working drive

   **B.** Restore the most recent backups to the array

   **C.** Use Disk Management to rebuild the array

   **D.** Replace both drives; the other drive will probably fail right away as well

2. A 1-TB USB portable drive works fine on a desktop computer running Windows, but will not work when plugged into a Windows laptop computer on battery power. What is the most likely cause?

   **A.** Drive must be reformatted to be recognized by the laptop

   **B.** Drive is too large to be used by the laptop

   **C.** Laptop USB port is not providing enough power for the drive

   **D.** Laptop and desktop computers use different versions of Windows

3. A computer fails to reboot after a Windows update. The update was provided on a nonbootable USB drive. Which of the following should you try first to get the computer to boot?

   **A.** Reinstall the update from a bootable USB drive

   **B.** Reinstall the update from an optical disc

   **C.** Scan the USB drive for viruses

   **D.** Disconnect the USB drive and restart the computer

4. A customer's computer displays a "RAID not found" error on bootup. What can you do to troubleshoot this issue?

   **A.** Free up space on the system drive to achieve 10 percent more free space

   **B.** Reenable the RAID controller in BIOS/UEFI firmware or add-on card setup

   **C.** Repair the boot sector with OS utilities

   **D.** Add more RAM to the system

5. Which of the following indicates drive failure is imminent? (Choose the best answer.)

   **A.** S.M.A.R.T.

   **B.** BSoDs/pin wheels

   **C.** Loud clicking noises

   **D.** Event Viewer alerts

## 5.3 ANSWERS

1. **B**   RAID 0, despite the name, does not include any redundancy; the data is striped across both drives to improve performance, and thus the loss of a single drive wipes out the array's contents.

2. **C**   Some laptop USB ports do not provide the full power level needed for external hard drives when running on battery power; as a workaround, some drives include a Y-cable to pull power from a second port, or the drive can be plugged into a self-powered USB hub.

3. **D**   Some systems are configured to have a USB drive as the first bootable device to enable diagnostics or operating system installations; by disconnecting the drive, the system can use the next bootable device as set in the BIOS/UEFI firmware.

4. **B**   For "RAID not found" errors, you should reenable the RAID controller in the BIOS setup or add-on card setup. You can also try reconnecting or replacing data and power cables if you encounter loose or bad cables.

5. **A**   S.M.A.R.T. hard drive prediction errors indicate drive failure is imminent.

**Objective 5.4** # Given a scenario, troubleshoot video, projector, and display issues

Desktop and laptop computer users interact with their displays as much as with their keyboards or pointing devices. Getting display problems fixed quickly is a high priority.

## Troubleshooting Display Issues

The sections in this objective cover common symptoms of video, projector, and display issues, along with the typical causes and solutions.

### VGA Mode

| Corrupted video drivers | Reinstall the latest video drivers. |
|---|---|
| System booted in Safe Mode | Restart the system in normal mode. |

### No Image on Screen

| Loose or disconnected video cable | Power down the system and the display, reconnect the video cable, and restart the display and system. |
|---|---|
| Backlight failure | Replace the backlight or inverter. |
| Incorrect signal source setting | Select the correct signal source (input) setting on the display or projector. |

### Overheat Shutdown

| Projector overheated due to clogged air vents | Turn off the projector, vacuum out air vents, replace or clean filters if present, and restart. |
|---|---|
| Projector fan failure | Repair or replace the projector. |
| GPU (video card) fan failure | Replace the fan or video card. |

### Dead Pixels

| Pixels dead due to manufacturing defects | Replace the display under manufacturer's warranty. |
|---|---|
| Pixel stuck in "off" mode | Gently massage pixel with a pencil eraser to see if it turns on. |

### Artifacts

| Overheating video card (GPU) | Check the fan on the video card and replace the fan or card if defective. |
|---|---|
| | If the card is overclocked, reset it to normal operations. |
| Overheating computer | Check the fan on the CPU heat sink and replace the fan if defective. |
| | Clean case fans and air intakes. |

### Incorrect Color Patterns

| Overheating video card (GPU) | Check the fan on the video card and replace the fan or card if defective. |
|---|---|
| | If the card is overclocked, reset it to normal operations. |

### Dim Image

| | |
|---|---|
| Backlight failure | Repair or replace the display. |
| Inverter failure | Replace the inverter or display. |
| Display brightness too low | Increase brightness. |

### Flickering Image

| | |
|---|---|
| CCFL backlight failing | Replace the backlight or display. |

### Distorted Image

| | |
|---|---|
| Corrupted video card (GPU) drivers | Reinstall the latest drivers. |

### Distorted Geometry

| | |
|---|---|
| Overheating video card (GPU) | Check the fan on the video card and replace the fan or card if defective. |
| | If the card is overclocked, reset it to normal operations. |

### Burn-in

| | |
|---|---|
| Stationary design elements on screen leave "ghosts" behind on plasma displays | Don't use plasma displays as monitors. |
| | Play a full-screen slideshow for a few hours to remove moderate burn-in. |

### Oversized Images and Icons

| | |
|---|---|
| System running in VGA (640 × 480) or SVGA (800 × 600) resolutions | Reset the display resolution to preferred values. |
| Corrupted video card drivers | Reinstall the video card drivers. |
| Display scaling set too high | Reset the scaling to 100% (Windows 10: Display menu in Settings; Windows 7: Appearance and Personalization | Display; Windows 8/8.1: set *Change the size of all items* to Smaller). |

 **EXAM TIP**   Make sure you are familiar with the symptoms, explanations, and solutions covered in this objective and listed in the following Review section.

# REVIEW

**Objective 5.4: Given a scenario, troubleshoot video, projector, and display issues** Common symptoms of video, projector, and display issues include the following:

- VGA mode
- No image on screen
- Overheat shutdown
- Dead pixels
- Artifacts
- Incorrect color patterns
- Dim image
- Flickering image
- Distorted image
- Distorted geometry
- Burn-in
- Oversized images and icons

Keep in mind that many of these symptoms have multiple potential causes—and solutions.

# 5.4 QUESTIONS

1. A user has repositioned her desktop computer and now the display no longer has an image on the screen but the display and computer power lights are on. Which of the following would you have her check first?

   **A.** Loose power cord on display

   **B.** Press FN keys to go back to primary display

   **C.** Loose video cable

   **D.** Loose network cable

2. A Windows user reports very large text and icons on his screen. In the course of asking the user what might be the issue, the user reported there was "some sort of an error message" during startup. Which of the following is the most likely cause?

   **A.** System booted up in Safe Mode.

   **B.** Video card GPU fan has failed.

   **C.** CPU fan has failed.

   **D.** System booted up in STOP mode.

3. You are playing a 3-D game at home and have been experimenting with getting better performance from your video card, and now you see incorrect color patterns on screen. After checking the fan on your video card and determining it's working properly, what should you do next?

   **A.** Enable event logging

   **B.** Disable overclocking

   **C.** Enable Safe Mode

   **D.** Enable Airplane mode

4. How would you resolve a dead pixel display issue? (Choose two.)

   **A.** Replace the fan on the video card

   **B.** Replace the display if under warranty

   **C.** Gently message the pixel with a pencil eraser until it turns on

   **D.** Clean the case fans and air intakes

5. A customer is experiencing distorted images on a display. You believe this is a result of driver corruption. Which of the following is likely to fix this?

   **A.** Install or reinstall the latest video card drivers

   **B.** Replace the GPU

   **C.** Increase the display resolution

   **D.** Replace the inverter

## 5.4 ANSWERS

1. **C** Moving the computer could cause the video cable to become loose, causing the loss of picture.

2. **A** Some versions of Windows automatically boot in Safe Mode if the system didn't boot normally on the previous boot attempt; Safe Mode uses a low screen resolution, resulting in large icons and text.

3. **B** Overclocking video cards or other components can lead to overheating, which is a common cause of incorrect colors on screen.

4. **B C** Pixels may be dead due to manufacturing defects or stuck in "off" mode. Replace the display if it is under warranty or gently message the pixel with a pencil eraser to see if it turns on.

5. **A** A common cause for distorted images is corrupted video card (GPU) drivers. You should install or reinstall the latest video card drivers.

**Objective 5.5** # Given a scenario, troubleshoot common mobile device issues while adhering to the appropriate procedures

Mobile devices such as laptops, smartphones, and tablets, are essential tools for today's on-the-go workforce. When they stop working, companies stop working. This objective helps you understand typical mobile device problems and solutions.

## Troubleshooting Mobile Devices

The sections in this objective cover common symptoms of mobile device issues, along with typical causes and solutions.

### No Display

| Device Type | Cause | Solution |
|---|---|---|
| Laptop | LCD cutoff switch stuck | Free up the switch or have the unit serviced. |
| Laptop | System set to use external display | Use the display switching key on the keyboard to change to internal display. |
| Laptop | Inverter failure | Replace the inverter (applies to LCDs with CCFL backlights only). |
| Laptop | Backlight failure | Replace the backlight or LCD panel. |
| Smartphone, tablet | Backlight failure | Repair or replace the device. |
| Laptop | Inverter or backlight failure | Use an external display until the unit can be serviced. |
| Laptop, smartphone, tablet | System in sleep mode | Tap the keyboard, mouse button, or touchscreen to wake up system. |

### Dim Display

| Device Type | Cause | Solution |
|---|---|---|
| Laptop | Inverter failing | Replace the inverter (applies to LCDs with CCFL backlights only). |
| Laptop, smartphone, tablet | Display brightness set too low | Increase the display brightness. |

## Flickering Display

| Device Type | Cause | Solution |
|---|---|---|
| Laptop | Inexpensive displays with LED backlights turn them off and on rapidly when dim modes selected | Increase the display brightness or replace the display with a higher-quality LED-backlit LCD display. |

## Sticking Keys

| Device Type | Cause | Solution |
|---|---|---|
| Laptop, Bluetooth keyboard used with tablet or smartphone | Debris or sticky material between or behind keys | Use compressed air to clean between the keys; remove the keyboard to clean spills and be sure the keyboard is dry before reinstalling it. |

## Intermittent Wireless

| Device Type | Cause | Solution |
|---|---|---|
| Laptop | Wi-Fi antenna wire loose or disconnected | Check the Wi-Fi card in the laptop base for loose or disconnected antenna wires and reconnect. |
| Laptop | Wi-Fi card not properly installed | Check the Wi-Fi card in the laptop base for proper installation. If securing screws are loose, tighten. If securing screws are missing, replace them. |
| Laptop, smartphone, tablet | Low signal strength received by Wi-Fi radio | Adjust the position of the device or USB Wi-Fi adapter to help improve signal reception. |

## Battery Not Charging

| Device Type | Cause | Solution |
|---|---|---|
| Laptop, smartphone, tablet | Bad AC adapter | Replace the AC adapter and retry. |
| Laptop, smartphone, tablet | Failed battery | Replace the battery or device. |
| Laptop, smartphone, tablet | Damaged charging cable | Replace the charging cable or charger. |

### Ghost Cursor/Pointer Drift

| Device Type | Cause | Solution |
| --- | --- | --- |
| Laptop | Misconfigured touchpad | Use Control Panel mouse or touchpad settings or equivalent. |
| Laptop | Dirty touchpad sensors | Remove the keyboard to gain access to touchpad sensors and clean them. |
| Laptop | Incorrect refresh rate | Use Control Panel or Settings dialog to reset refresh rate to default (usually 60 Hz). |
| Laptop | Unintentional touches | Adjust the sensitivity of the touchpad. |

### No Power

| Device Type | Cause | Solution |
| --- | --- | --- |
| Laptop | Faulty peripheral device connected to USB, FireWire, and Thunderbolt ports | Disconnect the device and retry. |
| Laptop, smartphone, tablet | Bad AC power outlet | Try a different AC power outlet. |
| Laptop, smartphone, tablet | Bad AC adapter | Replace the AC adapter and retry. |
| Laptop | Bad laptop power jack | Have the laptop serviced. |

### NUM LOCK Indicator Lights

| Device Type | Cause | Solution |
| --- | --- | --- |
| Laptop | NUM LOCK or CAPS LOCK key turned on accidentally | Turn off the NUM LOCK or CAPS LOCK key as desired; if the problem persists, check BIOS setup, clean the keyboard, or replace the keyboard. |

### No Wireless Connectivity

| Device Type | Cause | Solution |
| --- | --- | --- |
| Laptop, smartphone, tablet | Wi-Fi radio turned off | Turn on the Wi-Fi radio; depending on the device, the radio might be controlled by an external switch or by OS settings. |
| Laptop, smartphone, tablet | Airplane mode turned on | Turn off airplane mode. |
| Laptop | Wi-Fi antennas not connected to Wi-Fi radio | If the laptop was recently serviced, check the Wi-Fi antenna connection to the Wi-Fi radio card. |

## No Bluetooth Connectivity

| Device Type | Cause | Solution |
|---|---|---|
| Laptop, smartphone, tablet | Bluetooth turned off | Turn on Bluetooth; pair the devices as needed. |
| Laptop, smartphone, tablet | Airplane mode turned on | Turn off airplane mode. |

## Cannot Display to External Monitor

| Device Type | Cause | Solution |
|---|---|---|
| Laptop | Display not plugged into laptop | Plug display into laptop. |
| Laptop | Laptop not configured to use external display | Use the appropriate laptop key or menu selection to use the external display or mirror internal/external displays as desired. |

## Touchscreen Non-Responsive

| Device Type | Cause | Solution |
|---|---|---|
| Laptop, smartphone, tablet | Dirty touchscreen | Clean the surface of the touchscreen with a microfiber cloth; do not use liquid directly on the touchscreen. |
| Laptop, smartphone, tablet | Touchscreen digitizer disconnected | Have the unit serviced. |
| Smartphone, tablet | System frozen | Use soft reset to restart the device. |

## Apps Not Loading

| Device Type | Cause | Solution |
|---|---|---|
| Laptop, smartphone, tablet | Too many apps running in memory | Close apps that are not in use. |
| Smartphone, tablet | Apps don't load after closing apps not in use | Perform a soft reset, then retry the app. |
| Laptop | App not compatible with device | Compare app requirements (OS, RAM, disk space, etc.) with laptop software/hardware specifications; uninstall app and replace if the app is not compatible. |

## Slow Performance

| Device Type | Cause | Solution |
|---|---|---|
| Laptop, smartphone, tablet | Too many apps running in memory | Close apps that are not in use. |

| Device Type | Cause | Solution |
|---|---|---|
| Laptop, smartphone, tablet | Not enough RAM | Install more RAM if possible. |
| Laptop, smartphone, tablet | Not enough free space on primary drive or internal storage | Free up space on the primary drive or internal storage. |
| Laptop, smartphone, tablet | Overheating device | Shut down device, allow it to cool down; restart the device. |

### Unable to Decrypt E-mail

| Device Type | Cause | Solution |
|---|---|---|
| Laptop, smartphone, tablet | E-mail app doesn't have correct software or decryption key | Install the correct software or decryption key to open e-mail. |

### Extremely Short Battery Life

| Device Type | Cause | Solution |
|---|---|---|
| Laptop, smartphone, tablet | Unneeded apps are running | Close or hibernate unneeded apps. |
| Laptop, smartphone, tablet | Battery not charged properly | Follow the manufacturer's suggestions for discharging and recharging the battery. |

### Overheating

| Device Type | Cause | Solution |
|---|---|---|
| Smartphone | Case or pocket causing overheating | Remove the device from pocket; take off the case if the problem persists. |
| Laptop, tablet | Vents on underside/rear of device are blocked | Place the device on a hard surface and clean dirty or clogged vents. |
| Laptop, tablet | Fans inside device have failed or are running too slowly | Check fan operation and have the device serviced if the fans have failed; clean the fans if they are running too slowly. |
| Laptop, smartphone, tablet | Battery defect | Remove the battery if possible; have the unit serviced or replaced. |
| Laptop | Thermal transfer material between CPU and heat sink has failed | Have the device serviced. |

## Frozen System

| Device Type | Cause | Solution |
|---|---|---|
| Laptop, smartphone, tablet | System software or app problem | Perform soft reset and retry app. |
| Laptop, smartphone, tablet | Incompatible or corrupt app | Remove and reinstall most recent app installed. |

## No Sound from Speakers

| Device Type | Cause | Solution |
|---|---|---|
| Laptop, smartphone, tablet | Speaker or headset wire not fully plugged into speaker jack | Turn off the unit, reconnect the speaker, and retry. |
| Laptop, smartphone, tablet | Bluetooth speaker or headset not working | Make sure the speaker or headset is turned on; pair with the mobile device if necessary. |
| Laptop | Incorrect audio output chosen | Open the audio mixer and choose the correct output device. |

## GPS Not Functioning

| Device Type | Cause | Solution |
|---|---|---|
| Smartphone, tablet | GPS turned off in device setting | Turn on GPS. |
| Smartphone, tablet | GPS turned off for an individual app | Change the app settings to use GPS. |
| Smartphone, tablet | Airplane mode enabled | Turn off airplane mode. |

## Swollen Battery

| Device Type | Cause | Solution |
|---|---|---|
| Laptop, smartphone, tablet | Overcharged battery | (Prevention) Disconnect the charger after the battery is fully charged. (Solution) Replace the battery and recycle the old battery safely. |
| Laptop | Charger output voltage too high | Check the charger voltage output; replace the charger if out of spec. |
| Laptop, smartphone, tablet | Defective battery | Replace the battery and recycle the old battery safely. |

 **EXAM TIP** Be sure to know the symptoms, explanations, and solutions covered in this objective and listed in the following Review section.

# Disassembling Processes for Proper Reassembly

Disassembling a portable device is usually pretty easy, if it was designed to be upgraded or serviced by casual users; reassembly is usually harder. Here's the four-step process you should know for the exam:.

1. *Document and label every cable and screw location.* There are few standards, and you can easily strip or jam a screw if you use the wrong one.

2. *Organize any parts you extract from the laptop.* Put a big white piece of construction paper on your work surface, lay each extracted piece out in logical fashion, and clearly mark every connection. You can also document your workspace with a webcam or smartphone camera in case something goes missing. Using magnetic trays can also be helpful to keep small screws from being lost.

3. *Refer to the manufacturer's resources.* Because few standards exist for portables, even two models from the same manufacturer can have both obvious and insidiously small differences.

4. *Use the appropriate hand tools.* You can do more harm than good without proper tools, such as pry bars, tiny-headed Phillips and Torx drivers, and so on. An entry-level laptop-tech toolkit, such as the one advertised by iFixit.com in Figure 5.5-1, is a good start.

**FIGURE 5.5-1**   Bare-minimum laptop repair tools

**EXAM TIP** Be sure to know the four steps for laptop repair: document and label cable and screw locations; organize parts; refer to manufacturer resources; and use appropriate hand tools.

# REVIEW

**Objective 5.5: Given a scenario, troubleshoot common mobile device issues while adhering to the appropriate procedures** Symptoms of common mobile device issues include the following:

- No display
- Dim display
- Flickering display
- Sticking keys
- Intermittent wireless
- Battery not charging
- Ghost cursor/pointer drift
- No power
- NUM LOCK indicator lights
- No wireless connectivity
- No Bluetooth connectivity
- Cannot display to external monitor
- Touchscreen non-responsive
- Apps not loading
- Slow performance
- Unable to decrypt e-mail
- Extremely short battery life
- Overheating
- Frozen system
- No sound from speakers
- GPS not functioning
- Swollen battery

Keep in mind that many of these have multiple potential causes—and solutions.

For many of these problems, you will need to perform some level of disassembly and reassembly. Follow these guidelines:

- Document and label cable and screw locations
- Organize parts

- Refer to manufacturer resources
- Use appropriate hand tools

## 5.5 QUESTIONS

1. A user is running a laptop computer in an office that also has an HDTV with a cable connected to the laptop. After dropping the laptop, the user can no longer see anything on the built-in display. What should you try first until you can get the laptop repaired or replaced?

   **A.** Connect the laptop to the network and try to use remote access

   **B.** Have the user press the appropriate key(s) to switch to the external display

   **C.** Tell the user to take a day off

   **D.** Find an identical laptop and clone the original laptop's Windows installation to it

2. A laptop's wireless connection is intermittent after it comes back from a screen replacement. Which of the following is the most likely cause of the problem?

   **A.** Antenna wires are not connected properly

   **B.** Keyboard is stuck

   **C.** Wi-Fi button on edge of laptop was turned off during repair

   **D.** Computer virus introduced in repair shop

3. A laptop with a user-upgradeable hard drive and RAM needs more RAM. Which of the following tools are you least likely to need to make this change?

   **A.** Anti-static mat

   **B.** Phillips-head drivers

   **C.** Torx drivers

   **D.** Pry bars

4. Which of the following is *not* part of the CompTIA four-step mobile device disassembly and reassembly process?

   **A.** Document and label cable and screw locations

   **B.** Organize parts

   **C.** Refer to general YouTube videos to figure out the disassembly/reassembly process

   **D.** Use appropriate hand tools

5. A customer is experiencing extremely short battery life on a mobile device. What recommendations should you make? (Choose two.)

   **A.** Close or hibernate unneeded apps

   **B.** Perform a hard reset on the mobile device

   **C.** Follow manufacture's suggestions for discharging and recharging the battery

   **D.** Free up space on the primary drive or internal storage

## 5.5 ANSWERS

1. **B** Most laptops can switch between the built-in display and the video port by using a Function key (sometimes requiring the user to also press the FN key).

2. **A** Laptops with built-in Wi-Fi use antennas mounted around the edges of the display panel and connected to the Wi-Fi card inside the body of the laptop; if these cables are not properly connected during reassembly, Wi-Fi connections will be poor or will completely fail.

3. **D** Pry bars are used for servicing smartphones, tablets, or other devices that are not designed for user upgrades.

4. **C** The CompTIA four-step process for mobile device disassembly and reassembly includes documenting and labeling cable and screw locations, organizing parts, referring to manufacturer resources, and using appropriate hand tools.

5. **A C** For extremely short battery life, close or hibernate unneeded apps and be sure to follow the manufacturer's suggestions for discharging and recharging the battery.

**Objective 5.6** # Given a scenario, troubleshoot printers

Although organizations have sought the so-called "paperless office" for decades, printing is still a vital part of computer use in offices of any size as well as home uses. Printer technologies vary, so it's essential to know both the symptoms and the printer type producing the symptoms to solve printing problems.

## Troubleshooting Printing Issues

The sections in this objective cover symptoms of common printing issues by printer type, along with typical causes and solutions.

### Streaks

| | |
|---|---|
| Impact: Horizontal white bars—dirty or damaged printhead | Clean the printhead. If the problem persists, replace the printhead. |
| Impact: Characters clipped off—head gap incorrect | Set the head gap to the recommended value for the media type. |
| Laser: Vertical white lines—toner clogged | Remove and shake the toner cartridge. |
| Inkjet: Colored bands through output | Enter the correct paper type setting in printer preferences. If the problem persists, clean the printhead. |

### Faded Prints

| | |
|---|---|
| Impact: Printer ribbon worn out or dried out | If the printer ribbon has extra an ink reservoir, activate it. Otherwise, replace the ribbon. |
| Impact: Fresh ribbon produces faint output | Adjust the head gap. If the head gap is OK, replace the printhead. |
| Impact: One side of printout is faded | The platen is out of adjustment; have the printer serviced. |
| Laser: Toner running low | Remove and shake or replace the toner cartridge. |

### Ghost Images

| | |
|---|---|
| Laser: Dark ghosting caused by damaged imaging drum | Replace the toner cartridge if the drum is built in, or replace the drum. |
| Laser: Dark ghosting caused by toner starvation | Prevention methods:<br><br>• Lower the resolution (print at 300 dpi instead of 600 dpi).<br>• Change the image/pattern completely.<br>• Avoid 50 percent grayscale and "dot-on/dot-off patterns."<br>• Change the layout so that grayscale patterns do not follow black areas.<br>• Make dark patterns lighter and light patterns darker.<br>• Print in landscape orientation.<br>• Adjust the print density and RET settings.<br>• Insert a blank page in the print job before the page with ghosting.<br>• Check the temperature and humidity in the printer location and adjust them if out of the recommended range. |
| Laser: Light ghosting caused by worn or damaged cleaning blade | Replace the toner cartridge if the cleaning blade is built in, or replace the blade. |

### Toner Not Fused to the Paper

| | |
|---|---|
| Laser: Fuser assembly dirty | Clean the fuser assembly with 90 percent or better denatured alcohol. |
| Laser: Fuser failure | Replace fuser, preferably with a maintenance kit that has other replaceable components. |

### Creased Paper

| | |
|---|---|
| Horizontal misalignment: Misaligned paper feed tray | Adjust the paper feed tray for the correct paper size. |
| Vertical misalignment: Paper picked up multiple sheets | Remove the paper, fan it, and make sure the appropriate paper is being used, and reinstall it. |

### Paper Not Feeding

| | |
|---|---|
| Wrong paper type for printer or paper tray | Use the recommended paper type; use a rear-mounted paper feed if possible. |
| Paper too damp | Replace the paper with dry paper. |
| Paper tray not loaded or inserted properly | Remove the paper tray, check the paper level and position, and reinsert the tray correctly. |

### Paper Jam

| | |
|---|---|
| Incorrect media type or printer setting | Check recommended media types for the printer and any special settings needed. |
| Paper jams when using duplex function because duplexer not installed correctly or not working | Check duplexer installation and paper separators; repair any broken parts. Print one side at a time as a workaround. |
| Worn separator pad | Replace the separator pad or use a scouring pad to add texture to the pad by removing the shiny surface. |

### No Connectivity

| | |
|---|---|
| Bad or loose printer or network cable | Check the printer or network cable and reconnect it if it loose or replace it if it is bad. |
| Printer set for incorrect data port | Check the printer input setting and set it to the correct source. |
| Bad network configuration | Check the wired or wireless network settings. |
| Printer taken offline | Put the printer back online at the printer or with the spooler app. |

### Garbled Characters on Paper

| | |
|---|---|
| Bad or loose printer cable | Check the printer cable and reconnect it if it's loose or replace it if it's bad. |
| Corrupt printer driver | Reinstall the printer driver. |

### Vertical Lines on Page

| | |
|---|---|
| Laser: Spots at regular intervals caused by a damaged drum or a dirty roller | Check the printer documentation to determine which markings are caused by which cause. Clean the printer rollers with 90 percent or higher denatured alcohol, replace the toner cartridge or drum, or service the printer as needed. |
| Laser: Random black spots and streaks caused by a worn or damaged cleaning blade | Replace the cleaning blade or toner, depending on where the cleaning blade is located. |
| Dirty rollers | Clean all rollers with 90 percent or higher denatured alcohol. |

### Backed-up Print Queue

| | |
|---|---|
| Printer has a number of print jobs waiting that are not progressing | Open the Print Spooler service and check the status of print jobs (see Figure 5.6-1); release print jobs that are waiting, delete print jobs that have errors, and resubmit. Bypass the print spooler and print directly to the printer (see Figure 5.6-2). Restart the Print Spooler service. |

### Low Memory Errors

| | |
|---|---|
| Laser: Too many fonts or graphics on page causes printer to run very slowly or print part of page after displaying an error message or error lights (user might need to eject page manually) | Upgrade printer memory if possible. Workarounds: Reduce printer resolution, simplify the page (fewer fonts, fewer or smaller graphics), and turn off RET or other print enhancements. |

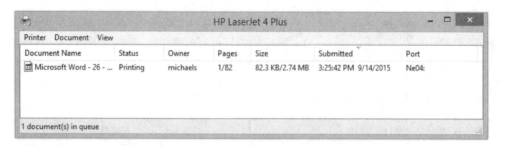

**FIGURE 5.6-1**   Print spooler's print queue

**FIGURE 5.6-2**   Print spool settings

## Access Denied

| Shared printer cannot be used | Verify user account has access to the printer (check Security tab in Printer properties). Some accounts might have access only during specified times. |
| --- | --- |

## Printer Will Not Print

| Incorrect paper in tray compared to printer setting in OS | Change the paper setting on the printer to match the OS paper setting. |
| --- | --- |
| Print queue backed up | See the "Backed-up Print Queue" symptom in this objective. |
| Printer set for incorrect data port | Check the printer input setting and set it to the correct source. |

### Color Prints in Wrong Print Color

| | |
|---|---|
| Printer may need calibration or realignment | Rerun automatic alignment or calibration. |
| Corrupt driver | Reinstall the latest printer driver. |
| Defective printer | Have the printer serviced or replace the printer. |
| Inkjet: printheads clogged | Run the printhead test and cleaning utility provided by the vendor. |

### Unable to Install Printer

| | |
|---|---|
| User lacks permission | Provide administrator or superuser credentials to install the printer. |
| Printer not detected | Local: check the printer cable and power to the printer. |
| | Network: check the network settings on the printer. |

### Printing Blank Pages

| | |
|---|---|
| Laser: Out of toner | Replace the toner cartridge or add toner as appropriate. |
| Laser: Not out of toner | Print the diagnostic page using self-test. If the page is blank, check the drum to see if the page image is visible there. If it is, the printer's transfer corona or power supply has failed. Replace or service as needed. |
| Blank page appears between print jobs | This is a normal spooler setting for networked printers, intended for privacy and security. Adjust the setting in the print spooler if not desired (after checking that corporate security policy doesn't require the blank page). |

### No Image on Printer Display

| | |
|---|---|
| Display frozen | Turn off the printer, unplug it for a few minutes, and turn it back on. If the display is still frozen, have the unit serviced. |

**Multiple Failed Jobs in Logs**

| Print jobs are not emerging from printer although the printer is online. | Examine print spooler logs for error details. Use the logs to determine possible causes for failures and solutions. |
|---|---|

**EXAM TIP**   Make sure you are familiar with the symptoms, causes, and solutions covered in this objective and listed in the following Review section. Note that to solve many of these problems, you need to correctly identify the printer type in use first.

# REVIEW

**Objective 5.6: Given a scenario, troubleshoot printers**   Common symptoms of problems with printers of all types include the following:

- Streaks
- Faded prints
- Ghost images
- Toner not fused to the paper
- Creased paper
- Paper not feeding
- Paper jam
- No connectivity
- Garbled characters on paper
- Vertical lines on page
- Backed-up print queue
- Low memory errors
- Access denied
- Printer will not print
- Color prints in wrong print color
- Unable to install printer
- Error codes
- Printing blank pages
- No image on printer display
- Multiple failed jobs in logs

## 5.6 QUESTIONS

1. A user is reporting that her print jobs are displaying dark ghost patterns. From this description, which of the following types of printers is in use?

   **A.** Virtual

   **B.** Laser

   **C.** Impact

   **D.** Inkjet

2. A user reports that when he prints envelopes, the envelopes are creased and misaligned. Which of the following steps is most likely to help?

   **A.** Change the printer to single-sided printing

   **B.** Adjust the tractor feed

   **C.** Adjust the paper guides

   **D.** Use RET in the printer preferences

3. A user reports paper jams at the rear of the printer when he tries to print double-sided pages. Which of the following components is most likely the cause?

   **A.** Rear paper feed

   **B.** Ink cartridges

   **C.** Duplexer

   **D.** RET

4. A laser printer is printing blank pages. Which of the following solutions should you apply to fix this problem? (Choose two.)

   **A.** Replace the printhead

   **B.** Bypass the print spooler and print directly to the printer

   **C.** Replace toner cartridge

   **D.** Attempt to print a diagnostic page using self-test

5. A user's printer has a number of print jobs backed up and waiting in the print queue. Which of the following measures should you take to get the print jobs printing again?

   **A.** Verify the user account has access to the printer

   **B.** Restart the Print Spooler service

   **C.** Calibrate the printer

   **D.** Reinstall the latest printer driver

## 5.6 ANSWERS

1. **B**  Dark ghost patterns only occur on malfunctioning laser printers.

2. **C**  Paper guides must be set correctly for the paper or media width installed; if they are set too wide, the paper/media will not feed straight.

3. **C**  The duplexer at the rear of the printer is used to flip the paper for printing on the reverse side.

4. **C D**  If a laser printer prints blank pages, you should replace the toner cartridge or add toner as appropriate. If it is not out of toner, print a diagnostic page using self-test. If the page is blank, check the drum to see if the page image is visible there. If it is, the printer's transfer corona or power supply has failed and should be replaced or serviced as needed.

5. **B**  Of the listed answers for addressing a backed-up print queue, restarting the Print Spooler service is the best option.

**Objective 5.7**  # Given a scenario, troubleshoot common wired and wireless network problems

Today's offices, home offices, and home entertainment systems rely on networking, so the odds of running into network problems are high.

## Troubleshooting Network Issues

Make the odds of solving network problems in your favor by learning the symptoms and solutions covered in the following sections.

### Limited Connectivity

| | |
|---|---|
| APIPA IP address only allows local LAN connections; DHCP server connection not available | Check the status of the DHCP server (often a function of the router or AP on the network). Restart the router or AP. Open a command prompt in Windows and use ipconfig/release and ipconfig/renew to obtain a new IP address, one from the DHCP server. Restart the device if necessary to get the DHCP IP address. |

### Unavailable Resources: Internet

| User or group not granted Internet access | Check the domain controller user/group configuration and change it if necessary. |
|---|---|
| APIPA IP addresses don't allow Internet connections | See the preceding "Limited Connectivity" symptom in this objective. |
| Router failure | Shut down and restart the router. Update the firmware. Release and review the IP address at each device. Replace the router if it fails again. |
| Broadband modem failure | Shut down and restart the modem, followed by the router. Update the modem firmware. Replace the modem if it fails again. |

### Unavailable Resources: Local Resources

| Unable to access local resource via network shortcut | Access the local resource through normal means, not as a network device. |
|---|---|
| Shares, printers: Incorrect user name/password for desired resource | Use the correct user name/password if the account is already set up on the device. If not, set up accounts for users on shared device. If the resource is shared via a homegroup, all users must use the homegroup password provided by the creator of the homegroup. For a domain resource, check with the network manager for a list of accessible shares. |
| Shares, printers: Incorrect network, homegroup, or domain settings | Check the workgroup, homegroup, or domain name setting in System properties and change it as needed. |
| E-mail: Incorrect user name/password for e-mail | Check with the e-mail provider to verify you are using the correct user name/password. Change the settings as needed. |
| E-mail: Incorrect configuration for e-mail provider | Check with the e-mail provider to verify you are using correct e-mail settings (server type [SMTP, POP, IMAP], port addresses, encryption, etc.). Change the settings as needed (see Figure 5.7-1). |

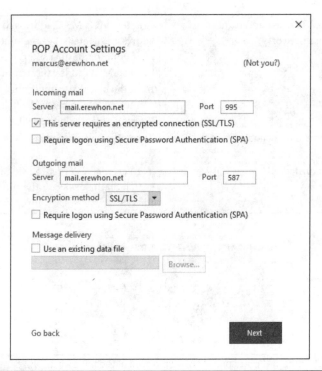

**FIGURE 5.7-1**   Changing POP account settings for an (imaginary) e-mail account

## No Connectivity

| | |
|---|---|
| Wired: Network cable might be loose or defective | Check the NIC or switch signal lights to see if they indicate physical connectivity (see Figure 5.7-2). If no lights are displayed, swap the patch cable. Use a known-good network port. |
| Wired: NIC might not be enabled or driver installed | Check Device Manager (see Figure 5.7-3) or the hardware listing for the NIC. If the NIC is not found, install the driver. If the NIC is disabled, enable it. |
| Wired: NIC might not be sending or receiving signals | Test the NIC with a loopback plug. Disconnect the network cable and insert the loopback plug. If the NIC is bad, replace it. |
| Wired: Cable might not be connected or might be defective | Check that the network cable is plugged into a wall socket; if it is, check the other end of the cable for a working connection. If it is connected at both ends, use a cable scanner to test the cable. Replace the cable if it's bad. |

| Wired: NIC MAC address doesn't have permission to use network | Add the NIC's MAC address to permitted addresses (whitelist) in the router configuration. If the router uses a blacklist of blocked MAC addresses, remove the address from the blacklist if applicable. If the device is connected to a managed switch, check MAC filtering settings on the switch. |
| --- | --- |
| Wireless: Airplane mode enabled (see Figure 5.7-4) | Turn off airplane mode. |
| Wireless: Wi-Fi turned off | Turn on the Wi-Fi radio using the physical switch on the device or the software switch in the OS. |

**FIGURE 5.7-2** Ethernet port connections on a typical Gigabit switch. The center port does not have a working connection (no signal lights).

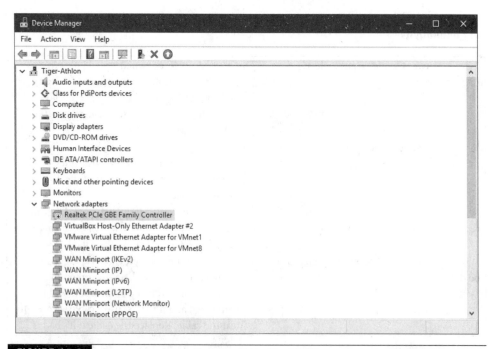

**FIGURE 5.7-3** Device Manager with nonworking Gigabit Ethernet adapter highlighted

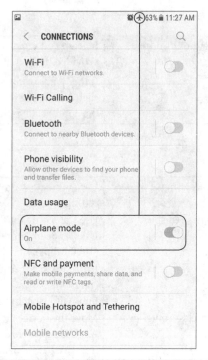

**FIGURE 5.7-4**   Airplane mode enabled on an Android smart phone prevents cellular, Wi-Fi, and Bluetooth connections.

## APIPA/Link Local Address

| | |
|---|---|
| The device has an IP address in the range 169.254.0.1–169.254.255.254 | DHCP server (provides IP addresses automatically) is not working. Check the device providing DHCP service (usually a router) and restart the DHCP server. Release and renew the IP address on each device with an APIPA address or restart them. |

## Intermittent Connectivity

| | |
|---|---|
| Bad or loose network cable | Reconnect the cable if it's loose or replace it if it's bad. |
| Bad NIC | Power down the system, remove the NIC, and reseat it in the slot (if it's a card). Replace the NIC if it's bad. Install the appropriate driver. |
| Marginal Wi-Fi signal | Change the position of the Wi-Fi antenna (move the laptop) to get closer to a wireless router or AP. Change to a less-crowded channel on the router or AP. |

### IP Conflict

| | |
|---|---|
| Two or more devices have same IP address | Release and renew the IP addresses if they are provided by DHCP.<br><br>If the IP addresses are set manually, change each conflicting device to its own IP address in the appropriate range. |

### Slow Transfer Speeds

| | |
|---|---|
| Wired: Manual speed/duplex settings can slow down network. | Use automatic negotiation of speed/duplex settings |
| Wired: marginal wiring for desired speed | Use Cat 5 only for Fast Ethernet (100 Mbps). Use Cat 5e or 6 for Gigabit Ethernet (1000 Mbps). |
| Wired: using a hub instead of a switch | Hubs broadcast to all connected devices and subdivide bandwidth. Replace any remaining hubs with switches. |
| Wireless: long distance to wireless router or AP | Move the device closer to the router or AP. Use repeaters or mesh networking to improve performance. |

### Low RF Signal

| | |
|---|---|
| Too much network congestion on selected channel (particularly with 2.4 GHz) | Choose the least-crowded channel of 1, 6, or 11. Use a Wi-Fi analyzer app on an Android or iOS device to find the network channels in use. |
| Long distance to wireless router or AP | Move the device closer to the router or AP. |
| Poor position of wireless antennas on device | Change the position of antennas (laptop display if built-in Wi-Fi). If USB Wi-Fi or Bluetooth, connect the adapter to a USB extension cable and move it as needed to improve signal. |
| More than one available SSID | Select the SSID with the strongest signal. Sign off the weaker network signal and sign into the stronger signal if permitted. |

### SSID Not Found

| | |
|---|---|
| Hidden SSID | Enter the correct name of the SSID and provide the encryption key. |
| Airplane mode enabled | Turn off airplane mode. If Wi-Fi is still turned off, turn it on again manually. |

**EXAM TIP**   Be sure to know the symptoms, causes, and solutions for the network issues covered in this objective and listed in the Review section.

# REVIEW

**Objective 5.7: Given a scenario, troubleshoot common wired and wireless network problems**   The following wired and wireless network problems can have multiple causes and, sometimes, more than one solution to try:

- Limited connectivity
- Unavailable resources:
  - Internet
  - Local resources: shares, printers, e-mail
- No connectivity
- APIPA/link local address
- Intermittent connectivity
- IP conflict
- Slow transfer speeds
- Low RF signal
- SSID not found

## 5.7 QUESTIONS

1. Enabling airplane mode does which of the following?
   - **A.** Enables wireless connections while flying
   - **B.** Disables wireless connections while flying
   - **C.** Disables wireless connections at any time
   - **D.** Turns off Wi-Fi but enables Bluetooth and cellular

2. A user reports that her system has an IP address of 169.254.0.230. She also reports that she can't connect to the Internet. Which of the following is the most likely issue?
   - **A.** DHCP server is not working.
   - **B.** DHCP server gave her system an invalid MAC address.
   - **C.** MAC address is blacklisted.
   - **D.** Broadband Internet connection has failed.

3. A home office user reports that he's lost his Internet connection due to a power failure. After the power comes back on, what is the best sequence to follow to bring up his network and get back online?

    A. Power up router, then broadband modem, then wireless printer, then computer

    B. Power up broadband modem, then computer, then router, then wireless printer

    C. Power up wireless printer, then router, then modem, then computer

    D. Power up modem, then router, then wireless printer, then computer

4. You are asked to upgrade the wiring in a SOHO network from 100 Mbps to 1000 Mbps. Which category of twisted pair Ethernet cable can you use for this project? (Choose two.)

    A. Cat 6

    B. Cat 5e

    C. Cat 5

    D. Cat 3

5. Which non-overlapping 2.4-GHz wireless channel should you set your wireless router to use in order to avoid congestion and low RF signal problems?

    A. 1, 6, or 11

    B. 2, 4, or 6

    C. 3, 5, or 7

    D. 8, 9, or 10

## 5.7 ANSWERS

1. **C** Airplane mode is not just for flying; when enabled, it turns off cellular, Bluetooth, and Wi-Fi features.

2. **A** IP addresses starting with 169. are assigned automatically when an IP address cannot be received from a DHCP server.

3. **D** By turning on devices in this order, the Internet connection is restored first and each subsequent device can use it via the LAN connection from the router.

4. **A B** Use Cat 5e or Cat 6 twisted pair cable for Gigabit Ethernet (1000 Mbps).

5. **A** To avoid low RF signal issues, choose the least-crowded non-overlapping channel of 1, 6, or 11.

# CompTIA A+
# Exam 220-1002

**Domain 1.0** Operating Systems

**Domain 2.0** Security

**Domain 3.0** Software Troubleshooting

**Domain 4.0** Operational Procedures

# Operating Systems

DOMAIN 1.0

## Domain Objectives

- **1.1** Compare and contrast common operating system types and their purposes
- **1.2** Compare and contrast features of Microsoft Windows versions
- **1.3** Summarize general OS installation considerations and upgrade methods
- **1.4** Given a scenario, use appropriate Microsoft command line tools
- **1.5** Given a scenario, use Microsoft operating system features and tools
- **1.6** Given a scenario, use Microsoft Windows Control Panel utilities
- **1.7** Summarize application installation and configuration concepts
- **1.8** Given a scenario, configure Microsoft Windows networking on a client/desktop
- **1.9** Given a scenario, use features and tools of the Mac OS and Linux client/desktop operating systems

### Objective 1.1 Compare and contrast common operating system types and their purposes

## 32-bit vs. 64-bit

32-bit operating systems can be used with either 32-bit or 64-bit processors. 32-bit processors, once common, are now used primarily by very low-performance tablets. Consequently, most computers and mobile devices use 64-bit operating systems.

### RAM Limitations

32-bit operating systems can address up to 4 GB of RAM, while 64-bit operating systems can address much higher amounts. For example, Windows 10 Home 64-bit edition can address up to 128 GB, while Windows 10 Pro, Education, and Enterprise 64-bit editions can address up to 2 TB. The maximum RAM size in a given system is also affected by the chipset and motherboard design. Current motherboards made for 64-bit processors support total RAM configurations much smaller than the maximum limits of these operating systems.

 **EXAM TIP**    Be sure to know differences between 32-bit and 64-bit operating systems (RAM sizes, software compatibility).

### Software Compatibility

64-bit operating systems are designed to run both 64-bit and 32-bit software, while 32-bit operating systems can use only 32-bit software.

## Workstation Operating Systems

Workstation operating systems are used on desktop and laptop computers. These include Microsoft Windows, Apple macOS, and Linux.

### Microsoft Windows

Current versions of Microsoft Windows are 7, 8/8.1, and 10. These are available in 64-bit and 32-bit versions. All versions support touch screen, keyboard, touchpad, and mouse interfacing.

**Cross-Reference**

To learn more about the differences between the Windows versions, see Objective 1.2, later in this domain.

# Apple Macintosh OS

The macOS interface (shown in Figure 1.1-1) has a *Desktop*, as you'd expect, though you'll access frequently used, running, and pinned applications through the *Dock*. The interface features *Spaces*—essentially multiple Desktops—that can have different backgrounds and programs. You can open *Spotlight* (COMMAND-SPACEBAR) to search for files and applications, and Apple keyboards use the F3 key (see Figure 1.1-2) to open *Mission Control* (see Figure 1.1-3), where you switch between desktops, applications, windows, and more. Launchpad displays apps in a grid, and Apple keyboards use the F4 key (refer to Figure 1.1-2) to open it. Apple macOS supports mouse, keyboard, and touchpad interfacing, but not touch screen interfacing.

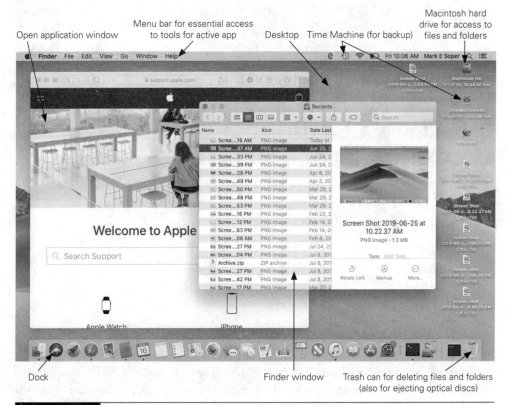

**FIGURE 1.1-1**    macOS Sierra desktop

**FIGURE 1.1-2**   Mission Control (F3) and Launchpad (F4) buttons on a keyboard

**FIGURE 1.1-3**   Mission Control showing two open apps on Desktop 1, another app in its own window, and three desktops

**EXAM TIP**   Be sure to know the major features of the macOS interface.

## Linux

There are many different *distributions (distros)* of Linux that offer a variety of graphical user interfaces, called *desktop environments (DEs)*, as well as the traditional Terminal command-line interface. The popular Ubuntu Linux 18.04 LTS distro (see Figure 1.1-4) comes with the GNOME 3 DE; frequently used utilities and applications are locked on the Launcher on the left side of the screen. Click Activities to search for new apps. The top-right corner of the desktop provides access to network, volume, and Shutdown options.

Apps locked
to Launcher
Essential utilities

Trash can for deleting
files and folders

Open application

Access to network, audio
levels, and shutdown options

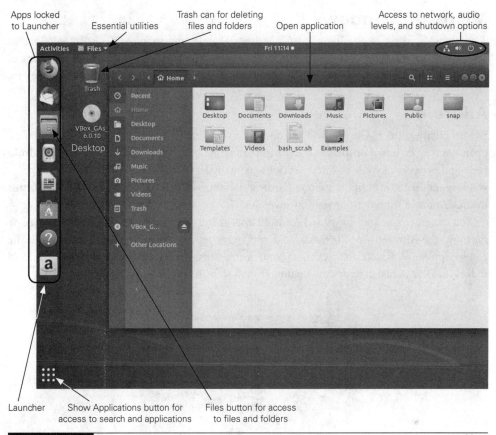

Launcher
Show Applications button for
access to search and applications
Files button for access
to files and folders

**FIGURE 1.1-4** Ubuntu Linux 18.04 LTS

---

> **EXAM TIP** Other popular Linux distros include Fedora, Red Hat Enterprise, CentOS, Debian, Arch Linux, and Raspbian, but the CompTIA A+ 220-1002 exam does not cover differences between distros; it does emphasize common Linux features and basic commands.

# Cell Phone/Tablet Operating Systems

Mobile operating systems (that is, OSs for cell phones and tablets) are substantially different than those made for workstations. These operating systems are optimized for touch input, long battery life, and small form factors.

## Microsoft Windows

Although Microsoft is phasing out its Windows Mobile smartphone OS, 32-bit versions of Windows 10 are used on low-cost tablets from a variety of manufacturers. 64-bit versions of Windows 10 are used on more powerful tablets such as the Microsoft Surface and Surface Pro.

## Android

For simplicity, think of Google Android and iOS as opposites. Android (see Figure 1.1-5) is an open-source OS, based on yet another open platform, Linux. Google writes the core Android code and occasionally releases new versions (named after a dessert or candy), at which point vendors modify it to support unique hardware features or customize the look and feel; this means "Android" differs from vendor to vendor.

You can purchase and download Android apps through various app stores, such as *Google Play* and the Amazon Appstore. Android app stores tend to be fairly open compared to the Apple App Store, which imposes tight controls on third-party app developers, and Android makes it easier to install apps downloaded from a website.

**FIGURE 1.1-5**   Android 7 (Nougat) on a Samsung smartphone

**EXAM TIP** Be sure to know the differences between Android (open source, often modified by hardware vendors) and iOS (closed source, controlled by Apple and used on Apple-branded devices only) for the exam.

# iOS

Apple's closed-source mobile operating system, iOS (see Figure 1.1-6), runs on the iPhone, iPad, and iPod Touch. Apple tightly controls the development of the hardware, OS, developer tools, and app deployment platform. Apple's strict development policies and controls for third-party developers contribute to its high level of security. iOS apps are almost exclusively purchased, installed, and updated through Apple's *App Store*.

**FIGURE 1.1-6** iOS 12.4 on an iPad Mini

## Chrome OS

Google Chrome OS is designed for low-cost laptops called Chromebooks that will be connected to the Internet at all times. Chrome OS is browser-based, so it's an easy OS to use if you've used a web browser on any device.

Most recent Chromebooks are also compatible with Android, enabling access to Google Play and its vast array of Android apps. A Chromebook that is Android compatible can also be used offline. Some Chromebooks also feature touch screens. For these reasons, it makes sense for CompTIA to classify Google Chrome OS as a mobile operating system.

# Vendor-specific Limitations

Some mobile device and operating system vendors place limitations on what can be done with their operating systems. Google exercises little control over how its open-source Android OS is used and who can modify it. Because Microsoft develops its closed-source Windows 10 OS and then licenses it to device makers, it knows the OS won't be modified and it controls which devices get a license. Apple doesn't even license its closed-source iOS, electing instead to retain control and tailor-fit the software to its own devices.

Companies building devices that use an open-source OS such as Android don't have to share the OS developer's philosophy. If the OS's license allows it, each of the device makers can modify the OS before installing it on their own closed-source devices—and never release those modifications. The modifications might only enable special hardware to work, but they can also install apps you don't want and can't remove, cause third-party apps to malfunction, or collect information.

 **NOTE**   Devices running "Android" with significant closed-source modifications can be so vastly different from familiar Android devices that you have to throw the rulebook out to manage them. We describe what is normal for Android devices, but none of these are rules.

## End-of-Life

The term "end-of-life" refers to an operating system or device that is no longer marketed or supported by the vendor. For example:

- Windows XP
- Windows Vista
- MacBook, Air, Pro (some 2011 models and all earlier models)

Hardware that is "end-of-life" might not even be upgradeable. For example, Windows 10 Mobile devices will not be supported after December 10, 2019, and no upgrades to a newer version of Windows will be available.

**NOTE**   Apple uses the term "vintage" to refer to products that have not been manufactured for more than five years and less than seven years ago, and uses the term "obsolete" for products that have not been manufactured for at least seven years. Most vintage products cannot be serviced by Apple (with a few geographic exceptions) and no obsolete products can be serviced by Apple.

## Update Limitations

Each vendor has its own specific update limitations:

- Android devices receive updates and upgrades from the hardware vendor. However, many hardware vendors don't offer updates and upgrades.
- iOS and macOS devices that are less than five years old generally can be upgraded to the latest versions, although in some cases, it might be necessary to upgrade to an older version first.
- Most devices running non-Mobile versions of Windows 7 or later can be updated or upgraded. However, some processors and chipsets don't support the latest releases of Windows 10.

# Compatibility Concerns Between Operating Systems

With very few exceptions, applications made for one operating system generally cannot be used on other operating systems. To make this possible, consider the following options:

- 32-bit versions of an app can usually be run in a 64-bit version of the supported OS, but not vice versa.
- Virtualization enables macOS or Linux to run Windows apps, and vice versa. Virtualization also enables Windows to run Android apps.
- Emulators enable Windows to run iOS apps.
- The Wine compatibility layer enables Linux, macOS, and BSD (a family of UNIX-like OSs) to run some Windows apps.

**ADDITIONAL RESOURCES**   Learn more about Wine at www.winehq.com.

# REVIEW

**Objective 1.1: Compare and contrast common operating system types and their purposes**

- 32-bit processors are found primarily in very low-performance tablets, but 32-bit software can be used by 64-bit processors.
- 32-bit processors are limited to 4 GB of addressable RAM.
- The memory limits of 64-bit processors are much higher than motherboard and RAM designs allow.
- Workstation operating systems are used on laptops and desktops. These include Microsoft Windows, macOS, and Linux. All three use GUIs as their primary user interface.
- Cell phone/tablet operating systems (also called mobile operating systems) include Android, iOS, and Google Chrome OS. Microsoft Windows Mobile is being phased out.
- Operating systems, applications, and devices reach end-of-life status when they are no longer supported by the vendor. Update options vary by vendor and device.
- To enable apps from one operating system to run on another operating system, virtualization, emulators, and compatibility layers can be used.

## 1.1 QUESTIONS

1. Your application needs 8 GB of RAM to work properly. Which of the following must be true as well about this application?

   **A.** It requires a 32-bit processor, but can use a 64-bit processor.

   **B.** It cannot run on Linux.

   **C.** It must be run on Windows.

   **D.** It requires a 64-bit processor.

2. A user has questions about using a Samsung smartphone after the company switched from Droid smartphones. Which is the most helpful response?

   **A.** They both use Android, so they should work the same way.

   **B.** Let's set up the Samsung so it looks like the Droid.

   **C.** Vendors can modify Android for their devices, so let me help you with what's new and different.

   **D.** Ask your boss to get you an iPhone.

3. A user has a pre-2011 MacBook that has a defective hard disk drive and wants to get it replaced. Which of the following options is the best response?

   **A.** Tell the user that the MacBook cannot be repaired.

   **B.** Contact Apple's vintage parts center for a replacement.

   **C.** Ask the user to call Apple and claim the MacBook has a lifetime warranty.

   **D.** Check third-party sources for compatible drives.

4. A user has asked you for a list of popular Linux distributions. Which of the following does not belong in this list?

   A. Fedora

   B. Ubuntu

   C. macOS

   D. Arch Linux

5. Your company's executive committee has asked you to modify iOS for company-provided smartphones. Which of the following accurately describes why this cannot take place?

   A. Apple is a closed-source software vendor.

   B. Apple is an open-source software vendor.

   C. iOS has no source code.

   D. iOS is short for "incomprehensible operating system" and therefore can't be modified.

## 1.1 ANSWERS

1. **D**   Only a 64-bit processor supports RAM amounts above 4 GB.

2. **C**   Android is an open-source operating system, so devices from different vendors running Android typically vary a great deal.

3. **D**   Because this device is too old for Apple to service, third-party parts sources are the only way to find a replacement drive.

4. **C**   Although macOS uses many command-line (Terminal) apps that are also supplied with Linux, it is actually based on UNIX.

5. **A**   Apple does not provide its source code to any other vendors.

# Objective 1.2   Compare and contrast features of Microsoft Windows versions

All current Windows versions share some structural features; we'll look at these features first, and then at specific versions.

> **EXAM TIP**   Be sure to know the differences between the Windows 7, 8/8.1, and 10 interfaces for the exam.

- Windows boots to the welcome (or login) screen, where you select a user account and provide credentials to log in.

- After logging in on most Windows systems, you'll be taken to the primary interface for traditional desktop and laptop computers—the Windows Desktop (see Figure 1.2-1). User accounts enable each user to personalize the interface with their own desktop icons and wallpapers, sound effects, color schemes, language and accessibility options, and so on.

 **NOTE** Windows 7, 8.1, and 10 all start at the Desktop, but Windows 8 starts instead at the mobile-friendly Start screen. Since Windows 8 is the lone exception, we'll cover its Start screen in the "Windows 8" section.

- The *taskbar*, at the bottom of the Desktop by default, has a *Start button* for quick access to the *Start menu*, favorite programs, running programs, and the *notification area* or *system tray*.

Desktop with a few icons running on it · · · · · · · Application running in the foreground

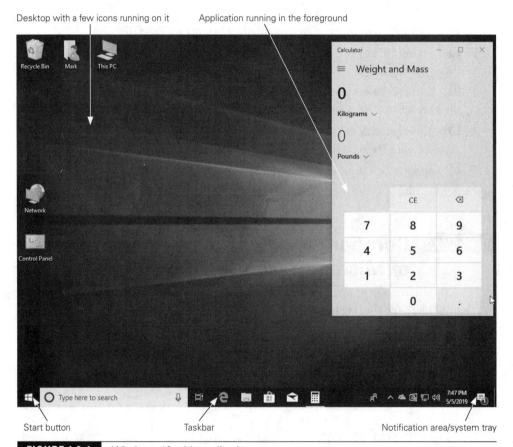

Start button        Taskbar        Notification area/system tray

**FIGURE 1.2-1**    Windows 10 with application open

**FIGURE 1.2-2**   Context menu for File Explorer (Windows 10)

- The Start menu provides compact access to most of your system's programs, settings, documents, and utilities, and enables you to search for other elements.
- The notification area or system tray contains icons for notifications, common settings, longer-running background programs, and a clock.
- You interact with an icon, button, or other interface element by moving the cursor to the element with your pointing device and clicking it. One left-click selects items on the Desktop itself (open them with a double-click) and items on the taskbar; a right-click opens a *context menu* (see Figure 1.2-2) with options that depend on what you clicked.
- Programs can be pinned to the taskbar. *Pinned programs* enable you to launch favorite programs with a left-click.
- Folders open in *Windows Explorer* (Windows 7), later renamed *File Explorer*, from which you can browse up or down the directory tree; copy, paste, move, create, and delete files and folders; view and modify file or folder properties and attributes; and access some other important *views*. File icons differ by extension and the program associated with that extension; Windows hides known extensions by default.
- File Explorer's *This PC* view (corresponds to the Windows 7 Computer view) shows accessible storage volumes (see Figure 1.2-3) and devices.

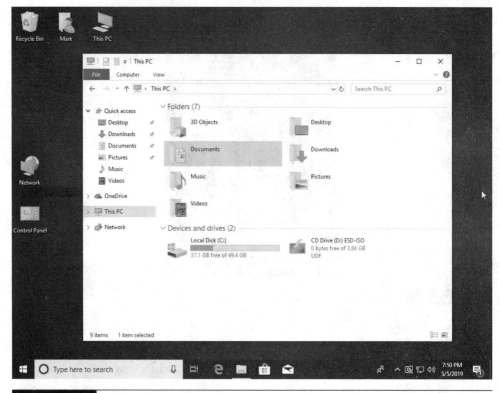

**FIGURE 1.2-3**   This PC in Windows 10

**FIGURE 1.2-3**   This PC in Windows 10

> **NOTE**   Microsoft changes UI options and features with *every* version of Windows and enables users to further customize the UI—having to hunt for specific files and folders is normal.
>
> Windows Explorer/File Explorer are available from the Taskbar in Windows 7 and later. The default locations/folders are consistent between Windows 7 and Windows 8: Favorites, Libraries, HomeGroup (if in a home network), Computer, and Network. But Microsoft changed the lineup in Windows 8.1 and again in Windows 10, compressing Libraries and Computer into This PC, adding OneDrive, dropping HomeGroup in later versions of Windows 10, and more.

- The *Network* view shows devices connected to your network as well as available remote networked resources.
- Windows can assign *drive letters* to storage drives and volumes (the primary drive is traditionally assigned "C:"), giving each its own directory tree with the drive letter as

the *root directory*. Windows creates a few special folders at the root (C:\) of the drive you install it on: *Windows*, *Program Files*, and *Users*. As you might expect, the OS itself is installed in the Windows directory.

**EXAM TIP**  The Windows directory is also called *SystemRoot*, which you may see written as a variable (%SystemRoot%) at the start of a longer path, such as %SystemRoot%\Fonts.

- 32-bit versions of Windows have a single C:\Program Files folder where many applications install by default. 64-bit versions have a second folder, in order to store 32-bit and 64-bit programs separately. 64-bit programs use C:\Program Files, whereas 32-bit programs use C:\Program Files (x86).

**EXAM TIP**  Be sure to know the differences between Program Files and Program Files (x86) on 64-bit Windows versions for the exam.

- The Users folder contains a folder for each user's files and programs as well as settings specific to the account. Windows creates a number of folders for *personal documents* here; you'll need to know a few of them: Desktop, Documents, Downloads, Music, Pictures, and Videos. The path to your user folders when viewed in Command Prompt mode is the same in any version of Windows. For example, C:\Users\Mark. However, the way this information is shown in Windows Explorer/File Explorer varies with the version of Windows in use. For example, in Windows 7, the path in Windows Explorer is Computer | Local Disk | Users | Mark, but in Windows 8 and later, the path in File Explorer is This PC | Local Disk (C:) | Users | Mark.

**EXAM TIP**  Know the personal directory paths (for example, C:\Users\Mark\Desktop).

- Windows sends a deleted file to the *Recycle Bin* folder until you empty the bin or restore the item (by right-clicking it and selecting Restore). Eventually, Windows will delete the file to make room for newly deleted files. If you need a deleted file that isn't in the Recycle Bin, a third-party recovery utility might work.
- Windows uses a portion of your hard drive space as *virtual memory*, a *slow* extension of system RAM that enables the size of loaded programs to exceed physical RAM capacity at the expense of performance.

**EXAM TIP** The terms virtual memory, swap file, and page file all refer to the same thing: space on the hard drive reserved as temporary storage for running programs.

# Windows 7

Windows 7 is the last version of Windows to have only a classic Desktop (although a few Windows 7 systems include touch screens).

- Open windows have an interface *transparency* feature called *Aero* or *Aero Glass*.
- Click the *Start button* to get access to applications, tools, files, and folders (see Figure 1.2-4).

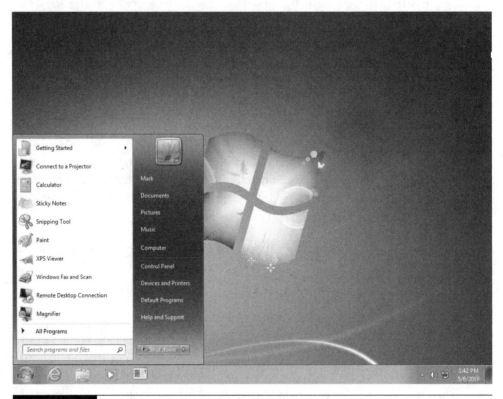

**FIGURE 1.2-4** Windows 7 Desktop with Start menu

# Windows 8

Windows 8 still has a classic Desktop, accessed by pressing the WINDOWS LOGO KEY, though it lacks a visible Start button (see Figure 1.2-5). Windows 8 also supports *side-by-side apps*, which streamline arranging windows to compare or reference documents.

Windows 8 and 8.1 have some hidden interface components that activate when you move the cursor to certain locations:

- The bottom-left corner activates the Start button while on the Start screen in Windows 8.
- The top- and bottom-right corners reveal the *Charms bar* (see Figure 1.2-6), a location for tools called *charms*: the combined Search charm searches both the computer and the Internet; the Share charm can share photos, e-mail messages, and more; the Settings charm opens Settings.

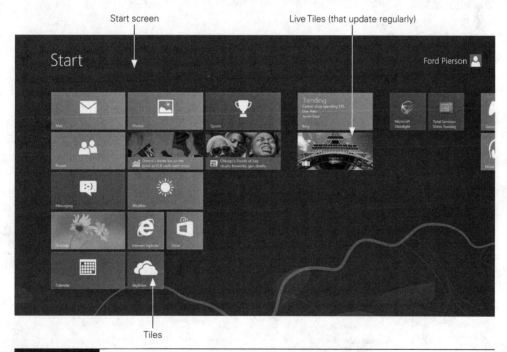

**FIGURE 1.2-5**   Windows 8 Start screen

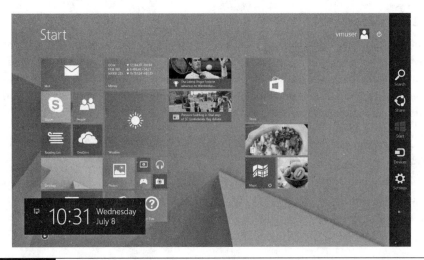

**FIGURE 1.2-6**   Charms accessed by moving the cursor to the upper- or lower-right corner

# Windows 8.1

With the Windows 8.1 update (see Figure 1.2-7), Microsoft brought back traditional features that it dropped in Windows 8, such as the Start button, easy access to a Close button for apps, and booting directly to the desktop.

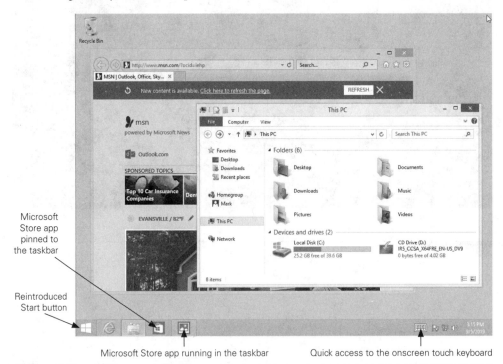

Microsoft Store app pinned to the taskbar

Reintroduced Start button

Microsoft Store app running in the taskbar

Quick access to the onscreen touch keyboard

**FIGURE 1.2-7**   Windows 8.1

# Windows 10

Windows 10 (shown in Figure 1.2-8) blends the Windows 7 interface with some progressive features from the Modern UI used in Windows 8/8.1. In particular, Microsoft refined the Start menu in Desktop mode (see Figure 1.2-9), removed the much unloved Charms bar, incorporated essential tools such as Search and its companion tool Cortana into the taskbar, further streamlined side-by-side apps, and added *Task View* to create *multiple desktops* for grouping applications by task.

Windows 10 can also run in Tablet mode, which resembles the Windows 8/8.1 user interface. Figure 1.2-10 shows Windows 10 running in Tablet mode. Windows 10 can be configured to open in Tablet mode on touch screen systems, or users can switch between Desktop and Tablet mode at any time.

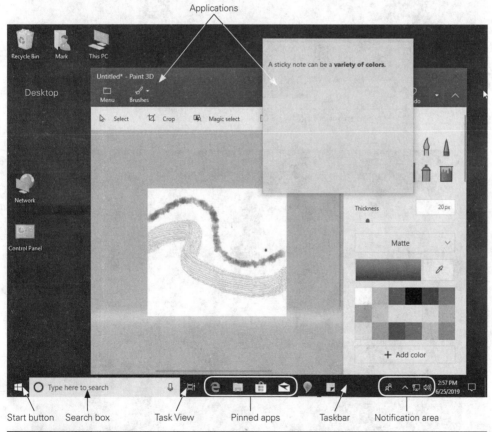

**FIGURE 1.2-8**   Windows 10 with a few applications open

**FIGURE 1.2-9** Start menu in Windows 10 Desktop mode

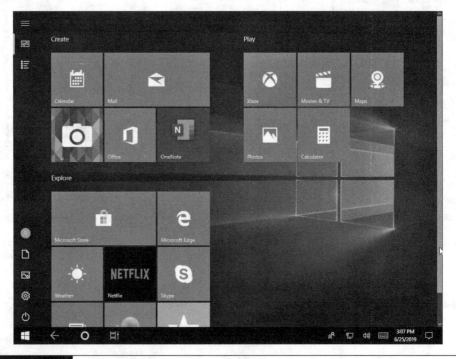

**FIGURE 1.2-10** Windows 10 Tablet mode

# Windows 7 Editions

Windows 7 was released in six editions: Starter, Home Basic, Home Premium, Professional, Ultimate, Enterprise. Table 1.2-1 provides a quick reference to some of the major differences between these editions. For the exam, concentrate on the business-oriented features that are not present in home editions.

**TABLE 1.2-1**   Select Windows 7 Features by Edition

| Edition<br>Feature | Starter | Home Basic | Home Premium | Professional | Ultimate | Enterprise |
|---|---|---|---|---|---|---|
| CPU support | x86 | x86, x64 | x86, x64 | x86, x64 | x86, x64 | x86, x64 |
| Aero | No | Limited | Yes | Yes | Yes | Yes |
| Max RAM size | 2 GB | 8 GB* | 16 GB* | 192 GB* | 192 GB* | 192 GB* |
| Windows Media Center | No | No | Yes | Yes | Yes | Yes |
| Domain networking | No | No | No | Yes | Yes | Yes |
| EFS | No | No | No | Yes | Yes | Yes |
| Backup to network | No | No | No | Yes | Yes | Yes |
| Remote desktop host | No | No | No | Yes | Yes | Yes |
| BitLocker disk encryption | No | No | No | No | Yes | Yes |
| UNIX app support | No | No | No | No | No | Yes |

* x64 (64-bit) editions; all x86 (32-bit) editions limited to 4 GB

**NOTE**   CompTIA uses the term "32-bit" for x86 (x86 is a reference to the 8086 CPU) and "64-bit" for x64. Using x86 and x64 makes Tables 1.2-1, 1.2-2, and 1.2-3 a little less cluttered.

# Windows 8/8.1 Editions

Windows 8/8.1 were released in four editions: RT, Standard, Professional, and Enterprise. Table 1.2-2 provides a quick reference to some of the major differences between these editions.

**TABLE 1.2-2**   Select Windows 8/8.1 Features by Edition

| Edition  Feature | RT | Standard | Professional | Enterprise |
|---|---|---|---|---|
| CPU support | ARM | x86, x64 | x86, x64 | x86, x64 |
| Max RAM size | 4 GB | 128 GB* | 512 GB* | 512 GB* |
| Domain networking | No | No | Yes | Yes |
| EFS | No | No | Yes | Yes |
| Boot from VHD images | No | No | Yes | Yes |
| Remote desktop host | No | No | Yes | Yes |
| BitLocker disk encryption | No | No | Yes | Yes |

* x64 (64-bit) editions; all x86 (32-bit) editions limited to 4-GB

# Windows 10 Editions

Windows 10 was released in several major editions: Standard, Pro, Enterprise, and Education. Table 1.2-3 provides a quick reference to some of the major differences between these editions.

**TABLE 1.2-3**   Select Windows 10 Features by Edition

| Edition  Feature | Standard | Pro | Enterprise | Education |
|---|---|---|---|---|
| CPU support | x86, x64 | x86, x64 | x86, x64 | x86, x64 |
| Max RAM size | 128 GB* | 2 TB* | 2 TB* | 2 TB* |
| Parental controls | Yes | No | No | No |
| Domain networking | No | Yes | Yes | Yes |
| Hyper-V virtualization | No | Yes | Yes | Yes |
| EFS | No | Yes | Yes | Yes |
| Group Policy Management | No | Yes | Yes | Yes |
| Remote desktop host | No | Yes | Yes | Yes |
| BitLocker disk encryption | No | Yes | Yes | Yes |

* x64 (64-bit) editions; all x86 (32-bit) editions limited to 4-GB

**EXAM TIP**   To see the Windows version and edition in the System applet:
Windows 7: Right-click Computer | Properties
Windows 8/8.1/10: Right-click This PC | Properties
In all versions, you can use WINDOWS KEY-PAUSE or access this information through Control Panel.

# Windows Corporate vs. Personal Needs

The various Windows 7, 8/8.1, and 10 editions have common core features but differ in their support for the following features intended to meet corporate needs:

- Domain access
- BitLocker
- BranchCache
- Encrypting File System (EFS)

CompTIA A+ 220-1002 objective 1.2 also lists one personal feature that is included in some home-oriented editions of Windows: Media Center (styled as Media center in objective 1.2).

Table 1.2-4 provides a quick reference to the different versions and editions of Windows that support these features.

## Domain Access

Workgroup networks, in which each computer can share folders or printers with other computers, are suitable when no more than 30 computers are connected. However, for larger networks, or networks that need more control and security, a Windows domain is preferable. A domain is a network that has centralized user accounts, passwords, and resources such as printers and folders.

A *domain controller* stores a set of *domain accounts*. A user logging on to any computer on the domain may use their one domain account to log on to the entire network. Domain access refers to the ability to join a network that uses Windows Server as a domain controller.

## BitLocker

BitLocker is Microsoft's full-disk encryption feature for internal drives. BitLocker To Go encrypts removable-media drives such as USB flash memory (thumb) drives. Editions that support BitLocker also support BitLocker To Go. BitLocker is supported on business-oriented editions of Windows because business computers often store proprietary and confidential information that needs to be encrypted.

**TABLE 1.2-4**  Personal and Corporate Windows Features by Version and Edition

| Technology | Windows 7 Support | Windows 8/8.1 Support | Windows 10 Support |
|---|---|---|---|
| Domain access | Professional<br>Ultimate<br>Enterprise | Pro<br>Enterprise | Pro<br>Enterprise<br>Education |
| BitLocker | Professional<br>Ultimate<br>Enterprise | Pro<br>Enterprise | Pro<br>Enterprise<br>Education |
| BranchCache* | Professional**<br>Ultimate<br>Enterprise | Pro**<br>Enterprise | Pro**<br>Enterprise<br>Education |
| EFS | Professional<br>Ultimate<br>Enterprise | Pro<br>Enterprise | Pro<br>Enterprise<br>Education |
| Media Center | Home Premium<br>Professional<br>Ultimate | Pro*** | N/A |

\* Enable using Group Policy settings or netsh command.
\** Works for BITS transfers only. HTTP and SMB transfers not supported with these editions.
\*** User must also purchase Windows Media Center Pack for Windows 8 Pro or Windows 8.1 Pro.

BitLocker's full-disk encryption normally requires a computer with a Trusted Platform Module (TPM). To use BitLocker on systems without a TPM, you must change Group Policy settings.

## Media Center

Windows Media Center is designed with an HDTV-friendly user interface for playback and recording of cable and broadcast TV, DVD and Blu-ray movie viewing (with the appropriate codecs), and CD music listening. Support for Media Center was removed as standard in Windows 8 and 8.1 and cannot be added to Windows 10.

## BranchCache

BranchCache is a Microsoft bandwidth optimization technology that fetches content from central servers and caches it on local servers or workstations to reduce the load on wide area networks.

# EFS (Encrypting File System)

Encrypting File System is a file and folder encryption technology that prevents encrypted files and folders from being used by anyone who does not have the original user's encryption credentials, even if the other user is an administrator. Just as with BitLocker, EFS is found in business-oriented versions of Windows because of business needs for the protection of confidential and proprietary information.

# Desktop Styles/User Interface

Windows 7, 8, 8.1, and 10 differ in a variety of ways, including desktop styles and user interfaces. Table 1.2-5 provides a comparison of these differences, some of which will be discussed in Objectives 1.5 and 1.6.

**TABLE 1.2-5** Windows Desktop Style/User Interface Comparison

| Feature | Windows 7 | Windows 8 | Windows 8.1 | Windows 10 |
|---|---|---|---|---|
| Lock screen | No | Yes | Yes | Yes |
| Start button | Yes | No | Yes | Yes |
| Boots to | Start button | Full-screen menu | Desktop | Start button (standard mode) or full-screen menu (Tablet mode) |
| Start menu | Opens when Start button is clicked | Opens full-screen when Windows starts | Opens full-screen when Start button on desktop is clicked | Opens when Start button is clicked (standard mode) or full-screen when Windows starts (Tablet mode) |
| Live tiles on Start menu | No | Yes | Yes | Yes |
| Control Panel | Yes | Yes | Yes | Yes |
| Settings menu | No | PC Settings | PC Settings | Settings |
| Access to Settings menu | N/A | Charms | Charms | Start menu |
| File Management | Windows Explorer | File Explorer | File Explorer | File Explorer |

# REVIEW

### Objective 1.2: Compare and contrast features of Microsoft Windows versions

- Windows 7 includes only a Desktop mode, regardless of the device type using it.
- Windows 8 uses a touch-oriented Start screen that occupies the entire Desktop, regardless of the device type using it.
- Windows 8.1 improves on Windows 8 by providing a Start button and the ability to boot directly to the Desktop.
- Windows 10 supports both Desktop and Tablet modes, with ability to detect which interface is in use for automatic switching between modes if desired.
- Most Windows editions support 32-bit (x86) and 64-bit (x64) processors. Business-oriented editions support BranchCache, EFS file and folder encryption, BitLocker full disk encryption, and domain networking, along with larger amounts of RAM than home-oriented versions. Home-oriented versions of Windows 7 include Media Center, which is an option in Window 8 and 8.1, but is not available for Windows 10.
- Windows versions also differ in menu display, how settings are managed, and how files are managed.

## 1.2 QUESTIONS

1. A Windows 10 Standard user wants to use BitLocker but cannot find it on the list of programs. The user should do which of the following?
   A. Upgrade from Windows 10 to Windows Server
   B. Open the Optional Features menu in Settings and add it
   C. Upgrade from Windows 10 Standard to Windows 10 Pro
   D. Downgrade to Windows 7

2. A Windows 8.1 user upgrades to Windows 10 and finds that the Start screen has been replaced by a Start menu that occupies only a portion of the screen. The user prefers the Start screen. What should the user do?
   A. Open Settings and configure Tablet mode
   B. Undo the upgrade and return to Windows 8.1
   C. Disconnect the keyboard to force the system to use the Start screen
   D. Upgrade to Windows 10 Pro

3. A Windows 10 user has heard about Cortana. Which feature of the Windows 10 Desktop provides access to Cortana?
   A. Task Manager
   B. Search
   C. Notifications
   D. Settings

4. In most cases, upgrading to a newer version of Windows will add features. However, sometimes newer versions of Windows drop features found in older versions. If a user upgrades from Windows 7 to Windows 10, which of the following features will no longer be available? (Choose two.)

   **A.** Media Center

   **B.** BitLocker

   **C.** Workgroup

   **D.** HomeGroup

5. A Windows administrator is looking for evidence of illegal files on a coworker's computer. She is unable to open some files in the user's Pictures folder. Which Windows feature did the coworker use to block access?

   **A.** BitLocker

   **B.** Hyper-V

   **C.** EFS

   **D.** Family Safety

## 1.2 ANSWERS

1. **C**   Business-oriented versions of Windows have BitLocker, but home versions do not.

2. **A**   Tablet mode enables Windows 10 to use the Windows 8.1 Start screen with either a touch screen or mouse interface.

3. **B**   Cortana uses the Search window in current versions of Windows 10.

4. **A D**   Media Center was removed as a standard feature in Windows 8/8.1, but could be added as an option. It was removed entirely in Windows 10. HomeGroup was available in early releases of Windows 10, but it was removed from Windows 10 in 2018.

5. **C**   Encrypting File System (EFS) prevents access by other users to encrypted files unless the other users are given a copy of the encryption certificate.

---

**Objective 1.3**   # Summarize general OS installation considerations and upgrade methods

One of the most common tasks for a computer technician is performing an operating system installation or upgrade. There are many ways to perform these, and this objective discusses how they work and helps you determine when you use a particular method.

# Boot Methods

To install or upgrade Windows, macOS, or Linux, a variety of boot methods are available. The following sections cover the boot methods you need to understand for the CompTIA A+ 220-1002 exam. (The installation choices are described a bit later in the "Type of Installations" section.)

## Optical Disc (CD-ROM, DVD)

To perform a clean install from an optical disc, follow this procedure:

1. Make sure the target computer is configured to boot from the optical disc.
2. With the bootable OS disc inserted, restart the computer.
3. Follow the onscreen prompts to boot from the disc and start the installation process.

To perform an upgrade install from an optical disc, follow this procedure:

1. Open the OS optical disc in the file navigation app of the current operating system.
2. Open the installation app on the disc and follow the prompts to perform the upgrade.

 **EXAM TIP**   Be familiar with the processes of booting from an optical disc, external drives, flash drives, PXE (network), internal hard drives, and hard drive partitions.

## External Drive/Flash Drive (USB/eSATA)

To boot from a USB or eSATA drive:

1. Start up the computer and configure the BIOS or UEFI firmware to boot from the desired drive.
2. With the bootable OS drive connected or inserted, restart the computer.
3. Follow the onscreen prompts to boot from the drive and start the installation process.

To perform an upgrade install from a USB flash drive, follow this procedure:

1. Open the OS USB flash drive in the file navigation app of the current operating system.
2. Open the installation app on the USB flash drive and follow the prompts to perform the upgrade.

# Network Boot (PXE)

Network boot is supported by Windows, Linux, and macOS. Windows and Linux refer to this feature as PXE, and macOS (and OS X) uses the term NetBoot and NetInstall.

The *Preboot Execution Environment (PXE)* can boot from a network location using protocols such as IP, TFTP (Trivial FTP), DHCP, and DNS. If your NIC supports PXE, you can enable it in the system setup utility from whichever screen has other options for your NIC (see Figure 1.3-1). While you're there, move network locations to the top of the boot sequence.

**EXAM TIP**   PXE (Preboot Execution Environment) refers to network boot.

On a Windows or Linux system, when you reboot, somewhere along the familiar boot process you'll see the instruction "Press F12 for network boot." (It's almost always F12.) If the system can find and connect to a server, you'll be asked to press F12 again to continue booting from the network (see Figure 1.3-2), at which point you'll see a selection screen if there are multiple images, or be taken directly to the Windows installer if there's just one.

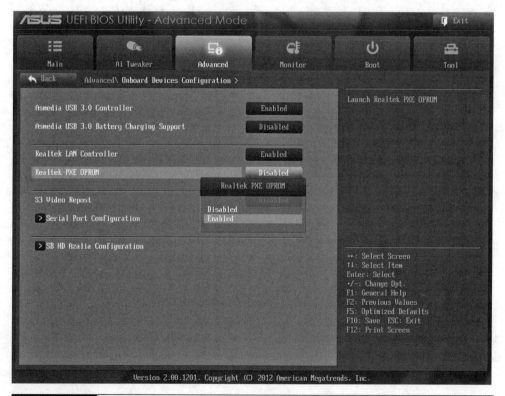

**FIGURE 1.3-1**   Selecting the PXE boot ROM option for the built-in Ethernet port on Mark's computer

```
Network boot from Intel E1000
Copyright (C) 2003-2008  VMware, Inc.
Copyright (C) 1997-2000  Intel Corporation

CLIENT MAC ADDR: 00 0C 29 D7 9B 6B  GUID: 564DCC2E-04EA-ACE1-381B-5148E8D79B6B
CLIENT IP: 10.12.14.51  MASK: 255.0.0.0  DHCP IP: 10.12.14.10
GATEWAY IP: 10.12.14.1

Downloaded WDSNBP...

Press F12 for network service boot
_
```

**FIGURE 1.3-2**   Network boot

 **ADDITIONAL RESOURCES**   To learn more about configuring PXE with Windows 10, go to docs.microsoft.com and search for "Configure a PXE Server to Load Windows PE." To learn more about using PXE in Linux, go to linuxconfig.org and search for "Network booting with Linux – PXE."

macOS supports NetBoot on Mac and iMac computers, produced in 2017 or earlier. Users can start NetBoot by holding down the N key at startup to go directly to the default NetBoot image or can use the Startup Disk preference pane to select the desired image.

 **NOTE**   Current models with the Apple T2 security chip don't support NetBoot, and macOS Server no longer includes UI tools for configuring NetBoot or NetInstall. As an alternative, Apple recommends using the open-source NetSUS or BSDPy tools.

 **ADDITIONAL RESOURCES**   To learn how to create a NetBoot, NetInstall, or NetRestore volume, and to learn which computers support booting from network volumes, see https://support.apple.com/en-us/HT202770. For a change list for macOS Server 5.7.1 and alternatives to no-longer-provided functions, see https://support.apple.com/en-gb/HT208312.

# Internal Fixed Disk (HDD/SSD)

The normal installation process for an operating system uses an internal fixed disk as its target. At the end of the process, you can boot from the internal fixed disk into the OS.

If you want to install the operating system onto the hard disk without using an additional drive, you can prepare the drive with installation files after you move it to a different computer. When you reinstall the drive into the original computer and set the computer to boot from the hard drive, the drive will start the installation process.

**ADDITIONAL RESOURCES**   For details, go to www.instructables.com and search for "Install Windows 8 Directly from Hard Drive." A similar procedure works for all current Windows versions. To learn how to install Ubuntu Linux directly from the hard drive, go to www.howtogeek.com and search for "How to Boot Linux ISO Images Directly from Your Hard Drive."

# Internal Hard Drive (Partition)

If you want to install the operating system onto the hard disk from a regular partition on the same hard disk, you can move the drive to a different computer, create an installation partition, assign it a drive letter, and copy the installation files to it. Copy the boot sector files to the new drive letter. When you reinstall the drive into the original computer and set the computer to boot from the hard drive, the drive will start the installation process. You can remove the drive letter and its contents after the installation process is complete.

To install Windows from a hidden recovery partition provided by some computer vendors, see the system documentation.

**ADDITIONAL RESOURCES**   For details for Windows, go to www .bleepingcomputer.com and search for "Clean Install Windows Directly from the Hard Disk Drive."

# Type of Installations

Operating systems can be installed using a variety of different methods. You need to understand these methods so that you can choose the right one for a particular situation (or exam question scenario).

## Creating Installation Media

Most of the time, you will need to create some type of installation media before performing an operating system installation or upgrade. Although this is not specifically an A+ exam topic, knowing how to create different media types is valuable as you practice installation and upgrading for the exams and in your day-to-day work as a technician.

## Creating a Bootable Optical Disc

To create a bootable optical disc:

1. Download an ISO image of the OS.
2. Burn the image to an optical disc large enough for the image (usually a DVD) using an ISO image burner app.

## Creating a Bootable USB Flash Drive or Hard Drive

To create a bootable USB flash drive or hard disk drive:

1. Download an ISO image of the operating system.
2. Transfer the image to a USB flash drive large enough for the image (an 8-GB drive is large enough for Windows; 4 GB is large enough for most Linux distros) using an ISO to USB imaging app. All files on the drive will be overwritten!

## Creating a Bootable eSATA Hard Drive

To create a bootable eSATA hard drive:

1. Disconnect all internal SATA drives.
2. Make sure the eSATA drive is connected and turned on.
3. Boot the system from an optical drive or USB flash drive that contains the OS.
4. Install the OS to the eSATA drive.
5. Turn off the system and reconnect all internal SATA drives.

# Unattended Installation

An unattended installation, also known as a scripted installation, uses a script file to provide answers to the prompts displayed during the installation process. Windows uses the Windows Assessment and Deployment Kit (Windows 8/8.1/10) or Window Automated Installation Kit (WAIK) to create scripts.

 **EXAM TIP**    Unattended (scripted) installations are very important for mass system installs.

With current versions of Ubuntu Linux and similar Debian-based distributions, you can use the unattended-upgrades package to perform an automated update. You can also use scripts to create an unattended installation of Ubuntu 16.04 LTS or later. macOS can use vendor-provided or third-party tools.

**ADDITIONAL RESOURCES**   To learn more about automated updates, go to https://linuxize.com and search for "How to set up automatic updates." To learn more about scripts for an unattended installation, go to https://github.com and search for "Linux unattended installation." To learn how to perform a silent installation or upgrade of macOS 10.13.4 (High Sierra update) or later, go to www.techrepublic.com and search for "How to silently upgrade or install macOS 10.13.4."

## In-place Upgrade

An in-place upgrade, also known as an upgrade installation, replaces the existing operating system with a new installation of either a newer version or the same version. On Windows systems, an in-place upgrade enables users of Windows 7 or 8/8.1 to upgrade to Windows 10 without losing data or needing to reinstall their apps.

To start an in-place upgrade with Windows, start the computer normally, insert/connect the installation media (ISO image file, DVD, or USB flash drive), and start the installation program. Follow the prompts until the process is complete.

**EXAM TIP**   In-place upgrades are also used for repair installations.

## Clean Install

A clean installation usually starts with an empty hard drive, but since the process partitions and formats the hard drive, it can also erase and install over an existing installation. A clean install won't carry over problems from the old OS, but you'll have to reconfigure the system and reinstall software. Begin by booting from installation media.

**EXAM TIP**   A clean install wipes out all existing operating system files, apps, and user data.

## Repair Installation

An in-place upgrade can also be used to repair an existing installation, again without losing data or reinstalling apps. To start a repair install with Windows, set the computer to boot from the installation media, insert/connect the same version of installation media (ISO image file, DVD, or USB flash drive) that was used to install Windows, start the computer, boot from the installation media, and start the installation program. When prompted, select *Repair your computer* (see Figure 1.3-3). Follow the prompts until the installation process is complete.

**FIGURE 1.3-3**    Repairing Windows from the installation media

**EXAM TIP**    Repair installations in Windows start the same way as in-place upgrades, but the user must select the Repair option when prompted. A repair installation is called Reinstallation in Linux.

Linux refers to a repair installation as Reinstallation. This option is available on some distributions, such as Ubuntu, when you start the computer with the same version of Linux on a Live CD or USB drive. The installation program detects the existing Linux install and asks you if you want to reinstall (keeping files and programs), or erase and install.

With macOS, start macOS Recovery (turn on the computer and immediately press COMMAND-R). From the macOS Utilities menu, select Reinstall macOS. You must have a working Internet connection to use Reinstall macOS.

## Multiboot

A multiboot (or dual-boot) installation configures your system with more than one OS to choose from, each in its own partition or volume. If you only have a single drive with one partition, you can use Disk Management in Windows to shrink your existing partition and create a new one in the reclaimed space.

**EXAM TIP**   For success, format the system partition using a file system that is common to all installed operating systems. You must install operating systems in order from oldest to newest, and you must install Windows before other operating systems. Any system with at least one hard drive can be configured for multibooting.

## Remote Network Installation

A remote network installation uses a network location as the installation media. Larger organizations may use this along with special scripts to automatically select options and answer all the prompts that us mere mortals have to deal with manually during the installation process. As previously covered, unattended installations can even install applications once the OS is in place.

**EXAM TIP**   Remote network installations use a network location for installation media, and can be scripted to run automatically.

## Image Deployment

Image deployment saves tons of time when you manage many systems. An image is a complete copy of a hard drive volume that includes an operating system and often includes preinstalled apps. You can use special software to set up a fully loaded system by copying the image over from removable media or the network.

**EXAM TIP**   An image used for image deployment can also contain software.

## Recovery Partition

Some prebuilt systems come with a factory recovery partition, other recovery media, or the ability to create recovery media. These can restore the active system partition or the entire hard drive to fresh-from-the-factory condition from a *recovery image*.

**EXAM TIP**   A recovery partition, recovery media, or the Reset Your PC/Remove Everything setting should be regarded as a last resort for fixing a computer, as it wipes out all apps and user data.

## Refresh/Restore

All modern versions of Windows include System Restore, which returns Windows to its condition as of a specified date and time using information stored in restore points.

**NOTE**  The Refresh/Restore options covered in this section aren't really a type of installation, but are included in this objective because they are used to fix issues with an installed operating system.

The Refresh/Reset options were introduced in Windows 8. They are available through the PC Settings | General menu or the Recovery Environment's Troubleshoot menu.

- **Refresh your PC**  Rebuilds Windows; preserves user files, settings, and Microsoft Store apps (but deletes all other applications)
- **Reset your PC**  Removes all apps, programs, files, and settings and freshly reinstalls Windows

In Windows 8.1, these options are located in PC Settings | Update and recovery | Recovery.

In Windows 10, the Refresh and Reset options are combined into a single menu, Reset this PC menu, which offers these options instead:

- **Keep my files** (removes apps and settings; equates to Refresh in Windows 8/8.1)
- **Remove everything** (removes apps, settings, and personal files; equates to Reset in Windows 8/8.1)

To access these Windows 10 options, go to Settings | Update & Security | Recovery | Reset this PC.

**EXAM TIP**  Refresh/Reset options are provided in Windows 8/8.1. In Windows 10, it's Reset this PC with two options (*Keep my files* or *Remove everything*).

# Partitioning

Partitioning is the process of electronically subdividing a physical drive into one or more units called partitions. Windows supports three partitioning schemes: the older *master boot record (MBR)* partitioning scheme, its own proprietary *dynamic storage partitioning* scheme, and the newer *GUID partition table (GPT)*. Microsoft calls an MBR-partitioned or GPT-partitioned drive a *basic disk* and a dynamic-storage-partitioned drive a *dynamic disk*. Windows doesn't mind if you mix schemes on different drives.

**EXAM TIP** A *globally unique identifier (GUID)* is a number with an almost-impossible chance of duplication that's used to uniquely identify different objects.

# Basic

MBR basic disk partition tables support up to four partitions. The partition table supports two types of partitions: primary and extended.

## Primary

Primary partitions support bootable operating systems (extended partitions don't). A single basic MBR disk supports up to four primary partitions, or three primary partitions and one extended partition. The partition table stores a binary *active* setting for each primary partition on the drive; at boot, the MBR uses it to determine which primary partition to boot to.

**EXAM TIP** A primary partition can be bootable.

## Extended

Each partition needs a unique identifier to distinguish it. Microsoft operating systems traditionally assign a drive letter from C: to Z:. Extended partitions do not get drive letters, but an extended partition can contain multiple logical drives, each of which can get a drive letter.

**EXAM TIP** An extended partition can contain one or more logical drives.

**Logical Drives**  After you create an extended partition, you must create logical drives within that extended partition. A logical drive traditionally gets a drive letter from D: to Z:.

Note that when you create partitions and logical drives in Windows, the OS prompts you to create *volumes*. Further, it creates logical drives automatically after you exceed four volumes on a single drive.

**EXAM TIP** Logical drives are found within extended partitions.

With the exception of the partition that stores boot files for Windows (always C:), primary partitions and logical drives can be assigned a drive letter or mounted as a folder on an existing primary partition. A *volume mount point* (or simply *mount point*) is the folder on one volume that points to another volume or partition. The mounted volume functions like a folder, but files stored in it are written to the mounted volume.

# GPT

MBR-partitioned disks have tangible limits such as a capacity no larger than 2.2 TB and no more than four partitions. The GUID partition table (GPT) partitioning scheme effectively overcomes these limits. GPT drives are basic drives, though you need a UEFI motherboard and a UEFI-compatible OS to boot to one.

 **EXAM TIP**    GPT drives can have more than four partitions, compared to the MBR limit of four.

# Dynamic

Windows' proprietary *dynamic storage partitioning*, better known as *dynamic disks*, uses the term *volume* to describe dynamic disk partitions. There is no dynamic disk equivalent to primary versus extended partitions. A volume is still technically a partition, but it can do things a regular partition can't, such as spanning. A *spanned volume* encompasses more than one drive (up to 32 drives in a single volume). Dynamic disks also support RAID 0 (striped), 1 (mirrored), and 5, though support differs among various Windows editions and versions (see Table 1.3-1).

 **EXAM TIP**    Dynamic disks are not bootable, but allow separate disks to be combined into various software RAID and spanned volumes.

**TABLE 1.3-1**    Dynamic Disk Compatibility

| Volume | Windows 7 (Professional/ Ultimate/Enterprise) | 8/8.1/10 Pro | Windows Server (2012 and newer) |
|---|:---:|:---:|:---:|
| Simple | ✓ | ✓ | ✓ |
| Spanned | ✓ | ✓ | ✓ |
| Striped | ✓ | ✓ | ✓ |
| Mirrored | ✓ | ✓ | ✓ |
| RAID 5 | | | ✓ |
| Storage Spaces | | ✓ | ✓ |

As Table 1.3-1 indicates, Windows 8/8.1/10 Pro also support Storage Spaces, which enables two or more non-system drives to be combined into RAID-like arrays to protect from drive failure. Objective 1.5 covers Storage Spaces in more detail.

**EXAM TIP**   Create basic and dynamic disks in Windows using Disk Management. Storage Spaces is a separate utility. The equivalent to Disk Management in macOS is Disk Utility.

# File System Types/Formatting

Formatting adds a file system to the drive—like a big spreadsheet that organizes each partition in such a way that the OS can store files and folders on the drive. Current Windows versions support these file systems: FAT32, NTFS, and exFAT/FAT64. Each has its own merits and limitations. Other file systems you need to understand for CompTIA A+ certification include CDFS, NFS, ext3, ext4, and HFS.

## FAT32

FAT32 supports partitions up to 2 TB—compared to the old FAT16 file system's limit of 2.1 GB—but it lacks local file security features found in NTFS such as permissions, compression, and encryption.

It also limits individual files to 4 GB. FAT32 stores files in clusters (also known as allocation units) which are multiples of the 512-byte block size used by standard drives. A file of any size must occupy at least one cluster, and cluster size in FAT32 increases as drive size increases, from a minimum of 4 KB (4096 bytes) for partitions up to 8 GB, and a maximum of 32 KB for partitions larger than 32 GB.

## ExFAT

As thumb drive and flash memory card capacities grow, the FAT32 file system has proven inadequate because it won't work on drives over 2 TB and limits files to 4 GB.

**EXAM TIP**   Be sure you known the differences between FAT32 and exFAT (file size limits, disk size limits).

Microsoft wisely developed a replacement called *exFAT* (aka *FAT64*) that supports files and partitions up to 16 exabytes (EB). Like FAT32, exFAT still lacks NTFS features such as permissions, compression, and encryption. Both FAT32 and exFAT are also supported by macOS and can also be accessed by Linux when appropriate support packages are installed.

**NOTE** The current implementation of exFAT limits partition size to 2 TB. Current hardware limits the maximum partition size to 2 PB. The theoretical maximum is some amazing figure, like 64 zettabytes (ZB). Here are the definitions of some big number terms. A *petabyte* is $2^{50}$ bytes, an *exabyte* is $2^{60}$ bytes, and a *zettabyte* is $2^{70}$ bytes. For comparison, a terabyte is $2^{40}$ bytes. Remember your binary: each superscript number doubles the overall number, so $2^{41}$ = 2 TB, $2^{42}$ = 4 TB, and so on.

## NTFS

Older versions of Windows ran well enough on FAT and FAT32, but you need New Technology File System (NTFS) to get the most out of modern versions. It supports partitions up to 16 TB, built-in compression and encryption, disk quotas, expanding dynamic partitions on the fly, and local file security.

**NOTE** By default, NTFS supports partitions of up to 16 TB minus 4 KB, but MBR-partitioned drives are still limited to 2.2 TB. Use GPT if you can.

NTFS uses an enhanced file allocation table, the *master file table (MFT)*, to track the file and folder locations. NTFS partitions keep a backup copy of the most critical MFT parts in the middle of the disk, reducing the chance a serious drive error will wipe out both the MFT and the partial MFT copy.

**EXAM TIP** Be sure you know the differences between FAT32, exFAT, and NTFS (security, MFT).

### Compression and Encryption

NTFS can compress individual files and folders to save space at the expense of slower data access; it can also encrypt files and folders to make them unreadable without a key. Microsoft calls the encryption utility in NTFS the *encrypting file system (EFS)*, but it's simply an aspect of NTFS, not a standalone file system.

### Disk Quotas

NTFS enables administrators to set disk quotas that limit drive space use per user. To set quotas, log in as Administrator, right-click the hard drive, and select Properties. In the Local Disk Properties dialog box, select the Quota tab (see Figure 1.3-4), click Show Quota Settings, and make changes. Disk quotas on multiuser systems prevent individual users from monopolizing storage space.

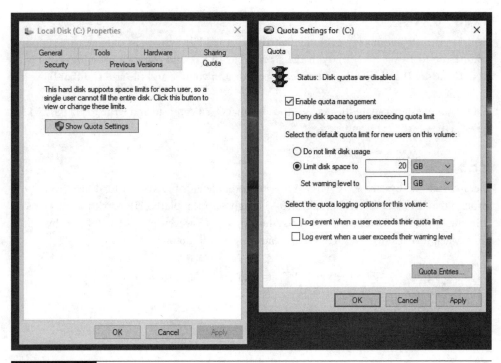

**FIGURE 1.3-4** Settings up disk quotas in Windows 10

# CDFS

Optical discs use a unique Compact Disc File System (CDFS), more accurately called the *ISO 9660 file system*. Microsoft's Joliet extension to ISO 9660 enables optical discs to support Windows 95-style long file names.

# NFS

The Network File System (NFS) enables Linux and UNIX systems to share files remotely and to use remote files as if they are stored locally. NFS has largely been replaced on Linux by *Samba* and SMB (Server Message Block), which are cross-platform file and printer sharing apps that work on Linux, macOS, and Windows.

 **EXAM TIP** Linux-supported file systems include NFS, ext3, and ext4.

### ext3, ext4

Most Linux distributions use ext4, the Fourth Extended File System, by default. ext4 supports volumes up to 1 exabyte (EB), with file sizes up to 16 TB, and is backward compatible with predecessors ext2 and ext3. Just know ext4's maximum volume and file size and that these are Linux file systems.

Linux file system capabilities exceed those of macOS; it can read and write to NTFS, FAT32, exFAT, HFS+, ext2, ext3, and ext4.

## HFS

Hierarchical File System Plus (HFS+) has been the default file system for Macs from 1998 through macOS 10.12 (Sierra). macOS 10.13 (High Sierra) replaced HFS+ with the new, more efficient Apple File System (APFS) for system drives. However, HFS+ is still used by Apple Time Machine backup drives. HFS+ has read-only NTFS support.

 **EXAM TIP**    HFS+ and APFS are both macOS file systems, but the recently adopted APFS is not listed in the CompTIA A+ exam 220-1002 objectives at the time of this writing.

## Swap Partition

A swap partition is an optional disk structure on a Linux installation. It is roughly equivalent to a Windows swap file/page file, enabling hard disk space to be used as a substitute for faster memory. The swap partition also supports hibernation, which stores the system's current state to disk (Windows uses a separate hibernation file for this purpose).

 **ADDITIONAL RESOURCES**    To learn how to size, create, and use a Linux swap partition, go to opensource.com and search for "An introduction to swap space on Linux systems."

## Quick Format vs. Full Format

The default format type for a Windows drive is a quick format. A *quick format* (also known as a high-level format) saves time by creating a FAT (file allocation table) and a blank root directory. A *full format* tests every drive sector for read/write integrity, marking unusable ones in the FAT, and can take many minutes when performed on a hard drive.

**EXAM TIP** Make sure you can describe the differences between quick format and full format.

# Load Alternate Third-Party Drivers When Necessary

Windows includes drivers for standard types of drives that are accessed through normal BIOS or UEFI firmware routines. However, if you are installing Windows to a drive that uses an expansion card or a third-party RAID chip, you may need to load drivers. If so, press the F6 key or click the Load driver option in the installation process (depending upon your version of Windows) to signal Windows that you have drivers. Nothing happens immediately when you respond to this request. You'll be prompted later in the process to insert a driver disc.

**EXAM TIP** Windows can't find devices for which it has no device drivers. Device drivers are often needed for storage cards or third-party RAID arrays.

With Linux, methods vary widely among distributions. To minimize problems, check for device compatibility before choosing a Linux distribution if you are planning to use RAID.

# Workgroup vs. Domain Setup

During the installation of Windows, any computer with a network adapter will prompt the user to choose a workgroup or a domain. In Windows 10, the prompt reads *Set up for personal use* (workgroup) or *Set up for an organization* (domain). So, what's the difference?

A workgroup is set up for personal use and requires each device that will share resources to be configured with authorized users.

A domain is set up for organizational use and requires a Windows Server configured as a domain controller.

The default Windows workgroup is WORKGROUP; enter a different name if your existing workgroup uses a different name.

**EXAM TIP** When a user on a workgroup connects to a different computer, the user must provide a username and password for the account on the remote computer. A domain account specifies which resources are available on a domain for that user. Those resources are available as soon as the user logs into the domain.

If your network uses a domain controller, select *Join a domain* when prompted, enter the domain name, username, and password, and select the account type when prompted. macOS, Windows, and Linux can join existing domains after installation.

**EXAM TIP**   Make sure you understand the differences between workgroups and domains.

# Time/Date/Region/Language Settings

During installation, operating systems prompt the user to select or confirm time, date, region, and language settings. U.S. users generally need to change only the time zone if they live in a non-default time zone. Defaults are generally Eastern or Pacific time. Users in other countries might need to change some or all settings.

**EXAM TIP**   You might need to know what setting or settings need to be adjusted depending upon your location.

# Driver Installation, Software, and Windows Updates

Immediately after installing Windows, install available OS updates to obtain the latest features and *patches* for known bugs and vulnerabilities. Use Windows Update (located in Control Panel, PC Settings, or Settings) to check for OS updates. Depending on how up-to-date the installed Windows version is, it might be necessary to run Windows Update several times to get all the updates.

**EXAM TIP**   A Windows installation isn't finished until you install all available updates.

Likewise, check for driver updates for important hardware (especially if you used default drivers during installation.). Early in the installation process, Windows checks to see if you have outdated apps installed that should be removed or updated. Be sure to follow the recommendations to keep your apps updated to avoid problems.

**ADDITIONAL RESOURCES**   Check the Microsoft Support website at https://support.microsoft.com for Windows and security update information. Check vendors' websites for your motherboard or add-on cards (LAN, video, sound, SATA, and so on) for driver updates.

To see if updates are available for macOS Mojave (10.14.6) or later, open System Preferences | Software Update, and click Update Now if updates are available. To see if updates are available for older macOS versions, open the App Store and check Updates. Any items (macOS or apps) that have updates available are listed. Click Update All to update all listed items. Click Update for a specific item to update it.

To see if updates are available for Linux, use the distro's command-line or GUI tools for updating the catalog and installed OS/apps.

# Factory Recovery Partition

Systems from major vendors that have Windows preinstalled generally have a factory recovery partition. This is a hidden partition that contains the vendor's customized Windows installation image. Systems with a factory recovery partition typically prompt the user to press a key during startup to restore the image if the system doesn't start properly.

 **CAUTION**  Restoring a factory recovery partition wipes out all user data and apps, restoring the system to its as-shipped condition. This feature should be used only if there is no alternative to restoring a system to operation. Before using this feature, the system should be booted with WinPE (Windows Preinstallation Environment) or other bootable media and a file manager should be used to copy all accessible data to a different drive.

# Properly Formatted Boot Drive with the Correct Partitions/Format

Using the normal clean installation process for a given operating system results in the proper formatting of the boot drive with the correct partitions and format. However, if you need to manually set up the partitions on a boot drive, make sure you understand the necessary partition scheme and partition sizes.

For example, these are the partitions needed on a Windows 10 drive according to Microsoft documentation:

- System partition (EFI system partition on a GPT drive)
- Microsoft reserved partition (MSR)
- Windows partition
- Recovery tools partition (Windows RE)

Windows 8/8.1 have the same types of partitions, but in a different order:

- Recovery tools partition (Windows RE)
- System partition (EFI system partition on a GPT drive)

- Microsoft reserved partition (MSR)
- Windows partition

Windows 7 uses a system partition and a Windows partition.

 **EXAM TIP**    Make sure you understand that the Windows partition is assigned the C: drive and that you can identify other partitions that Windows creates.

# Prerequisites/Hardware Compatibility

Before performing either a clean install or an upgrade of an operating system, you should verify that the computer has the necessary prerequisites and hardware compatibility. For a system you plan to upgrade, you can use the reporting tools built into the current OS to compare the computer's hardware with the minimum and recommended hardware for the upgraded OS:

 **EXAM TIP**    You don't need to know how to check for compatibility for the exam; just know that you should check for compatibility before you install an OS.

- **Windows**    System properties or System Information (msinfo32) (hardware and OS). For an example of Windows 10 requirements, see Table 1.3-2.
- **Linux**    Varies by distribution.
- **macOS**    Open Apple menu, About This Mac (hardware and OS).

**TABLE 1.3-2**    Windows 10 Hardware Compatibility

| Feature | Minimum Requirements |
| --- | --- |
| CPU | 1 GHz or faster |
| RAM | 1 GB (32-bit CPU) or 2 GB (64-bit CPU) |
| Hard drive size | 32 GB or larger recommended (smaller drives may work if enough space is available |
| Graphics card | Supports DirectX version 9.0 or greater using a WDDM 1.0 driver |
| Display | 800 × 600 |
| Internet connection | Required in all versions for installing updates and to install some features. Windows 10 S or Windows 10 versions running in S mode also require an Internet connection during initial installation. |

# Application Compatibility

Microsoft has developed various tools to help determine if installed applications will run properly in a particular operating system. The installers for Windows 7, 8/8.1, and 10 perform compatibility checks and will warn users of incompatible apps. The Mac App Store lists apps that are compatible with your Mac. The software repository for a given Linux distro lists apps that are compatible with your Linux PC.

 **EXAM TIP**   For the exam, don't worry about the details of how to check application compatibility; just know that checking it is necessary.

# OS Compatibility/Upgrade Path

Microsoft has a variety of upgrade paths that are officially supported (third-party tools support additional upgrade paths). In brief, here are the supported upgrade paths:

| Windows 7, 8/8.1 | can be upgraded to | Windows 10 |
|---|---|---|
| 32-bit versions | | 32-bit versions |
| 64-bit versions | | 64-bit versions |
| Home versions (Home, Home Basic, Home Premium) | | Windows 10 Home |
| Business versions (Ultimate, Business, Pro, Professional) | | Windows 10 Pro |

Note that users cannot upgrade to Enterprise and Education editions of Windows; their licenses do not support upgrades. For additional details, see the Microsoft website.

Linux upgrade paths in brief:

- Older 32-bit to newer 32-bit versions of the same distribution
- Older 64-bit to newer 64-bit versions of the same distribution

 **EXAM TIP**   Windows editions (except for Enterprise and Education, which do not support upgrades) can upgrade older 32-bit to newer 32-bit and older 64-bit to newer 64-bit editions. Linux also supports 32-bit to 32-bit and 64-bit to 64-bit upgrades.

By using manual installation processes, some Linux distros permit users to upgrade from a 32-bit to a 64-bit version.

macOS upgrade paths in brief:

- From 10.8 or later, upgrade to Mojave (10.14.x)
- From 10.6.8 (Snow Leopard) or 10.7 (Lion), upgrade to El Capitan (10.11), then upgrade to Mojave

# REVIEW

### Objective 1.3: Summarize general OS installation considerations and upgrade methods

- Boot methods that can be used for installing an OS include optical disc, external drive or flash drive, network boot (PXE), internal fixed disk, and internal hard drive partition.
- If installation media is not available, bootable optical discs, USB flash drives or hard drives, or eSATA hard drives can be created from downloadable OS ISO image files.
- An unattended installation uses a script file to provide answers to prompts that appear during the installation process. Windows, Linux, and macOS offer various utilities for creating a script file.
- Use an in-place upgrade to replace an older version of an OS with a newer one. Unlike a clean install, existing apps and files are preserved.
- To perform a clean install of Windows or Linux, the computer needs to be set to boot from the installation media (optical disc or USB). To create installation media for Windows or Linux, download the appropriate ISO disk image file and use a special image burner/transfer utility to create the installation USB drive or optical disc.
- An in-place upgrade can also be used for a repair install to fix problems with the OS. To perform a repair install, use the same version of the OS as is currently installed.
- A multiboot installation enables the user to choose from two or more different OSs at startup. Image deployment enables a single system image to be used for many similarly configured systems.
- A remote network installation uses a network location for the installation media and can be scripted.
- To restore a system to proper function, you can use a recovery partition. This method wipes out all user apps and files while returning the system to its original configuration.
- Windows 8 and above support PC reset, which, like a recovery partition, wipes out all user apps and files while returning the system to its original configuration). Windows 8/8.1 also features Refresh (preserving user files and Windows Store apps), and Windows 10 can keep user files or remove everything as part of its Reset function.

- Windows supports MBR partitions for drives up to 2.2 TB and GPT partitions for larger drives. MBR drives support no more than four partitions (one primary and up to three extended), while GPT supports many more partitions. Both are known as basic disks in Windows. Basic disks are bootable.

- Primary partitions are bootable, but extended partitions and the logical drives within them are not bootable.

- Windows dynamic disks are non-bootable, but can be configured as RAID or Storage Spaces configurations to improve drive performance or safety.

- NTFS is the native file system for Windows 7/8/8.1/10. It supports compression, encryption, security, and disk quotas. FAT32 is used primarily for flash drives or for drives shared with Linux or macOS. exFAT is used for 64-GB or larger flash drives and is also supported by macOS. ext4 is the native file system for modern Linux distributions. HFS+ is the native file system for most recent macOS editions and is used by Time Machine. Apple File System is used by High Sierra and newer versions as its default for system drives.

- A swap partition is an optical disc structure on a Linux installation.

- A quick format clears out the file allocation table or MFT; a full format rewrites all sector markings and determines if any sectors are unusable.

- Load alternate third-party drivers when necessary to support non-standard drive/host adapter hardware such as RAID.

- Workgroup setup, designed for personal use on smaller networks, requires you to specify the workgroup.

- Domain setup, designed for larger networks with Windows Server as a domain controller, requires that you specify the domain, user information, and user type.

- Time/date/region/language settings may not always be accurate, so check them and correct as needed.

- Driver installation, software, and Windows updates should be performed after the OS installation/upgrade process.

- A factory recovery partition is common on preinstalled systems so that the system can be reset to as-built condition.

- Properly formatted boot drive with the correct partitions/format—details vary according to Windows version.

- Check the prerequisites/hardware compatibility issues before installing an OS.

- Check application compatibility with the OS before buying/downloading an app.

- Windows and Linux 32-bit versions can be upgraded to newer 32-bit versions; 64-bit versions can be upgraded to newer 64-bit versions; old macOS versions might need two updates (one to the oldest version supported for updates, then to the current version).

## 1.3 QUESTIONS

1. You are preparing to upgrade a system running Windows 7 to Windows 10. To make sure the system meets the memory, processor, and disk space requirements for Windows 10, which of the following would you use?

   **A.** About This PC

   **B.** msinfo32

   **C.** uname –a

   **D.** DxDiag

2. Which of the following combination of settings would you use to prepare a 4-TB drive to be part of a software RAID array in Windows?

   **A.** FAT32, MBR, Basic

   **B.** Ext4, GPT, Dynamic

   **C.** NTFS, GPT, Dynamic

   **D.** HFT+, MBR, Basic

3. You are preparing to upgrade a 32-bit version of Windows 7 Home Premium to Windows 10. Which of the following Windows 10 editions can be used for the upgrade?

   **A.** Windows 10 Pro 32-bit

   **B.** Windows 10 Pro 64-bit

   **C.** Windows 10 Enterprise 64-bit

   **D.** Windows 10 Home 64-bit

4. You are reformatting an external hard disk for use with macOS Time Machine. Which of the following file systems should you use?

   **A.** NTFS

   **B.** ext4

   **C.** HFS+

   **D.** exFAT

5. You are examining a hard drive's layout using Disk Management. It contains a primary partition and an extended partition. It has four drive letters, C, E, F, G. Where are drive letters E, F, and G located?

   **A.** Primary partition

   **B.** Dynamic drive

   **C.** MSR

   **D.** Extended partition

## 1.3 ANSWERS

1. **B**  The command-line tool msinfo32 opens the System Information tool, which displays processor type, clock speed, installed memory size, available disk space, and many other hardware and software factors.

2. **C**  The NTFS file system is the only Windows file system to support software RAID. GPT is used for drives above 2.2-TB capacity, and dynamic supports software RAID.

3. **A**  Microsoft supports upgrades from older 32-bit versions to newer 32-bit versions. Third-party utilities would be necessary to upgrade from a 32-bit version to a 64-bit version.

4. **C**  HFS+ is a macOS-only file system still used by Time Machine.

5. **D**  A primary partition can only contain one drive letter, so additional drive letters are logical drives inside an extended partition.

 **Objective 1.4** # Given a scenario, use appropriate Microsoft command line tools

Although most routine operations in Windows are performed through the GUI, Windows retains a command prompt that is used for a variety of command-line tools. Table 1.4-1 provides a reference to the commands you need to know for the CompTIA A+ 220-1002 exam.

**TABLE 1.4-1**  Windows Command-Line Utilities

| Category | Command | Use | Examples/Notes |
|---|---|---|---|
| **Navigation** | dir | Lists files and folders in a directory | **dir *.jpg** <br> (displays all files with .JPG extension in current folder) |
| | cd | Changes your current location to the specified folder (subdirectory) | **cd \Myfiles** <br> (changes current location to the \Myfiles folder on the current drive/volume) <br> **cd yourfiles** <br> (changes current location to the yourfiles folder one level below the current folder on the current drive/volume) |

**TABLE 1.4-1**    Windows Command-Line Utilities *(continued)*

| Category | Command | Use | Examples/Notes |
|---|---|---|---|
| | .. | Works one level higher than the current folder; used as an option for cd, dir, and other commands | **cd ..** (changes current location to one level higher than the current folder) **dir ..** (displays contents of folder one level higher than the current folder) |
| **Network** | ipconfig | Displays Internet configuration (IP address, etc.) | **ipconfig /all** (displays all information for all installed network adapters) |
| | ping | Checks connectivity | **ping 8.8.8.8** (checks connectivity to the specified IP address) **ping www.evansville.net** (checks connectivity to the specified website; some websites block pings for security reasons) |
| | tracert | Traces route to the specified IP address or server | **tracert www.evansville.net** |
| | netstat | Displays network statistics | Lists TCP connections |
| | nslookup | Displays IP address of specified domain or server or displays domain or server associated with specified IP address | **nslookup microsoft.com** (displays the IP address for Microsoft.com) |
| | net use | Manages connections to shared network resources | **net use \\myserver\myfolder** (connects to the listed resource) |
| | net user | Manages and lists network users | **net user administrator /active:yes** (activates the local user account) |
| **System** | shutdown | Shuts down, hibernates, or restarts a local or network system | **shutdown /r** (shuts down and restarts) |
| | dism | Deployment Image Servicing and Management; repairs Windows images, including the image used by System File Checker | Requires elevated command prompt |

**TABLE 1.4-1** Windows Command-Line Utilities *(continued)*

| Category | Command | Use | Examples/Notes |
|----------|---------|-----|----------------|
| | sfc | System File Checker; verifies Windows system files, folders, and paths, and replaces corrupt versions | Requires elevated command prompt |
| | chkdsk | Scan, detects, and (optionally) repairs file and directory structure issues on drives | Requires elevated command prompt |
| | gpupdate | Immediately applies group policy updates | **gpupdate /Force** (reapplies all policy settings) |
| | gpresult | Displays current user's or computer's group policy settings | **gpresult /X GPRfilename** |
| | taskkill | Kills task specified by process ID (PID) or app name; use tasklist to see running tasks | **taskkill /f /im explorer.exe** (kills explorer.exe) **taskkill /pid 9898** (kills task with PID 9898) |
| **Disk/File Management** | format | Prepares a blank drive for use or clears the contents of a used drive | **format d: /FS:NTFS** (formats d: with NTFS) |
| | diskpart | Advanced disk management tool; opens diskpart> prompt when started <br><br> Some commands can cause data loss if misused (such as clean all) | **list disk** (displays connected drives) **select disk 3** (selects third disk) **clean all** (overwrites contents of the selected disk, disk 3) |
| | copy | Creates a copy of specified files on the target drive | **copy *.docx U:** (copies all .DOCX files to the current folder on U: drive) |
| | xcopy | Creates a copy of specified files and folders (directories) on the target drive | **xcopy *.docx U:\MyDOCS\ /S** (copies all .DOCX files in current folder and subfolders to the U:\MyDOCS folder) |
| | robocopy | Copies or moves files and folders with options to log, retry failures, use multithreading, and more; GUIs available to make use easier | **robocopy H:\MyDOCS\ U:\YourDOCS\ /MIR** (copies full directory tree from specified folder to specified folder) |
| **Help** | [command name] /? | Displays syntax for specified command | **format /?** (displays syntax for format command) |

**EXAM TIP** Be prepared to use the appropriate commands listed in Table 1.4-1 if you are "given a scenario" on the exam.

# Commands Available with Standard Privileges vs. Administrative Privileges

As noted in Table 1.4-1, some Windows commands will not function when a standard command prompt is opened. An elevated command prompt (also known as a command prompt with administrative privileges) is needed for these and other commands.

To open a command prompt with administrative privileges, use one of these methods:

- **Windows 7 and newer** Click Start, search for **command prompt** or **cmd**, right-click Command Prompt or cmd, and select *Run as administrator*.
- **Windows 8 and newer** Press WINDOWS KEY-X and select Command Prompt (Admin).

## REVIEW

**Objective 1.4: Given a scenario, use appropriate Microsoft command line tools** Windows command-line tools can be used for many purposes:

- Navigation (dir, cd, ..)
- Network reporting and troubleshooting (ipconfig, ping, tracert, netstat, nslookup, net use, net user)
- System management and repairs (shutdown, dism, sfc, chkdsk, gpupdate, gpresult, taskkill)
- Disk and file management (format, diskpart, copy, xcopy, robocopy)
- Help (available for almost any command-line tool by adding /? to the command)

An elevated (administrative) command prompt is required for some commands.

## 1.4 QUESTIONS

1. System File Checker (sfc) is unable to repair problem files. Which command will repair the image used by sfc?
   **A.** chkdsk
   **B.** gpupdate
   **C.** dism
   **D.** ipconfig

2. You are unable to remove all of the contents of an existing hard disk using Disk Management. Which command should you use instead?

   **A.** format

   **B.** diskpart

   **C.** taskkill

   **D.** dism

3. A user calls you to ask for help with her network connection. To find out what her network settings are, which of the following commands should be run?

   **A.** ping

   **B.** netstat

   **C.** net use

   **D.** ipconfig

4. You need to use ping to check the connectivity to a network server 164.172.1.150, also known as MyServer.net. Which of the following is the correct syntax?

   **A.** ping //MyServer.net

   **B.** ping 164-172-1-150

   **C.** ping MyServer.net

   **D.** ping theserverforthisnetwork

5. You are providing telephone support to a user named Miranda that needs to access her personal folders at a command prompt. From her Users folder, which of the following commands would she need to use to get to her personal folders?

   **A.** cd \Miranda

   **B.** Miranda.exe

   **C.** ls Miranda

   **D.** cd Miranda

## 1.4 ANSWERS

1. **C** The dism command repairs the SFC image file.

2. **B** The diskpart command has an option (clean all) to remove all contents from a connected drive.

3. **D** The ipconfig command can display various amounts of information about the user's network connection, depending on which options are used.

4. **C** You can use either the IP address or the URL with ping. However, the syntax must be correct.

5. **D** cd *foldername* drops the focus of the command prompt down one level, and Miranda is in the next level below the Users folder.

**Objective 1.5** # Given a scenario, use Microsoft operating system features and tools

Windows includes a variety of features and tools that help you to manage systems, users, drives, devices, policies, and updates. The ones you need to know for the CompTIA A+ 220-1002 exam are covered in this objective.

## Administrative

Most of the Administrative Tools covered in the following sections are available from the Administrative Tools folder in Control Panel (see Figure 1.5-1).

### Computer Management

Computer Management is a Microsoft Management Console (MMC) snap-in that provides access to Device Manager, Local Users and Groups, Event Viewer, Performance, Disk Management, and Services (refer to Figure 1.5-2). Most of these tools are also available separately from the Administrative Tools folder.

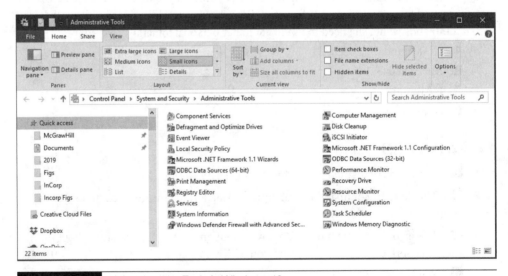

**FIGURE 1.5-1** Administrative Tools in Windows 10

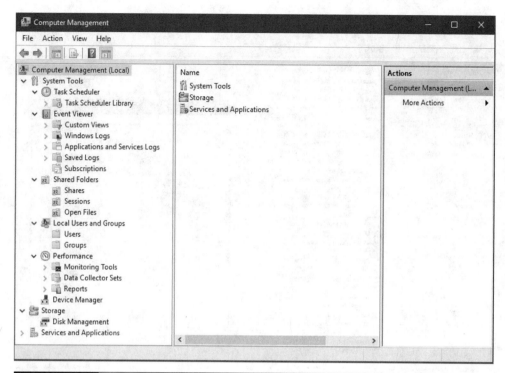

**FIGURE 1.5-2** Computer Management in Windows 10

**EXAM TIP** Computer Management is an MMC snap-in that collects several admin tools in one place, but these tools can be accessed individually in other ways that you should be able to identify.

**Cross-Reference**

To learn more about the Microsoft Management Console, see the "MMC" section later in Objective 1.5.

# Device Manager

Use Device Manager to view the status of system components and connected devices. You can use it to troubleshoot problem devices such as the disabled COM port in Figure 1.5-3. You can also update or roll back drivers, see power usage for USB devices, and view events for a particular device.

**EXAM TIP** Use Device Manager when a device has failed and causes problems for Windows. Device Manager is the first tool in Windows to use for hardware issues.

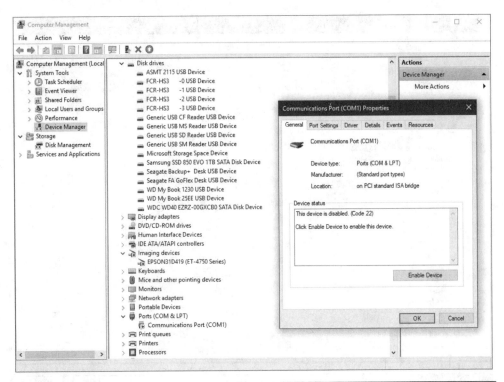

**FIGURE 1.5-3**    Device Manager window and device properties in Computer Management (Windows 10)

## Local Users and Groups

Professional editions of Windows include the Local Users and Groups tool (see Figure 1.5-4), a more powerful tool for working with user accounts—one that won't hold your hand like Control Panel applets do.

To add a group, right-click a blank spot in the Groups folder, select New Group, and enter a group name and description in the New Group dialog box. Click Add below the member list to open a dialog box that you can use to add multiple *object* types, such as user accounts, computers, and even other groups (see Figure 1.5-5).

You can also add or remove group membership through the user's properties. Just open the user's folder, right-click the user, select Properties, click the Member Of tab, and click Add below the group list.

**EXAM TIP**    Local Users and Groups is not available in Home editions of Windows.

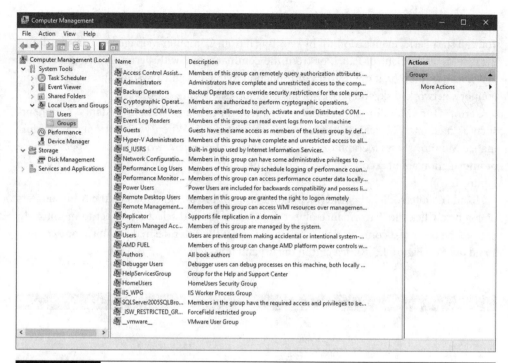

**FIGURE 1.5-4** The Local Users and Groups tool in Windows 10 Pro

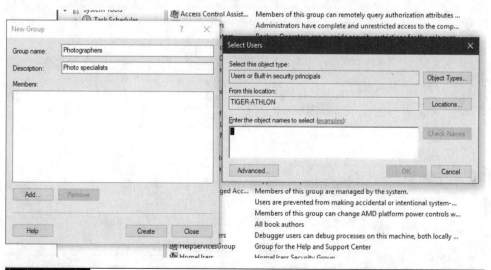

**FIGURE 1.5-5** Creating a new local group and selecting users in Windows 10 Pro

## Performance Monitor

You can start Performance Monitor by selecting it from Computer Management, from Administrative Tools in Control Panel, or from the command-line with perfmon. When you start Performance Monitor, it opens to an introduction to the tool and a System Summary showing memory, network, disk, and processor information (see Figure 1.5-6).

Performance Monitor gathers and graphs real-time data on *objects* (system components such as memory, physical disk, processor, and network). When you first open it, Performance Monitor shows a graph of data from the set of *counters*, which track a specific piece of information about an object, listed below the chart. The default is % Processor Time (see Figure 1.5-7).

To add counters, click the Add (plus sign) button or press CTRL-I to open the Add Counters dialog box. Click the Performance object drop-down list and select an object to monitor. To change the color of a counter, right-click it and select the color desired. To make one counter stand out (see Figure 1.5-8), select it in the list and press CTRL-H.

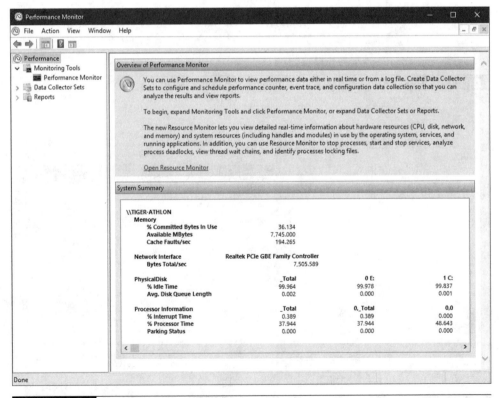

**FIGURE 1.5-6**    Initial Performance Monitor screen in Windows 10

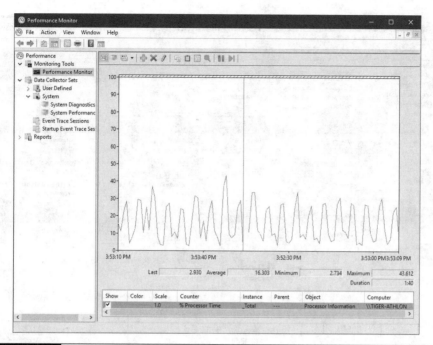

**FIGURE 1.5-7** Resource Monitor displaying % Processor Time

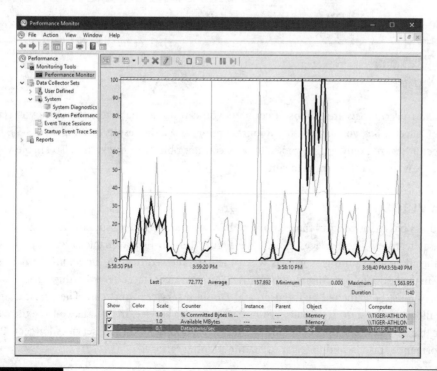

**FIGURE 1.5-8** Pressing CTRL-H makes one set of data stand out.

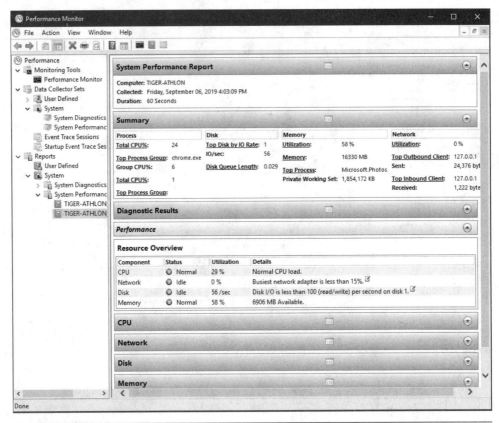

**FIGURE 1.5-9**    Sample report

*Data Collector Sets* are groups of counters you can use to make reports. Once you start a Data Collector Set, you can use the Reports option to see the results (see Figure 1.5-9). Data Collector Sets not only enable you to choose counter objects to track, but also enable you to schedule when you want them to run.

## Services

Windows has many *services* that run in the background, providing support for many of your system's features. The Services applet (see Figure 1.5-10) lists available services and shows whether they are running as well as when they are allowed to run: *Automatic* services start early in the boot process, *Automatic (Delayed Start)* services start after everything else, *Manual* services must be launched by the user, and *Disabled* services won't run. The Services applet also allows you to start, stop, pause, restart, or resume a service. In general, you use the applet to enable services to support something that isn't working, to disable services for security or performance reasons, and to restart a malfunctioning service.

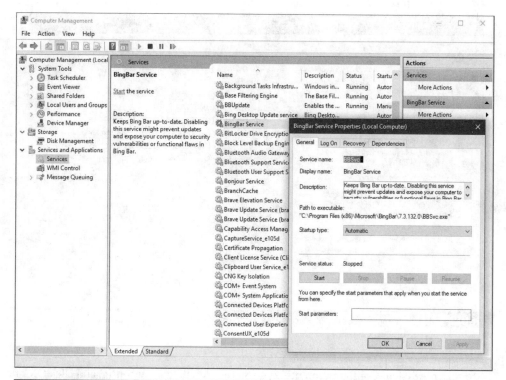

**FIGURE 1.5-10** Using Services to view the properties for the BingBar services

## Local Security Policy

Local Security Policy (shown in Figure 1.5-11) is used to view and configure a wide variety of policies including password, account lockout, Windows Defender Firewall, software restrictions, and many others.

### Cross-Reference

Understanding Local Security Policy is essential to doing well on the CompTIA A+ 220-1002 exam. For more information, see Part II, Domain 2.0, Objective 2.7.

## System Configuration/Msconfig

In Windows 7, techs use the System Configuration utility (also known by its executable name, msconfig) to edit and troubleshoot startup processes and services. From Windows 8 on, this functionality moves to the Startup tab in the Task Manager, which you'll see later in this objective.

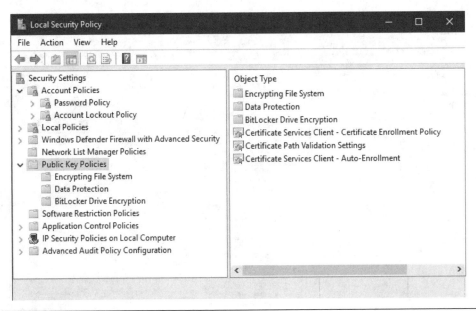

**FIGURE 1.5-11** Viewing available Public Key Policies objects in Local Security Policy (Windows 10)

To start the System Configuration utility, go Start | Search, type **msconfig**, and click OK or press ENTER. The System Configuration utility (shown in Figure 1.5-12) offers a number of handy features, distributed across the following tabs:

- **General**   For the next boot, select a normal startup with all programs and services, a diagnostic startup with only basic devices and services, or a custom boot called selective startup.

- **Boot**   See every copy of Windows you have installed, set a default OS, or delete an OS from the boot menu. You can set up a safe boot, or adjust options like the number of cores or amount of memory to use. While selected, Safe boot will always start the system in *Safe mode* with minimal, generic, trusted drivers for troubleshooting purposes.

- **Services**   Enable or disable services running on your system.

- **Startup**   Enable or disable any startup programs that load when you launch Windows.

- **Tools**   Lists many of the tools and utilities available elsewhere in Windows, including Event Viewer, Performance Monitor, Command Prompt, and so on.

**EXAM TIP**   Windows 8 and later also have the System Configuration utility with the same tabs as the Windows 7 version. However, the Startup tab in these versions has a link to Task Manager.

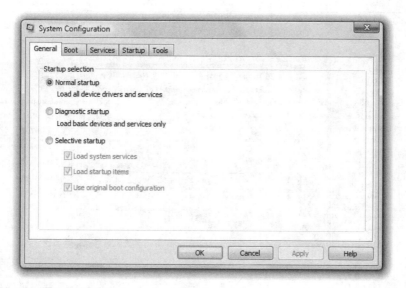

**FIGURE 1.5-12**   Windows 7 System Configuration utility

# Task Scheduler

Windows uses Task Scheduler to schedule its own automatic maintenance, and you can use its powerful options to create your own tasks or modify existing schedules. Among other useful settings, each task has *triggers*, *actions*, and *conditions* (see Figure 1.5-13) that, respectively, define when it runs, what it does, and criteria that must be met before it runs. The Windows default overnight maintenance schedules are fine for most of us—but they may be no good for users on the night shift.

 **EXAM TIP**   Task Scheduler illustrates why you need to know executable names and command-line options for common utilities—this is how a task action specifies the options a utility needs to run without user input.

# Component Services

Component Services is a tool administrators and developers use to configure systems to support specific applications (typically in-house or otherwise custom applications that take advantage of data-sharing tools with names such as COM, DCOM, and COM+). Professional software can typically handle all of this by itself. If you need to use this tool, you'll almost certainly have explicit directions for what to do with it.

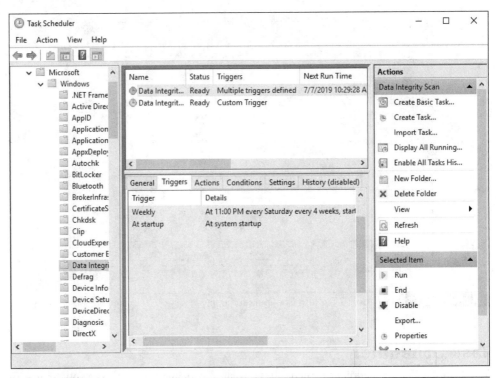

**FIGURE 1.5-13** Viewing Task Scheduler's Triggers tab (Windows 10)

## Data Sources

ODBC Data Source Administrator (shown in Figure 1.5-14) enables you to create and manage Open Database Connectivity (ODBC) entries called Data Source Names (DSNs) that point ODBC-aware applications to shared databases. Once again, you'll probably have explicit instructions if you need to use this.

## Print Management

Print Management (see Figure 1.5-15) enables the user to install, view, and manage printers, printer drivers, print jobs, and print servers. Print Management is available in the Administrative Tools applet and is an MMC snap-in. It can also be launched by pressing the WINDOWS KEY-R and entering **printmanagement.msc** in the Run command box.

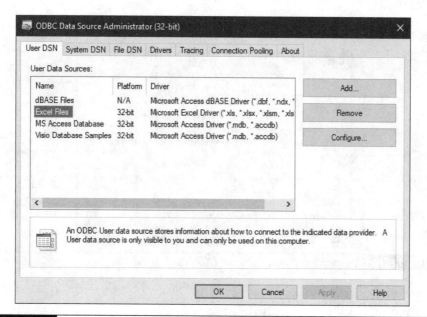

**FIGURE 1.5-14** ODBC Data Source Administrator in Windows 10

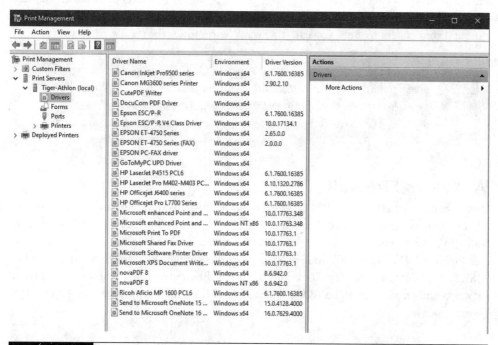

**FIGURE 1.5-15** Print Management in Windows 10

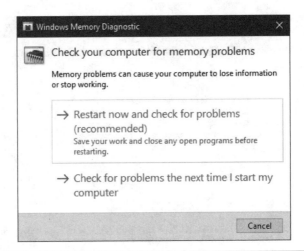

| **FIGURE 1.5-16** | Windows Memory Diagnostic Tool running |

## Windows Memory Diagnostics

Windows Memory Diagnostic runs on the next reboot when selected. During the next reboot, the diagnostic tool checks your RAM (see Figure 1.5-16) for the sorts of problems that can cause Blue Screens of Death (BSoDs), system lockups, and continuous reboots. After the tool runs and your system reboots, you can use Event Viewer to see the results.

**EXAM TIP**    You can launch the Windows Memory Diagnostic Tool from Administrative Tools or as **mdsched** at an administrative command prompt. It is available in the Windows Recovery Environment GUI in Windows 7. In Windows 8/8.1/10, it can be run from the Windows Recovery Environment command prompt.

## Windows Firewall

Windows includes a firewall that is designed to block unwanted inbound traffic. The standard Windows Firewall is configured through Control Panel | System and Security | Windows Firewall in Windows 7 and 8/8.1. In Windows 10, the firewall is called Windows Defender Firewall (see Figure 1.5-17), is part of Windows Security, and is configured through Settings | Update & Security | Windows Security. These firewalls offer different settings for public and private networks and enable apps to be added to or removed from the network permissions list (see Figure 1.5-18).

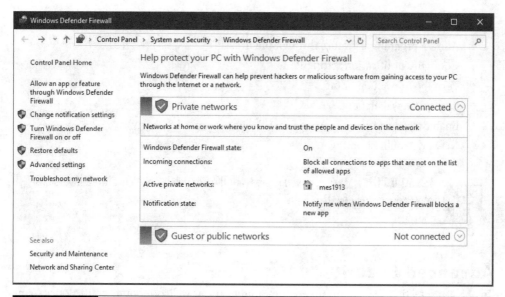

**FIGURE 1.5-17**   Windows Defender Firewall (Windows 10)

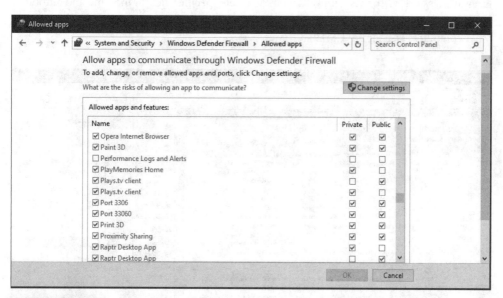

**FIGURE 1.5-18**   Preparing to add an app to the list of permitted apps

The task list on the left includes links to

- Allow a program or feature through the firewall
- Configure notification settings
- Turn the firewall on or off
- Restore firewall defaults
- Enable advanced settings (runs firewall with Advanced Security)
- Network troubleshooting

 **EXAM TIP** Make sure you know what the firewall is called in different versions of Windows and how to start it.

## Advanced Security

To enable protection against unwanted outbound traffic as well as inbound traffic, open Windows Defender Firewall with Advanced Security (Windows 10) or Windows Firewall with Advanced Security (Windows 7/8/8.1); click Advanced Settings from the Windows (Defender) Firewall's task list. With these firewalls, you can create specific rules for inbound and outbound traffic, import policies you have already created, or export policies you have created for use on other computers (see Figure 1.5-19).

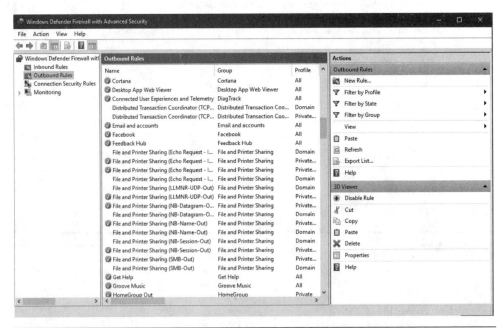

**FIGURE 1.5-19** Viewing current outbound traffic rules in Windows Defender Firewall with Advanced Security (Windows 10)

**EXAM TIP**   The Advanced Security versions of Windows Firewall can block outbound as well as inbound traffic.

# Event Viewer

With a little tweaking, Event Viewer (see Figure 1.5-20) records almost any system event you might want to know about, making it useful as both a troubleshooting tool and a security tool.

Note the four main bars in the center pane: Overview, Summary of Administrative Events, Recently Viewed Nodes, and Log Summary. The Summary of Administrative Events breaks down the events into different levels: Critical, Error, Warning, Information, Audit Success, and Audit Failure. You can click any event to see a description of the event.

 **EXAM TIP**   Be sure to know the four sections (Overview, Summary of Administrative Events, Recently Viewed Nodes, and Log Summary) as well as Application, Security, and System logs in Event Viewer.

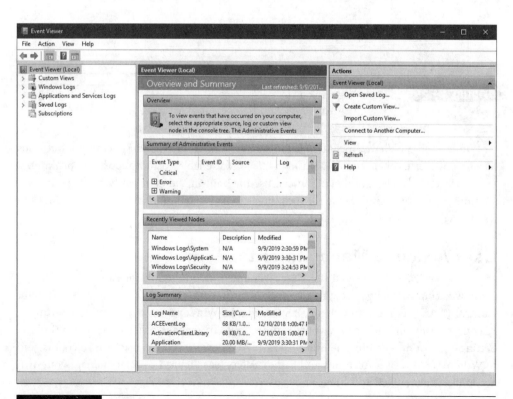

**FIGURE 1.5-20**   Windows 10 Event Viewer default screen

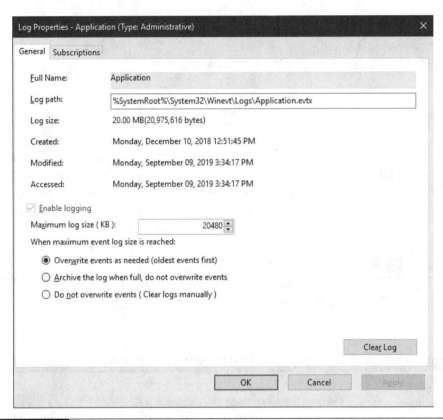

**FIGURE 1.5-21**  Log Properties dialog box in Windows 10

Windows Event Viewer includes classic Application, Security, and System logs, but leans heavily on filtering their contents through *Views* that enable custom reports by beginning/ end times, error levels, and more. You can use the built-in Views or easily create your own. Administrators can configure log file location as well as maximum size and what to do when it's reached, as shown in Figure 1.5-21.

## User Account Management

Manage user accounts through the User Accounts section of Control Panel. You can create new accounts, change account types (Standard, Administrator), change User Account Control (UAC) settings, and change passwords. In Windows 10, use Windows Settings | Accounts | Your info to change your own account. To manage other users, use Windows Settings | Accounts | Family and other users. In Windows 7, you can use User Accounts, and in Windows 8/8.1, User Accounts and Family Safety (see Figure 1.5-22) to manage your own account settings as well as those of other users.

**FIGURE 1.5-22**   Managing user accounts in Windows 8.1

 **EXAM TIP**   Be sure to know how user account management varies in Windows 7/8/8.1 and Windows 10.

# Task Manager

Half of the optimization battle is knowing what needs to be optimized. Current versions of Windows rely on the Task Manager to manage applications, processes, and services. Most users just use it to shut down troublesome programs, but it's a great tool for keeping tabs on how hard your system is working—and, if it's running slowly, what the cause may be. The quickest way to open the Task Manager is pressing CTRL-SHIFT-ESC. The Task Manager got a major update in Windows 8 and newer versions, so we'll look at the major variations separately.

 **EXAM TIP**   You can do a number of things you'd normally open the Task Manager for from the command line, or even with scheduled tasks. You can start and stop services with **net start <service>** and **net stop <service>**, list processes with **tasklist**, and kill them with **taskkill**.

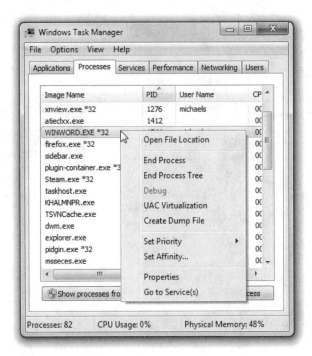

**FIGURE 1.5-23** Processes tab and context menu options

The Task Manager in Windows 7 enables you to control and review essential Windows components. It has six tabs:

- The *Applications* tab shows all the running applications on your system. If you're having trouble getting an application to close normally, this is the place to go.
- The *Processes* tab (see Figure 1.5-23) shows you every running process and enables you to kill it.

 **NOTE** Every program that runs on your system is composed of one or more processes.

- The *Services* tab enables you to work directly with services, the small programs that control various components of Windows (such as printing, sharing files, and so on). Here, you can stop or start services, and you can go to the associated process.
- The *Performance* tab (see Figure 1.5-24) enables you to see CPU usage, available physical memory, the size of the disk cache, commit charge (memory for programs), and kernel memory (memory used by Windows).

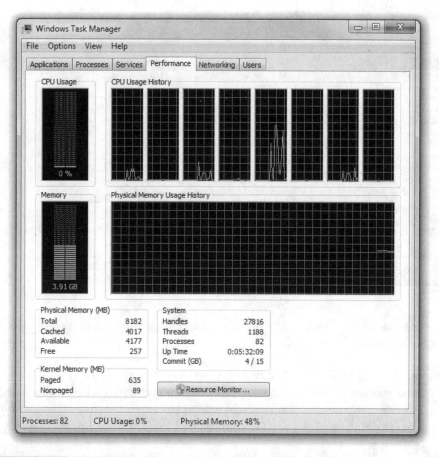

**FIGURE 1.5-24**    Task Manager Performance tab

- The *Networking* tab enables you to see network use at a glance and is a good first spot to look if you think the computer is running slowly on the network.
- The *Users* tab enables you to see which users' accounts are currently logged on to the local machine and, with the proper permissions, enables you to log off other users.

## Task Manager Tabs in Windows 8/8.1/10

With Windows 8 and later, Task Manager defaults to a simplified *Fewer details* view (left side of Figure 1.5-25) for listing and terminating running programs, but you can click *More details* to get the traditional tabbed view (right side of Figure 1.5-25). Even here, much changed from the Windows 7 version. While the Performance, Services, and Users tabs all still exist, the

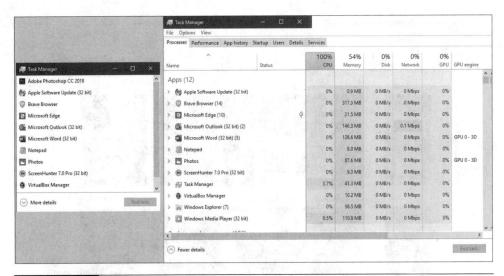

**FIGURE 1.5-25** Fewer details/more details views in Windows 10 Task Manager

Networking tab has been merged into the Performance tab, and the Task Manager gains three new tabs: App history, Startup, and Details.

- Task Manager's More details view opens on the *Processes* tab. When sorted by the Name column, it groups processes into three sections: Apps, Background processes, and Windows processes. Regardless of how you sort these processes, the view shows a color-coded breakdown of CPU, memory, disk, and network. Windows 10 adds GPU usage.

- The *Performance* tab (shown in Figure 1.5-26) serves the same purpose as in previous versions, but it is easier on the eyes and folds in performance information about disk (Disk I/O) and network use.

- The *App history* tab collects recent performance statistics regarding how heavily processes are hitting the CPU and network.

- The *Startup* tab, which moved over to Task Manager from System Configuration, enables you to control which programs load when Windows does, and assess what impact each has on the startup process.

- The *Users* tab serves the same basic purpose as in previous versions, but it also makes it dead simple to see what impact other logged-in users are having on system performance.

- The *Details* tab has all of the details that used to be in the Processes tab in the Windows 7 Task Manager.

- The *Services* tab is virtually unchanged, but it did receive some nice polish, such as a context-menu option to search for a process online as well as to restart a service with a single click.

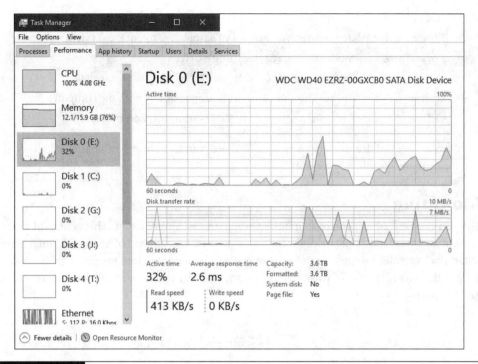

**FIGURE 1.5-26**   Performance tab in Windows 10 Task Manager showing a very active Disk 0

 **EXAM TIP**   Be sure to know the changes in Task Manager between Windows 7 and Windows 8/8.1/10 (more tabs, Details tab instead of Processes tab, More/Fewer Details option, etc.).

# Disk Management

Disk Management (located in the Computer Management MCC) is the go-to tool for adding drives or adding arrays to a Windows system, as well as for modifying them. To make changes to a drive, right-click its icon in Disk Management and choose the appropriate operation from the menu.

## Drive Status

Disk Management shows the *drive status* of every initialized mass storage device in your system, making it handy for troubleshooting. Hopefully, you'll see each drive listed as *Healthy*.

- **Unallocated**   The disk has no file system or has a file system that is not recognized by Windows (such as a Linux- or macOS-specific file system).

- **Active**    The disk partition used to boot the system.
- **Foreign drive**    Shown when you move a dynamic disk to another system.
- **Formatting**    Shown while you're formatting a drive.
- **Failed**    The disk is damaged or corrupt; you've probably lost some data.
- **Online**    The disk is healthy and communicating properly with the computer.
- **Offline**    The disk is either corrupt or having communication problems.

A newly installed drive is set as a basic disk; there's nothing wrong with basic disks, though you miss out on some handy features.

## Mounting

You can use Disk Management to mount a volume to an empty folder. This is helpful if you want to access an additional drive through an existing folder instead of as an additional drive letter. For example, a drive containing photos could be mounted into an empty folder called Photos that is a subfolder of your Pictures folder. A folder that is used to mount a volume is known as a *mount point*.

To create a mount point:

1. In Disk Management, right-click the volume you want to mount and select Change Drive Letter and Paths.
2. Click Add.
3. Click Browse.
4. Navigate to the empty folder you want to use, or click New Folder to create a folder.
5. After clicking the folder to use for the mount point, click OK.

## Initializing

A drive that has not been previously connected to Disk Management must be initialized before use in your system, even if it has been formatted and contains data. Don't worry—initialization in Disk Management-speak simply means that Disk Management identifies the drive and what its role is—such as whether it is part of a software RAID array or a spanned volume. No data is harmed. A drive is listed as Unknown until it is initialized (see Figure 1.5-27). To initialize the disk drive, right-click it and select Initialize Disk.

## Extending, Shrinking, Splitting Partitions

Disk Management can also be used to extend and shrink volumes in current versions of Windows without using dynamic disks; CompTIA calls this extending partitions and, oddly, shrinking partitions. You can shrink a volume with available free space (though you can't shrink it by the whole amount, based on the location of unmovable sectors such as the MBR), and you can expand volumes with unallocated space on the drive.

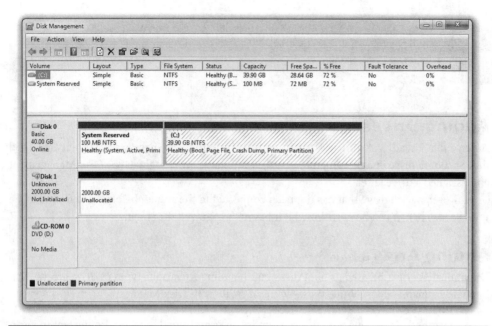

| FIGURE 1.5-27 | Unknown drive in Disk Management |

To shrink a volume, right-click it and select Shrink Volume. Disk Management calculates how much it can shrink and lets you choose up to that amount. Extending volumes is equally straightforward; right-click and select Extend Volume.

 **EXAM TIP**   The CompTIA A+ 220-1002 exam objectives mention "splitting" partitions, but there's no "split" option. To turn one partition into two, remove the existing partition and create two new ones, or shrink the existing partition and add a new one in the unallocated space. If you see "splitting" on the exam, know that this is what CompTIA means.

## Assigning/Changing Drive Letters

Drive letters are assigned automatically by Windows when fixed or removable storage drives are connected. You can see the drive letters assigned to existing drives using Disk Management, and you can also change them. Use the New Simple Volume Wizard to assign a drive letter to a volume when you create it. To change the drive letter used by an existing volume, right-click it and choose Change Drive Letter and Paths.

**CAUTION** When you change a drive letter, make sure that any apps that are using that drive letter for program or data storage are configured to use the new drive letter, or they will fail.

## Adding Drives

A drive that already has a file system recognized by Windows, such as an external USB hard disk or thumb drive or a flash memory card, is automatically recognized by Disk Management and assigned a drive letter.

However, a hard drive that has not been connected to the system before must first of all be initialized. Then, it can be partitioned if it has no recognized file system.

## Adding Arrays

Dynamic disks can't be used as boot disks but they support various types of drive arrays (also known as dynamic disk volume types) you can create with Disk Management:

- **Spanned** The capacities of two or more disks are added together. Equivalent to just a bunch of disks (JBOD) hardware array.
- **Striped** Data is written across two drives to enhance speed; a software version of a RAID 0 hardware array.
- **Mirrored** Data is written to two drives at the same time, so if one drive fails, the array can be rebuilt from the copy on the other drive; a software version of a RAID 1 array.
- **RAID 5** Data and parity (recovery) information is written across three or more drives, so the array can be rebuilt if one disk fails; software version of a RAID 5 hardware array.

To create any of these arrays, you start with empty or backed-up disks (existing contents will be wiped out during the creation process). Right-click the first drive to add to the array, select the type, and add additional drives to the array. After formatting the array, specify a drive letter or mount point and convert the disks to dynamic disks when prompted. In Disk Management, each array is color coded and identified as the type of array (mirror, spanned, or striped).

 **EXAM TIP** Be sure to know the differences between spanned, striped, mirrored, and RAID 5 arrays in Disk Management.

# Storage Spaces

The Storage Spaces utility offers a more flexible type of disk array. It was introduced in Windows 8 and also available in Windows 8.1 and 10. Storage spaces are created and managed from the System and Security menu in Control Panel (the drives used by storage spaces are listed as a single drive letter in Disk Management). Storage Spaces creates a *storage pool,* a collection of physical drives that enable you to flexibly add and expand capacity. From free space in the storage pool, Storage Spaces creates virtual drives that feature fixed provisioning (the space required for a virtual drive is immediately subtracted from the storage pool's free space) and resiliency, available in four configurations:

- Simple (similar to RAID 0 striping; two or more drives)
- Two-way mirror (similar to RAID 1 mirroring, two or more drives)
- Three-way mirror (five or more drives)
- Parity (similar to RAID 5, three or more drives)

Choose the drive(s) to use in the storage pool, and then create the storage space and select the type of resiliency (if any) to use (see Figure 1.5-28). Check Action Center for alerts about drives in Storage Spaces.

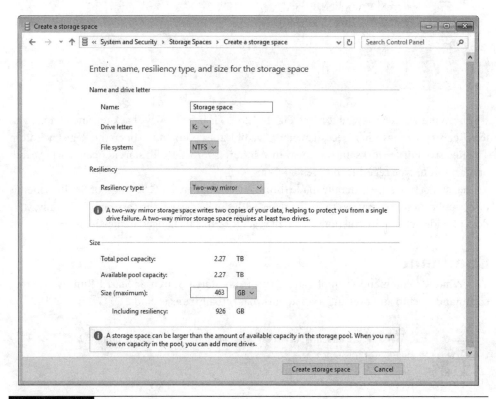

**FIGURE 1.5-28**   Creating a two-way mirror with Storage Spaces

**ADDITIONAL RESOURCES** To learn more about using Storage Spaces, go to techgenix.com and search for "Windows 10 Storage Spaces — A Comprehensive Guide."

# System Utilities

Windows includes a variety of system utilities for managing, configuring, and reporting on Windows. The following sections discuss the ones you need to understand for the CompTIA A+ 220-1002 exam.

## Regedit

The Windows Registry is a database that stores the Windows hardware, software, and user configuration data in the form of keys and values.

 **EXAM TIP** The five main keys to know are

- HKEY_CLASSES_ROOT
- HKEY_CURRENT_USER
- HKEY_LOCAL_MACHINE
- HKEY_USERS
- HKEY_CURRENT_CONFIG

The Windows Registry Editor (see Figure 1.5-29) is used to view, back up, and change system Registry settings when necessary, and regedit is the command to open the Registry Editor. The Registry Editor works the same way in Windows 7/8/8.1/10. To start it, open Start | Search or Start | Run, type **regedit**, and press ENTER.

Registry settings are generally made through Control Panel, PC Settings, or Settings menus or by applications, so changes to the Registry with the Registry Editor are rare. Generally, vendors provide detailed instructions or small regedit scripts if changes are needed.

## Command

The Windows command prompt can be run from Start | Search or Start | Run by entering **command** or **cmd** and pressing ENTER, but what actually runs is cmd.exe.

 **EXAM TIP** Launching command or cmd starts the command prompt with Standard user privileges.

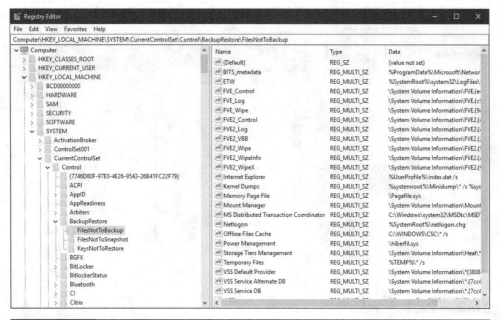

**FIGURE 1.5-29**   Using the Registry Editor to view files that Backup/Restore will not back up

## Cross-Reference

To learn more about standard versus elevated privileges for command prompt, see the "Commands Available with Standard Privileges vs. Administrative Privileges" section in Objective 1.4, earlier in this domain.

## Services.msc

As an alternative to opening Computer Management, then Services, you can go directly to Services via Start | Search by typing **services.msc** and pressing ENTER.

# MMC

Windows has so many utilities that it's hard to organize them all in a way that satisfies everyone, so *Microsoft Management Console (MMC)* is simply a shell program that enables you to build your own utility from individual *snap-ins*. To give you an idea of how powerful an MMC can be, the apps in Administrative Tools are just preconfigured MMCs. To start a blank MMC (see Figure 1.5-30), select Start | Search, type **mmc**, and press ENTER.

   **EXAM TIP**   Be sure to know how to create a blank MMC and how to add a snap-in.

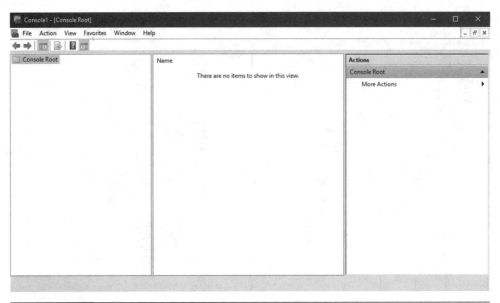

**FIGURE 1.5-30**    Blank MMC

You make a blank MMC console useful by adding as many snap-ins as you like, including utilities such as Device Manager. You can even buy third-party MMC snap-in utilities. To add one, select File | Add/Remove Snap-ins and then select one from the dialog box's list of available snap-ins (see Figure 1.5-31). Depending on the snap-in, you may need to configure some additional options before adding it. Once you've added the snap-ins you want, you can name the console (and put it somewhere accessible) by saving it.

## MSTSC (Remote Desktop Connection)

Microsoft's *Remote Desktop Connection*, available from the Windows Accessories menu, can connect to and control a remote Windows system with a fully graphical interface (see Figure 1.5-32). Because the Remote Desktop Connection executable is mstsc.exe, you can also open it from the CLI, Search bar, or Run command box by typing **mstsc** and pressing ENTER.

 **EXAM TIP**    Be sure to know how to open Remote Desktop Connection.

## Notepad

You might not think of Notepad as an important management tool, but you can use it to view the contents of a Registry patch, to view a log file created by some Windows functions, or as a

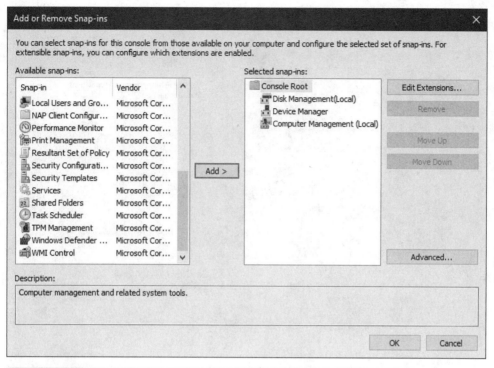

**FIGURE 1.5-31**    Adding snap-ins to a blank MMC console

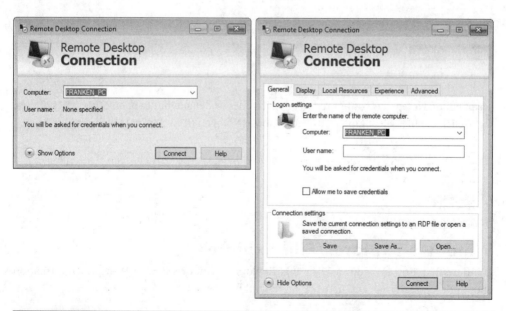

**FIGURE 1.5-32**    Windows Remote Desktop Connection dialog box in normal mode (left) and after clicking Show Options (right)

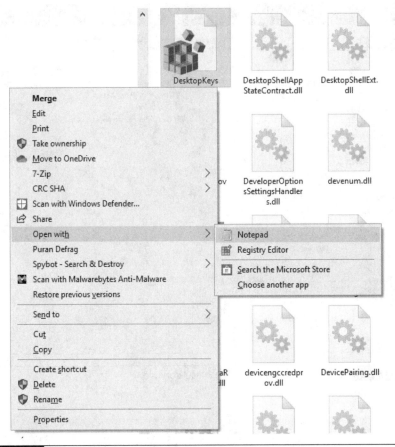

**FIGURE 1.5-33**   Selecting Notepad to open a Registry file with Open with

script editor. Notepad is configured to open .txt files by default, but to open other types of files, right-click the file, select Open with, and choose Notepad from the list (see Figure 1.5-33).

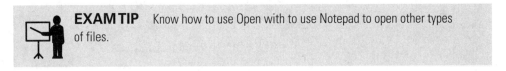

**EXAM TIP**   Know how to use Open with to use Notepad to open other types of files.

# Windows Explorer/File Explorer

Windows Explorer (Windows 7) or File Explorer (Windows 8/8.1/10) display information about internal, external, and network drives and folders.

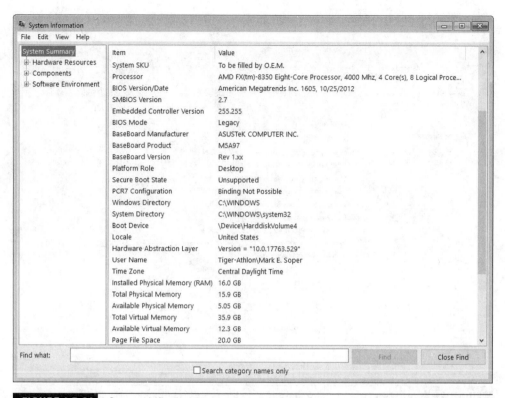

**FIGURE 1.5-34**   System Information

## Msinfo32

The *System Information tool* (shown in Figure 1.5-34), referred to by its executable, msinfo32, in CompTIA A+ 220-1002 objective 1.5, collects information about hardware resources, components, and the software environment into a nice report, enabling you to troubleshoot and diagnose any issues and conflicts. As with many other tools, you can access this tool from the Start | Search bar; simply enter **msinfo32** and press ENTER.

 **EXAM TIP**   Be sure to know how to start System Information (msinfo32).

## DxDiag

Microsoft created DirectX to prove a stable environment for running 3-D applications and games within Windows. DirectX includes many APIs (with names like Direct3D) that support direct access to audio and graphics hardware. Because specific cards and applications

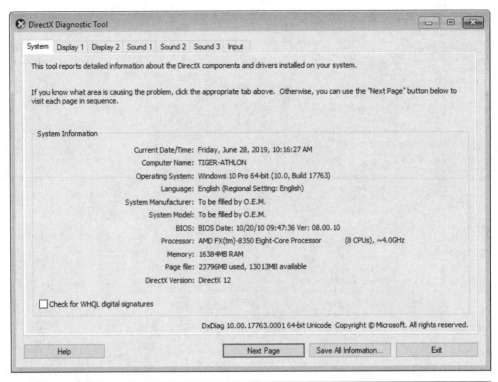

**FIGURE 1.5-35** DirectX Diagnostic Tool showing the system is running DirectX 12

support different DirectX versions, you'll eventually need the DirectX Diagnostic Tool (which CompTIA lists as DxDiag) to confirm a specific DirectX version is installed and working (see Figure 1.5-35). To access it, type **dxdiag** in the Start | Search bar and press ENTER.

**EXAM TIP** Be sure to learn the tabs that the DirectX Diagnostic Tool uses to show different parts of the computer (System, Display, Sound, and Input). There's a separate tab for each display and for each sound output.

## Disk Defragmenter

Fragmented blocks can increase drive access times, so it's a good idea to defragment (or *defrag*) your HDDs as regular maintenance. SSDs don't fragment like HDDs, so don't defragment them manually; let Windows handle the task.

You access the defrag tool, called Disk Defragmenter (Windows 7) or Optimize Drives (Windows 8/8.1/10) by right-clicking a drive in Computer, Windows Explorer, or File Explorer,

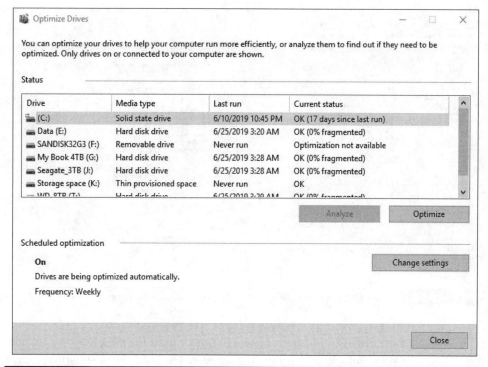

**FIGURE 1.5-36** Optimize Drives, the defragmentation tool in Windows 10

choosing Properties, and clicking the Defragment Now or Optimize button on the Tools tab to open the defrag tool (see Figure 1.5-36). Thanks to Windows running defragmentation auto-matically (the default is weekly), you hardly ever need to run it manually.

 **EXAM TIP** Know how to use Disk Defragmenter or Optimize Drives, but keep in mind it runs automatically.

## System Restore

System Restore provides a simple way to return to an earlier *restore point* (a snapshot of the system hardware and software configuration). Windows creates restore points automatically, but you also can create them manually before making changes to your system. If the computer malfunctions after new hardware or software is added, you can revert to a previous configuration. System Restore is available by clicking the System protection link in the System applet in the Control Panel. It is disabled by default in Windows 10, so if you want to use it, you must enable it.

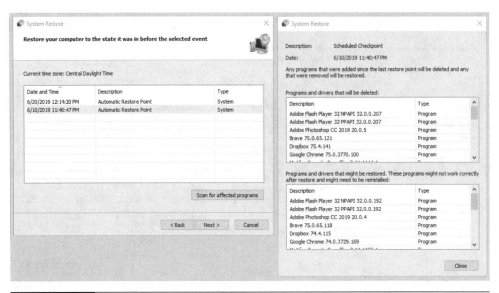

 **FIGURE 1.5-37**    Selecting a restore point and scanning for affected programs in Windows 10

To restore a particular snapshot, open System Restore, choose the most recent or an older restore point, click *Scan for affected programs* (optional; see Figure 1.5-37), and start the restore process. After the restore is complete and the system reboots, your system will be back to its configuration, with no data lost.

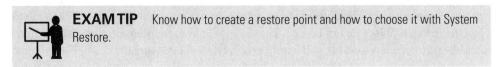

**EXAM TIP**    Know how to create a restore point and how to choose it with System Restore.

## Windows Update

Windows Update will check for available updates automatically, so you'll often see available updates as soon as you open the applet (see Figure 1.5-38). In Windows 7, there are *Important*, *Recommended*, and *Optional* updates, but Windows 8.1/10 download and install updates automatically without letting you pick and choose.

Windows Update is accessible in the Control Panel for Windows 7/8/8.1. Windows versions 8 and 8.1 also provide access to it from within the Settings app. Windows Update is only accessible through the Settings app (under Update and Security) in Windows 10 (see Figure 1.5-39).

**EXAM TIP**    The CompTIA A+ 220-1002 objectives cover many Microsoft system utilities and tools. Given a scenario on the exam, know how to access and use them all!

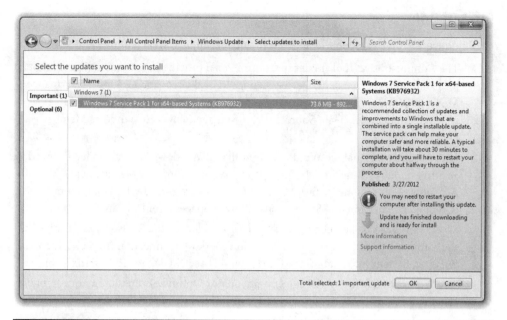

**FIGURE 1.5-38**   Important Windows 7 SP1 update in Windows Update

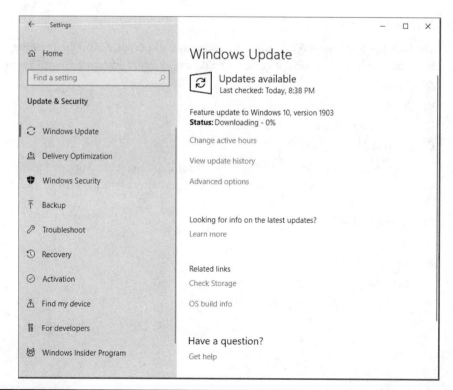

**FIGURE 1.5-39**   Windows Update in Windows 10

# REVIEW

## Objective 1.5: Given a scenario, use Microsoft operating system features and tools

- The Administrative Tools folder in Control Panel provides a convenient launching pad for Computer Management, Device Manager, Local Users and Groups, Performance Monitor, Services, Local Security Policy, System Configuration, Task Scheduler, Component Services, Data Sources, Print Management, and Windows Memory Diagnostics.
- Other useful tools include Windows Firewall and Windows Firewall with Advanced Security (Control Panel or Settings), Event Viewer (Computer Management), User Accounts (Control Panel), Task Manager (CTRL-SHIFT-ESC), Disk Management (Computer Management | Storage), and Storage Spaces (Control Panel).
- Several tools can be launched with Start | Run, including the Registry Editor (regedit), the command prompt (cmd), MMC, Remote Desktop Connection (mstsc), Notepad, Explorer, System Information (msinfo32), and DirectX Diagnostic Tool (dxdiag).
- The Windows defrag tool (Disk Defragmenter or Optimize) runs automatically, but it can also be run from the right-click drive properties sheet.
- System Restore and Windows Update can be launched from Control Panel or Settings.

# 1.5 QUESTIONS

1. You have just installed several programs, and now the computer is malfunctioning. How can you find out which programs would be removed if you run System Restore?

   **A.** Run msinfo32

   **B.** Use Windows Update

   **C.** Use Scan for affected programs

   **D.** Use Task Manager

2. You have created a two-way mirror to help protect data. However, it appears as only a single drive letter in Disk Management. Which tool shows which drives are used by the array?

   **A.** Storage Spaces

   **B.** RAID

   **C.** Device Manager

   **D.** Msconfig

3. To block unwanted outbound network traffic, you need to use the Advanced Security version of which of the following?
   A. Device Manager
   B. Windows Firewall
   C. Task Manager
   D. MMC

4. You are instructing a bench repair tech on how to view a downloaded Registry script. Which of the following methods should be used to view the script contents safely from within Windows/File Explorer?
   A. Double-click the Registry file
   B. Right-click the Registry file and select Properties
   C. Drag the Registry file into Microsoft Word
   D. Right-click the Registry file, select Open with, and choose Notepad

5. You have just upgraded a department's systems from Windows 7 to Windows 10. One of the users is having performance problems but only sees running apps when using the Task Manager. Which option will show other running processes?
   A. Click the Processes tab
   B. Click More details
   C. None in the Task Manager; must use another tool
   D. Click Performance

## 1.5 ANSWERS

1. **C** Clicking the *Scan for affected programs* button in System Restore reveals the programs (and device driver updates) that were installed after the specific restore point so that you can make a note about what might need to be reinstalled or replaced.

2. **A** You must use Storage Spaces to see the actual drives because the array was created with Storage Spaces.

3. **B** The Advanced Security version of Windows Firewall can be used to create rules for managing outbound traffic.

4. **D** Notepad is a safe way to view any text file (and a Registry script is a text file).

5. **B** The default configuration of the Task Manager in Windows 10 shows only running apps. You must click *More details* to see processes (which show on the same tab as apps).

**Objective 1.6** # Given a scenario, use Microsoft Windows Control Panel utilities

Although the Settings app in Windows 10 has replaced many of the traditional Control Panel utilities, the Control Panel is still used for much system management in Windows 10 as well as in Windows 7/8/8.1. The following sections discuss the Control Panel utilities you need to understand for the CompTIA A+ 220-1002 exam. In addition to accessing these functions from the Control Panel, you can also search for them using Start | Search (Windows 7, 10) or open the Charms menu and click Search (Windows 8/8.1).

 **EXAM TIP**   The CompTIA A+ 220-1002 exam specifically assumes Classic view with large icons, so you should do what every tech does: switch from Category view to Classic view. The following sections assume you are using Classic view.

## Internet Options

CompTIA refers to Internet Options, which is in fact a Control Panel applet, but the actual Windows dialog box that opens after clicking Internet Options in Control Panel is called Internet Properties. The Internet Properties tabs are used to configure Internet Explorer (IE) or Microsoft Edge. Thus, if you cannot make the configuration changes you need to in your browser, make them in Internet Properties.

 **NOTE**   You cannot configure non-Microsoft browsers with Internet Properties.

Internet Properties includes the following tabs in Windows 7/8/8.1/10:

- **General**   Set your home page, startup options, browsing history, and appearance settings
- **Security**   Set security levels for websites in different zones (Internet, Local intranet, etc.)
- **Privacy**   Configure the pop-up blocker, set up InPrivate browsing, per-site settings, and cookie management
- **Connections**   Set up Internet, VPN, LAN, proxy settings
- **Programs**   Select default programs for browsing, HTML editing, and file associations
- **Advanced**   Configure accessibility, graphics acceleration, multimedia, and other settings

**EXAM TIP**   Know how to access Internet Options and configure the various Internet Properties browser settings for a given scenario.

# Display/Display Settings

Beyond directly adjusting the display itself, the Display applet in Control Panel or Display Settings app enables you to adjust monitor resolution, refresh rate, driver information, color depth, and more. The specifics differ by operating system, although the options are fairly obvious once you know you can make these changes.

To adjust resolution in Windows 7, click the Adjust resolution link in the Display applet and then click the arrow in the Resolution drop-down list box (see Figure 1.6-1). Manually slide the marker to change resolution.

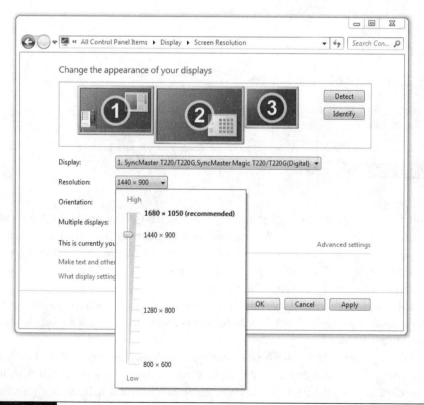

**FIGURE 1.6-1**   Screen Resolution options in Windows 7 Display applet

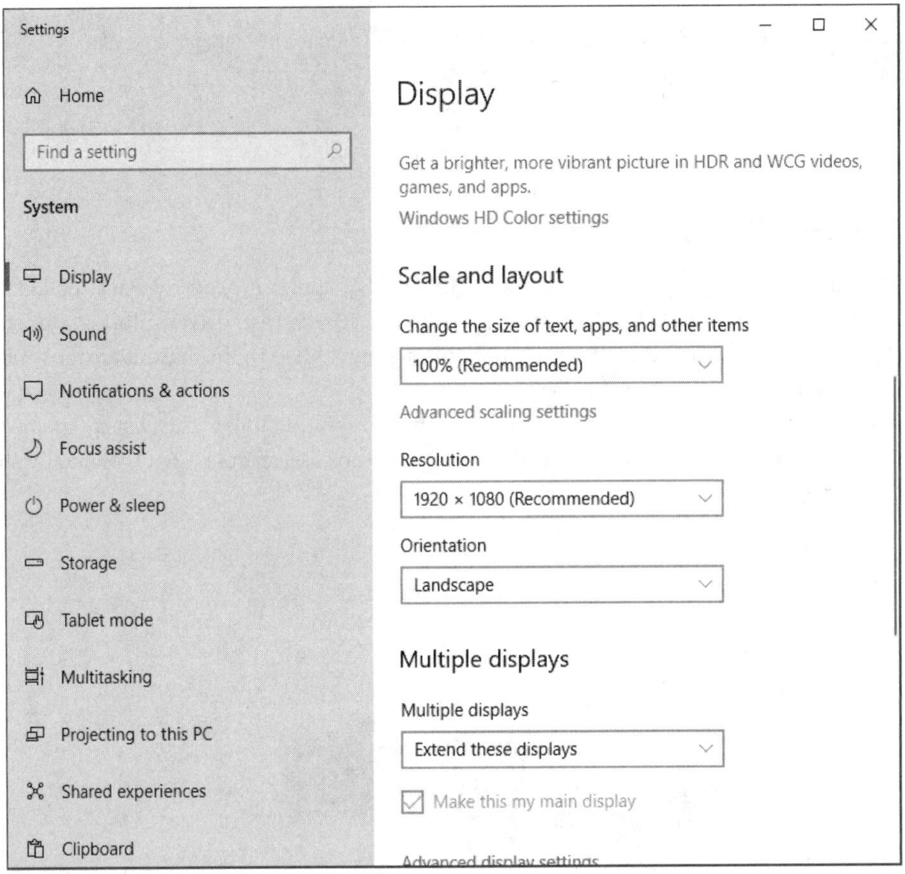

**FIGURE 1.6-2**   Display Settings in Windows 10

Similar options are in Display Settings in Windows 10 (see Figure 1.6-2). Windows displays only resolutions that your video card/monitor combination can accept. Normally, you should use the recommended value, which matches your monitor's native resolution. For those with trouble seeing small screen elements, Windows supports rescaling them to a larger size (though some applications don't handle this well).

The color quality, also called *color depth*, is how many colors the screen can display. Unless you have an older video card or a significant video speed issue, set your color depth to the highest supported value.

LCD displays use a fixed refresh rate (how quickly the screen redraws). However, if you are supporting old systems that use CRT displays, you can also adjust the refresh rate. If your CRT display can use refresh rates of 72 Hz or higher, flickering is reduced or eliminated. To change the refresh rate, click the Advanced settings link in the Display dialog, click Monitor, and choose a different refresh rate.

Another option you may see is multiple monitors or multiple displays (which CompTIA calls *dual displays*). Most systems can use two (or more) monitors like two halves of one large monitor, or to duplicate what's happening on the first. Multiple monitors are handy if you need lots of screen space but don't want to buy a really large, expensive monitor.

Each video card supports one or more monitors, so the first step is to confirm you have one or more video cards that, combined, can support the monitors you need. From here, it's easy. Just plug in the monitors and Windows should detect them. Windows will show each monitor in the Display applet (see Figure 1.6-3). Select the appropriate option to extend or duplicate your desktop on the new monitor. Each monitor can use different resolutions.

**EXAM TIP**   Be sure to know how to change resolution, color depth, and refresh rate.

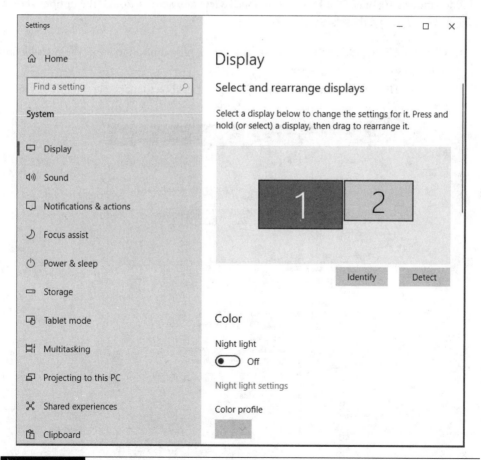

**FIGURE 1.6-3**   Using multiple displays in Windows 10

# User Accounts

The User Accounts applet in the Control Panel enables you to manage your own account (Windows 7/8/8.1), manage other accounts, or change User Account Control settings (refer to Figure 1.5-22 in the previous objective). In Windows 10, you manage your own account using Accounts in Settings.

## Cross-Reference

For more information, see the "User Account Management" section in Objective 1.5 earlier in this domain.

# Folder Options

To change how files and folders are viewed in Windows 7/8/8.1, open Folder options | View tab. In Windows 10, open File Explorer options | View tab. Scroll through the options shown in Figure 1.6-4 to find these settings:

- Click the **Show hidden files, folders, and drives** radio button to make them visible in Windows/File Explorer.
- Clear the **Hide extensions for known file types** checkbox to make file extensions visible.

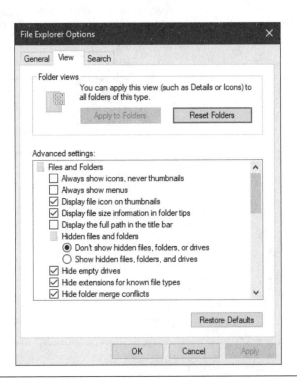

**FIGURE 1.6-4** Viewing folder standard and advanced attributes options in File Explorer

> **NOTE**   Folder options can also be changed in Windows Explorer (Windows 7) or File Explorer (Windows 8/8.1/10).

> **EXAM TIP**   Be sure you know how to show hidden files, folders, and drives in Windows/File Explorer by changing Control Panel settings.

# System

The System applet in Control Panel, in addition to displaying information about the hardware and Windows version in use, is also used for configuring performance and security settings.

## Performance (Virtual Memory)

From the System applet, you can access the Performance Options dialog box to configure CPU, RAM, and virtual memory (page file) settings. To access these options, click the *Advanced system settings* link in the Tasks list.

> **NOTE**   You can also open the System applet by right-clicking Computer or This PC in Windows/File Explorer and clicking Properties.

On the Advanced tab of the System Properties dialog box, click the Settings button in the Performance section. The Performance Options dialog box has three tabs:

- **Visual Effects**   Adjust visual effects for Windows.
- **Advanced**   Adjust processor scheduling for the best performance of programs or background services, and modify the size and location of virtual memory. Virtual memory is used as a substitute for RAM when there is not enough RAM for the currently running programs.
- **Data Execution Prevention (DEP)**   Control which programs are protected by DEP. DEP works in the background to stop viruses and other malware from taking over programs loaded in system memory.

## Remote Settings

To configure whether your Windows system can act as a Remote Assistance or Remote Desktop server, go to the System applet and click the Remote settings link. The Remote tab in System Properties has checkboxes for both Remote Assistance and Remote Desktop, along with buttons to configure more detailed settings.

## System Protection

System protection is used to configure the System Restore feature in Windows. To access it, click the System protection link in the task list. The System Protection tab provides options for turning on protection for each local drive connected to the system, overall system protection settings (enable/disable) and disk space to use, creating a restore point, and selecting a restore point to use when running System Restore.

**Cross-Reference**

To learn more about using System Restore, see the "System Restore" section in Objective 1.5 earlier in this domain.

## Windows Firewall

Windows (Defender) Firewall provides separate settings for private (Home/Work) and public networks. To access Windows (Defender) Firewall in Control Panel, open Windows (Defender) Firewall.

**Cross-Reference**

To learn more about Windows (Defender) Firewall, see the "Windows Firewall" section in Objective 1.5 earlier in this domain.

## Power Options

*Power management* refers to the ability of a system to shut down unused devices. To make this possible, the hardware, UEFI/BIOS, and OS in modern systems cooperate. The first power management standard, Advanced Power Management (APM) has been superseded by Advanced Configuration and Power Interface (ACPI). However, it's common to refer to both standards when discussing power management.

APM and ACPI require the following: a CPU that supports SMM (system management mode), capable of being slowed down or stopped to save power; a BIOS or UEFI/BIOS that supports APM and ACPI, enabling the CPU to turn off devices; Energy Star–compliant devices that can be turned off by the CPU; and an OS that can be configured to turn off unused devices and slow down the CPU when desired.

### Power Plans

In Windows, APM/ACPI settings are in the Power Options Control Panel applet (also accessible via the Power icon in the notification area—if it is present). Windows *power plans*—Balanced, High performance, and Power saver—enable better control over power (see Figure 1.6-5).

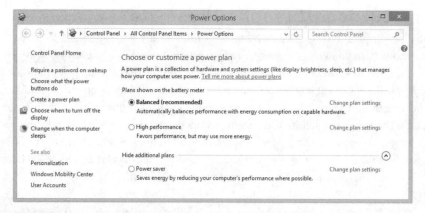

**FIGURE 1.6-5**    Windows Balanced, High performance, and Power saver power plan options

You can customize a power plan for your portable (see Figure 1.6-6) that will turn off the display or put the computer to sleep at different time intervals when on battery or AC power.

In Windows 10, you can also change display and sleep power settings: Settings | System | Power & sleep.

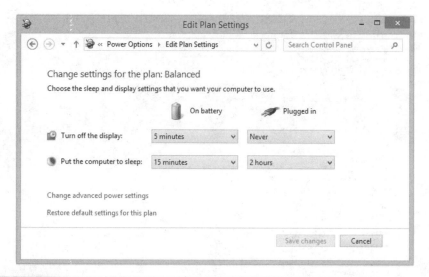

**FIGURE 1.6-6**    Customizing a laptop power plan in Windows

## Sleep/Suspend/Standby/Hibernate

Optional power plan settings include sleep, suspend, standby, and hibernate.

*Sleep* mode (also known as *suspend*) runs the system at very low power by saving the current system condition to RAM. This enables the system to be fully operational in just a few seconds. *Standby* runs the system at less power than normal, but more than sleep mode; standby mode is found mainly in older systems. *Hibernate* mode takes everything in active memory and stores it on the hard drive before the system powers down, and reloads it into RAM when the system wakes. To enable these modes, you might need to open Power Options | Choose what the power buttons do. Items that are checked in Shutdown settings are enabled. To change settings, click the *Change settings that are currently unavailable* link (Figure 1.6-7).

 **EXAM TIP**   Be sure to understand the differences between sleep/suspend, standby, and hibernate.

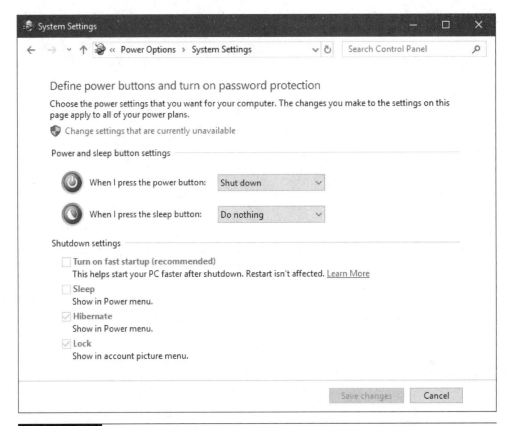

**FIGURE 1.6-7**   Power button and shut down settings dialog in Power Options

# Credential Manager

The Credential Manager Control Panel applet is used to store and manage credentials used by websites that require logins. Select the credential type and click the credential to view details. To view a credential's password, click Show and provide the user name and password for the credential. You can also edit or remove a credential.

# Programs and Features

Programs and Features (see Figure 1.6-8) is used to view and manage installed programs, uninstall or repair programs, and turn Windows features on and off. In Windows 10, you can use either Programs and Features in the Control Panel or Apps and features in Settings to perform program management.

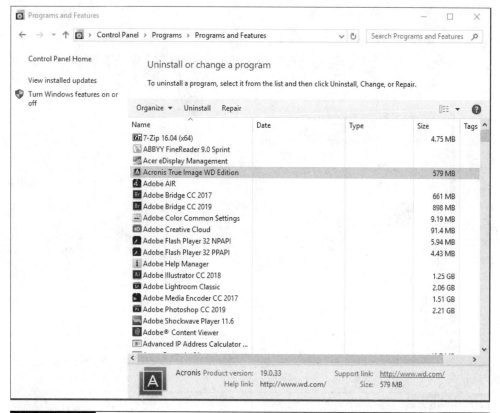

**FIGURE 1.6-8**   Using Programs and Features in Windows 10 to uninstall or repair an app

# HomeGroup

Windows 7, 8/8.1, and early releases of Windows 10 all support HomeGroup, a home networking technology for sharing folders and printers.

To create a homegroup, open the HomeGroup applet and click Create a homegroup. Select the libraries or printers you want to share with other users and note the password (all users of the homegroup use the same password). To join an existing homegroup, open the HomeGroup applet, click Join now, enter the password, choose which libraries you want to share with everyone else, and the new computer is in the homegroup!

A homegroup is set up on one computer on the network (see Figure 1.6-9), and the homegroup password that is generated during setup is used to add other computers to the homegroup. Use File Explorer or Windows Explorer to access the contents of a homegroup or conventionally networked devices.

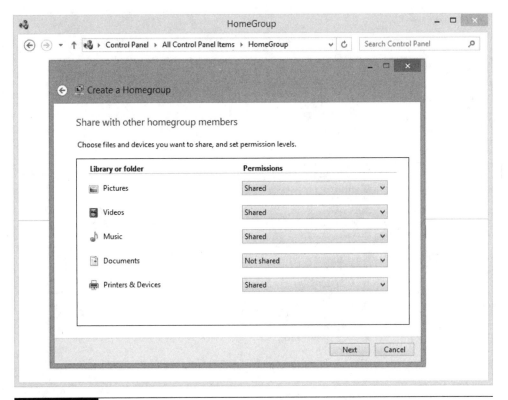

**FIGURE 1.6-9**   Creating a new homegroup in Windows 8.1

**NOTE**  Windows 10 dropped HomeGroup support starting with version 1803. To share files and printers from Windows 10 version 1803 and newer editions, right-click a folder or printer, select *Give access to*, and specify the user(s) to share with. Windows 7/8/8.1 can also share with Windows 10 version 1803 and newer with the right-click menu, choosing Share with.

# Devices and Printers

Devices and Printers provides centralized viewing and management of computers, monitors, printers, and peripherals (see Figure 1.6-10).

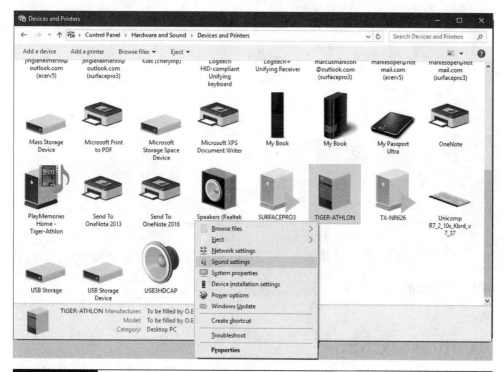

**FIGURE 1.6-10**  Using Devices and Printers to access computer settings

**NOTE** If Windows does not automatically detect a newly connected device or printer, you can use the corresponding toolbar option in the Devices and Printers applet.

# Sound

The Sound applet features a Playback tab for managing speakers and headset volume and balance (see Figure 1.6-11), a Recording tab for managing microphone volume and gain, a Sounds tab for selecting and modifying sound schemes (the sounds that play during events such as system startup or errors), and a Communications tab to specify what to do with sound volume during telephone calls. Click the Configure button to set up the selected device, the Set Default button to specify which device to use as default, and the Properties button to tweak additional volume or other properties.

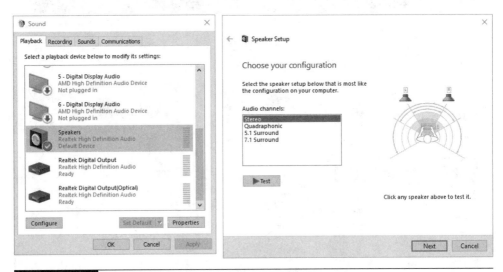

**FIGURE 1.6-11**  Selecting the speaker setup using the Configure button in the Sound applet

# Troubleshooting

Troubleshooting is located in Control Panel in Windows 7/8/8.1 (see Figure 1.6-12) and in Settings | Update & Security in Windows 10 (see Figure 1.6-13). Click the issue you are having problems with and follow the prompts or suggested tasks to resolve the problem.

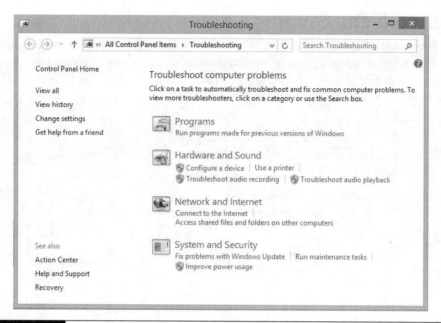

**FIGURE 1.6-12**   Selecting a troubleshooter in Windows 8.1

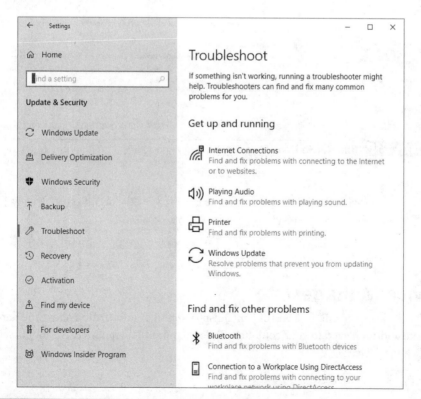

**FIGURE 1.6-13**   Selecting a troubleshoot tool in Windows 10

# Network and Sharing Center

The Network and Sharing Center applet allows you to set up a new connection or network, set up a homegroup on supported systems, troubleshoot network problems, change network adapter settings, and change advanced sharing settings. The Windows 7 version (see Figure 1.6-14) also allows you to see the status of your network.

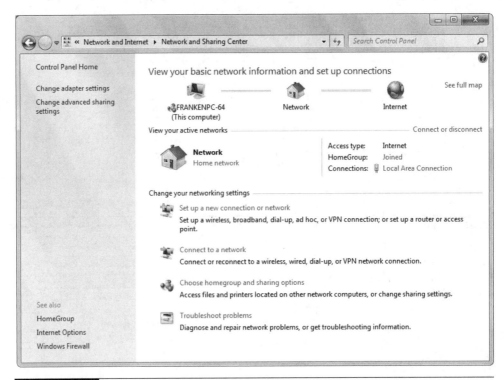

**FIGURE 1.6-14**    The Network and Sharing Center in Windows 7

---

**EXAM TIP**    To see the status of your network in Windows 10, go to Settings | Network & Internet | Status.

---

# Device Manager

The Device Manager link in Control Panel displays specific information about the hardware built into and connected to your computer. To learn more about a device, expand its category and click the device.

**Cross-References**

To learn more about using Device Manager, see the "Device Manager" section in Objective 1.5 earlier in this domain.

# BitLocker

BitLocker drive encryption is supported on Professional, Ultimate, and Enterprise editions of Windows 7; Pro and Enterprise editions of Windows 8/8.1; and Pro, Enterprise, and Education editions of Windows 10. Use it to encrypt the system drive or to enable BitLocker To Go encryption on USB drives.

 **NOTE**   To use BitLocker or BitLocker To Go on systems that don't have a Trusted Platform Module (TPM) chip, you will need to enable the option to use BitLocker without a TPM in the local security policy.

# Sync Center

Sync Center is used to set up and manage file sync between remote servers and local computers. Click the *Manage offline files* link in the task pane to enable/or disable offline files, view offline files, set up disk usage limits, encrypt offline files, and configure when to check for slow connections.

# REVIEW

**Objective 1.6: Given a scenario, use Microsoft Windows Control Panel utilities**   Control Panel and system utilities you need to be familiar with include

- Internet Options (aka Internet Properties)
- Display/Display Settings (resolution, color depth, and refresh rate)
- User Accounts
- Folder Options (view options)
- System (performance/virtual memory, remote settings, and system protection)
- Windows Firewall
- Power Options (power plans and sleep modes)
- Credential Manager
- Programs and Features

- HomeGroup (for Windows 7/8/8.1 and older Windows 10 versions)
- Devices and Printers
- Sound
- Troubleshooting (located in Settings in Windows 10)
- Network and Sharing Center
- Device Manager
- BitLocker
- Sync Center

## 1.6 QUESTIONS

1. A user has just upgraded from Windows 8.1 to the latest release of Windows 10 and can no longer connect to the homegroup. What should be done next?

   **A.** Repair HomeGroup

   **B.** Set up Folder sharing on the computers instead of HomeGroup

   **C.** Create a new homegroup using the Windows 10 computer

   **D.** Upgrade all of the other computers to Windows 10

2. The corporate network has just added a proxy server. Which utility is used to configure proxy settings for each Windows computer on the network?

   **A.** System properties

   **B.** Network and Sharing Center

   **C.** Internet Options

   **D.** Sync Center

3. A user has just switched from stereo speakers to a 5.1 surround sound setup, but there is no audio coming from the center or rear speakers. Which Sound applet option is used to set up the speakers?

   **A.** Playback

   **B.** Communications

   **C.** Set Default

   **D.** Configure

4. A user reports problems with a particular app in Windows 8.1. He considered using System Restore to fix the problem, but there would be many other apps and updates that may be lost using this method. Which of the following would you try instead?

   **A.** Uninstall and reinstall app

   **B.** Use Apps and features

   **C.** Use SFC

   **D.** Use Programs and Features

5. A new Windows user (who formerly used macOS) is looking for a quick way to get access to change settings for the major devices in a computer. Which of the following would you advise using?

    **A.** Computer Management

    **B.** System

    **C.** Devices and Printers

    **D.** Settings

## 1.6 ANSWERS

1. **B** Newer releases of Windows 10 do not support HomeGroup. Folder sharing works with any version of Windows.

2. **C** Proxy settings are configured by clicking the Internet Options applet in the Control Panel and going to the Connections tab of the Internet Properties dialog box that opens.

3. **D** Different speaker configurations are viewed and selected from the Sound applet by clicking the Configure button.

4. **D** The Programs and Features applet is used in Windows 7/8/8.1/10 to repair programs.

5. **C** Devices and Printers provides shortcuts to most options that are in separate Control Panel applets or Windows 10 Settings dialogs.

**Objective 1.7** # Summarize application installation and configuration concepts

After installing and updating an operating system, the next step in preparing a computer for use is installing applications. The exact procedure for installing an app depends on whether you are installing it on a Windows system (and which version), Linux system, or macOS system and whether the app is located in an app store or a repository, but there are fundamental procedures that should be followed with any of the operating systems covered on the CompTIA A+ 220-1002 exam.

## System Requirements

Before installing an application, compare its hardware requirements to the computer system where it will be installed (often called the target computer). Some of these requirements might include

- Processor type and speed
- Amount of available *drive space*

- Amount of *RAM*
- Graphics card and graphics memory
- Network features

**EXAM TIP** Drive space and RAM are the biggest concerns in application compatibility.

## Drive Space

The amount of drive space available on the system drive (C: in Windows) can be a big concern on systems with limited space, such as systems running SSDs. To find out how much space an app needs, check its installation requirements first.

With Windows 10, you can sometimes install an app on a non-system drive, but if you cannot and space is limited, you might need to remove seldom-used applications to make room for one you need, run Disk Cleanup to remove unnecessary temp files, old installation, and system files and so on.

**ADDITIONAL RESOURCES** To learn more about Disk Cleanup, go to https://support.microsoft.com and search for "Disk cleanup."

You can also use symbolic links in Windows 7 and newer to access software and data files on a different drive than C: and have them work properly.

**ADDITIONAL RESOURCES** For details, go to www.howtogeek.com and search for "The Complete Guide to Creating Symbolic Links (aka Symlinks) on Windows."

## RAM

The amount of RAM needed for an application is also a big concern on non-upgradeable systems, which now includes many laptops as well as tablets and 2-in-1 convertible devices. Although operating systems can use hard disk space as a RAM substitute (virtual memory), the application performance will leave much to be desired if the system lacks adequate RAM. Some applications will not install if RAM is inadequate.

Windows automatically configures virtual memory, but to improve system performance when you can't add more RAM, you can increase the size of virtual memory through the System applet: click Advanced system settings | Settings (Performance section) | Advanced | Change.

**ADDITIONAL RESOURCES** To learn more, go to https://support.microsoft .com and search for "Virtual memory."

# OS Requirements

Most applications made for Windows, macOS, or Linux are designed to run on a range of operating system versions. However, issues such as the following can prevent an app from working on a particular OS:

* App runs in 64-bit mode only—you couldn't run it on a 32-bit system.
* App made for a newer version of the OS than what is in use.
* App requires a newer version of DirectX 3D support than what the OS provides (Windows).
* App not compatible with the version of OS in use—some proprietary apps cannot run on Windows 10, etc.
* App cannot be expanded to full-screen—common behavior with apps made for early 32-bit Windows versions (Windows 9x/Me) when run on current versions of Windows.

# Compatibility

Windows includes the following tools to enable apps made for older versions of Windows to run on the installed version of Windows:

* Compatibility wizard in Control Panel (Windows 7/8/8.1)
* Program Compatibility Troubleshooter (Windows 10)
* Compatibility tab in program's Properties dialog box (see Figure 1.7-1)

Types of compatibility settings that can be used include

* Changing the version of Windows that the app detects
* Adjusting how the app uses the screen
* Running the app in administrator mode

The Compatibility wizard and Program Compatibility Troubleshooter can be used to determine the specific compatibility fixes needed for an app and apply them. The Compatibility tab (Figure 1.7-1) enables you to apply desired settings to the app before running it.

**EXAM TIP** Compatibility tools can help newer versions of Windows to run apps made for older versions.

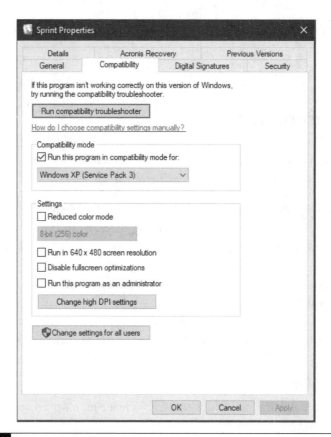

**FIGURE 1.7-1**    Using the Compatibility tab for an older app

# Methods of Installation and Deployment

Applications can be installed from two sources: *local (CD/USB)* and *network-based*. At one time, most applications for Windows and macOS were only installed from physical (CD/USB) media. However, with the rise of high-speed networking and Internet access and frequent software updates, most packaged software sold at retail now contains a key card used for validating and obtaining the application from a download source.

Network-based application installations in Windows may come from vendor websites or, with Windows 8 and later, from the Microsoft Store app store. In macOS, almost all apps are provided by the App Store.

In Linux, apps are provided primarily by the software repository provided by the distro in use. Typical distro ISO disk images include a large software repository, but updates to the repository are obtained online, so Linux uses a hybrid of local and network-based app installation.

Android and iOS apps can be installed through the app store or, in corporate environments, via mobile device management (MDM) and mobile applications management (MAM) software.

 **EXAM TIP**    Understand the differences between local (CD/USB) and network-based application installs.

# Local User Permissions

Before an application can be installed, the appropriate local user permissions must be configured. In Windows, administrator-level users can install apps. Depending on the app, the app can be installed for all users or the current user only. In macOS, apps are installed for the current user.

## Folder/File Access for Installation

Apps are generally installed into specific folders. On Windows, the default installation folder is \Program Files for 64-bit or 32-bit Windows. On 64-bit Windows, 32-bit apps are installed into \Program Files (x86).

In macOS, apps are installed into the Applications folder. In Linux, different folders are used for application binaries (/bin, /sbin), library files (/lib), optional application software packages (/opt), and more. The Filesystem Hierarchy Standard (FHS) is the standard directory structure used by Linux distributions.

 **ADDITIONAL RESOURCES**    Go to http://refspecs.linuxfoundation.org/fhs .shtml for details on FHS 3.0.

 **EXAM TIP**    Be sure to know where apps are installed on Windows and macOS.

# Security Considerations

Because apps need to interact with computer hardware, other apps, and network connections, an improperly designed app can be a security risk.

## Impact to Device and Impact to Network

Most apps require access to other parts of the device's hardware or software subsystems to work. Many apps also require access to the network to work. The Microsoft Store and Google

Play app stores provide information about the permissions an app needs, so you can review this information before you install it.

 **EXAM TIP**    Review what an app needs in the way of access to device and network resources before you install it.

# REVIEW

### Objective 1.7: Summarize application installation and configuration concepts

- Before installing an application, the device's hardware and software (including the operating system and other apps) should be checked for compatibility. Drive space can be an issue on mobile devices or on computers that use SSDs. Systems with non-upgradeable RAM might not be able to run some apps.
- To avoid compatibility issues with apps, Windows includes compatibility features to enable older apps to run on newer versions of Windows and newer hardware.
- Most current systems use network-based installations, either by direct download, app stores, or software repositories. Checking permissions needed by an app is useful to determine if an app is a security risk.

## 1.7 QUESTIONS

1. A 32-bit Windows app is being installed on two computers, a system running 32-bit Windows and a system running 64-bit Windows. Where will it be installed on the system running 64-bit Windows?
   
   **A.** Program Files
   
   **B.** Program Files (x64)
   
   **C.** Program Files (x86)
   
   **D.** Any of the above

2. A user is trying to install a 64-bit Windows app on a system running a 32-bit version of Windows. Which of the following recommendations should you make?
   
   **A.** Use the Program Compatibility Wizard
   
   **B.** Create a Program Files (x64) folder for the program
   
   **C.** Use the Compatibility tab
   
   **D.** Install a 32-bit version of the app

3. You are preparing a laptop for a trip that involves 12 hours of flight time. You have purchased a software key card from a retail store to use on the trip. When should you install the app?

   **A.** On the flight

   **B.** Before leaving for the airport

   **C.** While waiting for the flight

   **D.** Any of the above are acceptable

4. Your department is preparing to evaluate a new app that has a minimum requirement of 4 GB of RAM but recommends 8 GB of RAM. The systems you want to use have 4 GB of RAM and are expandable to 16 GB. Which of the following will help you evaluate the software most fairly?

   **A.** Set up a large pagefile on each system

   **B.** Install the software on all computers and see how slow they run

   **C.** Install upgrades to 8 GB on some systems and install the app on all systems for comparison

   **D.** Look for software that runs with 4 GB of RAM

5. Although your department is now running Windows 10, it relies on an application made for Windows 7. It doesn't run properly on Windows 10. Which of the following could be used to help it run correctly?

   **A.** Device Manager

   **B.** System properties

   **C.** Compatibility tab

   **D.** Virtual memory

## 1.7 ANSWERS

1. **C**   The Program Files (x86) folder is found only on 64-bit versions of Windows. It is used to enable both x86 (32-bit) and 64-bit apps to run properly (64-bit apps are installed into the Program Files folder).

2. **D**   32-bit apps work on 32-bit or 64-bit operating systems, but you cannot install a 64-bit app on a 32-bit operating system.

3. **B**   If you wait to install the app until you go to the airport or until onboard, you might not have access to an Internet connection or might need to pay a lot for a very slow connection needed to download and configure the software.

4. **C**   By upgrading some system to 8 GB and running the app on all systems, you can determine if the performance differences between systems with 4 GB and 8 GB of RAM justifies upgrading all computers in the department.

5. **C**   The Compatibility tab in the application's Properties dialog box provides access to the compatibility troubleshooter and to compatibility settings you can select manually.

### Objective 1.8 Given a scenario, configure Microsoft Windows networking on a client/desktop

Microsoft Windows is ready to connect to a network as soon as it is installed. However, a number of configuration settings need to be made, which vary depending on the network type. This objective covers the Windows network settings you need to understand.

## HomeGroup vs. Workgroup

The standard network type for Windows is a workgroup, which allows the computers on the network to share files, folders, and printers with each other. However, each computer on the network must have its local and remote users manually configured. The default name for a workgroup in Windows is WORKGROUP, but you can change it in the System applet.

HomeGroup technology, introduced in Windows 7 and also available in Windows 8/8.1 and early versions of Windows 10, provides easier security and setup than a workgroup. One user creates a homegroup, selects what to share with other users, and distributes the password to other users as desired. The homegroup uses a single randomly generated password, but each user decides what resources to share (printers, documents, pictures, music, or videos). To create or join a homegroup, use the HomeGroup applet.

A domain uses a domain controller (typically running some version of Windows Server and Active Directory) to provide centralized administration of all users on the network. With a domain server, a user logs into an account stored on the domain controller, rather than an account set up on an individual computer. Each user on a domain can be placed into a group of users, each of which can have different levels of access to network resources such as apps, folders, printers, and other network hardware.

**EXAM TIP** Make sure you can explain the differences between homegroups, workgroups, and domains.

## Domain Setup

To join an existing domain, open the System applet, click *Advanced system settings*, click the Computer Name tab, and click Change. Click Domain and enter the name of the domain you want to join (see Figure 1.8-1).

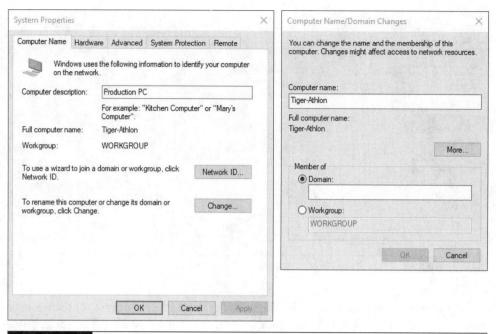

**FIGURE 1.8-1**   Preparing to join a domain (Windows 10)

# Network Shares/Administrative Shares/Mapping Drives

A *network share* is a folder that is shared with other users. Network shares require that File and Printer Sharing be enabled on each computer that will share folders with others. There are two ways to share a folder from its right-click menu:

- Choose Properties, click the Sharing tab, and click Advanced Sharing to open the Advanced Sharing dialog box (see Figure 1.8-2). You can specify the number of simultaneous users (20 is the max for non-server versions) and click Permissions to set up different permissions for different users or groups at the same time (shown on the right in Figure 1.8-2).

- Choose Share with | Specific people (Windows 7) or Give access to | Specific people (Windows 8/8.1/10). In the *Choose people to share with* dialog box (see Figure 1.8-3), you can choose individual users who have accounts on the system to share with.

- By default, new Windows shares only have Read permission; click the Permission Level drop-down to set your share to Full Control.

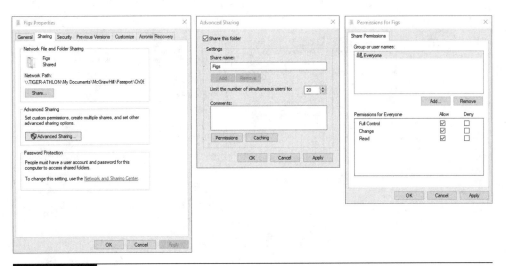

**FIGURE 1.8-2**   Advanced Sharing dialog boxes (Windows 10)

*Administrative shares* are hidden file shares. For example, the administrative share for the root folder of C: drive is C$. To access the share, a remote user must use the computer name and administrative share and provide a password and username (these must already be stored on the computer with the administrative share): \\server1\c$ opens the C: drive administrative

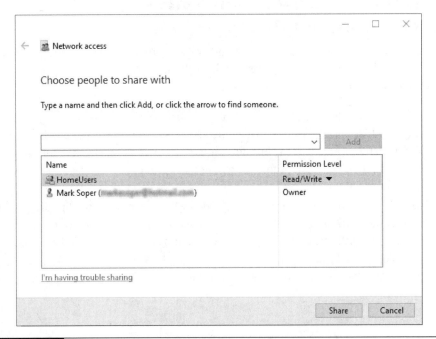

**FIGURE 1.8-3**   Choose people to share with dialog (Windows 10)

share on \\server1. Other administrative shares include admin$ (used to install software remotely) and IPC$ (used for the Server service to enable listing all shares, all users, and other remote procedure call commands), among others.

**EXAM TIP**   Make sure you understand what administrative shares are used for.

*Mapped drives* permit a network folder to be accessed with a drive letter. Some old apps must use drive letters, but they can also be used for convenience. To map a drive in Windows, use the *Map network drive* option in File Explorer/Windows Explorer or open a command-prompt session and use the **net use** command.

# Printer Sharing vs. Network Printer Mapping

Like network shares, printer sharing requires that File and Printer Sharing be enabled on each computer that will share printers with others. *Printer mapping* refers to setting up a shared remote printer on a networked computer. To map a printer, use Devices and Printers to add a printer, selecting the option to add a network printer. The process displays available shared printers (see Figure 1.8-4). Choose a printer, and the drivers are installed for you.

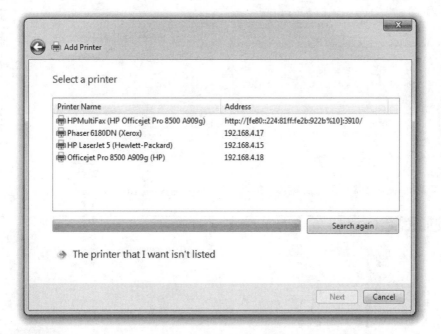

**FIGURE 1.8-4**   List of available shared printers on a network

While a manual printer mapping process is simple if you have only a few workstations, you will want to automate the process with a group policy setting (which works with either workgroup or domain networks) or a login script if you have a domain.

 **EXAM TIP**   Expect a question or two on the CompTIA A+ 220-1002 exam giving you a scenario where you need to choose printer sharing versus network printer mapping. Be careful on the exam if logon script is an option and group policy is not.

You can also browse your workgroup for printers or enter a printer's TCP/IP address or host name (see Figure 1.8-5).

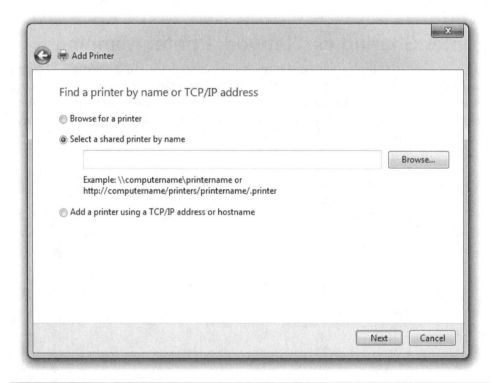

**FIGURE 1.8-5**   Options for setting up network printers

# Establish Networking Connections

Windows supports a wide variety of network connections, including VPN, dial-up, wireless, wired, and cellular (WWAN). The following sections provide a quick reference to each of these.

## VPN

To set up a virtual private networking (VPN) connection in Windows 7/8/8.1, open Control Panel in Classic mode | Network & Sharing Center | Set up a new connection or network | Connect to a workplace | Use my Internet connection (VPN).

In Windows 10, open Settings | Network and Internet | VPN | Add a VPN connection.

Enter the IP address of the VPN connection and a connection name, user name and password, and other information as prompted (Figure 1.8-6).

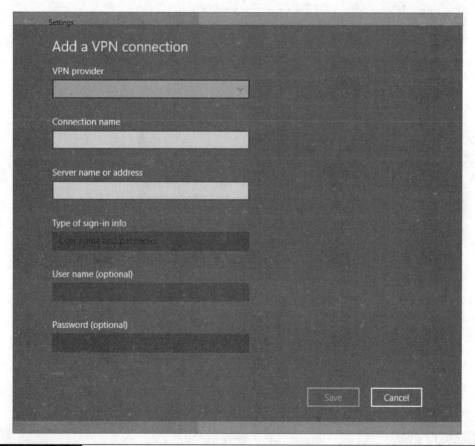

**FIGURE 1.8-6**  Add a VPN connection dialog (Windows 10)

## Dial-ups

To create a dial-up connection in Windows 7, open the Network and Sharing Center, click *Set up a new connection or network*, and click *Set up a dial-up connection*. To create a dial-up connection in Windows 8.1, open the Network and Sharing Center, click *Set up a new connection or network*, and click Connect to the Internet. To create a dial-up connection in Windows 10, open the Dial-up dialog box in the Network & Internet section of Settings and click *Set up a new connection*. Click Connect to the Internet, then click Dial-up.

You can set up the connection even if Windows can't detect your modem. When prompted, enter the phone number, user name, and password assigned by the ISP.

## Wireless

On a system with a Wi-Fi adapter installed and enabled, Windows automatically detects wireless networks. To connect to a network, click the wireless network icon in the taskbar (see Figure 1.8-7). If it's hidden, click the up-arrow icon first.

To connect, click the wireless network desired. To reuse the network connection, click the Connect automatically checkbox (see Figure 1.8-8). If the network is secured, enter the encryption key when prompted.

**FIGURE 1.8-7**   Selecting a wireless network (Windows 7)

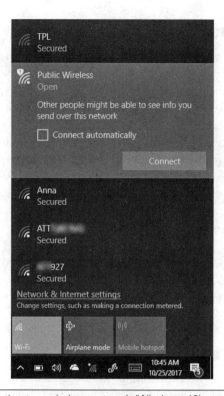

**FIGURE 1.8-8**    Connecting to a wireless network (Windows 10)

# Wired

Windows automatically connects to a wired network when a wired NIC in the computer is connected to a router, switch, or hub. However, it might be necessary to configure proxy or IP address settings to have a working connection.

# WWAN (Cellular)

To create a WWAN (cellular) connection in Windows, click the Network icon in the taskbar, and click the name of the network. If prompted, enter the user name, password, and APN (access point name). Provide any other information needed.

 **EXAM TIP**    Make sure you can explain the differences between the Windows configuration of VPN, dial-up, wireless, wired, and WWAN (cellular) connections.

# Proxy Settings

A *proxy server* is an intermediary between its users and the resources they request. Applications send requests to the proxy server instead of trying to access the Internet directly, and the proxy server fetches the resources on behalf of the users. This enables the proxy server to monitor usage; restrict access to or modify insecure or objectionable content; cache, compress, or strip out resources to improve performance; and more.

To set up manual proxy server settings, click the Internet Options Control Panel applet and then click the Connections tab in the Internet Properties dialog box. Click LAN Settings, click the empty *Use a proxy server* box, and enter the URL of the proxy server. It uses UDP port 80 by default; change the port as needed. If different proxy servers are used for different types of content (HTTP:, Secure[HTTPS], FTP:, and Socks:), click Advanced and enter the proxy server URLs and port numbers as needed. Click OK when done.

 **NOTE** In Windows 10, you can also set up a proxy server through Settings | Network & Internet | Proxy.

# Remote Desktop Connection

Remote Desktop Connection is a Windows feature used to host connections from other Windows computers (Remote Desktop support is also available for iOS and Android mobile devices).

**Cross-Reference**

For more information, see the "MSTSC (Remote Desktop Connection)" section in Objective 1.5 earlier in this domain.

# Remote Assistance

Windows Remote Assistance (shown in Figure 1.8-9) enables you to grant or assume control, enabling a user to request support directly from you. Upon receiving the support-request e-mail, you can log on to the user's system and, with permission, take the driver's seat.

The connecting system is a client and the remote system is a server providing access to its desktop. To configure whether your Windows system can act as a Remote Assistance or Remote Desktop server, go to the System applet and select the Remote settings link on the left. The Remote tab in System Properties has options for both Remote Assistance and Remote Desktop, along with some detailed settings.

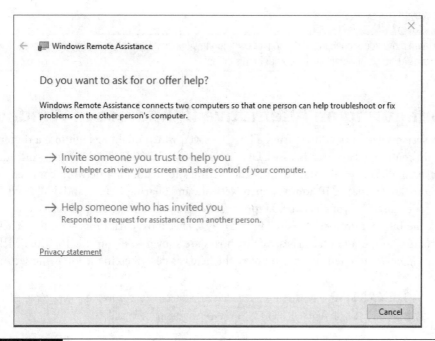

**FIGURE 1.8-9**  Windows Remote Assistance (Windows 10)

# Home vs. Work vs. Public Network Settings

You may be prompted to select a network type when you first connect to a network, or you can change it later using Network and Sharing Center. Home and Work networks are Private networks. A Private network is one in which you can trust the other computers and devices on the network and share folders and devices with them. A Public (or Guest) network, such as a network provided by a library, hotel, or coffee shop, is not secure. By default, folder and printer sharing is not enabled on a public network. These network types are used to configure Windows Firewall.

# Firewall Settings

Selecting Home, Work, or Public as the network type for a particular network connection configures Windows Firewall to block or unblock discovery and sharing services. When running on a Private (Home or Work) network, Windows enables Network Discovery and File and Printer Sharing as exceptions. When running on a Guest or Public network, Windows disables these exceptions.

*Exceptions* are apps or processes that are allowed to pass through the firewall. You can set up exceptions for inbound traffic with the standard Windows Firewall, or for outbound traffic with the Windows Firewall with Advanced Security.

> **Cross-Reference**
>
> To learn more about enabling, disabling, or configuring Windows Firewall, see the "Windows Firewall" section in Objective 1.5 earlier in this domain.

# Configuring an Alternative IP Address in Windows

Most systems get an IP address from a DHCP server, which might be built into a router or a domain controller. However, in case a DHCP server fails, Windows enables a network adapter to have an alternative IP address and other settings to maintain a network connection. To configure an alternative IP address, open Network and Sharing Center, and double-click the connection used by your network. From the General tab for the adapter, click Properties, check the Internet Protocol Version 4 (TCP/IPv4) checkbox, click Properties, then click the Alternate Configuration tab. These dialog boxes are shown in Figure 1.8-10. Then click the *User configured* radio button and complete the fields as described in the following sections.

 **EXAM TIP**    Make sure you understand the differences between an alternate IP address, an APIPA IP address, and a server-assigned IP address.

## IP Addressing

When a client cannot obtain an IP address automatically, the default alternate IP address is for Automatic Private IP Addressing (APIPA) to assign an IP address to the system. APIPA enables computers on a network to connect to each other but not to reach the Internet. An APIPA IPv4 address begins with the digits 169.254.

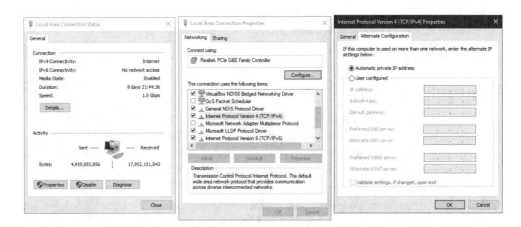

**FIGURE 1.8-10**    Getting ready to set up an alternate configuration for TCP/IPv4

If you want to set up an alternate IP address that will maintain an Internet connection, use a value that is not already assigned to another device on the network. Each computer must have a unique IP address in the same range. For example, if the DHCP server normally assigns values in the range 192.168.0.2–99, choose a value starting with 192.168.0.100 (up to 254).

## Subnet Mask

The subnet mask distinguishes which part of the IP address identifies the network ID and which part of the address identifies the host. The subnet mask blocks out (or masks) the network portion of an IP address. Use the same subnet mask for all the computers that will connect to each other, such as 255.255.255.0.

## Gateway

The default gateway is the IP address for your network's router. On private networks in a home or small office, a common value is 192.168.0.1. Check your network configuration for details.

## DNS

DNS servers translate host names (such as www.microsoft.com) into IP addresses. Google and other vendors offer freely available DNS servers you can use. Google's DNS servers are 8.8.8.8 and 8.8.4.4.

 **NOTE**    WINS Servers were used to provide a name service for computers that have NetBIOS computer names. WINS is a legacy technology which has been replaced by DNS.

# Network Card Properties

Network cards (wired or wireless) generally don't require configuration. However, some network implementations may benefit from taking a look at how the network card properties are set. To see the configuration for a network adapter, open Network and Sharing Center, and double-click the connection used by your network. From the General tab for the adapter, click Properties, and click the Configure button in the Local Area Connection Properties dialog box (shown in the center of Figure 1.8-10 in the previous section), then click the Advanced tab (see Figure 1.8-11). Scroll through the properties listed to find the ones discussed in the following sections.

 **EXAM TIP**    Make sure you know which dialog boxes contain the properties discussed in these sections.

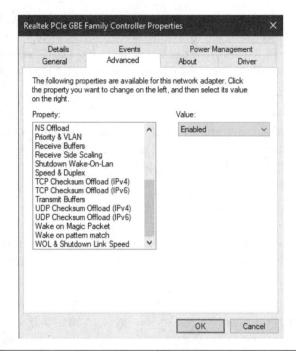

**FIGURE 1.8-11** Viewing the Advanced tab settings for a Gigabit Ethernet adapter

## Half Duplex/Full Duplex/Auto/Speed

Speed & Duplex are typically listed as a single property. Select this option and then choose the speed and duplex setting desired. When half duplex is selected, the network adapter must switch between sending or receiving data. Full duplex enables the network adapter to send and receive data at the same time.

Speed settings are designed to enable a faster adapter to work on a slower network. However, you should use Auto unless the device can't work properly on the network.

## Wake-on-LAN

Change the Wake-on-LAN (WOL) settings if the network adapter is not able to "wake up" the device after receiving a signal from another device on the network. To enable these settings, click the Shutdown WOL or WOL property and select Enable from the Value drop-down list. Then, click the Wake on Magic Packet property and select Enable from the Value drop-down list.

## QoS

QoS (quality of service) is used to prioritize streaming audio and video to make voice chatting and Voice over IP (VoIP) services provide better sound quality.

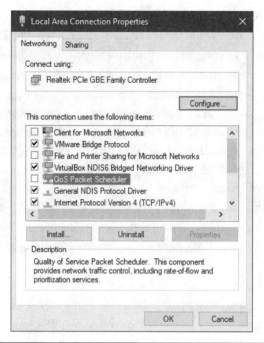

**FIGURE 1.8-12**   Check the QoS Packet Scheduler box to enable QoS.

To enable this, check the QoS Packet Scheduler checkbox in the Properties dialog box (refer to Figure 1.8-12). You can modify this setting by changing the Packet Priority & VLAN or Priority & VLAN property in the Advanced tab.

## BIOS (on-board NIC)

To enable the system to boot from an onboard NIC, enable the NIC's BIOS through the system BIOS or UEFI firmware configuration menu.

# REVIEW

**Objective 1.8: Given a scenario, configure Microsoft Windows networking on a client/desktop**   Network settings in this objective include

- HomeGroup is a Windows technology for easy and secure sharing. It is supported in Windows 7, 8/8.1, and early versions of Windows 10. A workgroup is a simple network supported by Windows 7 and newer versions. Unlike homegroups, each computer in a workgroup must have local and remote users manually configured.
- Domains use a domain controller running Windows Server and Active Directory to provide centralized control of users and resources.

- A network share is a folder shared with other users.
- Administrative shares are hidden file shares such as the root folder of a drive.
- A mapped drive is a network share that has been assigned a drive letter.
- A printer shared with other users is an example of printer sharing.
- Network printer mapping is connecting to a shared printer from another computer.
- Windows includes support for VPN, dial-up, wireless, wired, and WWAN (Cellular) connections. With Windows 7/8/8.1, these connections are created through Network and Sharing Center in Control Panel. With Windows 10, use Settings, Network & Internet.
- Proxy settings capture web page requests and provide the requested information from their proxy servers' copies. Proxy settings are configured through Internet Options.
- Remote Desktop Connection hosts connections from other Windows computers.
- Remote Assistance shares a desktop with a remote computer.
- Home vs. Work vs. Public network settings are used to configure the Windows (Defender) Firewall.
- Exceptions are used to permit traffic through a firewall.
- Windows (Defender) Firewall can be disabled if another firewall is used.
- The default alternative IP address in Windows is an APIPA (non-routeable) IP address.
- To set up a manual alternative IP address, use a non-duplicating IP address in the same range as other devices, the same subnet mask as other devices on the network, two DNS servers, and the IP address of the network's default gateway.
- To configure network card properties, open Network and Sharing Center, open the connection, click Properties. You can enable QoS from this dialog. To configure the following settings, click Configure, then the Advanced tab.
  - Half duplex/full duplex/auto
  - Speed
  - Wake-on-LAN
- The BIOS for an onboard NIC (used for PXE connections) is enabled through the system's UEFI/BIOS firmware dialog.

## 1.8 QUESTIONS

1. A documentation folder on a corporate intranet needs to be available to up to 20 users with different access levels. Which of the following sharing methods will permit this configuration?

   **A.** Share with

   **B.** HomeGroup

   **C.** VPN

   **D.** Advanced Sharing

2. A user needs to access a network printer but knows only the network printer's IP address. What should you tell the user?

   **A.** Find the printer brand and model.

   **B.** Use a wireless connection to the printer.

   **C.** The IP address is the only information needed to use the printer.

   **D.** Find out the host name.

3. A Windows user has just returned from a trip during which she connected to the Internet via Wi-Fi networks in coffee shops and airport lounges. The user wants to connect to the new wireless LAN to print a report to a network printer she has used before, but she can't connect to the printer. Which of the following is the most likely cause?

   **A.** Windows Firewall is set for a Private network.

   **B.** Windows Firewall is set for a Public network.

   **C.** The user must reinstall the printer driver.

   **D.** A printer app can't work on a wireless LAN.

4. You are performing telephone support with a user who has lost his Internet connection on a SOHO network. After running ipconfig, the user reports his IP address as 169.254.0.23. Which of the following should you check first?

   **A.** Broadband modem

   **B.** Network switch

   **C.** Network hub

   **D.** Network router

5. A user normally works at an office with a domain controller but has switched to working from home. The SOHO network has shared printers and a networked multifunction device, but the user cannot connect to it. Which of the following settings on the user's device need to be changed to permit access? (Choose all that apply.)

   **A.** Change the computer to use the SOHO workgroup

   **B.** Add the SOHO network to the domain

   **C.** Add the user account to each computer with a shared printer

   **D.** Add the domain to the SOHO network

## 1.8 ANSWERS

1. **D** Right-clicking the folder and choosing Properties | Sharing tab reveals the Advanced Sharing button, which leads to the Advanced Sharing dialog box in which folder sharing options can be configured.

2. **C** With the IP address of the printer, the user can find and set up the printer using Devices and Printers.

3. **B**    When Windows Firewall is set to Public, connections to LAN devices are blocked for security.

4. **D**    On most SOHO networks, the DHCP server that provides automatic IP addresses is a function built into the router. Thus, the router is the first device to check.

5. **A C**    The computer cannot connect to the SOHO network unless it is configured to connect to a workgroup instead of a domain. To use shared printers or folders, the user account must be added to each computer with a share the user wants to access.

## Objective 1.9  Given a scenario, use features and tools of the Mac OS and Linux client/desktop operating systems

Although macOS and Linux are not nearly as popular as Windows in most offices, chances are increasing that you will run into at least some computers that use these operating systems. Although macOS and Linux differ in many ways, they have some features in common—and both differ a lot from Windows. This objective covers the essential best practices and tools you need to understand for the CompTIA A+ 220-1002.

## Best Practices

As with Windows, macOS and Linux computers requires best practices such as scheduled backups, disk maintenance, system updates, and more.

## Scheduled Backups

macOS and most Linux distributions use one of two scripting tools to run all sorts of tasks automatically in the background. Apple developed launchd for automation; most Linux distros use cron. You can create custom launchd and cron jobs, but actually doing so is beyond the scope of the CompTIA A+ 220-1002 exam.

**EXAM TIP**    The CompTIA A+ 220-1002 Linux and macOS objectives include *scheduled disk maintenance* and *scheduled backups,* but each OS checks disks and drives automatically. If you're using common GUI backup utilities, you'll schedule backups within the utility itself. You can, of course, use the task schedulers to run other utilities or even custom backup scripts.

## Scheduled Disk Maintenance

macOS handles most chores automatically, and both macOS and Linux will occasionally run file system check (fsck) on reboot. Still, if you have reason to suspect a problem, it's worth running fsck from the CLI or using an included or third-party GUI tool. macOS includes *Disk Utility*, which can verify and repair file structures, partition and format drives, and even create disk images. Most Linux distros have one or more disk maintenance utilities, but if you keep the bootable installation media handy, you can just use its disk diagnostic (see Figure 1.9-1).

 **NOTE**   Linux and macOS don't include an equivalent to Disk Cleanup in Windows, but you can download third-party utilities for cleaning up junk files.

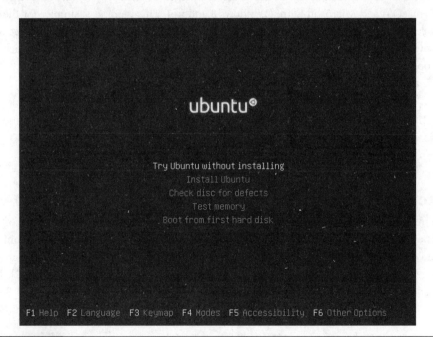

ubuntu

Try Ubuntu without installing
Install Ubuntu
Check disc for defects
Test memory
Boot from first hard disk

F1 Help   F2 Language   F3 Keymap   F4 Modes   F5 Accessibility   F6 Other Options

**FIGURE 1.9-1**   Ubuntu installation options, including one for disk diagnosis

## System Updates/App Store

Once upon a time, UNIX and Linux users largely downloaded and compiled their own software, which meant they were responsible for hunting down each dependency, a process called *dependency management*. This grew untenable, and long ago Linux distributions pioneered *package manager* programs that usually enable you to download and install a program and all its dependencies at once.

**NOTE** Most significant applications are built on the shoulders of other applications or software packages; these are called *dependencies* because the program depends on this other software to be present (and working!) to run.

Different distros have their own package managers and package-management interfaces, but the most common are the *advanced packaging tool (APT)*, which is used on Debian-based distros, and *Red Hat Package Manager (RPM)*. Later in this objective, we'll look at how to use the *apt-get* CLI tool (included in the CompTIA A+ 220-1002 objectives) to install and update software.

The other way of handling dependencies is to bundle them up with the application and distribute them together, which is generally what you get when you download an installer or use an *app store*. This applies to both mobile device stores and their desktop counterparts: the Apple App Store (macOS) and Microsoft Store (Windows 8 and up). This method is simpler for the user, but it can also be wasteful and less flexible. Imagine multiple apps on your system, all including their own copies of a few common dependencies—not only does this waste space, but each app's developers must also release a new version to include security patches to the dependency.

 **EXAM TIP** App stores and package managers aren't synonymous, but they do share some important features, such as giving users a central place to discover, install, and update software.

## Patch Management

Both macOS and Linux take an automated approach to patching and alert you when software needs an update. In macOS, you access app updates through the App Store and configure update settings with the App Store menu in System Preferences. Updates for macOS are now managed through the System Preferences | Software Update pane (see Figure 1.9-2). Most Linux distros have an updating tool like the Software Updater in Ubuntu (see Figure 1.9-3).

**FIGURE 1.9-2** System Preferences | Software Update pane for macOS updates

**FIGURE 1.9-3**   Software Updater in Ubuntu Linux

As useful as package managers are for installing single applications, that's not where their real power lies. These package managers can manage *all* the software (minus anything you compiled yourself) on the system, so you can upgrade installed packages from the CLI with two commands:

```
mike@server:~$ sudo apt-get update
mike@server:~$ sudo apt-get upgrade
```

## Driver/Firmware Updates

macOS will notify you about available system updates that contain driver updates for built-in components. Make a quick trip to the App Store to get updates installed, as described in the previous section. If the system has third-party devices, like a Wacom tablet, you will need to manually check and update any drivers for those devices.

Most Linux distros regularly check for updates and will signal any new updates. Download and install the updates using the Software Updater.

**EXAM TIP**   Unlike Windows Update, the macOS system updates will update drivers and the firmware of the Apple computer, if necessary.

Driver updates for Linux can be provided through package managers, as separate downloads from vendors (especially with GPUs), or, for printers, with the CUPS (Common Unix Printing System).

Firmware updates are provided by the motherboard or device vendor. In some cases, you might need to attach a device such as a printer or multifunction device to a Windows computer to update its firmware.

 **ADDITIONAL RESOURCES**   For more information on working with drivers in Linux, go to https://opensource.com and search for "How to Install a Device Driver on Linux."

## Antivirus/Anti-malware Updates

Antivirus/anti-malware updates are provided by the software vendors. Depending on the specific app, updates might be automatic or manual.

 **ADDITIONAL RESOURCES**   For more information on Linux antivirus/ anti-malware apps, go to www.tecmint.com and search for "The 8 Best Free Anti-Virus Programs for Linux."

# Tools

Use the tools described in the following sections to keep Linux or macOS systems in top working order.

## Backup/Time Machine

Systems running macOS use Time Machine to create full system backups (see Figure 1.9-4) called *local snapshots*. Time Machine requires an external HDD or SSD, or you can use a shared network drive.

As you should expect by now, Linux backup tools can differ by distro. Ubuntu uses Déjà Dup, though it's called Backups in System Settings (see Figure 1.9-5). Déjà Dup backs up a user's Home folder by default—just specify a location and it will permanently store file versions as long as the storage location has space. It isn't on the CompTIA A+ 220-1002 exam, but you can also download a drive imaging program such as Clonezilla.

 **EXAM TIP**   You can technically image your OS drive in both macOS and Linux with the **dd** command (covered later in this objective) at the Terminal, but the image will be as large as the drive's full capacity unless you compress it (ideally by piping it through a compression program before saving it). You can later use dd to apply this image to another drive (after decompressing it if necessary).

**FIGURE 1.9-4**    Time Machine

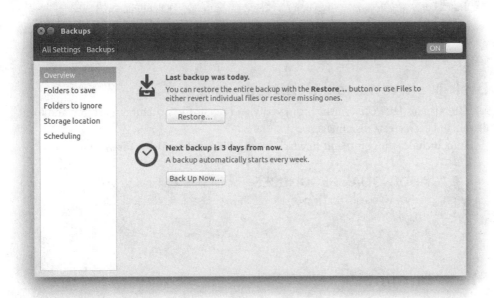

**FIGURE 1.9-5**    Backups under System Settings in Ubuntu

## Restore/Snapshot

The local snapshots created with Time Machine enable you to recover from a crash or even restore deleted files and previous versions. Configure it via Time Machine in System Preferences. You can also create and restore full disk images with Disk Utility, described next.

To create snapshots in Linux, you can use rsnapshot, based on rsync, or Timeshift.

**ADDITIONAL RESOURCES**    To try rsnapshot, go to rsnapshot.org. To download Timeshift, visit github.com. To learn more about using Timeshift, go to linoxide.com and search for "How to Take Linux System Snapshots with Timeshift."

## Image Recovery

Macs can be restored to proper operation by using the macOS recovery system. Press COMMAND-R at startup to display the macOS Recovery menu. You can restore from a Time Machine backup, reinstall macOS, or run Disk Utility.

Linux backups created with dd can also be restored using dd. Other popular image backup/recovery apps for Linux include clonezilla (clonezilla.org) and partimage (available via your distro's package manager).

**ADDITIONAL RESOURCES**    To learn more about dd, clonezilla, partimage, and other Linux image backup/recovery utilities, go to the nixcraft website at cyberciti .biz/open-source and search for "Top 6 Open Source Disk Cloning and Imaging Softwares."

## Disk Maintenance Utilities

macOS includes *Disk Utility*, which can verify and repair file structures, partition and format drives, and even create disk images.

Linux includes the command-line fsck for checking and repairing file systems.

**ADDITIONAL RESOURCES**    For an illustrated tutorial on using fsck, see www.tecmint.com and search for "How to Use 'fsck' to Repair File System Errors in Linux."

## Shell/Terminal

Linux uses its Terminal for command-line functions (see Table 1.9-1 later in this objective). Systems running macOS can also open a shell that has similar features, but most macOS commands run from the GUI.

## Screen Sharing

Screen sharing remotely in macOS is configured through System Preferences | Sharing. Screen sharing in Linux is typically known as VNC or Remote Desktop Viewing. Users might need to install it.

## Force Quit

The Force Quit feature is used to shut down malfunctioning apps. In macOS, press COMMAND-OPTION-ESC or open the Apple menu and select Force Quit. In Linux, open Terminal, run **ps** to see the process ID (PID for each app), and use **kill *PID*** to kill the app by specifying its PID.

# Features

macOS has a number of unique features, as described in the following sections. Where Linux has comparable features, they are also discussed.

 **EXAM TIP**    Make sure you know what the macOS features covered in this section are used for (multiple desktops/Mission Control, Key Chain, Spotlight, iCloud, Gestures, Finder, Remote Disc, Dock, and Boot Camp).

## Multiple Desktops/Mission Control

Mission Control enables users to see all of the open apps, switch between them, and move them to different desktops (Spaces in macOS-speak). In Linux, multiple sessions are managed with CTRL-ALT-function keys.

 **ADDITIONAL RESOURCES**    To learn more about using multiple desktop sessions in Linux, go to journalxtra.com and search for "Multiple Virtual Displays On One Linux Pc. Running Concurrently."

## Key Chain

*Keychain Access* securely manages passwords, accounts, certificates, and similar information on macOS devices. A comparable Linux app called keychain is available for most Linux distros from GitHub.com or from your distro's package manager.

## Spotlight

You can open Spotlight (COMMAND-SPACEBAR) in macOS to search for files and applications. It indexes your drive(s) for file names and other content, which means you can search for specific files plus all sorts of other things, like apps, e-mail messages, music, contacts, and even flight information. Cerebro, available from GitHub.com, offers similar features for Linux users and supports plugins for adding additional features.

## iCloud

Apple devices have built-in support for iCloud, which can synchronize pictures, documents, music, e-mail, contacts, calendars, bookmarks, login credentials, credit card information, and more. Some of iCloud's features can be used through client applications on Windows, Linux, and other non-Apple platforms—but one of its more unique features, *iCloud Keychain*, can only securely manage passwords and credit card information for macOS and iOS devices. Dropbox (www.dropbox.com) is one of a number of similar services available for Linux and other platforms.

## Gestures

macOS supports a wide variety of trackpad (touchpad) and Magic Mouse gestures. To see a list of supported gestures, open the System Preferences folder and Mouse or Trackpad. Linux users can use Touchegg, available through the software repositories of most distros, to add gesture support.

## Finder

macOS uses Finder (shown in Figure 1.9-6) to browse files on hard drives, removable media, and network locations. The trick with Linux is that, once again, this application varies. Rest assured that your distro or desktop environment comes with one—Ubuntu comes with Nautilus.

## Remote Disc

Apple doesn't provide optical drives on its computer, but macOS includes a Remote Disc feature that provides access to optical drives over a network connection. You can use this feature to view files or install an app, but not to burn a disc.

## Dock

The macOS Dock displays running apps along the bottom of the Desktop. You can add and remove apps from the Dock with a right-click. You also can adjust the magnification as desired. A variety of docks for Linux are available.

 **ADDITIONAL RESOURCES**   To learn more about docks for Linux, go to fossmint.com and search for "8 macOS Like Docks for Ubuntu."

**FIGURE 1.9-6**   Finder

# Boot Camp

Apple Boot Camp makes it pretty simple to install Windows on your Mac and choose which OS to load when you start the system; more recent versions of Boot Camp support only 64-bit versions of Windows.

# Basic Linux Commands

Table 1.9-1 lists common Linux commands run from Terminal. To get help with a specific command, enter **man** *commandname* to open the man page for that command.

 **EXAM TIP**   Make sure you know all the common Linux commands in Table 1.9-1 and the scenarios in which you would use them.

**TABLE 1.9-1**   Common Linux Commands

| Command | Use | Examples/Notes |
|---|---|---|
| ls | Lists files and folders in a directory | **ls -a**<br>(lists hidden as well as normal files in the current folder) |
| grep | Searches text files or command output | **grep 'thistext' myfile.doc**<br>(searches myfile.doc for thistext) |
| cd | Changes the focus of the command prompt | **cd ..**<br>(moves up one level from the current location) |
| shutdown | Brings down system | **shutdown -r**<br>(reboots machine) |
| pwd | Displays full path or working directory | **pwd**<br>/home/mark |
| passwd | Updates current user's password | **pwd**<br>Changing password for mark.<br>(current) UNIX password: |
| mv | Moves or renames files | **mv myfile.txt /home/Mark/Docs**<br>(moves myfile.txt to the /home/Mark/Docs folder) |
| cp | Copies files | **cp *.doc docfiles**<br>(copies all .doc files in current folder to docfiles folder one level below current folder) |
| rm | Permanently deletes files | **rm thisfile.doc**<br>(removes thisfile.doc)<br>**rm *.doc**<br>(removes all .doc files in the current folder) |
| chmod | Changes permissions for specified files | **chmod 664 thisfile.doc**<br>**chmod 750 thisapp**<br>(7=read, write, execute; 6=read/write; 5=read and execute; 4=read only; 0=no access<br>first digit = permissions for file owner<br>second digit = permissions for group<br>third digit = permissions for others) |
| chown | Changes ownership | **chown markesoper thisfile.doc**<br>(changes ownership of thisfile.doc to user markesoper) |
| iwconfig | Displays and configures wireless network settings | Enter **man iwconfig** for options |
| ifconfig | Displays and configures network settings | Enter **man ifconfig** for options |

| TABLE 1.9-1 | Common Linux Commands *(continued)* |

| Command | Use | Examples/Notes |
|---------|-----|----------------|
| ps | Lists processes | Use to display processes and their PIDs |
| su | Switches user to specified user account | **su - mark**<br>(switch to mark's account and mark's home folder) |
| sudo | Runs commands using root user access | **sudo apt-get update**<br>(use superuser account to update software packages; must enter your password) |
| apt-get | Updates and maintains list of software packages on Debian-based distributions (Ubuntu and many others) | **sudo apt-get install newpackage**<br>(installs newpackage)<br>**sudo apt-get upgrade**<br>(upgrades all installed packages) |
| vi | Standard Linux text editor | User switches between insert mode (enter/edit text) and command mode (save file, discard file, etc.)<br>In command mode, press the I key to enter insert mode; press ESC to return to command mode |
| dd | Creates an exact (bit-by-bit) copy of a storage volume | Also restores files and disk images, can overwrite disks with random data, and backup/restore master boot records) |
| kill | Stops a specified process | **kill 9999**<br>(kills PID 9999; to see the PIDs of current processes, use ps) |

# REVIEW

**Objective 1.9: Given a scenario, use features and tools of the Mac OS and Linux client/ desktop operating systems**

- macOS and Linux support best practices such as scheduled backups, disk maintenance, and system updates.
- Linux can use Terminal commands or GUI-specific features to perform these tasks, while almost all of macOS's functions can be performed from the GUI.
- macOS and Linux both support fsck for checking file systems. macOS uses launchd for automation, while Linux uses cron.
- The Linux package manager provides a reliable source for apps for a specific distribution, comparable to the App Store for macOS.
- Most macOS features have Linux counterparts, available either from a distro's package manager or from sources such as GitHub.com.

- Linux commands are documented through the use of man. For example, to learn more about chmod (changes file permissions), use **man chmod**.
- Basic Linux commands to know for the exam include ls, grep, cd, shutdown, pwd, passwd, mv, cp, rm, chmod, chown, iwconfig, ifconfig, ps, su, sudo, apt-get, vi, dd, and kill.

## 1.9 QUESTIONS

**1.** A Linux user is trying to update her system's apps with the command **apt-get update** and the command doesn't work. What did the user forget to do?

**A.** Restart in Safe Mode

**B.** Run the command from Terminal

**C.** Run the command as root user with sudo

**D.** Create an image backup first

**2.** A macOS user needs to search for a specific file. Which utility should he use?

**A.** Spotlight

**B.** Finder

**C.** Remote Disc

**D.** Dock

**3.** A Linux user needs to stop a process but doesn't know its PID. Which command from Terminal would show this information?

**A.** ifconfig

**B.** ps

**C.** ls

**D.** kill

**4.** Most macOS and Linux disk tools have different names, but the command-line (Terminal/shell) backup utility is available on both systems. Which of the following is it?

**A.** Time Machine

**B.** cron

**C.** dd

**D.** grep

**5.** A Linux user uses ls to perform the same task as which of these macOS GUI utilities?

**A.** Time Machine

**B.** Dock

**C.** Spotlight

**D.** Finder

# 1.9 ANSWERS

1. **C**   Many Linux commands must be run as root user (superuser) with sudo.

2. **A**   Spotlight is the macOS search tool.

3. **B**   The ps command lists the PID values for all running processes in Linux.

4. **C**   The dd command makes a byte-by-byte copy of the specified drive in both macOS and Linux.

5. **D**   Finder lists files and folders in macOS, so it is the equivalent of ls in Linux.

# Security

DOMAIN
2.0

## Domain Objectives

- **2.1** Summarize the importance of physical security measures

- **2.2** Explain logical security concepts

- **2.3** Compare and contrast wireless security protocols and authentication methods

- **2.4** Given a scenario, detect, remove, and prevent malware using appropriate tools and methods

- **2.5** Compare and contrast social engineering, threats, and vulnerabilities

- **2.6** Compare and contrast the differences of basic Microsoft Windows OS security settings

- **2.7** Given a scenario, implement security best practices to secure a workstation

- **2.8** Given a scenario, implement methods for securing mobile devices

- **2.9** Given a scenario, implement appropriate data destruction and disposal methods

- **2.10** Given a scenario, configure security on SOHO wireless and wired networks

 **Objective 2.1** # Summarize the importance of physical security measures

Physical security might seem like a mundane topic in a tech-oriented certification, but it's a vital first step in the security process. In this objective, you learn how physical security methods ranging from door locks to privacy tokens protect technology from tampering, theft, or misuse.

> **EXAM TIP**   Make sure you understand the role that each of the physical security measures covered in this objective has in overall physical security.

## Mantrap and Entry Control Roster

A mantrap is a small room with a set of two doors, one to the outer, unsecured area and one to the inner, secure area. The mantrap's outer door must be closed before the inner door can be opened, and the entrant must present authentication before the inner door is opened. The mantrap is often controlled by a security guard who records comings and goings on an *entry control roster*. Use a mantrap at the entrance to sensitive areas to keep intruders from tailgating in behind authorized entrants.

## Badge Reader

A badge reader is a fundamental physical security measure. Using radio frequency ID (RFID), magnetic strip, barcode, or Quick Response (QR) code technologies; a badge reader for ID badges, especially when combined with a mantrap, makes getting into secure areas much more difficult.

## Smart Card, Key Fob, and Hardware Tokens

Single-factor authentication requiring a password (something you know) can be greatly enhanced by adding a possession factor, making it two-factor authentication. *Smart cards* (see Figure 2.1-1) are credit-card-sized cards with circuitry that can identify the bearer of the card, and a *security token* (often in the form of a *key fob*) stores digital certificates, passwords, biometric data, and so on.

A hardware token (see Figure 2.1-2) is sometimes called an RSA token, although many different vendors produce similar products. One common type uses compatible authentication servers that use an initial random seed to regularly generate a time-based number the user must enter to authenticate. Another common type plugs into a USB port and is often thin enough to be carried on a key chain.

**FIGURE 2.1-1**  Keyboard-mounted smart card reader being used for a commercial application (photo courtesy of Cherry Corp.)

**FIGURE 2.1-2**  RSA hardware token (photo courtesy of EMC Corp.)

**ADDITIONAL RESOURCES**  For other vendors of multifactor authentication services, see themerkel.com and search for "7 Best Two-Factor Authentication Solutions." To learn more about multifactor authentication and its vulnerabilities, go to www.knowbe4.com and search for "Multi-factor Authentication Basics."

# Security Guard

Even if your organization uses badge readers, key fobs, or smart cards, the presence of one or more security guards provides an extra level of security and deterrence. A security guard with an entry control roster is needed to make a mantrap truly effective.

# Lock Types and Applications

One of the most basic types of physical security is a lock. The following sections cover the lock types you need to understand for the CompTIA A+ 220-1002 exam.

**EXAM TIP**   Be sure to know the different types of locks covered in this objective, including door locks, biometric locks, cable locks, server locks, and USB locks.

## Door Lock

Keyed door locks won't deter a determined intruder with a lock pick, but they will stop casual snoopers. Keyed door locks are also vulnerable if (when) keys are lost. Rekeying door locks can become quite expensive over time. A door lock combined with a mantrap improves security.

## Biometric Locks

Biometric door locks typically use fingerprint or hand readers to determine identity. These are very useful for controlling access to highly secure areas. Biometric door locks vary in the number of fingerprints or handprints they can store for recognition, how they are programmed, the physical lock type, and water-resistance factors.

## Cable Locks

A cable lock (see Figure 2.1-3) provides good physical security for portable devices such as laptop computers and external drives that have Kensington security lock connectors (see inset in Figure 2.1-3). Cable locks for individual users have combinations, while those made for use in organizations have keyed locks.

**FIGURE 2.1-3**   A cable lock on a laptop (inset shows Kensington security lock connector)

## Server Locks

Server locks are used to limit access to a server's ports and drives. Locks can be used to prevent access to the front or back of a server rack. Locks for server rack doors are available with electronic locks, keyed locks, support for a padlock, or TCP/IP interfacing to inform the network or status or breaches.

## USB Locks

USB ports' ease of use and omnipresence makes them a security headache. While Group Policy settings can be used to prevent certain types of USB devices from being connected to servers, it might be easier to use physical *USB locks* that insert into USB ports and are locked in place. These are available from many vendors. Locks are also available for USB flash drives and other types of external storage devices.

# Privacy Screen

To avoid shoulder surfing, position desks and screens where snoops can't see anyone's screen without the user's knowledge; in environments where this is hard, you can use privacy screens, also known as *privacy filters* (see Figure 2.1-4), to reduce the monitor viewing angle. For additional security, restrict access to a space or resource to just those who need it.

 **NOTE** Shoulder surfing is observing a user's screen or keyboard for information such as a password—usually over the user's shoulder.

**FIGURE 2.1-4**   Privacy filter

# REVIEW

**Objective 2.1: Summarize the importance of physical security measures**  Physical security measures include

- A mantrap at the entrance to a secure area (or an entire building) to limit access to authorized persons only and to prevent tailgating, with a security guard stationed next to the mantrap to check credentials based on an entry control roster.
- Badge readers can be used alone or in combination with a mantrap to limit access.
- Smart cards, key fobs, and hardware tokens can all be used as part of a two-factor authentication scheme.
- Door locks are available in various forms including keyed locks, smart card–enabled locks, or biometric locks that read hands or fingerprints. Keyed locks are the least expensive initially, but are harder and more costly to keep secure over time because of lost or stolen keys, duplicates, and rekeying locks.
- Security for equipment can be achieved by using cable locks for portable and desktop computers and peripherals, server locks to block access to servers in cabinets and racks, and USB locks to block access to USB ports or to prevent USB devices from being connected.
- Privacy screens on displays block "shoulder surfing" of passwords or confidential information by coworkers or visitors to an office, and can also be used on portable devices.

## 2.1 QUESTIONS

1. Which of the following is a useful feature in the use of mantraps and entry control rosters?
   - **A.** Key fob
   - **B.** Security guard
   - **C.** Biometric lock
   - **D.** Cable lock

2. An organization has contacted you for help in stopping security breaches on its servers. The latest breach involved the use of a flash drive to steal credentials. Which of the following is designed to stop this type of security breach?
   - **A.** Privacy screen
   - **B.** Server lock
   - **C.** Cable lock
   - **D.** USB lock

**3.** RFID, magnetic strip, barcode, and QR code technologies can all be used by which of the following?

**A.** Badge reader

**B.** Smart card

**C.** Mantrap

**D.** Biometric lock

**4.** A Kensington lock connector is used by which of the following devices?

**A.** Door lock

**B.** USB lock

**C.** Cable lock

**D.** Biometric lock

**5.** A mantrap is specifically designed to achieve which of the following?

**A.** Stop viruses from being introduced by users

**B.** Prevent multiple users from entering a secure area at the same time

**C.** Catch users who evade biometric locks

**D.** Stop shoulder surfers

## 2.1 ANSWERS

**1.** **B**    A security guard is helpful in making a mantrap more effective and to maintain the entry control roster.

**2.** **D**    A USB lock prevents unused USB ports from being "borrowed" for data theft.

**3.** **A**    Different types of badge readers use these technologies.

**4.** **C**    The cable lock connector was developed by Kensington, hence the name.

**5.** **B**    A mantrap is specifically designed to prevent tailgating. One door leads into the mantrap, and only when a single authorized person is present in the mantrap will the other door into the secure area be opened.

 **Objective 2.2** **Explain logical security concepts**

Logical security concepts revolve around the use of software- and technology-based security to protect computers and data. From features in Microsoft Active Directory to firewalls, logical security concepts are designed to help enforce the principle of least privilege.

# Active Directory

Active Directory is an integral part of Windows Server. It provides directory services to a Windows Server domain. Active Directory centralizes user accounts, passwords, and access to resources on a network via a domain controller. Valid domain accounts log in once to the domain and have access to all resources on the domain. This is called single sign-on.

 **EXAM TIP**   Be sure you can identify each of the Active Directory security features (login script, domain, group policy/updates, organizational units, home folder, folder redirection) covered in this section.

 **ADDITIONAL RESOURCES**   To learn more about Active Directory, go to https://blogs.technet.microsoft.com and search for "Understanding Active Directory for Beginners."

## Login Script

A login script (aka logon script) runs every time the user logs in to an Active Directory domain and is used to set up variables for the user, such as mapping folders to drive letters, setting a default printer for a specific user, capturing information about the user or device that is logged in, and much more.

 **ADDITIONAL RESOURCES**   To learn more about login scripts for Active Directory, go to https://redmondmag.com and search for "Exploring Logon Scripts for Active Directory."

## Domain

Larger networks use domains, in which a server running Windows Server controls access to network resources. An administrator creates a domain on the Windows Server system, making it the *domain controller (DC)*, and creates new *domain accounts* for the users. A domain controller must have the Active Directory Domain Server (AD DS) server role installed (see Figure 2.2-1).

 **EXAM TIP**   Login scripts and home folders (covered later) are two common methods for setting up users. Be sure you understand the differences between them.

**FIGURE 2.2-1**  Adding Active Directory Domain Services to Windows Server 2016

At a given time, a computer can be a member of a workgroup or a domain, not both. When a system joins the domain, it is automatically kicked off the workgroup. When you log on to any computer in the domain, Windows prompts you for a user name (see Figure 2.2-2) to log on directly to the domain. All user accounts are stored on the domain controller, which functions as the *authentication server*, though each system still creates a local user directory when you log on. You can log on using <domain>\<domain user name>, so the user Mike on the domain totalhome.local would log on with totalhome.local\Mike.

## Group Policy/Updates

If you want to apply *granular* policy settings *en masse*, you need to step up to Windows Active Directory domain-based group policy (see Figure 2.2-3) from Local Security Policy settings.

Group policy settings are a big topic on most of the Microsoft certification tracks, but for the purposes of the CompTIA A+ 220-1002 exam, you simply have to be comfortable with the concept behind group policy. To give you a taste, policies can be used to do the following,

**FIGURE 2.2-2**    Domain logon screen

among many other things: keep users from editing the Registry, accessing the command line, or installing software; define who can log on to or shut down a system; enforce minimum password length; configure account lockout after a number of failed logon attempts; and enable users to browse for printers on the network.

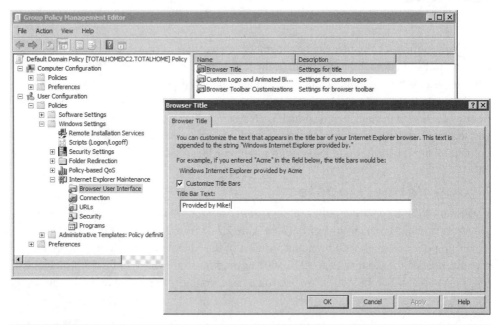

**FIGURE 2.2-3**    Using Group Policy to make the IE title bar say "Provided by Mike!"

# Organizational Units

An organizational unit (OU) is an Active Directory container that holds users, groups, and computers. A domain can manage multiple OUs, and each OU can have its own Group Policies. An OU can be used to collect the members of a department or division, and an OU can have its own administrator.

 **ADDITIONAL RESOURCES**   To learn more about the role of an OU in an Active Directory domain, go to www.varonis.com and search for "The Difference Between Organizational Units and Active Directory Groups."

# Home Folder

A home folder is used to store personal files on an Active Directory network. It can be used in place of login scripts to set up drives for users. One of the benefits of using a home folder is that each user's files can be stored in their own home folder on a remote server rather than having some files stored in each computer's Documents folder as users log into different computers in a domain. This feature is known as folder redirection.

 **ADDITIONAL RESOURCES**   For a discussion of pros and cons of login scripts versus home folders, see https://community.spiceworks.com and search for "Login Script vs. Home Folder (Connect:)." Microsoft doesn't provide guidance as to which method is recommended, so you should be familiar with both methods.

# Folder Redirection

Folder redirection is used to redirect users of a known folder to a different folder—for example, from a local Documents folder to the user's home folder on an Active Directory network. Folder redirection can be performed using group policy or manually.

# Software Tokens

A software token (also known as a soft token) is used as part of two-factor authentication security. For example, a would-be user of a secured network must provide their name and mobile phone number to start the authentication process. A software token is sent by the mobile network to the mobile phone. The user must interact with the software token to complete the login process.

 **ADDITIONAL RESOURCES**   For a definition and examples of soft tokens, visit https://searchsecurity.techtarget.com and search for "soft token."

## MDM Policies

Mobile device management (MDM) policies are security policies specifically tailored to mobile devices such as smartphones, tablets, laptop computers, e-readers, wearables, games, and other mobile devices that can connect to a network. With earlier versions of Windows 10, group policy settings override MDM policies. However, in the most recent versions of Windows 10, MDM settings can replace group policy settings. Some examples of MDM policies might include passwords must be stored in encrypted form on mobile devices; users cannot connect to insecure public Wi-Fi networks; devices must run up-to-date approved anti-malware apps; users cannot use recording, photo, or video features in the workplace without permission.

 **ADDITIONAL RESOURCES**    To learn more about Microsoft's support for MDM in Windows 10, go to https://docs.microsoft.com and search for "Mobile Device Management." For an example of a mobile device policy, go to https://drivestrike.com, click the Site map link, and search for "Mobile Device Acceptable Use Policy."

## Port Security

On a managed switch, enabling port security provides a way to specify which MAC addresses can connect to the switch. When port security is enabled and configured, a potential attacker who connects a device with an unknown MAC address to a switch is prevented from using it. Some vendors, such as Juniper, use the term port security to refer to a broader range of security features.

 **ADDITIONAL RESOURCES**    To learn more about port security in Cisco devices, see https://study-ccna.com and search for "port security." To learn more about different types of port security, go to www.netgear.com/support and search for "What is port security and how does it work with my managed switch?"

## MAC Address Filtering

Most wireless access points (WAPs) and many wired and wireless routers support MAC address filtering to limit access to your wireless network using the physical, hard-wired address of each wireless network adapter. A table stored in the WAP or router—the *access control list (ACL)*—lists MAC addresses permitted (*whitelist*) or excluded (*blacklist*) from the wireless network.

# Certificates

In order for a client and server—such as a web browser and web server—to encrypt data that the other can decrypt, they need to exchange the encryption keys they'll use. To do this, the server sends a public key to your browser in the form of a *digital certificate* signed by a trusted *certificate authority (CA)* to guarantee the public key it holds is actually from the web server and not from an attacker impersonating the web server.

Your web browser comes with a built-in list of *trusted root CAs* (see Figure 2.2-4), and if your browser receives a certificate signed by one of these highly respected root CAs from a website, the browser will seamlessly load the web page and display a small (usually green) secure-connection lock in the address bar. If your browser receives a fishy certificate— perhaps it's expired or doesn't use a trusted root CA—the browser will warn you (as shown in Figure 2.2-5).

What you do when you receive such a warning is up to you. There are a number of boring reasons you could see certificate warnings for a site that is secure, but the safe thing to do is to go back instead of entering the site—and you certainly don't want low-knowledge users naively clicking past certificate warnings. If the invalid certificate warning exists because a secure site on your corporate intranet uses a self-signed certificate instead of one from a trusted root CA, you may have to do additional user education about why they can ignore the certificate warning on the intranet, but not on the Internet.

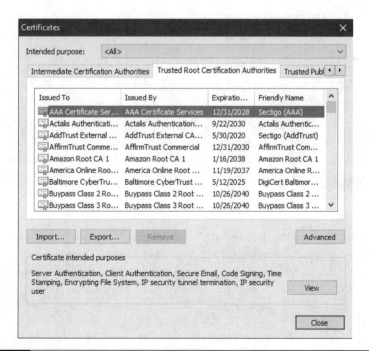

**FIGURE 2.2-4**   Trusted authorities built into Google Chrome

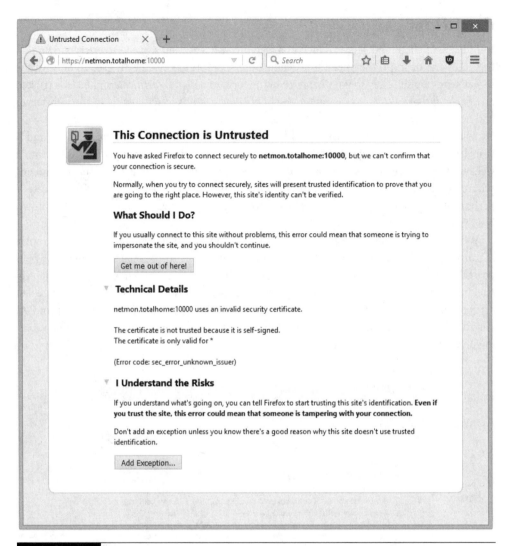

**FIGURE 2.2-5** Untrusted certificate

Another issue you may run into is that a browser may refuse to trust a site if its certificate suddenly differs from the one cached on a previous visit. If this is the problem, you can remedy it by clearing the SSL cache. The process varies by browser, but Internet Explorer and Chrome both use the Windows cache, which you clear by clicking the *Clear SSL state* button on the Content tab of the Internet Options applet.

# Antivirus/Anti-Malware

Antivirus/anti-malware features can be added to a network in several ways:

- Installed on individual clients
- Integrated into a router
- Built into a network appliance

Regardless of the method selected, the software and detection rules must be kept updated.

> **Cross-Reference**
>
> To learn more about antivirus and anti-malware, see the "Antivirus and Anti-Malware" section in Objective 2.4, later in this domain.

# Firewalls

Firewalls generally protect an internal network from unauthorized access to and from the Internet at large with methods such as hiding IP addresses and blocking TCP/IP ports, but firewalls at internal boundaries can also help limit the damage a compromised node can do to important resources. *Hardware firewalls* are often built into routers (or standalone devices), whereas *software firewalls* (such as Windows Firewall) run on individual systems.

 **EXAM TIP**   Make sure you can distinguish between hardware firewalls and software firewalls and understand where they are located.

> **Cross-Reference**
>
> To learn more about software firewalls as a logical security concept, see the "Software Firewalls" section in Objective 2.4, later in this domain.

# User Authentication/Strong Passwords

Authentication is the process of giving a user access to a system. An important factor in user authentication is the use of *strong passwords*. Strong passwords are reasonably resistant to a calculated attack by password-guessing programs—a good starting point is a minimum of eight characters, including letters (both upper- and lowercase), numbers, and symbols—but keep in mind that "strong" evolves along with processing power and password-guessing strategies.

## Multifactor Authentication

Multifactor authentication uses two or more different methods of authentication, such as user name/password and a key fob or smart card.

**Cross-Reference**

To learn more about authentication factors, see the "Authentication" section in Objective 2.3 of this domain.

## Directory Permissions

Directory permissions control which users or groups can access a folder (directory) and the files in it. Directory permissions prevent a standard user from viewing or opening folders or files that are in a different standard user's folders. An attempt to do so will trigger a Permission Denied error. However, an administrator can change ownership of a folder to view or change files. You can also use directory permissions to protect the OS and apps from being compromised by user-run scripts or programs. Directory permissions can also limit access to sensitive information on a shared file server.

## VPN

A *virtual private network (VPN)* sets up endpoints at each end of an encrypted tunnel between computers or networks to join them into a private network as if they were on a directly connected LAN (though they obviously won't perform like it). In order to pull this trick off, the endpoint on each LAN gets its own LAN IP address and is responsible for handling traffic addressed to and from the remote network (see Figure 2.2-6).

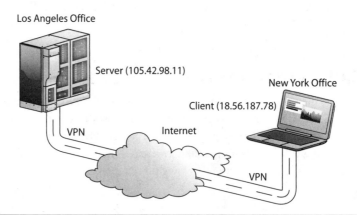

**FIGURE 2.2-6**    Typical tunnel

**NOTE**    When your mobile or portable device connects to an untrusted Wi-Fi hotspot, you can connect to another network with a VPN and do all of your browsing (or other work) through the secure tunnel.

# DLP

Many security appliances include context-based rules called *Data Loss Prevention (DLP)* to avoid data leaks. DLP scans outgoing packets and stops the flow if they break a rule.

# Access Control Lists

A table stored in the WAP—the *access control list (ACL)*—lists MAC addresses permitted (*whitelist*) or excluded (*blacklist*) from the wireless network. A different type of ACL is used on boot drive file systems as the basis for user and group permissions. While these different types of ACLs work in different ways, what they both have in common is their ability to permit or block access to a resource.

# Smart Card

A smart card is a credit card–sized card with circuitry that can identify the bearer of the card. It can be used as one factor in multifactor authentication. Some laptops and desktop keyboards include smart card readers. When the smart card reader is enabled as part of multifactor authentication, the user would need to insert a smart card as well as providing a user name and password to gain access to the network. A variant on smart cards that can be used without a card reader is a USB hardware token that can be plugged in to provide an authentication factor.

# E-mail Filtering

E-mail filtering enables easier e-mail message management as well as added security. By setting up rules for e-mail filtering, such as storing messages from company e-mail addresses in their own folder and sending messages with attachments into a folder for examination before opening, users can more easily find the most important e-mails and must also take an additional step to open possibly suspect messages. E-mail rules are available in Microsoft Outlook and most other e-mail clients.

## Trusted/Untrusted Software Sources

Tell your users to only install apps from trusted software sources, such as the manufacturer's website, or well-known app stores, such as Valve's Steam service—and teach them how to both identify and avoid untrusted software sources, such as free registry cleaners from some .support domain.

## Principle of Least Privilege

The number one consideration in network security is the principle of least privilege: accounts should have permission to access only the resources they need and no more. Access to user accounts should be restricted to the assigned individuals.

 **EXAM TIP**   The principle of least privilege states that users should have permission to access only the resources they need to perform their jobs.

## REVIEW

**Objective 2.2: Explain logical security concepts**   Active Directory security features include

- Login scripts are used to set up user-specific settings such as drive mappings, default printers, and more.
- Domains are used in Windows Servers to organize users, groups, and resources. A domain controller is used to create domain accounts and must have the Active Directory Domain Server (AD DS) role installed.
- Group policy/updates can be applied to multiple users and can be used to prevent user access to the Registry or command line, define users who can shut down the system, set password policies, and more.
- Organizational units (OUs) are Active Directory containers holding users, groups, and computers. A domain can manage multiple OUs.
- Home folders are used to store personal files on an Active Directory server. Folder redirection is used to enable users to store files into their home folder rather than storing files on a local Documents folder.

Other important logical security concepts include

- Software tokens (soft tokens) can be used as part of two-factor authentication; the user must interact with the token to complete the authentication process.

- Mobile device management (MDM) policies are security policies specially tailored to mobile devices that can connect to a network (smartphones, tablets, laptop computers, and other device types). MDM policies in the latest versions of Windows 10 can override group policy settings.

- Port security is a feature of managed switches. When enabled and configured, it uses a whitelist of approved MAC addresses to permit only authorized devices to connect.

- MAC address filtering is available in wired and wireless routers and APs. It can use a whitelist of approved MAC addresses or a blacklist of blocked MAC addresses to restrict access.

- Certificates, often referred to as digital certificates, are used to enable your web browser to exchange encrypted data with trusted websites. Certificates that are not issued by a trusted root certificate authority (CA), are outdated, or have other problems will display an error message.

- Antivirus/anti-malware can be installed on a network's clients, be integrated into a router, or be built into a network appliance.

- Firewalls are available in two forms: hardware firewalls used to protect networks, and software firewalls used to protect individual clients.

- One of the foundations of user authentication is strong passwords (at least eight characters with mixed letters, numbers, and symbols).

- Multifactor authentication uses two or more authentication methods. Smart cards are often used in multifactor authentication.

- Directory permissions control which users or groups can access a folder (directory) and the files in it.

- A virtual private network (VPN) sets up endpoints at each end of an encrypted tunnel between computers or networks to join them into a private network as if they were on a directly connected LAN.

- DLP is the collective name for context-based data loss prevention rules used by many security appliances.

- Access control lists (ACLs) are used by APs and routers to determine which MAC addresses are permitted (whitelist) or blocked (blacklist) from connecting. ACLs are also used by hard drives as the basis for user and group permissions.

- E-mail filtering can be used to separate company from other types of e-mail and to permit messages with attachments to be inspected for malware.

- Trusted software sources, such as a device vendor or operating system's app store or repository, are the preferred resource for software. Untrusted software sources should be avoided.

- The principle of least privilege states that accounts should have permission to access only the resources they need, and no more.

## 2.2 QUESTIONS

1. Which of the following violates the principle of least privilege?

   **A.** Making all users administrators

   **B.** Creating home folders

   **C.** Using smart cards to restrict access

   **D.** Using folder redirection

2. You are in charge of managing two different departments that need different types of access. Which of the following is the easiest way to provide the settings for each department?

   **A.** Put each department into a separate domain

   **B.** Write login scripts for each user in each department

   **C.** Put each department into its own OU

   **D.** Create special group policy settings for each department

3. You are creating an MDM policy for your department, which tests and uses a wide variety of devices. Which of the following device types does not need to be included in the MDM policy?

   **A.** Laptop

   **B.** Smart phone

   **C.** Portable media player

   **D.** Desktop

4. You are working on security for a router that is used with a defined list of devices. Which of the following should you create to restrict access?

   **A.** Whitelist

   **B.** Blue screen

   **C.** Blacklist

   **D.** MDM

5. Your network uses self-signed security certificates for its intranet. A new user is alarmed because her browser displayed a certificate warning when trying to connect to a website on the intranet. Which of the following should you tell the user?

   **A.** Never go to a website that displays a certificate warning.

   **B.** Always ignore certificate warnings.

   **C.** Company intranet sites are safe and you can proceed despite the warning.

   **D.** You must always use the clear SSL cache feature in your browser.

## 2.2 ANSWERS

1.  **A**   The principle of least privilege states that users should have permission to access only the resources they need to perform for their jobs—so making all users administrators is the opposite.

2.  **C**   Putting each department into its own organizational unit (OU) via Active Directory makes it easy to have separate settings for each department.

3.  **D**   Desktop computers are not mobile, so they don't need to be included in a mobile device management (MDM) policy.

4.  **A**   Creating a whitelist of MAC addresses allowed access is part of router security when it is used with a known list of devices. A blacklist is used to block specific computers by MAC address.

5.  **C**   The user needs to know the difference between intranet and Internet sites because it affects the rules for handling browser warnings.

 **Objective 2.3** ## Compare and contrast wireless security protocols and authentication methods

Although it's widely understood that wireless networks need to be secured, many people don't realize the huge differences in protection between technologies and authentication methods. After reviewing this objective, you'll be able to choose the best protocols and methods for your situation.

## Protocols and Encryption

Security protocols and encryption standards help safeguard wireless networks. Unfortunately, some "security" protocols aren't very secure. The following sections help you understand the differences between WEP, WPA, and WPA2, and the encryption methods that WPA and WPA2 use.

 **EXAM TIP**   Be familiar with the differences between WEP, WPA, WPA2, TKIP, and AES.

## WEP

Wired Equivalent Privacy (WEP) encryption was meant to secure wirelessly transmitted data with standard 40-bit encryption; many vendors also support 104-bit encryption (which some advertise as 128-bit). Unfortunately, WEP contains some serious security flaws. Shortly after it was released, hackers demonstrated that WEP could be cracked in a matter of minutes using readily available software. It's better than nothing, but it only stops casual snooping; it will not deter a serious attacker. Because WEP uses one key to encrypt traffic for all clients, other members of the network can read your packets.

## WPA and TKIP

*Wi-Fi Protected Access (WPA)* is a sort of interim security protocol upgrade for WEP-enabled devices. WPA uses the *Temporal Key Integrity Protocol (TKIP)* to protect from many attacks WEP was vulnerable to by providing a new encryption key for every packet sent. Other security enhancements include encryption key integrity checking and user authentication through the industry-standard *Extensible Authentication Protocol (EAP)*. TKIP is a deprecated standard now and should not be used if WPA2/AES is available.

## WPA2 and AES

The full IEEE 802.11i standard, WPA2, is the preferred way to lock down wireless networks. Current WAPs and wireless clients support (and require) WPA2, and most access points have a "backward compatible" mode for the handful of devices that still need WPA. WPA2 uses the *Advanced Encryption Standard (AES)*, among other improvements, to secure the wireless environment. AES, which uses 128-bit blocks and key lengths of 128 bits, 192 bits, or 256 bits, is the U.S. Government's preferred encryption standard.

# Authentication

Wireless security authentication uses one or more *authentication factors*:

- Something you know (e.g., a password, user name, or name of first childhood pet) is a *knowledge* factor.
- Something you have (e.g., a smart card, key, or driver license) is an *ownership* or *possession* factor.
- Something you are (e.g., your voice, fingerprint, or retinal pattern) is an *inherence* factor.

 **NOTE**    Less common factors exist: somewhere you are is a *location* factor, and *temporal* factors may restrict authentication to given times, or specify time relationships between different steps (like in the movies, when two people must turn two keys simultaneously).

## Single-Factor

Single-factor authentication requires the user to present only one factor. A user name and password are both knowledge factors, so this common authentication scheme is single-factor authentication. In wireless networking, the single-factor authentication is typically the pre-shared key (PSK) encryption code used by a particular wireless network: to connect to a typical encrypted wireless network, the user must provide the correct PSK before the connection can be completed.

## Multifactor

Multifactor authentication aims for better security by using more than one factor; you may hear *two-factor authentication* used to describe common authentication schemes that combine a user name and password (knowledge factor) with a code generated by or sent to your device (possession factor).

## RADIUS

SOHO and small-business wireless networks use a pre-shared key (PSK) to control access to the wireless network. However, larger networks, such as those with a domain server, need centralized wireless user authentication. One of the leading standards is the *Remote Authentication Dial-In User Service (RADIUS)* protocol. RADIUS is the most common authentication standard used by *WPA/WPA2 Enterprise* networks. In these networks, users log in with their user names and passwords, and the RADIUS server provides wireless access only to authorized users. This is much more secure than PSK because the user needs only their standard domain/network login to make connections. RADIUS is partially encrypted and uses UDP.

## TACACS

Another type of centralized remote authentication used on corporate networks is *Terminal Access Controller Access-Control System Plus (TACACS+)*, which the CompTIA exams refer to simply as TACACS. TACACS+ is primarily used for device administration. Thus, both RADIUS and TACACS+ are likely to be used on enterprise networks.

 **ADDITIONAL RESOURCES** To learn more about RADIUS versus TACACS+, enter the following into your browser: **www.networkworld.com RADIUS versus TACACS+**

 **EXAM TIP** WPA2 uses AES encryption, WPA uses TKIP encryption, and RADIUS and TACACS+ are both used on enterprise networks.

# REVIEW

**Objective 2.3: Compare and contrast wireless security protocols and authentication methods**   Wireless security protocols include

- The very weak Wired Equivalent Privacy (WEP) standard was introduced with early 802.11b networks. It was first replaced by Wi-Fi Protected Access (WPA) with its more powerful TKIP encryption, and both have now been replaced by WPA2, which uses virtually unbreakable AES encryption.

Authentication methods use the following factors (examples):

- Something you know (user name, password)
- Something you have (smart card)
- Something you are (voice, fingerprint)

Authentication types include

- Single-factor (username/password)
- Multifactor (typically adds a hardware or soft token or smart card to username/password)
- The RADIUS protocol is used to authenticate WPA/WPA2 Enterprise wireless networks, rather than a pre-shared key (PSK) as on SOHO networks.
- TACACS and TACACS+ are used for device administration.

# 2.3 QUESTIONS

1. If you log in to a server with your user name and password, which type of authentication is being used?

   **A.** Multifactor

   **B.** TACACS

   **C.** Single-factor

   **D.** WEP

2. WPA/WPA2 Enterprise uses which type of server for authentication?

   **A.** WEP

   **B.** TKIP

   **C.** AES

   **D.** RADIUS

3. If a wireless network uses both TKIP and AES encryption, which two types of wireless security is it using? (Choose two.)

   **A.** WPA

   **B.** WEP

   **C.** WPA2

   **D.** Multifactor

**4.** Entering a code sent to a device along with a user name and password constitutes which type of authentication?

   **A.** RADIUS authentication

   **B.** Multifactor authentication

   **C.** Single-factor authentication

   **D.** WEP

**5.** Which of the following is true of WEP encryption? (Choose all that apply.)

   **A.** Features 40-bit encryption

   **B.** Some versions feature 256-bit encryption

   **C.** Strongest wireless encryption standard

   **D.** Weakest wireless encryption standard

## 2.3 ANSWERS

**1.** **C**   This is single-factor authentication because the user name and password together are a single factor (knowledge).

**2.** **D**   A RADIUS server is used for authentication instead of storing the encryption key in the router (as with SOHO networks).

**3.** **A C**   Many routers support both WPA and WPA2 protocols by enabling the use of both TKIP and AES encryption.

**4.** **B**   This is multifactor authentication because the user name/password combo is one factor (knowledge) and the code is the second factor (possession).

**5.** **A D**   The original version of WEP encryption uses 40-bit codes, and WEP is by far the weakest and easiest-to-crack wireless encryption standard.

 Objective 2.4 # Given a scenario, detect, remove, and prevent malware using appropriate tools and methods

Malware is like a multipurpose tool, with every blade and gizmo designed to disrupt the computers, devices, and data you are responsible for. In this objective, we review the major types of malware and how to stop them.

# Malware

Malware, short for *malicious software*, is any program or code designed to do something on a system or network that you don't want done. Let's examine the forms and features of malware.

 **EXAM TIP** Malware types include worms (which replicate themselves through networks), viruses (which infect executable or data files), rootkits (hiding in protected parts of drives or OSs), keyloggers (recording keystrokes), Trojans (malware disguised as useful programs), ransomware (encrypts data until a ransom is paid), and spyware (collects information for misuse). Some types of malware can convert infected systems into zombies, which are controlled remotely and can be used as a botnet to attack other computers. Know these types of malware for the exam.

**Cross-Reference**

For details on the symptoms of malware infection, see Objective 3.2 in Domain 3.0 of Part II.

## Ransomware

Ransomware encrypts all the data it can gain access to on the system and its mapped network drives and then demands a ransom payment (often in bitcoins) in exchange for the decryption keys. To encourage fast payment, ransomware may present a countdown to the deletion of the encryption keys, which renders the scrambled data unrecoverable. Ransomware such as WannaCry has targeted both individual PC users and enterprise business and governmental networks.

 **NOTE** Bitcoin is a digital currency that supports global transactions and lacks the governmental control of most other currencies. These features make it a popular choice for ransomware payouts.

## Trojan

A Trojan (Trojan horse) doesn't replicate—it tricks users into installing it by appearing to do something useful (such as scan for malware [Trojan.FakeAV] or update a media player [Petya]) while it does something malicious.

## Keylogger

A keylogger records your keystrokes and is used to capture login information, banking or e-commerce transactions, and anything you do with a keyboard on your computer.

# Rootkit

A rootkit is a program that exploits root-level access to burrow deep into the system's OS or hardware, where it can often hide from all but the most aggressive anti-malware tools. Rootkits like ZeroAccess can be used to turn your computer into a cryptocurrency miner, a zombie in a botnet that is used to send spam, launch ransomware, and more.

# Virus

A virus is a type of malware that performs two tasks: replicating itself and activating its payload. When executed, a virus copies itself into existing executables or data files. A user action (such as opening a file, as with the ILOVEYOU virus, or inserting infected auto-run removable media, as in the case of Stuxnet) triggers the initial infection. Most viruses have a malicious payload capable of damaging the system or stealing data, but the payload may not be activated until the virus has had time to quietly spread.

# Botnet

Some malware enables remote control of infected *zombie* systems, which collectively become a *botnet* that the operators use (or rent out) to send spam, attack other systems and networks (e.g., the Mirai botnet of 2016), or do processing work such as mining bitcoins and breaking encryption keys.

# Worm

A worm functions similarly to a virus, except it does not need to attach itself to other programs to replicate. It can replicate on its own through networks, or even hardware like Thunderbolt accessories. If the infected computer is on a network, a worm will start scanning the network for other vulnerable systems to infect. One of the most famous worms of all time, Slammer, at one point doubled the number of infected servers every 8.5 seconds.

# Spyware

Spyware, which often sneaks in alongside legitimate software being downloaded, collects information on the system and its users. Many associate it with a subtype, *adware*, that attempts to make money by explicitly showing ads, redirecting searches, or replacing ads from other providers with its own—but this association is largely because most adware is obvious. The most dangerous spyware (such as MatCash) quietly collects private information without detection.

# Tools and Methods

There are plenty of different types of malware threats, and it's not surprising that there are several different types of tools and methods you can use to fight back.

## Antivirus and Anti-Malware

A classic antivirus program can actively scan for lurking malware or operate as a *virus shield* that passively monitors your computer's activity, checking for viruses in real time as your system runs programs or downloads files.

 **EXAM TIP**    Viruses are only a small component of the many types of malware. Many people continue to use the term antivirus as a synonym for anti-malware. However, CompTIA identifies antivirus and anti-malware as separate types of tools and expects you to know the differences.

Anti-malware programs use different techniques to combat different types of viruses:

- Because most boot sectors are the same, anti-malware programs detect boot sector viruses simply by comparing the drive's boot sector to a standard boot sector. If they detect a virus, most replace the infected boot sector from a copy.

- Executable viruses are difficult to find because they can lurk in any file, so the anti-malware program compares files against a library of signatures identifying the code pattern of a known virus. From time to time a perfectly clean program will match a signature, in which case the anti-malware program usually issues a patch to prevent further false alarms.

- Anti-malware programs search for *polymorphic malware* (malware that changes its signature to evade detection) by computing and storing a *checksum* from the contents of each executable file. Every time a program runs, the anti-malware program calculates a new checksum to see if the executable has changed.

## Recovery Console

The actual Windows tool called Recovery Console was found in Windows XP, but has been removed from later editions of Windows. The equivalent to the old Recovery Console is the Windows Recovery Environment (Windows RE), which can be launched from a Windows repair disc or by selecting *Repair your computer* from the Advanced boot options menu (Windows 7) or *Launch recovery environment* from Startup Settings (Windows 8/8.1/10).

**Cross-Reference**

To learn more about the special boot options menus in Windows 7 and later versions, see the "Safe Boot" section in Part II, Domain 3.0, Objective 3.1.

## Backup/Restore

Creating backups before a malware attack enables users to restore data to a cleaned system or another computer.

**Cross-Reference**

To learn more about backup and restore, see the "Backup and Recovery" section in Part II, Domain 4.0, Objective 4.3.

## End-user Education

Even the best anti-malware suite is imperfect—ideally it forms a rarely tested second line of defense. The first line of defense is educating your users—nobody wants their system infected with malware. Teach users to be cautious with e-mail from senders they don't recognize and to never click an attachment or URL in an e-mail unless they are 100 percent certain of the source. Explain the dangers of questionable websites and teach your users how to react when a site is trying to manipulate them or triggers their browser's built-in attack site warning (see Figure 2.4-1).

Depending on how much say your users have over their systems, you may need to reinforce the importance of having an anti-malware program, scanning regularly, and enabling the virus shield that automatically scans e-mail, downloads, running programs, and so on. Tell your users to only install apps from trusted sources, such as the manufacturer's website, or well-known app stores, such as Valve's Steam service—and teach them how to both identify and avoid untrusted software sources, such as free registry cleaners from some .support domain.

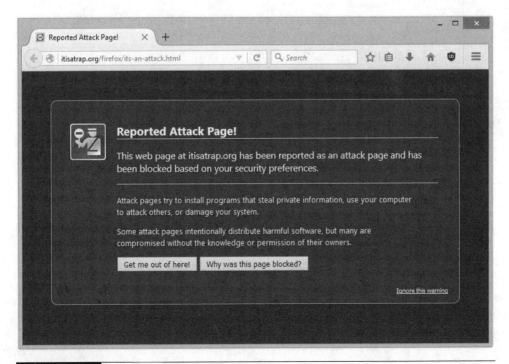

**FIGURE 2.4-1**   Attack site warning

Likewise, if your users have a say in whether their anti-malware software and its definitions automatically update, make sure they know how to enable these automatic updates to defend against new malware.

 **EXAM TIP** The best-laid security plans include end-user education.

## Software Firewalls

Software firewalls such as Windows (Defender) Firewall (shown in Figure 2.4-2) provide a variety of security features for computers, including the ability to block malware attacks originating from the network or the Internet. If you enable Windows Firewall with Advanced Security or use a third-party firewall that also checks outbound traffic, you can provide even more protection against malware for your network.

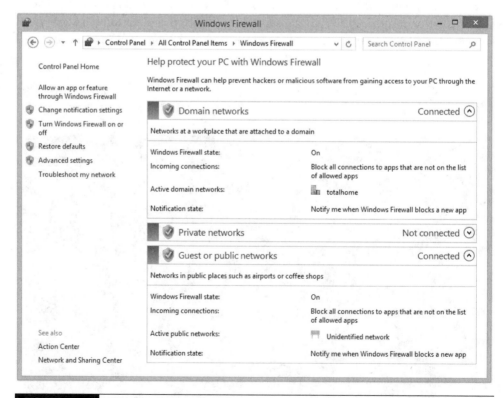

**FIGURE 2.4-2** Windows 7 Firewall applet

**Cross-Reference**

To learn more about Windows Firewall, see the "Windows Firewall" section in Part II, Domain 1.0, Objective 1.5.

# DNS Configuration

A DNS configuration issue will prevent effective use of the Internet. One way to tell if you have a problem is to see if you can ping a site; go to a command prompt and try pinging a known URL as follows:

```
C:\>ping www.cheetos1.com
Ping request could not find host www.cheetos1.com.
Please check the name and try again.
```

The ping fails, but we learn a lot from it. The ping indicates that your computer can't get an IP address for that website. This points to a DNS failure, which is a very common problem. DNS failures can be caused by malware as an attempt to prevent you from getting help with the infection. To fix DNS failures, follow these steps:

1. In Windows, go to a command prompt and type **ipconfig /flushdns**:

   ```
   C:\>ipconfig /flushdns
   Windows IP Configuration
   Successfully flushed the DNS Resolver Cache.
   ```

 **ADDITIONAL RESOURCES**   Despite the similarity, ifconfig and iwconfig aren't suitable for flushing the DNS cache, if it exists, in macOS or Linux. To flush the DNS cache in macOS Mojave, go to www.howtoisolve.com and search for "How to Reset DNS Cache in MacOS Mojave." Ubuntu doesn't cache DNS by default. To learn more, visit https://beebom.com and search for "How to Flush DNS Cache in Linux."

2. In Windows, go to the Network and Sharing Center and click *Change adapter settings*. Right-click your network connection and select Diagnose to run the troubleshooter (see Figure 2.4-3).

3. Try using a reputable public DNS server, such as Google's: 8.8.8.8 and 8.8.4.4.

4. Consider using a DNS web filter to help stop malware infections by blocking harmful or malicious websites.

 **ADDITIONAL RESOURCES**   To learn more about DNS web filtering and leading apps, go to www.expertinsights.com and search for "Top DNS Web Filtering Platforms."

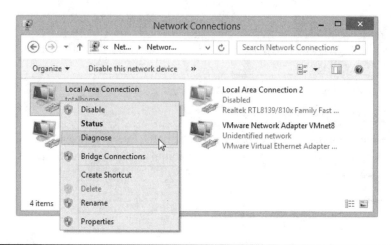

**FIGURE 2.4-3** Diagnosing a network problem in Windows 8.1

# REVIEW

**Objective 2.4: Given a scenario, detect, remove, and prevent malware using appropriate tools and methods** Types of malware include

- Worms (replicate themselves through networks).
- Viruses (infect executable or data files).
- Rootkits (hide in protected parts of drives or OSs where they are very hard to find and remove).
- Keyloggers (record keystrokes to steal information).
- Trojans (malware disguised as useful programs).
- Ransomware (encrypts data until a ransom is paid).
- Spyware (collects information for misuse).
- Some types of malware can convert infected systems into zombies which are controlled remotely and can be used as a botnet to attack other computers.

Tools and methods to fight malware include

- Antivirus (blocks virus infections and scans systems).
- Anti-malware (performs antivirus tasks, detects boot sector viruses and rootkits, creates checksums for executable files, compares stored checksums when a file is run to determine if it's been infected).
- Recovery console is a leftover Windows XP term that is better understood as referring to the Windows Recovery Environment (Windows RE).

- Backups made before a malware attack can be restored after a system is cleaned.
- End-user education is essential to avoid attacks from e-mail, links to dangerous websites, and other user-triggered threats.
- Software firewalls such as Windows (Defender) Firewall can stop malware attacks from other computers on the network or Internet.
- DNS configuration can be changed by malware, and users need to know how to repair DNS errors. DNS web filters can help protect against malware.

## 2.4 QUESTIONS

1. A client calls you for help: the company files are encrypted and they'll be deleted unless the company sends a payment in cryptocurrency. What type of attack has happened to your client's company?

   **A.** Malware

   **B.** Trojan

   **C.** Worm

   **D.** Ransomware

2. A single server on your network was infected with malware, but 24 hours later, over a hundred servers were infected. What type of malware infection has attacked the network?

   **A.** Trojan

   **B.** Spyware

   **C.** Worm

   **D.** Ransomware

3. Employees at Company Z have been navigating to a lot of malicious websites and infecting their network. Which of the following would best help prevent infections?

   **A.** Using a software firewall

   **B.** Using a DNS filter

   **C.** Running a DDoS attack on malicious websites

   **D.** Scanning for malware

4. Instructing individuals in your company not to click on URLs in suspicious e-mail is an example of?

   **A.** Social engineering

   **B.** Paranoia

   **C.** End-user education

   **D.** Untrusted software

5. A network server has been infected with malware that damages data. An up-to-date backup is available. When should the backup be restored?

  **A.** After the infection is removed.

  **B.** As soon as the infection is detected.

  **C.** It should not be restored.

  **D.** After another backup is run.

## 2.4 ANSWERS

1. **D** A ransomware attack combines file encryption and the demand for payment of a ransom before the files will be decrypted.

2. **C** A worm is a type of malware designed to spread through network connections.

3. **B** Using a DNS filter helps prevent users from navigating to questionable websites, so it's the best choice to prevent infections.

4. **C** Instructing users in how to avoid e-mail traps is an example of end-user education.

5. **A** The backup should be restored only after the infection is removed. A new backup should be created on the normal schedule after the server is restored to service.

 **Objective 2.5** Compare and contrast social engineering, threats, and vulnerabilities

Social engineering attacks networks by tricking users into providing access. Threats attack technological vulnerabilities found in networks. Understanding the differences between social engineering, threats, and vulnerabilities is an important part of improving security.

## Social Engineering

Attackers use social engineering to trick or manipulate people inside the organization into giving up access to its network or facilities. Social engineering attacks are rarely used in isolation.

Attackers may infiltrate facilities by posing as cleaning personnel, repair technicians, or messengers. Once inside, they may snoop around or talk with people to gather more information. Passwords are obvious targets, but information such as employee names, office numbers, and department names could all be useful for further social engineering attacks later. Social engineering can take place in person, via telephone calls, or via e-mail or messaging.

# Phishing

Phishing, the most common form of social engineering, is the act of trying to get people to give their user names, passwords, or other security information by pretending to be someone else electronically. It has the same goals as telephone scams but uses online methods, including e-mail and messages through social networks such as Facebook.

The more dangerous, targeted form, *spear phishing*, attacks individuals in an organization by pretending to be someone who has the authority to ask for a fund transfer, gain network access, and so on.

# Impersonation

Impersonation can take a variety of forms. For example, the attacker in a telephone scam attempts to impersonate someone inside the organization to gain information (such as a phone number, user name, blackmail material, or schedule) or help (perhaps a password reset or wire transfer). Impersonation can also rely on disguises such as cleaning personnel, repair technicians, messengers, employees with fake badges; anything that will help the attackers snoop around desks, chat with people inside the organization, gather names, office numbers, and department names—little things in and of themselves but powerful tools when combined later with other social engineering attacks.

# Shoulder Surfing

Shoulder surfing simply involves observing a user's screen or keyboard for information such as a password—usually over the user's shoulder.

# Tailgating

Tailgating is walking directly behind one or more people being admitted to a secure area and often includes impersonation techniques. Organizations use a *mantrap* (described earlier in Objective 2.1) to keep intruders from tailgating into the facility behind authorized entrants.

# Dumpster Diving

Dumpster diving is the generic term for searching through refuse for information. This is also a form of intrusion. Make sure unneeded documents are immediately shredded to reduce your vulnerability to dumpster diving.

# Threats and Vulnerabilities

Threats target technical vulnerabilities in organizations. Instead of targeting human weaknesses as with social engineering, threats are aimed at weaknesses in Internet firewalls, insecure connections, and inadequate passwords, among others.

**EXAM TIP**    Be able to compare and contrast all of the threats and vulnerabilities listed in the following sections.

## DoS and DDoS

A denial of service (DoS) attack is an attempt by a single device to disable another device by overwhelming ("flooding") its Internet connection with connection requests such as rapidly repeated pings, page requests, and so on. A distributed denial of service (DDoS) attack uses multiple coordinated devices to perform the attack. Devices involved in a DDoS attack often are compromised by malware that has turned them into zombie members of a botnet.

## Zero-day

A zero-day attack exploits a vulnerability that was previously unknown to the software's developers—they've had zero days to fix it. Systems running the software will be vulnerable until the developers release a patch and it is installed.

## Man-in-the-Middle

In a man-in-the-middle (MITM) attack, an attacker successfully taps into communications between two systems, covertly intercepting traffic thought to be only between those systems, reading or even changing the data before sending it on to the intended recipient, often leaving both parties unaware of the intermediary.

## Brute Force

Brute force is technically any attempt to find a useful value by trying many or all possibilities (typically with a program), but it most often refers to discovering a password by trying many possibilities. You can also use a brute-force search to find open ports, network IDs, IP addresses, or user names, or even to try a long list of known vulnerabilities.

## Dictionary

A dictionary attack is a form of brute force attack that essentially guesses every word in a dictionary. Don't think only of Webster's dictionary—a *dictionary* used to attack passwords might contain every password ever leaked online.

## Rainbow Table

A rainbow table attack is used to attack secured systems that store password hashes. A rainbow table stores precalculated password hashes and enters them until a match is found.

**EXAM TIP**    Make sure you know that rainbow tables are used to reverse password hashes.

 **NOTE**    A *hashed password* is a password that has been mathematically changed. The result of the change is called a *cryptographic hash*, and the hash is stored instead of the actual plaintext password. When a login attempt takes place, the password is hashed and compared to the stored hash; if they match, the login is successful.

 **ADDITIONAL RESOURCES**    To learn more about hashing, go to https:// tiptopsecurity.com and search for "What Is Cryptographic Hashing?"

# Spoofing

Spoofing is the process of pretending to be someone or something you are not by placing false information into your packets, such as a user name or MAC, IP, e-mail, or web address in order to trick other systems or users into aiding the attack.

 **EXAM TIP**    Be sure to know the difference between impersonation (pretending to be someone you are not—in person or by phone, e-mail, or messaging) and spoofing (adding false information to network data).

# Non-compliant Systems

A non-compliant system is a system that has not been updated with operating system updates and security patches, anti-malware updates and patches, or driver updates. A non-compliant system is not only vulnerable to attack itself, but could be used as an attack vector against other computers and devices on a network.

# Zombie

A zombie is a computer that is being controlled by malware to function as part of a *botnet*, a network of infected computers under the control of a single person or group. Botnets are used to send spam, launch DDoS attacks, and perform other types of unauthorized functions without the knowledge or consent of the users of the zombies.

# REVIEW

**Objective 2.5: Compare and contrast social engineering, threats, and vulnerabilities** Social engineering can use any of the following methods, and often uses them in combination:

- Phishing (pretending to be someone else electronically, via e-mail, social networks, etc, to get user names, passwords, and so on)
- Spear phishing (pretending to be someone who can ask a member of an organization for funds, network access, or other information)
- Impersonation (by phone deception, disguises, or just walking around to get information)
- Shoulder surfing (sneaking a peek at confidential information or a user's login process)
- Tailgating (walking in behind someone who has access to a secure area)
- Dumpster diving (picking up discarded information)

Other types of attacks include

- Denial of service (DoS) and distributed denial of service (DDoS) are attacks on a network or Internet resource.
- Exploiting a vulnerability the same day a vendor discovers it is a zero-day attack.
- Man-in-the-middle (MITM) attacks fool both ends of a connection into thinking they are communicating with the other end instead of an attacker.
- Brute force attacks try all possible passwords, user names, open ports, or other values.
- Dictionary attacks use a "dictionary" of possible, likely, or leaked passwords to gain access.
- Rainbow table attacks attack the rainbow table used to store password hashes to gain access.
- Spoofing places false information (MAC addresses, IP addresses, etc.) into network packets to trick other systems.

Non-compliant systems have not been brought up to standard in OS patches and updates, anti-malware updates, or driver updates and are vulnerable to being turned into zombies in a botnet.

## 2.5 QUESTIONS

1. A client reports that the organization's wireless network is being flooded with pings and page requests far beyond normal limits. The pings and page requests are coming from a wide variety of locations. Your client is dealing with what type of attack?

   **A.** DDoS

   **B.** Impersonation

    **C.** DoS

    **D.** Social engineering

2. You receive an e-mail purporting to be from the head of IT that is asking you to install a piece of malware. Which type of attack is being used?

    **A.** Impersonation

    **B.** Spoofing

    **C.** Rainbow table

    **D.** Brute force

3. Security cameras reveal that someone is walking by the server room and pulling reports out of the trash. What is going on?

    **A.** Dumpster diving

    **B.** Shoulder surfing

    **C.** Phishing

    **D.** Impersonation

4. The same day that your accounting software vendor is informed of a security vulnerability, you discover it was used to attack accounts payable. What type of vulnerability is being exploited?

    **A.** Phishing

    **B.** Man-in-the-middle

    **C.** Zero-day

    **D.** Dictionary

5. The RADIUS authentication server on your wireless network has been hacked and a list of old passwords has been leaked. Although none of the passwords are current, the list could still be used for which of the following attacks?

    **A.** Brute force

    **B.** Spoofing

    **C.** Impersonation

    **D.** Dictionary

## 2.5 ANSWERS

1. **A** A distributed denial of service (DDoS) is an attack coming from multiple locations that seeks to overwhelm a network resource so it can't respond.

2. **B** The use of a false sender on the e-mail makes this an example of spoofing.

3. **A** Dumpster diving is taking discarded information from any location, not just a dumpster.

4. **C**    A zero-day attack takes place before or immediately after the software vendor discovers or has been provided knowledge of a vulnerability. It's called zero-day because the vendor has had zero days to patch the vulnerability.

5. **D**    A dictionary attack uses a list of possible matches for passwords. Since many users who create their own passwords often recycle old passwords in whole or in part, a list of old passwords can be very useful in the hands of an attacker.

# Objective 2.6    Compare and contrast the differences of basic Microsoft Windows OS security settings

Microsoft Windows includes many security settings, from users and groups to EFS and BitLocker. In this objective, you learn what they do and how to put them to work.

## User and Groups

A *group* is a container holding user accounts that defines the capabilities of its members, such as file/folder permissions, printer access, and so on. If you make an Accounting group and add all users in the accounting department, you can easily grant or deny the whole group access to a given file or folder. By creating groups with specified roles and users for each group, and by providing each group with access to only files or folders relevant to their jobs, you improve the data security of the organization.

Windows provides built-in groups with predetermined access levels, but the following are the only ones you need to know for the exam.

**EXAM TIP**    Know the various Microsoft users and groups described in this section and what they can and cannot do.

## User and Group Types

Microsoft Windows includes the following user and group types:

- Administrator has complete control over a machine, and you can assign one or more users as Administrator.

- Power User is almost as powerful as an Administrator, but cannot install new devices or access other users' files or folders unless the file or folder permissions grant them access.

- Guest is an account that can be used by someone who does not have an individual account, and is granted very limited access.
- Standard User cannot edit the Registry or access critical system files; they can create groups, but can only manage ones they create.

# NTFS vs. Share Permissions

Each OS uses separate network sharing permissions to grant or restrict access to shared resources. Beyond these, file- or folder-level permissions (such as NTFS) also affect network shares. What are NTFS permissions? They are sets of rules that affect every folder and file in your system, and they define what any group or account can or cannot do with a file or folder.

Windows uses NTFS to authorize local and network users: even if you grant access via network share permissions, NTFS permissions still say what users can do with the resource.

If you share from an NTFS drive, you must set *both* network and NTFS permissions to grant access. The shortcut is to give everyone Full Control network permissions, and then use NTFS permissions to precisely control who has what access.

## Allow vs. Deny

To add or remove NTFS permissions, start by selecting the user or group you want to change, then click Edit to open the Permissions dialog box. Selecting the Allow checkbox next to an NTFS permission you want to add grants that permission. To remove an NTFS permission, clear the Allow checkbox.

NTFS permissions are inherited. In other words, if folder A provides permissions to everyone to have read/write access, any subfolder of A will have the same permissions.

**Cross-Reference**

To learn more about inheritance, see the "Inheritance" section later in this objective.

It might be necessary to turn off inheritance for a specific folder or file. Instead of shutting down inheritance completely, use the Deny checkbox. Clicking the Deny checkbox for an NTFS permission tells Windows to overrule inheritance and stop that NTFS permission.

 **EXAM TIP** Allow grants permissions; Deny overrules the inheritance of the selected permission.

# File Attributes

To view file attributes from Windows Explorer or File Explorer, right-click a file and select Properties. Typical attributes include Read-only and Hidden. Click Advanced to see additional attributes such as *File is ready for archiving, Allow this file to have contents indexed in addition to file properties, Compress contents to save disk space,* and *Encrypt contents to save data* (which uses EFS). From the command line, you can use attrib.

# Shared Files and Folders

To see the NTFS permissions for a shared file or folder, right-click it, choose Properties, and click the Security tab.

- **Full Control**   Complete access to contents of the file or folder. Full Control provides all of the following permissions.
- **Modify**   Change file or folder contents.
- **Read & Execute**   Access file or folder contents and run programs.
- **List Folder Contents**   Display folder contents.
- **Read**   Access a file or folder.
- **Write**   Add a new file or folder.

You can also select combinations of these settings.

## Administrative Shares vs. Local Shares

A local share is a share that is set up for a folder or a library in Windows. What if you want to share an entire hard drive across the network? Use a special administrative share set up by Windows for each local drive. On a system called MyPC, the C: drive's administrative share is called \\MyPC\C$. For the D: drive, it's \\MyPC\D$. Administrative shares are Windows default shares that give local administrators administrative access to all hard drives (not optical drives or removable devices) plus the %systemroot% folder (usually C:\Windows) and a couple of others, depending on the system.

Anyone who wants to connect to an administrative share must have an account (user name/password) on that system.

## Permission Propagation: Moving vs. Copying Folders and Files

Permission propagation determines which NTFS permissions are applied to files and folders you move or copy: their original permissions or those of their destination? Table 2.6-1 summarizes the results of moving and copying between NTFS volumes.

**TABLE 2.6-1**   Permission Propagation

|  | Same Volume | Different Volume |
|---|---|---|
| Move | Keeps original permissions | Inherits new permissions |
| Copy | Inherits new permissions | Inherits new permissions |

**ADDITIONAL RESOURCES**   To learn more about NTFS permissions, see support.microsoft.com and search for "How permissions are handled when you copy and move files and folders 310316." Although this article specifically refers to Windows 2000 and Windows XP, the information is accurate for current Microsoft Windows versions.

 **EXAM TIP**   Know what happens to permissions when you move or copy a file.

# Inheritance

Inheritance determines which NTFS permissions apply to new files or subfolders. The default rule is that new files or folders get the NTFS permissions of the parent folder. You can technically disable inheritance in the file or folder properties, but don't. Inheritance is good (and expected). Inherited permissions are grayed out and can't be changed (see Figure 2.6-1), but

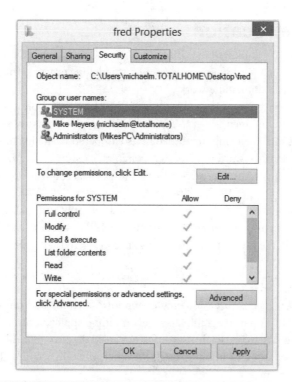

**FIGURE 2.6-1**   Inherited permissions

you can override them as needed with the Deny checkbox. These permissions are additive: if you have Full Control on a folder and only Read on a file in it, you still get Full Control on the file.

## System Files and Folders

By default, Windows Explorer (Windows 7) and File Explorer (Windows 8/8.1/10) hide system files and folders. This setting is intended to make it harder for standard users to accidentally or purposefully change or erase these files.

However, technicians and administrators might need to view these files to make configuration changes or repair problems. To make these files visible, open the Folder Options (Windows 7/8/8.1) or File Explorer Options (Windows 10) applet in Control Panel, click the View tab, and click the *Show hidden files, folders, and drives* radio button. Then, select *Hide protected operating system files (Recommended)* and clear its checkbox. Click Yes to continue. Click Apply, then OK. Normally hidden or protected files are now visible, using a paler version of the normal folder or file icon.

After making any changes necessary to the system, reverse these settings in Control Panel to hide the system and protected operating system files and folders.

## User Authentication

User authentication in Windows takes place in different ways, depending upon whether the account is managed on a per-system basis (as in a standalone or workgroup network) or by a domain controller (in a domain network).

On a standalone system or a system with shared folders on a workgroup, each computer has an individually maintained list of users and their associated passwords. When a local or workgroup user logs in to a computer, the login is compared to the list of users and access is granted if the user and password information match an existing account. Each account is set up as either an administrator or a standard user (a guest account is optional) and access is granted accordingly.

On a domain network, a list of users is maintained centrally and each user is assigned to a group. A login on any computer on the network is checked against the user list, and if the user and password match, the user is permitted access according to their group.

### Single Sign-On

Single sign-on (SSO) means to have a single Windows account that can log on to any system on the domain. SSO permits a user to access multiple applications or resources with one user name and one password. Each user does not need a separate local account stored on every computer. User authentication through the single domain account enables access to all machines on the domain.

# Run as Administrator vs. Standard User

In Windows, security settings will prevent you from running some commands as a standard user. To elevate the command prompt, right-click the cmd.exe icon and select *Run as administrator*.

You can also run executable files as administrator in the same way in Windows: right-click the executable icon and select *Run as administrator*. This is often necessary when running some installers or uninstallers or when running apps made for older versions of Windows.

 **EXAM TIP**   Know how to run commands and apps with elevated privileges.

# BitLocker and BitLocker To Go

Windows 7 Ultimate and Enterprise editions and Windows 8/8.1/10 Pro edition feature *BitLocker Drive Encryption*, which encrypts the whole drive, including every user's files. If the system has a *Trusted Platform Module (TPM)* chip, it can enhance security by validating on boot that the computer has not changed. Create a recovery key or password when you enable BitLocker and keep it somewhere secure (like a safe). To enable BitLocker, double-click the BitLocker Drive Encryption icon in the Control Panel and then click Turn on BitLocker (see Figure 2.6-2). *BitLocker To Go* enables you to encrypt removable media (such as a USB flash drive) and require a password to access its data.

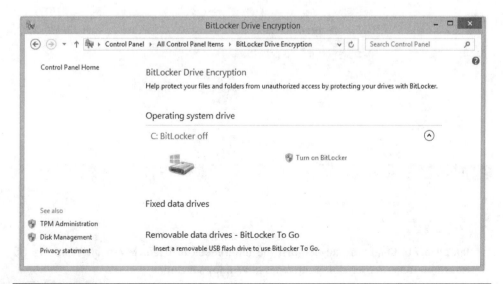

**FIGURE 2.6-2**   Enabling BitLocker Drive Encryption

# EFS

The professional editions of Windows support the *Encrypting File System (EFS)*, an encryption scheme any user can use to encrypt individual files or folders. To encrypt a file or folder, just right-click it and select Properties, click the General tab, click the Advanced button, and then check *Encrypt contents to secure data* (see Figure 2.6-3) in the Advanced Attributes dialog box. Close the open dialog boxes, and the file or folder is locked from other user accounts (unless you copy it to a non-NTFS drive).

 **CAUTION**    Data you encrypt with EFS is secure from prying eyes, but access to your encrypted files is based on that specific installation of Windows. If you lose your password or an administrator resets it, you're locked out of your encrypted files permanently. If you use EFS, make a password reset disk.

**FIGURE 2.6-3**    Selecting encryption

# REVIEW

**Objective 2.6: Compare and contrast the differences of basic Microsoft Windows OS security settings**    User and group types in Windows include

- Administrator (complete control over a machine)
- Power User (less powerful than an administrator)

- Guest (very limited access)
- Standard User (cannot edit files or Registry)

NTFS permissions are used for both local and network users, and affect what both types of users can do with a resource.

- Allow (grants permission to use a resource).
- Deny (overrides an inherited permission).
- File attributes (include read-only and hidden). Advanced attributes indicate if a file is ready for archiving (backup), if its contents can be indexed, or if it is compressed or encrypted with EFS.
- File attributes can be changed with attrib from the command line.

NTFS permissions for shared files and folders include

- Full Control (complete control)
- Modify (change file/folder contents)
- Read & Execute (access contents, run programs)
- List Folder Contents (display folder contents)
- Read (access file/folder)
- Write (add new file/folder)

Other security features in Windows include

- Administrative shares (for example, \\servername\C$) share an entire hard drive or %systemroot% (Windows folder); require user to have username/account on the system.
- Local shares share a folder or library.
- Permission propagation refers to how moving and copying files can change file permissions on NTFS volumes: move to same volume keeps original permission, move to different volume or copy to same or different volume inherits new permissions from new location.
- Inheritance refers to permissions inherited by new folders/files under an existing folder.
- System files and folders and protected operating system files are hidden by default. To make them visible, use Folder Options (Windows 7/8/8.1) or File Explorer Folder Options (Windows 10) in Control Panel.
- User authentication on workgroups is done at each computer with shares.
- On a domain, the domain controller performs user authentication for all resources in the domain.
- Single sign-on (SSO) enables domain accounts to log-in once to the domain and have access to all resources on the domain.

- Choosing *Run as administrator* provides access to commands and options not available to a Standard User.
- Encryption is available with BitLocker, BitLocker To Go, or EFS.

## 2.6 QUESTIONS

1. You need to run a command from the Windows command line as administrator. Which of the following methods will enable you to do this?

   **A.** Add su in front of the command

   **B.** Enter your user name and account when prompted

   **C.** Open the command prompt as sudo

   **D.** Right-click cmd.exe and select Run as administrator

2. A folder is configured with Full Control settings. However, there's a file in that folder that you want to make read-only. Which of the following would work?

   **A.** Change the security setting for the file to Read-only

   **B.** Move the file to a different folder at the same level as the current folder and set the folder as Read-only

   **C.** Use attrib

   **D.** None of the above

3. You want to view a file in a folder. Which of the following permissions is needed?

   **A.** List Folder Contents

   **B.** Modify

   **C.** Read & Execute

   **D.** Write

4. You have a SOHO workgroup at home but connect to a domain controller at the office. Your spouse wants to access a shared folder on your computer. Which of the following do you need to do?

   **A.** Send a request to the domain administrator

   **B.** Run BitLocker

   **C.** Set up an account for your spouse on your computer

   **D.** Share your password and user name with your spouse

5. Your computer is called \\MyPC. Your spouse's computer is called \\TheOtherPC. To log in to the administrative share on your spouse's C: drive, which of the following is the correct syntax?

   **A.** \\TheOtherPC\$C

   **B.** \\MyPC\C$

   **C.** \\TheOtherPC\DriveC$

   **D.** \\TheOtherPC\C$

## 2.6 ANSWERS

1. **D** To run command prompt commands as administrator, you must open the command prompt session as administrator.

2. **B** The parent folder permissions override the settings for a specific file in the folder.

3. **A** List Folder Contents will allow you to view the files in the folder.

4. **C** You control sharing on your workgroup, so you can make these changes.

5. **D** The correct syntax includes the remote computer name and the administrative share name.

**Objective 2.7** # Given a scenario, implement security best practices to secure a workstation

Keeping a workstation secure starts with passwords, but it doesn't end there. In this objective, you will also learn other methods for securing accounts and devices and when to use them.

 **EXAM TIP** Given a scenario, be ready to implement the appropriate security best practices listed in this objective.

## Password Best Practices

What does CompTIA mean by password best practices? Simply put, if you set up password policies that enforce the following practices, you will reduce the likelihood that attacks against password-protected resources, such as user accounts, will succeed.

 **EXAM TIP** Given a scenario, know how to implement the password best practices described in this section.

### Setting Strong Passwords

Strong passwords are passwords that are reasonably resistant to a calculated attack by password-guessing programs—a good starting point is a minimum of eight characters, including letters (both upper- and lowercase), numbers, and symbols—but keep in mind that "strong" evolves along with processing power and password-guessing strategies. The catch is that users react predictably to complex requirements by tacking punctuation and numbers onto either end of their otherwise weak passwords and/or by writing their passwords on sticky notes or scraps of paper kept somewhere close to their computers. Password-management apps can help mitigate this problem.

## Password Expiration

Setting passwords to expire regularly reduces how long a compromised password is useful, but users tend to cope with frequent change requirements by using a predictable template or formula. Assume an attacker who recovers an old password like #1SportsFan5 will try #1SportsFan6, and several more increments if it doesn't work. One way to overcome this problem is to have a password expiration policy that prevents identical or similar passwords from being reused for a period of time. Password policies are changed with Local Security Policy or group policy settings.

## Screensaver Required Password

If you must step away for a moment, manually lock the computer (or screen) with a hotkey or the primary OS menu to help prevent casual snooping at work. On a Windows system, just press WINDOWS-L on the keyboard to lock it. It's also a good idea to set up a screensaver with a short wait time and configure it to show the logon screen (Windows 7) or lock screen (Windows 8 or newer) on resume.

**EXAM TIP**    Windows does not enable screensavers by default but includes several to choose from.

## BIOS/UEFI Passwords

Passwords can also restrict access to internal resources to users who understand or need to use them. The BIOS/UEFI passwords discussed in Part I, Domain 3.0, Objective 3.5 are a great way to keep low-knowledge users from fiddling with the CMOS system setup utility.

## Requiring Passwords

Passwords are required for Windows accounts on standalone or workgroup computers as well as on computers belonging to a domain. However, local accounts can be set up without passwords. A local account without a password can be a major attack vector if the computer is connected to a network. When new accounts are created, require users to create passwords.

**CAUTION**    Make a password reset disk (can be a small USB drive or a CD) for every computer that has at least one local account. That way, if the local account passwords are forgotten, they can be recovered.

# Account Management

Account management refers to the creation and configuration of specific user accounts in Windows as well as the configuration of account settings, also known as *policies*. Policies can further restrict the actions a group or account can perform (such as opening a command prompt, installing software, or logging on at a given time of day). Every Windows client (except for Home versions) has its own *Local Security Policy* program (see Figure 2.7-1), but local policies are a pain if you want the same settings on multiple systems.

## Cross-Reference

To learn more about group policy settings, see the "Group Policy/Updates" section in Objective 2.2, earlier in this domain.

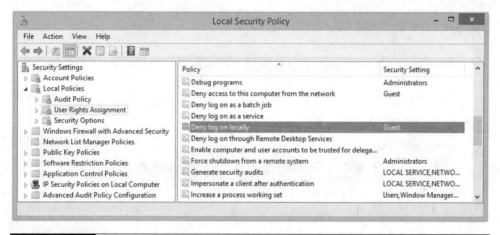

**FIGURE 2.7-1**   Local Security Policy

The Local Policy Editor also provides access to local security policies (see the upcoming examples). The aspects of account management you need to understand for the CompTIA A+ 220-1002 exam are covered in the following sections.

# Restricting User Permissions

User permissions are governed by the group a specific user account is assigned to. To see the current policies and the groups affected, click Local Policies | User Rights Assignment and scroll through the list of policies. To learn more about a policy, double-click it and then click the Explain tab (see Figure 2.7-2).

To prevent a group from performing a task, open the Local Security Setting tab, click the group, click Remove, then click Apply (see Figure 2.7-3).

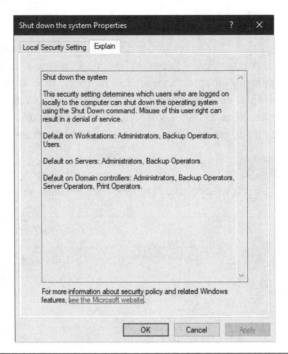

**FIGURE 2.7-2**    Viewing the description for the Shut Down the System policy

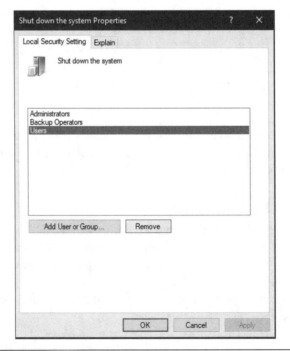

**FIGURE 2.7-3**    Preparing to remove the group Users from the Shut Down the System policy

## Logon Time Restrictions

Logon time restrictions for specific users can be set up with group policy on a domain controller, or by using the net user command on a workgroup or individual PC using an elevated command prompt. For example, to limit the user Geeksy to login between 11:00 AM and 8:00 PM (20:00 hours) on Monday–Friday, enter the following from an elevated command prompt:

```
net user Geeksy /time:M-F,11:00-20:00
```

 **ADDITIONAL RESOURCES**   To learn more about using net user for this process, see www.makeuseof.com and search for "How to Set Time Limits for User Accounts in Windows."

To set up time limits for children in Windows 10, you can set up their accounts as family members and use the Microsoft Account/Family dialog available online to restrict logon days, times, and maximum hours of usage. The similar Parental Controls feature is available for Windows 7 and Windows 8/8.1.

 **ADDITIONAL RESOURCES**   To learn more about family safety and parental controls in Windows, go to www.lifewire.com and search for "Microsoft Family Safety."

## Disabling Guest Account

The Guest account represents a potential security risk. To prevent it from being enabled, go to Local Policies | Security Options, double-click Accounts: Guest Account Status, and set it to Disabled.

## Failed Attempts Lockout

Set up account lockout policies to stop brute-force, rainbow table, or dictionary attacks from going on endlessly. To enable lockout duration or set account lockout threshold, go to Security Settings | Account Policies | Account Lockout Policy.

## Timeout/Screen Lock

By enabling the system to lock the screen after a period of inactivity and requiring a login to continue, you protect systems from casual snooping, even if the user forgets to lock the system manually. This feature is automatically enabled in Windows 8/8.1/10 for the screen lock. Windows 7 lacks a screen lock, but screensaver settings can be used the same way: in the local group policy editor, go to User Configuration | Administrative Templates | Control Panel | Personalization and enable and configure the following: Enable screen saver, Screen saver timeout, and Password protect the screen saver.

 **NOTE**    To change the timing for screen lock in recent and current versions of Windows 10, use the Lock Screen option in Settings | Personalization and click the Screen timeout settings link.

## Change Default Admin User Account/Password

As part of any operating system security best practice, it is recommended that you rename any default accounts such as the default administrator or Guest accounts that are created at installation and apply strong passwords. This practice also applies to routers, or any other devices that come "out of the box" with default accounts/passwords. It is also common practice to create a new account that has admin privileges and disable the default account.

## Basic Active Directory Functions

Managing a Windows Active Directory (AD) is beyond the scope of CompTIA A+ Certification, but you are expected to understand the functions covered in the following sections.

### Account Creation

The process of creating a user in an Active Directory uses the Active Directory Users and Computers Microsoft Management Console (MMC). Right-click the Users folder, select New | User, and enter the information requested (user's first name, initials, last name, full name, user logon name, password) and configure password settings (change on next login, etc.). Optional information to add after creating the account might include a logon script, profile path, and others.

### Account Deletion

To delete a user account in Active Directory, click the user account, click the red X in the menu ribbon, and click Yes when prompted. You can also right-click the user account, select Delete from the right-click menu, and click Yes when prompted.

Although an AD administrator can delete an account at any time, deleting an account can cause issues with resources connected to that account.

 **ADDITIONAL RESOURCES**    For a discussion of this topic, open a web browser, search for "adrian gordon" and "do not delete active directory user accounts." Click the article at www.itsupportguides.com.

### Password Reset/Unlock Account

To reset a password with Active Directory, right-click the user account, choose Reset Password, enter the new password (and confirm it) as directed in the Reset Password dialog box, and click OK. If a user is locked out, go to the same Reset Password dialog box, check the *Unlock the user's account* checkbox, and click OK.

### Disable Account

Many AD experts recommend disabling an account after a user leaves an organization. The user's e-mail can be forwarded to other users. To disable a user account in Active Directory, right-click the account and select Disable.

## Disable Autorun

AutoRun is a feature originally intended to make Windows software installation from optical discs (remember those?) easier: insert the CD or DVD into the drive, and an autorun.inf file told the computer what program to launch. The AutoPlay feature for removable media of all types doesn't even require a special file: Windows reads the contents of the optical disc or USB drive and displays programs that can be used to open the media's contents. The problem is that both of these features make it easy to introduce malware into a system.

To block AutoRun and AutoPlay with group policy, open Computer Configuration | Administrative Templates | Windows Components | AutoPlay Policies and set *Turn off Autoplay* to Enabled and set *Default behavior for AutoRun* to Disabled.

## Data Encryption

To enable data encryption with business editions of Windows 7 and later, you can use the following:

- BitLocker for fixed drives
- BitLocker To Go for portable drives
- EFS (Encrypting File System)

To configure BitLocker and BitLocker To Go settings in group policy, go to Computer Configuration | Administrative Templates | Windows Components | BitLocker Drive Encryption and make changes as desired. Anyone with the BitLocker credentials for a specific drive can view the contents of that drive.

 **ADDITIONAL RESOURCES** For details about setting BitLocker and BitLocker To Go options, go to https://docs.microsoft.com and search for "BitLocker Group Policy settings."

On the other hand, files or folders encrypted with EFS cannot be read unless the EFS certificate is available to the current user. For example, if User A uses EFS to encrypt a folder on her system drive, Administrator B cannot read the folder unless User A provides the EFS certificate to Administrator B.

# Patch/Update Management

Windows computers that receive their updates through Windows Server Update Services (WSUS) can have their updates managed by group policy. However, if you are not using WSUS, you need to know how to manage Windows patches and updates yourself through Windows Update.

**ADDITIONAL RESOURCES**   To learn more about WSUS and group policy, go to https://docs.microsoft.com, search for "Deploy Windows Server Update Services" and click the corresponding link, and read Step 4, "Configure Group Policy Settings for Automatic Updates."

Every OS has flaws, and the *Windows Update* applet (Windows 7/8/8.1) or Windows Update feature in Settings (Windows 10) is how Microsoft distributes updates to patch user systems easily and automatically. Microsoft makes unique patches available in Windows 7/8/8.1/10; plus the company provided a bundle of updates, called Service Pack 1 (SP1 for short), in Windows 7.

**EXAM TIP**   The CompTIA A+ exam objectives describe keeping a computer up to date on patches and updates as *patch/update management*. Techs do the job of patch/update management.

Windows Update will check for available updates automatically, so you'll often see available updates as soon as you open the applet. In Windows 7 there are *Important*, *Recommended*, and *Optional* updates (see Figure 2.7-4).

Windows 8/8.1 use Control Panel to access Windows Update, but they also support Windows Update through the PC Settings Recovery & Update menu. These versions of Windows install some updates automatically, but also offer Recommended and Optional updates you can select manually (Figure 2.7-5). In Windows 10, open Settings | Update & Security | Windows Update. Windows 10 downloads and installs updates automatically without letting you pick and choose, and lets you schedule updates that require a reboot after working hours and choose to delay updates for a period of time. All versions provide an update history you can view.

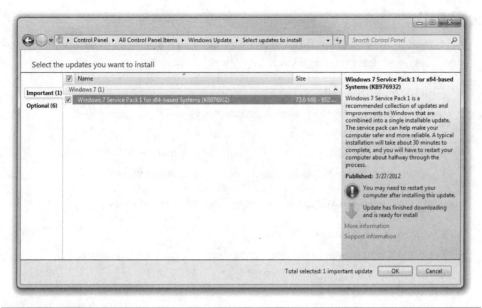

**FIGURE 2.7-4**   Important Windows 7 SP1 update in Windows Update

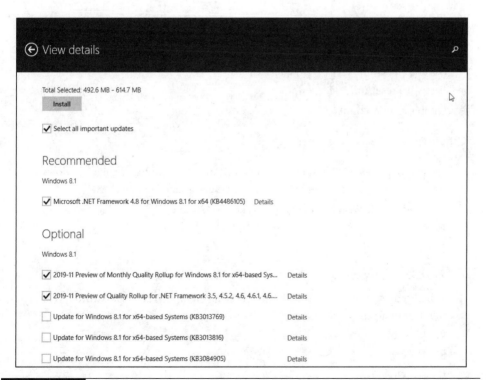

**FIGURE 2.7-5**   Selecting optional updates in Windows 8.1.

# REVIEW

**Objective 2.7: Given a scenario, implement security best practices to secure a workstation** Password best practices include

- Setting strong passwords
- Using effective password expiration policies
- Requiring passwords when screensavers are activated
- Using BIOS/UEFI passwords to protect computer firmware
- Requiring passwords on local accounts on Windows workstations

Account management in Windows uses group policy features such as

- Restricting user permissions
- Logon time restrictions (also can be performed using net user command)
- Disabling guest account
- Failed attempts lockout
- Timeout/screen lock settings
- Changing the default admin user account/password

You should also understand Active Directory functions such as

- Account creation
- Account deletion
- Password reset/unlock account
- Disabling an account

Other Windows security features include

- Using group policy to disable AutoRun and AutoPlay and to manage Windows updates that are performed by Windows Server Update Service (WSUS)
- Encrypting data with BitLocker, BitLocker To Go, and EFS
- Patch/update management through Windows Update

## 2.7 QUESTIONS

1. You are considering using one of the following eight-character passwords. Which is the strongest password?
   - **A.** 12345678
   - **B.** 1Z$#7j!~
   - **C.** 867530900
   - **D.** My$$Name

2. Your client is being plagued by a series of brute-force logon attacks. Which of the following group policy settings would best help stop them?

   **A.** Account Lockout Policy

   **B.** Security Options

   **C.** Password Policy

   **D.** Logon time restrictions

3. A user in your department is going on leave for six months. You don't want this user to have access to network resources while on leave. What should you do with their account?

   **A.** Merge it with yours

   **B.** Delete it

   **C.** Take no action

   **D.** Disable it

4. Your department was recently attacked by malware that was automatically loaded from a consultant's USB drive when it was inserted for diagnostic purposes. Which of the following needs to be disabled?

   **A.** AutoRun

   **B.** Explorer

   **C.** AutoPlay

   **D.** Autoexec.bat

5. Some of the computers in the organization need to use BitLocker. Which of the following is the correct path in group policy to configure BitLocker settings?

   **A.** User Configuration | Administrative Templates | Control Panel | BitLocker Drive Encryption

   **B.** Computer Configuration | Administrative Templates | Windows Components | BitLocker Drive Encryption

   **C.** Computer Configuration | Administrative Templates | Windows Components | BitLocker Policies

   **D.** Computer Configuration | Windows Settings | Security Settings | BitLocker Policies

## 2.7 ANSWERS

1. **B**  The strongest passwords use a mixture of upper- and lower-case letters, numbers, and symbols without recognized words.

2. **A**  The Account Lockout Policy prevents login attempts after a specified number of incorrect logins.

3. **D**  Disabling an Active Directory account prevents logins by that user while not disrupting security or other settings involving that user.

**4.** **C**    AutoPlay is the feature that opens an app or lists a choice of apps based on the contents of the removable media.

**5.** **B**    BitLocker Drive Encryption is a Windows component.

## Objective 2.8  Given a scenario, implement methods for securing mobile devices

**M**obile devices are convenient for carrying around data and apps; and communicating via voice, e-mail, and text from anywhere in the world. But convenience means that if unsecured, mobile devices can be a malware superhighway. In this objective, you learn how to implement the appropriate methods to prevent mobile devices from becoming security headaches.

## Screen Locks

*Screen lock* generally refers to any security mechanism that is used to prevent unauthorized users from viewing and using a mobile device. You need to be able to identify the following four types of screen lock. Most mobile devices provide at least two different types of screen lock.

### Fingerprint Lock

A fingerprint lock requires the user to touch a fingerprint sensor button or screen area to have their fingerprint scanned. If it matches a stored fingerprint, the device is unlocked. Typically, this feature is used along with a passcode lock, so if the user cannot provide a readable fingerprint, a passcode lock code can be provided instead. To implement a fingerprint lock on an Android device, open Settings | Lock Screen and Security | Fingerprints, and follow the prompts. To implement a fingerprint lock (known as Touch ID) on an iOS device, open Settings | Touch ID & Passcode, and follow the prompts. To implement a fingerprint lock on a Windows 10 device with Windows Hello fingerprint support, open Settings | Accounts | Sign-in options | tap Set up in the Windows Hello fingerprint section, and follow the prompts (you must have a PIN enabled to use Windows Hello).

### Face Lock

A face lock uses your device's camera to capture an image of the user's face. The captured image is compared to a previously stored image. If it matches, the device is unlocked. Apple's version, Face ID, is supported on iPhone X-series phones and on some iPad Pro models. To enable it, open Settings | Face ID & Passcode, and tap Set Up Face ID. Follow the prompts to complete setup. Face ID uses 3-D face mapping for high security.

Windows Hello supports facial recognition on devices that have a built-in or add-on pair of infrared cameras. To implement a face lock on a Windows 10 device with Windows Hello face support, open Settings | Accounts | Sign-in Options | tap Set Up in the Windows Hello Face section, and follow the prompts (you must have a PIN enabled to use Windows Hello).

Android's version, Trusted Face, is available on a variety of high-end smartphones from various vendors. To see if your phone supports it, open Settings | Security | Smart Lock. After supplying login information, Trusted Face appears on supported phones. Note that Trusted Face doesn't use 3-D face mapping, so it's not as secure as Face ID or Windows Hello.

## Swipe Lock

A swipe lock compares a swiping pattern across the lock screen to the stored swiping pattern. If the swipe is performed the same way as the stored pattern, the device is unlocked. Swipe locks, when available, are configured through Settings | Security.

## Passcode Lock

A passcode lock (also known as a PIN) requires entering a series of digits in order and is the fundamental protection for a mobile device; all other lock methods are used as alternatives. At a minimum, a passcode is four digits. However, many devices support six digits and alphanumeric characters, making the passcode much harder to guess (see Figure 2.8-1).

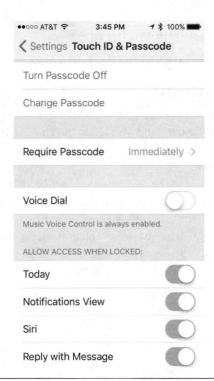

**FIGURE 2.8-1**   Passcode option in Settings on an iPhone

# Remote Wipes

If you keep your data backed up locally and remotely, you're free to *remotely wipe* (see Figure 2.8-2) your mobile device to safeguard data such as credit card numbers from a sustained attack if your mobile device is lost or stolen.

 **EXAM TIP**   Know how to implement mobile device screen locks and how to perform a remote wipe.

**FIGURE 2.8-2**   Select Erase iPad to perform a remote wipe.

# Locator Applications

Locator applications and services (Android Device Manager or Find My Device, Lookout for iOS or Android, Find My iPhone, or Find My Device in Windows 10) enable users to find lost devices (see Figure 2.8-3). When enabled in a device, it periodically sends its location to the OS vendor so you can locate it.

Be sure to enable this feature in the device's setup. In Windows 10, enable Find My Device in the Update & Security section of Settings. In iOS, open Settings, tap your Apple ID, tap iCloud, and tap Find My iPhone or Find My iPad. Slide the switch to on. In Android, open Settings and look for Android Device Manager (older devices), Find My Device or Find My Mobile (the name varies with the version of Android used by your device; you might need to download Find My Device or Find My Mobile from Google Play). Follow the prompts to enable it or set it up.

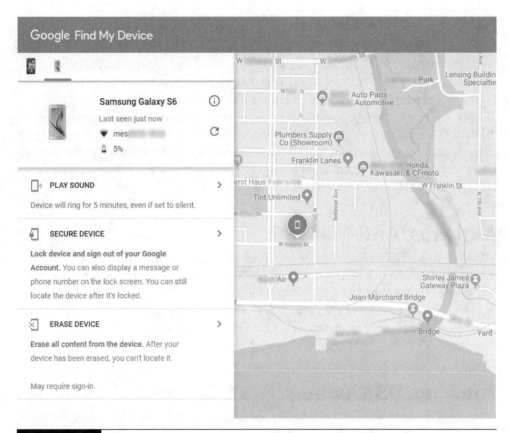

| FIGURE 2.8-3 | Locating an Android smartphone using Find My Device |

# Remote Backup Applications

Remote backup applications are built into iOS, Android, and Microsoft Windows. For Apple devices, you back up and restore with services such as iCloud and iTunes, or use the Apple Configurator to handle a whole fleet. Android devices use Google Sync to back up and restore. Windows 10 mobile devices can use OneDrive for file backup and restore.

 **ADDITIONAL RESOURCES**   To learn more about setting up OneDrive and your documents or other folders for automatic backup, go to https://answers.microsoft .com and search for "Using One Drive to automatically Back Up My Documents Folder."

# Failed Login Attempts Restrictions

*System lockout* occurs when too many consecutive login attempts fail, the purpose being to protect the device from brute-force attacks. Both iOS and Android devices have restrictions on failed login attempts built into their operating systems. Group policy can be used on a Windows computer to set up account lockout duration and threshold.

With Android devices, options to change these settings depend on the version of Android the device uses and whether the device uses stock or modified Android. With iOS, the length of the timeout between login attempts increases with each unsuccessful attempt that is made. If you enable the Erase Data option in Settings | Passcode, your device will be erased after ten failed passcode attempts.

# Antivirus/Anti-Malware

Windows 10 mobile devices include Windows Defender for antivirus and anti-malware protection. However, iOS and Android do not include antivirus/anti-malware protection. You can obtain antivirus and anti-malware for iOS and Android from many of the major security software vendors in the devices' app stores. Some products are free, while others offer free detection-only products and charge for virus- and malware-removal versions of their apps.

# Patching/OS Updates

Windows 10 mobile devices and iOS devices have updates available from Microsoft and Apple, respectively. However, Android smartphones and cellular-equipped tablets receive OS and firmware updates from mobile service providers (iOS devices receive cellular-specific updates from mobile telecom vendors).

Android tablets without cellular service, unlike Windows 10 or iOS devices, are updated only by the device vendors. Some vendors provide updates, while others do not.

# Biometric Authentication

Devices that use fingerprint readers, face recognition, or iris scanning all incorporate biometric authentication. Starting with the iPhone 5s, for example, Apple's Touch ID (see Figure 2.8-4) can unlock the device with a fingerprint.

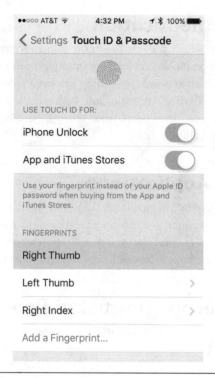

**FIGURE 2.8-4**   Touch ID options

# Full Device Encryption

iOS devices automatically use full device encryption when you assign a passcode to your device. With Windows 10 mobile devices, use BitLocker to encrypt onboard storage and Bit-Locker To Go to encrypt removable storage.

With Android devices, that familiar phrase "that depends" is in order. You might need to set up a PIN or password first, or go straight to encryption. Some recent devices automatically encrypt their contents, but with most Android devices, you must run encryption yourself. Make sure your phone is connected to a charger and is charged to the minimum required by the vendor before you can start the process, which can take an hour or so.

# Multifactor Authentication

Multifactor authentication, which uses two or more authentication factors, can be implemented in a variety of ways on mobile devices. For example, most mobile devices include fingerprint readers, so user name/password (something you know) plus a fingerprint (something you are) provides strong multifactor authentication. Because mobile devices include GPS and other types of location services, user name/password can be combined with geofencing to provide multifactor authentication.

# Authenticator Applications

Corporate networks may require you to authenticate with their own application to access a corporate VPN. Generic authenticator apps can provide a similar service for multiple sites or networks. Authenticator apps for multifactor authentication act as tokens or issue temporary session PINs. The key to these apps is proper initial configuration and setup.

# Trusted Sources vs. Untrusted Sources

Getting software from trusted sources—legitimate app stores run by the major vendors, such as Apple, Google, Microsoft, and Amazon—is easy and mostly secure. App stores have their own requirements (including security) that developers must meet in order to get an app into the vendor's store. Remember that modified versions of Android can change which stores and sources a device will or won't trust.

Untrusted sources are a different beast, and have a higher risk of malware and spyware. Apple has strict controls to block untrusted sources (though organizations can deploy inhouse apps to their own devices). Android blocks untrusted sources by default, but you can install apps from wherever you like with a simple settings change. Some apps are forced to use untrusted sources because they require elevated access to your OS or hardware that the trusted source forbids.

# Firewalls

Software firewalls on individual devices protect them from network-based threats. Mobile devices generally don't use a firewall because they don't listen for the traffic a firewall blocks; think of them as having a firewall by design. Cellular and Wi-Fi networks also employ firewalls to protect networked devices. You can find firewall apps (see Figure 2.8-5) for individual or enterprise use to filter specific traffic coming into the host, which may also include anti-malware and basic intrusion detection.

**FIGURE 2.8-5** An Android firewall app

# Policies and Procedures

Policies and procedures relating to mobile devices can be more complex than those for other types of computing devices because of the following questions:

- Who owns the device (the user or the organization)?
- Who manages the device?

## BYOD vs. Corporate-owned

With the omnipresence of mobile devices in the workplace, there are two approaches that companies take: Bring Your Own Device (BYOD) and corporate-owned devices.

A BYOD policy covers if and how individually owned devices can be used within the organization. Some companies prohibit access to corporate data and resources with personal devices, particularly in high-security environments; others encourage use of personal devices to cut costs and keep employees happy. Most fall in the middle. The BYOD policy answers questions such as who pays for device service, who owns and can access the device's data, and how privacy is handled.

For organizations that prefer to own their employees' mobile devices, an alternative to BYOD is corporate-owned personally enabled (COPE) devices. Organizations that use this model provide their employees with mobile devices such as smartphones, tablets, or notebook computers but permit employees to use them as if they personally own them.

**EXAM TIP**   The two critical issues with BYOD are personal data privacy versus protection of corporate data as well as the level of organizational control versus individual control.

## Profile Security Requirements

A *profile* is a collection of configuration and security settings that an administrator can create to apply to almost any user or device category (see Figure 2.8-6). Profiles, created through the mobile device management (MDM) software or a program such as Apple Configurator, are typically saved in eXtensible Markup Language (XML) format and pushed out to the correct devices. A common use is to restrict or grant access to apps, connections, and servers based on whether the user is a manager, executive, or external contractor, works in a given department, and so on. Profiles for a given device or OS can address device- or platform-specific risks.

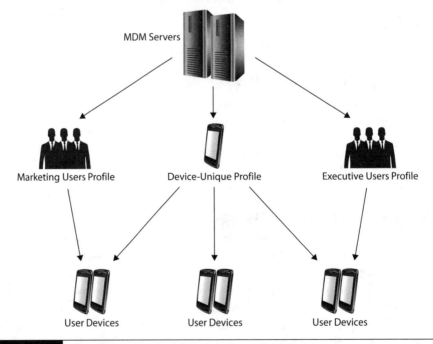

**FIGURE 2.8-6**   Applying profiles to different device and user groups

**Cross-Reference**

For more details about MDM, see the "MDM Policies" section in Objective 2.2, earlier in this domain.

# REVIEW

**Objective 2.8: Given a scenario, implement methods for securing mobile devices**   Mobile devices are secured by screen locks. Types include

- Fingerprint lock
- Face lock
- Swipe lock
- Passcode lock

Other mobile devices security features include

- The capability to remotely wipe device data
- Locator applications to locate lost or stolen devices
- Remote backup applications to ensure device data is recoverable
- Restrictions on failed login attempts to counter brute-force password guessing
- Adding antivirus/anti-malware protection
- Installing patches and performing OS updates when available
- Biometric authentication features such as fingerprint readers
- Full device encryption
- Multifactor authentication and authenticator apps
- Availability of trusted sources of software
- Firewall apps
- Policies and procedures covering BYOD versus company-owned devices and profile security requirements

# 2.8 QUESTIONS

1. An Android phone with confidential company information was lost. The information on the phone began to be used for attacks on company resources, although the user had set up a passcode. Which of the following Android settings could have prevented attacks using the information in the phone? (Choose all that apply.)

   **A.** Remote wipe

   **B.** Firewall

   **C.** Device encryption

   **D.** BYOD

2. Your company policy for mobile devices prohibits the use of untrusted software sources. Which of the following sources would be prohibited?

   **A.** App store

   **B.** Freeware website

   **C.** Vendor-supplied utilities

   **D.** Company intranet utilities

3. You receive a message on your smartphone that someone is attempting to log in to your e-mail from an unrecognized device. You are asked to approve or deny it. This is an example of which type of security mechanism?

   **A.** Multifactor authentication

   **B.** Firewall

   **C.** Trusted source

   **D.** Single-factor authentication

4. Your client is very forgetful, and while away from home is trying to log in to her iPhone. The client has tried eight times already to log in and is frustrated because it takes longer between login attempts each time. What should you advise her to do?

   **A.** Keep trying to log in

   **B.** Stop trying until she can get back home and check to see if she has the information available there

   **C.** Use a hacking tool

   **D.** Run antivirus

5. You are part of a team developing a BYOD policy for smartphone usage. Which of the following topics are most likely to be part of the policy? (Choose two.)

   **A.** Approved case colors

   **B.** Company reimbursement for mobile service charges

   **C.** Ownership of charging cables

   **D.** Ownership of data stored on device

## 2.8 ANSWERS

1. **A** **C**    Remote wipe could wipe out the device's contents after it was determined to be lost or stolen; device encryption (a manual process on many devices) could prevent the device's contents from being accessed.

2. **B**    Freeware websites might have software that has been compromised with hidden malware.

3. **A**   Multifactor authentication is being used because an additional confirmation beyond user name/password is needed to permit access.

4. **B**   If the option to wipe data after ten unsuccessful logins has been enabled in Settings | Passcode, the user is very close to losing her data.

5. **B D**   Deciding who pays for mobile service and who owns the data on a BYOD device are typical issues in a BYOD policy.

## Objective 2.9   Given a scenario, implement appropriate data destruction and disposal methods

Although a device might have reached its end-of-life status, the data it contains can still be valuable—and ready to be exploited by thieves or hackers. Data that is no longer needed on a device should be rendered inaccessible, and in this objective you learn the methods to use and when to use each method.

## Physical Destruction

If you want to make sure that absolutely nobody can recover data from a magnetic, optical, or flash storage device, physical destruction is the way to go. The following sections describe the methods you can use.

**EXAM TIP**   Know the appropriate data destruction or disposal method, described in this section, to use in a given scenario.

## Shredder

A few heavy-duty office paper shredders can make hash out of optical media, but certified data destruction firms have shredders that can also take on hard drives, flash drives, magnetic tape, and any other type of storage around.

## Drill/Hammer

If you don't want to take your devices to a third-party data disposal facility, a power drill and a hammer can do a bang-up job (pun intended) of getting rid of data. Smash drive platters and read write heads, run drill bits through flash memory chips and optical discs, and your data isn't around anymore.

## Electromagnetic (Degaussing)

Degaussing tools reduce or remove the magnetic fields that store data on HDDs. Using a degausser is great for situations in which you want to have a device that looks intact but no longer has a readable magnetic pattern. It's useful for blasting data off floppy disks, magnetic tape, and other types of magnetic media.

## Incineration

Incineration is a good choice for paper, magnetic tape, and optical media, and should be performed by a third-party data disposal facility. Don't try this at home (or in an office wastebasket)!

## Certificate of Destruction

If you use a data destruction facility (usually one of the services provided by an electronics recycler), be sure to get a certificate of destruction confirming they have destroyed the drive. Inquire first; if a company doesn't offer certificates of destruction, go to one that does.

# Recycling or Repurposing Best Practices

As an alternative to destroying data storage devices, you might prefer to recycle or repurpose them. Just as with destroying devices, the objective is to make sure that no one else can read the data.

## Low-level Format vs. Standard Format

A standard format leaves data in place but inaccessible through the file system. Keep in mind, though, that there are many third-party apps and data-recovery services that would have no difficulty retrieving data from a formatted drive.

A "low-level" format rewrites sector markings on the media. This is possible with some types of removable media, but not with modern SATA drives.

## Overwrite

You can also attempt to sanitize the drive without rendering it unusable by overwriting data. A *zero-fill* or *overwrite* operation fills the drive with zeros—but sensitive tools can still recover the data.

## Drive Wipe

A *drive wiping* utility fills the drive with junk data many times over; this is better than simply overwriting or zero-filling a drive, but not perfect. Some recommendations include using ATA Secure Erase (supported by many SATA magnetic and SSD drives) and Darik's Boot and Nuke (DBAN). It's important to realize that the wear-leveling feature in SSDs might leave some data on small portions of the drive.

 **ADDITIONAL RESOURCES**   For the latest National Institute of Standards and Technology (NIST) recommendations for sanitizing data, download Special Publication 800-88, Rev. 1, "Guidelines for Media Sanitization," from https://csrc.nist.gov.

## REVIEW

**Objective 2.9: Given a scenario, implement appropriate data destruction and disposal methods**   Physical data destruction methods include

- Shredder
- Drill or hammer
- Degaussing
- Incineration

Be sure to get a certificate of destruction if you have a third-party firm perform data destruction for you.

Methods for recycling or repurposing storage devices include

- Zero-filling (overwriting) a drive
- Drive wiping

## 2.9 QUESTIONS

1. A 64-GB flash memory card contains confidential information. Which of the following methods assures that data cannot be read from the card (which will not be reused)?

   **A.** Drill

   **B.** Zero-fill

   **C.** Drive wiping

   **D.** Degaussing

2. After the completion of a government contact, your firm must prove that the media used to store data have been destroyed. Which of the following do you need?

   **A.** Drill/hammer

   **B.** Certificate of destruction

   **C.** Shredder

   **D.** Degausser

3. Your client is panicking because a disgruntled employee performed some type of command on an important hard drive before leaving the premises. Which of the following would make the data the most difficult to recover?

   **A.** Standard format

   **B.** Zero-fill

   **C.** Drive wiping

   **D.** Low-level format

4. You are in charge of a project to remove hard drives from end-of-life systems and prepare them for donation to schools for reuse. You discover that one of your assistants is running the Format command on each drive before removing it. Which of the following is the best reaction to this discovery?

   **A.** "Good job! No one can get to that data now."

   **B.** "Did you use quick or standard format?"

   **C.** "Using Format isn't drive wiping."

   **D.** "You should be using a hammer or drill."

5. Your firm has a large amount of magnetic tape from old mainframe systems. Which of the following is the quickest way to render this tape unreadable?

   **A.** Drill/hammer

   **B.** Zero-fill

   **C.** Drive wiping

   **D.** Degaussing

## 2.9 ANSWERS

1. **A** Drilling through the memory chip(s) will render the contents unrecoverable.

2. **B** A certificate of destruction from a third-party data destruction facility is what you need; the facility will decide the best methods and tools to use.

3. **C** Drive wiping would be the biggest concern.

4. **C** Formatting doesn't remove or overwrite data, so it is no substitute for drive wiping.

5. **D** Degaussing is the only suitable method of those listed for destroying data on magnetic tape.

 **Objective 2.10** Given a scenario, configure security on SOHO wireless and wired networks

A network without security is like leaving the doors and windows of your home or office open at all hours: anyone can enter and help themselves to whatever they can find. In this objective, you learn the methods you can use to secure your small office/home office (SOHO) network and when to use them.

> **EXAM TIP**   Know how to configure all of the SOHO wireless and wired network security–related settings listed in this objective.

# Wireless-Specific

Some security settings apply only to wireless networks. For details, keep reading.

## Changing Default SSID

Wireless devices want to be heard, and APs are usually configured to broadcast their *service set identifier (SSID)* or *network name* to announce their presence. Unfortunately, this default SSID can give away important clues about the AP's manufacturer (and maybe even model) that make it easier for attackers to exploit known vulnerabilities in the hardware.

Always change the default SSID to something unique, and change the password right away. Older default SSID names and passwords are well known and widely available online. When you pick a unique SSID, think about whether the name makes your network a more interesting target or gives away information an attacker could use to physically locate the AP. Most newer APs require you to create a unique SSID, user name, and password.

## Setting Encryption

Use the strongest encryption supported by the devices on your wireless network. In order from strongest to weakest: WPA2, WPA, and WEP.

### Cross-Reference

To learn more about wireless encryption, see the "Protocols and Encryption" section in Objective 2.3, earlier in this domain.

## Disabling SSID Broadcast

Disabling the SSID broadcast is regarded by CompTIA as a method for securing your wireless network. However, in practice, even simple wireless scanning programs can discover the name of an "unknown" wireless network, and disabling the SSID broadcast is useful only as a way to help avoid the attention of someone targeting known vulnerabilities with specific hardware and default settings.

## Antenna and Access Point Placement

You can hide your network from outsiders to limit risk by keeping your signal from extending outside your home or office. Place omni-directional antennas that send and receive in all directions near the center of the physical space.

 **EXAM TIP**    Most APs have physical Ethernet ports that are not password-protected or encrypted. Place the AP where unscrupulous folks can't get to it.

## Radio Power Levels

If your WAP enables you to adjust the radio power levels of the antenna, decrease radio power until you can get reception inside the target network space, but not outside.

## WPS

The developers of Wi-Fi created *Wi-Fi Protected Setup (WPS)* to make secure connections easier for novice users to configure with a button (see Figure 2.10-1), password, or code. For example, you could connect a WPS-capable WAP and wireless printer by pressing the WPS button on the printer and then on the WAP within a set time. Sadly, WPS codes are very easy for a program to guess. The only protection is disabling WPS; check the WAP manufacturer's website for instructions.

**FIGURE 2.10-1**    WPS button on an e2500 router

## Change Default Usernames and Passwords

Each AP (or router) includes a web server that hosts a browser-accessible configuration utility (see Figure 2.10-2) at the AP's default IP address (often 192.168.1.1). It will prompt you to log in with an administrator password, which you create during installation or find in the AP or router's documentation.

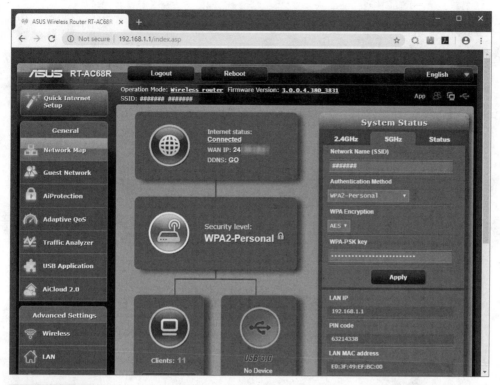

**FIGURE 2.10-2**    ASUS wireless main setup screen

**NOTE**    These configuration utilities vary by vendor and model.

By changing the default SSID and the default user name and password for the administrator account, you make your AP or router more secure against attack because the default values are widely known and can easily be looked up.

# Enable MAC Filtering

Configure MAC filtering (see Figure 2.10-3) if you have known MAC addresses to allow or deny.

**Cross-Reference**

To learn more about MAC filtering, see the "MAC Address Filtering" section in Objective 2.2, earlier in this domain.

**FIGURE 2.10-3** MAC filtering configuration screen for a Linksys WAP

# Assign Static IP Addresses

Why would you need to set up static IP addresses? In some cases, you need a static IP address for your broadband connection. Or, one or more of your devices might need a static IP address. Let's take a closer look.

When you connect to your ISP, your broadband modem receives a dynamic IP address using DHCP, just like the computers on your LAN get. For some users, these occasional IP address changes cause trouble, so most ISPs enable you to pay for a static IP address. You may need to change your connection type from Automatic/DHCP to Static IP and manually enter this information into your router (see Figure 2.10-4).

Likewise, some devices—servers in particular—may need a static IP address within your LAN. You can manually configure the device's TCP/IP settings to use a static address, but it isn't ideal—it doesn't, for example, guarantee the DHCP server won't give its address out to another system. Some routers have DHCP settings that enable you to reserve IP addresses and

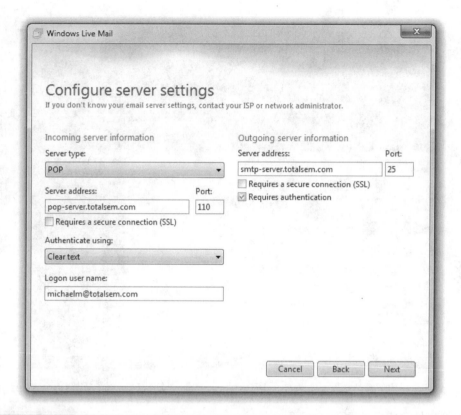

**FIGURE 2.10-4**    Entering a static IP address

assign specific hosts to them via DHCP; in other cases, you may just need to turn DHCP on or off depending on your needs (but turning DHCP off is rare).

# Firewall Settings

Hardware firewalls protect a LAN from outside threats by filtering packets before they reach your internal machines. You can configure a SOHO router's firewall from the browser-based settings utility (see Figure 2.10-5). Hardware firewalls use *Stateful Packet Inspection (SPI)* to inspect individual packets and block incoming traffic that isn't a response to your outgoing traffic. You can even disable ports entirely, blocking all traffic in or out.

**FIGURE 2.10-5**   SPI firewall settings

# Port Forwarding/Mapping

Since Network Address Translation (NAT) hides the true IP address of internal systems, a common configuration task is to enable devices outside of your LAN to reach a server inside it. *Port forwarding* (see Figure 2.10-6) enables you to open a port in the firewall and direct incoming traffic on that port to a specific IP address on your LAN.

 **EXAM TIP**   Port mapping is sometimes used as a synonym for port forwarding and CompTIA might use either terms.

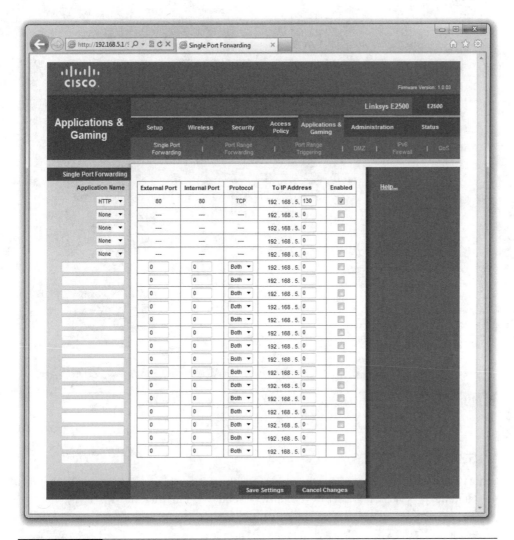

**FIGURE 2.10-6**   Port forwarding configured to pass HTTP traffic to a web server

*Port triggering* (see Figure 2.10-7) automatically opens incoming connections to one computer based on its outgoing connections. If you set the outgoing *trigger port* to 3434 and the incoming *destination port* to 1234, a system sending outgoing traffic on port 3434 will trigger the router to open port 1234 and send received data back to the same system.

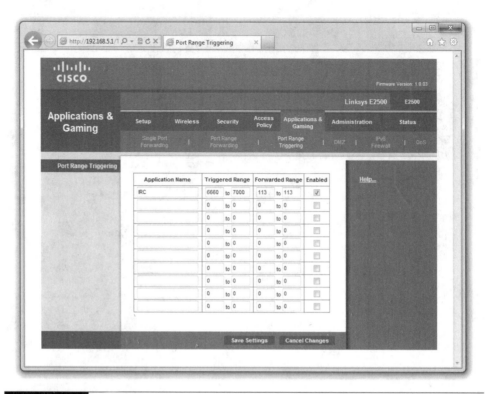

**FIGURE 2.10-7** Port triggering for an Internet Relay Chat (IRC) server

# Disabling Ports

Some wireless routers have options to disable the Ethernet ports. Be cautious about using this option, though, because it is safer to administer a router via Ethernet than wirelessly.

 **EXAM TIP** Disabling ports can also refer to disabling TCP or UDP ports on a firewall. Be sure to look at the full question to determine which meaning is appropriate.

# Content Filtering/Parental Controls

Content filtering and parental controls are important to some institutions and families as a way to limit exposure to potentially harmful online content. Content filtering and parental controls can be added at the client, by using a web-based service (Windows Family combines these approaches), or by using a router that support these features. Be sure to consider the cost of renewing the subscription for the router's content filtering/parental controls software, just as you would for any subscription-based service, when you calculate the long-term cost.

# Update Firmware

A router is only as good as its firmware, so keeping router firmware up to date is an important consideration. There are two approaches you can take:

- Update the router with the vendor's firmware
- Use third-party firmware such as DD-WRT, OpenWrt, and others

 **CAUTION**   A firmware update can kill ("brick") your router, so be careful to follow all of the instructions and make sure you choose the correct firmware update for your router brand, model, and revision. Many mass-market routers use different hardware for different revisions of the same model, so choosing, for example, a firmware update for revision 1.0 of a router when you have revision 2.0 could destroy the router.

Using the vendor's firmware updates provides bug fixes and maintains your device warranty, but might not provide full support for everything your router can do. Third-party firmware puts the support responsibility on you but might give you access to hidden features in your router.

 **ADDITIONAL RESOURCES**   To learn more about leading third-party router firmware sources, go to www.maketecheasier.com and search for "4 Great Alternative Firmwares to Install on Your Router."

# Physical Security

Keeping your network's router physically secure is as important as protecting your network from malware or social engineering attacks. Consider using these methods as they apply to your home or office:

- Keep the router in a locked room or enclosure. Just make sure it has sufficient ventilation to avoid overheating.
- If you can't lock up the router, make sure it's in a location where it's easy to keep an eye on it.
- Change the default password!
- Disable IP directed broadcasts.
- Disable HTTP configuration for the router, if possible.
- Block ICMP ping requests.
- Disable IP source routing.
- Determine your packet filtering needs.

- Establish ingress (inbound) and egress (outbound) address filtering policies.
- Maintain physical security of the router.
- Take the time to review the security logs.

# REVIEW

**Objective 2.10: Given a scenario, configure security on SOHO wireless and wired networks**    Wireless-specific security settings include

- Changing default SSIDs
- Setting encryption
- Disabling SSID broadcast
- Proper placement of antennas and access points
- Adjusting radio power levels
- Avoiding the use of WPS

Security issues for both wired and wireless networks include

- Changing default user names and passwords
- Enabling MAC filtering
- Assigning static IP addresses as needed
- Configuring the hardware firewall
- Using port forwarding and mapping
- Disabling Ethernet ports if not used
- Enabling content filtering and parental controls
- Updating router firmware
- Securing your router location (physical security)

## 2.10 QUESTIONS

1. The default SSID for a SOHO router can be used to look up which of the following? (Choose all that apply.)

   **A.** Brand and (sometimes) model

   **B.** Default administrator name and password

   **C.** Location

   **D.** Default encryption

2. WPS is easy to use. Which of the following terms best describes its other features?

   **A.** Secure

   **B.** Vulnerable

   **C.** Recommended

   **D.** Mandatory

3. Which of the following programs are you most likely to use when you set up your SOHO router?

   **A.** Web browser

   **B.** Paint program

   **C.** FTP program

   **D.** Word processor

4. You need to set up your router to open a certain range of ports based on outgoing traffic. What is this feature known as?

   **A.** Port forwarding

   **B.** DMZ

   **C.** Disabling ports

   **D.** Port triggering

5. Because you live in an apartment building, you would like to adjust the power of your router's Wi-Fi radio. You've heard it's possible, but you can't find any setting for it when you log in to your router. After updating your firmware, you're still coming up empty-handed. What should you try next?

   **A.** Replacing the router as defective

   **B.** Buying a different router

   **C.** Researching third-party firmware

   **D.** Putting up with the problem

## 2.10 ANSWERS

1. **A B D**   Documentation for a typical SOHO router lists its default SSID, and from this the other information can be found.

2. **B**   Wi-Fi Protected Setup (WPS) is very vulnerable to hacking, so it is not recommended.

3. **A**   A web browser is the standard method for configuring and managing a router's settings.

4. **D**   Port triggering changes the setting for some ports depending on traffic to other ports.

5. **C**   Third-party firmware often makes "hidden" features available.

# Software Troubleshooting

DOMAIN
3.0

# Given a scenario, troubleshoot Microsoft Windows OS problems

Microsoft Windows is, by far, the most common family of desktop operating systems you will be working with. Keeping Windows working is essential to knowledge workers, SOHO workers, and gamers alike. This objective helps you discover common symptoms and solutions.

## Common Symptoms of Windows Problems

The following sections review the common symptoms of Windows problems that you are expected to know for the CompTIA A+ 220-1002 exam.

### Slow Performance

Some of the causes for slow performance of Windows include

- Applications and processes consuming high CPU, RAM, or disk resources
- Running a system with limited RAM, requiring swapping of RAM contents to and from a hard drive
- Malware infestation

### Limited Connectivity

The default IP addressing method used by Windows is to get an IP address from a DHCP server on the network. In a SOHO network, for example, the DHCP server is normally built into the router. When the DHCP server can't be reached:

- Windows generates a random APIPA IP address (169.254.x.y, where x.y is the computer's ID).
- An APIPA IP address enables local networking only.

An APIPA address isn't routable, so computers cannot access the Internet.

### Failure to Boot, No OS Found

If the system powers on and the POST succeeds, the computer will try to load an OS. Failure to boot can be caused by hardware, BIOS/UEFI firmware configuration, or Windows faults. The challenge is to determine which of these is the actual cause.

- If you're staring at a dire error message such as *Operating System not found* or *No boot device detected*, keep in mind that the hard drive might not have proper connectivity and power.

**Cross-Reference**

For more information about hard drive installation, see Part I, Domain 3.0, Objective 3.4.

- There are a variety of ominous messages that are less clear: a critical boot file or component is missing, corrupt, damaged, invalid, can't be found, and so on. The specific critical files and components you should know for the exam are bootmgr and Boot Configuration Data (bcd), but this is far from a comprehensive list.
- Another possible cause is that the boot order in the UEFI/BIOS firmware is not configured correctly.

**Cross-Reference**

For more information about BIOS/UEFI settings, see Part I, Domain 3.0, Objective 3.5.

If simple hardware and system settings don't appear to be the cause, it's time to roll up your sleeves and use the repair and recovery tools that come with Windows.

## Application Crashes

Some programs, often games rushed to market near the winter holidays, are released with code errors that render them unstable. These errors can produce symptoms such as a crash to desktop (CTD), freeze, or even an unexpected shutdown or restart. These improper shut-downs can cause other problems, including damage to open files and folders. Keep an open mind, because hardware or driver problems could also be the cause; think in terms of what the system is using.

Think about what could cause this scenario: your whole system freezes while you're playing a huge, graphically intensive game that eats RAM like candy. For starters, it could be an error in the game code, an overwhelmed video card, a problem with the video card driver, a hardware problem on the video card, or a bad section of RAM. But what if the system didn't freeze; what if it was just slow and jerky? After checking for malware, check other possibilities such as poor programming, or hardware that just isn't powerful enough to run the game properly.

## Blue Screens

A blue screen is a classic sign of a non-maskable interrupt (NMI), better known as the Blue Screen of Death or Stop error in Windows (see Figure 3.1-1). The BSoD appears only when something causes an error from which Windows can't recover.

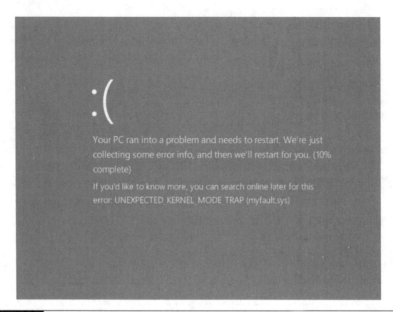

**FIGURE 3.1-1**    The Blue Screen of Death (BSoD) in Windows 10

Although this is a Windows error report, that doesn't mean the cause is Windows itself. To find out the reason for the error, look up the error code.

**CAUTION**    Bad RAM can trigger different error codes, so if the system keeps crashing but displays different Stop errors, the problem could be bad RAM.

## Black Screens

A black screen (or blank screen) can have several causes:

- Lost connection to display; check display cable connections. On a laptop or tablet, try toggling between displays.
- Peripherals preventing proper startup; a reversed IDE cable on a system drive can stop the boot process before the display is working, as can a loose or missing video card.
- Graphics driver problems; try booting in Safe Mode or WinRE. If the system boots correctly in these modes, update the graphics driver.
- System in sleep mode; wake up the system.

**ADDITIONAL RESOURCES**    See the article "Troubleshoot Black Screen or Blank Screen Errors" at https://support.microsoft.com.

## Printing Issues

Some typical printing issues that have an operating system component include

- No connectivity
- Backed-up print queue
- Color prints in wrong print color
- Access denied

**Cross-Reference**

For details on these and other printing problems and solutions, see Part I, Domain 5.0, Objective 5.6.

## Services Fail to Start

Windows uses a wide variety of services, some of which start automatically when Windows starts, while others are started only when they are called upon to start by a specific application or circumstance.

When Windows services fail to start, the feature provided by the service fails. Depending upon the service, you might see an error message at system startup or the problem might not be noticed until you attempt to use a service. For example, if the services used for wireless networking don't start, you can't connect to a wireless network. Services might fail to start if they depend upon other services that didn't start, if a specific user account is used to run the account has a different password than when the service was set up, or for other reasons.

 **ADDITIONAL RESOURCES**   To learn more about why Windows services might not start, go to www.coretechnologies.com and search for "Why doesn't my Windows Service Start at Boot?"

## Slow Bootup

Different Windows systems boot at different speeds, due to variables such as Windows version installed, the number of startup apps, processor type and speed, onboard RAM, and hard drive speed. This is normal. What isn't normal is for a Windows system to boot up more slowly than usual. Some of the causes for slow bootup include

- Outdated drivers
- Lack of free space on system drive
- File fragmentation on system drive
- Faulty antivirus

- Malware
- Fast startup (ironic, isn't it!)
- Programs with high startup impact running at startup

## Slow Profile Load

When you select a user and log into that profile with Windows, the startup process runs at about the same speed on the same system. However, if it runs much more slowly than usual, consider one or more of the following possible causes:

- Malware
- System file corruption
- Profile corrupted

# Common Solutions for Windows Problems

The solutions in the following sections can be used to solve multiple symptoms. Use the best practices troubleshooting methodology covered in Objective 5.1 of Domain 5.0 in Part I to evaluate the symptoms and choose the best solution(s) to try. Be sure to try one solution at a time until you find the answer.

## Windows Repair and Recovery

Windows needs two critical files to boot: bootmgr and bcd. If they are damaged, you can fix them with a tool called bcdedit. But bcdedit isn't just hanging out in Control Panel, so first we need to take a step back and look at where bcdedit lives and how you get there.

 **NOTE**   Boot Configuration Data (BCD) contains information about installed operating systems.

## Windows Recovery Environment

The *Windows Preinstallation Environment* (*WinPE* or *Windows PE*) supports booting a limited graphical OS directly from the Windows installation media—one that includes troubleshooting and diagnostic tools alongside the installer. These troubleshooting, diagnostic, and repair tools are collectively (and confusingly) called the *Windows Recovery Environment* (*WinRE* or *Windows RE*) or the *System Recovery Options* (see Figure 3.1-2).

In case your installation media is lost or damaged, create a system *repair disc* before you have problems. In Windows 7, go to Control Panel | System and Security | Backup and Restore and select *Create a system repair disc*.

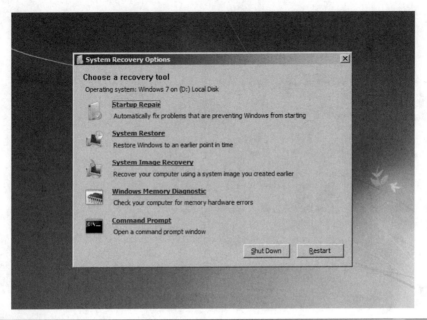

**FIGURE 3.1-2**   Windows 7 Recovery Environment main screen

**NOTE**   WinPE can also assist unattended installations, network installations, and booting diskless workstations on a network.

Depending on your Windows version, a few different paths lead to WinRE:

- In any version, boot from the Windows installation media, recovery drive, or repair disc, and select *Repair*.
- Select *Repair Your Computer* on Windows 7's Advanced Boot Options (F8) menu (see Figure 3.1-3).

I recommend you access WinRE from the installation media because it works in each OS, doesn't require an administrator password, and isn't vulnerable to interference from malware or hard drive issues. No matter how you choose to access the Windows Recovery Environment, you have a few options:

- **Startup Repair**   Performs a number of repairs on the Registry, critical boot, system, and driver files. Rolls back or uninstalls incompatible drivers and patches. Runs chkdsk and a RAM test. Saves diagnostic and repair details to *srttrail.txt*.
- **System Restore**   Provides a simple way to return to an earlier *restore point* or snapshot.

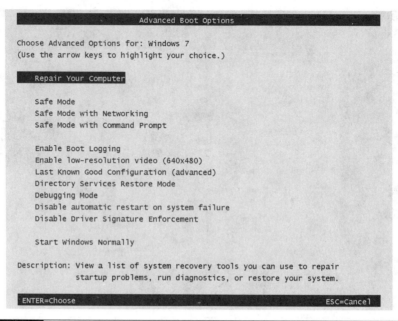

```
                    Advanced Boot Options

Choose Advanced Options for: Windows 7
(Use the arrow keys to highlight your choice.)

  Repair Your Computer

    Safe Mode
    Safe Mode with Networking
    Safe Mode with Command Prompt

    Enable Boot Logging
    Enable low-resolution video (640x480)
    Last Known Good Configuration (advanced)
    Directory Services Restore Mode
    Debugging Mode
    Disable automatic restart on system failure
    Disable Driver Signature Enforcement

    Start Windows Normally

Description: View a list of system recovery tools you can use to repair
            startup problems, run diagnostics, or restore your system.

 ENTER=Choose                                        ESC=Cancel
```

**FIGURE 3.1-3**     Selecting Repair Your Computer in the Advanced Boot Options menu

- **System Image Recovery**    Enables you to select and restore from a full system image. It includes an option to format and repartition disks so the restored system will get the same partitions that the backed-up system had.

**EXAM TIP**    Most prebuilt systems come with a *factory recovery partition,* other recovery media, or the ability to create recovery media. These can restore the active system partition or the entire hard drive to fresh-from-the-factory condition from a *recovery image.*

- **Windows Memory Diagnostic**    During the next reboot, the diagnostic tool checks your RAM for the sorts of problems that can cause Blue Screens of Death (BSoDs), system lockups, and continuous reboots. After the tool runs and your system reboots, you can use Event Viewer to see the results.

**EXAM TIP**    You can also launch the Windows Memory Diagnostic Tool from Administrative Tools or with **mdsched** at an administrative command prompt.

- **Command Prompt**    A true 32- or 64-bit command prompt with useful recovery and repair tools (though it lacks a number of commands you would have at a regular Windows command prompt).

Windows 8 and above not only introduce a new look (the Metro/Modern UI) to WinRE, but offer some significant changes. First, a new Troubleshoot menu is now available with two new options:

- **Refresh your PC**  Rebuilds Windows; preserves user files, settings, and Microsoft Store apps (but deletes all other applications)
- **Reset your PC**  Removes all apps, programs, files, and settings and freshly reinstalls Windows

The Troubleshoot menu also has an Advanced options button, which is where you'll find most of the utilities from the earlier version of WinRE (the Memory Diagnostics option is available from the command line). The Advanced options menu includes a link to your UEFI firmware settings if you have a UEFI motherboard.

With Windows 8/8.1/10, you can start WinRE from the logon screen:

1. Hold down either SHIFT key and click/tap the onscreen power button.
2. Continue to hold down the SHIFT key and click/tap Restart (Figure 3.1-4).
3. Continue to hold down the SHIFT key until the WinRE dialog opens.

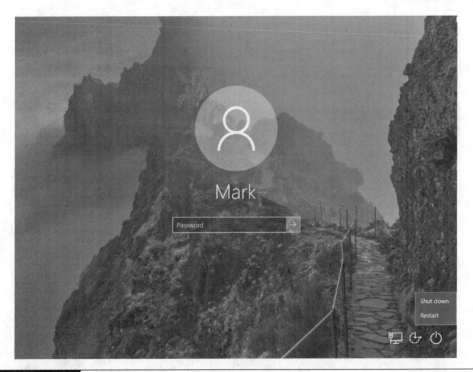

**FIGURE 3.1-4**  Selecting the Restart to WinRE option in Windows 10

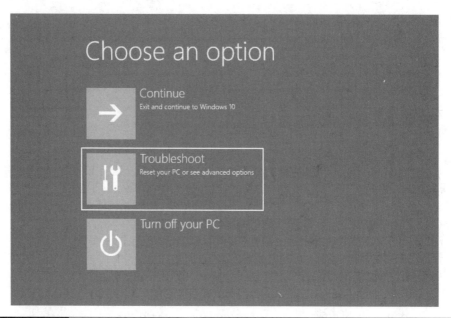

**FIGURE 3.1-5**     Selecting the Troubleshoot option in Windows 10 WinRE

**4.** Click/tap Troubleshoot (Figure 3.1-5).

**5.** Click/tap Advanced options (Figure 3.1-6).

**6.** Click/tap Startup repair (Figure 3.1-7).

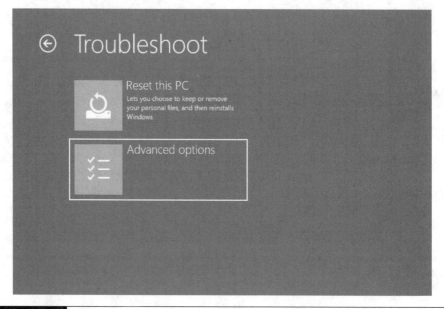

**FIGURE 3.1-6**     Selecting the Advanced options setting in Windows 10 WinRE

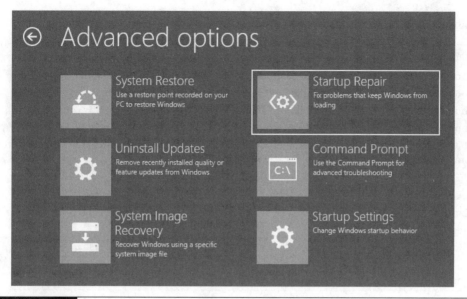

**FIGURE 3.1-7**   Running Startup Repair in Windows 10 WinRE

You can also create a recovery drive as well as a repair disc in Windows 8 and above.

**NOTE**   A repair disc is a CD with WinRE. A recovery drive is a USB flash drive that includes WinRE plus Windows installation files. Both can be used to start your system and perform repairs.

In Windows 8 and up, go to Control Panel | Click large or small icons view | Recovery | Create a recovery drive. (Connect an empty USB flash drive with at least 16 GB capacity before continuing.) With Windows 8.1, you have the option to copy the files in the hidden recovery partition (if present) to the media as well.

## Command-Line Recovery and Repair Tools

The CompTIA A+ exams won't expect you to know everything about these utilities—the goal is for you to use them with higher level support—but you should know roughly what the tools listed in Table 3.1-1 do, how to access them, and some of the basic switches. Keep in mind that these commands are in addition to basic CLI commands such as copy, move, del, format, and so on.

**TABLE 3.1-1**   Useful Recovery and Repair CLI Commands

| Command | Description |
| --- | --- |
| bcdedit | See and edit the BCD store that controls how Windows boots. |
| bootrec /fixboot | Rebuild boot sector for active system partition. |
| bootrec /fixmbr | Rebuild MBR for the system partition. |
| bootrec /scanos | Find and report Windows installations not in the BCD store. |
| bootrec /rebuildmbr | Like scanos, but can optionally add found installs to the BCD store. |
| diskpart | Advanced drive partitioning tool (lacking most of Disk Management's safety features). |
| expand | Expand one or more compressed files. |
| fsutil | Perform advanced queries, changes, and repairs on the file system. |
| reg | Query, copy, change, and restore the Registry. |
| sfc | Scan, detect, and restore important Windows system files and folders. Short for System File Checker. |
| mdsched | Runs Windows Memory Diagnostics. |

# Defragment the Hard Drive

A fragmented system drive can slow down many aspects of Windows, including boot, user profile loading, and application loading. Fragmentation takes place when a file cannot be stored in a single contiguous location on a drive but must be stored in sections at different locations on the drive. A drive that stores frequently changed files or temporary files, such as the system drive used by Windows, is more likely to be fragmented than a drive that has few changes to its contents.

Although Windows automatically defragments drives as needed, you can run defragmentation manually if necessary.

**Cross-Reference**

For more information about Disk Defragmenter, see Part I, Domain 1.0, Objective 1.5.

# Reboot

One of the simplest solutions to any type of Windows—or hardware—problem is rebooting the system. If Windows or application code is corrupt, devices are incorrectly set, or memory is being filled up, rebooting the system provides a clean workspace to use after restart.

- Be sure to close all apps before rebooting.
- If an app is still open, this prevents the system from rebooting. Windows displays a warning if there are open files when you select the reboot option, so you can choose to close them (recommended) or force a reboot.

- Forcing a reboot could cause the app to become corrupted, or you could lose unsaved data.

 **EXAM TIP**   For a Windows troubleshooting scenario, be sure to know common solutions such as defragment, reboot, kill tasks, and restart services.

## Kill Tasks

If too many tasks (including apps and services) are open, Windows can slow down. To speed up Windows and important tasks, shut down tasks you don't need. If you cannot shut down an app normally, or if you need to close a task, use the Task Manager in the Windows GUI or use **taskkill** from the command line.

**Cross-References**

For more information about Task Manager, see Objective 1.5 in Domain 1.0 of Part II. For more information about taskkill, see Objective 1.4 in Domain 1.0 of Part II.

## Restart Services

If a service has stopped running or is not working properly, open Services, select the service you want to restart, stop it, and restart it. You can also use the Services dialog to start a service that failed to start automatically.

**Cross-Reference**

For more information about Services, see Objective 1.5 in Domain 1.0 of Part II.

## Update Network Settings

To force Windows to check for an IP address from a DHCP server, open a command prompt and run **ipconfig /release**, followed by **ipconfig /renew**. If a DHCP server is now available, Windows will receive a normal IP address and you will be able to connect to the Internet as well as to other computers on your network.

To enable Windows to have connectivity without an IP address, you can set up an Alternate Configuration in the Local Area Connections properties for the connection. The default is to use Automatic Private IP Addressing (APIPA). Click the User configured radio button instead and enter the information needed:

- IP address
- Subnet mask
- Default gateway
- Preferred DNS server

- Alternate DNS server
- Preferred WINS server
- Alternate WINS server

Be sure to use an IP address that is not normally assigned by the DHCP server. Each computer in the network needs a unique IP address. This information will be used to set up a network connection if the DHCP server cannot be reached.

**Cross-Reference**

For more information about IP address configuration, see Part I, Domain 2.0, Objective 2.6.

## Reimage/Reload OS

The ultimate solution for a defective Windows installation is to restore the original Windows image from an image backup. This step should be held back as a last resort, as it results in all system updates, application updates, and user data on the system being wiped out. If it isn't backed up, it's gone!

 **EXAM TIP** Be sure to know the differences between reimage and reload OS.

Before restoring the original Windows image, use other methods to install a fresh copy of Windows. These include

- Repair installation (reload OS); preserves your apps as well as data
- Reset this PC (Windows 10); choose Keep Your Personal Files to keep your data
- Windows refresh (Windows 8/8.1); keeps your personal files

With these options, you can keep your existing data and, in some cases, apps.

**Cross-Reference**

For more information about repair installation, refresh/restore, and Reset this PC, see Objective 1.3 in Domain 1.0 of Part II.

## Roll Back Updates

If Windows malfunctions can be traced back to right after an update was installed, the update is almost certain to be the cause. System Restore is the key to rolling back updates that don't work, as it records the system configuration as part of a restore point so you can go back to it if an update fails.

**Cross-Reference**

For more information about System Restore, see Objective 1.5 in Domain 1.0 of Part II.

## Roll Back Device Drivers

Device drivers are the "glue" that connects your hardware with Windows. Faulty device drivers can prevent devices from working or can affect Windows in other ways. Device drivers are installed as part of initial device setup, and might be updated by Windows or manually by the user.

If Windows starts malfunctioning after a device is installed or its drivers are updated, the device drivers might be at fault. To roll back device drivers, open Device Manager, right-click the device and choose Properties, click the Driver tab in the Properties dialog box, and click Roll Back Driver (if available). The previous version of the device driver will be installed.

 **EXAM TIP**   Be sure to understand the differences between Roll Back Driver and Roll Back Updates.

If the device is newly installed or has not had a driver update, the Roll Back Driver button won't be available. In that case, use Update Driver to check for updated drivers that might work better.

**Cross-Reference**

For more information about Device Manager, see Objective 1.5 in Domain 1.0 of Part II.

## Apply Updates

Although updates can cause problems, more often than not, updates can resolve problems with Windows or drivers. Windows Update is the place to check for updates.

**Cross-Reference**

For more information about Windows Update, see Objective 1.5 in Domain 1.0 of Part II.

## Repair Application

Windows apps can become corrupt for a variety of reasons, including disk errors, poor coding, errant updates, or apps left open when Windows is shut down or restarted. To get a faulty application working again, repair the application.

You can repair an application through Control Panel's Programs and Features applet. To start the process, click the application, then click Uninstall/Change. If a repair option is available, select it to repair the app. If an app lacks a repair option, uninstall the app and reinstall it instead.

In Windows 10, you can also open Apps & features in Settings, choose an app, and click Modify to start the process.

**NOTE**   The Windows 10 Apps & features menu doesn't always offer repair options for apps that have them. Try the Programs and Features applet in Control Panel instead.

## Update Boot Order

If Windows can't boot, the problem might be the boot order in the system UEFI/BIOS firmware.

- Check your external ports (USB, Thunderbolt, eSATA, and so on) for errant drives.
- Check optical drives and flash card readers as well.
- Disconnect, eject, or unplug drives you don't need for booting.
- Confirm your boot sequence is correct, and check settings to boot from USB or other sources.
- Check power and data cables for the OS drive.
- Check the appropriate settings if your system uses RAID or multiboot.

If you want the fastest boot possible, put your system drive as the first boot device. However, keep in mind that if you occasionally boot from an OS disc or USB drive or run other self-booting drives, you need to change the boot order again to use them.

**Cross-Reference**

For more information about boot options, see Part I, Domain 3.0, Objective 3.5.

## Disable Windows Services/Applications

Sometimes, Windows services and applications can slow down your system or interfere with other apps you're using. Services run in the background and are used for network connections, printing, encryption, device installation, and many other tasks. To view Microsoft and third-party Windows services and disable unwanted services, open Services.msc or open the Services node from the Microsoft Management Console.

**ADDITIONAL RESOURCES**   For a list of Windows services you might not need, go to https://windowsreport.com and search for the article "Disable apps in Windows 10/8.1 to improve performance."

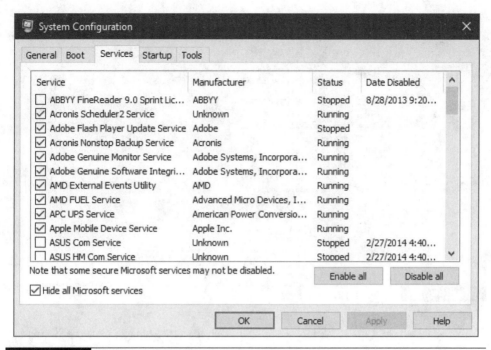

**FIGURE 3.1-8**   Disabling third-party services with MSConfig

To disable unwanted third-party services, use the Services tab in the System Configuration utility (aka MSConfig and **msconfig**). First, check the Hide all Microsoft services checkbox, then click Disable all, then clear the checkboxes for the services you want to keep (see Figure 3.1-8). When you restart, the checked services won't run.

Windows features are optional components such as Hyper-V virtualization service, Windows Subsystem for Linux, Internet Information Services, and more. To disable unwanted Windows features, open Windows Features from Control Panel (see Figure 3.1-9) and clear the checkboxes for the features you don't need. Click OK, and restart the system if prompted.

 **EXAM TIP**   Be sure to understand the differences between services and Windows features and how to disable them.

## Disable Application Startup

Apps that run at startup can eat up memory and processor cycles, and sometimes can interfere with other apps. To disable application startup in Windows 7, start MSConfig, click the Startup tab, and clear the checkbox for each startup app you want to disable.

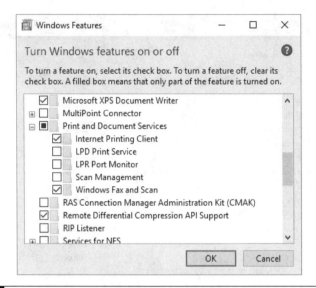

**FIGURE 3.1-9**    Selecting Windows features

To disable a startup app in Windows 8 or later, open the Task Manager, click the Startup tab, right-click the app, and choose Disable (see Figure 3.1-10). Disabling apps that have a High status in the Startup impact column has the biggest potential to improve startup time.

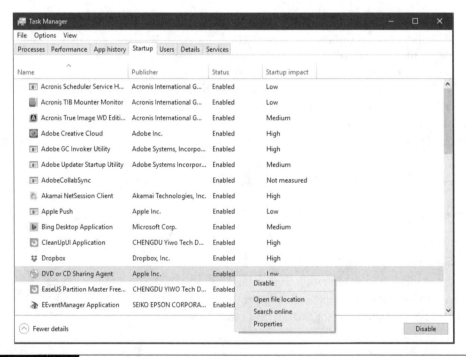

# Safe Boot

Safe boot, better known as Safe Mode, offers a way to fix a lot of problems that prevent a system from booting normally…by loading only essential services. If you can boot your system in Safe Mode, but not normally, it means that at least one startup app or service that is normally run is causing your startup headaches. In Safe Mode, you can use Device Manager and other tools to locate and fix problems. You can also choose to start your system in Safe Mode with Networking services enabled or to start your system in Safe Mode with the command prompt rather than the Windows GUI.

To choose from these or other startup options with Windows 7, press the F8 key repeatedly after the POST messages but before the Windows logo screen until the Advanced Boot Options menu appears (see Figure 3.1-11). To go directly to Safe Mode, press the F5 key at boot up.

To start your system in Safe Mode with Windows 8/8.1/10, boot the computer. At the login screen:

1. Hold down the SHIFT key.

2. Click the Power button on the login screen.

3. Click Restart.

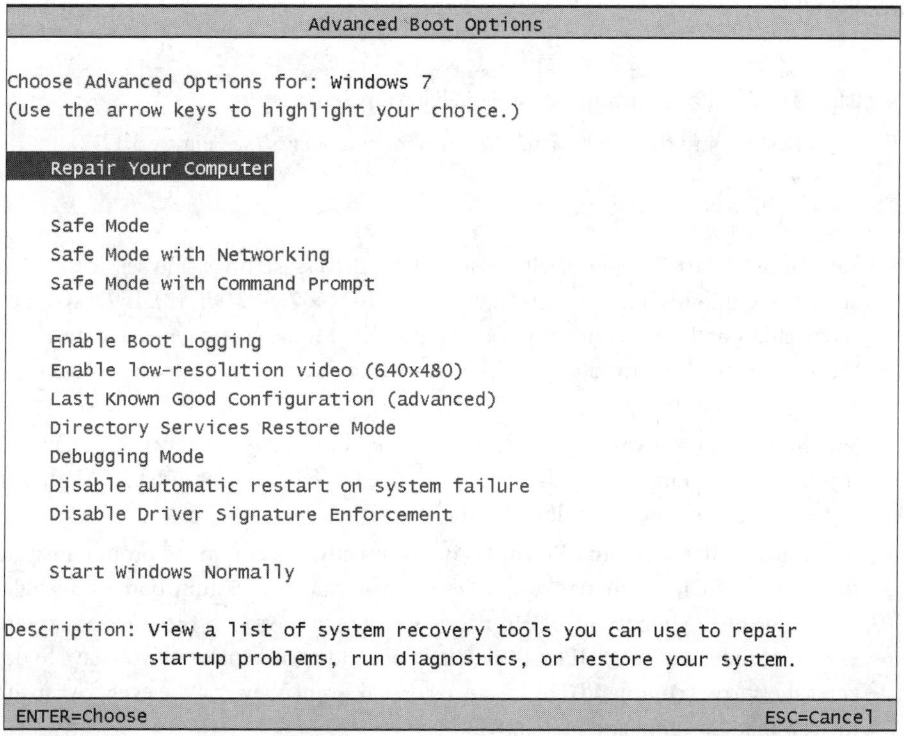

```
                         Advanced Boot Options

Choose Advanced Options for: Windows 7
(Use the arrow keys to highlight your choice.)

    Repair Your Computer

    Safe Mode
    Safe Mode with Networking
    Safe Mode with Command Prompt

    Enable Boot Logging
    Enable low-resolution video (640x480)
    Last Known Good Configuration (advanced)
    Directory Services Restore Mode
    Debugging Mode
    Disable automatic restart on system failure
    Disable Driver Signature Enforcement

    Start Windows Normally

Description: View a list of system recovery tools you can use to repair
            startup problems, run diagnostics, or restore your system.

ENTER=Choose                                          ESC=Cancel
```

**FIGURE 3.1-11**   The Advanced Boot Options menu in Windows 7 provides access to Safe Mode and related startup modes.

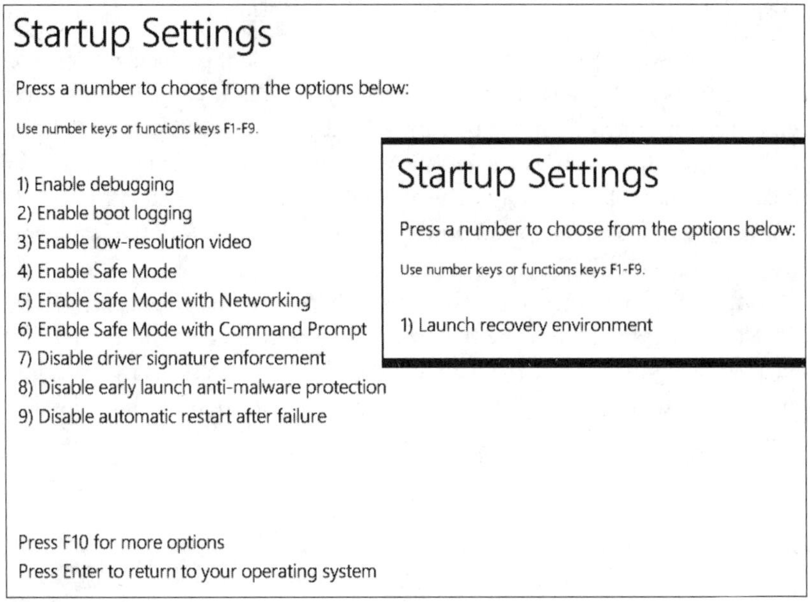

Startup Settings

Press a number to choose from the options below:

Use number keys or functions keys F1-F9.

**FIGURE 3.1-12**   The Startup Settings menu in Windows 10. Press the F10 key to switch to the second screen of choices (inset).

**4.** Click Troubleshoot | Advanced Options | Startup Settings.

**5.** Click Restart, and then the Startup Settings menu appears (see Figure 3.1-12).

Choose one of the following:

- **Safe Mode**   Starts Windows with basic/default drivers, settings, and services. Screen resolution is limited to 800 × 600 (7) or 1024 × 768 (8/8.1/10). If the system is repeatedly and unintentionally booting into Safe Mode, you may need to deselect the Safe boot or Boot to Safe Mode check box (see Figure 3.1-13) in the System Configuration utility.

- **Safe Mode with Networking**   Identical to Safe Mode, but with networking support. If your system boots into regular Safe Mode fine but fails to boot into Safe Mode with Networking, check network devices for driver issues.

- **Safe Mode with Command Prompt**   Boots directly to a command prompt instead of the Explorer GUI, which may succeed even if you can't successfully boot into regular Safe Mode due to buggy video drivers or corrupt Windows GUI files such as explorer. exe. You can load other GUI tools that don't depend on Explorer. All you have to do is enter the correct command. For instance, to load Event Viewer, type **eventvwr.msc** at the command prompt and press ENTER.

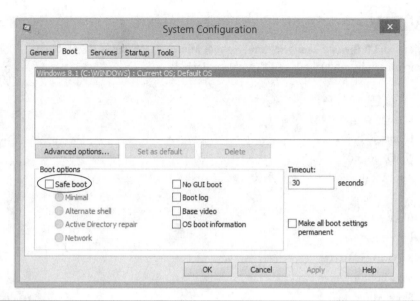

FIGURE 3.1-13 Uncheck Safe boot if the system is repeatedly and unintentionally booting into Safe Mode.

**EXAM TIP** Be sure to understand the differences between Safe Mode, Safe Mode with Networking, and Safe Mode with Command Prompt.

# Rebuild Windows Profiles

A corrupted user account profile prevents you from logging in to your system. There are two ways to fix this problem:

- Fix the user profile settings in the Registry with Regedit
- Create a new user account and copy the files from the corrupt one to the new one

**ADDITIONAL RESOURCES** To learn more about rebuilding Windows profiles, see www.easeus.com and search for "Fix a Corrupted User Profile."

# REVIEW

**Objective 3.1: Given a scenario, troubleshoot Microsoft Windows OS problems**   Common symptoms indicating Windows OS problems include

- Slow performance
- Limited connectivity
- Failure to boot
- No OS found
- Application crashes
- Blue screens
- Black screens
- Printing issues
- Services fail to start
- Slow bootup
- Slow profile load

Common solutions to Windows OS problems include

- Defragment the hard drive
- Reboot
- Kill tasks
- Restart services
- Update network settings
- Reimage/reload OS
- Roll back updates
- Roll back device drivers
- Apply updates
- Repair application
- Update boot order
- Disable Windows services/applications
- Disable application startup
- Use Safe boot (Safe Mode)
- Rebuild Windows profiles

## 3.1 QUESTIONS

**1.** To change the boot order, which of the following is necessary?

  **A.** Start Windows in Safe Mode

  **B.** Restart the system and open the UEFI/BIOS firmware setup

    **C.** Use the Task Manager

    **D.** Use MSConfig

2. Which of the following is the best way to recover from a bad device driver update?

    **A.** Roll back the system

    **B.** Restart the system and open UEFI/BIOS firmware setup

    **C.** Roll back the device driver

    **D.** Restart in Safe Mode

3. Your client needs to restart her system to solve a problem. Which of the following should she do first?

    **A.** Create a registry backup

    **B.** Run System Restore

    **C.** Create a full system backup

    **D.** Unplug USB drives

4. Your personal computer used to load your desktop in about ten seconds. Now it takes ten minutes. Which of the following is *not* a likely cause?

    **A.** Too many tasks running

    **B.** Malware

    **C.** System file corruption

    **D.** User profile corrupted

5. You need to start your computer in Safe Mode. Which of the following do you need to know to do this?

    **A.** Your APIPA network address

    **B.** Your screen resolution

    **C.** The version of Windows you use

    **D.** The location of the temporary files

## 3.1 ANSWERS

1. **B** You must use the UEFI/BIOS firmware dialog to change the boot order.

2. **C** Rolling back the device driver will not affect other parts of the system, so it is the preferred method.

3. **D** USB drives that are plugged in could prevent the system from restarting.

4. **A** The other items listed are likely causes; the number of tasks running has a small impact on load time, but not as much impact as the others.

5. **C** You need to know the version of Windows so that you can choose the proper method of starting in Safe Mode.

## Objective 3.2  Given a scenario, troubleshoot and resolve PC security issues

Security issues, regardless of the effectiveness of e-mail filters and anti-malware apps, are likely to be around for a long time. In this objective, you will learn about common symptoms of PC security issues, from pop-ups and slow performance to invalid security certificates and access denied errors. This objective sets the stage for the upcoming Objective 3.3, where you learn how to remove malware, a frequent cause of security issues.

## Common Symptoms of PC Security Issues

The following sections describe how to identify common PC security problems.

### Pop-ups

*Pop-ups*, or browser windows that pop up when you visit a site or click elements, used to be very common on websites. Many of these are simple ad windows, but others are malware that emulate alerts from the OS in an attempt to infect your system, sometimes with drive-by downloads, and often attempt to circumvent efforts to close them.

Abuse of automatic pop-ups led to the use of pop-up blockers, which have since been integrated directly into browsers; sketchy modern pop-ups need to trick the user into clicking something to open the pop-up.

### Browser Redirection

Browser redirection, in which an incorrect URL is opened when the user clicks a legitimate link, is a common sign of a malware infection that has overwritten your hosts file. A variation on browser redirection is when your normal home page is changed to a different home page, a malware action known as home page hijacking.

To stop browser redirection, use anti-malware apps. Keep your browser updated and check whether your browser has an option to lock your home page.

### Security Alerts

Systems with real-time protection from malware can display security alerts when malware is detected. However, false security alerts are caused by malware embedded in a website. Some of these alerts can look remarkably like actual security alerts, so how can you tell the difference?

- Actual security alerts use the anti-malware app installed on your system; fake security alerts use names that are similar to, but not the same as, actual anti-malware apps such as Windows Defender, AVG Antivirus, and so on.

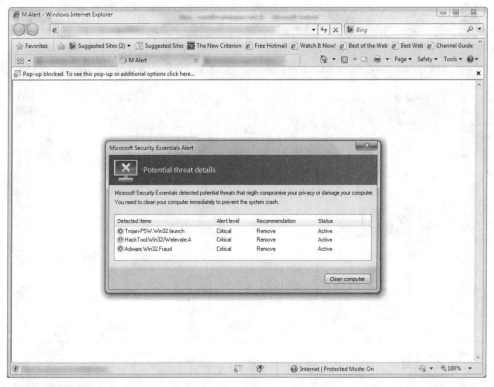

**FIGURE 3.2-1**    Fake security alert in a browser tab

- Fake security alerts look like malware scans, but are displayed in a web browser window. Actual malware scans run in their own window.
- Actual real-time security alerts don't take over your screen.

Figure 3.2-1 shows a fake security alert in a browser tab. If you were to click the alert, the next step would prompt you to pay for the full version of the app to "clean" your system. Actually, only your wallet would be cleaned (of money)—the system was not infected and there's nothing to clean up.

Figure 3.2-2 shows an actual malware scan performed using Windows Defender that found actual malware. You would need to click the Show details link to see the malware discovered.

Figure 3.2-3 shows a malware warning displayed by Window Defender's real-time protection module.

To get rid of a fake security alert like the one shown in Figure 3.2-1, close the browser window/tab, and if you can't close it the normal way, use the Task Manager or a similar tool.

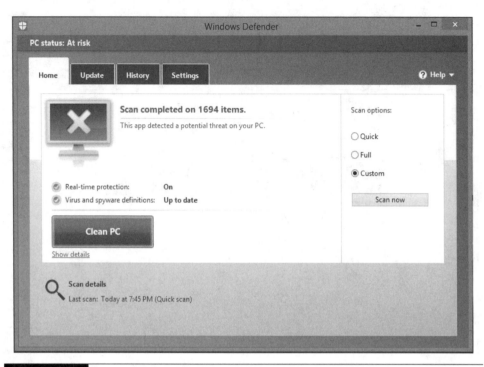

**FIGURE 3.2-2** Windows Defender preparing to clean a PC of malware

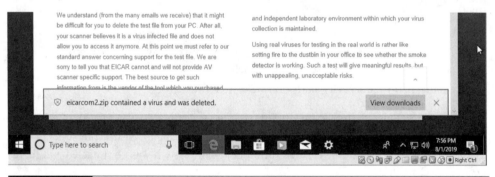

**FIGURE 3.2-3** Windows Defender's real-time protection stops malware from infecting a system.

## Slow Performance

Computers can slow down as more programs are opened, especially if you have marginal amounts of RAM installed for the workload. However, if a system is abnormally slow, sluggish, or prone to crashes and lockups given the programs you have open, especially if it persists after you close busy programs or reboot, it's time to scan for malware.

# Internet Connectivity Issues

If a system loses its Internet connection but the network itself and the network hardware appear to be working, malware may be the culprit. To prevent users from accessing anti-malware apps, online scanning, or updates, malware often disables a system's Internet connection.

# PC/OS Lockup

Computer or operating system lockups can have many causes, but if you rule out potential causes such as overheating, power quality, file corruption, or user error, suspect a malware infection.

> **Cross-Reference**
>
> For a comprehensive discussion of hardware troubleshooting, see Part I, Domain 5.0.

# Application Crash

Similar to lockups, application crashes can have many causes, but if you rule out potential causes such as overheating, power quality, file corruption, or user error, suspect a malware infection. Before assuming a malware infection, try to repair the application.

> **Cross-Reference**
>
> See the "Repair Application" section in Objective 3.1 of this domain for details.

# OS Updates Failures

Operating systems are actually the first line of defense against malware, and many of the updates to Microsoft Windows in particular are rolled out to patch weaknesses to help stop malware. Thus, it's not surprising that malware can interfere with OS updates.

If you are unable to run Windows Update or other OS update routines and are unable to repair those routines, it's time to check for malware.

# Rogue Antivirus

So-called "rogue antivirus" apps are a sinister development of the fake security alerts discussed earlier in this objective. Like them, they pretend to be antivirus apps. The difference is that some of them directly threaten data by encrypting user information and demanding a ransom payment. Malware that appears or pretends to be beneficial while attacking your system or data is a Trojan horse.

 **ADDITIONAL RESOURCES**   Other types of ransomware use different aliases. For example, Bad Rabbit purports to be an Adobe Flash installer. Cerber attacks Office 365 with an infected Microsoft Office document as part of a phishing e-mail. For more details about recent ransomware attacks, see the www.allot.com network security website.

# Spam

Attackers and scammers send tens or hundreds of millions of *spam* e-mails (often from a bot-net or compromised servers) just to exploit the fraction of a fraction of a percent of recipients who fall for the bait. Some of these are simple ads for real products of questionable value, but many are outright attempts to scam, steal personal information, or deliver malware. Limit spam by not posting your e-mail address on the Internet and by using an e-mail service with robust spam filtering. Also consider blocking senders, unsubscribing from mass e-mails, reporting spam, and manually moving unwanted e-mail to your spam folder.

 **CAUTION** Most spam is from addresses you won't recognize, but some of the more dangerous spam spoofs an entity you recognize, or uses the compromised system/account of a friend to send spam—perhaps claiming your friend has run into trouble abroad and urgently needs you to wire cash.

# File Issues

Renamed system files, disappearing files, and files that have unexpected file permission changes may indicate that malware is modifying or destroying files and data.

 **EXAM TIP** Be ready to identify renamed system files, unexpected file permission changes, and disappearing files as signs of malware infection.

# E-mail Issues

If you receive an e-mail (CompTIA refers to this as email) response from a contact who you haven't e-mailed or receive an undeliverable mail notification referencing a message you didn't send, that indicates someone's e-mail account has been hijacked. CompTIA describes these symptoms of hijacked e-mail accounts with two unwieldy phrases: *responses from users regarding e-mail* and *automated replies from unknown sent e-mail*. When either of these takes place, it's time to change your e-mail password.

 **NOTE** These symptoms of a hijacked e-mail account don't guarantee a device with access to the account is compromised; there are tons of potential causes. Other explanations include the following: you leave your system unlocked, lose a device configured with account credentials, or leave your account logged in on a public system; someone spoofs your e-mail address, hijacks your webmail session, or discovers your account credentials; an app or extension you have granted permission to manage e-mail on your behalf is compromised; or you use a browser with a malicious extension installed.

## Access Denied

Malware might prevent you from accessing its files to prevent file deletion. If you get an "access denied" message when trying to delete malware-infected files, you could try to take over ownership of the files. However, it is usually easier to bypass the normal file management processes to delete those files.

In Windows, open a command prompt and use the attrib command to remove the attributes from the file (replace *infected_filename.ext* with the actual filename):

```
attrib -r -s -h infected_filename.ext
```

Or, boot the system with a malware-removal disc or USB drive that includes a file manager.

## Invalid Certificate (Trusted Root CA)

Digital certificates are used by web browsers and operating systems to validate websites and applications (in other words, to prove that the alleged owner or developer is actually valid). Digital certificates are issued by a certificate authority (CA), such as Symantec, Comodo, IdenTrust, and others.

A digital certificate error can be caused by various issues, but one possible cause is that malware has attempted to sneak a bad certificate onto your system or has changed the system date (a date mismatch is the cause of many certificate errors).

 **ADDITIONAL RESOURCES**   To learn more about certificate errors in browsers, go to https://support.microsoft.com and look up Certificate errors: FAQ.

## System/Application Log Errors

Windows creates various types of logs that can be viewed in Event Viewer. To see errors that might be caused by malware, open Event Viewer from the Microsoft Management Console (MMC) and filter for errors.

In macOS, open the Console app and use it to filter for errors and faults. In Linux, open a terminal session and use dmesg to view kernel messages.

**Cross-Reference**

To learn more about using Event Viewer in Windows, see the "Event Viewer" section in Objective 1.5 of Domain 1.0 in Part II.

# REVIEW

**Objective 3.2: Given a scenario, troubleshoot and resolve PC security issues**   Common symptoms indicating PC security problems include

- Pop-ups
- Browser redirection
- Security alerts (real vs. fake)
- Slow performance
- Internet connectivity issues
- PC/OS lockups
- Application crash
- OS updates failures
- Rogue antivirus
- Spam
- Renamed system files
- Renamed or disappearing files
- Unexpected file permission changes
- Hijacked e-mail
- Access denied
- Invalid certificates
- System/application log errors

## 3.2 QUESTIONS

1. If your browser is displaying pop-up windows, what should you do first?

   **A.** Run a scan with your anti-malware app

   **B.** Update the OS

   **C.** Check browser settings

   **D.** Use a different browser

2. You have just returned from a business trip during which you temporarily misplaced your smartphone and laptop. You also used a public library's computer to check e-mail. You can't log in to your e-mail now that you're back in the office. What should you do?

   **A.** Contact your e-mail vendor for a new password

   **B.** Scan for malware

   **C.** Quarantine your system

   **D.** Restart your system in Safe Mode

3. You have received an urgent e-mail from a casual acquaintance stating they need $500 to get home after a serious car breakdown. What should you do?

   **A.** Wire the money

   **B.** Unfriend your friend

   **C.** Reply to the e-mail

   **D.** Assume it's spam

4. Your browser is displaying a security alert that there are several malware apps running on your system. Which of the following should you do?

   **A.** Note the name of the malware and then scan for it

   **B.** Close the browser window

   **C.** Follow the instructions on-screen

   **D.** Panic

5. Your favorite application has stopped working. After investigation, you have determined that your system was infected with malware. How can you get your application working after you remove the malware? (Choose two.)

   **A.** Update your OS

   **B.** Reboot

   **C.** Repair the application

   **D.** Restart in Safe Mode

## 3.2 ANSWERS

1. **C**  Your browser's built-in pop-up protection is probably turned off, so turn it on.

2. **A**  Change your password so others can't use your e-mail.

3. **D**  It's probably spam. Use other means of contact to check with anyone before sending them money or confidential information.

4. **B**  A security alert in a browser window is a fake, so close the browser window.

5. **B C**  Rebooting might get your app working again. If not, use the repair application feature in your operating system.

 **Objective 3.3** # Given a scenario, use best practice procedures for malware removal

CompTIA recommends a seven-step process for malware removal. This objective covers the process.

# Best Practice Malware Removal Process

Despite your best efforts, your computer or a computer you are responsible for is likely to become infected with malware. To get rid of computer viruses or other malware infections, follow the best practice steps in this section.

**Step 1: Identify and Research Malware Symptoms**   The first step is to recognize (identify) that a potential malware outbreak has occurred and act swiftly to keep it from spreading. Network monitoring, security event logs, and user reports may all tip you off to the malware symptoms described in the previous objective. Many networks employ software such as the open source PacketFence to monitor network traffic and automatically isolate systems that start sending suspicious packets.

**Step 2: Quarantine the Infected Systems**   To quarantine a computer, take it off the network by disconnecting the network cable or disconnecting/disabling its Wi-Fi radio. Depending on how the malware spread, you may need to take additional steps to keep other systems from contracting it. For example, don't allow removable drives or media from that system to be connected to other systems unless the drives or media are scanned for malware first.

**Step 3: Disable System Restore (in Windows)**   Once you're sure the machine isn't capable of infecting other systems, disable System Restore to keep the malware from being included in (and potentially restored later from) saved restore points. To turn off System Restore in Windows, go to Control Panel | System applet | System protection. In the Protection Settings section, you'll need to individually select each drive, click Configure to open the System Protection dialog, and select Turn off system protection.

**Step 4: Remediate the Infected Systems**   Follow these best practices to remediate a system:

- **Update the anti-malware software**   If you have removed the system from the network, you need to use different methods to update the anti-malware software than usual. Most providers have downloadable files that can be copied to media and then used on the infected system.

- **Scan and use removal techniques (Safe Mode, Windows Preinstallation Environment)**   Once you get to a clean boot environment, update your anti-malware software and definitions, run its most comprehensive scan, and remove any malware it discovers. Next, repeat this process for all removable media exposed to the system, and any other machine that might have received data from it.

Remediation sometimes requires a third step: Repair any damage done to the system.

If you can't start Windows after the malware scan is finished, you need to boot to the Windows Preinstallation Environment and use the Windows Recovery Environment/System Recovery Options.

These recovery options include useful remediation utilities such as Startup Repair, System Restore, System Image Recovery, Refresh, and Command Prompt. Run the appropriate option for the situation, and you should have the machine properly remediated in a jiffy.

**EXAM TIP**   Remember to re-enable System Restore and create a new restore point once the system has been repaired.

**Step 5: Schedule Scans and Run Updates**   One of the reasons that systems become infected is because anti-malware updates and scans were disabled or never set up. Set up a schedule for scans and run updates.

**Step 6: Enable System Restore and Create a Restore Point (in Windows)**   By creating a restore point after re-enabling System Restore, you establish a new baseline to return to after cleaning up the system.

**Step 7: Educate the End User**   Even the best anti-malware suite is imperfect—ideally it forms a rarely tested second line of defense. The first line of defense is educating your users—nobody wants their system infected with malware. Teach users to be cautious with e-mail from senders they don't recognize and to never click an attachment or URL in an e-mail unless they are 100 percent certain of the source. Explain the dangers of questionable websites (for example, warez websites distribute illegal copies of software that are often laden with malware) and teach your users how to react when a site is trying to manipulate them or triggers their browser's built-in attack site warning (see Figure 3.3-1).

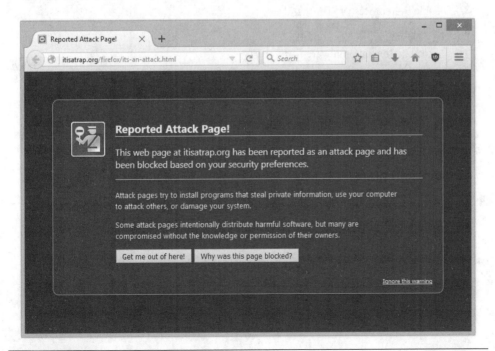

**FIGURE 3.3-1**   Attack site warning

Remind users to

* Install, use, and update anti-malware programs regularly.
* Enable automatic updates for anti-malware programs.
* Install apps only from trusted sources.
* Avoid untrusted software sources (warez, registry cleaners from obscure websites).
* If a malware attack takes place, analyze weaknesses in prevention and work to improve user education.

 **EXAM TIP** Be sure to know the steps for best practice procedures for removing malware.

# REVIEW

**Objective 3.3: Given a scenario, use best practice procedures for malware removal** Removing malware involves a seven-step process:

1. Identify and research malware symptoms.
2. Quarantine the infected systems.
3. Disable System Restore (in Windows).
4. Remediate the infected systems:
    a. Update the anti-malware software.
    b. Scan and use removal techniques (Safe Mode, Windows Preinstallation Environment).
5. Schedule scans and run updates.
6. Enable System Restore and create a restore point (in Windows).
7. Educate the end user.

## 3.3 QUESTIONS

1. After updating anti-malware software and scanning/using removal techniques, what is another step that might be necessary in remediation?
    A. User education
    B. Repairing damage from malware
    C. Re-enabling system restore
    D. Creating a restore point

2. Which of the following is a reason to use a clean boot environment in removing malware?

   **A.** Makes computer run faster

   **B.** Makes user education easier

   **C.** Prevents reinfection

   **D.** Helps prevent malware from interfering with removal

3. When should you enable System Restore and create a restore point?

   **A.** Before removing malware

   **B.** Before scheduling scans and running updates

   **C.** After scheduling scans and running updates

   **D.** As the last step in the process

4. As part of user education, you have taught your users to install apps only from trusted sources. Which of the following is not a trusted source?

   **A.** A website offering warez

   **B.** Valve's Steam service

   **C.** Apple App Store

   **D.** Microsoft Store

5. Determining that a system has probably been infected with malware is which step in the malware removal process?

   **A.** Step 7

   **B.** Step 2

   **C.** Step 3

   **D.** Step 1

## 3.3 ANSWERS

1. **B**  Software can be damaged by malware, so repairing it may be a part of remediation on some systems.

2. **D**  Clean booting or booting from a USB or optical disc before running malware removal helps prevent malware from running and interfering with the removal process.

3. **C**  The restore point needs to remember the system configuration after it's been remediated and protected against threats.

4. **A**  Warez is untrustworthy, illegal, and may be filled with malware.

5. **D**  Determining that a malware infection is present is included in Step 1. Identify and research malware symptoms.

# Objective 3.4 Given a scenario, troubleshoot mobile OS and application issues

Mobile operating systems and applications have some issues in common with desktop and laptop operating systems and applications, but because of how mobile devices work, some OS and application issues are unique. In this objective, you learn how to deal with them.

## Common Symptoms of Mobile OS and Application Issues (with Solutions)

The following symptoms commonly plague mobile devices, operating systems, and applications. After each symptom is provided, you will also learn some typical solutions.

### Dim Display

Mobile devices have a *brightness control* that you set to auto mode or control manually. A dim display might be a panel problem, but you need to rule out display settings. Follow these steps:

1. Disable auto-brightness and manually change from the dimmest to brightest setting.
2. If adjusting the setting doesn't cover an appropriate range, suspect the display panel.
3. If it does cover an appropriate range, suspect auto-brightness and try the following:
   a. Ensure front-facing sensors and cameras are clean and unobstructed.
   b. Check the environment for bright lights that may confuse the sensor.
   c. Perform a soft reset to clear up issues with apps that tinker with system brightness.

> **NOTE** Power saving settings to extend battery life can also cause a dim display.

### Intermittent Wireless

The biggest wireless connectivity problem for mobile devices is a weak signal caused by distance or interference; symptoms are dropped connections, delays, slow transmission speeds, and frequent no-signal indicators. There's not much you can do on the device end except move. Cellular signal boosters exist, but they're best in a fixed low-signal location.

Some tricky connectivity problems can occur despite a good signal:

- An *overloaded network* is common when large public events or emergencies cause a surge in network use, leaving users with a good signal unable to place calls, send texts, or transfer data.

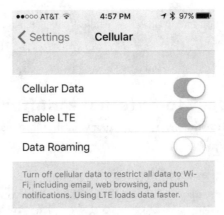

**FIGURE 3.4-1**   Option to disable cellular data in iOS

- You may experience slow data speeds while roaming just because the carrier of the network you are roaming on limits data rates for nonsubscribers.

- Exceeding *data usage limits* your carrier sets can lead to slow data speeds, overage charges, or a hard data cap. To resolve this last problem, which CompTIA calls *data transmission over limit*, either pay your carrier to raise the data limits or monitor data use and disable cellular data (see Figure 3.4-1) as needed.

Symptoms depend on how the carrier handles the overage, so check these limits when dealing with unexplained good-signal connection problems.

## No Wireless Connectivity

If you have no cellular or Wi-Fi connectivity, regardless of your location relative to cell towers or Wi-Fi APs, the problem might be with your mobile device itself: Airplane mode, when enabled, turns off all wireless connections. Airplane mode, developed originally to enable fliers with mobile devices to keep them on without interfering with navigation systems, can be easily triggered on some mobile devices.

To determine if your device is in Airplane mode, look at the status bar on your smartphone, tablet, or laptop for an airplane icon. To restore connection, turn off Airplane mode and reconnect to a Wi-Fi AP (cellular reconnection is automatic).

## No Bluetooth Connectivity

Bluetooth connectivity is also affected by Airplane mode, but Bluetooth can also be turned off manually.

To restore connection with Bluetooth devices, turn off Airplane mode (if applicable), turn on Bluetooth, and see if your previous pairing is still active. If not, re-pair your mobile device with the other device (headset, speaker, keyboard, mouse, and so on).

**EXAM TIP**    Be sure to know how wireless connections can be turned off and affect battery life.

## Cannot Broadcast to External Monitor

Here are a few tried-and-true things to check when your mobile device cannot broadcast to an external monitor:

- Is your input source correct on the external monitor?
- Do you have the right adapter for your device? Make sure you have an adapter known to work for your device.
- Does your adapter need its own power source?
- For HDMI: Did the HDMI recognize your device and your external monitor? Try resetting one or both devices to give the HDMI time to see connections and set up.
- For laptops: Did you use the correct key combination to switch to the external display or to mirror the built-in display to an external display? There is no standard keystroke, and some systems require the user to press the FN key along with the function key toggle, while others don't.
- For HDTVs: Did you make sure the display is set to the correct port? Most HDTVs have two or more HDMI ports.

## Touchscreen Nonresponsive or Responds Inaccurately

If the touchscreen is nonresponsive or responds inaccurately, consider the following:

- Touch sensors can register an accidental touch, often where you grip the device. Show the user how the sensors pick up an accidental touch, and how to hold the device to avoid them.
- Sometimes you can restore responsiveness by cleaning the touchscreen with a dry microfiber cloth to get rid of fingerprints, dust, dirt, grease, and so on.
- Performance issues can make a touchscreen inaccurate, sluggish, or inoperable. Clues include incorrect time, jumpy lock screen or wallpaper animations, out-of-date weather or stock widgets, slow or no response to hardware buttons, failure to receive texts or calls, and so on. If you can't regain control after a few minutes, perform a soft reset and see if the touchscreen works.
- If a soft reset doesn't work, look online to see if the device has a hidden *diagnostics menu* or *service menu*. You reach these by typing a code into the device's dialer or by holding specific buttons while the device boots. A touchscreen diagnostic makes hardware problems obvious. Some Android and Windows Phone devices may have a touchscreen calibration routine in either the primary OS settings menu or a hidden device menu.

**FIGURE 3.4-2**   Pristine LCI sticker (top) and LCI sticker after absorbing a drop of water (bottom)

- If the touchscreen is still not responding properly, look for signs it has physical damage and needs service or replacement. You can ask the device user whether it was dropped or exposed to liquid, but don't expect much; the cause is often embarrassing. Even if the glass is fine, impacts can break internal connections, so check for scuffs and dings. Liquid can cause shorts and disorient sensors, so check for *liquid contact indicator (LCI)* stickers (see Figure 3.4-2) on the battery or in the battery compartment and external ports; look up additional locations online.

- A poorly applied protective cover can affect touchscreen responsiveness. If the protective cover is peeling away or has air bubbles, remove it and use a different one.

## Apps Not Loading

If a mobile device app is not loading, try these steps:

1. Start with a soft reset.
2. If the app still won't load, it may be incompatible with some combination of the mobile device's hardware, OS version, or vendor/carrier customizations to the OS.
3. Confirm the device meets the app's hardware requirements, including RAM, storage space, processor type, specific sensors or radios, required camera features, and so on.

## Slow Performance

Add the following to what you already know about poorly performing mobile devices:

- A mobile device with performance issues will often be running hot, but a hot device could be using *thermal throttling* to protect the device's CPU from heat damage; see if performance picks up as it cools.
- Performance issues can be caused by storage space being almost filled up on a mobile device, making it struggle to efficiently save data or install apps; free some space and see if the problem resolves.
- Performance can also suffer when there are too many apps running at the same time, eating up RAM.
- A soft reset often resolves the immediate symptoms, and you can use the device settings or third-party apps to measure the device's performance, separate hardware from software causes, and decide whether you should take the device to an authorized repair facility.

**EXAM TIP**   Be sure to note the many symptoms for which you can use soft reset, such as apps not loading, slow performance, frozen system, and others.

## Unable to Decrypt E-mail

Securing an e-mail requires encrypting it—scrambling it with a unique key using some standard, such as Pretty Good Privacy (PGP) or Secure/Multipurpose Internet Mail Extensions (S/MIME)—so that only the recipient can decrypt or unscramble it with software and a related unique key. Each *key* is a string of bits that software uses to encrypt or decrypt data.

In practice, the most common reason a mobile device is unable to decrypt an e-mail is that the e-mail client or app doesn't support the encryption standard used to encrypt the message. The fix is a plugin or a new e-mail client or app:

- Download a plugin or e-mail client or app that supports this encryption method and follow any steps to configure the client to use it.

- Provide the e-mail client with a decryption key. Some standards require manual key exchange; contact the sender to exchange keys. Other standards may exchange keys automatically if you meet certain criteria, such as being part of the same organization.

## Extremely Short Battery Life

Modern mobile devices use Li-ion batteries, and it's important to manage them well to ensure the device lives a long life. Before good management can help, you need to meet the user's power needs. Know how long a given user's device needs to last on a charge, and try to provide a device that can last at least 20 percent longer, to account for dwindling capacity over the battery's lifetime.

Mobile devices are rated in terms of how long their battery should power the device during "normal" use, how long the device can go between battery charges, and how much power the battery provides and needs to charge. Start with the device maker's numbers, and follow up with benchmarks on mobile device review sites. If no devices meet the user's needs, make sure they have a removable battery and spares, or a portable external battery recharger. You can plug a mobile device into a *portable battery recharger* (also called an *external battery*, *power pack*, or *portable charger*) to recharge.

There are two ways to think about battery life: how long it will last on each charge, and how long the battery can meet your needs before you have to replace it. When you waste battery life on unused device features, you shorten both. Here's a list of power-hungry components with tips for managing them, but there's no need to guess; check your device's battery usage monitor (see Figure 3.4-3).

- **Display**   The fastest way to drain most modern mobile devices is leaving the screen on. Keep the display off when you can, and use the lowest acceptable brightness setting or automatic brightness. Other settings control how soon the screen turns off without

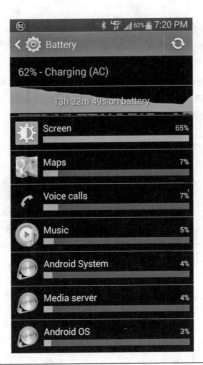

**FIGURE 3.4-3**   Battery usage for a smartphone

input and whether notifications turn it on. Enable *power-saving modes*—some of which can even go grayscale. OLED displays, which use less power for darker colors, can reduce drain with black wallpapers and dark app themes.

- **Wireless communication**   Cellular voice, cellular data, Wi-Fi, Bluetooth, NFC, and so on, all have a radio inside the device, and each draws power while enabled. Additionally, searching for a signal is expensive, and some apps will do more work when a radio is available. You may be able to dodge signal-search drain with settings to limit or disable device roaming and searching for new wireless networks. You can likewise restrict drain from overeager apps with app or OS settings.

- **Location services**   The power drain caused by these services can vary widely between an app that occasionally checks low-accuracy location based on nearby cellular or Wi-Fi networks in the background, and an app that constantly requests high-quality GPS updates. The simple solution is keeping location services off unless needed, but you may find a happy medium with per-app restrictions. An app should prompt you to turn location services on when it needs them.

 **EXAM TIP**   Be familiar with the factors that can reduce battery power and battery life.

# Overheating

Some mobile devices, such as laptops or some tablets, have cooling vents or fans; make sure these fans and cooling vents are not blocked. With smartphones, avoiding overheating is trickier because they are usually turned on, carried in our hands or pockets, and might be inside a hard or semi-hard case for protection against impact. Tips to avoid overheating include

- Avoid very hot environments or turn the device off.
- If the device is hot to the touch in a cool environment, put it into airplane mode, close all running programs, and see if it cools. If not, turn it off until it cools and try again.

Beware if the device overheats for no obvious reason, or gets hot enough to burn someone. These problems are usually caused by a defective battery or other power circuit within the device. There's not much you can do other than turn it off to protect the device from further damage; keep it out of pockets, away from people, and take it to a service center.

# Frozen System

A mobile device that won't respond to key or screen presses is a frozen system. The immediate goal is getting it to a usable state:

- If the device isn't responding, follow the manufacturer's steps for performing a soft reset.
- If the device is partially responsive, close the offending app, save work in other open apps, and perform a soft reset. When the device is usable again, look for a solution.
- If the device froze when you opened a new or updated app, use a soft reset, then try the app one more time. If the device freezes up again, uninstall it and wait for an update or find a replacement app.
- OS issues can also cause a freeze, especially after an update; look for follow-up OS patches. If you haven't recently updated and the device starts freezing when you use any app that activates a component (such as the GPS or camera), your device needs service.
- If the device is unusable after the soft reset, find documentation on how to boot into any special modes that enable you to remove an offending app, repair the OS installation, or reset the device to factory default. If this too fails, send it to a service center.

# No Sound from Speakers

If your mobile device has no sound, check the following:

- If a headset or external speaker is plugged in, unplug it if you want to use the device's internal speakers.
- Check volume and mute settings in the OS and apps as well as hardware controls. Expect the OS to have multiple settings for calls, music, notifications, and so on.
- Try a soft reset.
- If none of these steps works, the speakers have likely been damaged or disconnected inside the device; it needs service.

# System Lockout

System lockout occurs when too many consecutive login attempts fail, to protect the device from brute-force attempts to guess the password. Differing lockout mechanisms may prevent further login attempts for some period of time, require login with full account credentials, or even wipe user data. Configure options like this on the device itself, or through the organization's central mobile device management (MDM) software, but advise users not to exceed a certain number of login attempts and to keep their devices away from anyone (e.g., children) who might trigger the mechanism.

The company should securely store PINs and maintain current backups of all its own mobile devices, and instruct those with their own devices to keep backups. The MDM software can unlock the device, but it won't help if it has already been wiped. If no one can unlock a device, you'll have to restore from a backup or perform a reset to factory default.

# App Log Errors

Mobile device operating systems track app errors in a log that you can check to help track down system problems:

- Windows mobile devices use the Event Viewer available from the Microsoft Management Console (MMC).
- Use the Console app on macOS to read logs for connected iOS devices. Logs for iOS devices are also synced to iTunes.
- On Android, use third-party developer tools to see Android logs.

 **NOTE**   iOS logs are stored in the following directories:
**macOS**   ~/Library/Logs/CrashReporter/MobileDevice/
**Windows**   C:\Users\username\AppData\Roaming\Apple Computer\Logs\
CrashReporter\Mobile Device\DeviceName

# REVIEW

**Objective 3.4: Given a scenario, troubleshoot mobile OS and application issues**   Common symptoms of mobile OS and application issues include

- Dim display
- Intermittent or no wireless connectivity
- No Bluetooth connectivity
- Can't broadcast to external monitor
- Touchscreen nonresponsive or responds inaccurately

- Apps not loading
- Slow performance
- Unable to decrypt e-mail
- Extremely short battery life
- Overheating
- Frozen system
- No sound from speakers
- System lockout
- App log errors

A common solution for some of these problems is a soft reset.

## 3.4 QUESTIONS

**1.** Which of the following would not be affected by airplane mode?

   **A.** Wi-Fi connections

   **B.** Cellular connections

   **C.** Display brightness

   **D.** Bluetooth connections

**2.** You have connected an HDTV with your laptop and you can't see your desktop on the HDTV. You have set your display properties to mirror. What should you do next?

   **A.** Restart in Safe Mode

   **B.** Check the HDTV input setting

   **C.** Restart in normal mode

   **D.** Set your display properties to HDTV

**3.** Your client is afraid that her smartphone has come in contact with water. Which of the following should you have her check?

   **A.** LCI

   **B.** Moisture sensor in Settings

   **C.** Bluetooth

   **D.** Airplane mode

**4.** Which of the following issues can be helped by performing a soft reset of a mobile device? (Choose two.)

   **A.** Extremely short battery life

   **B.** Frozen system

   **C.** Moisture

   **D.** No sound from speakers

5. Your smartphone is down to 10 percent battery life but you're expecting an important phone call. Which settings can you safely change to improve battery life? (Choose two.)

   **A.** Enable airplane mode

   **B.** Disable NFC

   **C.** Disable GPS

   **D.** Enable navigation

## 3.4 ANSWERS

1. **C** The other settings are disabled by airplane mode, but it has no effect on screen brightness.

2. **B** The HDTV must be set to use the correct HDMI input before it can be used with the laptop.

3. **A** A liquid contact indicator (LCI) is a moisture-sensitive sticker used by many vendors to determine if a device has come in contact with liquid.

4. **B D** A frozen system and no sound from speakers are two of the many problems that can be solved by performing a soft reset.

5. **B C** Disabling NFC and GPS will save power without affecting your ability to make and receive phone calls.

 **Objective 3.5** # Given a scenario, troubleshoot mobile OS and application security issues

With mobile devices becoming more and more common as primary computing devices, mobile OS and application security issues are more important than ever. With the rise of BYOD (bring your own device) policies, it can be harder than ever to keep mobile devices working securely.

## Common Symptoms of Mobile OS and Application Security Issues (with Solutions)

The following sections discuss common symptoms of mobile OS and application security issues and their corresponding solutions.

## Wi-Fi, Wireless Cellular, and Bluetooth Issues

Malware is just software that uses your device against your will, so a simple sign is unexpected resource use. Because many resource issues are benign problems fixed by a soft reset, it's easy to shrug them off; be suspicious, especially of unexplained patterns such as the following:

- A hot phone, *high resource utilization*, and excessive *power drain* might mean your device is doing a malware developer's bidding, such as uploading recorded audio in real time or smuggling networked files out.
- *Slow data speeds* might mean your device is busy uploading or downloading data without your knowledge, or might be a clue that it is using an illegitimate WAP or cell tower with less capacity than its official counterpart.
- A device uploading stolen data might unexpectedly exceed cellular data transmission limits.

*Unintended Wi-Fi connections* and *unintended Bluetooth pairing* enable malicious people to access, steal, or modify data. Configure your mobile device not to automatically connect or pair; doing these manually is worth the trouble. If the device is centrally managed, MDM software can enforce these protections via profile settings.

In addition to their impact on battery life, power management, and running apps, *signal drop* and *weak signal* are some of the few clues you'll get that your device is interacting with a spoofed cell tower or rogue Wi-Fi access point. If signal quality suddenly changes in either direction, be curious. See if the cellular provider has known tower issues nearby. Fire up a cell tower analyzer and compare nearby signals with what you've seen in the past, or with third-party resources online. To prevent automatic connections to a rogue Wi-Fi access point, disable the automatic connection setting for SSIDs. It's a bit more work to click the SSID you want to connect to, but it helps prevent connecting to a bogus wireless network.

## Leaked Personal Files/Data

Device locks and remote wipe can prevent unauthorized users from accessing data on a mobile device—if you wipe the device in time. Data can also leak out through apps and removable storage cards. Encrypt portable devices and removable storage if it contains sensitive data. App and device security and privacy settings can protect personal data, but there's always risk here.

No matter the source, *leaked personal files and data* can pose a direct privacy or security risk, indicate an ongoing security issue, and suggest what that issue might be. A full audit of ways an important file could've leaked out of a networked environment is beyond what can be expected of a CompTIA A+ tech, but be curious—you may well get the first chance to escalate the issue, or write it off as a compromised login and make the user change passwords.

# Unauthorized Account Access

For convenience, mobile devices are often set to automatically authenticate with networks, VPNs, e-mail servers, online services, and so on, granting unauthorized account access to anyone who can unlock the device. To keep sensitive accounts and connections secure, don't store credentials for automatic entry. When a device is lost, change the user's credentials. Unauthorized account access can also indicate an attack or malware has compromised a device, creating an ongoing threat to the organization.

 **EXAM TIP**   Be sure to know that unauthorized account access, unauthorized location tracking, and unauthorized camera/microphone activation are significant security threats.

# Unauthorized Location Tracking

Depending on settings, the OS and geotracking apps may send a user's location to third parties. Prevent this by disabling GPS or location services until needed; otherwise, configure the OS and geotracking apps to prevent unauthorized tracking. Some apps or specific features won't work until geotracking is enabled (see Figure 3.5-1).

Both legitimate networks and some of the network attacks listed earlier in this objective can also be used to locate or track a device. Tracking when devices cross invisible boundaries, or *geofencing*, is used for advertising, customer tracking, and employee tracking.

 **CAUTION**   People tend to enjoy privacy, so tracking them can have legal consequences, especially if they didn't opt in.

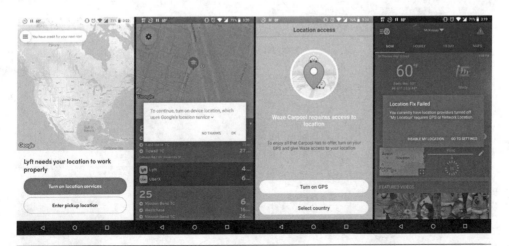

**FIGURE 3.5-1**   Android apps prompting the user to enable location services

## Unauthorized Camera/Microphone Activation

App features, malware, and unauthorized network connections can potentially be used to toggle device features such as built-in cameras and microphones, enabling attackers to spy on anyone nearby. You can limit risk by restricting camera and microphone permissions in apps or OS settings, preventing unauthorized network connections, and using anti-malware solutions. With camera and microphone permissions, even popular apps (see Figure 3.5-2) by trustworthy developers could have a vulnerability that enables an attacker to watch or listen in.

 **CAUTION** Sophisticated network attacks can reportedly *appear* to power down a device but leave its microphone active. Be on the lookout for strange behavior.

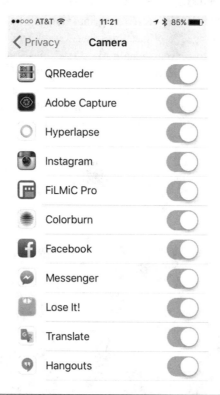

**FIGURE 3.5-2** Apps with permission to access an iPhone's camera

# REVIEW

### Objective 3.5: Given a scenario, troubleshoot mobile OS and application security issues

- High resource utilization, power drain, and slow data speeds are all clues that point to a possible malware infection.
- Unintended Wi-Fi connections and unintended Bluetooth pairing can lead to data theft or unauthorized changes.
- Signal drop and weak signal can indicate a spoofed cell tower or rogue WAP is being used.
- To prevent leaks of personal files and data, use encryption and app settings that enforce privacy.
- Avoid unauthorized account access by using manual logins.
- Turn off geotracking when not needed.
- Disable camera and microphone permissions in all apps except those that need them to function.

## 3.5 QUESTIONS

1.  Which of the following mobile features can be set up for use by specified apps only?
    - **A.** Wi-Fi connections
    - **B.** Browser
    - **C.** GPS
    - **D.** Airplane mode

2.  High resource utilization when no apps are open could be a sign of which of the following?
    - **A.** Dying battery
    - **B.** Malware
    - **C.** Airplane mode
    - **D.** GPS enabled

3.  A user wants to use Google Maps to navigate to a meeting. Which function does he need to enable to make this possible?
    - **A.** Wi-Fi
    - **B.** Bluetooth
    - **C.** GPS
    - **D.** NFC

4. Your CEO is conducting sensitive negotiations with another firm. In addition to using a passcode on his device, which of the following steps can prevent his device from revealing confidential information if lost? (Choose two.)

    **A.** Encrypting the drive

    **B.** Enabling airplane mode

    **C.** Enabling GPS

    **D.** Enabling remote wipe

5. Which of the following common features can be used to snoop on a user's conversations?

    **A.** Microphone

    **B.** NFC

    **C.** Panorama

    **D.** Browser

## 3.5 ANSWERS

1. **C**  GPS access can be granted to specific apps.

2. **B**  Malware can use a lot of resources because it captures and sends data without the user's permission or knowledge.

3. **C**  GPS must be enabled to permit navigation. Without it, you can only view maps.

4. **A D**  Encrypting the drive prevents its contents from being accessed by others, while enabling remote wipe will make the device useless and protect its contents from being decrypted when the wipe command is activated.

5. **A**  A microphone can be used to record conversations.

# Operational Procedures

**Domain Objectives**

- **4.1** Compare and contrast best practices associated with types of documentation
- **4.2** Given a scenario, implement basic change management best practices
- **4.3** Given a scenario, implement basic disaster prevention and recovery methods
- **4.4** Explain common safety procedures
- **4.5** Explain environmental impacts and appropriate controls
- **4.6** Explain the processes for addressing prohibited content/activity, and privacy, licensing, and policy concepts
- **4.7** Given a scenario, use proper communication techniques and professionalism
- **4.8** Identify the basics of scripting
- **4.9** Given a scenario, use remote access technologies

**Objective 4.1** Compare and contrast best practices associated with types of documentation

Accurate documentation is a great aid to managing and troubleshooting devices, peripherals, and networks. Inaccurate documentation is frustrating because you never know which parts are accurate and which aren't. That being said, many networks and individual workstations have no documentation at all. This objective helps you understand the best practices needed to create accurate and useful documentation.

 **EXAM TIP** Be ready to compare and contrast best practices for the various types of documentation listed in this section.

## Network Topology Diagrams

A network topology diagram provides a visual guide to the hardware on the network, from routers and switches to workstations, printers, and WAPs. A simple diagram is useful for showing how the components connect, while more complex diagrams provide connection types, speeds, and specific component brand/model information. Figure 4.1-1 illustrates a simple network diagram created with Microsoft Visio and Cisco network diagram icons.

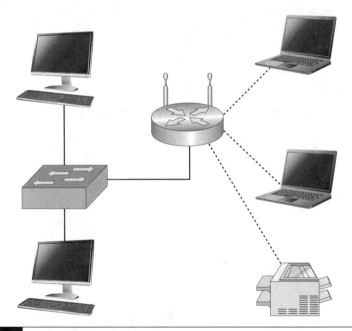

**FIGURE 4.1-1**   A simple network diagram

# Knowledge Base/Articles

A network topology diagram is just the beginning of your company's *knowledge base*—a collection of documents that identifies the equipment and software in use, problems detected, and solutions to those problems; along with links to vendors and third-party websites with relevant information. Every time a technology-related event happens in an organization, there's an opportunity to build up your knowledge base. Ideally, an organization's knowledge base should start with the official documentation for each computer, component, and peripheral. These days, if the paper manual isn't available, it's no big deal because product manuals are almost always available for download.

 **ADDITIONAL RESOURCES**   If you need to identify the specific motherboard, CPU, GPU, and other components in a custom-built system, there are a number of free and commercial apps available that can help, such as Belarc Advisor (personal use only), SiSoftware Sandra, CPU-Z, GPU-Z, SIW, and others. Find links to these and others by visiting the https://alternativeto.net website and searching for "Belarc Advisor."

Add documentation for the operating systems and apps used, supplemented by third-party e-books and patch and update information. To track down the information you need, make sure you have searchable PDF or e-book versions of your documentation.

Your knowledge base is not complete until you capture information as covered in the CompTIA six-step best practice methodology. Make sure you identify the device(s) or software affected, the theories that were discarded and the one that was accurate, how the solution was applied, and how to avoid similar problems in the future.

## Cross-Reference

To learn more about the best practice methodology, see Part I, Domain 5.0, Objective 5.1 of this book.

To summarize, here's what your organization needs in its knowledge base:

- Official documentation, including patch and update information
- Third-party resources (websites, forums, e-books)
- Documentation of the organization's own troubleshooting solutions

# Incident Documentation

Incident documentation should include

- Devices or software involved
- Event logs when appropriate
- Symptoms and solutions

> ### Cross-Reference
> To learn more about the full scope of incident response and use of documentation, see the "Incident Response" section in Objective 4.6, later in this domain.

# Regulatory and Compliance Policy

Larger organizations, such as government entities, benefit greatly from organizing their data according to its sensitivity and minimizing surprises by keeping computer hardware and software as uniform as possible. This also helps maintain *compliance* with government and internal regulations; common examples are rules on approved software and regulations on how you must handle *personally identifiable information (PII)* such as health or academic records. Templates for regulatory and compliance policies are widely available online.

**EXAM TIP**    CompTIA A+ 220-1002 exam objective 4.6 uses specific language regarding compliance. People must *follow all policies and security best practices.* Follow the rules, in other words.

> ### Cross-Reference
> To learn more about software compliance in terms of licensing, see the "Licensing/DRM/EULA" section in Objective 4.6, later in this domain.

# Acceptable Use Policy

Most organizations require employees to sign an Acceptable Use Policy (AUP) that defines what actions employees may or may not perform with company equipment and systems, including computers, phones, printers, and the network itself.

**EXAM TIP**    You might see a question on Acceptable Use Policy. An organization's Acceptable Use Policy (AUP) defines what actions employees may or may not perform with the organization's property.

The AUP covers the handling of passwords, e-mail, and many other issues, and it guides what actions or content should be identified as prohibited.

**ADDITIONAL RESOURCES**    The SANS Institute provides a boilerplate AUP at www.sans.org. Search for "Information Security Policy Templates" to find the link.

# Password Policy

Organizations need a password policy. Why? In an ideal world, all of the users in your organization would have impossible-to-guess passwords that they change often and never write down or reuse elsewhere. In reality, users often choose passwords that are easy to hack—often including the name of a relative or pet—and practice poor security hygiene that exposes the organization's systems and networks to risk, such as leaving their passwords on sticky notes next to their keyboards.

> ### Cross-Reference
> For practical tips on developing a password policy, see the "Password Best Practices" section in Part II, Domain 2.0, Objective 2.7.

# Inventory Management

Computers and common peripherals are relatively inexpensive, but when a computer or printer is misplaced, the cost of the hardware is trivial compared to other questions:

- What information is stored on the device?
- Where is it?
- Is it being stored?
- Was it stolen?
- Is it being used for unauthorized tasks?

The use of asset tags and barcodes can help organizations to track their technology inventory in an inventory management system.

## Barcodes

A *barcode* asset tag contains a barcode that can be scanned. A barcode asset tag might be a vendor-applied tag or could be applied by the equipment owner. The use of a barcode asset tag makes tracking equipment faster and easier than with a strictly manual system because the barcode can be scanned rather than the asset tag code number being recorded manually or by typing.

 **ADDITIONAL RESOURCES**   The Camcode barcode website (www .camcode.com) has many articles on the use of asset tags, including "50 Asset Tracking Tips: Solutions and Strategies to Help Successfully Track Your Business's Most Valuable Assets."

## Asset Tags

An asset tag with RFID capabilities provides much more equipment management capabilities than a barcode system. With an RFID-based system, it's easier to update inventory and update location and other information, and RFID tags don't need to be scanned individually.

 **EXAM TIP** If a client needs to control inventory without handling each piece, RFID asset tags are the way to go. You might see a question about how these systems compare.

# REVIEW

**Objective 4.1: Compare and contrast best practices associated with types of documentation** Elements of documentation best practices include

- Creating network topology diagrams
- Creating a knowledge base from vendor and third-party documentation of hardware and software along with in-house troubleshooting information
- Gathering incident documentation
- Developing regulatory and compliance policy
- Developing an Acceptable Use Policy
- Creating a password policy
- Using asset tags and barcodes as part of inventory management

## 4.1 QUESTIONS

1. At a minimum, a network topology diagram should record which of the following?
   **A.** Connections between network components such as routers, switches, and WAPs
   **B.** Usernames and accounts
   **C.** Routing details
   **D.** DHCP address ranges

2. You have been tasked with creating a knowledge base for the Windows-based equipment in your department. Some of the computers were hand-built by a computer shop and you need to find out the motherboard, chipset, CPU, and RAM information. Which of the following will enable you to find the most information about each system?
   **A.** Contacting the computer shop
   **B.** Dismantling each custom-built PC

**C.** Running a third-party system information app

**D.** Viewing the System Properties dialog box

**3.** Which of the following is *not* likely to be covered in an Acceptable Use Policy?

**A.** Password handling

**B.** Keyboard lighting

**C.** Using e-mail

**D.** Personal print jobs

**4.** You are creating an asset tag design for your employer, which plans to use a hand-held scanner as part of the company's inventory system. Which of the following must be on the asset tag?

**A.** Company slogan

**B.** Barcode

**C.** Company logo

**D.** Asset number

**5.** You visit a department to prepare for a training class that will deal with issues you observe. As soon you open the door to the department, you see sticky notes on each computer display. Which of the following topics do you need to address in training?

**A.** Decluttering the office

**B.** Shutdown procedures

**C.** Choosing sticky note colors that harmonize with the décor

**D.** Security

## 4.1 ANSWERS

**1.** **A**   A network topology diagram must record the network's physical layout. The other items are desirable to know, but not essential.

**2.** **C**   A third-party system information app can provide much more information than the System Properties dialog box in Windows.

**3.** **B**   Keyboard lighting is a feature found mainly on gaming keyboards and some laptops and won't affect typical operations covered in an AUP.

**4.** **B**   An asset tag that will be used with a hand-held scanner needs a barcode.

**5.** **D**   The sticky notes are almost certainly used for passwords, so security training is top priority.

**Objective 4.2** **Given a scenario, implement basic change management best practices**

"Change" is a frightening word to most organizations. Whether it's a change from one brand of printer to another, from an old Windows version to the latest Windows 10, or a change from local to cloud-based apps, people are usually comfortable with the status quo and resist change. Managing change helps ease the shock of the new and makes it easier for an organization to cope when the inevitable happens.

## Change Management Best Practices Overview

Change management best practices include

- Documented business processes
- Purpose of the change
- Scope the change
- Risk analysis
- Plan for change
- End-user acceptance
- Change board
  - Approvals
- Backout plan
- Document changes

 **EXAM TIP** Be sure you are familiar with the order of the best practices in this objective.

## Documented Business Processes

Step 1 is to document existing business processes that will be affected by the change. For example, how users back up files, print documents, share documents, and so forth. The specific business processes to analyze depend on the changes being considered.

# Purpose of the Change

The next step is to determine and document the purpose of the change. Some examples might include

- Improve compatibility with the latest software
- Make backups more reliable
- Standardize hardware platforms

# Scope the Change

Scope the change means to identify who and what will be affected by the change. Specifically, which personnel will be affected by the change, which systems will be replaced, what software will be replaced, how long the change will take, and how much the change will cost (including support staff, training, and other indirect costs).

# Risk Analysis

What are the risks of the proposed change? Some of the questions to consider in creating a risk analysis include

- Will existing data backups be compatible post-change?
- How much time will employee training require?
- Will proprietary software or systems continue to work or will they need to be updated?
- What are the security risks of the change?

**EXAM TIP**   Be sure you understand the difference between risk analysis (what can go wrong) and scope the change (what you are planning to change).

# Plan for Change

Planning for change should include

- Creating a timeline for the process
- Developing a transition strategy
- Running old and new procedures in parallel if appropriate (for example, for accounting or database changes)
- Building in time for training and practice
- Determining where to store surplus equipment

# End-user Acceptance

End users sometimes are the last to be consulted about proposed changes, although their acceptance is critical to the success of any change. To help promote end-user acceptance, consider

- Having end-user involvement in the planning process
- Making sure end-users are properly trained
- Asking for feedback and carefully considering it
- Addressing concerns over proposed changes

# Change Board

A committee known as a change board or change control board is typically in charge of evaluating a proposed change to the organization's technology, particularly software. It should include technical experts and subject matter experts.

## Approvals

The change board should consider a range of possible alternatives to any suggested change. Some possibilities might include

- Change approved
- Further study needed
- Reschedule change to (specify date)
- Reject change
- Modify change to (specify modifications)

# Backout Plan

Some people believe that change = improvement, but in the real world, changes don't always improve a situation. Having a backout plan, sometimes referred to as a rollback plan, is a change management best practice. Its purpose is to be able to return to the pre-change condition if needed.

Some parts of a backout plan might include

- Backing up the operating system, apps, and data before applying a change
- Using restore points, versioning, snapshots, or other options to capture the state of the system before and during changes.
- Creating a checklist of expectations for the change; if the change doesn't meet expectations, the checklist also needs to establish at what point changes should be backed out

# Document Changes

After a change has been implemented successfully, the change should be documented in its final form. This should incorporate the documentation generated throughout the change process, as previously discussed, as well as receipts, overtime records, systems, users, and so on.

# REVIEW

**Objective 4.2: Given a scenario, implement basic change management best practices**   Elements of basic change management best practices include

- Document business practices
- Identifying the purpose of the change
- Scoping the change
- Developing a risk analysis
- Planning for the change
- Working to get end-user acceptance
- Submitting a proposed change to the change board for approval
- Creating a backout plan
- Documenting the changes made

# 4.2 QUESTIONS

1. A backout plan is used to perform which of the following tasks?
   - **A.** Gain change board approval
   - **B.** Analyze the effects of change
   - **C.** Return to pre-change conditions
   - **D.** Aid end-user acceptance

2. You are helping to choose the members of the change board for a technology upgrade to the art department. Which of the following do not need to be involved? (Choose two.)
   - **A.** IT
   - **B.** Human resources
   - **C.** Executive management
   - **D.** End users

3. Which of the following is a good example of change management?
   - **A.** End users are introduced to a new technology without training
   - **B.** The change board is not consulted during the process
   - **C.** Rumors abound about the reasons for the change
   - **D.** Risk analysis is performed

4. Six months after a software change was made in a department, you are asked to troubleshoot a problem. The only related information you can locate refers to the old software system. Which of the steps in change management was not performed?

   **A.** Document changes

   **B.** End-user acceptance

   **C.** Risk management

   **D.** Plan for change

5. Your organization is proposing a change that will have a big impact on its salespeople in the field. Which of the following steps is most likely to enable the field reps to provide input about the proposed change?

   **A.** Plan for change

   **B.** Risk management

   **C.** End-user acceptance

   **D.** Document changes

## 4.2 ANSWERS

1. **C**   A backout (rollback) plan is designed to help an organization return to pre-change conditions if a change has an adverse impact.

2. **B C**   Neither human resources nor executive management are directly involved in the department's day-to-day operations.

3. **D**   Risk analysis is a necessary part of change management.

4. **A**   Without documenting changes, the knowledge of what has changed will fade over time.

5. **C**   End-user acceptance should include the opportunity for end users to address potential changes.

**Objective 4.3** ## Given a scenario, implement basic disaster prevention and recovery methods

Ready for a disaster? If you haven't made preparations, the answer is "No." When a disaster that affects IT resources occurs, data is the most critical asset to recover. In this objective, you review the basic processes needed to preserve and recover user data.

# Backup and Recovery

System maintenance starts with preparation. Conducting regular backups of critical system files and personal data protects the system and its users from accidents and hardware failures. Having backups available also protects you from losing data if problems happen during maintenance. It's best if you're always positioned to restore both the OS and personal data quickly, but you can ultimately reinstall Windows and programs; personal data, on the other hand, is often irreplaceable.

**EXAM TIP**   Know the difference between an image-level backup and a file-level backup and know how to back up critical applications as described in the following sections.

## Image Level

An image-level backup stores the entire contents of the specified drive in one or more files in a different location (local drive or network drive). Contents include the operating system, apps, data files, settings, boot sector, and so on. An image-level back is also known as a *drive clone*. Image-level backup software is included in Windows 7, 8/8.1 and early releases of Windows 10 (Backup and Restore [Windows 7]). For current versions of Windows 10, third-party image backup apps can be used. For Apple systems running macOS or OS X Lion or later, Time Machine can be used as an image backup, using Recovery Mode to restore. For Linux, the built-in dd utility can be used.

## File Level

File-level backup creates copies of data files in a different location (local drive, network drive, or cloud service). File-level backups can be performed as part of image backup, but are most often performed by file backup utilities. File backups typically support *versioning*, enabling users to restore the latest or earlier versions of specific files or folders.

The *Backup and Restore* applet in Windows 7 orients the options (see Figure 4.3-1) around the automatic *Let Windows choose (recommended)* and manual *Let me choose*. If you let Windows do the picking (and your backup location has enough space), it will back up each user's data and create a full system image. Alternatively, you can use granular controls to include or exclude any of these system-level and account-level options (see Figure 4.3-2). Backup and Restore is also included in Windows 8/8.1 and early releases of Windows 10. Current releases of Windows 10 support restoring from a Backup and Restore backup, but not the creation of a new backup using this tool.

**FIGURE 4.3-1**   Who chooses what to back up?

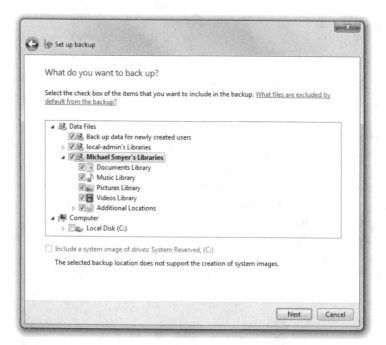

**FIGURE 4.3-2**   Granular backup options include libraries/folders for each account.

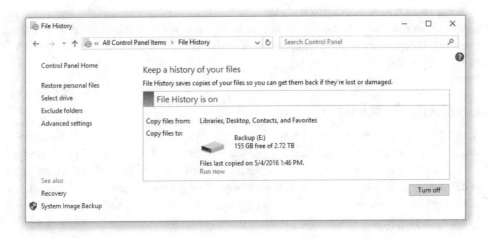

**FIGURE 4.3-3**   File History in Windows 10

Windows 8/8.1/10 all have the *File History* applet (see Figure 4.3-3), where you can enable continuous backup of any personal files in your user account's libraries (both the default libraries and any custom libraries you add) to another storage volume. File History doesn't replace full-system backups, but it does link to the Backup and Restore tool in Windows 8/8.1 and early releases of Windows 10.

# Critical Applications

Obviously, backing up user data is the most important first step in backups, but a great deal of time is also consumed if critical applications must be reinstalled manually after a drive failure or other data-loss scenario takes place.

Image backups back up the operating system and installed applications as well as the current state of user files. For complete protection, consider a two-step backup process:

- Periodic image backup of the entire system (monthly if the OS and apps don't change much)
- File-by-file backups of data files daily to weekly

If an image backup isn't feasible, be prepared to reinstall apps. Have ready license keys, account information or credentials, and app sources (application installers or physical media).

 **EXAM TIP**   Be prepared to identify what's needed to restore critical applications.

What about restore points in Windows? A *restore point* records a snapshot of the operating system, drivers, and app configuration as of the date and time of the restore point. You can use a restore point to recover from a bad software or driver update, but it should be used along with image backups, not in place of them.

## Backup Testing

A data-loss event is highly stressful, but it becomes disastrous if you discover that the backups you've been counting on to "save the day" can't be recovered or don't include the files needed.

The easiest way to test a backup is to use an option to restore the backup to a different folder. This feature is included in most backup apps. To test a backup that stores different versions (such as File History or Time Machine), look for an older version of a file and restore it to a different folder.

 **NOTE**   Perform backup testing regularly to ensure your data is actually being backed up!

## UPS

An *uninterruptible power supply (UPS)* protects your computer from brownouts and blackouts, which can cause data loss in addition to shutting down computers. A UPS (see Figure 4.3-4) has built-in batteries that supply power to your system when the electricity traveling through the power line drops below a certain level. Most UPS devices have an integrated alarm that tells you when your computer is running on battery power. Many techs call a UPS a *battery backup*. Note that a UPS does not provide unlimited power to keep working while the city lights are out; it simply gives you a short window of opportunity to save your data and shut down the system properly.

**FIGURE 4.3-4**   A typical UPS has some battery-backed AC outlets (right two outlets) and some outlets that are surge protected only: use these for printers.

**TABLE 4.3-1**   UPS Battery Backup Types

| UPS Type | How It Works |
|---|---|
| Standby power system (SPS) | An SPS actively monitors the electricity traveling through the power line and begins supplying power as soon as the unit detects a sag. It takes a split second for the SPS to come online, however, and therein lies the main disadvantage. The brief lapse of time can result in data loss or damage before the SPS has kicked in. |
| Online UPS | An online UPS, in contrast to an SPS, acts as a power source to the system, using the electricity from the AC outlet simply to recharge its internal batteries. If an electrical brownout or blackout occurs, your computer doesn't even flinch! As an added bonus, most online UPS boxes act as power conditioners—that is, they regulate the flow of electricity to your computer to even out any fluctuations your power line might experience. An online UPS costs more than an SPS, but in the long run its benefits justify the expense. |
| Line-interactive UPS | A line-interactive UPS is similar to a standby UPS but has special electronic inverter/converter circuitry that can handle moderate AC sags and surges without the need to switch to battery power. This allows for faster response to a power loss than a standby UPS. Due to the circuitry that adapts to undervoltage and overvoltage conditions, a line-interactive UPS may draw more or less electrical current for a device than is normally needed. As a result, when using a line-interactive UPS, be aware of the impact an increase in current consumption might have on any fuses or circuit breakers in the electric supply. |

The different types of UPS are explained in Table 4.3-1.

 **CAUTION**   Don't plug a laser printer into a UPS. Laser printers draw massive amounts of electricity and may interfere with the function of the UPS and prevent your computer equipment from shutting down safely.

# Surge Protector

Surge protectors (also known as surge suppressors) help to absorb power surges so that your computer does not feel their effects (data corruption, lockups, crashes). They come either as separate modules or integrated into the UPS. Good surge protectors come with a long-term or lifetime guarantee against damage to your computer. Avoid purchasing or using cheap surge protectors. These are usually little more than power strips and provide virtually no protection against power surges or spikes.

**EXAM TIP**   The CompTIA A+ 220-1002 exam calls power surges, brownouts, and blackouts *environmental impacts*. Using an appropriate surge suppressor/surge protector and battery backup *applies the appropriate controls* to counter those impacts.

# Cloud Storage vs. Local Storage Backups

Both cloud storage and local storage backups can be used to back up users' data files. Cloud storage offers easier backup than local storage: as long as your device is connected to the Internet and you have synchronization enabled, your backup takes place.

Some cloud storage vendors combine cloud and local backup into a single service so that you can recover data instantly from local backup while having cloud backup provide offsite backup as well.

Cloud storage is the default backup for iOS and Android users. However, the amount of free backup space is limited, and may need to be supplemented by purchasing more space, especially for users with 32-GB or larger-capacity storage devices.

- Cloud storage offers easier backup and a wide variety of capacities. However, restoring all of your files from cloud storage can take weeks.
- Local backups require the purchase of a backup drive and present the risk of backup loss if the backup drive fails. However, restoring files from local backup is very speedy.

**EXAM TIP**   Understand the differences between cloud storage and local storage backups.

# Account Recovery Options

Account recovery has become a new concern with the rise of mobile devices and the increasing use of non-local accounts on laptops and desktops. Here are some typical account recovery options to set up before a device is lost or stolen:

- Set up security questions. In case of a lost password, you might need to provide the answers to several security questions to get access to your account or reset the account to a temporary password. Make sure you choose questions and answers that may be difficult for others to guess. Rule of thumb: If info is posted on social media, it's not safe to use for a question or answer!
- Use your mobile phone as part of two-factor authentication (also known as two-step verification). If you are unable to use your normal authentication process via e-mail or login, having your mobile phone as a second authentication method prevents you from being locked out of your account.

- Have a secondary e-mail address as part of two-factor authentication. If you are unable to use your normal authentication process and if you lose your phone, having a secondary e-mail address can be a lifesaver for your account.
- For local accounts, create a password recovery disk (you can use either a small flash drive or recordable CD).

# REVIEW

**Objective 4.3: Given a scenario, implement basic disaster prevention and recovery methods**   Elements of basic disaster prevention and recovery methods include

- Performing scheduled image- and file-level backups
- Identifying and backing up critical applications
- Testing backups to verify that they are usable
- Using power protection devices such as UPSs and surge protectors
- Using cloud storage and/or local storage backups depending on requirements
- Configuring account recovery options before a device is lost or stolen

# 4.3 QUESTIONS

1. You need to restore a proprietary app that was lost in a system crash. Which type of backup will enable you to restore this information?

   **A.** Time Machine/File History

   **B.** Cloud backup

   **C.** Restore point

   **D.** Image backup

2. Which of the following statements most correctly describes power protection devices and issues?

   **A.** A surge protector provides protection against brownouts.

   **B.** A battery backup does not include surge protection.

   **C.** A battery backup also incorporates surge protection.

   **D.** A power surge is a type of ESD.

3. Which of the following is an example of a bad account recovery option?

   **A.** Using the name of your high school as a security question when you have a complete Facebook profile

   **B.** Using your mobile phone as part of two-factor authentication

   **C.** Using the name of your first-grade teacher as a security question when you don't use social media

   **D.** Having a secondary e-mail address

4. SPS and UPS are examples of which type of solution?

   **A.** Delivery couriers

   **B.** Cloud-based backups

   **C.** Battery backups

   **D.** Image backups

5. You are helping a user running the latest edition of Windows 10 to recover from the loss of archive information stored with the Windows 7 Backup and Restore app. What should you tell the user?

   **A.** You must roll back to an early edition of Windows 10 to restore the backup.

   **B.** You can restore the backup from your current Windows 10 system.

   **C.** You must roll back to Windows 7 to restore the backup.

   **D.** The backup can't be recovered.

## 4.3 ANSWERS

1. **D**   An image backup stores app information as well as the operating system.

2. **C**   Battery backups also include surge protection hardware.

3. **A**   This is a poor choice for a security question because anyone with access to the Facebook account can learn the answer.

4. **C**   Standby power systems and uninterruptible power supplies are terms for battery backups.

5. **B**   All editions of Windows 10 include restore support for Windows 7 Backup and Restore, but backup support was dropped in recent and current editions.

 **Objective 4.4** **Explain common safety procedures**

Safety is of paramount importance when working as an IT tech. You need to protect yourself and others from the dangers of high-voltage equipment, toxic materials, and workplace hazards; and you need to protect valuable equipment from electrostatic discharge (ESD) and other environmental risks. Use this objective to learn the basic safety procedures you need to follow to go home safely after a long day in the IT trenches.

## Equipment Grounding

Any AC-powered equipment that uses a three-prong cable (hot, neutral, ground) needs to be properly grounded. Surge suppression depends on having a working ground as a safe place to send power surges.

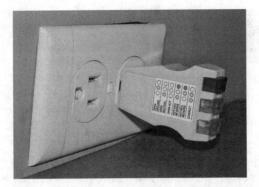

**FIGURE 4.4-1**   A typical AC outlet tester indicating the outlet is wired properly

Unfortunately, some three-wire plugs are improperly wired or have no ground at all. To determine which outlets are working and which have wiring faults, use an outlet tester such as the one shown in Figure 4.4-1. Some surge suppressors also feature wiring fault testing in their circuitry.

# Proper Component Handling and Storage

Even when your computer is not in use, heat, moisture, and dirt are still hazards. Heat causes plastics to fade and become brittle, moisture encourages rust and corrosion, and dirt is, well, *dirty*. For these reasons, components and peripherals should be stored indoors in a climate-controlled environment.

## Antistatic Bags

Antistatic bags have a special coating or contain small filaments that help dissipate any static charge. Always store adapter cards and drives in antistatic bags when they're not in use and when transporting them—even if you're just going down the hall or across the room. Antistatic bags dissipate charge most effectively when they're closed, so it's a good idea to fold the end over and tape it down with an antistatic sticker if possible.

   **EXAM TIP**   The safest way to store any electrical component is in—not on—an antistatic bag.

Do not place components on top of antistatic bags, as charge is directed from the inside of the bag to the outside. Note that regular plastic or paper bags will *not* protect your components. In fact, plastic baggies conduct static electricity rather than preventing it, so don't use them!

**NOTE** Special antistatic sprays dissipate static charges built up in your clothing. Commonly used to prevent unsightly static "cling," they are also good to use before you start working on a computer. Some folks also use these sprays to try to protect their work areas from the effects of ESD, but this is not an effective or recommended procedure. Never use these sprays directly on your components!

## ESD Straps

Electrostatic discharge (ESD) occurs only when two objects that store different amounts (or *potential*) of static electricity come in contact. ESD straps, commonly known as antistatic wrist and ankle straps, avoid ESD by keeping you at the same relative electrical ground level as the computer components on which you're working. An ESD strap consists of a wire that connects on one end to an alligator clip and on the other end to a small metal plate that secures to your wrist (or ankle) with an elastic strap. You snap the alligator clip onto any handy metal part of the computer and place the wrist strap directly on either wrist (not over a shirt sleeve). Figure 4.4-2 shows an antistatic wrist strap grounded to a computer chassis. Others have a prong that you plug into the ground wire of an electrical wall outlet.

**CAUTION** Antistatic wrist (and ankle) straps use a 1-megohm resistor that is suitable for protection against only very low-level static electricity. They are unsuitable as protection against high voltage and can even make high-voltage shocks more dangerous! Make sure you always remove your antistatic strap before you work on or near high-voltage components.

By the way, don't forget to remove your antistatic strap (or at least detach it from the computer) before walking away from your work area!

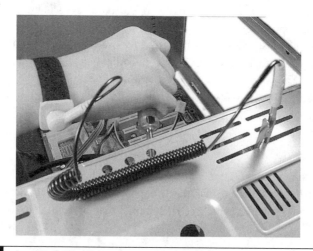

**FIGURE 4.4-2**   An antistatic wrist strap grounded to a computer

## ESD Mats

Portable antistatic mats (see Figure 4.4-3) provide a work surface that dissipates ESD. They have a small metal clip that you can attach to an antistatic strap to ground out ESD. In addition to helping prevent ESD, these mats help keep your work area organized by giving you a place to put your tools and components while you work.

Antistatic floor mats are basically the same as portable antistatic mats, except much larger. Instead of placing them on top of your work area, you place them on the floor and stand on them while you work.

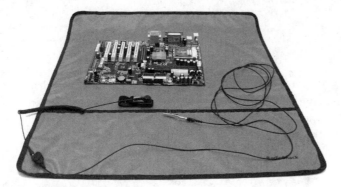

**FIGURE 4.4-3**   A typical ESD kit contains a mat and an ESD bracelet.

## Self-Grounding

One of the most important steps you can take to prevent the effects of ESD is to ground yourself before you handle computer components. Self-grounding is accomplished by touching a metal surface, such as the exterior of the power supply, before touching any of your system components.

## Toxic Waste Handling

Many computer components, such as batteries, CRTs, chemical solvents, and toner kits, contain harmful ingredients. Don't throw these items in the garbage, as this is wasteful, environmentally damaging, and possibly illegal. Recycle, recycle, recycle! If you can't recycle an item, dispose of it properly. We all share the same planet.

 **ADDITIONAL RESOURCES**   Most cities in the United States have one or more *environmental services centers* that you can use to recycle electronic components. For your city, try a Google (or other search engine) search on the term "environmental services" and you'll almost certainly find a convenient place for e-waste disposal. Use these centers to comply with local governmental regulations on disposal.

Different cities and counties have different requirements for safe disposal of materials such as computer components. Always check with the appropriate authorities before tossing that old Pentium 4 on the curb! Proper compliance to local government regulations is essential. Visit your city's official website for more information.

 **EXAM TIP**    Make sure you know the proper disposal procedures for each of the items described in the following sections prior to taking the exam. Check the material safety data sheet (MSDS) documentation (discussed in the next objective) for handling and disposal of any electronic equipment.

## Batteries

Batteries often contain lithium, mercury, nickel-cadmium, and other hazardous materials. If they are thrown in the garbage and carried off to a landfill, they will contaminate the water and soil. Take batteries to a recycling center or send them back to the manufacturer. Most batteries have disposal instructions printed on them (see Figure 4.4-4). Familiarize yourself with these instructions and follow them.

**FIGURE 4.4-4**    Typical warning on the label for a lithium-ion battery

# Toner

You have a couple of options when dealing with depleted toner and inkjet cartridges. You can refill them yourself, which saves on environmental wear, but an improperly refilled cartridge can wreak havoc on your printer. You can also search the Web to see if commercial toner recyclers service your area. Alternatively, many toner cartridge manufacturers have a recycling program. Check with your vendor and see if this is an option for you.

# CRT

Many CRT monitors contain lead and mercury. Both materials are poisonous, so CRTs must be disposed of properly to avoid contamination. To dispose of nonfunctional CRTs, send them to a commercial recycler or contact your city's hazardous waste management department. They will give you the proper procedure for disposing of them. Don't be surprised if recycling of CRTs isn't free—many electronics recyclers charge by the pound.

# Cell Phones and Tablets

Cell phones and tablets, although small, should not be thrown away when they have outlived their usefulness. They might contain mercury from their backlights and have rechargeable batteries. Have them recycled by a certified e-waste disposal firm. If a mobile device is still working and is not too old, it may have some trade-in value. Be sure to wipe all data from phones and tablets before recycling or trading them in.

# Personal Safety

Whoever told you that IT is a "desk job" didn't know very much about the actual work of an IT tech. In the course of a typical day, you might find yourself under a desk wrestling with stubborn wiring, plunging into the guts of a malfunctioning PC, cleaning out a computer that looks like the inside of a wet-dry vacuum, or fighting an electrical fire! Here's how to stay safe at work.

## Disconnect Power Before Repairing PC

In the old days, the conventional thinking was that you should leave the computer plugged in while working inside it, to ensure electrical grounding. The opposite is true for modern computers, because modern motherboards always have a small amount of voltage running any time the system is plugged in, even if it's not running. Therefore, you should completely unplug the system before servicing it or you'll likely toast something!

Unplugging power supplies does not make them safe enough to work on. The capacitors inside can hold a dangerous electrical charge even when the unit is unplugged, making power supplies extremely risky to open. As the label says, "No serviceable components inside." With that in mind, the safest method of repairing power supplies is not to repair them at all. It's better to dispose of them properly and install a brand-new power supply (see Figure 4.4-5).

**FIGURE 4.4-5**    Typical warning on the label for a computer power supply

 **CAUTION**    As electricians will tell you, it's amperage (the amount of electricity) that's dangerous, not voltage. Power supplies have relatively low voltages, but high amperage. It's not worth the risk for you to attempt to service a power supply.

## Remove Jewelry

Rings, bracelets, necklaces, watches, and other metal adornments can short out devices if they touch the wrong part of a computer. They can also scratch (or be scratched) by scraping against the computer's surfaces. Remove jewelry and watches before working on or inside of a computer.

## Lifting Techniques

It seems that everything we use—computers, printers, monitors—comes to us in heavy boxes. Remember never to lift with your back; lift with your legs, and always use a hand truck if available. If the box says "team lift," remember: you are not a team—get some help! You are never paid enough to risk your own health.

## Weight Limitations

Weight limitations also apply to yourself, carts, and other moving equipment. Take a look at the gross weight on a package or look up the weight of an unboxed device. If it's beyond your comfort zone, get help. Pay attention to weight limitations on the devices you use to move anything heavy. Also pay attention to weight limitations when wall-mounting monitors. Even relatively light LCD monitors require a mounting arm strong enough to support them.

## Electrical Fire Safety

Thankfully, the risk of fire occurring inside your computer is relatively low. If, however, you do experience a computer fire, or any electrical fire for that matter, never try to extinguish it with water. This can cause the electrical current to travel up and straight into you! Instead, use a fire extinguisher certified for fighting electrical fires. These are Class C and Class ABC fire extinguishers (see Figure 4.4-6).

**FIGURE 4.4-6**   A typical fire extinguisher. Be sure to read the label before using!

 **EXAM TIP**   You need to use a Class C or Class ABC fire extinguisher to put out a computer fire.

## Cable Management

A disorderly computing environment invites problems, so successful techs keep it neat. People place computers or peripherals in crazy places: on rickety desks, cardboard boxes, and other places where they could easily fall. Arrange your computer and peripherals safely on the floor or on a sturdy desk. Tape or cover cords (using cable raceways or trays) running along the ground or walls (Figure 4.4-7) to avoid people tripping on them or accidentally ripping a computer off a desk. If you see a potential hazard at a work site—even one that's not yours—report it or fix it. You're the expert, so take charge!

**FIGURE 4.4-7**   A cable raceway in use in a small office

If you are responsible for running network cable, make sure that plenum-grade (aka plenum) cable is used when routing cables through airspace such as a suspended ceiling. Plenum cable doesn't produce noxious fumes when burned. Standard network cable, by contrast, has a PVC jacket that burns easily, producing a lot of noxious fumes.

## Safety Goggles

If you need to cut a bit of aluminum to rig up a part for an old PC or use compressed air or a vacuum cleaner to clean out an old PC, put on safety goggles. A tiny shard of metal or bit of dust can ruin your day—and if your eyes are damaged, a lot of upcoming days will also be ruined.

## Air Filter Mask

You need to protect yourself (and your coworkers) from dust and debris when servicing, storing, or disposing of equipment. Everyone in the work area should wear an air filter mask that is designed to handle appropriate environmental risks.

 **EXAM TIP**   Although the CompTIA A+ 220-1002 exam doesn't deal with specific requirements for air filter masks and safety goggles, be aware of the circumstances for which they should be worn.

# Compliance with Government Regulations

Be sure to follow applicable OSHA or other safety regulations when building, repairing, cleaning, or dismantling equipment. These regulations might address issues such as ventilation, protection against dust, cable management, and other issues. Proper compliance with government regulations is essential.

# REVIEW

**Objective 4.4: Explain common safety procedures**   Common safety procedures include

- Equipment grounding
- Proper component handling and storage through the use of antistatic bags, ESD straps, and ESD mats
- Using proper handling and disposal procedures for anything containing toxic waste, such as batteries, toner, CRTs, and mobile devices
- Taking personal safety precautions, which include (among others) disconnecting power before repairing a PC, removing jewelry before working inside a computer case,

using safe lifting techniques, noting weight limitations of moving equipment, using Class C or ABC fire extinguishers for computer equipment fires, practicing good cable management, and wearing safety goggles and an air filter mask when appropriate

- Complying with government regulations regarding occupational health and safety

## 4.4 QUESTIONS

1. An electrical fire has broken out in an old laser printer. Which of the following should be used to put out the fire?

   **A.** Class A fire extinguisher

   **B.** Water

   **C.** Class ABC fire extinguisher

   **D.** Sprinkler system

2. What are two environmental threats found in CRT displays? (Choose two.)

   **A.** Lead

   **B.** Lithium-ion batteries

   **C.** Mercury

   **D.** MSDS

3. Which of the following is not recommended before working on a PC?

   **A.** Disconnecting the power supply from the AC outlet

   **B.** Using an ESD strap

   **C.** Using an ESD mat

   **D.** Spraying antistatic spray on the PC

4. You are walking through a work area where computers and components are being prepared for storage. You notice that a network interface card has been placed on top of an antistatic bag. What should you do?

   **A.** Connect an ESD strap to the bag

   **B.** Move the card to a piece of paper

   **C.** Place the card inside the bag after self-grounding

   **D.** Nothing; it's OK to use an antistatic bag this way

5. A network cable running across the floor of a busy hallway is an example of which of the following:

   **A.** ESD grounding

   **B.** Poor cable management

   **C.** Cable testing

   **D.** A practical joke setup

## 4.4 ANSWERS

1. **C**  An electrical fire is a Class C fire, so a Class ABC fire extinguisher is the best choice.

2. **A C**  Lead and mercury are contained in typical CRTs as well as more recent technology.

3. **D**  Spraying the hardware can damage it.

4. **C**  The ESD bag can only protect a NIC placed inside it.

5. **B**  This is an example of poor cable management, because the cable presents a tripping hazard.

**Objective 4.5** # Explain environmental impacts and appropriate controls

Environmental impacts are the results of any changes in the environment that can affect computer equipment such as heat, humidity, and lightning; or can be caused by servicing, using, or disposing of technology. This objective covers the details of how to have minimal environmental impact when using technology.

## MSDS Documentation for Handling and Disposal

All batteries, chemicals, and other hazardous materials come with a *material safety data sheet (MSDS)* that documents any safety warnings about the product, safe methods of transportation and handling, and safe disposal requirements. If you have any doubts or questions about how to handle or dispose of chemicals or compounds, check the applicable MSDS. If the MSDS for a product or substance is missing, you can obtain a copy from the manufacturer or locate it on the Internet.

**ADDITIONAL RESOURCES**   For more information about MSDSs, go to www.osha.gov and search for "OSHA 3514." To search for a specific MSDS, visit www.msds.com.

## Temperature, Humidity Level Awareness, and Proper Ventilation

Good techs keep up with weather conditions. The temperature and humidity level *outside* can dramatically affect the risk of ESD *inside*. If the weather is cold and dry, the potential for a computer-killing zap is greatly increased. Take extra precautions to prevent ESD when the weather calls for it.

Proper environmental controls help secure servers and workstations from the environmental impact of excessive heat, dust, and humidity. Such environmental controls include air conditioning, proper ventilation, air filtration, and monitors for temperature and humidity. A CompTIA A+ technician maintains an awareness of temperature, humidity level, and ventilation so that he or she can tell very quickly when proper levels or settings are out of whack.

Dust and debris aren't good for any electronic components. Equipment closets filled with racks of servers need proper airflow to keep things cool and to eliminate dusty air. Make sure that the room is ventilated and air-conditioned and that the air filters are changed regularly. This provides protection from airborne particles as well as heat and humidity.

# Power Surges, Brownouts, and Blackouts

Your computer needs power to run properly, but various factors can turn what should be a steady stream of electricity from the wall socket into either a trickle or a fire hose. Power fluctuations can wreak havoc on an unprotected system. Surges and sags can damage power supplies and components and cause file corruption. It's important that you know how to protect your computing environment from electrical power spikes, power sags, and power losses. Related issues that CompTIA doesn't specifically list as environmental impacts—but that might appear on the exam—are lightning strikes and electromagnetic interference, which are discussed separately after the specified impacts.

*Power spikes* or *power surges* occur when the voltage on your power line rises suddenly to above-normal levels. Power spikes are extremely dangerous and can destroy computers, monitors, and any other component plugged into the affected power line.

A *brownout* occurs when the supply of electricity drops dramatically but does not go out completely. During a brownout, you'll notice lights flickering or growing dim. When the power rises back up to its original level, your computer might not be able to handle the drastic change, and damage may occur.

*Blackouts* occur when power goes out completely. The danger of a blackout is twofold. First, you may have data loss or corruption when the power goes out. Second, the power surge when the electricity comes back on may damage your system's electronics.

As you learned in the "UPS" and "Surge Protector" sections in Objective 4.3 of this domain, uninterruptable power supplies (battery backups) are the solution to brownouts, sags, and blackouts, while high-quality surge suppressors (surge protectors) help mitigate the damage that can be caused by power surges. The cost of a good UPS or surge suppressor is nothing compared to the cost in time and money caused by lost components or corrupted files that you may have to endure if you don't use either one.

**EXAM TIP**   You need to know the differences among power surges, brownouts, and blackouts and the devices that help to protect your equipment in each situation: surge suppressors and battery backups such as a UPS.

## Lightning

Lightning storms are an underrated hazard. Leaving a computer plugged in during a lightning storm is asking for trouble. A surge suppressor won't protect your plugged-in computer (or any other electronic device) from the massive electrical discharge of a lightning strike.

## EMI

A magnetic field interfering with electronics is *electromagnetic interference (EMI)*. EMI isn't nearly as dangerous as ESD, but it can cause permanent damage to some components and erase data on some storage devices. Long cable runs tend to pick up EMI, especially if a power cable is running alongside a data cable. You can prevent EMI by keeping magnets away from computer equipment.

EMI can be controlled by using cables with a Mylar coating and through the use of special EMI and RFI noise filters, typically built into better quality surge suppressors, UPS units, or available as stand-alone products. You can also minimize EMI by moving data cables away from power cables and by shortening the cables you use.

# Protection from Airborne Particles

When you use canned air to blast dust and hair from air vents and other openings in a computer or peripheral, you're helping keep the hot air flowing out and cool air flowing in to maintain the appropriate temperature inside the computer or peripheral. This will extend the life of your computer. When you're using canned air, remember the words of Corporal Hicks from the *Aliens* movie, and use "short, controlled bursts." If you haven't dusted the computer or peripheral in a while, take it outside before spraying. Otherwise, you'll spread dust everywhere.

However, you want to prevent the dust, dirt, and grime inside the computer or peripheral from winding up where it doesn't belong—your lungs, nose, and mouth, for example. Here's how.

## Enclosures

Ensuring proper protection from airborne particles encompasses devices and people. Put your electronics into the right enclosures with good air filters. When you're cleaning very dirty equipment, if you have an enclosure with a built-in vacuum, consider using that to catch the dust you shake loose.

## Air Filters/Mask

When shopping for air filters/masks, be sure to look for masks and air filters with appropriate ratings. Masks with N95 ratings are designed to filter out 95 percent of particles of at least 0.3 microns in size (N97 = 97 percent, N100 = 100 percent). Note that most dust particles that you might encounter in technology or buildings (such as copier toner, fiberglass, sawdust, asbestos) have particle sizes in excess of 0.3 microns. N-series masks do not provide any protection against oil, however.

**ADDITIONAL RESOURCES** To learn more about dust masks and for a list of common particulate sizes, go to www.envirosafetyproducts.com and search for "Dust Masks, What's in a Rating."

# Dust and Debris

Dust and debris are bad news for electronic components. Ideally, you'd like to stop dust and debris from getting into systems because they can clog air intakes and air exhausts, cause overheating, and in some cases, "kill" a system.

## Compressed Air

You can use canned air to loosen dirt and dust from delicate components. Canned air comes in a couple of forms: the liquid propellant kind and the kind that uses small cartridges of compressed $CO_2$. You can find both at computer stores, office supply stores, camera shops, and big-box stores that sell electronics (see Figure 4.5-1).

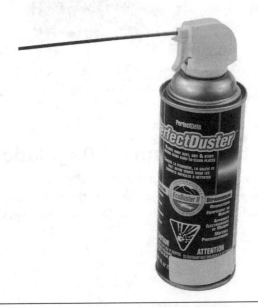

**FIGURE 4.5-1** Typical canned air with extension tube attached

Follow three rules when using canned air:

- Never breathe this stuff in. It's not *that* kind of air, and inhaling it can, quite literally, kill you!
- With regard to the liquid propellant type of canned air, always keep the can upright. Tilting or turning the can upside down causes the liquid inside to come squirting out. This liquid can cause frostbite to the tech and irreparable damage to any computer components that it touches.
- Don't shake canned air cans. They don't need to be shaken to work, and you run a small but real risk of the can exploding in your hand.

## Vacuums

Small, hand-held vacuums designed specifically for use on electronics (such as shown in Figure 4.5-2) suck up dirt and dust loosened by a brush or canned air. Note that you should definitely *not* use a common household vacuum cleaner. These create static electricity and can toast your computer! Some computer vacuums can also act as blowers. Some stand-alone blower products go by names such as "electric dusters." They can be used as alternatives to canned air and do not create condensation or contain harmful liquid propellants.

**FIGURE 4.5-2**    A non-static vacuum

# Compliance to Government Regulations

Whether you are disposing of unwanted equipment or supplies or cleaning equipment, follow the rules! Specifically, use cleaners that are approved for the job and follow government regulations for ventilation, filters, air masks, and the like. Don't let a visit from OSHA or the EPA ruin your day.

# REVIEW

**Objective 4.5: Explain environmental impacts and appropriate controls**    To control environmental impacts, understand the following methods:

- Consulting MSDS documentation for proper handling and disposal of chemicals and other substances
- Maintaining temperature and humidity level awareness and proper ventilation to avoid ESD, equipment overheating, and other issues
- Protecting computer equipment from the dangers of power surges, brownouts, and blackouts by using battery backups and surge suppressors
- Protecting people and equipment from airborne particles by using enclosures, air filters, and air masks
- Protecting computer equipment from dust and debris by using compressed air and an electronics vacuum
- Complying with government regulations regarding environmental issues

## 4.5 QUESTIONS

1. You are helping to clean out an office that has a chemical you are unfamiliar with stored in a closet. Which of the following is most useful in determining safe disposal and handling procedures?

    **A.** Government regulations

    **B.** MSDS

    **C.** Product labeling

    **D.** Guesswork

2. As a member of the environmental controls team, you are helping to set up an unfinished building as a hot site for IT use in case of a disaster affecting the primary IT location. Which of the following does not fit into your team's responsibilities?

    **A.** Networking

    **B.** Ventilation

    **C.** Air filtration

    **D.** Temperature monitoring

3. A client is reporting problems with her computer. Using a multimeter, you determine that the electricity available at the client site is about 87-V AC (the standard for the location is 115-V AC). Which of the following conditions most accurately describes the electrical problem?

    **A.** Power surge

    **B.** Blackout

    **C.** Brownout

    **D.** EMI

4. While working on a motherboard with an overheating processor, you decide to clean the fan and heat sink on top of the CPU. Which of the following should you do while using canned air for this job?

   A. Shake the can before using

   B. Turn the can to get a better angle

   C. Sniff the air coming from the can

   D. Keep the can upright

5. You are considering whether to remove components from a working PC on a day that is cold and very dry. You feel a spark when you touch the doorknob to go into the workroom. Which of the following would be the best move to make?

   A. Wait for a day with more humidity

   B. Keep touching metal as you move around the room

   C. Use an ESD mat

   D. Use an ESD wrist strap

## 4.5 ANSWERS

1. **B**   The material safety data sheet (MSDS) for the chemical has the most information about proper handling and disposal procedures.

2. **A**   Networking is not an environmental control issue.

3. **C**   Low electrical voltage is considered a brownout.

4. **D**   Keeping the can upright is the only recommended procedure of the ones listed.

5. **A**   Because the choice of when to remove equipment is up to you, waiting for a day with more humidity (and thus less risk of ESD) is the best option.

**Objective 4.6** **Explain the processes for addressing prohibited content/activity, and privacy, licensing, and policy concepts**

Sooner or later, you'll probably come face-to-face with a user who is misusing their computer or network access. Maybe they're storing pornography or running a BitTorrent server, or cranking out posters of their children's favorite bands on the company color printer. In this objective, you learn how to deal with prohibited content or activity. And, you also learn about privacy, licensing, and policy concepts that can help to keep users and companies out of trouble.

# Incident Response

The incident response process is a series of guidelines that help you properly deal with prohibited content or activity.

 **EXAM TIP**  Be able to explain the incident response process.

# First Response

As a tech, you'll need to deal with people who use company computers in prohibited ways. Because you're not a police officer, in most you cases you should not get involved, but if you encounter something bad—really bad—on a system or device you support, everyone may turn to you for action if you're the first tech person on the scene. For the most part, avoid reading any personal information, whether confidential or not, on a user's computer or device—but if you identify an obvious felony or dangerous behavior in the course of your job duties, you've just become the first line of defense and need to act accordingly.

Depending on the type of incident, you might detect it yourself by examining log files, by servicing a computer, or by listening to talk around the office coffee maker. No matter how you determine there's a problem, the incident response process needs to start right away.

## Identify

When confronted with a potential incident, you need to determine if it's really an incident. Use common sense, but keep in mind that most organizations have an Acceptable Use Policy (AUP) that employees must read and sign that defines what actions employees may or may not perform on company equipment. Remember that these polices aren't just for obvious issues such as using a computer for personal use. These policies cover use of computers, phones, printers, and even the network itself. The AUP will define the handling of passwords, e-mail, and many other issues.

## Report Through Proper Channels

You report violations through the proper channels: directly to a security officer or *incident response leader* if your organization has one, and to your supervisor otherwise. Do *not* speak to the person making the infraction unless your supervisor approves it.

## Data/Device Preservation

To prevent changes to a system after a violation has been detected, you must isolate the system: take it off the network and store it in a secure location.

## Use of Documentation/Documentation Changes

When an incident is detected or reported, be sure to document the relevant facts, such as

- What account was used?
- What devices were used?
- What software was used?
- What types of content were discovered?
- When did the violation take place?

# Chain of Custody

The chain of custody depends, in part, upon careful documentation of the computer's location before the violation was detected, who had access to it after the violation was detected, and what steps were taken to isolate it.

A device's data must be preserved in case it becomes evidence, so the device's location and who has touched it needs to be recorded to prove the data hasn't been tampered with; you need to establish a *chain of custody* documenting this history. You should have a legal expert to guide you, but the following are fairly common rules:

1. Isolate the system. Shut down the system and store it in a place where no one else can access it.

2. Document when you took control of the system and the actions you took: shutting it down, unplugging it, moving it, and so on. Don't worry about too much detail, but you must track its location.

3. If another person takes control of the system, document the transfer of custody.

## Tracking of Evidence/Documenting Process

Record information that indicates the illegal or unauthorized use of the computer or device. Some clues to look for include

- Dates of illegal files
- Event logs
- Dates unauthorized software was installed or updated
- Browser cache
- Recently visited IP addresses
- Dates of and contents of deleted files
- Print server logs
- Proxy server logs

**ADDITIONAL RESOURCES**   Special forensic software and hardware can be used to examine a computer without changing its contents. This software can make a byte-by-byte copy of the hard drive's contents for analysis. To learn more about forensic software tools, see https://resources.infosecinstitute.com and search for "Computer Forensics."

# Licensing/DRM/EULA

Software compliance is simple enough if you have an explicit list of allowed software and strict controls on who can install programs, but less restrictive regimes require more effort to stay in compliance with software licenses.

**EXAM TIP**   Noncompliant systems are also at increased risk of malware infections or other vulnerabilities introduced by the unapproved software.

Like other creative acts worthy of copyright protection, software developers are granted copyright to software they create, enabling them to decide how or if others can obtain a license to use the software. The licensing can be commercial or noncommercial, personal or enterprise. The software can be closed source or open source. You have a legal obligation to use the software in compliance with its license, which typically entails the following:

- Paying money for software released under a *commercial license* and complying with terms that indicate whether the license supports personal or private use.

- Complying with any *End User License Agreement (EULA)* you agree to when you open or install software, which typically specifies how you may use the software and whether you may share it. If the software uses *digital rights management (DRM)* techniques to protect the application or its files, the EULA typically forbids you from breaking, reverse-engineering, or removing these protections (or helping anyone else do so).

- Observing stipulations in noncommercial software licenses that specify whether the software is free for all uses, free only for personal/educational use, or requires a special commercial license for commercial use.

- Complying with additional stipulations in *open-source software* licenses that specify how you may use the source code. These licenses commonly give you the right to modify the source, but may require you to release your modifications for free as well.

## Open-Source vs. Commercial License

Generally, Windows, iOS, and macOS operating systems and apps are closed-source software and require a commercial license. Android and Linux, by contrast, are open-source operating systems. Although most Android apps are closed source and require a commercial license, Linux apps are typically open source and free to use.

 **NOTE**    The "open-source vs. commercial license" distinction of this objective is not always clear in the real world. There are plenty of open-source programs with licensing fees, such as server versions of Linux. Many "free" programs are likewise closed source.

Observe stipulations in *closed-source software* licenses regarding whether you may modify the software and whether you may include it in or distribute it with one of your own products.

## Personal License vs. Enterprise Licenses

Software that is licensed to an individual for a single computer cannot be used on multiple computers: it's a violation of the license agreement. Enterprise licenses may (depending on the specific license agreement) permit individuals to use company-licensed software on their personal systems.

Given the high potential penalties for pirated software, it just makes sense to make sure that users understand what the license on a particular program permits and use it per that agreement.

# Regulated Data

Larger organizations, such as government entities, benefit greatly from organizing their data according to its sensitivity and minimizing surprises by keeping computer hardware and software as uniform as possible. This also helps maintain *compliance* with government and internal regulations; common examples are rules regarding approved software and regulations on how you must handle *personally identifiable information (PII)* such as health or academic records.

A common *data classification* scheme that flags documents as public, internal use only, highly confidential, top secret, and so on, helps employees (including techs) know what to do with documents and hardware containing them (such as using different rules to recycle hard drives that hold top secret data). Your strategy for recycling a computer system no longer being used, for example, will differ a lot if the data on the drive is classified as internal use only or top secret.

Table 4.6-1 identifies different types of regulated data.

| TABLE 4.6-1 | Types of Regulated Data |

| Regulated Data Type | Meaning | Notes |
| --- | --- | --- |
| PII | Personally identifiable information | Sensitive PII refers to information that can specifically identify a person, such as full name, Social Security number, and so on. CompTIA refers to this simply as PII.<br><br>Search for "Personally Identifiable Information (PII)" at www.investopedia.com for more information. |
| PCI | Payment Card Industry | PCI is an industry that has a specific Data Security Standard (PCI DSS) that applies to all organizations that accept payment cards and requires protection of PII and other security measures. To learn more about PCI DSS, see www.pcicomplianceguide.org. |
| GDPR | General Data Protection Regulation | GDPR is the European Union (EU) standard for data protection; it applies to any organization that handles the PII of EU citizens, regardless of the organization's geographic location. It took effect in May 2018 and regulates handling of PII, browser cookie use disclosures, and other types of personal data. See the www.csoonline.com article "General Data Protection Regulation (GDPR): What You Need to Know to Stay Compliant" for more information. |
| PHI | Protected health information | Also known as "personal health information," PHI includes data such as patient demographics, test and lab results, insurance information, and so on. PHI is regulated under the Health Insurance Portability and Accountability Act (HIPAA). PHI is not the same as PII. To learn more, go to https://searchhealthit.techtarget.com and search for "protected health information." |

**EXAM TIP** Be sure you can distinguish between PHI and PII, as you might see a question pertaining to these.

# Follow All Policies and Security Best Practices

As you can see from Table 4.6-1, different industries must protect different types of information about their clients. The one key to follow consistently is this: whatever the regulations are in your industry, follow them—and maintain the specific security best practices for that industry.

# REVIEW

**Objective 4.6: Explain the processes for addressing prohibited content/activity, and privacy, licensing, and policy concepts** The incident reporting process includes the following steps:

- First response—Identifying whether an incident has occurred and, if so, reporting it through proper channels and securing any data or devices related to the incident
- Use of documentation/documentation changes—Documenting the details about the incident (where, when, equipment, account, and so on)
- Chain of custody—Tracking what happens to a system after an incident is reported, including the evidence/documenting process: looking for clues without affecting the system's contents

Licensing issues include

- Understanding the details of a specific program's licensing agreement
- Understanding the differences between open-source, closed-source, and commercial licenses and the differences between personal and enterprise licenses

Be prepared to identify the following types of regulated data and how they are regulated:

- PII (personally identifiable information)
- PCI DSS (Payment Card Industry Data Security Standard)
- GDPR (General Data Protection Regulation that applies to any organization that handles PII of EU citizens)
- PHI (protected health information regulated by HIPAA)

Make sure you follow all policies and security best practices.

## 4.6 QUESTIONS

1. You are evaluating a program's source code to see if it can be modified for your company's needs. The program is free for personal use but must be licensed with a fee for company use. Which of the following phrases best describes its company licensing arrangement?

    **A.** Free open source

    **B.** Closed source

    **C.** Commercial open source

    **D.** Noncommercial

2. You are attempting to determine if an incident involving company IT resources qualifies as a violation. Which of the following should you consult?

   **A.** PII

   **B.** AUP

   **C.** HIPAA

   **D.** GDPR

3. You are attempting to determine if illegal websites were accessed by an employee. Which of the following would be the most useful source to discover this information?

   **A.** Browser cache

   **B.** Event logs

   **C.** Print server logs

   **D.** Windows installation logs

4. Which of the following is an example of PII?

   **A.** ZIP code

   **B.** Phone number

   **C.** Gender

   **D.** Citizenship

5. A U.S.-based healthcare company has operations in the UK and France. It accepts credit and debit card payments. Which of the following types of regulated data must it protect?

   **A.** PHI

   **B.** GDPR

   **C.** PCI DSS

   **D.** All of the above

# 4.6 ANSWERS

1. **C**   The software has a licensing fee (making it commercial), but the source code can be modified (open source).

2. **B**   The Acceptable Use Policy is an organization's guide to unacceptable IT resource use.

3. **A**   The browser cache should be checked. Although it can be deleted, it can be recovered to see which websites were visited.

4. **B**   A phone number is PII because it can be used to identify an individual.

5. **D**   The company is involved in health care (PHI), has business dealings in the UK and France (GDPR), and handles payment cards (PCI DSS).

 **Objective 4.7** # Given a scenario, use proper communication techniques and professionalism

Y ou will encounter all sorts of people as a tech. Emotions will run from anger, to fear, to frustration. You'll find bluster, smiles, patience, impatience, and much more. Treat the customer with respect. This objective helps you focus on the specifics to make that happen.

> **EXAM TIP**   Don't underestimate the importance of this objective! Given a scenario on the exam, be ready to use proper communication and professionalism skills.

## Communication Techniques

Knowing how to communicate with customers is a key "soft skill" for anyone who works with the public. For IT workers in particular, communicating with customers is vital to solving their problems and developing a good long-term professional relationship. Here are some tips to help you achieve these goals.

### Use Proper Language and Avoid Jargon, Acronyms, and Slang, When Applicable

We live in a vulgar and informal age, but that's no excuse for sounding like you've overdosed on reality programs when you are speaking with your customers. Slang is out, and proper language is in.

You're the technology expert, but if you don't avoid jargon and acronyms when speaking with your customers, you'll sound like an arrogant jerk, not an expert, and your customers won't understand your tech speak. Make sure you understand technology well enough to translate it into ordinary language—if you don't, you're not as knowledgeable as you think you are. Practice effective communication. The best techs know both technology and how to talk with users.

### Maintain a Positive Attitude/Project Confidence

Maintain a positive attitude when dealing with a difficult customer or situation. Project confidence that you can solve the problem efficiently and get the user back to work. Don't argue with the customer or get defensive if he or she implies that the computer problem is somehow your fault. It happens!

## Actively Listen (Taking Notes) and Avoid Interrupting the Customer

Effective communication in "computerese" requires active listening to get to the heart of the problem, which in turn calls for the proper use of language. You know and speak tech. Chances are that your customer doesn't. Getting through this language barrier is essential for solving problems.

Actively listening means focusing your attention on the customer's words. They might not make sense at first, so take notes. The customer might say something like, "I was working away, but a clock started ticking inside the CPU, then my screen went blue and I can't get the computer to start at all." Oy! Don't interrupt the customer. Let him or her tell you the story. Because you wrote it down, you likely can interpret the non-technical language into something that potentially makes sense.

Many users call the case or system unit a CPU. A ticking sound inside a case often points to a dying hard drive. A blue screen is a classic sign of a non-maskable interrupt (NMI), better known as the Blue Screen of Death (a term you don't want to use in front of a customer, by the way!) in Windows (see Figure 4.7-1). The user's hard drive might have just died. If the user has burned his hand on the case, that could point to an overheating issue that caused the problem—and potentially a lot more than just a dying drive.

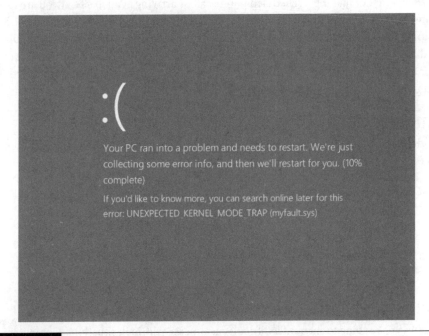

:(

Your PC ran into a problem and needs to restart. We're just collecting some error info, and then we'll restart for you. (10% complete)

If you'd like to know more, you can search online later for this error: UNEXPECTED_KERNEL_MODE_TRAP (myfault.sys)

**FIGURE 4.7-1**   The Blue Screen of Death (BSoD) in Windows 10

## Be Culturally Sensitive

With a diverse population needing help from tech experts like you, you need to deal graciously with cultural differences. If a customer's religious holiday conflicts with your work schedule, the customer wins. If the customer wants you to take off your shoes, take them off. If the customer wants you to wear a hat, wear one. If a person's title happens to be in a language you don't speak, figure out how to say it before arriving on the scene. That's what Google Translate is for! Be culturally sensitive. Always use the appropriate title, personal or professional. Never assume that using a customer's first name establishes rapport. In fact, you shouldn't use a customer's first name unless the customer requests that you do so.

# Professionalism

Professionalism is a way to describe someone who is in control of an unexpected situation. From traffic jams to customer frustrations, you are likely to encounter less-than-ideal situations. Here are some ways to defuse potential trouble spots so you can solve customer problems.

## Be on Time (if Late, Contact the Customer)

*Be on time*, whether making a scheduled phone call or arriving at a job site. If you are driving, plan ahead to ensure you know the route to the customer's premises, and build in extra time for traffic congestion or other unforeseen issues. If you are running late, contact the customer immediately, apologize, and provide an estimated time of arrival. We live in the future: call, text, or alert your dispatcher to notify the customer. This is more than common courtesy; it's an essential skill for the professional tech.

## Avoid Distractions

Avoid distractions that take your focus away from the user and addressing his or her computer problem.

- Don't take a personal call when interacting with a customer.
- Don't text or tweet or respond to messages on other social media sites.
- Don't chat with coworkers; keep your focus on interacting with the customer.
- Avoid any kind of personal interruption that doesn't deal directly with fixing the computer; it will only irritate the customer.

## Dealing with Difficult Customers or Situations

Inevitably, you're going to encounter difficult customers in difficult situations. Computer issues tend to cause stress, and some people become difficult to deal with when they are stressed out. As a professional tech, you need to know how to defuse the tension and get the job done.

**Do Not Argue with Customers and/or be Defensive**   You want to fix the customer's problem—and the customer really wants it fixed. You have the same goal. Don't argue or be defensive. Assure the customer that you're here to help—and be helpful!

**Avoid Dismissing Customer Problems**   What might be an easy, five-minute fix to you might be the potential "end of the world" for the customer. Don't dismiss their problems, no matter how many times you've seen a similar problem before. Remember, this one might be different!

**Avoid Being Judgmental**   Customers would fix their problems themselves if they knew how. They don't—and that's why they call you. If you discover that a customer caused the problem, don't be judgmental about how the device was damaged or files were deleted. Keep an even, nonaccusatory tone. You've probably made a few mistakes in your professional life too. Fix the problem and be thankful the customer called you—and not somebody else—for help. It's good job security.

**Clarify Customer Statements (Ask Open-Ended Questions to Narrow the Scope of the Problem, Restate the Issue, or Question to Verify Understanding)**   Customers with technology problems are likely to be long on fear and frustration and short on clarity when you first talk to them. So, it's up to you to clarify customer statements. Ask open-ended questions, such as "What other strange or unusual things about the computer have you noticed recently?" A "nothing, really" response from the customer has a wildly different meaning than "I burned my hand on the CPU a couple of days ago." Open-ended questions help narrow the scope of the problem.

Also, *restate the issue or question to verify your understanding*, but use proper, simple language. Avoid jargon and acronyms. Definitely skip the silly computer guy slang, like calling a Windows PC "the comp" or a motherboard a "mobo." That stuff just makes customers defensive. Once you think you understand both the scope and nature of the problem, go back to your notes and you might find a good explanation.

**Do Not Disclose Experiences via Social Media Outlets**   After you finish a job (or even during one in progress), never share any "funny" stories about the customer or the activities around you. Certainly share professional and technical details with coworkers and any personal issues with your supervisor, but definitely *do not disclose experiences via social media outlets* such as Facebook and Instagram. Someone knows someone without fail, and your words will come back to haunt you.

## Set and Meet Expectations/Timeline and Communicate Status with the Customer

*Expectations management* means to give a customer as accurate an estimate as possible regarding how long it will take you to fix the computer problem. Plus, it means providing status updates if you expect to finish more quickly than your initial estimate or if things seem to be taking longer than first predicted. Also, many times with a computer issue, you can fix the problem and avoid a similar problem in the future in several ways. These options boil down to money.

**Offer Different Repair/Replacement Options, if Applicable**   If applicable, offer different repair/replacement options and let the customer decide which route to take.

**Provide Proper Documentation on the Services Provided**   At the completion of work, provide proper documentation of the services provided. Describe the problem, include the time and day you started work and completed work and the number of hours you worked, provide a list of parts you replaced, if applicable, and describe the solution.

**Follow up with Customer/User at a Later Date to Verify Satisfaction**   Follow up with a customer/user at a later date to verify satisfaction. This can be a simple follow-up, usually just a phone call, to confirm that the customer is happy with your work.

## Deal Appropriately with Customers' Confidential and Private Materials (Including Those on Computers, Desktop, Printers, etc.)

You have a lot of power as a tech at someone else's computer. You can readily access files, browsing history, downloads, and more. Don't do it! You need to deal appropriately with customers' confidential and private materials. This includes files on the computer, items on a physical desktop, and even pages sitting in a printer tray. If you are caught violating a customer's privacy, you not only will lose credibility and respect, but you could also lose your job.

# REVIEW

**Objective 4.7: Given a scenario, use proper communication techniques and professionalism**   The keys to effective communications with customers include

- Using proper language
- Avoiding jargon, acronyms, and slang
- Maintaining a positive attitude and projecting confidence
- Actively listening, taking notes, and avoid interrupting the customer
- Being culturally sensitive, including using professional titles when appropriate

Maintaining professionalism as an IT tech at all times requires

- Being on time or contacting the customer before you're late
- Avoiding distractions such as personal calls, texting, social media sites, talking to coworkers while interacting with customers, and personal interruptions

- Dealing with difficult customers or situations by following these practices:
  - Don't argue or be defensive
  - Avoid dismissing customer problems
  - Avoid being judgmental
  - Clarify customer statements by asking open-ended questions
  - Don't disclose experiences on social media
- Setting and meeting (or exceeding) expectations/timeline and communicating status with the customer, including
  - Offering different repair/replacement options when applicable
  - Providing proper documentation on the services provided
  - Following up to verify satisfaction
- Dealing appropriately with confidential and private materials, including print jobs, material on desktops, data on computers, and so on

## 4.7 QUESTIONS

1. You allowed plenty of time to reach your destination, but a massive traffic jam caused by a couple of accidents has disrupted your schedule. You will be late to your next appointment. What should you do?

   **A.** Don't worry about it. The customer listens to traffic reports every ten minutes and will know why you're late.

   **B.** Abandon your vehicle and call a taxi to pick you up from the service drive.

   **C.** Call your supervisor and ask her to call the customer.

   **D.** Call the customer yourself and explain the situation, apologizing for being late.

2. You open the customer's computer, a four-year-old system running a Core i3 that is no longer being produced, only to find that smoke is coming from the motherboard. What should you do?

   **A.** Quote the customer a price for replacing the entire computer

   **B.** Offer the customer the option to repair or replace the system

   **C.** Find out if a similar motherboard is available and order it

   **D.** Try to replace the burnt chip

3. You are planning a date with your spouse and haven't heard back about what time you are meeting. You get a text message while you are discussing repair options with your client. What should you do?

   **A.** Check the message while trying to conceal the phone from your client

   **B.** Ask your client if you can excuse yourself while you view the message

   **C.** Check the message after the meeting with the client is over

   **D.** Tell your client you can't stay late because you're going out to dinner that night

4. You have just heard another technician's phone conversation with a client. It went like this: "Dude, your mobo is shot and your distro is dead! Your burner is burned up. Howzabout I get you a deal on a sweet little laptop! Is that OK, Doc?" Which of the following did you hear? (Choose all that apply.)

   **A.** Use of slang

   **B.** Use of jargon

   **C.** Proper use of titles

   **D.** Customer offered options to repair or replace computer

5. You have just completed a diagnostic test on your client's computer, identified a defective memory module, replaced it, and removed three of the most dangerous current malware threats. You now need to provide documentation on the services you provided. Which of the following best describes the work you did?

   **A.** Fixed your PC

   **B.** Broke RAM, replaced with good RAM

   **C.** Turned your frown upside down

   **D.** Diagnostics, defective memory replaced, malware removed

## 4.7 ANSWERS

1. **D** Always call the customer yourself if you're going to be late. If you don't have the right contact information, get it from your supervisor.

2. **B** Even if you think it's cheaper to replace the computer, offer a repair option. For example, some older systems must be maintained because of compatibility issues with newer hardware or operating systems.

3. **C** The message can wait. If necessary, excuse yourself after the meeting and head to the restroom to read it.

4. **A B** Slang and jargon abounded, not good communication techniques!

5. **D** This represents a professional, accurate, concise description of services rendered.

 **Objective 4.8** **Identify the basics of scripting**

A *script* is a small program used to help automate computing tasks. Scripts are written in a text editor and executed from a command prompt. Scripting, which is a kind of programming, has the power to make complex or repetitive data manipulation and machine configuration easier. For purposes of the CompTIA A+ 220-1002 exam, you don't need to be a scripting expert, but you do need to be able to identify the basic scripting concepts covered in this objective.

# Script File Types

Scripts are stored as text files using the extensions discussed in the following sections. Because they are stored as text files, scripts can be created using a text editor such as Notepad. However, some scripting languages include some type of integrated development environment (IDE) or integrated scripting environment (ISE) that can be used to edit and run scripts.

## .bat

The .bat file extension is used by the simple scripting language originally developed for MS-DOS and still used from the command prompt in Windows. In addition to running commands in sequence, a .bat file (also known as a batch file) can also display each command as it runs (using echo) and include remarks that explain the purpose of the file (using REM).

Use Notepad or a word-processing program that can save files as plain-text files to edit a .bat file. There are no restrictions on .bat files, so a potentially harmful .bat file can be run without being blocked by Windows. Be sure to view the contents of an unfamiliar .bat file before running it.

This simple batch file creates a list of subfolders of C: drive's root directory (folder) after pausing and redirects the output to a text file:

```
@echo off
REM preceding line prevents commands from being echoed to display
REM A statement preceded by REM is a remark statement that can be used to explain a
step
REM Create this file in your default Documents folder and change to that folder to
run it
echo This batch file will create a sorted list of your system drive's root folder's
folders
pause
REM The pause statement makes the batch file wait until you press a key to continue
REM The following 3 lines explain the command that is used to create the list
REM dir C:\ Displays the contents of the root folder (directory) of C: drive
REM /AD Lists folders (directories) only; /ON Sorts folders by name
REM >folders.txt Redirects output that normally goes to the screen to a file called
folders.txt
dir C:\ /AD /ON>folders.txt
pause
REM Following opens the file in Notepad
notepad folders.txt
```

Figure 4.8-1 is a typical example of the folders.txt file being opened in Notepad.

## .ps1

The .ps1 file extension is used by PowerShell scripts. PowerShell is an object-oriented scripting language built into Windows 7 and later. Windows 10 can be configured to use PowerShell instead of cmd.exe as its default command interpreter. You can also run PowerShell from within its ISE (integrated scripting environment).

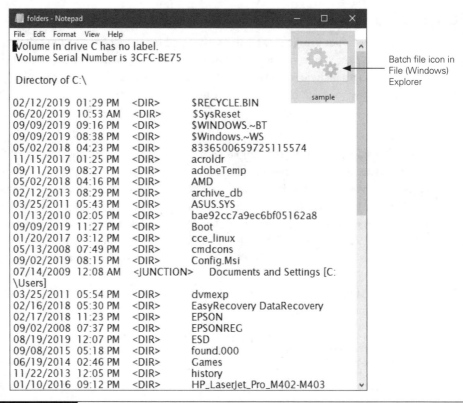

Batch file icon in File (Windows) Explorer

**FIGURE 4.8-1** Notepad viewing the directory list file created by sample.bat

PowerShell includes support for variables, looping, cmdlets (small .NET-based apps), and consistent syntax using a verb-noun command structure. To make transition easier to PowerShell, it supports aliases. Users can enter commands from cmd.exe or a Linux terminal and PowerShell will run its matching command.

**ADDITIONAL RESOURCES** An open-source version called PowerShell Core is available for macOS and for Ubuntu and CentOS Linux distributions. Learn more about PowerShell at https://docs.microsoft.com.

The following script displays the aliases for various cmd.exe commands, counts the number of cmdlets available on the author's computer, displays the number of cmdlets available, and displays Windows version and hardware information obtained with the command-line systeminfo program.

```
Get-Alias cls
Get-Alias chdir
Get-Alias dir
```

```
Get-Alias ls
Get-Alias write
(get-command).count
$numberofcmdlets=(get-command).count
Write-Host "The number of cmdlets on Mark's computer is $numberofcmdlets"
systeminfo /fo csv | ConvertFrom-Csv | select OS*, System*, Processor*, Hot-
fix* | Format-List
```

## .vbs

The .vbs file extension is used for Visual Basic Script, also known as VBScript. This is a Microsoft scripting language derived from Visual Basic. The macro functions of Microsoft Excel and other Office apps with macro support refer to it as Visual Basic for Applications (these use the .vba file extension). VBScript can also be run outside of Microsoft Office by using Windows Script Host, and it supports HTML applications such as Internet Explorer and Microsoft IIS. You can use Notepad or another plain-text editor to create VBScript files.

Here's a simple VBScript that adds the total of the numbers from 1 to 34 and displays the answer in a GUI message box. After you close the first message box, the script multiplies the result by 2.3 and displays the answer in another GUI message box.

```
' Comment - DIM declares a variable
Dim N
' Sets value of N to 0
N = 0
' For/Next loop
For i = 1 to 34
   N = N + i
Next
' Msgbox displays text and variables in a GUI box.
' Click OK to close the box and continue.
Msgbox "Sum from 1 to 34 = " & N
Msgbox "N x 2.3 = " & N * 2.5
```

Alternatively, you can use document.write (as in JavaScript, covered a bit later) to display the messages in a normal display.

Figure 4.8-2 illustrates the output from this script along with the icon used by File Explorer for Visual Basic Script files.

If you incorporate VBScript into HTML (supported by Internet Explorer 11 and earlier versions), be sure to place the following at the beginning of the script:

```
<script language = "vbscript" type = "text/vbscript">
```

Place this at the end of the script:

```
</script>
```

## .sh

The .sh file extension is used for Bash shell files, a type of executable file used originally on UNIX systems and now used on Linux or macOS in Terminal mode.

VBScript icon                    Second output window

**FIGURE 4.8-2**    VBScript file as shown in File Explorer and second output window

 **EXAM TIP**    Bash scripts use echo to print text to the screen and use $ as part of variable names for both text and numeric variables.

Bash files require execute permission to run. The easiest way to gain access to run a .sh file is to use the sudo command (sudo enables the current user to run as root, or superuser) in front of the bash command:

```
sudo bash script.sh
```

 **EXAM TIP**    As with any sudo command, the user is prompted to type their password before continuing.

Here's a simple .sh script that includes a statement that prints text onscreen using echo, gets the user's name, uses comments (#), and performs math:

```
#!/bin/bash
echo "Enter your name"
read name
echo "$name is running a Bash script!"
echo "Now let's add 120 and 87"
# Addition command
((sum=120+87))
# The next line displays the result
echo $sum
```

Bash Script file as shown
in Ubuntu file manager

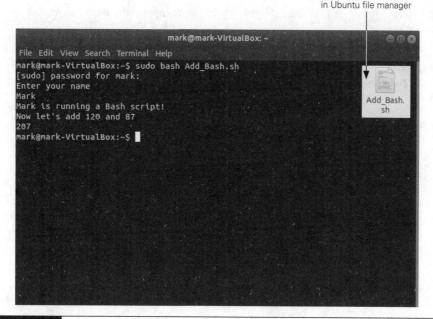

FIGURE 4.8-3 | Terminal window in Ubuntu Linux running Add_Bash.sh as superuser

**CAUTION** Linux, UNIX, and macOS consider uppercase and lowercase filenames and commands to be different. So, if you use the wrong case in a script or when referring to a filename, you will see an error.

Figure 4.8-3 illustrates the output from this file as displayed in Ubuntu Linux's terminal.

## .py

A .py extension is used for Python scripts. Python is a versatile programming language that is included in macOS and most Linux distros. The current version is Python 3, although Python 2 is still in wide use. Python versions are available for Windows as well as macOS and Linux.

If you are not using a system with Python already installed, you can download the Python IDLE (which combines a text editor with a Python interpreter) from the Python.org website. You can also run Python in your browser at various websites such as Code Academy (www.codeacademy.com) or Code the Blocks (https://codetheblocks.com).

**EXAM TIP** Python scripts include simple variable statements (n = 5) and # at the start of each comment.

Here's a simple .py script that includes a statement that prints text onscreen, gets the user's name, inserts comments (#), and performs math. Compare it to the Bash (.sh) script shown in the previous section.

```
# Python program showing
# a use of raw_input(), variables, and sum
n = raw_input("Type your name: ")
print (n, "is running a Python script!")
print ("Now let's add 120 and 87")
# Addition command
z = (120,87)
y = sum (z)
# The next line displays the result
print (y)
```

Figure 4.8-4 illustrates how this script appears when entered and run at the Code the Blocks website (the Sandbox tab is used for your own scripts) along with the icon used by File Explorer for Python script files.

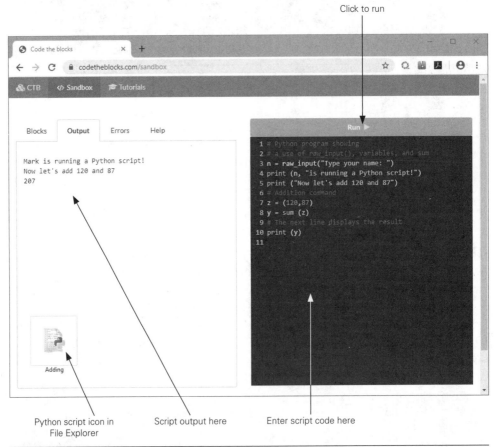

**FIGURE 4.8-4**   Running Adding.py at the Code the Blocks website

# .js

A .js extension is used for JavaScript scripts. JavaScript is widely used in web development and web applications, web servers and server apps, smartwatch and mobile apps, and more. It is an object-based, interpreted language that, despite its name, has no connection to Java.

A free JavaScript IDE is available for Windows, macOS, and Linux from Visual Studio Code (https://code.visualstudio.com). You can also run JavaScript in your browser at various websites such as Code Academy or JavaScript Editor (https://js.do). Because JavaScript is used in web development, you can use HTML tags for text enhancement.

 **EXAM TIP**   JavaScript scripts start with <script> and end with </script>.

Here's a simple .js script that can be inserted into HTML code. It includes statements that set up variables, print text, and insert comments (//), includes some HTML, and performs math.

```
<script>
// JavaScript program showing
// printing, variables, and sum
// <br> is a line break in HTML
// <b> starts bold in HTML; </b> ends bold
// <i> starts italic in HTML; </i> ends italic
document.write("JavaScript Example<br>")
// Setting up text variables
var variable1 = '<b>Mark wrote a</b> ';
var variable2 = '<i>JavaScript example.</i><br>';
// combines variable text together into a phrase
var phrase = variable1 + variable2
document.write(phrase)
var a = 120; var b = 87; var result = a + b;
document.write(result)
</script>
```

Figure 4.8-5 illustrates how this script appears when entered and run at the JS.do website along with the icon used by File Explorer for JavaScript files.

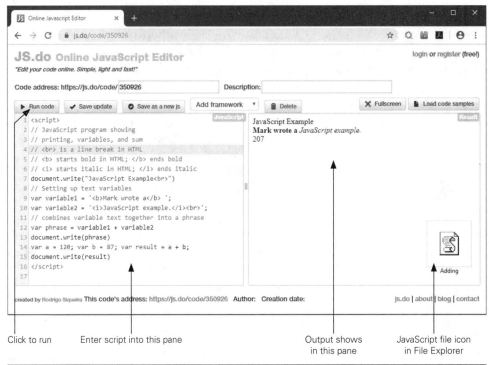

**FIGURE 4.8-5**    Running Adding.js at the JS.do website

# Environment Variables

Environment variables are used by all modern operating systems' scripting languages to provide shortcuts to common locations and features.

Examples of environment variables in Windows include %USERPROFILE%, which can be used to display the current user's profile folder (directory), and %PATH%, which displays the locations the command interpreter will look for an executable file. Although you can incorporate these and other variables into batch files, you can simply use echo *variablename* from a command prompt to see the current value:

```
echo %userprofile%
echo %path%
```

Examples of similar environment variables in Linux include $HOME, which can be used to display the current user's Home directory, and $PATH, which displays the locations the command interpreter will look for an executable file.

**ADDITIONAL RESOURCES**   For a list of environment variables in Windows, go to the AskVG website at www.askvg.com and search for "List of Environment Variables in Windows Operating System."

For a list of environment variables in Linux, check the documentation for your preferred distribution. For example, go to https://help.ubuntu.com and search for "Environment Variables for Ubuntu."

Additional environment variables can be added by using variable=*variable* (Linux) and set variable=*value* (Windows). To create a permanent environment variable in Linux, use export *variable* to add it to the Linux kernel after creating it.

# Comment Syntax

As you have seen in this objective, comment syntax varies between scripting languages. While comments are not essential to script operation, they are extremely important to debugging, maintenance, and documentation. Table 4.8-1 lists the comment syntax used by the scripting languages covered in this objective.

**TABLE 4.8-1**   Comment Syntax by Scripting Language

| Scripting Language (File Extension) | Comment Syntax |
|---|---|
| Batch (.bat) | REM |
| PowerShell (.ps1) | # |
| VBScript (.vbs and .vba) | ' |
| Shell (.sh) | # |
| Python (.py) | # |
| JavaScript (.js) | // |

**EXAM TIP**   Given a scenario, be able to identify the scripting languages and their associated file extensions and comment syntax.

# Basic Script Constructs

Basic script constructs (CompTIA-speak for the features that scripts have in common) include loops and variables. The following sections introduce you to these concepts.

## Basic Loops

Basic loops tell the computer to run the code over and over until the condition is (or is not) met. There are many variations on loops in all of the scripting languages covered on the CompTIA A+ 220-1002 exam.

 **ADDITIONAL RESOURCES** To learn more about loops, go to https:// docs.microsoft.com/ and search for "Loop Structures." Click the Loop Structures (Visual Basic) link.

Here are a couple examples of basic loops:

**For/Next (VBScript Example)**   The logic of this loop is

1. Set up a range of values and the value to change using FOR:

```
For i = 1 to 34
   N = N + i
```

2. The NEXT statement goes back to the N = N + i statement until i = 34, and then the script moves on:

```
Next
```

A For/Next loop must have a counter and runs a specified number of times.

**Do/While (JavaScript Example)**   The logic of this loop is

1. The value of z, since it is not defined, is 0 and it will be incremented by a value of 1 each time the loop runs (z++):

```
do {
 text += "The number is " + z;
 z++;
}
```

2. The WHILE statement goes back to the z++ statement while z <77, and then the script moves on:

```
while (z < 77);
```

A Do/While loop always uses an increment of +1 as it runs and it keeps running as long as the Do statement is true.

 **EXAM TIP**   Make sure you understand that a loop is a way for a script to run until a task is finished, and recognize the differences between For/Next and Do/While loops.

# Variables

A *variable* is a value that can be changed by a script, such as a=999 or $a="Mark". With few exceptions, scripting languages must set up, or *declare*, the meanings of the text or number variables that will be used in a program. By using variables, all that is needed to change a program to work with different data is to change the variable statements. Table 4.8-2 compares how variables are declared in the scripting languages covered in this objective.

**TABLE 4.8-2**   Variable Syntax by Scripting Language

| Scripting Language (File Extension) | Numeric Variable | Text Variable |
|---|---|---|
| Batch (.bat)* | SET /A= | SET= |
| PowerShell (.ps1) | $value = 3 | $value = 'Mark3' |
| VBScript (.vbs) | a = 25 | Text1 = "Mark" |
| Shell (.sh) | let a=1 (use $a to use the variable) | TEXT="Mark" (use $TEXT to use the variable) |
| Python (.py) | a = 1 | b = "Mark" |
| JavaScript (.js) | var a = 1; | var writer = "Mark"; |

*Use SETLOCAL at the beginning of a batch file to make the variables set in the batch file temporary; they will expire when the batch file is over.

# Basic Data Types

To be able to treat numbers and words differently, computers need a new concept—data types. A data type is a defined category, like number or word. As you have seen in earlier parts of the objective, there are two basic data types used by scripting languages: integers and strings.

 **EXAM TIP**   Know the differences between integers and strings.

## Integers

Integers are whole numbers: 5, 22, 37. Integers can have mathematical operations performed upon them, such as adding, dividing, averaging, and so on.

## Strings

Strings are text, or numbers being treated as text such as telephone numbers or Zip Codes. Strings are usually surrounded with double quotes (") or, in PowerShell, single quotes ('). A string can be combined textually with other strings. For example, if $a = "Mark Edward " and $b = "Soper", then $a + $b = "Mark Edward Soper".

# REVIEW

### Objective 4.8: Identify the basics of scripting     Script file types include

- .bat (batch files, used by Windows command prompt)
- .ps1 (PowerShell files, used by Windows PowerShell command environment or by the PowerShell ISE)
- .vbs (VBScript [Visual Basic Script] files, used by Windows Script host, CSCRIPT.exe, and Internet Explorer)
- .vba (Visual Basic for Applications files, used by Microsoft Office apps from the VBA editor)
- .sh (Bash shell files, used by Linux and macOS in Terminal mode)
- .py (Python files, used by Python interpreters)
- .js (JavaScript files, used by web apps and browsers and by JavaScript IDEs)

Script files use the following features:

- Environmental variables (shortcuts to common locations and features in operating systems)
- Comments (indicated by characters such as REM, #, or '; used to explain program logic and features)
- Loops (such as For/Next, Do/While, and others; used to repeat operations)
- Variables (used to store numeric or text values that can be changed by a script)

The basic data types used in scripting include

- Integers (whole numbers)
- Strings (text, or numbers being treated as text)

## 4.8 QUESTIONS

1. You are using a Windows computer and need to create a list of files stored on a Linux server. Which of the following scripting languages can you use without special setup or installation?

    **A.** Batch

    **B.** JavaScript

    **C.** PowerShell

    **D.** Shell

2. The fundamental data types used in scripting include which of the following? (Choose two.)

   **A.** Floating point

   **B.** Integers

   **C.** Binary

   **D.** Strings

3. JavaScript script files sometimes contain paired codes such as <br>…</br> or <i>…</i>. What do these represent?

   **A.** Placeholders for HTML code

   **B.** The beginning and end of comments

   **C.** HTML code used in browsers

   **D.** Placeholders for data imported from Python or PowerShell

4. A new tech is puzzled by the # signs at the beginning of several lines in a scripting language. Which of the following most accurately describes what they mean?

   **A.** Comments in a batch language follow.

   **B.** Explanatory notes for a language such as Python or Bash follow.

   **C.** They are placeholders for numbers that are too wide for the current display.

   **D.** Comments in JavaScript follow.

5. Which scripting language uses a $ sign and single quotes for a text variable, such as $value = 'Smith'?

   **A.** Batch

   **B.** JavaScript

   **C.** Shell

   **D.** PowerShell

## 4.8 ANSWERS

1. **A**  Batch files can be created in Notepad and run from the command prompt; no setup is needed.

2. **B D**  Integers (numbers) and strings (text) are the data types used in scripting.

3. **C**  Paired codes like these and others are HTML code, indicating the script will be used in a web environment.

4. **B**  The hashtag (#) symbol is used for comments in Python, Bash, and PowerShell.

5. **D**  PowerShell uses single quotes for text variables, while other languages use double quotes.

**Objective 4.9** # Given a scenario, use remote access technologies

Remote access technologies allow technicians to diagnose and fix many computer problems, including malware removal and data recovery, without going to the client site. Understanding the technologies and the potential security issues they pose are important for technicians and their clients.

## RDP

Remote Desktop Protocol (RDP) is the protocol that supports Microsoft's remote desktop software. Remote desktop software enables you to use another system's GUI as if you were sitting in front of that computer. Microsoft's *Remote Desktop Connection* can connect to and control a Windows system with a fully graphical interface (see Figure 4.9-1).

 **EXAM TIP** Because the Remote Desktop Connection executable is mstsc.exe, you can also open it from the CLI or search bar by typing **mstsc** and pressing ENTER.

**FIGURE 4.9-1** Windows Remote Desktop Connection dialog box with Options displayed

Similar programs enable techs to see what a client sees on their screen and use the client's system to resolve the issue. *Windows Remote Assistance* (shown in Figure 4.9-2) enables you to grant or assume control, enabling a user to request support directly from you. Upon receiving the support-request e-mail, you can log on to the user's system and, with permission, take the driver's seat.

In all these methods, the connecting system is a client and the remote system is a server providing access to its desktop. To configure whether your Windows system can act as a Remote Assistance or Remote Desktop server, go to the System applet and select the Remote settings link on the left. The Remote tab in System Properties has checkboxes for both Remote Assistance and Remote Desktop, along with some detailed settings.

 **EXAM TIP** Windows can also run applications hosted on another machine. Think of it as Remote Desktop without the desktop—a single application runs on one machine (a server) but the GUI appears on another desktop (a client). Set it up in the RemoteApp and Desktop Connections applet.

To make RDP more secure, find out the IP address or range of addresses of the remote computer(s) connecting with your computer. Then, use Windows Firewall with Advanced

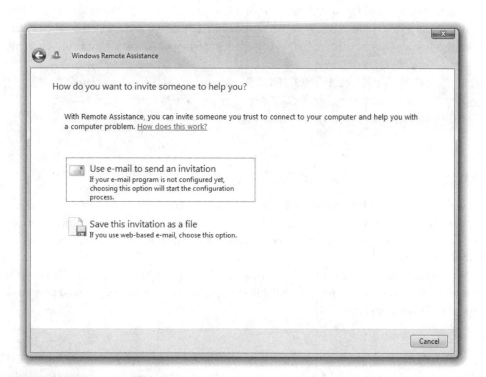

**FIGURE 4.9-2** Remote Assistance in action

Security to restrict access to the RDP port to that IP address or range, a process known as *scoping*. You can also use a VPN (virtual private network) with RDP connections.

**ADDITIONAL RESOURCES**   To learn more about protecting an RDP session, go to www.liquidweb.com, click Knowledge Base in the navigation pane on the left, and search for "Improving Security for Your Remote Desktop Connection" (without quote marks).

## Telnet

Telnet is a terminal (as in CLI) emulation program that enables authenticated users to run commands on a remote system (such as a server or router) that is running the Telnet Server service.

**EXAM TIP**   Telnet is insecure. SSH provides a secure connection and is preferred whenever possible.

Telnet is an optional feature in Windows. If it is not installed, open the Programs and Features Control Panel applet, click *Turn Windows features on or off*, and check the Telnet Client checkbox to add it to your system. Telnet is a standard feature of almost all Linux distributions.

**ADDITIONAL RESOURCES**   For examples of using Telnet for troubleshooting in Linux (many examples also work with Windows), go to www .linuxjournal.com and search for "Troubleshooting with Telnet."

## SSH

Secure Shell (SSH) has largely replaced Telnet because it encrypts the entire connection to prevent eavesdropping. SSH has one other trick up its sleeve: it supports *tunneling* files or any type of TCP/IP network traffic through its secure connection, enabling SSH to secure an insecure protocol such as FTP.

Windows 10 includes the OpenSSH client as of the Fall Creators Update (2017). It is enabled by default starting with the April 2018 release. To run it, open a command prompt or PowerShell session and type:

```
ssh username@hostIP
```

Replace *username* with your username on the remote computer and *hostIP* with its IP address. You will be prompted for your account password on the remote computer. If SSH uses a different TCP port than the default 22, add -p *portnumber* to the ssh command, replacing *portnumber* with the actual port number.

If OpenSSH is not installed, open Settings | Apps. From the Apps & features menu, click *Manage optional features*. Click OpenSSH Client.

 **ADDITIONAL RESOURCES**   The www.sshe.com website provides information about using SSH on Linux or Windows.

# Third-Party Tools

Third-party remote access tools offer a number of advantages over the command-line SSH and Telnet clients. These tools might include one or more of the following features:

- Support for Windows, macOS, and Linux clients and remote access (GUI or command line)
- Easier configuration than CLI apps
- Support for remote access to mobile devices running Android or iOS
- Screen sharing
- File sharing

The following are some examples of third-party remote access tools:

- PuTTY (Windows GUI-based Telnet and SSH client; can connect to other OSs via Telnet and SSH; available from www.chiark.greenend.org.uk/)
- GoToMyPC (macOS or Windows GUI from macOS, Windows, Android, iOS; https://gotomypc.com)
- TeamViewer (cross-platform Windows, Linux, macOS, iOS, Android, Blackberry; www.teamviewer.com)

# Screen Share Feature

One of the advantages of many GUI-based remote clients is the ability to share screens. Depending on the app, screen sharing can run in either or both directions.

A client who needs help can share their screen with a remote helpdesk worker so that the worker can diagnose and solve the problem far faster than trying to describe the solution to a user who is unfamiliar with the diagnostic features of their operating system.

Another application of screen sharing is for a trainer to share screens with students so that students can learn by watching as the instructor explains the settings needed for an app, a document, or another use.

## File Share

File sharing is also a major benefit of third-party remote access apps. Although current e-mail systems can handle much larger file sizes than they could a few years ago, there are still occasions when e-mailing files just won't do. With built-in drag-and-drop file transfers included in some remote access apps, file transfers are as easy as moving files between folders in Windows.

# Security Considerations of Each Access Method

The best remote access method is the one that provides the best balance of speed, power, ease of use—and security. Here's how the major methods stack up:

- RDP is relatively secure because it uses encryption, but its default settings make it vulnerable to unwanted connections. Changing the RDP port, using a VPN, and adjusting firewall settings make an RDP setting more secure.
- Telnet is insecure and sends passwords and user names as clear text, so you should use it only within your own LAN.
- SSH is very secure, using encryption for the entire connection and supporting tunneling (VPN) connections.
- Third-party remote access apps are typically very secure because they offer advanced encryption and (some) support for one-time passwords. The latter feature generates a list of passwords, each of which can be used just once. Use the list if you need to connect remotely from public network connections to prevent shoulder surfers or keyboard loggers from gaining access to the remote computer. Check the specifications for the specific third-party app to determine its security features and how to improve them.

# REVIEW

**Objective 4.9: Given a scenario, use remote access technologies**    Major types of remote access technologies include

- RDP (Remote Desktop Connection and Windows Remote Assistance, Microsoft)
- Telnet (Linux, macOS, and Windows—command line)
- SSH (Linux, macOS, and Windows—command line)
- Third-party tools (PuTTY, GoToMyPC, TeamViewer, and others)
- Screen sharing, offered by third-party tools and RDP
- File sharing, offered by third-party tools

Telnet is the least secure, with third-party apps being the most secure.

## 4.9 QUESTIONS

1. You are preparing to run Remote Desktop Connection to perform remote troubleshooting. From the command line or Search bar, which of the following commands would you use to start it?

   **A.** RDC

   **B.** DeskConn

   **C.** mstsc

   **D.** WRA

2. You are helping a client configure her system for Remote Assistance. Which Windows configuration option is used to make these changes?

   **A.** Remote Access in Settings

   **B.** Remote tab in System Properties

   **C.** Remote Assistance in Computer Management

   **D.** Connections tab in Internet Explorer

3. You need to use Telnet to remotely access another computer on the company network, but you cannot locate Telnet on your Windows 10 system. How do you get access to Telnet?

   **A.** Install it from the Microsoft website

   **B.** Open Settings | Apps and click *Manage optional features*

   **C.** Set up a Linux VM and run Telnet from there

   **D.** Click *Turn Windows features on and off* in the Programs and Features Control Panel applet

4. A new tech is attempting to use SSH to connect to IP address 192.168.4.19 as user newbie. Which of the following commands is the appropriate syntax?

   **A.** ssh newbie@192.168.4.19

   **B.** ssh 192.168.4.19@newbie

   **C.** https://192.168.4.19 ssh-newbie

   **D.** None of the above; run SSH from a GUI by clicking the remote computer

5. Your organization is looking for a remote access application that can be used securely from public Internet terminals. What security feature should this app include?

   **A.** Cross-platform support

   **B.** One-time passwords

   **C.** Screen sharing

   **D.** File sharing

## 4.9 ANSWERS

1. **C** mstsc is the command to launch Remote Desktop Connection.

2. **B** System properties, Remote (tab) is the correct answer.

3. **D** Enable Telnet with the Add and Remove Windows Features dialog.

4. **A** The correct syntax is ssh *username@ipaddress,* as shown in choice A.

5. **B** One-time passwords are used only once, so although a shoulder surfer or keystroke app might see the login, the password cannot be used again.

# About the Online Content

This book comes complete with the following:

- TotalTester Online practice exam software with practice exam questions for both exam 220-1001 and 220-1002, as well as a pre-assessment to get you started
- More than 25 sample TotalSim interactive simulations from Total Seminars
- More than an hour of video training episodes from Mike Meyers' CompTIA A+ Certification Video Training series
- A link to a collection of Mike's favorite tools and utilities for PC troubleshooting
- A PDF Glossary for reference

## System Requirements

The current and previous major versions of the following desktop browsers are recommended and supported: Chrome, Microsoft Edge, Firefox, and Safari. These browsers update frequently, and sometimes an update may cause compatibility issues with the Total Tester Online or other content hosted on the Training Hub. If you run into a problem using one of these browsers, please try using another until the problem is resolved.

## Your Total Seminars Training Hub Account

To get access to the online content, you will need to create an account on the Total Seminars Training Hub. Registration is free, and you will be able to track all your online content using your account. You may also opt in if you wish to receive marketing information from McGraw-Hill Education or Total Seminars, but this is not required for you to gain access to the online content.

### Privacy Notice

McGraw-Hill Education values your privacy. Please be sure to read the Privacy Notice available during registration to see how the information you have provided will be used. You may view our Corporate Customer Privacy Policy by visiting the McGraw-Hill Education Privacy Center. Visit the **mheducation.com** site and click on **Privacy** at the bottom of the page.

# Single User License Terms and Conditions

Online access to the digital content included with this book is governed by the McGraw-Hill Education License Agreement outlined next. By using this digital content you agree to the terms of that license.

**Access**   To register and activate your Total Seminars Training Hub account, simply follow these easy steps.

1. Go to this URL: **hub.totalsem.com/mheclaim**
2. To Register and create a new Training Hub account, enter your e-mail address, name, and password. No further personal information (such as credit card number) is required to create an account.

 **NOTE**   If you already have a Total Seminars Training Hub account, select **Log in** and enter your e-mail and password. Otherwise, follow the remaining steps.

3. Enter your Product Key: `g2kz-9ng0-z9qg`
4. Click to accept the user license terms.
5. Click **Register and Claim** to create your account. You will be taken to the Training Hub and have access to the content for this book.

**Duration of License**   Access to your online content through the Total Seminars Training Hub will expire one year from the date the publisher declares the book out of print.

Your purchase of this McGraw-Hill Education product, including its access code, through a retail store is subject to the refund policy of that store.

The Content is a copyrighted work of McGraw-Hill Education, and McGraw-Hill Education reserves all rights in and to the Content. The Work is © 2020 by McGraw Hill LLC.

**Restrictions on Transfer**   The user is receiving only a limited right to use the Content for the user's own internal and personal use, dependent on purchase and continued ownership of this book. The user may not reproduce, forward, modify, create derivative works based upon, transmit, distribute, disseminate, sell, publish, or sublicense the Content or in any way commingle the Content with other third-party content without McGraw-Hill Education's consent.

**Limited Warranty**   The McGraw-Hill Education Content is provided on an "as is" basis. Neither McGraw-Hill Education nor its licensors make any guarantees or warranties of any kind, either express or implied, including, but not limited to, implied warranties of merchantability or fitness for a particular purpose or use as to any McGraw-Hill Education Content or the information therein or any warranties as to the accuracy, completeness, correctness, or results to be obtained from, accessing or using the McGraw-Hill Education Content, or any material referenced in such Content or any information entered into licensee's product by users or other persons and/or any material available on or that can be accessed through the licensee's product (including via any hyperlink or otherwise) or as to non-infringement of third-party rights. Any warranties of any kind, whether express or implied, are disclaimed. Any material or data obtained through use of the McGraw-Hill Education Content is at your own discretion and risk and user understands that it will be solely responsible for any resulting damage to its computer system or loss of data.

Neither McGraw-Hill Education nor its licensors shall be liable to any subscriber or to any user or anyone else for any inaccuracy, delay, interruption in service, error or omission, regardless of cause, or for any damage resulting therefrom.

In no event will McGraw-Hill Education or its licensors be liable for any indirect, special or consequential damages, including but not limited to, lost time, lost money, lost profits or good will, whether in contract, tort, strict liability or otherwise, and whether or not such damages are foreseen or unforeseen with respect to any use of the McGraw-Hill Education Content.

# TotalTester Online

TotalTester Online provides you with a simulation of the A+ exams 220-1001 and 220-1002. Exams can be taken in Practice Mode or Exam Mode. Practice Mode provides an assistance window with hints, references to the book, explanations of the correct and incorrect answers, and the option to check your answer as you take the test. Exam Mode provides a simulation of the actual exam. The number of questions, the types of questions, and the time allowed are intended to be an accurate representation of the exam environment. The option to customize your quiz allows you to create custom exams from selected domains or chapters, and you can further customize the number of questions and time allowed.

To take a test, follow the instructions provided in the previous section to register and activate your Total Seminars Training Hub account. When you register you will be taken to the Total Seminars Training Hub. From the Training Hub Home page, click the Study drop-down menu at the top of the page, click CompTIA A+ Certification, and then click A+ (220-100x) TotalTester (or, alternatively, find the exam on the list of Your Topics on the Home page). Select the TotalTester Online item on the right and then click the Tester! icon. You can then select the option to customize your quiz and begin testing yourself in Practice Mode or Exam Mode. All exams provide an overall grade and a grade broken down by domain.

## Pre-assessment Test

In addition to the exam questions, the TotalTester also includes a pre-assessment test that covers topics from both exams to help you assess your understanding of the topics before reading the book. To launch the pre-assessment test, click A+ (220-100x) TotalTester, select the Assessment item on the right, and click the Tester! icon. The A+ pre-assessment test has 50 questions and runs in Exam mode. When you complete the test, you can review the questions with answers and detailed explanations by clicking See Detailed Results.

# Other Online Book Resources

The following sections detail the other resources available with your book. You can access these items by selecting the Resources tab or by selecting CompTIA A+ Certification from the Study drop-down menu at the top of the page or from the list of Your Topics on the Home page. The tabs at the top and the menu on the right side of the screen outline all of the available resources.

## TotalSims for A+

 From your Total Seminars Training Hub account, select TotalSims for A+ (220-100x) from the list of Your Topics on the Home page. Click the TotalSims tab. The simulations are organized by chapter, and there are over 25 free simulations available for reviewing topics referenced in the book, with an option to purchase access to the full TotalSims for A+ (220-100x) with over 200 simulations.

## Mike's Video Training

Over an hour of training videos, starring Mike Meyers, are available for free. Select CompTIA A+ Videos (220-100x) from the list of Your Topics on the Home page. Click the TotalVideos tab. Along with over an hour of free videos, you'll find an option to purchase Mike's complete video training series.

## Mike's Cool Tools

Mike loves freeware/open source networking tools! Access the utilities mentioned in the text by selecting CompTIA A+ Certification from the list of Your Topics on the Home page. Click the Resources tab, and then select Mike's Cool Tools.

## PDF Glossary

To access the free online CompTIA A+ Glossary, select CompTIA A+ Certification from the list of Your Topics on the Home page. Click the Resources tab, and then select CompTIA A+ Glossary.

# Technical Support

For questions regarding the Total Tester software or operation of the Training Hub, visit **www.totalsem.com** or e-mail **support@totalsem.com**.

For questions regarding book content, visit **www.mheducation.com/customerservice**.

# Index

# total**tester**
### Certification Exam Prep

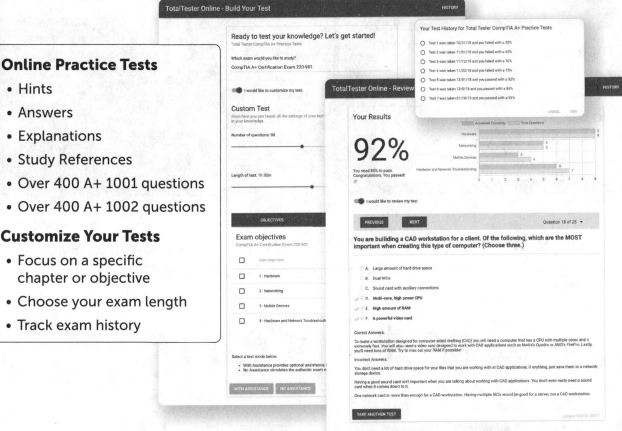

## Online Practice Tests

- Hints
- Answers
- Explanations
- Study References
- Over 400 A+ 1001 questions
- Over 400 A+ 1002 questions

## Customize Your Tests

- Focus on a specific chapter or objective
- Choose your exam length
- Track exam history

**Buy Now** - use coupon code *APP2019TT* at totalsem.com/a2019test
Save 10% on A+ practice tests

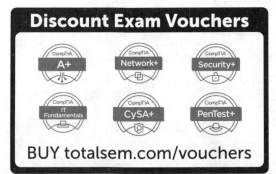

## Discount Exam Vouchers

CompTIA A+
CompTIA Network+
CompTIA Security+
CompTIA IT Fundamentals
CompTIA CySA+
CompTIA PenTest+

BUY totalsem.com/vouchers

## Attention Educators

✓ Comprehensive Mike Meyers Curriculum

✓ Classroom in a Box Equipment Solutions

✓ Special Educator Pricing

www.totalsem.com • (800) 446-6004

# total**video**
### Certification Exam Training

## Includes

- A+ 1001 & 1002 exam coverage
- Over 16 hours of A+ 1001 training
- Over 15 hours of A+ 1002 training
- Free episodes at hub.totalsem.com
- Mike Meyers' dynamic teaching style

**Buy Now** - use coupon code *APP2019V* at totalsem.com/a2019video
Get the Full Version at a **SPECIAL PRICE!**

# total**sims**
### Performance-Based Exam Prep

 **Type!**
Interactive Command-Line Windows Exercises

 **Click!**
Interactive Graphical Windows Exercises

 **Show!**
Operating System and Application Training Demonstrations

 **Challenge!**
Interactive Configuration and Identification Exercises

### Interactive simulations that reinforce critical concepts
Try free TotalSims at hub.totalsem.com

**Buy Now** - use coupon code *APP2019TS* at totalsem.com/a2019sims
Save 10% on A+ TotalSims

## www.totalsem.com • (800) 446-6004